A THEORY OF CONSTITUTIONAL RIGHTS

A Theory of
Constitutional Rights

ROBERT ALEXY
translated by Julian Rivers

OXFORD
UNIVERSITY PRESS

OXFORD

UNIVERSITY PRESS

Great Clarendon Street, Oxford OX2 6DP

Oxford University Press is a department of the University of Oxford.
It furthers the University's objective of excellence in research, scholarship,
and education by publishing worldwide in

Oxford New York

Auckland Bangkok Buenos Aires Chennai
Dar es Salaam Delhi Hong Kong Istanbul Karachi Kolkata
Kuala Lumpur Madrid Melbourne Mexico City Mumbai Nairobi
São Paulo Shanghai Singapore Taipei Tokyo Toronto
with an associated company in Berlin

Oxford is a registered trade mark of Oxford University Press
in the UK and in certain other countries

Published in the United States
by Oxford University Press Inc., New York

British Library Cataloguing in Publication Data

Data available

Library of Congress Cataloging in Publication Data
Alexy, Robert.
[Theorie der Grundrechte. English]
A theory of constitutional rights/Robert Alexy; translated by Julian Rivers.
p. cm.
Includes bibliographical references and index.
1. Civil rights. 2. Constitutional law. I. Title.
K3240.A4213 2002
342'.085—dc21   2002074272
ISBN 0-19-825821-6

1 3 5 7 9 10 8 6 4 2

Typeset in Sabon by
Cambrian Typesetters, Frimley, Surrey
Printed in Great Britain
on acid-free paper by
T.J. International Ltd, Padstow, Cornwall

For
Georg Corbin
and
Julia

Preface

It can hardly be unusual for an author to take pleasure in the publication of his work in another language. But this general pleasure becomes a particular one when the book is translated by someone who is not only fully at home in both languages, but who has also completely mastered the subject-matter. I consider it a matter of the greatest good fortune to have found in Julian Rivers such a translator. I thank him not only for the fact that he has so beautifully recrafted this book, which first appeared in German in 1985, but also for his encouragement to write a new Postscript, in which I attempt, in response to some of my critics, to bring the book up to date on the current discussion.

R.A.

Kiel
October 2001

In preparing this translation, I have incurred a number of debts of gratitude. To Stanley Paulson, who first suggested that it would be a good idea; to John Louth at Oxford University Press, who enthusiastically adopted and has supported the project throughout; to my own Department of Law at the University of Bristol, whose enlightened study leave policy allowed me time free from teaching and administration to complete the work; to colleagues at Bristol, Oxford Brookes, and Kiel, who endured, and responded to, earlier versions of the sketchy integration of the *Theory of Constitutional Rights* into the British context; to friends who commented in detail on drafts of the text of that essay, in particular Trevor Allan, Patrick Capps, Aileen McHarg, Tonia Novitz, and Henrik Palmer Olsen; and finally, to Robert Alexy himself, whose lucid prose and patient explanations have made the work even more instructive and enjoyable than I ever anticipated. Responsibility for the remaining faults—and it is impossible to believe that there are not some—remains entirely my own.

J.R.

Bristol
October 2001

Contents

Abbreviations

ABlKR	Amtsblatt des Kontrollrats
AC	Law Reports Appeal Cases
AcP	Archiv für die civilistische Praxis
All ER	All England Law Reports
Am Phil Q	American Philosophical Quarterly
AöR	Archiv des öffentlichen Rechts
ARSP	Archiv für Rechts- und Sozialphilosophie
BAGE	Entscheidungen des Bundesarbeitsgerichts
BGH	Bundesgerichtshof
BGHSt	Entscheidungen des Bundesgerichtshofes in Strafsachen
BGHZ	Entscheidungen des Bundesgerichtshofes in Zivilsachen
BVerfGE	Entscheidungen des Bundesverfassungsgerichts
BVerwGE	Entscheidungen des Bundesverwaltungsgerichts
Cal L Rev	California Law Review
CLJ	Cambridge Law Journal
ČSAV	Československé Akademie Věd
DÖV	Die Öffentliche Verwaltung
DR	Decisions and Reports (European Commission of Human Rights)
DRiZ	Deutsche Richter-Zeitung
Duke LJ	Duke Law Journal
DVBl	Deutsches Verwaltungsblatt
ECHR	European Convention for the Protection of Human Rights and Fundamental Freedoms
ECR	European Court Reports
EHRLR	European Human Rights Law Review
EHRR	European Human Rights Reports
EuGRZ	Europäische Grundrechte-Zeitschrift
ICLQ	International and Comparative Law Quarterly
Ill LQ	Illinois Law Quarterly
IR	Irish Reports
Jahrb. d. Ak. d. Wiss.	Jahrbuch der Akademie der Wissenschaften
JBl	Jahresblatt
JöR	Jahrbuch des öffentlichen Rechts der Gegenwart
Jur Rev	Juridical Review
JuS	Juristische Schulung

JZ	Juristenzeitung
KB	Law Reports King's Bench
L Ed	Lawyers' Edition United States Supreme Court Reports
LGR	Knight's Local Government Reports
LQR	Law Quarterly Review
MLR	Modern Law Review
NF	Neue Fassung
NJW	Neue Juristische Wochenschrift
NVwZ	Neue Zeitschrift für Verwaltungsrecht
OJLS	Oxford Journal of Legal Studies
ÖZöR	Österreichische Zeitschrift für öffentliches Recht und Völkerrecht
Phil Q	Philosophical Quarterly
PL	Public Law
Proc Aris Soc	Proceedings of the Aristotelian Society
QB	Law Reports Queen's Bench
QBD	Law Reports Queen's Bench Division
SA	South African Law Reports
St Tr	State Trials
Tul L Rev	Tulane Law Review
US	United States Supreme Court Reports
VerwArch	Verwaltungsarchiv
VVDStRL	Veröffentlichungen der Vereinigung der Deutschen Staatsrechtlehrer
WLR	Weekly Law Reports
Yale LJ	Yale Law Journal
YBEL	Yearbook of European Law
ZGesStW	Zeitschrift für die Gesamte Strafrechtswissenschaft
ZSR	Zeitschrift für Schweizerisches Recht

A Theory of Constitutional Rights *and the British Constitution*

JULIAN RIVERS

Robert Alexy's *Theorie der Grundrechte* is a rational reconstruction of German constitutional rights reasoning. His primary subject-matter, the judgments of the German Federal Constitutional Court, represents one of the most resourceful bodies of constitutional rights case-law in the liberal democratic tradition.[1] So this work provides both a general introduction to a rich and interesting body of case-law and a theoretically attractive account of the structure of constitutional rights within liberal democracy.

The prime locus of constitutional rights in the United Kingdom is now the Human Rights Act 1998,[2] which gives further legal effect to the European Convention on Human Rights and Fundamental Freedoms. While discussion of the Act has been carried on in an explicitly comparative atmosphere,[3] the tendency, for obvious linguistic and cultural reasons, has been to look to other common law jurisdictions for guidance, in particular Canada and New Zealand. Attitudes towards the value of continental European jurisprudence in general, and German constitutional jurisprudence in particular, vary from the enthusiastic,[4] through the cautiously open,[5] to the positively sceptical.[6]

---

[1] A useful collection of the most important judgments can be found in *Entscheidungen des Bundesverfassungsgerichts: Studienauswahl*, 2 vols. (Tübingen: J. C. B. Mohr (Paul Siebeck), 1993). An English-language account of substantive German constitutional rights can also be found in S. Michelowski and L. Woods, *German Constitutional Law: The Protection of Civil Liberties* (Aldershot: Ashgate/Dartmouth, 1999).

[2] 1998 Chapter 42. The main provisions of the Act came into force on 2 Oct. 2000: Human Rights Act 1998 (Commencement no. 2) Order 2000/1851.

[3] See e.g. The Constitution Unit, *Human Rights Legislation* (London, 1996); R. Clayton and H. Tomlinson, *The Law of Human Rights* (Oxford: Oxford University Press, 2000). For a general account of the problems raised by this phenomenon, see C. McCrudden, 'A Common Law of Human Rights?: Transnational Judicial Conversations on Constitutional Rights', OJLS 20 (2000), 499 ff.

[4] See Basil Markesinis, 'Privacy, Freedom of Expression and the Horizontal Effect of the Human Rights Bill: Lessons from Germany', LQR 115 (1999), 47 at 47: 'when it comes to balancing competing values, German jurists have, in my view, constructed one of the most sophisticated and rational systems that has ever been devised'.

[5] See David Feldman, 'The Human Rights Act 1998 and Constitutional Principles', Legal Studies, 19 (1999), 165 at 205; id., 'Human Dignity as a Legal Value—Part I', PL 1999, 682 at 698–9.

[6] See Lord Hoffmann, 'Human Rights and the House of Lords', MLR 62 (1999), 159 at

For there are, of course, a number of significant differences in the constitutional arrangements of both countries. The German catalogue of constitutional rights is unambiguously 'higher law', binding all three powers of
the state. There is a separate constitutional court, whose judges are the
guardians of the constitution, and whose powers can be invoked in defence
of constitutional rights by affected individuals. Furthermore, Alexy himself
expressly disavows any suggestion that he is creating a theoretical account
of constitutional rights generally;[7] the task he sets himself is to rationalize
one specific state's constitutional tradition. Nevertheless, there are ample
grounds for the thesis that his theory is applicable more widely.

That thesis is made at least plausible by the formal abstraction and
substantive openness of his theory. Key to the entire theory is the argument
that constitutional rights are principles, and that principles are qualitatively
different from rules, being optimization requirements relative to what is
factually and legally possible. This feature of constitutional rights explains
the logical necessity of the principle of proportionality and exposes constitutional reasoning as the process of identifying the conditions under which
one of two or more competing principles takes precedence on the facts of
specific cases. Perhaps the most contentious feature of the theory is its rejection of a notion of rights as anti-utilitarian 'trumps'[8] which can be identified in any other way than through a process of reasoning taking account
of the arguments for and against constitutional protection.[9]

Alexy's theory is open to a range of possible substantive contents at a
number of significant points. No distinction is drawn between individual
rights and collective goods: both can be the subject-matter of optimization
requirements. Constitutional rights need not be limited to the classic liberties, or defensive rights against public authorities: equality rights, rights to
protection and procedure, and social rights are all conceivable as constitutionally protected rights. Nor need constitutional rights be limited to relationships between the individual and the state; the precise degree of third
party, or horizontal, effect is also a matter of substance. Finally, the theory
manages a (partial) reconciliation between democracy and human rights,
once again, not in any substantive sense, but in showing how the structure
of constitutional rights reasoning can be sensitive to both concerns. More
or less latent in the original work, this reconciliation is developed at length
in a discussion of legislative discretion in the Postscript.

Thus, from the perspective of the *Theorie der Grundrechte*, many of the
distinguishing features of different constitutions are contingent, and trans-
ferability between systems is at least plausible. Whether it can ultimately be

159–60. For more general scepticism, see P. Legrand's self-explanatory, 'European Legal
Systems are not Converging', ICLQ 45 (1996), 52 ff.

[7] 5 below.
[8] See R. Dworkin, *Taking Rights Seriously* (London: Duckworth, 1977), 90 ff.
[9] 178–181, 210 ff. below.

successfully carried out depends on a detailed conceptual reconstruction of the constitution along these lines. Such reconstructions would require works at least as long as the original, but some preliminary points of contact can, at any rate, be established. That is what will be attempted in the context of the British Constitution in the remainder of this essay. To the extent that this argument succeeds, it is *likely* to apply, with some adjustments, to other common law jurisdictions as well. But of course, that, too, would require substantial reconstructive work.

1. HUMAN RIGHTS AND CONSTITUTIONAL RIGHTS

Is it correct to see the human rights set out in Schedule 1 to the Human Rights Act ('Convention rights') as *constitutional* rights? Undoubtedly, rights become constitutional because of their perceived substantive significance as expressions of an underlying political morality. But substantive significance alone does not secure legal recognition. Most obviously, certain rights are constitutional because they have a status which is higher in the hierarchy of legal norms than ordinary legal rights. This in turn gives rise to an expectation that they have relevance to the whole of law. Constitutional rights in Germany are constitutional in all three respects. They represent a rejection of Nazi ideology in favour of liberal democracy, they bind all three powers in the state, and, according to the long-standing case-law of the Federal Constitutional Court, they express an objective order of values which permeates the entire legal order.[10] However, the position under the Human Rights Act 1998 is, at first sight, far from clear. Convention rights are ultimately at the disposal of Parliament, since incompatibility with them does not affect the validity, continuing operation, or enforcement of any statutory provision in question.[11] They appear only relevant to statute law and the acts of subordinate public authorities, not to Parliament, the common law, or private individuals.[12] Arguably then, they have neither the status nor relevance necessary to justify calling them 'constitutional'.

Constitutions exist on a spectrum from the purely formal or procedural to the purely substantive.[13] Under Diceyan conceptions of parliamentary supremacy, the constitution of the United Kingdom is as near purely procedural as possible.[14] It is open to any content, so long as that content is made legal in a certain form, through certain procedures of Parliamentary legislation. There are no constitutional rights (except perhaps procedural rights

---

[10] Lüth Judgment, BVerfGE 7, 198 (205).   [11] Human Rights Act 1998 sect. 6(4).
[12] Sects. 6(3)(*b*), 3(1), and 6(1) respectively.   [13] See 349 ff. below.
[14] A. V. Dicey, *Introduction to the Study of the Constitution*, 10th edn. (London: Macmillan, 1959), 39–40.

to enforce the ordinary legislative process[15]), and the danger of this is that the legal system is open to unjust content. On the other hand, a constitution such as the German one which makes human rights enforceable as supreme law risks becoming purely substantive. All law becomes an outworking of the resolutions of competing constitutional rights and principles, resolutions which are reviewable for their correctness by the judiciary. The legislature ceases to have any autonomous law-making function, which renders the commitment to on-going democratic legitimacy practically meaningless. Clearly some sort of mediating solution is appropriate. The first solution is to conceive of constitutional rights as setting jurisdictional limits to legislative activity: the legislature can do as it pleases so long as it does not infringe certain definitive rights. The limits of these rights are absolute. The alternative is to conceive of constitutional rights as imposing extra procedural constraints on legislation which falls within their scope. The limits that rights impose are in that sense only relative, because they can always be surmounted in certain ways.

The absolute, or jurisdictional, view is supported by the fact that if there are constitutional rights at all, there must be some things the legislature cannot do by way of ordinary legislative process. However, such jurisdictional limits are rarely absolute in any full sense of the word; the constitution can always be amended. The relative, or procedural, view recognizes that it is not impossible for the legislature to limit constitutional rights; rather, extra procedural constraints are legally imposed if it wishes to do so. Such procedural constraints can be more or less restrictive. In Germany, the legislature is required to form special majorities and formally to amend an inconsistent constitutional text if it wishes to pass legislation incompatible with existing constitutional rights.[16] This is obviously a stronger form of obstacle than requiring a mere notwithstanding clause in ordinary legislation which infringes rights as in Canada.[17] And where the procedure for amending the constitution is highly complex, as in the United States, one

---

[15] The 'manner and form' argument holds that Parliament is limited in its composition and procedure: see I. Jennings, *The Law and the Constitution*, 5th edn. (London: University of London Press, 1959), 151 ff.; R. F. V. Heuston, *Essays in Constitutional Law*, 2nd edn. (London: Stevens & Sons, 1964), ch. 1; G. Marshall, *Constitutional Conventions* (Oxford: Oxford University Press, 1984), ch. 12. Heuston suggested that an injunction might issue to prevent the procedurally improper statute being brought into force. Although contrary to established orthodoxy (see *Pickin v British Railways Board* [1974] AC 765), the decisions of the House of Lords in the Factortame litigation (*R v Secretary of State for Transport ex p Factortame (no. 1)* [1990] 2 AC 85; *R v Secretary of State for Transport ex p Factortame (no. 2)* [1991] 1 AC 603) have made this suggestion less implausible. See also David Feldman's suggestion at fn. 30 below.
[16] Under art. 79 Basic Law an act to amend the constitution must do so expressly and requires two-thirds majorities in both houses of the legislature.
[17] See Canadian Constitution Act 1982 sect. 33(1) and (2). Under sect. 33(3) such legislation passes automatically out of force five years after being passed. The requirement repeatedly to renew incompatible legislation is, of course, another procedural constraint.

will admittedly tend to think more easily of constitutional rights as 'absolute' jurisdictional limits. But the distinction is better seen as one of degree. Even the so-called eternity clause[18] of the German Constitution, which protects core elements of human rights from constitutional amendment, can be seen as a procedural constraint which can be surmounted by an entirely new constituent act.

A further advantage of the 'relative' view is that it can explain the fact that both the German Basic Law and the European Convention permit certain legislative interferences within the scope of rights, but subject these to formal constraints, such as the requirement that they must be 'according to law'. Thus in practice constitutional rights give rise to a range of procedural obstacles to legislative and executive action depending on the extent to which that action departs from the presumptions of political morality expressed in the constitutional rights catalogue. It is these procedural constraints, beyond those implicit in the normal legislative process, which give constitutional rights their higher status, a status which is revealed whenever they conflict with norms of ordinary law and lead to an outcome which is different from the one which would have been reached in their absence.

Convention rights under the Human Rights Act are not 'absolute' jurisdictional limits, but they do give rise to procedural constraints. The weakest extra procedural obstacle of all can be found in the new interpretative rule of section 3. This requires that 'so far as it is possible to do so', legislation be 'read and given effect'[19] in a way which is compatible with Convention rights. Far from being 'deeply mysterious',[20] the section is phrased this way because of judicial attitudes to Convention rights prior to the Act. These supposedly required a two-stage analysis. First, an ambiguity in the statute had to be established; secondly, Convention rights could be used to determine the correct meaning.[21] Justification for this process could be found in the UK's dualist approach to international obligations.[22] The executive should not distort the judicial construction of legal meaning by entering into international agreements without submitting them to Parliamentary approval in the form of legislation. However, this two-stage process of reasoning should be contrasted with the position as regards

[18] Art. 79(3) protects the federal structure, participation of the *Länder* in the legislative process, and the principles set out in arts. 1 and 20 from constitutional amendment.

[19] The draftsman obviously shrank from inserting the requisite preposition: one can only give effect *to* something. Grammar triumphed towards the end of sect. 6(2)(*b*).

[20] See Geoffrey Marshall, 'Interpreting Interpretation in the Human Rights Bill', PL 1998, 167; id., 'Two Kinds of Compatibility: More about Section 3 of the Human Rights Act 1998', PL 1999, 377. See also Francis Bennion, 'What Interpretation is Possible under Section 3(1) of the Human Rights Act 1998', PL 2000, 77 at 88.

[21] *Salomon v Commissioners of Customs & Excise* [1967] 2 QB 116 at 143 (per Diplock LJ); *R v Secretary of State for the Home Department ex p Brind* [1991] 1 AC 696 at 747–8 (per Lord Bridge).

[22] See e.g. *Rayner (Mincing Lane) Ltd v Department of Trade* [1990] 2 AC 418.

'common law fundamental rights'. The courts in the United Kingdom have long accepted that certain rights are fundamental, in that they give rise to a process of strict statutory construction.[23] In determining the meaning of a statute in the light of common law fundamental rights, it is assumed that Parliament does not intend to authorize infringements of such rights unless the clear words of the statute make no other conclusion possible. The purpose of section 3 is thus simply to bring the situation as regards Convention rights into line with the existing role of common law fundamental rights.[24] The effect of both sets of rights is to place a procedural obstacle—albeit a minor one—in the way of Parliament's expression of legislative intent, by forcing it expressly and in detail to infringe the right in question. Conflicts between broad statutory rules and Convention rights are to be resolved in favour of the latter. Both Convention rights and common law fundamental rights can thus properly be called constitutional.

The system for dealing with primary legislation which cannot be interpreted in conformity with Convention rights, and which thus appears to the judiciary to be incompatible with those rights, confirms their higher status. The constitutional innovation of the declaration of incompatibility[25] empowers the judiciary to evaluate legislation against human rights standards and if necessary declare it incompatible with Convention rights. This fact alone implies a higher status. If the Human Rights Act were an ordinary statute, incompatibilities with other statutes would be resolved by way of the doctrine of implied repeal.[26] They are not. The Human Rights Act remains in force, and the incompatibility—whether the offending statute predates or postdates the Human Rights Act—is 'resolved' by formally declaring it. Thereafter, admittedly, the executive has a choice; it may either remove the offending law by the so-called 'fast track procedure'[27] or it may seek re-enactment of the legislation with the statement that in spite of the incompatibility, 'the government nevertheless wishes the House to proceed with the Bill',[28] or it may of course do nothing, in which case the unconstitutional law remains in force.[29] But the power of the judiciary to evaluate all law against the standards of Convention rights is clear.

It may be that the procedural constraints on Parliament infringing

<hr>

[23] See e.g. *Chertsey UDC v Mixnam's Properties* [1965] AC 735; *Morris v Beardmore* [1981] AC 446; *Raymond v Honey* [1983] AC 1; *R v Secretary of State for the Home Department ex p Leech* [1994] QB 198 at 209; see also T. R. S. Allan, *Law, Liberty and Justice* (Oxford: Clarendon Press, 1993), ch. 4.
[24] *R v Secretary of State for the Home Department ex p Simms & O'Brian* [1999] 3 WLR 328 per Lord Hoffmann (obiter) at pp. 341–2.
[25] Human Rights Act 1998 sect. 4(2).
[26] *Vauxhall Estates Ltd v Liverpool Corporation* [1932] 1 KB 733; *Ellen Street Estates Ltd v Minister of Health* [1934] 1 KB 590.
[27] Human Rights Act 1998 sect. 10 and Schedule 2.
[28] Sect. 19(1)(*b*). Sect. 19 has been in force since 24 Nov. 1998: Human Rights Act 1998 (Comencement no. 1) Order 1998, 2882.
[29] Sect. 4(6).

Convention rights are not quite as weak as at first sight seems. David Feldman has suggested that the statement of compatibility or incompatibility supplied with each statute could be treated by the courts as a procedural necessity, meaning that failure to supply it would render the statute procedurally ultra vires.[30] But the real practical problem concerns situations in which the government fails to take action after a judicial declaration of incompatibility, either because it disagrees with the judiciary, considering the law in question to be compatible with constitutional rights, or because it wishes to see the law remain on the statute book notwithstanding its incompatibility. The first option is fundamentally inconsistent with the Separation of Powers, which requires the executive to defer to the judiciary on disputed questions of law; the second is procedurally improper, because the Human Rights Act provides a procedure for the enactment of laws incompatible with constitutional rights. The problem is that the Act appears explicitly to prevent the judiciary from requiring the executive to use the proper legislative procedure for incompatible legislation.[31] But although there is no remedy for an inactive government in this respect, there is at least a strong political expectation that one of the two appropriate courses of action will be followed, and the existence of a joint Parliamentary Committee on Human Rights will surely strengthen that expectation. In short, Convention rights are rights of a higher status, but with a very weak system of enforcement. It is thus appropriate to talk about constitutional rights in the United Kingdom.

2. CONVENTION RIGHTS AS SUBJECTIVE RIGHTS AND OBJECTIVE LAW

There is a familiar distinction within German jurisprudence between objective law and subjective rights (the adjectives being made necessary by the ambiguity of the word *Recht*). The distinction corresponds to one between norms on one hand and the positions or relations of legal persons on the other. As applied to the term 'constitutional rights', the distinction gives rise to two meanings, 'constitutional rights' in the sense of the legal positions of constitutional right-holders, and 'constitutional rights' as the label for

---

[30] 'The Human Rights Act 1998 and Constitutional Principles', Legal Studies, 19 (1999), 165 at 185. A more ambitious, and rather less plausible, extension of this argument would be that the formal executive statement of incompatibility is a procedurally necessary requirement for the validity of legislation the judiciary consider to be incompatible. Since the executive is hardly likely to make such a statement, this would destroy the purpose of the judicial declaration of incompatibility, which is designed *not* to affect the validity of legislation.

[31] On the assumption that the introduction of legislation into Parliament is a 'function in connection with proceedings in Parliament': see sect. 6(1) and (3). This may not be true in relation to unconstitutional Orders in Council: see S. Grosz, J. Beatson, and P. Duffy, *Human Rights: The 1998 Act and the European Convention* (London: Sweet and Maxwell, 2000), 75.

norms of a certain content, namely constitutional rights norms. The latter
term may sound awkward, but it differs little from the term 'human rights
law', which is common enough. Exactly how the distinction is to be drawn
depends in large measure on one's concept of a (subjective) right.[32] In
Chapter 4 Alexy considers the nature of subjective rights, and sets out a
taxonomy of constitutional rights.

The distinction between subjective rights and objective law takes on
practical significance in German constitutional doctrine as a result of
section 93(1) no. 4*a* Basic Law, which establishes the constitutional
complaint procedure.[33] This enables individuals who consider their constitutional rights to have been breached by a public authority (including a
court or the legislature) to seek review of the relevant act before the Federal
Constitutional Court. Such individuals have subjective constitutional rights
in the fullest possible sense. This protection is often contrasted with
'merely' objective constitutional law, which might impose duties on state
bodies, but which gives rise to no individual cause of action. Thus although
it is clear that constitutional rights norms impose certain duties on the state
with respect to foetuses, it is not clear that the foetus itself has subjective
rights, in the sense of a power to bring proceedings (by a next friend) to
enforce those duties.[34] The constitutional duty can only be enforced by
procedures allowing state organs such as the opposition party in Parliament
to test the constitutionality of legislation. Much of the debate about constitutional entitlements—protective rights, procedural rights, and social
rights—which Alexy considers at length in Chapter 9 concerns whether
they are rights in this sense, or only a matter of objective law.

The distinction between objective law and subjective rights is of the first
importance under the Human Rights Act, because Convention rights are
not unambiguously part of objective law. The only routes by which they
enter the legal system is by the obligation to interpret legislation compati-
bly with them so far as it is possible to do so (section 3(1)) and a rule
making it unlawful for public authorities to act incompatibly with them
(section 6(1)). On a 'subjectivist' reading, both the interpretative provision
of section 3 and the illegality provision of section 6 are all subject to the
victim test of section 7.[35] This means that only victims of breaches of rights
can argue for interpretations of legislation that are Convention rights-

---

[32] A problem which is still subject to vigorous jurisprudential debate. For the latest round,
see M. H. Kramer, N. E. Simmonds, and H. Steiner, *A Debate over Rights* (Oxford: Clarendon
Press, 1998).

[33] See Appendix; for a brief discussion of the procedural background, see J. Rivers,
'Stemming the Flood of Constitutional Complaints in Germany', PL 1994, 553.

[34] BVerfGE 39, 1; 88, 203. Note that one can still usefully talk about the constitutional
rights of the foetus, so long as one remembers that this right does not include a power to bring
enforcement proceedings.

[35] M. Supperstone and J. Coppel, 'Judicial Review after the Human Rights Act, EHRLR
1999, 301 at 308–9.

compatible or that acts of public authorities are unlawful; only they are Convention right-holders. On this account, the law has only been modified to the extent that there is a new overriding obligation not to breach subjective Convention rights. On an 'objectivist' reading, the correct interpretation of legislation or the lawfulness of an act of a public authority is a matter of general law, and so long as a party can surmount any procedural obstacles to get before a court, all Convention points can be raised and argued. This is the effect of the suggestion that as a public authority itself, a court has the duty to consider relevant Convention rights issues even if these are not raised by the parties.[36]

Both positions are problematic. To see section 3 as a *right* that all legislation be interpreted in a certain way would be an odd way to approach the problem of legal meaning. A statutory norm can only have one legal meaning; what that meaning is may be disputed—the linguistic meaning may be unclear—but the search is for *the* legal meaning.[37] The meaning of a statutory norm is a matter of objective law, and the issue of Convention-compatible interpretations can be raised *by anybody* whenever the meaning of a norm is in dispute. The idea that a norm might mean one thing when applied to one party and another when applied to another party breaches one of the most fundamental aspects of the principle of equality. On the other hand, if section 6 is objective law in the same sense, a party before the court in judicial review proceedings could argue that the executive act in question is unlawful not only because it infringes their own Convention rights, but also because it infringes quite different rights of somebody else. The attempt to exclude public interest groups from constitutional review proceedings may be retrograde given the current state of general administrative law,[38] but unless there is to be a subjective right to the Rule of Law there must be some limits to the (good) reasons individuals can give for

---

[36] Clayton and Tomlinson, *Law of Human Rights*, paras. 22.10–13. The authors appear not to draw the full implications of this at paras. 22.46–9. The important point is that standing for judicial review purposes cannot be considered in the abstract but only in relation to the matter to which the application relates (Supreme Court Act 1981 sect. 31(3) and *R v IRC ex p National Federation of Self-Employed and Small Businesses* [1982] AC 617). The issue is whether a party who is before the court for other reasons is permitted to argue a Convention point at all.

[37] Of course, the legal meaning will be expressed in a natural language, and the process of making connections between those words and the real world may not be reviewable. See *R v Hillingdon Borough Council ex p Puhlhofer* [1986] AC 484. In this context, the law–fact distinction can be explained by way of Frege's distinction between sense and reference. The legal meaning of a norm is its sense; how it relates to the real world is a matter of reference. See G. Frege, 'Sense and Reference', in P. Geach and M. Black (eds.), *Translations from the Philosophical Writings of Gottlob Frege* (Oxford: Blackwell, 1960).

[38] This is the effect of the 'victim test' under sect. 7(1). See I. Leigh and L. Lustgarten, 'Making Rights Real: the Courts, Remedies and the Human Rights Act', CLJ 58 (1999), 509 at 521–2. For various other critiques of the mismatch between Human Rights Act procedure and principles of ordinary administrative law, see D. Nicol, 'Limitation Periods under the Human Rights Act and Judicial Review', LQR 115 (1999), 216; D. B. Squires, 'Judicial Review of the Prerogative after the Human Rights Act', LQR 116 (2000), 572.

impugning acts of public authorities. In general, it is not unreasonable that
those reasons should be self-regarding.[39]

In German constitutional thought, the problem becomes particularly
acute in the context of the general right to liberty, which requires that all
norms limiting liberty in any way be constitutionally justifiable. This means
that in theory a person can seek review of practically any norm which
applies to them. This in turn raises the spectre of the *actio popularis*,
because in most cases, laws are only really constitutionally suspect because
they breach the specific rights of a few people. It would be easy to use the
general (subjective) right to liberty to overcome the procedural obstacles in
the way of complaining to the constitutional court, but then rest the
substance of one's complaint on the fact that the law is objectively unconstitutional because it breaches the rights of others. Alexy argues in Chapter
7 that a consideration of the constitutional rights of others must be
excluded in such a context. The purpose of the constitutional complaint
procedure is to vindicate the complainant's own rights, not objective constitutional law. In the British context, the obvious middle road between the
two extremes, which fits well with the structure of the Human Rights Act
in its close association of section 6 with section 7, is to suppose that the
interpretative provision of section 3 is the route by which the general law is
changed, while sections 6 to 9 make Convention rights enforceable as a
matter of subjective right alone. The purpose of these latter sections is to
enable victims of breaches of Convention rights to vindicate their own
rights, either by judicial review, or as a defence to civil or criminal proceedings taken against them.[40] However, none of this prejudices any existing
procedures to determine the general law as it is affected by section 3.[41]

Although attractive at first sight, even this solution is problematic. Such
a distinction between objective law and subjective rights would make the
precise route by which public law powers are 'read down' or rights 'read in'
crucial. If an apparently broad statutory power is interpreted less gener-
ously to be compatible with Convention rights, then anyone can raise the
issue, because it concerns the true legal meaning of the provision. If,
however, the public authority in question is only prevented legally from
making limited use of what is acknowledged to be a broad statutory power,
because of the need to respect the rights of potential victims, then the point
can only be raised by a victim of the broader use. This distinction is of no
practical significance where the public authority has made over-extensive

---

[39] On the question of appropriate tests of standing, see J. Miles, 'Standing under the Human
Rights Act 1998: Theories of Rights Enforcement and the Nature of Public Law Adjudication',
CLJ 59 (2000), 133.

[40] Gordon Nardell, 'Collateral Thinking: the Human Rights Act and Public Law Defences',
EHRLR 1999, 293.

[41] Clayton and Tomlinson, *Law of Human Rights*, paras. 22.46–9; Grosz *et al.*, *Human
Rights*, 87. See also Human Rights Act sect. 11.

use of its power to the detriment of a person's Convention rights. Either way, the person suffering detriment is a Convention rights victim. By contrast, it is of great significance if a public authority has made under-extensive use of its power to the detriment of another individual's, or even public body's, non-Convention interests, and if that person wants to argue in the course of ordinary judicial review proceedings that the authority was not required by Convention rights to act as cautiously as it thought it had to. It is not just victims who have an interest in raising Convention points. The procedural restrictions of the section 6 route may thus have an unjustifiable, and irremediable, chilling effect on public authorities.

A particular instance of the potentially irremediable chilling effect can be found in the relationship between Convention rights and the common law. This is usually treated as part of the problem of horizontal effect, which will be considered below. But common law is also to be found in non-private law contexts, common law criminal offences being the most conspicuous example. The fact that the Act does not expressly regulate the relationship between Convention rights and the common law is often overlooked. However, it would be bizarre if the Convention were not relevant to judge-made law at least to the same extent as to statute law. The most obvious way of extending Convention rights to the common law is by way of the section 6 duty on all public authorities (including courts) not to act incompatibly with Convention rights. Thus, if a common law criminal offence is incompatible with the Convention, it is unlawful for the Director of Public Prosecutions to bring a prosecution, and unlawful for the court to convict.[42] But if the only person who can 'rely' on the Convention right is a victim, the courts ought to refuse to review a decision of the DPP not to prosecute made in a mistaken belief about the impact of Convention rights on the criminal common law.[43] Since such a refusal is practically inconceivable,[44] the proposed distinction between sections 3 and 6 is unsustainable.

The only satisfactory solution is thus substantially an 'objectivist' interpretation whereby anyone can raise the correct interpretation of statute law, the effect of Convention rights on the common law, and their effect on discretionary powers of public authorities in the course of legal proceedings. Proceedings under section 7, with all their constraints, are thus a separate and distinct cause of action in addition to existing ones. The problem of the *actio popularis*, or subjective right to the Rule of Law, can be

---

[42] Although since the compatibility of the common law with Convention rights is likely to be uncertain, it may be appropriate for the DPP to bring a prosecution and allow the court to determine the question. See *R v DPP ex p Kebilene* [1999] 3 WLR 972.

[43] Unless, of course, the victim of the crime could find a protective right in the European Convention giving rise to a constitutional duty to prosecute.

[44] The House of Lords in *R v DPP ex p Kebilene* [1999] 3 WLR 972 at 983, had no doubt that judicial review was available in principle for failure to prosecute.

adequately addressed by the ordinary rules of standing in judicial review. In short, the better view of the correct balance between subjective rights and objective law under the Human Rights Act parallels the position set out in Chapter 7 below.

3. THE THEORY OF PRINCIPLES AND RULES

The heart of Alexy's thesis can be found in Chapter 3. In this chapter, he argues that rules are definitive norms, which if they are valid are to be followed precisely. By contrast, principles compete with each other as a result of their nature as optimization requirements. Principles are to be optimized, or realized to the greatest extent possible given empirical and normative constraints. One significant set of normative constraints is that of all other competing principles. This gives rise to the Law of Competing Principles, which can be stated as follows: 'The circumstances under which one principle takes precedence over another constitute the conditions of a rule which has the same legal consequences as the principle taking precedence'.[45] The judicial function is to establish the conditions under which one principle takes precedence over another. In establishing these conditions judges must seek to balance and optimize all the competing principles, and this requirement gives rise to the Law of Balancing: 'The greater the degree of non-satisfaction or limitation of one principle, the greater must be the importance of satisfying the other.'[46] This corresponds, in economic terms, to the law of diminishing marginal utility. However, it is important to note that constitutional rights norms are not just principles. They can contain rules as well, although the obligation to follow rules itself derives from underlying formal principles.

   A good example of the distinction between rules and principles can be found in the context of sections 12 and 13 Human Rights Act, which seek to address situations in which freedom of expression and collective aspects of freedom of thought, conscience, and religion respectively compete with other Convention rights. Sections 12(4) and 13(1), which require the court to have 'particular regard for the importance' of the right in question, increase the abstract weight of the underlying principles. Interference with such rights requires a correspondingly greater justification than would otherwise be the case.[47] By contrast, section 12(2) establishes a set of rules which are to be followed if a person's freedom of expression is likely to be

---

[45] 54.   [46] See 102 below.
[47] The view that these provisions are meaningless (see J. Wadham and H. Mountfield, *Blackstone's Guide to the Human Rights Act 1998* (London: Blackstone Press, 1999), 55), cannot be sustained in the light of the decision of the Court of Appeal in *Douglas v Hello! Ltd* [2001] 2 WLR 992.

affected: no relief is to be granted unless they are present or represented, or unless all practicable steps have been taken to notify them, or unless there are compelling reasons for not notifying them.[48]

The theory of principles has a number of more general consequences for the nature of constitutional rights which flow through the rest of the work. The most immediate is that the principle of proportionality as understood by the German Federal Constitutional Court follows logically from the nature of constitutional rights norms. Another consequence, which Alexy develops in more depth in Chapter 6, is that a wide conception of the scope of constitutional rights, which embraces all the reasons counting in favour of constitutional protection, and a correspondingly wide conception of limits, which embraces all the competing reasons,[49] are both analytically necessary consequences of the theory of principles and normatively preferable to alternative attempts to constrain the extent of constitutional rights. This latter consequence will be considered first.

3.1 THE SCOPE AND LIMITS OF CONVENTION RIGHTS

Rights protected under articles 8 to 11 European Convention are explicitly structured into an initial statement of the scope of a right, followed by a subsequent power to limit the enjoyment of the right in question. Such qualified rights can be contrasted with apparently unqualified rights, for example, the prohibition of torture in article 3, which appear simply to prohibit some acts and not others. As regards qualified rights, the European Court of Human Rights has shown a tendency to expand both the initial scope of the right and the reasons justifying limitation. Applications tend not to fail because they are excluded from the scope of the first paragraph, but because they are justified under the second.[50]

However, more interesting is the widening of both scope and limits in so-called unqualified Convention rights. A good example can be found in

---

[48] The last clause contains a term ('compelling reasons') which itself requires a balancing of principles. The rule is therefore structurally identical to the German constitutional human dignity norm discussed at 62 ff. below, in that it is a rule containing a term which is itself given content by reference to a balance of principles.

[49] At this point, it is worth clarifying the sense in which public goods, pursuit of which can justify the limitation of a right, are principles. The legislature is not obliged by the second paragraphs of qualified Convention rights to limit rights for the sake of such goods. In that sense they are not optimization requirements, or principles. However, in working out whether the legislature has acted disproportionately in pursuing a public good, one must treat them—like the rights they limit—as if they were optimization requirements. If the legislature has done more than it would be permitted to do were it *required* to optimize the enjoyment of public goods, then it has done more than it is permitted to do given that it is only *permitted* to optimize the enjoyment of public goods.

[50] See e.g. *Handyside v UK* A 24 (1976) (freedom of information applicable to any information or ideas); *Niemietz v Germany* A 251–B (1992) (privacy includes the right to establish and develop relationships with other human beings).

Kröcher & Möller v Switzerland.[51] Two convicted terrorists were held in
conditions which they argued were inhuman and degrading contrary to
article 3 European Convention. The Commission held that one could not
state whether conditions of imprisonment were inhuman and degrading in
the abstract, but only in the light of the special characteristics of the situation, the stringency of the measure, its duration, purpose, and effect on the
prisoner. On the facts, the measures adopted by the Swiss prison authorities
were justified by the security risk posed by the two terrorists. This means
that the evaluation of the conditions of punishment did not depend solely
on features intrinsic to that punishment. Rather conditions which would
have been inhuman and degrading when applied to an ordinary criminal,
ceased to be inhuman and degrading when justified by certain overriding
public interests. Thus we should think of article 3, in spite of its language,
as containing a scope of state action which is prima facie inhuman and
degrading, and limits justifying (or not) such action in particular cases.[52]

Some rights contain express exceptions or definition clauses, but exactly
the same process of simultaneous expansion of scope and limits can be
found in these contexts as well. A good example is article 4 and the question of whether certain conditions of service attached to membership of a
profession amount to 'forced or compulsory labour'. In *Van der Mussele v
Belgium,*[53] the European Court of Human Rights had to consider the terms
of service attached to pupil advocates. They evaluated them under the
rubric of hypothetical voluntariness: was the burden, 'so excessive or
disproportionate to the advantages attached to the future exercise of profession that the service could not be treated as having been voluntarily
accepted'?[54] Once again, some of the criteria seem to relate to the nature of
the work itself, such as the amount of time spent doing obligatory unpaid
advocacy and the experience gained in doing so, but others relate to good
public interest reasons for imposing the conditions, such as the availability
of cheap advocates. It seems appropriate to reconstruct article 4 as having
a wide scope. Specific professional conditions of service which are not
voluntarily accepted (except—from the perspective of the professional—as
an unnecessary prerequisite for gaining recognition) are prima facie
compulsory labour, but they may be justified by an implicit limiting clause,
referring to a wide range of public interests.[55]

If 'unqualified' rights appear at first to guarantee too much, then some
rights appear to guarantee too little. Articles 5(1) and 12 ECHR contain

---

[51] 34 DR 25 (1982).

[52] Other rights which appear absolute but which can be divided into scope and limits
include the presumption of innocence (art. 6(2) and *Salabiaku v France* 13 EHRR 379) and
the prohibition of discrimination (art. 14 and *Rasmussen v Denmark* A87 (1984)).

[53] A70 (1983).   [54] Ibid., at para. 37.

[55] Similar reasoning can be found in the context of the 'peaceful enjoyment of possessions'
(art. 1 First Protocol and *Sporrong & Lönnroth v Sweden* A52 (1982)).

rights which are subject to national law. In the case of article 5(1), lawful-ness of detention is determined by reference to procedural and substantive criteria, which include a consideration of whether the detention is 'arbi-trary'.[56] This enables a consideration of the purpose of the detention on grounds similar to the 'necessary in a democratic society' formula of arti-cles 8 to 11.[57] Similarly in the context of the right to marry under article 12, which is guaranteed 'according to the national laws governing the exer-cise of this right', the Commission has held that a complete restriction on prisoners' rights to marry in national law is unjustifiable.[58]

Thus at least as a rule of thumb it would seem that no Convention right is unqualified and no right fully at the disposal of national law. The expand-ing tendency of both the scope and the limits of Convention rights is consis-tent with the theory of principles, which requires all the reasons counting in favour of the court's intervention on behalf of a victim to be weighed against all the reasons for upholding the state action in question. Rights are only absolute or unqualified—Alexy would say, 'definitive'—once that process of balancing has been completed.[59]

3.2 PROPORTIONALITY

The theory of principles entails the 'principle'[60] of proportionality. In German public law, proportionality comprises three tests of suitability, necessity, and proportionality in the narrow sense. State action which limits the enjoyment of a right must be capable of achieving the end desired (suit-able), it must be the least restrictive means of doing so (necessary), and it must be justified given the 'cost' to the right in question (proportionate). Alexy argues that necessity is to be understood as the requirement to opti-mize the relevant principles in the light of what is empirically, or factually, possible, and that the test of proportionality in the narrow sense is to be understood as the requirement to optimize the relevant principles in the light of what is legally possible. Necessity asks whether any less intrusive means would achieve the same end, which is essentially an empirical ques-tion of prognosis and causation, and proportionality asks whether the end is worth pursuing, given what it necessarily costs. It is important to see that necessity and proportionality (in the narrow sense) are different tests: a measure may be the least intrusive means to achieve a certain end, and yet

---

[56] *Winterwerp v Netherlands* A33 (1979).

[57] D. J. Harris, M. O'Boyle, and C. Warbrick, *Law of the European Convention on Human Rights* (London: Butterworths, 1995), 105.

[58] *Hamer v UK* 24 DR 5 (1979); *Draper v UK* 24 DR 72 (1980).

[59] For a discussion of different models for the limitation of rights in the public interest, see A. McHarg, 'Reconciling Human Rights and the Public Interest: Conceptual Problems and Doctrinal Uncertainty in the Jurisprudence of the European Court of Human Rights', MLR 62 (1999), 671.

[60] It is really a set of rules. See 66 ff. below.

even the least intrusion necessary may be too high a price to pay in terms of the interference with other legally recognized interests.

The test of suitability can thus be subsumed under the test of necessity. Any state action which is necessary, in the sense of being the least intrusive means of achieving some end must, by definition, be capable of achieving the end in the first place. It has to be suitable. Nevertheless, the test of suitability serves a practical function as an initial filter. Any state action which is not even capable of achieving a given end is unlawful, regardless of the existence of other alternative means. The test of proportionality in the narrow sense also has its threshold counterpart. Proportionality presupposes that the state action in question be directed towards the pursuit of an end which is generally legitimate. If the end is illegitimate, then no limitation of any right is justifiable. So any state action which is proportionate in the narrow sense, that is, which correctly balances the gains achieved by the measure in question with the cost to other interests, must, by definition, pursue a legitimate end. If it did not, there would be no gains to offset the costs. In short, the entire principle of proportionality can be seen as consisting of two threshold requirements (pursuit of a legitimate end by an effective means) and two optimization requirements (the use of the least intrusive means to achieve something worth achieving given the costs involved).

Although it will use the language of necessity and proportionality, the case-law of the European Court of Human Rights is not entirely clear about what this entails, and the problem is compounded by the cultural variation permitted to states under the doctrine of the margin of appreciation, which can mask the point at which the balancing requirement should take place. For this reason, appeals are often made in the British literature to the Canadian case-law. But the leading Canadian decision of *R v Oakes*[61] is not as clear as it could be either. In discussing the general limiting clause contained in section 1 of the Canadian Charter of Rights and Freedoms, Dickson CJ insisted both that the objective pursued by the state be of 'sufficient importance to warrant overriding a constitutionally protected right or freedom', and that the principle of proportionality be satisfied. The first test already set a 'high standard'; it had to relate to concerns which are 'pressing and substantial in a free and democratic society'. Taken literally, this test seems to imply a degree of balancing, and its relationship to the final element of the proportionality test is uncertain. In practice however, the first element has not played a large role. In *R v Big M Drug Mart*,[62] the Supreme Court held that the purpose of upholding the Christian sabbath was not sufficiently important to justify infringing freedom of religion. This is the only case which has fallen at the first hurdle, and one could equally

[61] [1986] 1 SCR 103.   [62] [1985] 1 SCR 295.

say that it is not a legitimate governmental purpose at all.[63] So in practice the fourfold test in *Oakes* seems to be applied exactly in line with the scheme which has just been set out; Dickson CJ's first test is a threshold requirement, not a balancing requirement. However, in *de Freitas v Permanent Secretary of Ministry of Agriculture, Fisheries, Lands and Housing*,[64] the Privy Council failed adequately to replicate the fourfold structure of the *Oakes* test. The court had to consider whether restrictions on the freedom of expression of a civil servant in Antigua and Barbuda were 'reasonably justifiable in a democratic society'. After considering a South African case, which correctly summarized the Canadian position, Lord Clyde went on to adopt an analysis which amalgamated the third and fourth criteria, corresponding to the first three elements only of the Canadian test. Although the first criterion (sufficiently important objective) was correctly applied by the Privy Council as a simple threshold criterion, the amalgamated account of necessity/proportionality risks[65] missing out an important point: even the least intrusive means factually necessary to achieve an end which is desirable in principle may have costs which are unbearable on the facts of the case.

There can be little doubt that the two threshold requirements form part of the general principles of British public law. Administrative action that fails to pursue a legitimate end is illegal, vitiated by an improper motive or irrelevant consideration.[66] Likewise, action that is incapable of achieving the end desired would be Wednesbury unreasonable.[67] The debate about proportionality concerns whether the two optimization requirements are also part of public law. Here, explicit denial by the House of Lords[68] has to be balanced with implicit reliance in other cases,[69] along with the increasing

---

[63] Although preserving a common day of rest is: *R v Edwards Books and Art* [1986] 2 SCR 713.

[64] [1998] 3 WLR 675.

[65] The Court described the third element (necessity) as raising a question of proportionality, and held that the failure to distinguish different grades of civil servant meant that the law was unnecessarily restrictive. It is not clear whether this was because preventing the political speech of junior civil servants was not necessary to preserve the impartiality of the civil service (necessity) or because even if it did undermine impartiality to some extent that loss was preferable to preventing political participation (proportionality in the narrow sense).

[66] See e.g. *Congreve v Home Office* [1976] QB 629; *R v Ealing LBC ex p Times Newspapers* (1986) 85 LGR 316; *R v Lewisham LBC ex p Shell* [1988] 1 All ER 938.

[67] *Associated Provincial Picture Houses v Wednesbury Corporation* [1948] 1 KB 223.

[68] *CCSU v Minister for Civil Service* [1985] AC 374; *R v Home Secretary ex p Brind* [1991] 1 AC 696. But see now *R (Alconbury Developments Ltd) v Secretary of State for the Environment, Transport and the Regions* [2001] 2 WLR 1389 per Lord Slynn at 1407.

[69] To give just one example, it is hard to see how the refusal to renew the rugby club's licence in *Wheeler v Leicester City Council* [1985] AC 1054 was not in pursuit of a legitimate aim (improving race relations) and at least capable of achieving that end. It was, however, arguably neither a necessary nor a proportionate way of going about this. Thus the judgments in the Court of Appeal are more principled than those of the House of Lords, whether in their denial of relief (per Ackner LJ and Sir George Waller), or in their granting of review on grounds of breach of fundamental rights (per Browne-Wilkinson LJ).

impact of the existence of proportionality as part of European Community Law.[70] Writers understandably differ in their assessment of exactly how far acceptance has progressed.[71]

In the specific context of human rights, there is clear authority for the imposition of stricter standards on the exercise of executive discretion. But the discussion is not helped by a failure to distinguish carefully enough between three quite different issues. For example, one well-known statement of the obligation of public authorities in the human rights context is that of Sir Thomas Bingham MR in *R v Ministry of Defence ex parte Smith*:

> The court may not interfere with the exercise of an administrative discretion on substantive grounds save where the court is satisfied that the decision is unreasonable in the sense that it is beyond the range of responses open to a reasonable decision-maker. But in judging whether the decision-maker has exceeded this margin of appreciation the human rights context is important. The more substantial the interference with human rights, the more the court will require by way of justification before it is satisfied that the decision is reasonable in the sense outlined above.[72]

The problem with such statements, which is compounded by phrases such as 'anxious scrutiny',[73] 'sliding scale of review',[74] or 'intensity of review',[75] is that they risk confusing three issues. The first issue is the identification of the legal norms controlling the exercise of executive discretion. The second issue is the set of reasons which a public authority must have if it wishes to limit a constitutional right. The third issue is the role of the court in reviewing a public authority's decisions. The first issue—whether the norms of proportionality apply to the exercise of discretion—is not a matter of degree. Either they do or they do not. Alexy's argument is that they must apply, as a consequence of the nature of constitutional rights, and the tendency of recent British case-law is clearly also in this direction. As a result, the more intensively an act of a public authority interferes with constitutional rights, the greater must be the importance of the end being pursued by the authority. So the second issue—the reasons for interfering with constitutional rights—is a matter of degree, requiring proportionately greater reasons to justify proportionately greater interferences with consti-

[70] *Hauer v Land Rheinland-Pfalz* [1979] ECR 3727; *R v Minister for Agriculture, Fisheries and Food ex p Fedesa* [1990] ECR 4023.
[71] Cf. S. De Smith, H. Woolf, and J. Jowell, *Judicial Review of Administrative Action*, 5th edn. (London: Sweet & Maxwell, 1995), 600–6, with H. W. R. Wade and C. F. Forsyth, *Administrative Law*, 8th edn. (Oxford: Oxford University Press, 2000), 368–70.
[72] [1996] QB 517 at 554. The statement is counsel's, but was adopted by the Master of the Rolls as an 'accurate distillation' of previous case-law.
[73] *R v Home Secretary ex p Bugdaycay* [1987] AC 514 per Lord Bridge.
[74] *R (Mahmood) v Home Secretary* [2001] 1 WLR 840 per Laws LJ at para. 19.
[75] In *R (Daly) v Home Secretary* [2001] 2 WLR 1622, Lord Steyn seems to use 'intensity of review' to refer to the choice between Wednesbury standards of review and proportionality (at 1635–6). Laws LJ in *R (Mahmood) v Secretary of State for the Home Department* [2001] 1 WLR 840 at 848–9 uses it to refer to the strength of reasons needed to justify an infringement with a constitutional right.

tutional rights, in accordance with the Law of Balancing. The third issue is what the proper attitude of courts should be when faced with claims by public authorities (both executive and legislative) that their actions are indeed proportionate. Should the courts consider for themselves whether these claims are correct, or should they defer in some way to public authorities? It is this issue which is properly raised by the idea of 'intensity of review'. The robust answer is that disproportionate executive and legislative action is unlawful, and that the courts cannot assess the lawfulness of such action without engaging in a consideration of the balance of reasons implicit in the proportionality test for themselves. If constitutional rights are legal rights, the question is not whether a public authority reasonably believes that it is not breaching those rights, but whether they are actually being breached. However, concerns for a 'discretionary area of judgment'[76] linger on, and it is not clear at first sight how these can be reconciled with the principle of proportionality.

Much of the Postscript to this book is concerned with precisely this issue. Alexy points out that a certain amount of discretion is implicit within the structure of the proportionality test itself ('structural discretion'). For example, where two principles compete with each other, there is a range of permissible options, from serious interference justified by the protection of a very important interest, to minor interference justified by the protection of a minor interest. There is no way in which the principle of proportionality presupposes just one right answer where constitutional rights compete, and judicial deference to the democratically legitimated legislature requires respect for legislative choices. Furthermore, there will be cases in which it is not possible to tell whether elements of the test are satisfied ('epistemic discretion'). Here once again, judicial deference is required by a commitment to the formal principle of democratically legitimated legislation. But the extent of that deference is determined by the weight of the interests at stake. Uncertain empirical evidence is not a good ground for a serious interference with constitutional rights, although merely plausible evidence might be for a relatively trivial interference.

This argument can be extended in respect of executive decision-taking as well, although slightly different formal principles are at stake. The courts can accept that executive bodies might have greater expertise at the necessity stage (for example, prognosis of the likely impact of different courses of action), and legislative bodies at the stage of proportionality in the narrow sense, imposing stronger or weaker burdens of argumentation on

---

[76] See A. Lester and D. Pannick, *Human Rights: Law and Practice* (London: Butterworths, 1999), 74. Another term used is 'margin of discretion' (see Laws LJ in *R (Mahmood) v Home Secretary* at 855). This risks confusion with the European Court's doctrine of a margin of appreciation (see e.g. *Handyside v UK* (1976) A 24 paras. 48–9), which has no place in a single political community: see Clayton and Tomlinson, *Law of Human Rights*, paras. 6.82–4, *R v DPP ex p Kebilene* [1999] 3 WLR 972 at 993–4 (per Lord Hope).

those seeking to impugn the decision as is appropriate. In this way, it is possible to insist that all acts of all public authorities must be proportionate, but that the type of evidence and argument needed to prove this can be sensitive to the context and expertise of the decision-taker, and the weight of the interests at stake.[77]

4. HORIZONTAL, OR THIRD PARTY, EFFECT [*DRITTWIRKUNG*]

One of the most controversial elements of the Human Rights Act is the question of its horizontal effect. Do Convention rights apply to private law and bind private actors or not? The tendency in most of the literature is to set out a range of possible different forms of horizontal effect, and then to argue that the Act is best seen as establishing one or more of these forms.[78] Some of these forms of so-called horizontal effect are in reality unproblematic instances of vertical effect. The expansive definition of a public authority in section 6 Human Rights Act explicitly brings certain private bodies within a new definition of the state, and so the effect of Convention rights is, by definition, vertical. Furthermore, where private law courts exercise discretionary public power, either in their structuring of private law procedure, or in granting discretionary remedies, they are acting as organs of the state and effect is again unproblematically vertical. But this still leaves a range of questions: Does the requirement that all statutes be interpreted in line with Convention rights imply a form of horizontal effect? Is there a distinction between indirect effect, in which Convention rights only affect the interpretation of existing private law, and direct effect, in which Convention rights are held by one private individual against another? What is the relationship between protective duties and horizontal effect?

Alexy's thesis at this point is striking. In the context of the German legal system, there is, he argues in Chapter 10, a single phenomenon of horizontal effect. Different constructions, such as direct horizontal effect favoured by the Federal Labour Court and indirect horizontal effect favoured by the Federal Constitutional Court, are outcome-neutral, in the sense that the same outcome can be reached whichever account of horizontal effect one adopts. There might be some reason for thinking that this argument is restricted to German law. The German Civil Code has general clauses which

---

[77] *Brown v Stott* [2001] 2 WLR 817 at 842 (per Lord Steyn). See also on this point, D. Pannick, 'Principles of Interpretation of Convention Rights under the Human Rights Act and the Discretionary Area of Judgment', PL 1998, 545; R. Singh, M. Hunt, and M. Demetriou, 'Is there a Role for the "Margin of Appreciation" in National Law after the Human Rights Act?' EHRLR 1999, 15; and in the context of EC law, G. de Búrca, 'The Principle of Proportionality and its Application in EC Law', YBEL 13 (1993),105.

[78] The best account of this type is I. Leigh, 'Horizontal Rights, the Human Rights Act and Privacy: Lessons from the Commonwealth', ICLQ 1999, 57.

can be used to protect the values underlying constitutional rights. Not only is the fulfilment of all private obligations subject to requirements of 'good faith',[79] but the basic tort provision[80] is open in the interests it protects.[81] The Human Rights Act has none of this. However, Alexy's argument is independent of these contingent features of private law and it is equally valid in the British context.

The case against the Human Rights Act having any sort of horizontal effect is stronger than is often assumed. The mere fact that all statutes must be interpreted in conformity with Convention rights and that courts are public authorities for the purposes of the Act does not necessarily create any form of horizontal effect. It all depends on the content of the rights in question.[82] Constitutional rights are primarily defensive rights; they impose (negative) duties on the state not to affect individuals in certain ways. If an individual makes use of private liberty in a way which adversely affects somebody else, the state has not breached its own duty not to affect the victim. Of course, private liberty is hedged about with a 'protective perimeter' of rights and duties. But even if the state creates and upholds this protective perimeter, that fact alone does not implicate the state in the use of liberty either.[83] In Alexy's example, even assuming that one person's smoking infringes his neighbour's constitutional right to bodily integrity, enforcing the law of assault, which protects the smoker from the non-smoker's violent attempts to prevent him smoking, does not make the state responsible for the violation of the non-smoker's bodily integrity through the act of smoking.[84] If one wants to make the state responsible for failing to do something to protect the non-smoker, one has to assume that Convention rights are protective rights, or positive state duties to take certain forms of action to protect private individuals from each other.

It is true that in a limited set of circumstances, defensive rights can give rise to horizontal effect. Where private law imposes duties on individuals which restrict their constitutionally guaranteed liberties, then those private law duties (and the corresponding private law rights) are unconstitutional, since the state, in the form of the private law legislature and private law courts, has illegitimately affected citizens, albeit only potentially and indirectly. For example, suppose the private law of defamation to be overly restrictive of freedom of speech. The state has created a private law cause of action which implies a duty not to speak in circumstances which are constitutionally protected. That breaches freedom of speech as a defensive

---

[79] § 242 Civil Code.   [80] § 823 Civil Code.

[81] In effect this gives rise to a tort of breach of constitutional duty, as, apparently, in Ireland: see *Meskell v Coras Iompair Éireann* [1973] IR 121 and the brief discussion in M. Hunt, 'The Horizontal Effect of the Human Rights Act', PL 1998, 423 at 428–9.

[82] Correctly, in this respect, Sir Richard Buxton, 'The Human Rights Act and Private Law', LQR 116 (2000), 48 at 50, 56.

[83] See below at 304 ff.   [84] See below at 307.

right against the state. By contrast, suppose that the private law of defamation is non-existent in a way which fails to respect privacy rights. There is therefore a liberty to defame people where there should be none. By failing to create an appropriate cause of action, the state has not breached any defensive right—one cannot breach defensive rights by doing nothing—it can only have breached a protective right to give causes of action to private individuals to protect their privacy from third parties who breach it. Thus the most that the defensive right construction of horizontal effect can do is to *remove* private law causes of action which restrict constitutionally protected interests. Since most issues of horizontal effect concern attempts to restrict the private liberty of others by binding private power to the same standards as public power, and thus in practice *expanding* private law causes of action, the defensive right route to horizontal effect does not have much relevance.[85]

However, Convention rights are not simply defensive rights that the state refrain from doing certain nasty things to its citizens. They are also protective rights that the state protect its citizens from the nasty things other citizens do to them. Even this is not entirely conclusive of the matter, since most commentators locate the protective aspect of Convention rights in article 1,[86] which is not included in the Human Rights Act. However, the better view must be that each substantive right contains defensive and protective elements.[87] Again, the state is necessarily given a certain discretion in how it protects its citizens. There are more ways of positively protecting a person than of negatively refraining from injuring them.[88] One could argue that the protective duty can always be fulfilled through criminal and other public law measures. There might be no need to achieve protection through structuring private law. But the case-law of the European Court of Human Rights gives rise to a few situations in which structuring private law is so obviously the best way of protecting citizens that it is required by Convention rights. The illegality of closed shop agreements in *Young, James and Webster v UK*[89] is a good example. Thus if there is a risk that the principles underlying Convention rights are threatened by private actors, and if a certain structuring of private law is a good way of reducing that risk, then the legislature is under a duty to pass appropriate legislation and the courts are under a duty at least to interpret legislation and shape the common law in that way. Protective duties give rise, at least, to indirect horizontal effect.

Murray Hunt has argued that prohibiting the courts from enforcing

---

[85] But it does explain why the US Supreme Court, which is generally hostile to horizontal effect, could decide the way it did in *New York Times v Sullivan* (1964) 376 US 254 11 L.Ed. 2nd 686, which *removed* a putative private law cause of action.

[86] See e.g. Harris *et al.*, *Law of the European Convention*, 21–2.

[87] See the discussion of protective rights below.

[88] See below at 308.   [89] A44 (1981).

private law rights where they would infringe constitutional rights of the other party is a stronger version of indirect horizontal effect which falls short of direct horizontal effect.[90] Following the dissenting judgment of Kriegler J in *Du Plessis v De Klerk*[91] he argues that private individuals are not bound to respect Convention rights in their relations with each other, but that they cannot call the law in aid to support their unconstitutional behaviour. Thus, assuming that it is a breach of Convention rights for an all-male golf club to exclude women, the golf club is not obliged to admit women, but they could not use the law to exclude one who succeeded in gaining access.[92] This argument is deeply problematic.[93] According to Hunt, the club has no duty to admit the woman applicant to membership and she therefore has no right of entry. However, if she succeeds in gaining entry, the club has no right to deprive her of physical use and possession of club property. This trades on an ambiguity in the concept of a 'right of entry'. Non-members have a duty not to enter club premises; they would be trespassers. But if the woman physically gains entry she also gains a liberty to use the premises (the correlative, in Hohfeld's terms, of the club's no-right to stop her using the premises:[94] a liberty to use must include a liberty to enter). But a liberty to enter is the opposite of a duty not to enter, so by her physical act of entry the woman has created for herself a liberty in place of a duty with identical content. Since there is no practical distinction between a liberty all the time, and a liberty which one only has when one exercises it,[95] we can say not only that she has a liberty to enter whenever she enters, but that she has the liberty to enter *tout court*. Thus Hunt's example contains a logical contradiction. He is asserting both that the woman applicant has no liberty to enter and that she has a liberty to enter. If she has no liberty, her non-discrimination rights have not had any effect on her private law relationship with the club; if she has the liberty, they have removed the club's liberty, replacing it with a no-right, which is directly effective on her private rights.

Hunt also trades on a dangerous distinction between the woman applicant's liberty to enter and use club property and her right to membership. If she only has a liberty to use, this can lawfully be thwarted by the club's taking appropriate physical precautions. The only difference is that the club cannot legally complain when she in turn uses physical force to surmount

---

[90] M. Hunt, 'The Horizontal Effect of the Human Rights Act' PL 1998, 423. For a critique on different grounds see G. Phillipson, 'The Human Rights Act, "Horizontal Effect" and the Common Law: A Bang or a Whimper?' MLR 62 (1999), 824.

[91] 1996 (3) SA 850. The majority accepted only indirect horizontal effect.

[92] At 442.

[93] Sir William Wade candidly confessed he could not follow the example: 'Horizons of Horizontality', LQR 116 (2000), 217 at 222.

[94] Alexy amply demonstrates the value of Hohfeld's analysis in the course of Chapter 4.

[95] One cannot avoid exercising liberties both to φ and ~φ all the time; here we are only interested in her liberty to enter (φ), which she does not exercise by not entering (~φ).

those obstacles. The club has the right to lock the doors, but no right to sue if she breaks them down. What the woman applicant really wants—and needs if the situation is not to collapse into a trial of brute force—is a *right* to membership which imposes a *duty* on the club to let her in. If Convention rights are only defensive rights, they may prevent the state from giving private individuals rights to exclude trespassers in discriminatory circumstances, but they cannot require the state to give any rights to other private individuals suffering discrimination. To achieve this, Convention rights must also be protective rights, or rights that the state take positive action to protect private individuals from each other. As we have seen, they are at least capable of giving rise to such protective rights, so if constitutional principles indicate that the woman applicant has at least a liberty to use club premises, commitment to the Rule of Law would indicate that she must also have a right to membership.

Thus the various types of horizontal effect collapse into a distinction between indirect and one specific form of direct effect. The interpretation of private law statutes and the development of the common law are required consequences of the state's protective duties arising from constitutional rights. These give rise to new private law rights between private individuals, and the effect is in that sense direct. The only remaining difference is that under the Human Rights Act, there is no new private law cause of action purely for breach of constitutional rights. How significant is this? Indirect horizontal effect is clearly constrained by formal principles. Most obviously, the principles of legal clarity, democratic legitimacy, and legislative intent constrain the extent to which statute law can be interpreted to give effect to Convention rights. Likewise, the development of the common law is constrained above all by a requirement of legal certainty. Even if private law needs reworking to express better the balance of constitutional principles, that reworking may be too far removed from the existing state of private law to count as 'interpretation' or legitimate development. A specific statutory cause of action for breach of constitutional rights by private individuals would have removed these formal constraints by opening up the private law to any new content. So the key question concerns the nature of the relationship between the substantive principles indicating a new content to private law, and the formal principles constraining development. If one takes the view that in certain circumstances formal principles can never be outweighed by substantive ones, then there is a real difference between direct and indirect horizontal effect. Some private law developments will simply not be 'possible'. However, if one takes the view that formal and substantive principles are equally ranked in the abstract, the question of whether recognizing a radical change to existing private law is 'possible' depends on how substantively important that change is. On the first view, for example, the judicial creation of a tort of privacy must be left to Parliament, because it represents too ambitious a development; on the second view, the judiciary could develop a new tort, if there were circumstances in which the protection of privacy was so important that it outweighed not only competing substantive principles, such as freedom of expression, but also competing formal principles, such as the consistent application of existing private law. It is clear that Alexy takes the latter position, as is implied by his account of the Law of Competing Principles, which denies hard abstract rankings, and by his caveat that statutory interpretations *contra legem* must be possible for his argument about the collapse of indirect into direct horizontal effect to work.[96] In reality, since constitutional principles indicate, at best, only a modification of existing private law within the scope of statutory interpretation and common law development, the distinction between direct and indirect horizontal effect becomes practically irrelevant.[97]

5. THE GENERAL RIGHT TO LIBERTY

In spite of some controversy, the Federal Constitutional Court has maintained its long-standing position that the German Basic Law contains a general right to liberty, making the substantive extent of constitutional rights protection in this respect as wide as it can be. In Chapter 7, Alexy considers the nature of this right. The right is useful in two respects. As a general right, subsidiary to specific liberty rights, it requires the justification of all state infringements of liberty. State action which cannot be brought within the scope of a specific express liberty right can still be reviewed. In assessing the weight of the interest in liberty as against other interests, the Court has recourse to the concept of human dignity, protected in article 1 Basic Law. The Federal Constitutional Court has thus incorporated a dynamic element into the protection of constitutional rights, enabling the protection of new interests not expressly identified by the makers of the Constitution.[98] So the Constitution contains both express specific liberties and implied specific liberties. Examples of the latter include the rights to privacy, confidentiality, and intimacy, the right of personal reputation, the right to control the representation of one's own person, and the right to one's own picture and spoken word.[99]

---

[96] See below at 357.

[97] Thus in *Venables v News Group Newspapers Ltd* [2001] 2 WLR 1038, Dame Elizabeth Butler-Sloss P reworked the tort of breach of confidence in the light of competing constitutional principles to grant novel injunctions against newspapers to protect two vulnerable ex-prisoners.

[98] But only in its liberty-enhancing aspect. Feldman's concerns about the liberty-reducing potential of the concept of dignity do not therefore apply in the German context. See id., 'Human Dignity as a Legal Value—Part I', PL 1999, 682 at 699–702.

[99] See 242 below.

It has been argued that the common law, while protecting specific liberties, does not give any weight to liberty in general.[100] Liberty is residual, in
the sense that what is not prohibited is permitted, but when liberty comes
into conflict with other values it has no weight apart from its association
with a more concrete interest. The mere fact that liberty has been limited
gives rise to no need for justification. The debate about the weight (if any)
of general liberty is considered by Alexy in Chapter 7. The answer which
he gives, and it is equally applicable in the British context, is that general
liberty has weight *in connection with* other principles. In the context of the
German Constitution, the single most significant other principle is 'human
dignity' found in article 1(1) Basic Law. But the point is that any restriction
of liberty still requires justification, although the success of that justification
depends on the weight of competing specific interests. The residual nature
of general liberty is thus not merely an analytical truth (that which is not
forbidden must be permitted); on its own it already creates a reason against
the restriction in question.[101]

The protection of a general right to liberty is not only useful, it is also
necessary once one accepts that constitutional rights have horizontal effect.
Horizontal effect is characterized by the fact that the parties have private
rights derived from the constitution against each other. The commonest
situation discussed in the UK has involved one party's privacy rights
competing with another party's freedom of expression rights, but it is
largely fortuitous that both interests can be found in the Convention. Most
of private law involves interests only partly expressed in Convention
rights.[102] One might be able to read the right to peaceful enjoyment of
possessions in First Protocol article 1 widely enough to grant a general right
to property, but it is hard to locate freedom of contract in the Convention,
for example. One obvious difficulty that this gives rise to is in employment
law. If an employer wishes to impose constraints on what employees wear,
or say, in the course of their employment, it is easy enough to find a
Convention right protecting the interests of the employee, but where do we
locate the competing interests of the employer? It would be hard to argue
that employers have no legitimate interests at all in this respect. Some
progress can be made by way of an expansive reading of Convention rights.
Article 8 is a particularly rich ground for the development of implied
specific liberty rights such as those recognized by the Federal Constitutional
Court over the years.[103] But there are limits to this approach, which mean

[100] See the discussion in T. R. S. Allan, *Law, Liberty and Justice* (Oxford: Clarendon Press,
1993), 135–43.
[101] See Allan, *Law, Liberty and Justice*, 139. The Dworkinian distinction between limitable
general rights and specific anti-utilitarian ones is questionable. All abstract rights are limitable.
Once they have been limited, they give rise to definitive (illimitable, 'anti-utilitarian') rights.
[102] I. Leigh, 'Horizontal Rights, the Human Rights Act and Privacy: Lessons from the
Commonwealth', ICLQ 1999, 57 at 73.
[103] See Feldman, 'Human Dignity as a Legal Value', 694–5.

that important elements of the political morality of private law are unprotected by the Convention.

Although the problem is not much discussed in the literature, there appear to be two potential solutions under the Human Rights Act itself, but both are unsatisfactory. The first solution points out that Convention rights are not unlimited, but may be limited to protect all sorts of legitimate interests, including the 'rights and freedoms of others'.[104] This solution is unsatisfactory because it transfers conditions for the limitation of rights from state actors to private actors. This is particularly inappropriate in the case of procedural constraints, such as 'according to law'. It is one thing to require that a state wishing to limit a right does so by law that is sufficiently clear and precise, quite another to require that a private individual, who has no control over the law-making process, should do the same. The other solution considers that it might be possible to contract out of protection from constitutional rights. This may reach the right outcome, but involves a certain doctrinal sleight of hand. No plausible contracting-out theory is going to permit people to contract out of rights in their entirety. It will have to determine which elements of constitutional rights protection can be contracted-out of, and which not. Those limits will be set by the strength of the interests of both parties, so it will necessarily involve a balancing exercise between substantive rights on each side. Consent is only one relevant factor.

It is suggested that the most fruitful place to locate competing interests within private law is in the concept of common law constitutional rights. The courts have long been willing to recognize that the common law protects certain rights as constitutional, and the status of these rights is broadly similar to rights protected under the Human Rights Act. Most importantly, they indicate a narrow interpretation of limiting statutes. Moreover, although there is some overlap with Convention rights, such as rights of personal liberty,[105] access to justice,[106] freedom of expression,[107] and freedom of association,[108] common law constitutional rights have a markedly private law bias. Rights to property[109] and freedom of contract[110] are clearly protected. One only needs to accept a willingness on the part of the common law to recognize and give weight to new threats to private liberty in order for it to be appropriate to conceptualize the common law as containing both a general right to liberty and certain specific liberties. The structural similarity between common law rights and

---

[104] See arts. 8(2), 9(2), 11(2), and, to similar effect, 10(2) European Convention.
[105] *R v Home Secretary ex p Khawaja* [1984] AC 74.
[106] *R v Lord Chancellor ex p Witham* [1998] QB 575.
[107] *Derbyshire CC v Times Newspapers* [1993] AC 534.
[108] *Beatty v Gillbanks* (1882) 9 QBD 308.
[109] *Entick v Carrington* (1765) 19 St Tr 1030; *Burmah Oil v Lord Advocate* [1965] AC 75.
[110] *Mixnams v Chertsey UDC* [1965] AC 446.

Convention rights is only broad, because there are probably fewer procedural limitations on the ability to invoke common law rights, but the remedies are more restricted. For example, it is unlikely that the courts will feel able to grant declarations of incompatibility in respect of statutes which disproportionately limit common law constitutional rights, at least in the near future. But these rights are not to be treated *as a matter of substantive law* as having any different status from Convention rights. On the facts of different cases they may take precedence or not, as determined by the Law of Competing Principles.

This means that when considering the impact of Convention rights on, for example, employment law or family law, the courts ought to take into account the opposing common law constitutional rights of parties.[111] The impact of Convention rights is constrained not only formally, by the requirement to interpret statute and develop the common law incrementally, but also substantively, by the common law's constitutional commitment to the private liberty of the citizen. Convention rights do not take precedence over common law rights in the abstract. Rather, the function of the courts in accordance with the Law of Competing Principles, is to establish the conditions under which now one, now the other, takes precedence. In this process the general right to liberty establishes a prima facie reason against limiting an individual's existing private law rights. But it is only a prima facie reason, and it may be outweighed. That process of balancing requires the court to assign a weight to general liberty which is determined by general and specific features of the case. In that process, the contours of more precise liberties, such as freedom of contract, will become apparent.

6. THE GENERAL RIGHT TO EQUALITY

The counterpart to a general right to liberty is a general right to equality. This too is an accepted part of German constitutional rights jurisprudence. In Chapter 8, Alexy argues that the general right to equality protected in the German Constitution should be understood in terms of two rules,

> If there is no adequate reason for permitting an instance of differential treatment, then similar treatment is required;
> If there is an adequate reason for requiring differential treatment, then differential treatment is required.[112]

The question is how this relates to the European Convention's protection of equality and to traditional British conceptions of discrimination.

---

[111] A good example in which the principles of testamentary and religious liberty took precedence over that of non-discrimination can be found in *Blathwayt v Lord Cawley* [1976] AC 397.

[112] At page 271 f. below.

In understanding the Convention right to equality, it is important to distinguish between the scope of an equality right and the criteria by which discrimination is prohibited. Article 14 ECHR only prohibits discrimination in 'the enjoyment of the rights and freedoms set forth in this Convention'. In practice, the Court has expanded the scope of article 14 beyond the narrow confines of each specific right. Thus article 14 prevents discrimination in the statutory limitation of rights and within the broader 'ambit' of a right.[113] In *Abdulaziz, Cabales and Balkandali v UK*,[114] the applicants claimed on the basis of sex discrimination in the UK's immigration law. While the Convention contains no right to immigrate, the fact that the applicants were claiming in respect of spouses wishing to enter the UK brought them within the ambit of article 12 (right to family life), and thus permitted the Court to consider the discrimination. This may be justifiable enough on pragmatic grounds, but in principle it is objectionable, because the applicants' marital status was irrelevant to the substance of their claim, which was that immigration law drew an unjustifiable distinction between men and women. The only function of the ambit test is to allow the Court to consider, or refuse to consider, alleged discrimination, and the boundaries of this jurisdiction are essentially arbitrary. For this reason, Protocol no. 12 prohibits discrimination in the enjoyment of 'any right set forth by law'.[115] Of course, even this has a limited scope: it is not intended to cover the use of purely private liberty.[116] But at least the arbitrariness of the current application of article 14 will be avoided. Regardless of the precise scope of equality, both article 14 and Protocol no. 12 are general in the criteria by which discrimination is prohibited. The list of characteristics is exemplary only, containing those which are particularly common and objectionable as bases of discrimination.[117] In this respect, the Convention right to equality is general, not specific, and this has significant consequences for its structure.

In the British context, discrimination is usually discussed in terms of direct, indirect, or positive discrimination. The words 'discrimination' and 'equality' are ambiguous, referring both to the mere fact of difference (or similarity) of treatment and also to unjustified difference (or justified similarity, or indeed justified difference) of treatment. The descriptive and normative components need to be carefully distinguished. Direct discrimination becomes an issue when a norm expressly draws a distinction

---

[113] See already *Belgian Linguistics Case* A6 (1968) at para. 33; *Rasmussen v Denmark* A87 (1984) at para. 29

[114] A94 (1985).

[115] This protocol opened for signature on 4 Nov. 2000. The British Government unfortunately, and, as will appear below, unjustifiably, appears to have no interest in signing.

[116] See the Explanatory Report, para. 28.

[117] See the words at the end of art. 14, 'or other status' (French: *sans distinction aucune*), and see *Salgueiro da Silva Mouta v Portugal* appl. no. 33290/96, 21 Dec. 1999, for an example of discrimination on a criterion not listed in art. 14 (sexual orientation).

between two classes of people. The question is then whether such a distinction is justifiable. There are many different ways of justifying the drawing of distinctions even against suspect criteria. Sub-cultural homogeneity may be one—Chinese restaurants are allowed to discriminate in favour of Chinese waiters, for example[118]—and there are others. Indirect discrimination is usually defined as arising when a norm does not draw a distinction between two classes of people, but which when applied has a differential impact in fact on two classes of people. The stock example is the obligation of motorcycle riders to wear helmets, which impacts differentially on Sikhs. In fact, most cases of indirect discrimination[119] reaching the courts have been different and more complex. In *R v Employment Secretary ex parte Equal Opportunities Commission*,[120] the House of Lords assumed that there was indirect discrimination in the fact that part-time workers (who are mostly women) had fewer employment rights than full-time workers (who are mostly men). This consists of a combination of direct discrimination between full-time and part-time workers which also has a differential impact on men and women, because of the relative proportions of each gender among each type of employee. The difference between the Sikh-motorcycle helmet situation and the EOC case is that in the former a general law *fails to draw* a distinction between classes of people, which failure makes life harder for one class, but in the latter the law *does draw* a distinction which *in addition* has a differential impact on two classes of people, differently defined. It is worth calling the EOC type of discrimination 'implicit direct discrimination', rather than indirect discrimination, since men and women are in law being treated differently, although one needs statistical evidence to show this. The difference of treatment is only implicit, not express.

Instances of implicit direct discrimination can always be considered from two perspectives. From the direct perspective, what matters is the differentiation drawn by the law, and it matters particularly because of the additional differential impact on classes defined by suspect criteria (sex, race, etc.). From an indirect perspective, the differential impact on classes defined by suspect criteria is at the forefront of consideration, but this still cannot avoid assuming that the explicit differentiation is also suspect. No one sees implicit discrimination in the fact that the male to female ratio among motorcycle riders is higher than among car drivers, thus making the helmet rule impact more harshly on men than women. The reason we do not see this is that applying the helmet rule only to motorcycle riders, and not to car drivers, is obviously justified. But structurally this is as much an

[118] See Race Relations Act 1976 sect. 5(2)(*c*).
[119] Above all on grounds of sex and race, although see now Council Directive 2000/78/EC of 27 Nov. 2000 (OJ L 303/16) establishing a general framework for equal treatment in employment and occupation.
[120] [1995] 1 AC 1.

instance of (potential) implicit discrimination as differential treatment of full and part-time workers. If it were obvious that full-time and part-time employees should have different employment rights, we would not even spot the gender discrimination. Because the current law prohibits indirect discrimination on grounds of sex and race, but contains no general prohibition on direct discrimination, some cases which are litigated are really a rather artifical means of attempting to remedy direct discrimination which would otherwise go unremedied. For example, a government minister appoints one of his friends as an adviser and a potential woman appointee threatens to sue on grounds of indirect sex discrimination, because his friends are more likely to be male than female.[121] The allegation here is principally one of direct discrimination, with the gender dimension being secondary only. The adoption of Protocol no. 12 would allow such claims to be considered on their proper basis.

Positive discrimination is simply one form of direct differentiation which is justified by appeal to the factual similarity it achieves. Although normally restricted to the conferring of benefits, there is no reason why it should not also cover the exemption from obligations as well. Creating an exception for Sikhs who wish to ride motorcycles without helmets is thus as much positive discrimination as preferring one for a job over an otherwise better qualified non-Sikh would be.

The key concepts are thus on one hand difference and similarity of treatment, and on the other differences/similarities on the face of the law, and those caused by the application of the law. The latter pair of concepts can be called legal and factual differences/similarities respectively.[122]

Thus Alexy's two rules of general equality can be recast in more familiar language as follows:

(Prohibition of direct discrimination) If there is no adequate reason for permitting the law expressly to draw a distinction between two classes of people, then it must not draw that distinction;

(Right to positive discrimination) If there is an adequate reason for requiring the law expressly to draw a distinction between two classes of people, then it is required to do so.

This contains a bias against direct differentiation, since it is easier to show that there is no reason for *permitting* an express differentiation than it is to show that there is a positive constitutional reason for *requiring* one. It also shows that the general right to equality contains no bias against indirect discrimination. The reason for this lies both in the open-ended nature of the factual consequences of legal norms, and also in the fact that a general right to equality prohibits discrimination *on any ground*. No norm which appears to treat two or more people in the same way actually treats them

---

[121] See *Lord Chancellor v Coker*, *The Times*, 23 Jan. 2001, EAT.

[122] See below at 276 ff.

in the same way, because their life circumstances are different. Every person will experience the same legal obligation as more or less onerous depending on their character, resources, and so on. If the right to equality required all indirect differentiation to be justified, this would make norms treating two people identically as constitutionally suspect as norms expressly distinguishing between them. Not only would that destroy the 'equality bias' of the right to equality, it would be tantamount to a requirement that the factual consequences of every legal norm be justified in a process of constitutional review, in short, that the law be just so and not different. There cannot be a general right to protection from indirect discrimination.

However, from what has been said above, it should be clear that this neither excludes implicit direct discrimination from the scope of a general equality right, nor does it say that a specific equality right, such as racial equality, could not treat indirect differentiation in the same way as direct differentiation.[123] One could even derive a set of specific equality rights prohibiting indirect discrimination on certain criteria from a general equality provision such as article 14 ECHR. The point is simply that the general right to equality does not necessarily require this.

7. CONSTITUTIONAL ENTITLEMENTS

In spite of all the developments of the past fifty years, German constitutional rights are still first and foremost liberties, or defensive rights against the state. They set limits to what the state may do. Nevertheless, the Federal Constitutional Court has developed various other types of right on the basis of the Constitution, which can loosely be called positive rights or entitlements, since they require the state to take positive action to fulfil them. In Chapter 9, Alexy discusses the nature of such entitlements under a threefold division into protective rights, organizational and procedural rights, and what could be called rights to services, entitlements in the narrow sense, or social rights.

As has been demonstrated, the first group of entitlements, rights that the state protect individuals from the actions of other non-state actors, is of particular significance to the question of horizontal effect, although their impact is not limited to the private law sphere. The acceptance of protective rights is clearly established in the case-law of the European Court of Human Rights. The protective aspects of Convention rights can impose obligations as regards the exercise of executive discretion,[124] the structure

---

[123] Although the law accepts that indirect differentiation is easier to justify than direct differentiation: cf. sect. 1(1)(*a*) with 1(1)(*b*) of both the Sex Discrimination Act 1975 and the Race Relations Act 1976.
[124] *Plattform Ärzte für das Leben v Austria* A139 (1988) (lack of police protection of demonstrators a potential breach of art. 11).

of criminal procedure,[125] the content of criminal law,[126] and, as we have seen, the content of private law obligations[127] as well. It is by definition harder to demonstrate a breach of protective rights, since states always have a choice of means as to how they go about protecting private individuals from each other, but this has not prevented the Court from finding a breach in appropriate circumstances. As has already been indicated, the precise location of the protective aspect of rights in the Convention is controversial. Some have found it in article 1, which obligates states party to the Convention to 'secure' the rights to everyone, and which is omitted from the Human Rights Act 1998. Article 1 either adds something to the nature of Convention rights or it does not. One could take the view that Convention rights are interests not intrinsically binding on anybody, which article 1 then makes binding on the state, requiring the state both to respect those interests itself and to ensure that they are adequately respected by other private individuals. If this view is correct, by omitting article 1, the Human Rights Act has no legal effect at all. So each Convention right must be at least intrinsically a defensive right and article 1 is in that respect simply declaratory. If one still wants to argue that the protective aspect of Convention rights is only *added* by article 1, one has to recognize that article 1 then has two fundamentally different meanings depending on the type of right in question, declaratory in respect of defensive aspects, constitutive in respect of protective aspects. Since that would be very odd, it is better to assume that if Convention rights are protective rights at all (and they are), they are so intrinsically and not by virtue of article 1. They thus apply under the Human Rights Act as well.

The procedural nature of Convention rights is also well established. Conor Gearty has argued that Convention rights are to be seen primarily as procedural in nature and that ' "due process" is the core unifying concept in the Convention and its case-law'.[128] One can remain agnostic about this thesis and still accept the importance of procedural rights as one element of Convention rights. For example, there is nothing to stop the British judiciary developing individual media participation rights on the basis of article 10 ECHR *in addition* to its substantive guaranteeing of freedom of expression in a negative sense.[129] Recent German experience shows that in many complex cases, a procedural solution may be the only practicable way

---

[125] *X and Y v Netherlands* A91 (1985) (lack of standing to complain of criminal behaviour a breach of art. 8).

[126] *A v United Kingdom* 1998–VI, 2692 (lack of effective criminal sanction for corporal punishment by a stepfather a breach of art. 3).

[127] *Young, James and Webster v UK* A44 (1981).

[128] 'The European Court of Human Rights and the Protection of Civil Liberties: an Overview', CLJ 52 (1993), 89.

[129] The Court has accepted that rights can be protected through procedure; see e.g. *Johansen v Norway*, 1996–III, 979. However, this does not preclude a review of the substantive compatibility of the outcome, a conclusion with which Alexy would concur. See below at 328.

of protecting constitutional rights. In this light it is instructive to note the partial procedural solution to the balancing of privacy and freedom of expression adopted in section 12(2) Human Rights Act.

Finally, it is usually assumed that the derivation of social rights is not possible under the European Convention,[130] although the argument is by no means conclusive.[131] Certainly, the Court has resisted going down that road.[132] But once again, there is no reason why the British judiciary should not be more innovative, and the German debate on this provides many fruitful points of contact. Even in the case of social rights, it is not as if there are no textual 'pegs' in the Convention which could not give rise to such a development. In this sense, the Convention is little different from the German Basic Law, so arguments in that context are equally relevant in the United Kingdom.

In respect of constitutional entitlements, the German Basic Law and the European Convention are largely similar. Both focus primarily on the classic defensive rights of citizens against the state, but both are capable of jurisprudential development to embrace protective, procedural, and social rights. These, together with the more conventional defensive rights, constitute the potential structure of the 'complete constitutional right'.[133]

8. CONCLUSION: THE CONSTITUTIONALIZATION OF THE LEGAL SYSTEM

Alexy's conclusion is—to a common lawyer—comfortingly familiar: all law is ultimately constitutional.[134] This does not mean that there is no role for settled areas of public and private law, which appear at first sight to have little to do with constitutional principle. They represent the large set of resolutions of competing constitutional principles about which there is little practical doubt; they are only potential constitutional cases, not actual ones. But as perceptions of the weight of the various principles at play change over time, so potential constitutional cases, in any area of law, can become actual ones. Their resolution requires lawyers to return to the underlying principles at stake in a continual process of reconstruction. In A. W. B. Simpson's memorable metaphor, 'the point about the common law is not that everything is always in the melting-pot, but that you never quite

---

[130] See e.g. K. D. Ewing, 'Social Rights and Constitutional Law', PL 1994, 104.

[131] See e.g. V.-P. Viljanen, 'Abstention or Involvement? The Nature of State Obligations under Different Categories of Rights', in K. Drzewicki, C. Krause, and A. Rosas (eds.), *Social Rights as Human Rights: A European Challenge* (Turku and Åbo, 1994).

[132] The right to property does not include a right to acquire property, see *Marckx v Belgium* A31 (1979); the Convention does not guarantee even minimum social welfare rights, see Harris *et al.*, *Law of the European Convention*, 519.

[133] See below at 159 ff.

[134] See 365 f. below.

know what will go in next'.[135] The same can be said about constitutional rights.

This conclusion is problematic for a centralized, 'European' model of constitutional review, which seeks to confine questions of constitutional law to a specialist court.[136] It risks undermining the procedural distinction between constitutional and ordinary law. However, for decentralized, 'American'—one can now write 'Anglo-American'—models of constitutional review the conclusion is unsurprising. It is this, the broadest possible perspective of the nature of Alexy's *Theorie der Grundrechte*, which makes it more than merely plausible that it can inform constitutional reasoning in common law jurisdictions. Intellectually, it is as much at home, possibly even *more* at home, in the gradualist, precedential tradition of the English-speaking world as it is in what we stereotypically consider to be the systemic, codified, legal atmosphere of continental Europe. There is thus every reason for hoping that this translation can help inform the common law tradition as it increasingly finds itself in the heady world of human rights. And it is in that hope that it is offered now to the English-speaking reader.

---

[135] 'The Common Law and Legal Theory', in A. W. B. Simpson (ed.), *Oxford Essays in Jurisprudence*, 2nd series (Oxford: Clarendon Press, 1973), 77 at 91.

[136] On the distinction between centralized and decentralized constitutional review, see Vicki C. Jackson and Mark Tushnet, *Comparative Constitutional Law*, (New York: Foundation Press, 1999), ch. 6.

A Note on this Translation

Apart from a very few minor corrections and amendments,[1] which have been agreed with the author, the translation follows the third edition of *Theorie der Grundrechte* (Frankfurt a. M.: Suhrkamp, 1996). The Postscript was specially written for this English edition.

Obviously, an attempt has been made to develop and use a consistent technical vocabulary to match the original German. On the few occasions where it was felt that a knowledge of the German term would assist understanding, it has been included in square brackets. Furthermore, for those readers who wish to refer to the German text in parallel, the headings, their numerical structure and the footnote numbering, which is sequential within each chapter, are identical between the two versions. *Bund* and *Länder* have been translated as 'Federation' and 'Regions' respectively, and the corresponding adjectives, federal and regional, should be understood accordingly. In case the German court structure is not familiar, *Landesgericht* (which is the court of first instance for more serious cases, organized on a regional basis) has been translated as 'Regional Court', *Oberlandesgericht* (which is the immediate court of appeal) as 'Upper Regional Court', and *Bundesgerichtshof* (which is the court of final appeal for all Regions) as 'Federal Civil Court' or 'Federal Criminal Court' depending on the division which heard the case. The word 'jurisprudence' as it is used here is also worth clarifying. It refers neither to *Rechtsprechung* (case-law) nor to *Rechtsphilosophie* (philosophy of law), but to *Rechtswissenschaft*, which is the academic study of law.

The Appendix contains a translation of the constitutional rights provisions of the German Basic Law for ready reference. According to conventional practice in Germany, provisions of the Basic Law are referred to by article, paragraph, and sentence (e.g. 'Artikel 5 Absatz 3 Satz 2'). This translation has used a simplified mode of citation throughout, with the second and third numbers in parentheses referring to the paragraph and sentence (if there is more than one) respectively (e.g. 'article 5(3)(2)'). References to the official versions of judgments of the Federal Constitutional Court follow the standard mode of citation by volume number, first page number, and page referred to (e.g. BVerfGE 7, 198 (205)). In practice, judgments are often known informally by name, and, except in the case of proper names, those names have been translated. No distinction has been drawn between *Urteil* and *Beschluss*, both of which have simply been translated as 'Judgment'.

---

[1] See, in particular, the sentence inserted in brackets on p. 134.

Some dozen or so German texts which Alexy engages with have already been translated, not least his own *Theory of Legal Argumentation* (trans. Ruth Adler and Neil MacCormick, Oxford: Clarendon Press, 1989). Where possible, footnote references to these texts have been 'translated' as well, referring to the equivalent English versions and page numbers. Quotations follow these translations, even if the translation uses a slightly different technical vocabulary. This is generally unproblematic, but perhaps worth noting in respect of one work, Max Knight's 1967 translation of Hans Kelsen's *Pure Theory of Law*.

J. R.

Introduction

Questions of what rights the individual has as a human being and citizen of a political community, what principles bind state law-making, and what the realization of human dignity, liberty, and equality requires represent major themes in practical philosophy and central points of political dispute, both past and present. They become legal problems when a constitution such as the Basic Law of the Federal Republic of Germany binds the legislature, executive, and judiciary to constitutional rights norms as directly applicable law and subjects this obligation to comprehensive review by a constitutional court.

Where the constitutional rights catalogue is written, the legal problem of constitutional rights is first and foremost a problem of the interpretation of authoritative formulations of positive law. In this respect it is no different from problems of interpretation which arise generally in law. But a glance at the debate about the constitutional rights of the Basic Law shows that while the dispute about human and civil rights may have changed its character as a result of their enactment as directly applicable law, it has hardly become less sharp or less complex.

One reason for this, which is often commented upon, lies in the textual openness of the constitutional rights catalogue. Descriptions such as 'elliptic formulae and maxims, which in themselves largely lack clarity of content',[1] 'shorthand',[2] 'an agglomeration of general clauses and plastic concepts',[3] a lack of 'conceptual sufficiency',[4] 'empty formulae under which almost any facts may be subsumed'[5] abound. More precisely, we can distinguish between more or less open-textured constitutional rights provisions,[6] but in general it is true that the constitutional rights catalogue, along with

---

[1] E.-W. Böckenförde, 'Grundrechtstheorie und Grudrechtsinterpretation', NJW 1974, 1529; see also M. Kriele, *Theorie der Rechtsgewinnung*, 2nd edn. (Berlin, 1976), 197, who speaks of 'elliptic general clauses'.

[2] H. Huber, 'Über die Konkretisierung der Grundrechte', in P. Saladin and L. Wildhaber, *Der Staat als Aufgabe: Gedenkschrift für M. Imboden* (Basle and Stuttgart, 1972), 197.

[3] R. Dreier, 'Zur Problematik und Situation der Verfassungsinterpretation', in id., *Recht— Moral—Ideologie* (Frankfurt a. M., 1981), 112.

[4] W. Leisner, *Von der Verfassungsmäßigkeit der Gesetze zur Gesetzmäßigkeit der Verfassung* (Tübingen, 1964), 5.

[5] K.-D. Opp, *Soziologie im Recht* (Reinbek, 1973), 124, 232. On the empty-formula thesis, see also E. Denninger, *Staatsrecht*, i (Reinbek, 1973), 25 ff., 117; E. Topitsch, 'Die Menschenrechte', JZ 1963, 3 f.; G. Degenkolbe, 'Über logische Struktur und gesellschaftliche Funktionen von Leerformeln', *Kölner Zeitschrift für Soziologie und Sozialphilosophie*, 17 (1965), 327 ff.

[6] The fact that we can distinguish not only between more or less open-textured constitutional rights provisions, but also between different types of open-texture, will only be of interest later on.

other substantive constitutional provisions, above all those concerning state goals and state structure, represents the 'regulatory structure with the least regulatory density'[7] within the German legal system.

Open-texture alone is admittedly an inadequate explanation for the intensity of constitutional rights controversy. A norm can be as open as possible, but if there is wide consensus on the matter in question there will hardly be much discussion about it. But if the openness of a norm combines with fundamental disagreements about its subject-matter, then the stage has been set for a major dispute. And this is precisely what has happened in the case of constitutional rights. The constitutional rights catalogue regulates in a highly open manner what are in part deeply controversial questions about the basic normative structure of state and society. This is clearest in the case of the constitutional rights concepts of dignity, liberty, and equality. If one adds to these concepts the state goals and structural ideas of democracy, the Rule of Law, and the social state, one ends up with a conceptual system which embraces the main ideas of early modern rational law,[8] as extended by the social state principle, which expresses the requirements of the social movements of the nineteenth and twentieth centuries. These concepts remain the basic concepts of political philosophy. At the same time they serve as the semantic weapons of ideological warfare. The phrase, 'the battle for the Basic Law', relates primarily to such terms.[9]

If the discussion of constitutional rights were only to be based on the text of the constitution and the uncertain ground of the history of its enactment, we would have to reckon with an endless and almost limitless to-ing and fro-ing in the battle of opinions. The fact that this is to a considerable extent not true, is in large measure due to the case-law of the Federal Constitutional Court. In the course of fifty years of decision-taking it has established ever more fixed points within the scope of the constitutionally possible. What constitutional rights are today, they are above all because of the case-law of the Federal Constitutional Court. The study of constitutional rights has become—notwithstanding the dispute about the precedential nature of decisions of the Federal Constitutional Court[10]—to a significant extent the study of constitutional adjudication.

The ever-thickening network of precedent has given the dispute about constitutional rights certain fixed points, but it has not been able to deprive

---

[7] O. Bachof, 'Contribution to Debate', VVDStRL 39 (1981), 175.

[8] See Dreier, *Recht—Moral—Ideologie*, 124. As the main ideas of early modern rational law, the concepts mentioned here are based on older traditions. See e.g. C. Starck, 'Menschenwürde als Verfassungsgarantie', in L. Lombardi Vallauri and G. Dilcher (eds.), *Christentum, Säkularisation und modernes Recht* (Baden-Baden and Milan, 1982), 814 ff., who speaks of the 'initial biblical–classical ignition of the idea of human dignity'.

[9] See P. Römer (ed.), *Der Kampf um das Grundgesetz* (Frankfurt a. M., 1977); M. Kriele, 'Das Grundgesetz im Parteienkampf', in id., *Legitimationsprobleme der Bundesrepublik* (Munich, 1977), 131 ff.

[10] See below at 373 f.

it of its vitality. This is not simply a result of the large number of old unde-cided questions, as well as new ones in ever-increasing measure. Nor is it simply a result of the fact that decisions of the Federal Constitutional Court can be challenged in the course of academic debate. It is above all a result of the fact that the Federal Constitutional Court itself has repeatedly prompted basic discussion about constitutional rights by its general and sometimes ambiguous comments. Examples of such judicial initiations of fundamental discussion about constitutional rights are its thesis of the objective order of values enacted in the constitutional rights section of the Basic Law,[11] its assertion of the priority of exercises of liberty for political purposes over those serving purely private interests,[12] its reading of consti-tutional rights provisions as guarantees of 'institutional liberties',[13] its assumption that constitutional rights norms impose protective duties on the state even to the extent of requiring the criminalization of certain acts,[14] its discussion of entitlements, which are supposed to secure the factual precon-ditions for the enjoyment of liberties,[15] and its increasing emphasis in more recent times on the procedural content of constitutional rights.[16] These examples show what a great variety of things are mixed up in the picture the Federal Constitutional Court paints of constitutional rights. Practically every position in the dispute about constitutional rights can appeal to this or that decision or leading judgment of the Court. Even if debate were only concerned with establishing what applies as a result of the decisions of the Federal Constitutional Court, very different views could still be adopted on numerous issues. So in addition to the open-texture of constitutional rights provisions there is the open-texture of constitutional rights case-law. While the case-law has reduced the problem of open-texture to some extent, in no way has it been entirely resolved.

This is the situation in which the jurisprudence of constitutional rights sets itself the task of giving rationally justifiable answers to constitutional rights questions. The theory of constitutional rights offered here attempts to contribute to the fulfilment of this task. The first chapter expands further on its content and nature, so it can be read as a continuation of this intro-duction. The only point to make at this stage is that the theory is a legal, and indeed a general legal, theory of the constitutional rights of the Basic Law. Thus it is neither a philosophy of constitutional rights independent of positive law, nor a sociological, historical, or political theory. The classical term for it would be the general part of constitutional rights doctrine. Its basis is the theory of principles found in Chapter 3 and the theory of basic

---

[11] See e.g. BVerfGE 7, 198 (205).
[12] See e.g. BVerfGE 7, 198 (212); 42, 163 (170).
[13] See e.g. BVerfGE 12, 205 (264); 31, 314 (326).
[14] BVerfGE 39, 1 (41 f.).
[15] See BVerfGE 33, 303 (331 ff.).
[16] See BVerfGE 37, 132 (148); 45, 297 (322); 48, 292 (297 f.); 51, 150 (156).

legal positions developed in Chapter 4. The theory of principles is a theory of values purified of unsustainable presuppositions. It will be shown that an adequate theory of constitutional rights is not possible without a theory of principles. Thus one aim of this investigation is the rehabilitation of the much-despised theory of values. The theory of basic legal positions traces the variety of constitutional rights relationships back to positions and relations of the most basic type, and in this way it makes it possible to represent them precisely, which is the necessary precondition of a clear doctrine of constitutional rights. It follows the spirit of Jellinek's status theory, which is clarified and refined with its help. On the basis of the theory of principles and positions, some key issues within constitutional rights doctrine are considered, in particular the theory of scope and limits, general rights to liberty and equality, protective, organizational, and procedural rights, social constitutional rights, and horizontal, or third party, effect. The final chapter considers the role of constitutional rights and constitutional rights norms in the legal system, as well as constitutional rights argumentation and decision-taking. It will be shown that the enactment of constitutional rights binding all state powers entails the opening of the legal system to the system of morality, an opening which is both rational and can be mastered by rational means.

It should be obvious that only some of the large number of questions associated with constitutional rights could be considered here. To the extent that these questions have received correct answers, it can be hoped that they will also be useful in resolving the problems which are not covered.

1

The Content and Purpose of a Theory of Constitutional Rights

I. THE CONCEPT OF A GENERAL LEGAL THEORY OF THE CONSTITUTIONAL RIGHTS OF THE BASIC LAW

There are many different types of constitutional rights theory. Historical theories, which explain the development of constitutional rights,[1] philosophical theories, which are concerned with their justification,[2] and sociological theories as to the function of rights within the social system[3] are just three examples. There is hardly a discipline within the humanities which could not have something to contribute to a theory of constitutional rights from its own perspective and with its own methods.

The purpose of this book is to develop a general legal theory of the constitutional rights of the Basic Law. The content and nature of this theory is determined by three characteristics: it is first of all a theory of the *constitutional rights of the Basic Law*; secondly, it is a *legal* theory, and finally, it is a *general* theory.

1. A THEORY OF THE CONSTITUTIONAL RIGHTS OF THE BASIC LAW

A theory of the constitutional rights of the Basic Law is a theory of certain specific enacted constitutional rights. This distinguishes it from theories of constitutional rights which were valid in the past (legal-historical theories), and also from theories about constitutional rights *per se* (philosophical theories). It also distinguishes it from theories of constitutional rights not part of the Basic Law, such as the constitutional rights of other states or of the German Regions.

The fact that these alternative theories are to be distinguished does not mean that there are no connections between them. Historical and comparative

---

[1] See e.g. the essays collected in R. Schnur (ed.), *Zur Geschichte der Erklärung der Menschenrechte* (Darmstadt, 1964), in particular those of G. Jellinek and E. Boutmy.

[2] From more recent times see e.g. J. Rawls, *A Theory of Justice* (Cambridge, Mass., 1971) on one hand and R. Nozick, *Anarchy, State and Utopia* (New York, 1974), on the other.

[3] See N. Luhmann, *Grundrechte als Institution*, 2nd edn. (Berlin, 1974).

accounts have an important role to play in the interpretation of the constitutional rights of the Basic Law.[4] There is a connection with philosophical
theories because such theories are concerned (among other things) with the
contingent and necessary structure of all constitutional rights, that is, with
a theory of their general form. The fact that certain constitutional rights
have been enacted means that the necessary structure and one of the contingent structures of constitutional rights have been realized. Thus, on one
hand, a theory of certain specific enacted constitutional rights can benefit
from the insights of legal philosophy, and, on the other, it can make its own
contribution to legal philosophy by analysing its subject-matter. It is important to distinguish the two approaches precisely in order to see the connections.

2. A LEGAL THEORY OF THE CONSTITUTIONAL RIGHTS OF THE BASIC LAW

As a theory of the enacted law of a particular legal system, a legal theory of
the constitutional rights of the Basic Law is doctrinal. Exactly what it is that
makes a theory doctrinal, and hence legal, is far from clear.[5] It seems appropriate primarily to orientate ourselves according to legal practice and to
what is sometimes called 'legal doctrine' or 'jurisprudence', that is, to legal
science in its narrow and most basic sense.[6] If we do this, three dimensions
of legal doctrine—analytical, empirical, and normative—become apparent.[7]

---

[4] On these forms of interpretation, see R. Alexy, *A Theory of Legal Argumentation*
(Oxford, 1989), 239 f.
[5] On the concept of legal doctrine see E. J. Thul, 'Die Denkform der Rechtsdogmatik',
ARSP 46 (1960), 241 ff.; T. Viehweg, 'Zwei Rechtsdogmatiken', in U. Klug (ed.), *Philosophie
und Recht, Festschrift für C.A. Emge* (Wiesbaden, 1960), 106 ff.; L. Raiser, 'Wozu
Rechtsdogmatik?' DRiZ 1968, 98; F. Wieacker, 'Zur praktischen Leistung der
Rechtsdogmatik', in R. Bubner, K. Cramer, and R. Wiehl (eds.), *Hermeneutik und Dialektik,
Festschrift für H.-G. Gadamer*, ii (Tübingen, 1970), 311 ff.; J. Esser, 'Möglichkeiten und
Grenzen des dogmatischen Denkens im modernen Zivilrecht', AcP 172 (1972), 97 ff.; id.,
'Dogmatik zwischen Theorie und Praxis', in F. Baur *et al.* (eds.), *Funktionswandel der
Privatrechtsinstitutionen, Festschrift für L. Raiser* (Tübingen, 1974), 517 ff.; K. Adomeit,
'Zivilrechtstheorie und Zivilrechtsdogmatik', *Jahrbuch für Rechtssoziologie und
Rechtstheorie*, 2 (1972), 503 ff.; H. Albert, 'Erkenntnis und Recht', *Jahrbuch für
Rechtssoziologie und Rechtstheorie*, 2 (1972), 80 ff.; S. Simitis, 'Die Bedeutung von System
und Dogmatik', AcP 172 (1972), 131 ff; W. Krawietz, 'Was leistet Rechtsdogmatik in der
richterlichen Entscheidungspraxis?' ÖZöR 23 (1972), 47 ff.; U. Meyer-Cording, *Kann der
Jurist heute noch Dogmatiker sein?* (Tübingen, 1973); D. de Lazzer, 'Rechtsdogmatik als
Kompromißformular', in R. Dubischar *et al.* (eds.), *Dogmatik und Methode, Festschrift für J.
Esser* (Kronberg, 1975), 85 ff.; G. Struck, 'Dogmatische Diskussionen über Dogmatik', JZ
1975, 84 ff.; E. v. Savigny, U. Neumann, and J. Rahlf, *Juristische Dogmatik und
Wissenschaftstheorie* (Munich, 1976); R. Dreier, *Recht—Moral—Ideologie* (Frankfurt a. M.,
1981) 51 ff., 85 ff., 109 ff.
[6] See G. Radbruch, *Legal Philosophy*, trans. K. Wilk (Cambridge, Mass., 1950), 140 ff.
[7] On the three-dimensionality thesis see Dreier, *Recht—Moral—Ideologie*, 10 ff., 51 ff., 88
f.; Alexy, *Theory of Legal Argumentation*, 251 ff. Here the three-dimensionality thesis will be
applied to legal doctrine. For an application in the context of distinguishing legal theory, legal

The *analytical* dimension is concerned with the systematic and conceptual elucidation of valid law. The range of tasks stretches from the analysis of basic concepts (such as the concepts of a rule, a right, liberty, and equality) through legal constructions (such as the relationship between the scope of a constitutional right and its limits, and the issue of horizontal effect) to an examination of the structure of the legal system (such as the so-called radiating effect of constitutional rights) and constitutional justification (such as the process of balancing interests).

The *empirical* dimension of constitutional rights doctrine can be understood in two senses. It can be understood, first, in connection with the knowledge of validly enacted law, and, secondly, in connection with the use of empirical premises in the course of legal argument,[8] for example in the context of causation.[9] Only the former is of interest here.[10]

Those who think that the knowledge of validly enacted law is an empirical matter have to presuppose a broad and multifaceted concept of law and legal validity. The empirical dimension is concerned not only with describing enacted law, but also with describing and predicting judicial practice, not merely with statute but also with judge-made law. The effectiveness of law is also part of the empirical dimension, at least to the extent that it is a precondition of its positive validity.[11] In other words, the empirical dimension is broader than a positivistic concept of law and legal validity. The reasons for this are easy to see, certainly in the area of constitutional rights. Precisely because the norms are so open-textured, little is gained by the mere knowledge of enacted law on its own. The moment someone who maintains a positivistic concept of law and legal validity writes a commentary as an academic, or prepares a brief as a practitioner, or gives a judgment as a judge, they cannot avoid knowing and digesting the case-law of the Federal Constitutional Court. Exactly where this case-law is to be located as a source of valid law can be left open for the moment.[12] The point is simply that there must be a broad concept of what counts as validly

---

sociology and legal philosophy see H. Rottleuthner, *Rechtstheorie und Rechtssoziologie* (Freiburg and Munich, 1981), 13 ff., who apart from that draws the same distinction in the context of legal doctrine as here (ibid. 16 f.). See also M. Rehbinder, *Rechtssoziologie* (Berlin and New York, 1977), 5 ff., who relates three-dimensionality to the distinction between legal philosophy, legal doctrine, and legal sociology.

[8] See on this K. J. Philippi, *Tatsachenfeststellungen des Bundesverfassungsgerichts* (Cologne, Berlin, Bonn, and Munich, 1971); G. Winters, 'Tatsachenurteile im Prozeß richterlicher Rechtssetzung', *Rechtstheorie*, 2 (1971), 171 ff.; C. Starck, 'Empirie in der Rechtsdogmatik', JZ 1972, 609 ff.; H. Rottleuthner, *Rechtswissenschaft als Sozialwissenschaft* (Frankfurt a. M., 1973), 205 ff.

[9] See H.-J. Koch and H. Rüßmann, *Juristische Begründungslehre* (Munich, 1982), 227 ff.; T. W. Wälde, *Juristische Folgenorientierung* (Kronstein, 1979).

[10] So we are only concerned with what Kant called 'a merely empirical doctrine of right'; see his *Metaphysics of Morals*, trans. M. Gregor (Cambridge, 1991), 55.

[11] See here, in place of many, H. Kelsen, *Pure Theory of Law*, trans. M. Knight (Berkeley, 1967), 208 ff.

[12] See on this 373 below.

enacted law which no one who wishes to satisfy the requirements of legal practice can avoid.

The characterization of this second dimension as 'empirical' is not meant to imply that the recognition of validly enacted law is exhausted by the perception of observable phenomena, or that it can be reduced to these. It is common ground that no conclusions as to valid law can be drawn *merely* by establishing, for example, that a group of people have come together in a room, that speeches have been made and hands raised.[13] If we want to arrive at statements of valid law on the basis of such facts[14] we have to interpret them in the light of certain assumptions, which assumptions turn them into legislative facts.[15] The details of this interpretative process are controversial.[16] The only point to make here is that its starting-point is always a set of facts in the narrow empirical sense, and this makes it appropriate to speak of an 'empirical dimension'.

The third, or *normative*, dimension goes beyond the mere establishment of validly enacted law by an empirical process, to the explanation and critique of legal practice, above all of adjudicative practice. The key question here is, what is the correct decision on the basis of validly enacted law given any concrete set of facts? In all controversial cases, the answer to this question will incorporate the speaker's value-judgments.[17] To a large extent, legal doctrine is the attempt to give rationally defensible answers to the evaluative questions which have been left open by the authoritative materials at hand. This confronts legal doctrine with the problem of the rational justification of value-judgments,[18] but it will be argued below that rational justification is in principle possible.[19]

The evaluative problem emerges primarily in the interpretation of empirically ascertainable authoritative material and the filling of its gaps. To this extent, it is permissible to speak of a '*problem of elaboration*'. In addition to this problem, the '*problem of foundation*' arises to the extent that value-judgments are necessary to identify authoritative material in the first place. The problem of foundation becomes significant in constitutional law, for example in connection with the issue of unconstitutional norms of the constitution,[20] or in the question of the precedential nature of the judg-

[13] See, in place of many, Kelsen, *Pure Theory of Law*, 2 ff.

[14] Such facts are 'brute facts' in Searle's sense. These must be distinguished from 'institutional facts', of which passing a law is an example; see J. R. Searle, *Speech Acts* (Cambridge, 1969), 50 ff.

[15] See N. MacCormick, 'Law as Institutional Fact', LQR 90 (1974), 102 ff.; O. Weinberger, 'Das Recht als institutionelle Tatsache', *Rechtstheorie*, 11 (1980), 427 ff.

[16] For a model of the interpretative process, see A. Aarnio, R. Alexy, and A. Peczenik, 'The Foundation of Legal Reasoning', in A. Aarnio and D. N. MacCormick (eds.), *Legal Reasoning*, i (Aldershot, 1992), 235 ff.

[17] See Alexy, *Theory of Legal Argumentation*, 1 ff.

[18] Ibid. 14 ff., 33 ff., 211 ff.   [19] At 369.

[20] The problem of foundation is clearly raised when the Federal Constitutional Court states that it is conceivable that the judiciary, which 'gains its authority not merely externally from

ments of the Federal Constitutional Court. In the final analysis, the problem of foundation is also connected to the question of why the constitution
is binding at all,[21] even if this aspect plays practically no role in constitutional rights doctrine.[22]

In the history of legal thought, and even more so in the history of legal
theory, the relative weight of these three dimensions is always changing.
The shift from analytical to interest-based and then to evaluative jurisprudence is an impressive example of this.[23] What is understood as narrowly
and essentially 'legal' varies according to the understanding of the relationship between the three dimensions. In order to arrive at an understanding
of this relationship, some overarching perspective is necessary. This is
provided by the character of legal thought as a *practical* discipline.
Jurisprudence, as it is carried out today, is in the first instance a practical
discipline, because it asks the question, what ought to happen in real or
hypothetical situations. This question is asked from a perspective corresponding to the judicial one.[24] This does not mean that jurisprudence
cannot adopt other perspectives, nor that it is always directly concerned
with the solution of concrete cases. However, it does mean that the judicial
perspective is the prime characteristic perspective of jurisprudence, and that
the statements and theories propounded from this perspective, however
abstract they are, are always ultimately directed to the solution of cases,
that is, to the justification of concrete legal ought-judgments.[25]

In contrast to the three dimensions, the character of jurisprudence as a
practical discipline proves to be a unifying principle. If jurisprudence is
rationally to fulfil its practical function, it must find some way of connecting the three dimensions. It must be an integrative multidimensional discipline. Relating the three dimensions to each other is a necessary condition
for the rationality of jurisprudence as a practical discipline.

The reasons for this are easy to see. In order to answer the question of

the Constitution, but which is to a certain extent based on the very idea of law and corresponds with the nature of their function, . . . [should examine] constitutional norms according
to the standards of suprastatutory law incorporated in and presupposed by the Constitution'
(BVerfGE 3, 225 at 235). For a critique and numerous references see F. Müller, *Die Einheit der
Verfassung* (Berlin, 1979), 50 ff., 128 ff.

[21] See on this MacCormick's theory of 'underpinning reasons' in his *Legal Reasoning and
Legal Theory* (Oxford, 1978), 62 ff., 138 ff., 240 ff., 275 ff.

[22] Peczenik's distinction between deep and, in the legal context, sufficient, justification is
instructive in this respect. See A. Peczenik, *Grundlagen der juristischen Argumentation* (Vienna
and New York, 1983), 1 f.

[23] See F. Wieacker, *Privatrechtsgeschichte der Neuzeit*, 2nd edn. (Göttingen, 1967), 433 ff.,
574 ff.

[24] On jurisprudence as a practical discipline in this sense, see P. Heck, *Das Problem der
Rechtsgewinnung*, 2nd edn. (Tübingen, 1932), 3; H. Coing, *Die juristischen Auslegungs-
methoden und die Lehren der allgemeinen Hermeneutik* (Cologne and Opladen, 1959), 23; M.
Kriele, *Theorie der Rechtsgewinnung*, 2nd edn. (Berlin, 1976), 39 ff.

[25] See K. Engisch, *Logische Studien zur Gesetzesanwendung*, 3rd edn. (Heidelberg, 1963),
5.

what legally ought to be, one has to know the law in force. The recognition of validly enacted law is the function of the empirical dimension. Authoritative material ascertainable in the empirical dimension is not sufficient in all moderately problematic cases fully to determine concrete legal ought-judgments. That leads to the necessity for additional value-judgments and hence the normative dimension. Conceptual clarity, consistency, and coherence[26] are preconditions for the rationality of any field of knowledge. The many conceptual and systematic problems in the area of constitutional rights show what a significant role the analytical dimension has to play in any practical science of constitutional rights which wishes to fulfil its function in a rational manner.

Connecting the three dimensions in a way which is oriented towards the practical function of jurisprudence defines the doctrinal and also the legal in its narrow and most basic sense. If we define legal theory in this way, a legal theory of the constitutional rights of the Basic Law is a theory located in the relationship between the three dimensions of legal theory and oriented towards its practical function.

3. A General Legal Theory of the Constitutional Rights of the Basic Law

A general legal theory of the constitutional rights of the Basic Law is a theory which is concerned with problems common to all constitutional rights, or to all constitutional rights of a certain sort, such as all liberties, equality rights, or entitlements. Its counterpart is a specific theory, which deals with specific problems of specific rights. The distinction turns on the extent of the theory, which is a matter of degree. So a theory which deals with problems common to all liberties is a general theory, but is not as general a theory as one which deals with problems common to all rights. The distinction between general and specific theories gives rise to problems in the case of constitutional rights which are themselves general in character, such as the general right to liberty and the general right to equality. In such cases, generality is already a characteristic of the subject-matter. But even here we can distinguish between general theories of these rights as constitutional rights of a certain type, and specific theories which concern themselves with specific problems in the interpretation of such rights.

---

[26] On the concept of coherence, see N. Rescher, *The Coherence Theory of Truth* (Oxford, 1973); id., *Cognitive Systematization* (Oxford, 1979); on the role of coherence in jurisprudence, see Peczenik, *Grundlagen der juristischen Argumentation*, 176 ff.; A. Aarnio, *Philosophical Perspectives in Jurisprudence* (Helsinki, 1983), 191; N. MacCormick, 'Coherence in Legal Justification', in W. Krawietz, H. Schelsky, G. Winkler, and A. Schramm (eds.), *Theorie der Normen, Festgabe für O. Weinberger* (Berlin, 1984), 37 ff.

II. CONSTITUTIONAL RIGHTS THEORY AND CONSTITUTIONAL RIGHTS THEORIES

The concept of a general legal theory of constitutional rights expresses a theoretical ideal. It aims at an integrative theory which contains the most extensive set of true or correct statements formulated in terms of the three dimensions, and which connects these in optimal fashion. One can legitimately speak of an ideal constitutional rights theory here. Every existing, and in that sense real, theory of constitutional rights can only approximate this ideal.

The idea of an integrative theory is to be preserved from two misconceptions. The first suggests that the requirement to connect the various elements leads to an all-embracing mishmash. The aim is exactly the opposite. Our concern is to create as clearly ordered a system of correct or true general statements of constitutional rights as possible. The second misconception suggests that the integrative programme overloads the development of constitutional rights theory, and rejects every proposed theory of constitutional rights as inadequate or valueless, when in fact they are true, or correct, but simply not all-embracing. This also is not the case. The concept of an integrative theory is a regulative idea which can connect with the creation of constitutional rights theory in many different ways. Every theory of constitutional rights which contributes to its realization is valuable because of its contribution. To treat it as valueless, because it does not fully realize the ideal, is to ignore the character of the integrative programme as a regulative idea. In order to realize as far as possible *the* theory of constitutional rights (in the sense of the ideal theory), many true or correct theories of constitutional rights have to be brought together. Of course, these have to be evaluated in terms of their potential contribution to the ideal theory.

In the light of these comments, it is helpful to look at the accounts characterized as 'theories of constitutional rights' in the current literature. The most influential collection is that of Böckenförde. He distinguishes five theories: 'the liberal, or civic/Rule of Law, theory of constitutional rights, the institutional theory, the value theory, the democratic-functional theory and the social state theory'.[27] The status of these theories will be discussed in more detail below.[28] Here, we are only interested in their 'function as normative guiding principles for interpretation'[29] as emphasized by

---

[27] E.-W. Böckenförde, 'Grundrechtstheorie und Grundrechtsinterpretation', NJW 1974, 1530 ; similarly K. Kröger, *Grundrechtstheorie als Verfassungsproblem* (Baden-Baden, 1978), see also M. Kloepfer, *Datenschutz als Grundrecht* (Königstein im Taunus, 1980), 20; E. Schmidt-Jortzig, *Die Einrichtungsgarantien der Verfassung* (Göttingen, 1979), 63 ff.

[28] 377 ff.

[29] E.-W. Böckenförde, 'Die Methoden der Verfassungsinterpretation', NJW 1976, 2096; similarly Kröger, *Grundrechtstheorie als Verfassungsproblem* 1: 'definitive orientation-point for the interpretation of constitutional rights'.

Böckenförde. From *this* point of view, these theories are basic perspectives of the most general kind on the purpose and structure of constitutional rights.

Theories of constitutional rights which have the character of basic perspectives of the most general kind are dogged by two problems. The first results from their level of abstraction.[30] They are, by definition, undeveloped in all three dimensions. To start with, they are merely hypotheses which might lead to a complete theory. If they are confirmed in this process, they could take on the character of the most general set of worked-out theories. Theories of constitutional rights which take the form of basic perspectives of the most general kind cannot therefore replace a worked-out theory of constitutional rights. They can only be a starting-point, and possibly a conclusion.

The second problem is more serious. If one adopts the theories identified on their own terms, each of them expresses just *one* basic thesis. We can call theories that try to derive all constutional rights from a single basic thesis, '*one-point*' theories. One candidate for a one-point theory not included in Böckenförde's list is the thesis that constitutional rights are procedural guarantees.[31] Everything tends to the suspicion that constitutional rights cannot be adequately explained on the basis of a one-point theory, whichever one-point theory we may prefer. The justification for this suspicion will become apparent in the course of this investigation. The only reason offered for the moment is the general consideration that it would be quite amazing if, in the light of the variety and complexity of the subject-matter regulated by constitutional rights, and in the light of the experience that in practical matters of any weight a whole bundle of conflicting perspectives have to be considered, constitutional rights could be derived from a single principle. The only exception applies to one-point theories of a very high level of abstraction, such as the theory that the ultimate purpose of all constitutional rights is the preservation of human dignity.[32] In fact, even this is not a true exception, because such highly abstract accounts are not actually one-point theories at all, since they can embrace all the divergent accounts identified.

The counterpart to a one-point theory is a *combined theory*. A combined theory forms the basis of the case-law of the Federal Constitutional Court, which has adopted all the perspectives identified here.[33] It is also main-

---

[30] See on this J. Schwabe, *Probleme der Grundrechtsdogmatik* (Darmstadt, 1977), 5.

[31] See, with numerous further references, H. Goerlich, *Grundrechte als Verfahrensgarantien* (Baden-Baden, 1981).

[32] See also formulations such as those of W. Schmidt, 'Grundrechtstheorie im Wandel der Verfassungsgeschichte', *Jura*, 1983, 180, according to which the protection of 'the individual's freedom of action between state authority and social power' is supposed to be the central point of a modern theory of constitutional rights.

[33] See e.g. BVerfGE 50, 290 at 337 (liberal theory); BVerfGE 12, 205 at 259 ff. (institutional theory); BVerfGE 7, 198 at 205 (value theory); BVerfGE 42, 163 at 170 (democratic theory); BVerfGE 33, 303 at 330 ff. (social state theory); BVerfGE 53, 30 at 64 f. (procedural theory).

tained by the countless writers who speak of many functions,[34] aspects,[35] or purposes[36] of constitutional rights. The immediate objection to a combined theory is that it cannot give any guidance to legal decision-taking and justification, but simply represents a collection of highly abstract arguments, which one can adopt at will. It is in this context that Böckenförde accuses the Federal Constitutional Court of 'basing itself inconsistently on diverse theories of constitutional rights as the starting-point of its interpretations, without any system being recognizable in the diversity'.[37] It is quite true that one cannot do much with a theory which consists principally of a list of the most general assumptions about the purpose and structure of constitutional rights. This is not simply a function of their abstraction, but above all because in concrete cases the theories can conflict with each other in many different ways.[38]

If we were faced only with a choice between one-point theories or ill-defined combinations of abstract and potentially conflicting basic assumptions, the theory of constitutional rights would face a real dilemma. But the possibilities for theory-construction in the field of constitutional rights are in no way exhausted by this alternative. The inadequacy of both versions merely shows that constitutional rights theory cannot rest on the superficial basis of general assumptions, either in the form of a one-point theory, or in the form of a combined theory. Of course, the combined theory expresses cogently the point that many aspects of constitutional rights are relevant, but in order to make use of these aspects, a model is necessary which can deliver more than mere juxtaposition. It is the purpose of an integrative theory to create such a model.

III. CONSTITUTIONAL RIGHTS THEORY AS STRUCTURAL THEORY

The route to an adequate integrated theory lies through a structural theory of constitutional rights. A structural theory, which is part of an integrated theory, is primarily analytical. It is primarily, and not purely, analytical, because it investigates structures such as constitutional rights concepts, the influence of constitutional rights on the legal system, and constitutional justification with reference to the practical function of an integrated theory. Its most important subject-matter is the case-law of the Federal

---

[34] See E. Stein, *Staatsrecht*, 8th edn. (Tübingen, 1982), 250 ff.; E. Denninger, *Staatsrecht*, ii (Reinbek, 1979), 138; A. Bleckmann, *Allgemeine Grundrechtslehren* (Cologne, Berlin, Bonn, and Munich, 1979), 155 ff.

[35] See P. Häberle, 'Grundrechte im Leistungsstaat', VVDStRL 30 (1972), 75.

[36] See M. Kriele, *Einführung in die Staatslehre*, (Reinbek, 1975), 336 ff.

[37] Böckenförde, 'Grundrechtstheorie und Grundrechtsinterpretation', 1536.

[38] See Denninger, *Staatsrecht*, ii 182.

Constitutional Court. To this extent it has an empirical-analytical character. But it is guided by considerations of correct decision and rational justification, and to that extent has a normative-analytical character.

Structural theory is not simply the first part of an integrated theory of
constitutional rights; it is the basis and framework for everything else that
follows. There is a whole host of reasons for this. Conceptual and analytical clarity is an elementary prerequisite for the rationality of any field of
knowledge. In practical disciplines, which are only indirectly controlled by
empirical experience, this requirement has even greater significance. This is
particularly true for constitutional rights, which are characterized by an
analytical tradition to a much lesser extent than, say, private law, and which
are subject to ideological influences to a much greater extent.

As a practical discipline, constitutional rights doctrine is directed
towards the rational justification of concrete constitutional ought-judgments. The rationality of the justification requires that the route from the
statement of constitutional right to the concrete ought-judgment is as
accessible to inter-subjective control as possible. But this presupposes clarity about the structure of constitutional rights norms and also about all the
concepts and forms of argument relevant to the decision. It is simply not
the case that such clarity already exists to a sufficient degree. A glance at
the structural characterization of constitutional rights and norms in the
case-law and the literature reveals a confused jumble. Even the simple
point that constitutional rights are both 'individual rights' and 'objective
principles'[39] is problematic on closer inspection. What is meant by 'objective' and 'principle'? The misleading appearance of simplicity hardly first
arises when constitutional rights are characterized not only as 'defensive
rights' but also as 'participation rights' or 'participation entitlements'.[40]
And what is meant when 'legal power'[41] is mentioned? Particular difficulties are associated with the various designations of the concept of value
associated with the objective aspect of constitutional rights. Examples are:
'value-deciding basic norm',[42] 'value-decision',[43] 'objective-legal value-
decision',[44] 'evaluative content',[45] 'constitutional value(s)',[46] and 'commu-
nity-constitutive value'.[47] It is almost impossible to gain an oversight over
other terms not belonging to the family of value-terms, such as 'principles
of social ordering',[48] 'directives',[49] 'influences',[50] 'structural principles',[51]

[39] BVerfGE 50, 290 at 337.   [40] BVerfGE 35, 79 at 112, 128, 115.
[41] BVerfGE 24, 367 at 396.
[42] BVerfGE 6, 55 at 71; 35, 79 at 112; 39, 1 at 47.
[43] BVerfGE 27, 195 at 201.   [44] BVerfGE 49, 89 at 142.
[45] BVerfGE 7, 198 at 208; 27, 104 at 109.
[46] BVerfGE 35, 202 at 225.   [47] BVerfGE 12, 45 at 54.
[48] BVerfGE 7, 198 at 215.   [49] BVerfGE 39, 1 at 41.
[50] ibid.   [51] BVerfGE 31, 58 at 69.

'basic principles',[52] 'guiding norm',[53] 'benchmark norm',[54] 'benchmarks',[55] 'postulates',[56] 'functions',[57] and 'protective duties'.[58] And the terminological variety of the case-law is trumped by the literature. To pick just one example—remarkable, but not untypical—in *one* article[59] in connection with constitutional rights, Scheuner uses the following twenty-one expressions with structural connotations: 'guarantees of liberty', 'principles of social formation', 'elements of social ordering',[60] 'constitutional principles', 'limit' (on legislative discretion), 'goal', 'task', 'binding guideline',[61] 'principles and determinations in their institutional-functional aspect', 'principles',[62] 'objective determinations', 'framework', 'constitutional freedoms', 'constitutional goals',[63] 'participation',[64] 'social rights', 'determinations of state goals', 'conceptions of goals', 'obligatory goal', 'legislative task', and 'directives'.[65]

Against the background of these lists, the words of Hohfeld take on particular significance: 'in any closely reasoned problem, whether legal or non-legal, chameleon-hued words are a peril both to clear thought and to lucid expression'.[66] If there is no clarity in the structure of constitutional rights and constitutional rights norms, then there will be no clarity in constitutional adjudication either. The same applies to all concepts in constitutional rights doctrine. Doctrinal statements such as, 'liberty is not liberty from the law, but liberty in and under law',[67] or, 'according to the laws of pure logic [there are] no limits to constitutional rights provisions, but only definitions of those provisions'[68] or that 'from a logical and legal perspective' rights to positive state action stand in 'opposition'[69] or even 'contradiction'[70] to liberties, are not accessible to rational discussion without clarity about the concepts of liberty, limits, and rights to positive state action.

A broad consensus on the need for conceptual clarification and hence theorizing in the analytical dimension should be achievable. There is no lack of voices arguing in this direction. Thus Lerche notes 'the value of each

---

[52] BVerfGE 31, 58 at 70.   [53] ibid.   [54] BVerfGE 21, 73 at 85.

[55] BVerfGE 42, 143 at 148.   [56] BVerfGE 35, 79 at 114.

[57] BVerfGE 35, 321 at 331.   [58] BVerfGE 39, 1 at 42.

[59] U. Scheuner, 'Die Funktion der Grundrechte im Sozialstaat. Die Grundrechte als Richtlinie und Rahmen der Staatstätigkeit', DÖV 1971, 505 ff.

[60] ibid. 506.   [61] ibid. 507.   [62] ibid. 508.

[63] ibid. 510.   [64] ibid. 512.   [65] ibid. 513.

[66] W. N. Hohfeld, 'Some Fundamental Legal Conceptions as Applied in Judicial Reasoning', in id., *Fundamental Legal Conceptions as Applied in Judicial Reasoning and Other Legal Essays* (New Haven, 1923), 35.

[67] P. Häberle, *Die Wesensgehaltgarantie des Artikel 19 Abs. 2 Grundgesetz*, 3rd edn. (Heidelberg, 1983), 226.

[68] H. v. Mangoldt and F. Klein, *Das Bonner Grundgesetz*, i, 2nd edn. (Berlin and Frankfurt, 1957), *Vorbemerkung* B XV 1 b (122).

[69] C. Schmitt, *Verfassungslehre*, 5th edn. (Berlin, 1970), 169.

[70] W. Schätzel, 'Der internationale Schutz der Menschenrechte', in *Festschrift für F. Giese* (Frankfurt a. M., 1953), 218.

formal, straight contour, that is the value of constitutional clarity',[71] Kloepfer warns of a 'dangerous undervaluing of form',[72] and Forsthoff's critique of an 'informalizing of the constitution' is, in connection with his references to the 'mathematical school of macro-economics' and the 'logical direction of modern philosophy',[73] also to be understood as a demand for conceptual-systematic clarification. However, one can reckon on controversy, when debate turns to the relative value of the analytical as against the empirical and the normative in the jurisprudential enterprise. This dispute leads straight back to long-standing disagreements about legal method.

Work in the analytical dimension corresponds closely to what conceptual jurisprudence[74] called 'the logical treatment of law'. A classic formulation of this programme can be found in Laband,

I know perfectly well that *exclusive* mastery of the logical treatment of law would be a most disadvantageous one-sidedness, and one which would lead in certain contexts to an atrophy of our science. I do not overlook the significance of legal historical research, or the value that history, economics, politics and philosophy can have for our understanding of law. Doctrine is not the *only* aspect of jurisprudence, but it is one aspect. The scientific function of a *doctrinal* analysis of a certain area of positive law lies in the construction of legal institutions, in the tracing of individual legal propositions to more general concepts, and then in the derivation of conclusions from these concepts. Apart from the process of establishing valid positive legal propositions, that is, the complete identification and mastery of the material to be processed, this is a purely logical activity of the mind. There is no other means to the fulfilment of this task than logic, which cannot be replaced by anything else for this purpose. All historical, political and philosophical considerations—however valuable they may be in and of themselves—are for the doctrinal analysis of concrete legal material without relevance, and often only serve to mask a lack of reconstructive work.[75]

What Laband describes as the 'logical treatment of law' has been the subject-matter of vigorous critique, principally among private lawyers, since the methodological controversy of the turn of the nineteenth

[71] P. Lerche, 'Review of Peter Häberle, Die Wesensgehaltgarantie des Art. 19 Abs. 2 Grundgesetz', DÖV 1965, 213.

[72] M. Kloepfer, *Grundrechte als Entstehenssicherung und Bestandsschutz* (Munich, 1970), 26.

[73] E. Forsthoff, 'Die Umbildung des Verfassungsgesetzes', in *Festschrift für C. Schmitt* (Berlin, 1959), 52.

[74] See the references in the article by W. Krawietz, 'Artikel: Begriffsjurisprudenz', in J. Ritter (ed.), *Historisches Wörterbuch der Philosophie*, i (Basle, 1971), cols. 809 ff., as well as in Krawietz (ed.), *Theorie und Technik der Begriffsjurisprudenz* (Darmstadt, 1976).

[75] P. Laband, *Das Staatsrecht des Deutschen Reiches*, i, 2nd edn. (Freiburg, 1888), p. x f. See also R. v. Ihering, 'Unsere Aufgabe', *Jahrbücher für Dogmatik*, 1 (1857), 7 ff.; C. F. Gerber, *System des Deutschen Privatrechts*, 2nd edn. (Jena, 1850), p. v ff., as well as the more comprehensive account in W. Wilhelm, *Zur juristischen Methodenlehre im 19. Jahrhundert* (Frankfurt a. M., 1958).

century.[76] The same discussion also took place within public law after some delay, mainly in the 1920s.[77]

Such different writers as Smend, Kaufmann, Heller, and Schmitt were united in their rejection of the positivist-analytical tradition of Gerber, Laband, Jellinek, and Kelsen. Smend characterized the 'Jellinek-Kelsen-line' as a 'cul-de-sac without purpose or goal'[78] and argued for a dissolution of 'juristic formalism' through a public law theory founded on the 'methods of the humanities'.[79] Kaufmann accused the analytical approach, with its neo-Kantian tendencies, of trying to 'eliminate the substantive content of legal concepts'[80] and of being responsible for the 'unusually low cultural status of a large part of our jurisprudence'.[81] Heller spoke of a 'formalism from top to bottom insubstantial and irresponsible'[82] and a 'mistaken path that our theory of state has taken for the past two generations in the belief that it must avoid all sociological and ethical problems'.[83] Carl Schmitt stated that 'only philosophical, economic, ethical and political stupidity is left as the single identifying characteristic of a doubtless pure, nothing-but-juristic, intellectual process'.[84][85]

To the extent that these viewpoints criticize a reduction of jurisprudence to the analytical dimension, they can be accepted. Jurisprudence can only fulfil its practical task as a multidimensional discipline. Windscheid's famous maxim, that 'the final decision is the result of a calculation in which the legal concepts are the factors'[86] expresses an overvaluation of logic's potential. It is precisely logical analysis which shows that the decision in moderately difficult cases cannot be derived from the legal norms and

---

[76] On this, see in place of many, K. Larenz, *Methodenlehre der Rechtswissenschaft*, 5th edn. (Berlin, Heidelberg, New York, and Tokyo, 1983), 43 ff.

[77] See M. Friedrich, 'Die Grundlagendiskussion in der Weimarer Staatsrechtslehre', *Politische Vierteljahresschrift*, 13 (1972), 582 ff.; K. Sontheimer, 'Zur Grundlagenproblematik der deutschen Staatsrechtslehre in der Weimarer Republik', ARSP 46 (1960), 39 ff.

[78] R. Smend, 'Verfassung und Verfassungsrecht' (1928), in *Staatsrechtliche Abhandlungen und andere Aufsätze*, 2nd edn. (Berlin, 1968), 124.

[79] ibid. 119 ff.

[80] E. Kaufmann, *Kritik der neukantischen Rechtsphilosophie* (Tübingen, 1921), 75.

[81] ibid. 76.

[82] H. Heller, 'Die Krisis der Staatslehre' (1926), in id., *Gesammelte Schriften*, ii (Leiden, 1971), 9.

[83] ibid. 15.

[84] C. Schmitt, *Über die drei Arten des rechtswissenschaftlichen Denkens* (Hamburg, 1934), 39 f.

[85] Ehrlich's polemic against 'fruitless sharp-wittedness' lies outside of this group. However, it is worth mentioning, because it is characteristic of an anti-analytical tendency that is never quite laid to rest: 'Sharp-wittedness is the most fruitless of the talents of the human spirit; there is deep wisdom in the fact that the devil of German folklore is so often a sharp-witted dialectician' (E. Ehrlich, 'Freie Rechtsfindung und freie Rechtswissenschaft', in id., *Recht und Leben. Gesammelte Schriften zur Rechtstatsachenforschung und zur Freirechtslehre* (Berlin, 1967), 202).

[86] B. Windscheid, *Lehrbuch des Pandektenrechts*, i, 9th edn., ed. T. Kipp (Frankfurt a. M., 1906), 111.

concepts identified through logic in the first place.[87] Additional values, and empirical knowledge as the basis of these values, are essential. A logical technique which reaches conclusions without such additional premises, and which wants in this sense to be *productive*, can only create the illusion of logic, which masks the necessary normative premises that—logically speaking—really do lead to the conclusions. This is what the later Ihering had in mind when he turned against the 'cult of the logical, which thinks it can twist jurisprudence into a mathematics of law'.[88]

But however justified the objections to a reduction of jurisprudence to the analytical dimension and every attempt to base judicial decision-taking on logic *alone* might be, the noticeable undervaluing of the analytical in the quotations cited is not. Without a conceptual-systematic exposition of law, jurisprudence is not possible as a rational enterprise. The measure of rationality of jurisprudence depends to a large extent on the standard it reaches in the analytical dimension. Without analytical clarity, we could not even make precise and justifiable statements about the relationship of the three dimensions. There could be no talk of a rationally controlled appropriation of the value-judgments indispensable to jurisprudence or the methodologically controlled use of empirical knowledge. To the extent that the study of constitutional rights can distance itself at all from political rhetoric and the vacillating battle of world-views, this is the work of the analytical dimension. If one adds to this, first, that the analytical dimension makes possible discoveries in jurisprudence which cannot be delivered by any other field of knowledge, and, secondly, that these belong to some of the most reliable of jurisprudential insights, then we have reason enough to characterize and engage in the conceptual-systematic exposition of law as the '*opus proprium*' of jurisprudence.[89]

For all the faults of the 'logical treatment of law', we must not abandon its correct emphasis on what is jurisprudentially essential. There is even less reason for this, given that modern logic, theory of method, and practical philosophy all provide tools which hold out the hope of a fruitful development of existing conceptual research[90] and of its location in a complete model of an integrative theory. In this sense, the structural theory propounded here stands in the great analytical tradition of conceptual jurisprudence.

[87] See Alexy, *Theory of Legal Argumentation*, 221 ff.
[88] R. v. Ihering, *Geist des römischen Rechts*, part 3, 5th edn. (Leipzig, 1906), 321 f. See also E. Ehrlich, *Die juristische Logik* (Tübingen, 1918), 299 ff.; as well as P. Heck, *Begriffsbildung und Interessenjurisprudenz* (Tübingen, 1932), 94 ff.
[89] Dreier, *Recht—Moral—Ideologie*, 112.
[90] As an example of which, reference can be made to Jellinek's status theory discussed at 163 ff. below.

2

The Concept of a Constitutional Rights Norm

There is a close connection between the concept of a constitutional rights norm and the concept of a constitutional right.[1] Whenever anyone has a constitutional right, there must be a valid constitutional rights norm which grants them that right. It is questionable whether the reverse applies. It does not apply in the case of constitutional rights norms which do not grant subjective rights. One could answer the question of whether such norms exist by defining the problem away: only norms which grant constitutional rights are constitutional rights norms. Constitutional rights norms and constitutional rights would then simply be two sides of the same coin. However, this way out is inappropriate for a theory which relates to positive law. Norms are included in the text of the constitutional rights catalogue which do not correspond directly to any subjective right. Whether these norms have any legal effect is a question of the interpretation of positive law and should not be ruled out as a matter of mere definition. A definition by which only those norms which grant subjective rights are to be classed as constitutional rights norms could have the consequence that there might be norms enacted as part of the catalogue of constitutional rights which could not be called 'constitutional rights norms'. Such terminology seems awkward. It seems more appropriate to treat the concept of a constitutional rights norm as wider than that of a constitutional right. This point,

---

[1] The fact that there are close connections does not mean that no distinction is to be drawn between constitutional rights norms and constitutional rights. Many examples can be given of inadequate differentiation, of which two will suffice for present purposes. The Federal Constitutional Court has stated that it '[can] only consider whether the legal regulation in question is compatible with the *norms* of the Basic Law, *in particular* with constitutional *rights*' (BVerfGE 21, 73 (78), emphasis added), and Breuer uses the phrase 'constitutional rights as claim-norms' as the title of an essay concerning 'constitutional claim-rights' (R. Breuer, 'Grundrechte als Anspruchsnormen', in O. Bachof, E. Heigl, and K. Redeker (eds.), *Verwaltungsrecht zwischen Freiheit, Teilhabe und Bindung, Festgabe aus Anlaß des 25jährigen Bestehens des Bundesverwaltungsgerichts* (Munich, 1978), 89). A clear distinction between constitutional rights norms and constitutional rights is drawn, for example, by W. Schmidt-Rimpler, P. Giesecke, E. Friesenhahn, and A. Knur, 'Die Lohngleichheit von Männern und Frauen', AöR 76 (1950/1) 172, and E. Friesenhahn 'Der Wandel des Grundrechtsverständnisses', in *Verhandlungen des fünfzigsten Deutschen Juristentages*, ii (Munich, 1974), G 4, as well as by F. Klein, in H. v. Mangoldt and F. Klein, *Das Bonner Grundgesetz*, i, 2nd edn. (Berlin and Frankfurt, 1957) *Vorbemerkung* A VI (79).

together with the fact that every assertion of the existence of a constitutional right presupposes the existence of a valid constitutional rights norm, justifies our starting with the analysis of the concept of a constitutional rights norm.[2]

I. ON THE CONCEPT OF A NORM

Constitutional rights norms are norms. They thus share all the problems associated with the concept of a norm. The concept of a norm is one of the most, if not *the* most, fundamental in all jurisprudence. This does not mean that the use of the term is limited to law alone. This expression, along with associated ones, such as 'rule', 'command', and 'regulation', have an established place apart from general usage in other disciplines such as sociology, ethnology, moral philosophy, and linguistics. The use of the term 'norm' in all these areas is characterized by the fact that it is used with a variety of meanings,[3] most of which are rather vague, and that endless controversy ensues whenever the term is roused from the slumber of unreflective usage.

1. ON THE CONTROVERSY ABOUT THE CONCEPT OF A NORM

It is hardly surprising that being the fundamental concept of jurisprudence which it is, discussion about the concept of a norm seems endless. Every definition of this concept includes decisions about the content and method of the discipline, and hence about its character. What one is concerned with, and how one justifies it, depends on whether a norm is understood as the objective 'meaning of an act by which a certain behavior is commanded, permitted, or authorised',[4] or as 'counter-factually stabilised behavioural expectations',[5] or as a command,[6] or as a model of behaviour which is either followed, or if not followed has a social reaction as a consequence,[7] or as an expression having a certain form,[8] or as a social rule.[9] The problems raised

---

[2] This takes no position on the classic problem of whether rights or duties, or objective norms or subjective rights, have priority. This problem turns primarily on substantive issues. See on this, J. Finnis, *Natural Law and Natural Rights* (Oxford, 1980), 205 ff.

[3] An impressive account of both the terminological variation as well as the variety of associated meanings in sociology can be found in R. Lautmann, *Wert und Norm. Begriffsanalysen für die Soziologie*, 2nd edn. (Opladen, 1971), 54 ff. One of the most fruitful attempts to systematize the matter is to be found in G. H. v. Wright, *Norm and Action* (London, 1963), 1–16.

[4] H. Kelsen, *Pure Theory of Law* trans. M. Knight (Berkeley, 1967), 5.

[5] N. Luhmann, *A Sociological Theory of Law*, trans. E. King and M. Albrow (London, 1985), 33.

[6] J. Austin, *Lectures on Jurisprudence*, i, 4th edn. (London, 1873), 98.

[7] T. Geiger, *Vorstudien zu einer Soziologie des Rechts*, 2nd edn. (Neuwied and Berlin, 1964), 61 f., 68 ff.

[8] J. Wróblewski, 'The Problem of the Meaning of the Legal Norm', in id., *Meaning and Truth in Judicial Decision* (Helsinki, 1979), 15.

[9] H. L. A. Hart, *The Concept of Law* (Oxford, 1961), 54 ff.

by this list of definitions are significant for the current discussion, albeit to a variable extent. Having said that, they are not the subject-matter of this discussion. This suggests that we should look for a model of norms which, on one hand, is rich enough to form the basis for further discussion, but which, on the other, is weak enough to be consistent with as many positions in the conceptual debate as possible. These requirements are satisfied by a semantic model which is consistent with a great variety of theories concerning legal validity.

2. THE SEMANTIC CONCEPT OF A NORM

The starting-point of this model is the distinction between a *norm* and a *normative statement*.[10] Take as an example of a normative statement the statement:

(1) No German may be extradited to a foreign country (art. 16(2)(1) Basic Law).

This statement expresses the norm that it is forbidden to extradite a German to a foreign country. That it is forbidden to extradite a German to a foreign country is what the statement 'no German may be extradited to a

---

[10] In reality this distinction is drawn by numerous authors, although the terminology varies considerably and there is great variety both in the justification for the distinction and in the consequences which are taken to flow from it. The terms adopted here correspond to those of C. and O. Weinberger (see C. and O. Weinberger, *Logik, Semantik, Hermeneutik* (Munich, 1979), 20, 108). Ross distinguishes between the 'linguistic form which expresses a directive' and the 'directive' itself (A. Ross, *Directives and Norms* (London, 1968), 34 ff.). The 'directive' is what is here called a 'norm'. By 'norm' Ross understands something else, as will be shown later. According to H. J. Wolff, the expression 'norm' stands for the 'imperative content (sense) expressed by a "legal proposition" ' (H. J. Wolff and O. Bachof, *Verwaltungsrecht*, i, 9th edn. (Munich, 1974), 115). G. H. v. Wright speaks of 'norm formulation' and 'norm', but he does not agree with the thesis concerning the relationship between normative statement and norm put forward here (Wright, *Norm and Action*, 93 f.). Rottleuthner adopts von Wright's terminology (H. Rottleuthner, *Rechtstheorie und Rechtssoziologie* (Freiburg and Munich, 1981), 42). Following Kelsen, he uses the expression 'normative statement' [*Normsatz*] for statements that norms apply. Kelsen calls such statements 'legal statements' [*Rechtssätze*] and contrasts them with 'legal norms' (Kelsen, *Pure Theory of Law*, 73). Kelsen uses the expression 'norm' differently from the way it is used here, as can be seen already from the fact that for Kelsen something is only a norm if it has 'objectively the sense of ought', which for Kelsen means that it can be derived from a basic norm giving rise to objective validity (ibid. 7 f.). Quite apart from that point, it is hard to incorporate Kelsen's view in the model used here. According to Kelsen, the norm is the 'meaning of a willing, or act of will' (*General Theory of Norms*, trans. M. Hartney (Oxford, 1991), 2; see also his *Pure Theory of Law*, 4 ff.) which appears to be something quite different from the sense or meaning of a sentence. The meaning of an act of will is characterized by Kelsen in the following way: 'that the other person should behave in a certain way' (*General Theory of Norms*, 39). In this sense he states, 'by "norm" we mean that something ought to be or ought to happen, especially that a human being *ought to* behave in a specific way' (*Pure Theory of Law*, 4). But this is precisely what is meant here by 'norm'. So apart from the mentalistic elements (will, act of will), there does seem to be a close connection between the model adopted here and the view of Kelsen.

foreign country' means. A norm is thus the meaning of a normative state-ment.[11]

The fact that it is right to distinguish between a norm and a normative statement can also be seen in the fact that the same norm can be expressed by other formulations. So the norm that it is forbidden to extradite a German to a foreign country instead of being expressed as in (1) can also be expressed:

(1')   It is forbidden to extradite Germans to a foreign country

or

(1")   Germans may not be extradited to a foreign country

or through a corresponding statement in some other language. It is easy to spot that these statements express norms because they contain expressions such as 'forbidden' and 'may not'. But norms can also be expressed with-out using such terms. Take for example, the formulations of the Criminal Code, such as section 223(1): 'whoever physically abuses another or injures their health will be punished with imprisonment for up to three years or with a fine'. As the context shows, this formulation is not intended to express what is the case, but what ought to be the case. The norm that it is forbidden to extradite Germans to a foreign country could also be expressed in a similar way, such as:

(1''')   Germans will not be extradited to a foreign country.

It should also be noted that norms can be expressed without the use of words at all, such as by traffic lights.

This makes it clear that the concept of a norm is prior to that of a norma-tive statement.[12] It is therefore appropriate to look for criteria for the iden-tification of norms not at the level of statements but at the level of the norm itself. Such a criterion can be established with the help of deontic modes, and at this point only the basic deontic modes of command, prohibition, and permission need be considered. What exactly deontic modes are, how many there are, their structure, and their relationship to each other will be considered at greater length below. To clarify the point at issue, we only need to consider the mode of prohibition used in the examples above. By using this mode we can say that the statement 'Germans will not be extra-dited to a foreign country' (1''') expresses a norm and is therefore a norma-tive statement because it expresses a prohibition on extraditing Germans to a foreign country.

This leads to the question of what a prohibition is and how one tells that a statement such as the one just given expresses a prohibition. One could

---

[11] Thus also Weinberger and Weinberger, *Logik, Semantik, Hermeneutik,* 20, 108, as also in connection with the 'linguistic form which expresses a directive' and the 'directive', Ross, *Directives and Norms,* 34.

[12] See on this Wright, *Norm and Action,* 102 f.

say in answer to the first question that a prohibition is the negation of a permission. But what is a permission? Saying that a permission is the negation of a prohibition is objectionable circular reasoning. And this objection can easily be combined with another, namely that if no better definition of prohibition is possible, then the idea should not be used to explain the concept of a norm. In reply, it can be pointed out that the demand for a definition of each and every concept by some new concept leads to an infinite regress and is impossible to fulfil. If anything is to be said at all, we have to proceed on the basis of concepts which are not further defined within the conceptual system presupposed. This does not mean that one can do as one pleases at the level of basic concepts. An attempt will be made to show that the basic deontic concepts used here relate to each other in a well-defined order. They can also be tested to see if their structure adequately replicates the language of law. In addition, their suitability is demonstrated by their ability to ground a fruitful theory of constitutional rights.

As regards the second question, how one can tell that a statement such as an indicative statement in the Criminal Code expresses a norm, the answer is simply that we can tell from the context. 'Context' includes both the statements that are connected with the one in question and its use, that is, the circumstances and rules concerning its application. The fact that pragmatic considerations thus become indispensable in the identification of something as a norm does not affect the fact that what is identified is a semantic entity, namely a meaning which includes a deontic mode.[13]

Every norm can be expressed by a normative statement. As has been shown, there are various ways of expressing a norm. It is useful to identify one particular way of expressing norms which is represented when the norm that it is forbidden to extradite Germans to a foreign country is expressed by the statements, 'No German may be extradited to a foreign country' (1), 'It is forbidden to extradite Germans to a foreign country' (1'), or 'Germans may not be extradited to a foreign country' (1″). Statements such as these are characterized by the use of *deontic expressions* such as 'may', 'forbidden', and 'shall'. They should therefore be referred to as *deontic statements*.[14]

---

[13] In this connection, Ross states that just as expressions contain a specific indicative element, 'so it is', so also directives contain a 'specific directive element "so it ought to be" ' (Ross, *Directives and Norms*, 13, 34.). In a development of his well-known distinction between neustic and phrastic (R. M. Hare, *The Language of Morals* (London, Oxford, and New York, 1952), 18), Hare calls these elements 'tropic' to which what is said belongs, and not what is done, as with the neustic (R. M. Hare, 'Meaning and Speech Acts', in id., *Practical Inferences* (London and Basingstoke, 1971), 90); see also R. Alexy, *A Theory of Legal Argumentation* (Oxford, 1989), 58 ff. What is here called the 'deontic mode' belongs to what Hare calls the 'tropic' and corresponds to Ross's 'specific directive element "so it ought to be" '.

[14] On this expression, see Wright, *Norm and Action*, 96. It should be emphasized that deontic statements are not different from normative statements, but are a sub-category of norma-

The expression, 'has a right to . . .', is also a deontic expression.[15] As will be discussed in more detail below, terms such as 'has a right to . . .' express complex deontic modes. Thus the statement, 'all Germans have the right to form corporations and associations' (art. 9(1) Basic Law) is also a deontic statement. By contrast, *imperative statements* such as, 'a German shall never be extradited to a foreign country!' and *indicative statements without deontic expressions*, such as 'Germans will not be extradited to a foreign country' (1''') are not deontic. Whenever such statements do express norms, they can be reworked into deontic statements expressing the same norm. Not every normative statement is a deontic statement, but every normative statement can be reformulated into a deontic statement. The significance of this should not be underestimated, because standard forms of deontic statements can be created which expose the structure of the norms being expressed. Standard forms of deontic statements are the final stage of development before one reaches the representation of the logical structure of norms in a formal language.

The relationship between normative statements and norms corresponds to that between expressive statements and expressions.[16] Instead of 'expression', the meaning of an expressive statement is sometimes termed 'thought'[17] or 'proposition'.[18] The significant distinction between normative statements and norms on the one hand and propositional statements and propositions on the other is generally said to be the fact that it can only sensibly be said of propositions and propositional statements that they are true or false, whereas this cannot be said of norms or normative statements.[19] This epistemological assumption will not be made here. In grasping the distinction, it is sufficient to say that propositional statements express the idea that something is the case, while normative statements

---

tive statements. All deontic statements are normative statements, but not all normative statements are deontic statements. The expression 'deontic statement' is used in quite a different sense by Weinberger and Weinberger. There it stands for propositions about norm-systems, that is, for what will be termed 'norm-assertion statements' (see Weinberger and Weinberger, *Logik, Semantik, Hermeneutik*, 99, 111 ff.). In what follows the expression 'deontological' will be used instead of 'deontic' as a counterpart to expressions such as 'axiological'.

[15] See on this Ross, *Directives and Norms*, 36.

[16] The structural correspondence is exploited by Ross with great care, although he admittedly speaks of 'directive' instead of 'norm'. See his *Directives and Norms*, 9 ff., 34 ff. See also Weinberger and Weinberger, *Logik, Semantik, Hermeneutik*, 19 f., as well as H. J. Wolff, in Wolff and Bachof, *Verwaltungsrecht*, i, 115, according to whom the distinction between norm and legal statement corresponds to that between 'logical judgment' and 'logical statement'. Wright (*Norm and Action*, 93 f.) is critical of the assumption of structural correspondence.

[17] Thus G. Frege, 'Thoughts' in *Logical Investigations*, trans. P. T. Geach and R. H. Stoothoff (Oxford, 1977), 5, who in addition speaks in terms of 'sense' rather than 'meaning' (reference). Weinberger speaks of norms as thoughts: see O. Weinberger, *Logische Analyse in der Jurisprudenz* (Berlin, 1979), 97, 'the norm is a thought'.

[18] R. Carnap, *Meaning and Necessity*, 2nd edn. (Chicago and London, 1956), 27.

[19] Frege, 'Thoughts' 6 (in the context of commands); Weinberger and Weinberger, *Logik, Sernantik, Hermeneutik*, 20.

express the idea that something is required, prohibited, and so on. If one gathers the various deontic modes under the single concept of 'ought',[20] one can say simply that propositional statements express the idea that something *is the case*, and normative statements the idea that something *ought to be the case*.

The analogy that has just been drawn between normative statements and norms on one hand and propositional statements and propositions on the other is commonly expressed in the choice of terminology as well. This occurs for example when instead of the four terms used here one finds 'normative statement', 'normative expression', 'empirical statement', and 'empirical expression'. These terms will be used from time to time here as well.

3. THE SEPARATION OF SEMANTIC QUESTIONS FROM QUESTIONS OF VALIDITY

The semantic conception of the idea of a norm adopted here distinguishes strictly between the concept of a norm and the concept of its validity. As an example of a definition of a norm which combines semantic elements with issues of validity consider that of Alf Ross. According to Ross, a norm is 'a directive which corresponds to certain social facts in such a way that the pattern of behaviour expressed in the norm (1) is in general followed by members of the society, and (2) is felt by them as binding (valid)'.[21] By 'directive' Ross understands the same idea as is here expressed by 'norm'. The adoption of criteria of validity, in this case empirical criteria, in the definition of a norm is said to be necessary so that one can 'say that certain norms actually *exist* or *are in force*'.[22] But Ross's definition goes too far. It does not just make it *possible* to speak of the existence or validity of a norm, it makes it *necessary*, since only valid or existing norms are, on his definition, norms at all. If there is an interest in speaking of the validity or existence of norms—and there is indeed such an interest—then there is also an interest in speaking of invalid and non-existent norms. But in that case the concept of a norm must not be defined in such a way as to include its validity or existence. Just as it is possible 'to express a thought without laying it down as true',[23] so also it has to be possible to express a norm without assuming that it is valid.

Relieving the concept of a norm from the burden of validity seems at first glance to have the disadvantage that the universe of norms suddenly becomes overpopulated. Everybody can express as many norms with whatever content they please. But this does not give rise to any serious difficulty.

---

[20] See on this, e.g. Kelsen, *General Theory of Norms*, 97.
[21] Ross, *Directives and Norms*, 93.   [22] ibid. 79.
[23] Frege, 'Thoughts', 7.

It does not in practice make any difference whether in order to establish that something is a norm one has to ask from the outset whether it fulfils a certain criterion of validity, or whether to establish that something is a valid norm one asks first whether it is a norm and then whether it fulfils the criterion of validity. There would be a more serious objection if the semantic definition corresponded less well than the validity-enhanced definition with general or legally expert usage. This is the case in a whole series of contexts. The statement of a bank robber, 'you should not give me any coins' would hardly be characterized in general usage as a norm.[24] On the other hand, there are many expressions which correspond better to the semantic definition. If one understands 'norm' as 'valid norm', the simple statement, 'this norm no longer applies' becomes inconsistent. Even statements such as 'the following norm shall apply' become problematic. It should also be noted that in the case of the bank robber, it is not just the issue of validity but also its logical structure which leads us to pause before calling it a norm. General usage tends to resist calling individual norms,[25] such as are found in legal judgments, 'norms'. If the bank robber had said, 'on the first of every month banknotes are to be ready prepared at every counter' there would be fewer objections to terming this an (invalid) norm. In general, one can say that the objection that this definition does not correspond to common and legally expert usage is not so much related to the question of validity, but to the inclusion of norms which have a certain logical structure, such as individual norms. General usage and existing technical usage are important but not essential perspectives for the creation of intellectual concepts. What is decisive is their usefulness. The semantic definition of a norm is certainly not equally suitable for all purposes, nevertheless, in questions of legal doctrine and the application of law, it is more useful than any other. These areas are concerned with issues such as the logical compatibility of two norms, the consequences of a norm, how it is to be interpreted and applied, if it is valid, and, sometimes, if it is not valid whether it should be. The semantic definition of a norm is tailored to just these sorts of question.[26]

---

[24] In this situation, Kelsen's model, according to which such an expression has only 'subjectively the meaning of ought' (because the bank robber lacks authority), and not objectively, and is thus not the expression of a norm (Kelsen, *Pure Theory of Law*, 8 f.), fits general usage better than the semantic model. Ross also takes the view that the bank robber does not express a norm. He justifies this by pointing out that it only concerns a transitory event (Ross, *Directives and Norms*, 80).

[25] On the concept of the individual norm see Ross, *Directives and Norms*, 106 ff.; Kelsen, *Pure Theory of Law*, 19.

[26] See on this H. Yoshino, 'Zur Anwendbarkeit der Regeln der Logik auf Rechtsnormen', in *Die Reine Rechtslehre in wissenschaftlicher Diskussion, Schriftenreihe des Hans Kelsen-Instituts*, vii (Vienna, 1982), 146 ff.

4. THE CONNECTION OF SEMANTIC QUESTIONS WITH QUESTIONS OF VALIDITY

A further strength of the semantic definition consists in the fact that it is not only consistent with many different theories of legal validity, but it is also presupposed by them. By a theory of validity is meant a theory which sets out criteria for when a norm is valid. The formal structure of the core of various theories of validity can be simplified and expressed as follows: when in respect of norm N the criteria $C_1, \ldots C_n$ apply, then norm N is valid. The various theories of validity can be distinguished by the criteria they adopt. To the extent that social facts, such as regular obedience connected with a feeling of obligation,[27] or the alternatives of obedience and punishment of disobedience,[28] are adopted, one can speak of *sociological* theories of validity. To the extent that the creation of the norm by an authority empowered to do so by a higher norm is appealed to,[29] one can speak of *juridical* theories of validity. And to the extent that moral reasons, such as 'natural law'[30] are seen as determinative of validity, one has an *ethical* theory of validity.[31] The many and varied issues associated with these three groups of theories of validity need not detain us here.[32] The only

---

[27] See Ross, *Directives and Norms*, 82 ff., 93.

[28] See Geiger, *Vorstudien zu einer Soziologie des Rechts*, 68 ff.

[29] See Kelsen, *Pure Theory of Law*, 198 ff.

[30] See I. Kant, *The Metaphysics of Morals*, trans. M. Gregor (Cambridge, 1991), 51.

[31] On the threefold division of concepts of validity into sociological, juridical, and ethical, see R. Dreier, *Recht—Moral—Ideologie* (Frankfurt a. M., 1981), 194 ff., and also J. Wróblewski, 'Three Concepts of Validity of Law', *Tidskrift, utgiven av Juridiska Föreningen i Finland* (1982), 408 ff., who distinguishes between systemic, factual, and axiological validity.

[32] The problem that needs mentioning in particular is the question of whether the three concepts of validity lie on the same categorical level. It is the juridical concept of validity which provides the stimulus for this question. According to this concept, the validity of a norm rests on the validity of another norm which is higher in the legal hierarchy, which authorizes the creation of the first norm. If one questions the validity of the authorizing norm, then one can only appeal to a further norm etc. Since this process cannot be carried on indefinitely, the regress has to be blocked by some sort of basic norm. If one wants to avoid seeing this Grundnorm as a purely transcendental-logical, or fictional, condition of validity (cf. Kelsen, *Pure Theory of Law*, 201 ff., 'transcendental-logical presupposition'; id., *General Theory of Norms*, 256, 'fictitious norm') for which a whole set of reasons can be given (see R. Dreier, 'Bemerkungen zur Rechtserkenntnistheorie', *Rechtstheorie*, Beiheft 1 (1979), 95 ff.; A Peczenik, 'On the Nature and Function of the Grundnorm', *Rechtstheorie,* Beiheft 2 (1981), 279 ff.) one can only justify the Grundnorm in the context of a sociological or an ethical concept of validity. But then the significance of the juridical concept of validity shrinks to its application to norms in systems of norms, which are created on the basis of norms which authorize their creation. Of course, such norms created on the basis of other norms are a typical hallmark of modern legal systems, but they are also present in norm-systems which are not legal systems. This might seem to suggest that instead of three concepts of validity, we should really only talk of two, a sociological and an ethical, and distinguish in the context of each between direct and indirect (i.e. with reference to authorizing norms) justifications of validity. Nevertheless, maintaining the threefold division is justified by the fact that in jurisprudence justifying validity by reference to social facts and moral reasons is less important than a reference to proper enactment together with substantive conformity with higher status law.

comment to make is that the semantic definition of a norm does not presuppose or exclude any of these theories, but that each theory which wants to say of something that it is valid, must have an idea of the thing of which it wants to say this. The best candidate for this thing is the norm as understood on the semantic definition.

5. THE ASSERTION AND CREATION OF NORMS

Until now we have only considered norms and the statements which express them. Asserting the validity of a norm and creating a norm are to be distinguished from both of these. Someone who asserts that a norm is valid or who creates a norm undertakes an act. Such acts can be called 'speech acts' after J. L. Austin.[33] In considering acts of norm-assertion and acts of norm-creation we are leaving the field of semantics for the field of pragmatics.

Whether we are dealing with an act of norm-assertion or an act of norm-creation can often not be determined from the content of the expression alone. If someone answers, 'you may park here', to the question, 'may I park here?', they could be doing many different things. They might be telling the questioner about the law currently in force, that is, informing them about a valid norm, or they might be granting permission, say if the questioner wishes to park on their land. In that case they would be creating a norm.[34] What is actually being done can only be determined by the circumstances surrounding the expression. Suppose we are concerned with the provision of information. In that case the statement expressed is to be understood as a statement concerning what is permissible within the boundaries of the current legal order, that is, as regards which norm is valid. Statements which are intended to express which norms are valid will be called '*statements of normative validity*'. Depending on the particular criteria of validity adopted, different things will be said by such statements. Generally speaking, in cases such as the one just cited, we are not concerned with the factual consequences or enforcement of the parking law, nor with what considerations of rationality require or permit, but with what has been laid down in the context of an existing and largely functioning legal order as regards the problem of parking. Statements of normative validity of this nature are capable of truth: they are either true or false.[35]

---

[33] See J. L. Austin, *How to do things with Words* (London, Oxford, and New York, 1962), as well as J. R. Searle, *Speech Acts* (Cambridge, 1969). For a brief account of speech act theory, see Alexy, *Theory of Legal Argumentation*, 53 ff.

[34] See on this Wright, *Norm and Action*, 104 f.

[35] Kelsen uses the expression 'legal statements' ('rules of law', "propositions of law') for statements of normative validity (Kelsen, *Pure Theory of Law*, 71). Here, the expression 'legal statement' is reserved for normative statements which express legal norms. According to Kelsen, statements of normative validity which are related to juridical validity and capable of truth are *the* statements of jurisprudence, since according to him, jurisprudence should be limited to the description of law (ibid. 73). In reality, as will soon be seen in this text, state-

Statements of normative validity of the form indicated above give rise to no particular problems. Problems start arising however if an ethical conception of validity is presupposed, or when (which is more likely to be the case) moral criteria are incorporated within the juridical concept of validity. These problems are related to those associated with *interpretative assertions*, which are to be seen as a subdivision of statements of normative validity. What is the status of an assertion such as 'the rights and freedoms contained in particular in article 2 (free personal development), article 5 (freedom to form and express opinions) and article 12 (freedom of profession) Basic Law [also contain] a right to education and higher education'?[36] This statement is significantly different from the one above about parking, yet it too is to be included as a statement of normative validity. The reasons which can be advanced for (or against) it are certainly different in nature from those in the parking case. References to acts of legislation or to other empirical facts will not suffice. In order to reach a complete justification (whether applicable or not) of a statement concerning a right to education and higher education, normative resources are necessary which cannot be drawn from existing authoritative material or empirical statements. This does not affect the character of the statement as a statement of normative validity, and its assertion as an assertion of normative validity. Just as normative statements can be turned into statements about valid norms on the basis of a variety of theories of normative validity, so also can assertions of normative validity be based on various criteria of correctness.

It has already been noted that a statement such as, 'you may park here', can be used not only to assert a norm but also to create one. There is a great variety of acts of norm-creation. A similarly simple one is the situation where a father forbids his children to drink anything before they have

---

ments of normative validity which are not capable of truth in this sense also appear in jurisprudence. It will be shown that they are correct so to appear.

Statements of normative validity about what applies socially must be distinguished from statements of normative validity about what applies juridically. Such a statement would arise if there were indeed a prohibition on parking in the parking case, but if the answer, 'you can go right ahead and park here' were given, coupled with the observation, 'we all do it, and the police drive past every day and have never done anything'.

The distinctions adopted here are relatively crude. Further distinctions need not be drawn. They could refer, for example, to whether the person making the statement in the case in question has legal competence (such as a judge or a policeman) or not, and whether a private person is simply making the statement as a matter of neutral information, or is expressing an expectation, or requirement, of obedience. There are some grounds for accepting that there is a normative assertion in all these cases, and in some cases either qualifying this in some way, or coupling it with a further speech act.

Explicit assertions of validity must be distinguished from the normative assertions we have considered already, such as might appear in a law textbook and which can be made by replicating normative statements. Statements expressed by explicit assertions of validity have the form, 'in society S (legal system L), norm N is valid at time t' (see Rottleuthner, *Rechtstheorie und Rechtssoziologie*, 47). Non-explicit statements of normative validity can be reconstructed in terms of such explicit statements of normative validity.

[36] K. Grimmer, *Demokratie und Grundrechte* (Berlin, 1980), 285.

emptied their plates. By contrast there can be highly complex acts of norm-creation such as the adoption of the Basic Law by the Parliamentary Council on 8 May 1949, its ratification by the occupying forces on 12 May 1949, its adoption by the popular representatives of ten of the eleven Regions in the week 16–22 May 1949, and after these acts of adoption had been certified by the Parliamentary Council on 23 May 1949, its signature and publication by the Council as represented by its President. Acts of norm-creation of this form are not the same as those which jurisprudence engages in. In such matters, assertions about acts of norm-creation, and the *statements of norm-creation*[37] expressed in these assertions, play an important role, in particular as arguments for assertions of validity. Of course, in the area of constitutional rights doctrine, such statements are of secondary importance. It can be assumed that the norms which were created by the particular act of norm-creation just referred to are indeed valid.

II. THE CONSTITUTIONAL RIGHTS NORM

Until now we have been considering norms in general; now we must consider what *constitutional rights* norms are. This question can be considered in both abstract and concrete forms. In the abstract, the question seeks to identify the criteria by which a norm can be considered a constitutional rights norm independently from its position in any given legal system or constitution. In the concrete, the question tries to establish which norms in any given legal system or constitution are constitutional rights norms. Here we are concerned with a theory of the *constitutional rights of the Basic Law*. We are therefore interested in the second question as it relates to a particular constitution, namely the Basic Law.

There is a simple answer to the question which goes as follows: constitutional rights norms are those norms which are expressed by provisions relating to constitutional rights, and constitutional rights provisions are those statements, and only those statements, contained in the text of the Basic Law. This answer gives rise to two problems. The first is that, since not all statements of the Basic Law express constitutional rights norms, it presupposes some criterion by which it is possible to divide the statements of the Basic Law into those which express constitutional rights norms and those which do not. The second problem concerns whether it is true that the constutional rights norms of the Basic Law are only those norms which are directly expressed by statements of the Basic Law.

---

[37] On this concept, see F. v. Kutschera, *Einführung in die Logik der Normen, Werte und Entscheidungen* (Freiburg and Munich, 1973), 13.

1. Constitutional Rights Norms and Constitutional Rights Provisions

In formulating both problems, the concept of a statement of the Basic Law plays a significant role. An example of a statement of the Basic Law is, 'no German shall be extradited to a foreign country' (art. 16(2)(1)). This statement expresses a norm and is therefore a normative statement. All articles of the Basic Law contain normative statements or parts of normative statements. The norm expressed by the example above is a constitutional rights norm. The statement could therefore be termed a 'normative statement relating to a constitutional right', but rather than using this rather unwieldy expression, we will refer to a *constitutional rights provision* in what follows. So the question is, what makes any given statement of the Basic Law a constitutional rights provision? And the answer to this question can turn on substantive, structural, and/or formal characteristics.

One criterion which combines *substantive* and *structural* elements can be derived from Schmitt's definition of a constitutional right. According to this definition, rights are only constitutional 'if they form part of the foundation of the state itself and are recognised as such in the Constitution'.[38] The fact that a right belongs to 'the foundation of the state itself' is a substantive requirement. According to Schmitt, only a certain group of rights belong to the foundation of the liberal state under the Rule of Law, namely the 'individual liberties'.[39] 'Constitutional rights, or rather constitutional rights in the proper sense of the word'[40] are thus only rights which demonstrate a certain structure, that of the individual rights to liberty.

There are disadvantages in trying to determine the concept of a constitutional right by reference to such substantive and structural criteria. It ties the concept of a constitutional right from the very beginning to a particular theory of the state which is only controversially that of the Basic Law. A right such as the guarantee of a basic minimum material support necessary for existence,[41] even if it can be derived from the norms of the constitutional rights catalogue,[42] could not be called a constitutional right, since it has a structure different from that of the liberties of the classic liberal state.[43] It is therefore inadvisable to limit the idea of a constitutional right, and thus also of a constitutional rights norm, in the way that Schmitt does.

Schmitt's criterion is characterized by the way it combines substantive

---

[38] C. Schmitt, 'Grundrechte und Grundpflichten' (1932), in *Verfassungsrechtliche Aufsätze*, 2nd edn. (Berlin, 1973), 190.

[39] ibid. 206.   [40] ibid. 207.

[41] On such a generally accepted right, see G. Dürig in T. Maunz and G. Dürig, *Grundgesetz Kommentar*, 5th edn. (Munich, 1983), Art. 1 Abs. 1 Rdnr. 43 f., Art. 2 Abs. 2 Rdnr. 26 f., with further references. See also below at 334.

[42] On the various possibilities of derivation—art. 1(1), 2(2)(2) or the social state principle of the Basic Law—see Dürig, in Maunz and Dürig, *Grundgesetz Kommentar*.

[43] See below at 126 f.

and structural aspects. One could try to avoid the undesirable limitation of the concept of a constitutional rights norm by asking simply whether the norm expressed by a constitutional provision guarantees some sort of subjective right. This would be a purely *structural* criterion. According to this purely structural criterion, article 7(1) Basic Law, 'the entire school system is under the oversight of the state', would not be a constitutional rights provision and would not express a constitutional rights norm. This would have the advantage that, as the term itself seems to indicate, a 'constitutional rights norm' would only be applied to those norms protecting subjective rights. But it would have the disadvantage of excluding norms related systemically and textually very closely to those protecting subjective rights. This close relationship is well expressed by a single idea. This point, together with the fact that a wider use of expressions such as 'constitutional rights norm' and 'constitutional rights provision' corresponds to the tradition of constitutional doctrine,[44] suggests that the purely structural criterion is unacceptable.

Rather than basing the concept of a constitutional rights norm on substantive and/or structural criteria, it is more useful to adopt a *formal* criterion which looks to the manner and form of enactment. On this basis, to start with, all the statements contained in that section of the Basic Law headed 'the constitutional rights' (arts. 1 to 19) are constitutional rights provisions, quite independently of their content and structure. The range of material covered by this is of course still too narrow. There can be no doubt that a whole series of further provisions of the Constitution, such as article 103(1), which says that everyone has a right to a fair hearing before a court, express constitutional rights norms. To identify such provisions, which F. Klein has appropriately termed 'associated orbiting provisions',[45] there is the formal criterion of the list of 'rights' contained in article 93(1) no. 4 on the basis of which constitutional review may be sought by the individual citizen. If we combine these two criteria as they appear in the text of the Constitution, we end up with the following definition: constitutional rights provisions are the statements formulated in articles 1 to 19 and those which guarantee the individual rights contained in articles 20(4), 33, 38, 101, 103, and 104 Basic Law.[46] Constitutional rights norms are the norms directly expressed by these statements.

---

[44] See e.g. R. Thoma, 'Die juristische Bedeutung der grundrechtlichen Sätze der deutschen Reichsverfassung im allgemeinen', in H. C. Nipperdey (ed.), *Die Grundrechte und Grundpflichten der Reichsverfassung* (Berlin, 1929), 3 ff.; Klein, in Mangoldt and F. Klein, *Das Bonner Grundgesetz*, i, Vorbemerkung A VI (78 ff.).

[45] Klein, in Mangoldt and Klein, *Das Bonner Grundgesetz*, i, Vorbemerkung A VII 3 (83).

[46] On the characterization of the right of resistance in art. 20(4) Basic Law as a constitutional right, see J. Isensee, *Das legalisierte Widerstandsrecht* (Bad Homberg, Berlin, and Zurich, 1969), 81 f. Apart from the right of resistance, a corresponding list of orbiting provisions of the constitutional rights catalogue can be found in K. Hesse, *Grundzüge des Verfassungsrechts der Bundesrepublik Deutschland*, 14th edn. (Heidelberg, 1984), para. 277.

All that is said of this definition is that it is useful in building a theory of the constitutional rights of the Basic Law. When one realizes that many different further distinctions are possible within the scope of this definition, then it has four advantages: (1) it relates as closely as possible to the Constitution, (2) without ruling out more general perspectives, (3) it is not predisposed for or against any particular substantive or structural thesis, and (4) it basically includes all those provisions which are treated as having significance for constitutional rights in general discussion on the matter.

2. DERIVATIVE CONSTITUTIONAL RIGHTS NORMS

According to the definition just developed and qualified as provisional, constitutional rights norms are only those norms directly expressed by statements of the Basic Law (constitutional rights provisions). We have to consider if this is too narrow. In order to answer this question we must cast a glance at article 5(3)(1) Basic Law, of which the following part is of interest:

(2)   '. . . science, research and teaching are free'.

There can be no doubt that this statement is normative, not descriptive, as the context shows, in particular article 1(3) Basic Law which binds the legislature, executive, and judiciary to the subsequent constitutional rights as directly applicable law. What the quotation states can therefore be reformulated into the following deontic statement:

(2′)   It is required that science, research, and teaching be free,

or

(2″)   Science, research, and teaching shall be free.

It can be said of these three statements that in different ways they express *directly* the norm established by the text of the Constitution. Of course, this norm is deeply indeterminate. Its indeterminacy is of two kinds; it is both semantically as well as structurally open-textured.

The norm is *semantically open* on the grounds of the indeterminacy of the expressions 'science', 'research', and 'teaching'.[47] This indeterminacy can be countered by the adoption of semantic rules.[48] The Federal Constitutional Court creates such semantic rules when it defines scientific activity as everything 'in substance and form to be regarded as a serious and

---

What T. Maunz, *Deutsches Staasrecht*, 23rd edn. (Munich, 1980), 111 ff. includes as a constitutional right outside of the constitutional rights catalogue is significantly more comprehensive. His account includes, to give two examples, the rights of Members of Parliament under arts. 46 to 48 Basic Law and the independence of the judiciary (art. 97 Basic Law).

[47] A more precise analysis of semantic openness is unnecessary at this point. See on this H.-J. Koch and H. Rüßmann, *Juristische Begründungslehre* (Munich, 1982), 191 ff.; R. Alexy, 'Die logische Analyse juristischer Entscheidungen', ARSP, Beiheft NF 14 (1980), 190 ff.

[48] See on this Alexy, *Theory of Legal Argumentation*, 223 ff.

structured attempt to attain to truth'[49] or when it says that there is no scientific activity if 'discoveries made by scientific method are adopted into the programme of a political party, that is, a group committed in its very nature to active participation in the life of the state, and turned into a guiding basis for its political activity'.[50]

At this point we are only interested in the first rule identified. This rule can be stated as follows:

(3)   Everything which in substance and form is a serious and structured attempt to attain to truth is science.

Combining (3) with (2″) produces:

(4)   Everything which in substance and form is a serious and structured attempt to attain to truth shall be free.

Statement (4) expresses a norm, and one can properly ask whether this norm is a constitutional rights norm. But before this question is answered we need to consider structural open-texture, where the corresponding question is particularly pressing.

The *structural open-texture* which is characteristic of many constitutional rights provisions is seen in the case of article 5(3)(1) Basic Law in the fact that the mere requirement that science, research, and teaching be free does not tell us whether this state of affairs is to be actively brought about by the state, or simply ensured by non-intervention, and whether the maintenance or establishment of this state of affairs presupposes subjective rights of academics in relation to scientific freedom. In its judgment on the interim law for comprehensive university education in Lower Saxony, the Federal Constitutional Court gave (among other things) the following answers to the questions just raised:

(5)   'The state must enable and support the fostering of free science and its transmission to future generations by making personal, financial and organizational means available',[51]

and

(6)   'Everyone active in science, research and teaching has—apart from the duty imposed by article 5(3)(2) Basic Law to uphold the constitutional order—a defensive right against every state influence on the process of gaining and transmitting scientific insight.'[52]

There can be no doubt that these statements express norms, but are they constitutional rights norms?

Counting against seeing these norms as constitutional rights norms is the fact that they neither correspond to the norm directly formulated by article 5(3)(1) Basic Law nor do they derive solely from that provision. One would

---

[49] BVerfGE 35, 79 (113).   [50] BVerfGE 5, 85 (146).
[51] BVerfGE 35, 79 (114 f).   [52] BVerfGE 35, 79 (112 f).

not be contradicting the words of article 5(3)(1) Basic Law if one only interpreted it to contain a prohibition on state influence, that is, if one rejected
statement (5). Nor does the text on its own give any particular grounds for
holding that it guarantees a subjective right, that is, that statement (6)
applies. This makes quite plain the consequences of holding the position
that only norms directly expressed in the text of the Constitution are constitutional rights norms. In the case of article 5(3)(1) Basic Law it would lead
to the conclusion that in the field of science, research, and teaching there is
precisely one constitutional rights norm, namely that which is expressed by
the statement:

(2″)   Science, research, and teaching shall be free.

This position can hardly be called false, yet there are strong grounds for
maintaining the other position. In order to decide a case such as that raised
by the comprehensive university education act of Lower Saxony, the structural indeterminacy of this norm has to be resolved. The adoption of norms
such as (5) and (6) is indispensable for this purpose. This shows that the
relationship of such norms to the constitutional text is more than merely
accidental. They are necessary if the norm expressed in the text of the
Constitution is to be applied to cases. If norms of this nature are not
adopted, it would not be clear what is commanded, prohibited, or permitted on the basis of the constitutional text (or the norms directly expressed
in it). This type of relation between the norms cited and the constitutional
text can be termed a *'clarifying relation'*.[53] In addition to this relation, there
is a second special connection to the text of the Constitution, or to its
directly expressed norms. In that the Federal Constitutional Court adopts
the norms cited, it assumes that they are to be adopted, *because* the
Constitution contains article 5(3)(1). In other words, we are dealing with a
justifying relation between the norm in need of clarification and the clarifying norm. These two relations justify us in treating as constitutional rights
norms not only norms directly expressed in the Constitution, but also
norms of the type advanced.

 Norms such as (4), (5), and (6) are not directly established by the text of
the Constitution, but are ordered under and derived from directly expressed
norms. This permits us to call them *'derivative norms'*. Constitutional
rights norms can thus be divided into two classes: those directly established
by the text of the Constitution and derivative constitutional rights norms.

 By terming derivative norms constitutional rights norms one admittedly
opens the door to a whole host of difficulties. A great variety of norms get
ordered under the norms directly established by the constitutional rights

---

[53] To this extent the situation here is different from the adoption of an 'unwritten constitutional right'. An unwritten constitutional right is characterized by the fact that the constitutional rights norm which expresses it does not stand in a clarifying relation to a constitutional
rights norm directly expressed in the text of the constitution.

provisions. The debate about constitutional rights is in large measure a dispute about which norms are to be derived from directly expressed constitutional rights norms. Should all proposed norms thrown up by this controversy be seen as constitutional rights norms, for example, even those which are rejected by almost everybody and which are poorly justified? In such a case the statement advanced by some person, perhaps not totally seriously, that 'on the basis of article 13 Basic Law, university administrations must provide every student with at least two-room accommodation in the proximity of the university' would be a constitutional rights norm.

This difficulty can only be resolved if there is some criterion which enables us to distinguish among the potentially boundless class of candidates for derivative norms between those which are really constitutional rights norms and those which are not. On one hand an empirical criterion is worth considering, on the other, a normative one. Those who say that derivative norms are all those in fact adopted as such by case-law and legal scholarship are adopting an empirical criterion. But such an empirical criterion cannot be used from the perspective of a legal theory of constitutional rights. This is concerned with the question of which identifications are *properly* adopted. Judgments and doctrinal consensus are of course important factors in answering that question.[54] But the question cannot be answered by reference to what has been decided or said alone.

Derivation is legitimate when the derivative norm can be classified as valid. In order to classify a directly established constitutional norm as valid it is sufficient to refer to its creation as a legal text. In the case of derivative norms, such a reference is by definition not possible. Their identification as such is simply not possible within the juridical concept of legal validity. The same applies for the sociological or ethical concepts of validity. Just because a norm is valid sociologically or ethically does not mean that it can be ordered as a derivative norm under a directly established constitutional rights norm. None of the three concepts of validity is suitable to identify derivative norms. Nevertheless, all three are represented in the following criterion: a derivative norm is valid and is a constitutional rights norm when it is possible to provide *correct constitutional justification* for its ordering under a directly established norm. The fact that all three concepts of validity play a part can be seen in the role that the text of constitutional rights provisions, the case-law of the Federal Constitutional Court, and general practical arguments play in constitutional rights reasoning.

So, whether a derivative norm is a constitutional rights norm depends on the constitutional reasoning which can be found to support it. At first sight this has fatal consequences. In many cases the existence of correct constitutional justification for a derivative norm is thoroughly controversial. The rules of constitutional justification do not set out a procedure which infal-

---

[54] See Alexy, *Theory of Legal Argumentation*, 266 ff., 274 ff.

libly delivers an answer in every case,[55] and anyway those rules are themselves controversial.[56] This means that in many cases it is uncertain whether certain norms are constitutional rights norms.

However, this uncertainty is not so very serious. For a start it does not affect all derivative norms to the same extent. For example, there is hardly any doubt about the justification of a norm derived from article 5(3)(1) Basic Law granting a defensive right. Beyond that it is a problem which is simply unavoidable. We could do away with the idea of a derivative constitutional rights norm proposed here, but then the problem of what is required by constitutional rights provisions would remain just as pressing. Since there are good grounds for keeping the concept of a derivative norm, and since no uncertainty is thereby added, everything is in favour of using it.[57]

The definition of a constitutional rights norm as dependent on correct constitutional justification has until now only been applied to derivative constitutional rights norms. But it can be extended to directly established constitutional rights norms and hence generalized. Such a general definition would state that constitutional rights norms are all those norms for which correct constitutional justification is possible. For directly established constitutional rights norms a reference to the text of the constitution is usually adequate. Any deeper justification which seeks to address the issue of why what the Constitution says is valid is in practice only generally of theoretical interest. This makes it clear that the generalization of the definition based on correct constitutional justification does not blur the distinction between directly and indirectly established constitutional rights norms.

[55] This applies quite generally to the rules of legal justification; see on this R. Alexy, 'Die Idee einer prozeduralen Theorie der juristischen Argumentation', *Rechtstheorie*, Beiheft 2 (1981), 180 ff.

[56] Thus the case may arise in which equally good reasons are available for two mutually incompatible norms N_1 and N_2. Does this mean that both N_1 and N_2 are valid constitutional rights norms? That has to be denied. In order to deny it, the idea of correct constitutional justification used in the criterion above must be understood in the sense that justification for the derivation of N_1, which in itself would be correct, ceases to be correct if N_2 can also be correctly derived. In this case neither of the two candidates applies as a derivative norm. A court which considers both N_1 and N_2 to be equally well justified, can thus not rely on one of the norms, which it is able to characterize as valid on account of its correct justification, but must take a decision in an area which is open as regards validity. But on account of the force of precedent, which is significant for justification, the decision may make the preferred norm appear better justified in the future. This situation, in which two mutually incompatible norms appear equally justified to an adjudicator, must be distinguished from the situation in which two adjudicators have different views about the justifiability of a norm. This latter situation is much more common than that in which an adjudicator cannot tell which of two justifications is the better.

[57] One advantage of this concept will only be noted in passing: it makes it possible to speak of the discovery of new constitutional rights norms. In this connection one is reminded of the fine picture drawn by Thoma, which with some moderation can be applied equally well to the Basic Law. 'One could say that German jurisprudence treats the Imperial Constitution like a mountain in the depths of which the divining rod of exegesis reveals ever new, hitherto hidden, seams of valid norms' (Thoma, *Die juristische Bedeutung*, 4).

Correct constitutional justification is different in the case of directly established constitutional rights norms from what it is for indirectly established ones.

3. ON FRIEDRICH MÜLLER'S THEORY OF CONSTITUTIONAL RIGHTS NORMS

The definition of a constitutional rights norm which has been developed above has a threefold character. It proceeds from the distinction between normative statement and norm which distinguishes the semantic conception of a norm. At the first level, the concept of a constitutional rights norm is defined by reference to normative statements which have been established by a certain authority, namely the makers of the constitution. These normative statements, the provisions containing constitutional rights, are to be identified by formal criteria such as presence in the constitutional rights section of the Basic Law and in the provision concerning the constitutional complaint (art. 93(1) no. 4*a* Basic Law). This guarantees the orientation of the theory to the actual form of the Constitution, without excluding necessary structural and substantive distinctions. At the second level, that of derivative constitutional rights norms, this orientation is continued in that the concept of a derivative norm is tied to the correctness of relationship to authoritative formulations. The freedom necessary in the process of attributing derivative norms is taken adequate account of by the idea of a constitutional rights norm proposal. Anyone can maintain, of any given norm, that it is derived from a constitutional rights provision. The proposal only actually contains a constitutional rights norm if it is correct, that is, if correct constitutional justification is possible for its derivation. In a third stage, the idea of constitutional justification is generalized, in that it is applied both to directly established and to derivative norms.

   This theory of the constitutional rights norm, along with the semantic conception of a norm which underlies it, is paralleled by the norm theory of Friedrich Müller. Müller's conception is of particular interest here first, because it was developed with particular reference to constitutional law[58] and secondly, because it enjoys a growing number of adherents.[59]

   Müller characterizes his theory as 'a theory of norms which puts legal positivism behind itself'.[60] The principal contention of his, as he puts it, 'post-positivist structural theory of the legal norm',[61] is the thesis of the 'non-identity of norm and norm-text'.[62] What Müller is saying by this

---

[58] F. Müller, *Juristische Methodik*, 2nd edn. (Berlin, 1976), 24, 26 ff.
[59] See Müller's summary, *Juristische Methodik*, 116 f.
[60] ibid. 126.   [61] ibid. 265.
[62] id., 'Rechtstaatliche Methodik und politische Rechtstheorie', *Rechtstheorie*, 8 (1977), 75; id., *Juristische Methodik*, 55, 61, 147, 202, 265.

thesis is that 'a norm is more than its literal meaning'.[63] The idea that a legal norm is 'only linguistically constituted' is the 'fundamental lie of a purely formalistic conception of the Rule of Law'.[64] A post-positivist, and that means for Müller an adequate, theory of legal norms must proceed from the assumption that 'legal norms are also defined by social reality, by their area of operation'.[65] The literal meaning of a norm, according to Müller, 'expresses the "normative programme", traditionally understood as a "legal command". Of equal status with this is the field of normative operation, that is that section of social reality in its basic structure which the normative programme "points to" as its area of regulation, or has even itself created.'[66] Accordingly, 'the legal norm is to be understood as a binding proposal, which embraces the ordering and what is to be ordered in equal measure'.[67] The opposition of is and ought is in this way overcome.[68] The consequence for constitutional rights is, once again in Müller's own words, as follows:

constitutional rights are substantively shaped protective guarantees for certain individual and social complexes of action, organization and subject-matter. These 'areas of subject-matter' are turned into 'fields of normative operation' by constitutional recognition and the protection of freedom in the context of the normative order, the 'normative programme' of constitutional rights. The fields of normative operation play a part in practical normativity, that is, they are constituent elements of legal adjudication.[69]

This theory of norms in general, and constitutional rights norms in particular, is not compatible with the semantic theory of norms which formed the starting-point for our understanding of the constitutional rights norm. This is clear in the case of directly established constitutional rights norms. These are constituted, and are only constituted, by what is expressed in constitutional rights provisions. The term 'constitutional rights provision' corresponds to what Müller calls 'literal text', and a 'norm' here is what Müller calls a 'normative programme'. The concept of a 'field of normative operation', which is central to Müller's thesis, does not appear here. This also applies to derivative constitutional rights norms. Does this mean that a theory of constitutional rights which rests on the concept of a norm and a constitutional rights norm as developed here must fail to explain 'legal normativity, and thus also the character of jurisprudence as a

---

[63] id., *Juristische Methodik*, 117; id., *Normstruktur und Normativität* (Berlin, 1966), 147 ff.
[64] id., 'Rechtsstaatliche Methodik und politische Rechtstheorie', 74.
[65] ibid. 75.
[66] id., *Juristische Methodik*, 117.
[67] ibid., 194, 121; See also id., *Normbereiche von Einzelgrundrechten in der Rechtsprechung des Bundesverfassungsgerichts* (Berlin, 1968), 9.
[68] id., *Juristische Methodik*, 60, 193.
[69] id., *Die Positivität der Grundrechte* (Berlin, 1969), 11.

normative science, because [it is] based on reasons which fail to escape the influence of positivistic theory'? Or does it mean that it has 'a restrictive influence on the understanding of the process of concretization' as Müller accuses a wide variety of positions such as 'positivism, formalism, decisionism and sociologism'?[70] In order to answer these criticisms, we need to consider Müller's reasons for adopting his non-identity thesis.

The crucial reason lies in Müller's understanding of the connection between a theory of law and a theory of adjudication. The theory of law and the theory of adjudication are for Müller only distinguished by their perspectives; they are two sides of the same coin: 'this conception can on one hand be seen as a general structural model of legal *norms*, and on the other hand as a structuring of legal *decision-taking processes*, indeed in the final instance as a *work-programme* for lawyers'.[71] In this regard, Müller uses a three-stage argument. The first stage consists of the point that 'general legal norms cannot fully determine the creation of precise norms by adjudicative bodies';[72] 'legal concepts do not have reference, and legal statements do not have sense, if by that one means something conclusively given in advance'.[73] Given a bit more precision, and indeed a little weakening, one would hardly want to deny this point.[74] Where the argument gets interesting is at the second stage. This second stage consists of the statement that theories such as the semantic norm-theory developed here, which see legal norms as linguistic entities to be identified by certain criteria of validity, are forced 'to develop the decision-determining norm with the help of linguistic data'.[75] But it is claimed that following the first stage of the argument this is not possible. Thus theories based on semantic concepts of a norm are supposedly inadequate. The third stage consists of Müller's solution to the problem. In order to reach a decision 'real data (the field of normative operation)' is above all other elements determinative alongside 'linguistic data (the normative programme)' and thus in principle of equal significance.[76] Thus the field of normative application belongs to the norm.

This argument is subject to three objections. The first challenges the idea that theories oriented towards a semantic conception of a norm are forced to justify legal decision-taking exclusively with the help of semantic arguments (linguistic data). The second objection concerns the general statement that every argument necessary to justify a decision must be included in the concept of a norm. The third objection is directed specifically to the thesis

---

[70] id., *Juristische Methodik*, 194.

[71] id., *Juristische Methodik und Politisches System* (Berlin, 1976), 94; see also id., *Juristische Methodik*, 271; id., *Strukturierende Rechtslehre* (Berlin, 1984), 230 ff.

[72] id., *Normstruktur und Normativität*, 148.

[73] id., 'Rechtsstaatliche Methodik und politische Rechtstheorie', 73.

[74] See Alexy, *Theory of Legal Argumentation*, 1 f.

[75] Müller, 'Rechtsstaatliche Methodik und politische Rechtstheorie', 75.

[76] id., *Juristische Methodik*, 200 ff. Only in determining the limits of permissible outcomes may linguistic data take precedence over real data (ibid. 202).

that the arguments to be included in the concept of a norm are precisely those related to the field of normative regulation ('real data'). Since these objections are closely related they will be discussed together.

The thesis that a theory based on a semantic conception of a norm is forced to justify judicial decisions solely on the basis of semantic arguments would only be true if it were true that resources not to be found in the norm could not be used in legal reasoning. Not even Müller's theory holds to this proposition, since alongside directly norm-related elements (methodological elements properly so called, elements relating to the area of normative protection, and some doctrinal elements) it permits elements only indirectly related to the norm (some other doctrinal elements, technical, constitutional, and moral-political elements) as part of legal reasoning,[77] without characterizing them as belonging to the norm. If one were to adopt the statement that only what was part of a norm could be used in judicial decision-taking, then either one would have to incorporate the entire arsenal of legal reasoning in the concept of a norm, or one would have to limit legal reasoning, which would be both hypersensitive and restrictive of rationality. Thus the independent value-judgments (and sometimes even the underlying values themselves) which are a necessary part of legal justification must either be included in the concept of a legal norm, or banned from legal reasoning altogether. Neither alternative is acceptable.

In response to Müller's thesis, we have to differentiate carefully between the concept of a norm, the concept of normative significance, and the concept of a reason for a norm. Normative significance applies to everything that may appropriately be used as an argument for or against a legal decision.[78] The most significant things for or against a legal decision are valid legal norms. It is therefore the case that all legal norms are normatively significant. However, it is not true that everything normatively significant is a norm or part of one. The latter proposition is required neither on conceptual nor Rule of Law grounds. It is not required on conceptual grounds, because it is entirely possible to distinguish between a norm as a linguistic entity and the various evaluative, empirical, precedential, doctrinal, and other reasons which may be put forward for a particular interpretation of a norm. It is not only possible, it is desirable. Without distinguishing between the norm, the proposed interpretation, and its supporting arguments, we cannot attain to a clear understanding of legal justification. The Rule of Law also points to the value of a strict distinction between the norm and the normatively significant. It is of course very attractive to include all, or at least the decisive, reasons for interpretation in

---

[77] id., *Juristische Methodik*, 199 ff.

[78] This definition of the concept of normative significance corresponds to a central aspect of Müller's conception of normativity, expressed, among other things, in the following way: ' "normative" sensibly refers to everything belonging to the case in hand, which gives some direction to its resolution' (Müller, *Normbereiche von Einzelgrundrechten*, 10).

the concept of a norm, since one can then characterize interpretation as an instance of strict obedience to the norm. But very little is gained in this process. A clear distinction between what the legislator has established as a norm and what the interpreter puts forward as reasons for a particular interpretation serves the ideal of the Rule of Law better than an artificial obedience manufactured by manipulating the definition of a norm.

Of course, we have to take account of the fact that Müller only wants to include elements from the field of normative operation in the norm and not all possible legal arguments. But the expansion of norms even under this limitation is unacceptable. In the case of elements of the field of normative operation, or 'real data', we could be concerned either with purely empirical arguments, or with empirical connected with evaluative or normative arguments. If we are dealing with purely empirical arguments, then not much is gained by their problematic inclusion within the concept of a norm. A relatively open-textured norm (so far as the case in hand is concerned) together with empirical arguments will not give us the answer to a case. In addition, evaluative or normative arguments making the empirical information significant are necessary. But if the idea of the field of normative operation includes such evaluative and normative elements, then since these are not apparent from the text of the norm and the empirical information, a whole range of complex and controversial arguments are introduced into the definition of the norm, and against which the argument against including everything normatively significant in the concept of a norm applies. This is not to say that empirical analysis in the light of the statutory rule is insignificant. Valuable and even decisive arguments can be made in this way. What is being countered is their inclusion in the concept of a norm.

Everything that has been said so far applies equally to derivative constitutional rights norms, which have a certain affinity to Müller's decision-norms.[79] A norm is a derivative constitutional rights norm if correct

---

[79] At this point no more than a certain affinity is to be established. As a matter of detail, Müller's concept of a decision-norm gives rise to some difficulties. These are instructively revealed in the following formulation: 'finally, the provision is only to be treated as a completed decision-norm (and even then only for this one case) when the case is resolved' (Müller, *Juristische Methodik*, 132). The clause in brackets seems to indicate that the decision-norm is only a norm for the case to be decided, i.e. an individual norm in Kelsen's sense (see Kelsen, *Pure Theory of Law*, 250 ff.; id., *General Theory of Norms*, 226) or a concrete legal ought-judgment in Engisch's sense (see K. Engisch, *Logische Studien zur Gesetzesanwendung*, 3rd edn. (Heidelberg, 1963), 3 ff.). A comment of Müller's in which he identifies the decision-norm with the linguistic formulation of the individual decision speaks in favour of this interpretation: 'the derivation of the individual decision and its linguistic formulation (the "decision-norm")' (Müller, *Juristische Methodik*, 278). Counting against this reading, which closely follows Müller's own words, is not only the fact that he speaks of the provision as a decision-norm, but above all that on this version, a legal norm can hardly 'be substantively determined, modified and expanded by the decision-norms derived from it on a case by case basis in the course of its existence' (ibid. 272 f.). This presupposes a universalizing adjudicative practice which combines relatively general legal norms with relatively specific, but none the less universal, decision-norms. This version of the decision-norm, which Larenz also has in

constitutional justification is possible for its derivation from a constitutional rights provision. One might suppose that this requires a connection between norm and reasoning quite similar to Müller's. However, it should be noticed that it is possible in the case of derivative norms to distinguish without difficulty between the norm as a linguistic entity and its supporting reasons; indeed, such a distinction must be made. The possibility of correct constitutional justification for derivation from a constitutional provision is the *criterion* by which the norm in question is a constitutional rights norm. A clear distinction is to be drawn between the criterion for a particular characteristic and the object which either fulfils the criterion or not, and thus either has the characteristic or not. A criterion for something is different from a component of something. All the same, the existence of derivative norms makes it clear that constitutional reasoning plays a significant role in determining what applies as a matter of constitutional rights. To the extent that Müller makes this point with his theory of norms, it is a point well made.

mind when he comments that 'like Fikentscher's "case-norm" Müller means by "decision-norm" a norm which has been concretized by those required to decide the case to such an extent that it can now be applied to the case in hand without intermediate steps' (K. Larenz, *Methodenlehre der Rechtswissenschaft*, 4th edn. (Berlin, Heidelberg, and New York, 1979), 495) is not only to be preferred for substantive reasons, but it also corresponds to Müller's point that the decision-norm is the 'aggregated state of the legal norm, "concretized" in the light of specific cases and directed towards their authoritative resolution' (Müller, *Juristische Methodik*, 119).

3

The Structure of Constitutional Rights Norms

I. RULES AND PRINCIPLES

Up to this point, we have been concerned with the concept of a constitutional rights norm; now its structure needs to be considered. Innumerable theoretical distinctions may be made for this purpose, but the most important for the theory of constitutional rights is that between rules and principles. This distinction is the basis for a theory of constitutional justification and a key to the solution of central problems of constitutional rights doctrine. Without it there can be neither an adequate theory of the limitation of rights, nor an acceptable doctrine of the conflict of rights, nor a sufficient theory of the role of constitutional rights in the legal system. It constitutes a basic element not only of rights to liberty and equality, but also of protective rights, of rights to organization and procedure, and of entitlements in the narrow sense. Problems such as horizontal effect and the division of competence between constitutional court and Parliament can be clarified with its assistance. In addition, the distinction between rules and principles constitutes the framework of a normative-substantive theory of constitutional rights and is the starting-point of an answer to the question of the possibility and limits of rationality in the field of constitutional rights. All in all, the distinction between rules and principles is a basic pillar in the edifice of constitutional rights theory.

There is no lack of references to the role that the distinction between rules and principles plays in the context of constitutional rights. Constitutional rights norms are not infrequently characterized as 'principles'.[1] Even more frequently, the character of constitutional rights as principles is asserted less directly. As will be shown, this occurs, for example, whenever people speak of values,[2] goals,[3] short formulae,[4] or burdens of

---

[1] See e.g. E. v. Hippel, *Grenzen und Wesensgehalt der Grundrechte* (Berlin, 1965), 15 ff.; D. C. Göldner, *Verfassungsprinzip und Privatrechtsnorm in der verfassungskonformen Auslegung und Rechtsfortbildung* (Berlin, 1969), 23 ff.; U. Scheuner, 'Die Funktion der Grundrechte im Sozialstaat' DÖV 1971, 507; E.-W. Böckenförde, 'Die Methoden der Verfassungsinterpretation', NJW 1976, 2091.

[2] See the examples from the case-law of the Federal Constitutional Court listed at 14 above.

[3] See e.g. P. Häberle, 'Grundrechte im Leistungsstaat', VVDStRL 30 (1972), 135.

[4] See e.g. BVerfGE 32, 54 (72); H. Huber, 'Über die Konkretisierung der Grundrechte', P.

argumentation.[5] By contrast, constitutional rights norms are treated as rules when it is claimed that the constitution is to be taken seriously as law,[6] or if reference is made to the possibility of deductive reasoning even in the field of constitutional rights.[7] For the most part, these characterizations remain suggestive only. What is lacking is a precise differentiation and systematic application of rules and principles. That is what will be attempted here.

1. TRADITIONAL CRITERIA FOR DISTINGUISHING RULES FROM PRINCIPLES

The distinction between rules and principles is not new. But in spite of its age and frequent usage, it is still dogged by confusion and controversy. A confusing variety of distinguishing criteria are on offer, their relationship to other things, such as values, is obscure, and the terminology is inconsistent.

In many cases it is not rule and principle, but norm and principle, or norm and basic provision,[8] which are opposed to each other. Here, rules and principles are to be brought together under the concept of a norm; they are both norms because they both say what ought to be the case. Both can be expressed using the basic deontic expressions of command, permission, and prohibition. Principles are reasons for concrete judgments as to what ought to happen just as much as rules are, even if they are reasons of a very different nature. The distinction between rules and principles is thus a distinction between two types of norm.

There are many suggested criteria for distinguishing rules from principles. Probably the most common is that of generality.[9] According to this, principles are norms of relatively high generality, and rules are norms of relatively low generality. An example of a norm of relatively high generality is the norm that everyone enjoys freedom of religion. By contrast, a norm which states that every prisoner has the right to seek to persuade

---

Saladin and L. Wildhaber (eds.), *Der Staat als Aufgabe* (Basle and Stuttgart, 1972), 197: 'abbreviated'.

[5] B. Schlink, *Abwägung im Verfassungsrecht* (Berlin, 1976), 195; A. Podlech, *Gehalt und Funktionen des allgemeinen verfassungsrechtlichen Gleichheitssatzes* (Berlin, 1971), 90.

[6] E. Forsthoff, *Zur Problematik der Verfassungsauslegung* (Stuttgart, 1961), 34.

[7] H.-J. Koch and H. Rüßmann, *Juristische Begründungslehre* (Munich, 1982), 97 ff.

[8] See e.g. J. Esser, *Grundsatz und Norm*, 3rd edn. (Tübingen, 1974). Occasionally the Federal Constitutional Court speaks of 'norms and principles of the Basic Law' (BVerfGE 51, 324 (350)).

[9] See e.g. J. Raz, 'Legal Principles and the Limits of Law', Yale LJ 81 (1972), 838; G. C. Christie, 'The Model of Principles', in Duke LJ 1968, 669; G. Hughes, 'Rules, Policy and Decision Making', Yale LJ 77 (1968), 419; A. Simonius, 'Über Bedeutung, Herkunft und Wandlung der Grundsätze des Privatrechts', ZSR, NF 71 (1952), 239. Against generality as a distinguishing criterion are J. Esser, *Grundsatz und Norm*, 51, and K. Larenz, *Richtiges Recht* (Munich, 1979), 26: 'it is not the degree of generality which is decisive for something being a principle, but its nature as a justifying reason.'

other prisoners to abandon their faith is a norm of relatively low generality.[10,11] One might think that one could divide norms into rules and principles according to this criterion of generality. Other alternative criteria considered in the literature are the 'ability to state precisely the situations in which the norm is to be applied',[12] the manner of creation, perhaps in the distinction between 'created' and 'evolved' norms,[13] the explicitness of evaluative content,[14] connection with the idea of law[15] or with a higher legal statute,[16] and significance for the legal order.[17] Principles and rules have also been distinguished by whether they are reasons for rules or rules themselves,[18] or whether they are norms of argumentation or norms of behaviour.[19]

[10] See on this BVerfGE 12, 1 (4).

[11] The concept of the generality of a norm is to be strictly distinguished from its universality. In spite of their different degrees of generality, both 'everyone enjoys freedom of religion' and 'every prisoner has the right to persuade other prisoners to abandon their faith' express universal norms. This is because these norms relate to all individuals within an open class (human beings/prisoners; on the concept of an open class, see A. Ross, *Directives and Norms* (Oxford, 1930), 109 f.). The counterpart to a universal norm is an individual norm. The statements, '*x* enjoys freedom of religion' and 'prisoner *x* has the right to persuade other prisoners to abandon their faith' both express individual norms, of which one has a relatively high, the other a relatively low, degree of generality. The counterpart to generality is the concept of specificity. The first of the two norms can thus be called 'relatively general' and the second 'relatively specific'. A norm is always either universal or individual. By contrast generality, and its counterpart, specificity, is a matter of degree. On the pairs of concepts universality/individuality and generality/specificity, see R. M. Hare, *Freedom and Reason* (Oxford, 1963), 39 f.; id., 'Principles', Proc Aris Soc 73 (1972/3), 2 f.

The expressions, 'individual', 'universal', 'specific', and 'general' are used in many different ways apart from the meaning adopted here. Other terms such as 'abstract' and 'concrete' can be added. The description of a norm divisible into preconditions and consequences applicable on an unpredictable number of occasions to an unpredictable number of people as 'abstract-general' is widespread (see e.g. D. Volkmar, *Allgemeiner Rechtssatz und Einzelakt* (Berlin, 1962), 74 ff.). Where further precision is not necessary use will be made in what follows of this relatively well-established mode of speech. On further differentiations, see Ross, *Directives and Norms*, 106 ff.; G. H. v. Wright, *Norm and Action* (London, 1963), 70 ff.

[12] Esser, *Grundsatz und Norm*, 51; Larenz, *Richtiges Recht*, 23. See also H. T. Klami, *Legal Heuristics* (Vammala, 1982), 31 ff.

[13] S. I. Shuman, 'Justification of Judicial Decisions', in *Essays in Honour of Hans Kelsen*, Cal L Rev 59 (1971), 723, 729; T. Eckhoff, 'Guiding Standards in Legal Reasoning', in *Current Legal Problems* 29 (1976), 209 f.

[14] C.-W. Canaris, *Systemdenken und Systembegriff in der Jurisprudenz*, 2nd edn. (Berlin, 1983), 50.

[15] K. Larenz, *Methodenlehre der Rechtswissenschaft*, 5th edn. (Berlin, Heidelberg, New York, and Tokyo, 1983), 218, 404.

[16] H. J. Wolff, 'Rechtsgrundsätze und verfassungsgestaltende Grundentscheidungen als Rechtsquellen', in O. Bachof, M. Drath, O. Gönnenwein, and E. Walz, *Festschrift für W. Jellinek* (Munich, 1955), 37 ff.

[17] Larenz, *Methodenlehre der Rechtswissenschaft*, 461; A. Peczenik, 'Principles of Law', *Rechtstheorie*, 2 (1971), 30; see also S. Wronkowska, M. Zieliński, and Z. Ziembiński, 'Rechtsprinzipien: Grundlegende Probleme', *Zasady prawa* (Warsaw, 1974), 226.

[18] Esser, *Grundsatz und Norm*, 51: 'the principle is . . . not itself an "instruction", but the reason, criterion and justification for the instruction'; Larenz, *Richtiges Recht*, 24 f.; J. Raz, 'Legal Principles and the Limits of Law', 839; N. MacCormick, ' "Principles" of Law', Jur Rev 19 (1974), 222; id., *Legal Reasoning and Legal Theory*, (Oxford, 1978), 152 ff.

[19] H. Gross, 'Standards as Law', *Annual Survey of American Law 1968/69*, 578.

Three quite different theses about the difference between rules and principles are possible on the basis of such criteria. The first maintains that every attempt to divide norms into two classes, rules and principles, fails in view of the diversity which exists in reality. This can be seen, for example, in the fact that the criteria suggested, of which some are only distinctions of degree anyway, can be pretty well indiscriminately combined with each other. It is not at all difficult to conceive of a norm which shows a high degree of generality, which is not applicable without further input, which has not explicitly been enacted, which wears its evaluative content on its sleeve, which has a close relation to the idea of law, is of great importance for the legal order, and is a reason for rules as well as being a criterion for the evaluation of legal arguments. In addition to all this, what these criteria taken on their own terms distinguish can again take many forms.[20] In view of all these similarities and dissimilarities, distinctions and differences, within the class of norms, perhaps it is better to group them all together under a Wittgensteinian concept of *family resemblances*[21] rather than a division into two classes. The second thesis maintains that those who accept that norms can be divided into rules and principles also end up showing that this is really only a distinction of *degree*. The proponents of this thesis are the many authors who look to the criterion of generality as the decisive one. The third thesis states that norms can be divided into rules and principles and that this distinction is not simply a matter of degree but is *qualitative*. This latter thesis is correct. There is a criterion which allows us to distinguish strictly between rules and principles. This criterion is not to be found in the list given above, but it does show most of the traditional criteria to be typical, if not decisive. It must now be explained.

2. Principles as Optimization Requirements

The decisive point in distinguishing rules from principles is that *principles* are norms which require that something be realized to the greatest extent possible given the legal and factual possibilities.[22] Principles are *optimization requirements*,[23] characterized by the fact that they can be satisfied to

---

[20] So e.g. Esser distinguishes between axiomatic, rhetorical and dogmatic, immanent and informative, juristic principles and legal principles, as well as constructive and value principles (Esser, *Grundsatz und Norm*, 47 f., 73 ff., 90, 156). Peczenik divides principles into 'principles or "laws" of logic', 'principles of justice', 'semi-logical', 'instrumentally formulated legal principles', 'principles similar to the instrumentally formulated', and 'all the other principles' (Peczenik, *Principles of Law*, 17 ff.).

[21] L. Wittgenstein, *Philosophical Investigations*, trans. G. E. M. Anscombe, 2nd edn. (Oxford 1958), 31–2 (§§ 66, 67).

[22] See on this R. Alexy, 'Zum Begriff des Rechtsprinzips', in: *Rechtstheorie*, Beiheft 1 (1979), 79 ff.; id., 'Rechtsregeln und Rechtsprinzipien', Lecture before the Eleventh World Congress of the International Association for Philosophy of Law and Social Philosophy (Helsinki, 1983, reproduced in the conference proceedings).

[23] The concept of requirement is used here in a wide sense to embrace commands, permissions, and prohibitions.

varying degrees, and that the appropriate degree of satisfaction depends not only on what is factually possible but also on what is legally possible. The scope of the legally possible is determined by opposing principles and rules.[24]

By contrast, *rules* are norms which are always either fulfilled or not.[25] If a rule validly applies, then the requirement is to do exactly what it says, neither more nor less. In this way rules contain *fixed points* in the field of the factually and legally possible. This means that the distinction between rules and principles is a qualitative one and not one of degree.[26] Every norm is either a rule or a principle.[27]

3. COMPETING PRINCIPLES AND THE CONFLICT OF RULES

The distinction between rules and principles becomes most apparent in the case of competing principles and conflicts of rules.[28] What they have in

---

[24] Two cases in the limitation of the realization or satisfaction of principles by rules can be distinguished: (1) rule R, which limits principle P, applies strictly. This means that a validity *rule R'* applies, which states that R takes precedence over P regardless of how important it is to satisfy P and how unimportant R is. It can be assumed that at least in modern legal systems at least not every rule is subject to such a strict validity rule. (2) R does not apply strictly. This means that a validity *principle P'* applies, which under certain conditions permits P to take precedence over, or limit, R. These conditions cannot be satisfied simply whenever the fulfilment of P is more important in a concrete case than the *substantive* principle PR supporting R, because then P' would have no role to play. It would simply raise the question of the relationship between P and PR. P' has a role to play, when the precedence of P is not only a consequence of P's taking precedence over the principle PR, which supports R substantively, but when it is required that P be stronger than PR *together with* principle P', which requires the satisfying of rules and in this sense supports R *formally*.

[25] § 5(1) Traffic Code ('Vehicles must overtake on the left') is a rule which makes this particularly clear. One can only ever overtake on the left or the right. The characteristic of only being capable of being followed or not followed is not limited to rules of this simple type. It is not dependent on whether the act required (prohibited, permitted) can only ever be carried out or not carried out. Rules prescribing acts which can be satisfied to varying extents can also have this characteristic. They have this characteristic if a certain level of act or performance is required (prohibited, permitted). An example would be the provisions relating to negligent actions. What is required is not the highest possible standard of care, but a certain level of care differentiated according to different areas of law. Of course, doubts can arise in individual cases about the level of care required, but this is possible in the application of any norm and is nothing special. In resolving these doubts, the question is always whether the level of care required by the provision has been met or not. This question is the hallmark of a rule.

[26] Similarly, in outcome, Esser, *Grundsatz und Norm*, 95.

[27] The distinction just drawn is similar to that of Dworkin (see R. Dworkin, *Taking Rights Seriously*, 2nd edn. (London, 1978), 22 ff.). However, it differs from Dworkin's at one significant point, namely in the characterization of principles as optimization requirements. On the dispute with Dworkin, see Alexy, 'Zum Begriff des Rechtsprinzips', 59 ff.

[28] The terminology varies. Thus Paulson uses generally the expression, 'conflict of norms', without distinguishing between rules and principles (S. Paulson, 'Zum Problem der Normenkonflikte', ARSP 66 (1980), 487 ff.), and the Federal Constitutional Court speaks occasionally of 'collisions of norms' without further differentiation (BVerfGE 26, 116 (135); 36, 342 (363)). The terminology adopted here is supposed to express the idea that in spite of important similarities, competing principles and conflicting rules are fundamentally different from each other.

common is that two norms, each taken on their own, lead to inconsistent results when applied, that is, they lead to two mutually incompatible concrete legal ought-judgments. What separates them is the way the conflict is resolved.

3.1 The Conflict of Rules

A conflict between two rules can only be resolved in that either an appropriate exception is read into one of the rules, or at least one of the rules is declared invalid. An example of a conflict of rules which can be resolved by the inclusion of an appropriate exception is the conflict between the prohibition on leaving the classroom before the bell goes, and the requirement to leave it on hearing the fire alarm. If the bell has not rung, but the fire alarm goes, these rules lead to mutually incompatible ought-judgments. The conflict is to be resolved in that an exception is read into the first rule in the case that the fire alarm sounds.

If such a solution is not possible, then at least one rule must be declared invalid and thereby excised from the legal system. Unlike the social validity of a norm or its substantive importance, the concept of legal validity does not admit of degrees. Legally speaking, a rule is valid or it is not. The fact that a rule is valid and applicable to a certain set of facts means that the legal consequence is valid. However one justifies it,[29] the possibility that two mutually incompatible ought-judgments might apply has to be excluded. If the application of two rules results in mutually incompatible outcomes on the facts of any given case, and if an exception cannot be read into one of them, then at least one must be declared invalid.

The mere fact that in a case involving a conflict of rules which cannot be removed by reading in an exception at least one of the rules has to be declared invalid does not determine which rule must be treated this way. The problem can be solved by maxims such as '*lex posterior derogat legi priori*' or '*lex specialis derogat legi generali*', but it is also possible to proceed according to the substantive importance of the conflicting rules. What is significant is that the decision is a decision concerning validity. An example of a conflict of rules which the Federal Constitutional Court resolved in just this way according to the conflicts rule of article 31 Basic Law (federal law overrides regional law) was the one between section 22(1) Working Time Act of 1934 and 1938 (applicable as federal law), which according to the Court permitted the opening of shops on weekdays from 7 a.m. to 7 p.m., and section 2 of the 1951 Baden Region Law concerning closing times, which among other things prohibited the opening of shops on Wednesdays after 1 p.m.[30] Both rules could not be valid, because then

---

[29] See e.g. Wright, *Norm and Action*, 135, 141 ff.; Ross, *Directives and Norms*, 169 ff.; C. and O. Weinberger, *Logik, Semanitk, Hermeneutik* (Munich, 1979), 133 f.
[30] BVerfGE 1, 283 (292 ff.).

opening on a Wednesday afternoon would be both permitted and prohibited. The incorporation of the regional rule in the federal rule was excluded by article 31 Basic Law. And so the only option was to declare the invalidity of the regional norm.

3.2 Competing Principles

Competing principles are to be resolved in quite a different way. If two principles compete, for example if one principle prohibits something and another permits it, then one of the principles must be outweighed. This means neither that the outweighed principle is invalid nor that it has to have an exception built into it. On the contrary, the outweighed principle may itself outweigh the other principle in certain circumstances. In other circumstances the question of precedence may have to be reversed. This is what is meant when it is said that principles have different weights in different cases and that the more important principle on the facts of the case takes precedence. Conflicts of rules are played out at the level of validity; since only valid principles can compete, competitions between principles are played out in the dimension of weight instead.[31]

As examples of the solution of competing principles one can point to many cases in which the Federal Constitutional Court has balanced interests.[32] Here we will focus on just two of those decisions, the decision concerning unfitness to stand trial, and the Lebach Judgment. An analysis of the first judgment will provide an insight into the structure of the resolution of conflicts, which can be summarized as a Law of Competing Principles, and the second judgment will extend this insight and lead to an understanding of the outcome of balancing exercises as derivative constitutional rights norms.

3.2.1 The Law of Competing Principles

The decision concerning unfitness to stand trial concerned the permissibility of the trial of an accused person, who was in danger of suffering a stroke and heart attack from the stress of the trial.[33] The Court established that in such cases there was 'a tension between the duty of the state to maintain a properly functioning criminal justice system and the interest of the accused in his constitutionally guaranteed rights, which the state is also obliged to

---

[31] On the concept of a dimension of weight, see Dworkin, *Taking Rights Seriously*, 26 f.

[32] The balancing of interests is the clearest sign that the Federal Constitutional Court understands constitutional rights norms (at least, in addition) as principles. This can be seen even more clearly when the Court explicitly formulates optimization requirements, such as in the KPD Judgment (BVerfGE 5, 85 (204)): 'the most extensive development of personality *possible*', in the Pharmacists Judgment (BVerfGE 7, 377 (403)): 'the choice of profession must be as undisturbed by state interferences as *possible*', and in the decision on trade regulations (BVerfGE 13, 97 (105)): 'the greatest *possible* liberty in choosing a profession' (emphasis added).

[33] BVerfGE 51, 324.

protect under the Basic Law'.[34] This tension was not to be resolved by giving one of these duties absolute precedence, for neither principle enjoyed 'precedence *per se*'.[35] On the contrary, the conflict was to be resolved by balancing the conflicting interests. The question in this balancing process was, which of the requirements having *equal status in the abstract* had the *greater weight* in the *concrete case*: 'if this balancing process leads to the conclusion that the interests of the accused weigh obviously and significantly more heavily than the requirements indicating the need for state intervention, state action undertaken in spite of this would breach the principle of proportionality and hence the accused person's constitutional rights under article 2(2)(1) Basic Law'.[36] This decision corresponds fully to a competition of principles; the differences are only terminological. The judgment does not refer to 'competition' but to 'tension' and 'conflict', and that which competes and is to be balanced is not called 'principle' but 'duty', 'requirement', 'constitutional right', 'claim', and 'interest'. It is entirely possible to represent the decision as a competition between principles. That is what it is when the court speaks, on one hand, of the maximum possible degree of functionality of the criminal justice system, and on the other hand, of the requirement to leave the life and bodily integrity of the accused inviolate to the greatest extent possible. These requirements are to be applied according to what is factually and legally possible. If the only principle at stake were the proper functioning of the criminal justice system, then the trial would be required, or at least permitted.[37] If there were only the principle of the protection of life and bodily integrity, then the trial would be prohibited. So each principle on its own leads to a contradiction. This means that each limits the legal possibility of satisfying the other. This situation is not resolved by declaring one of the principles invalid and hence excluding it from the legal system. It is also not resolved by building an exception into one of the principles, such that this principle is in all further cases to be seen as a rule that is either satisfied or not. Rather, the solution

---

[34] BVerfGE 51, 324 (345).   [35] ibid.
[36] BVerfGE 51, 324 (346).
[37] At this point we will only consider the possibilities arising from the case to be resolved and both principles. If one of the competing principles on these facts were to fall away, the reference to what is legally possible would lose its significance. The remaining principle would cease to be an optimization requirement and become a maximization requirement related only to what is factually possible. This leads to the general point that principles on their own or in isolation, that is, independently from their relationship with other principles, are maximization requirements. One could therefore consider defining principles as such rather than as optimization requirements. But such a definition would not express the constitutive relation that principles have with other principles. One would either have to expand it by adding an optimization rule to maximization requirements, or extend the definition of isolated principles as maximization requirements by a definition as optimization requirements to embrace the relationship with principles. By contrast, the general definition as optimization requirements adopted here has the advantage of simplicity. But it does not exclude the assumption of a perspective which considers principles in themselves or isolated where this is useful, and this will occur frequently in what follows.

of the competition consists in establishing a *conditional relation of precedence* between the principles in the light of the circumstances of the case.
The relation of precedence is conditional because in the context of the case
conditions are laid down under which one of the principles takes precedence. Given other conditions, the issue of precedence might be reversed.

The idea of a conditional relation of precedence which has just been used
is of fundamental importance in understanding competing principles and
thus for the theory of principles in general. In order to investigate this
further, let the two competing principles in the fitness to stand trial case be
designated P_1 (right to life and bodily integrity) and P_2 (proper functioning
of the criminal justice system). Taken independently, P_1 and P_2 lead to
mutually contradictory concrete legal ought-judgments, P_1 to 'it is forbidden to conduct the trial' and P_2 to 'it is required to conduct the trial'. This
conflict can be resolved either by establishing an unconditional or a conditional relation of precedence. The sign **P** will be used to symbolize the relation of precedence.[38] For the conditions under which one principle takes
precedence over the other we shall use 'C'. There are thus four ways of
deciding the case by resolving the competing principles:

(1) P_1 **P** P_2
(2) P_2 **P** P_1
(3)   (P_1 **P** P_2) C
(4)   (P_2 **P** P_1) C

(1) and (2) are unconditional relations of precedence; one could also refer
to them as abstract or absolute relations of precedence. The court excludes
the adoption of such unconditional relations of precedence with the words,
'neither of these requirements enjoys precedence *per se* over the other'.[39]
This statement is true generally for competing principles in constitutional
law. It is only at first sight that the principle of human dignity, which we
will have to come back to, seems to be an exception. So, only possibilities
(3) and (4) of a conditional, or as we might say, a concrete, or relative, relation of precedence remain. The key question is thus under what conditions
does which principle take precedence over the other. At this point the Court
uses the very common metaphor of balancing. In the Court's words, it all
depends on whether 'the interests of the accused in the concrete case weigh
obviously and significantly more heavily than the requirements which state
action is supposed to preserve'.[40] Such interests and requirements cannot
have weight in any quantifiable sense. One can therefore ask what is
supposed to be meant by this talk of weight. The idea of a conditional relation of precedence gives us a straightforward answer. On any set of concrete

---

[38] See on this, G. H. v. Wright, *The Logic of Preference* (Edinburgh, 1963), 19.
[39] BVerfGE 51, 324 (345).
[40] BVerfGE 51, 324 (346).

facts principle P_1 has greater weight than the opposing principle P_2 when there are sufficient reasons for supposing that in the circumstances of the concrete case, P_1 takes precedence over P_2. A more precise formulation follows.

The balancing undertaken by the court follows precisely the pattern that has just been set out in naming the conditions of precedence (C) and in maintaining the thesis that under these conditions, P_1 takes precedence over P_2. The conditions of precedence for P_1 (that is, for the principle established by art. 2(2)(1) Basic Law) in their most general formulation are as follows: 'if there is a proximate and specific danger that if the trial is continued, the accused person will lose his life or suffer serious injury to his health, then continuing the legal process breaches his constitutional rights under article 2(2)(1) Basic Law'.[41] This statement takes us to an important point in the theory of the conditional relation of precedence. It should be observed that the court is no longer speaking about the precedence of a principle, requirement, interest, claim, right, or any other such object; rather *conditions* are being identified under which there is a *breach of constitutional rights*. The fact that some action breaches constitutional rights means that it is prohibited. The sentence cited can thus be reformulated as a rule of the form: 'if some act fulfils condition C then it is constitutionally prohibited'.

Thus what has been called here the condition of precedence, and identified by the letter 'C' plays a twofold role. In the preferential statement

(3) $(P_1 \, \mathbf{P} \, P_2) \, C$

C is the condition for a relation of precedence. In the formulation of the rule

(5)   If an act A fulfils condition C, then A is constitutionally prohibited

C is the protasis of a norm. The fact that C has a twofold character is an unavoidable consequence of the structure of the preferential statement, for P_1's taking precedence over the competing principle under condition C means that the legal consequences of P_1 apply in the case that circumstances C are present.[42] Thus a preferential statement concerning a conditional relation of precedence gives rise to a rule requiring the consequences of the principle taking precedence should the conditions of precedence apply. This enables us to formulate the following law concerning the connection between conditional relations of precedence and rules:

---

[41] ibid.

[42] The case under discussion is concerned with whether the legal consequences flowing from P_1 are to apply in their full extent or not. There can also be cases in which exceptions are necessary from the legal consequences of the principle taking precedence. In this case, P_1 only takes precedence over P_2 in the circumstances of the case (C) in respect of a limited legal consequence Q'. This can be symbolized as '$(P_1 \, \mathbf{P} \, P_2) \, C, \, Q'$'. The question of precedence in respect of a limited legal consequence is to be distinguished from problems of suitability and necessity to be discussed below, which relate to the possibilities of factual realization of principles.

(LCP)   If principle P_1 takes precedence over principle P_2 in circumstances
         C: $(P_1 \; \mathbf{P} \; P_2) \; C$, and if P_1 gives rise to legal consequences Q in
         circumstances C, then a valid rule applies which has C as its prota-
         sis and Q as its apodosis: $C \rightarrow Q$.

A rather less technical formulation goes:

(LCP′)   The circumstances under which one principle takes precedence
         over another constitute the conditions of a rule which has the same
         legal consequences as the principle taking precedence.

This law, which we can call the *Law of Competing Principles*, is one of
the foundations of the theory of principles being established here. It reflects
the character of principles as optimization requirements between which
there is, first, no relation of absolute precedence, and which concern,
secondly, acts and situations which are not quantifiable. At the same time
it constitutes a basis from which to deal with objections to the theory of
values,[43] which lies close to the theory of principles.[44]

3.2.2 Results of Balancing Principles as Derivative Constitutional Rights Norms

All this can be made clearer in the context of the Lebach Judgment.[45] This
case concerned the following facts: ZDF, a television channel, planned to
broadcast a documentary, 'The Soldiers' Murder at Lebach'. This
concerned a crime in which four sleeping soldiers at the munitions depot of
the Federal Army at Lebach were murdered and weapons were stolen for
the purpose of committing further criminal offences. At the time of the
intended broadcast, a person who had been convicted as a secondary party
to the offence was shortly to be released from prison. He was of the view
that the broadcast of the programme in which he was named and in which
his picture was given, would breach his constitutional rights under article
1(1) and article 2(1) Basic Law, mainly because it would endanger his resocialization. The regional court rejected his application for an injunction and
the upper regional court rejected his appeal. He brought a constitutional
complaint against these decisions.

At this point we are only interested in the part of the judgment dealing
with the resolution of competing principles. Other problems, such as horizontal effect, will be dealt with later. The court's reasoning can be broken
down into three stages of particular interest for the relation of precedence.
At the first level, 'a tension [is established] between the protection of

---

[43] See on this 86 ff. below.

[44] It only needs pointing out here that in establishing concrete relations of precedence, the
Law of Competing Principles leads to a differentiated doctrine of constitutional rights, that is,
not to a simple process of preferred and secondary rights. Thus the question of setting limits
is not all-or-nothing, but a problem of the 'suppression of constitutional rights in individual
relationships' (BVerfGE 28, 243 (263)).

[45] BVerfGE 35, 202.

personality in article 2(1) in connection with article 1(1) Basic Law and the freedom of media reporting under article 5(1)(2) Basic Law'.[46] Once again, let us call the first principle P_1 and the second P_2. P_1 on its own would lead to the banning of the broadcast, P_2 to its permission. This 'conflict', as the court calls the competition, is not resolved by declaring one of the principles invalid, but by 'balancing' in which neither of the two principles—the Federal Constitutional Court talks at this point of 'constitutional values'— 'can claim basic precedence'. On the contrary, 'one must decide in the light of the characteristics of such cases and the circumstances of this particular case which interest has to give way'.[47] A clearer description of competing principles is hardly possible. Two norms lead to mutually incompatible results. Neither is invalid, neither takes absolute precedence. The law applicable depends on how one should determine precedence in the light of the facts of the case.[48] It should merely be observed in passing that here is yet another term for what is to be balanced: 'constitutional values'.

After establishing a competition between two principles of equal status at an abstract level, in a second stage the Court holds that there is general precedence for the freedom of media reporting in cases of 'up-to-date reporting of crime' (C_1),[49] in other words $(P_2 \text{ P } P_1) \ C_1$. This relation of precedence is interesting because it is only a precedence in general or in principle. This means that not every up-to-date report is permitted. The conditions of precedence, and hence the legal rule which corresponds to the preferential statement under the Law of Competing Principles, include a *ceteris-paribus* clause which permits exceptions.

The decision itself is made at the third level. Here the Court establishes that in the case of a 'repeated report of a serious criminal act, no longer covered by the interest in up-to-date information, which endangers the resocialization of the criminal' (C_2), the protection of privacy takes precedence

---

[46] BVerfGE 35, 202 (219).   [47] BVerfGE 35, 202 (225).

[48] There can be no doubt that the Court resolves the case by way of balancing principles. But one can well ask whether this was the only possible way. The question is provoked by comments of the Court in which it considers whether the broadcast challenged by the plaintiff was suitable and necessary in pursuit of ZDF's goals. These goals included, among other things, informing the general public about the effectiveness of criminal sanctions, a deterrent effect on potential wrongdoers, and 'strengthening of public morals and social responsibility' (BVerfGE 35, 202 (243)). One could therefore take the view that the case was not to be decided on the level of balancing between constitutional values or principles, that is, not at the third stage of the principle of proportionality (see on this, L. Hirschberg, *Der Grundsatz der Verhältnismäßigkeit* (Göttingen, 1982), 2 ff. as well as below at 66 ff.), but at the prior stages of suitability and necessity (thus, Schlink, *Abwägung im Verfassungsrecht*, 34). On this approach, only the name and the picture of the individual would have needed excluding. Since the Court assumed that the plaintiff's rights would be infringed even without his name and picture being broadcast (BVerfGE 35, 202 (243)), a decision at the third stage of the principle of proportionality was unavoidable. Only if the Court had not proceeded from this premiss would it have been possible to resolve the case merely by way of the principles of suitability and necessity.

[49] BVerfGE 35, 202 (231).

over the freedom of media reporting, which in this case meant that the report was prohibited.[50] In other words, the preferential statement $(P_1 \; \mathbf{P} \; P_2)$ C_2 applied. C_2 consists of four conditions (repetition, no current interest, serious criminal offence, endangering resocialization). The rule $C_2 \to Q$ corresponding to the preferential statement is thus a rule with four conditions and the following structure:

(6) F_1 and F_2 and F_3 and $F_4 \to Q$

It goes: a repeated (F_1) media report, no longer required by the interest in current information (F_2), concerning a serious criminal offence (F_3), which endangers the resocialization of the offender (F_4) is constitutionally prohibited (Q).

It has already been argued that both directly established and derivative norms are to be considered constitutional rights norms.[51] A derivative constitutional rights norm is a norm for whose derivation correct constitutional justification is possible. If correct constitutional justification is possible for the norm just stated, which can be assumed to be the case for present purposes, then it is a constitutional rights norm. At the same time it is a rule under which the facts of the case can be subsumed as under any statutory norm, which is just what happened in the Lebach Judgment.[52] Thus the following proposition applies: the result of every correct balancing of constitutional rights can be formulated in terms of a derivative constitutional rights norm in the form of a rule under which the case can be subsumed. Thus even if all directly established constitutional rights norms were principles, which as will be shown is not the case, there would still be constitutional rights norms which are principles and those which are rules.

Those last comments lead already to the application of a theory of principles to the theory of the constitutional rights norm. But before we go down that road, the theory of principles needs to be extended somewhat. Hitherto, principles have been defined as optimization requirements and rules as norms which are either satisfied or not. This distinction gave rise to a difference of treatment in cases of conflict. It is now appropriate to consider some further characteristics which result from this basic distinction and to discuss various objections which can be made directly against the ideas of conflict and competition outlined above. Objections of a more general nature to the ideas of values and balancing, which are closely related to the theory of principles, will not be dealt with until that theory has been applied to constitutional rights norms.

---

[50] BVerfGE 35, 202 (237).
[51] At 33 ff.
[52] On the structure of this subsuming process, see R. Alexy, 'Die logische Analyse juristischer Entscheidungen', ARSP, Beiheft NF 14 (1980), 195 ff.

4. THE DIFFERENT PRIMA FACIE CHARACTER OF RULES AND PRINCIPLES

The first significant characteristic which arises from what has been said is the different prima facie character of rules and principles.[53] Principles require that something be realized to the greatest extent legally and factually possible. They are thus not *definitive* but only *prima facie* requirements. It does not follow from the fact that a principle is relevant to a case that what the principle requires actually applies. Principles represent reasons which can be displaced by other reasons. How the relation between reason and counter-reason is to be stated is not decided by the principle itself. Principles lack the resources to determine their own extent in the light of competing principles and what is factually possible.

This is quite different in the case of rules. In that rules insist that one does exactly as required, they contain a decision about what is to happen within the realm of the legally and factually possible. This decision can run up against legal and factual impossibility, which can lead to the rule's invalidity. But if it does not run up against impossibility, then what the rule requires applies definitively.

One could take the view that principles always have the same prima facie character and rules always the same definitive character. Dworkin seems to make this assumption when he says that valid rules apply in an all-or-nothing way, but that principles only contain reasons pointing in a certain direction but not necessarily requiring a particular decision.[54] But this model is simplistic and needs to be more nuanced. However, even under this more nuanced model the different prima facie character of rules and principles is to be maintained.

The necessity for a more nuanced model arises, as far as rules are concerned, from the fact that it is possible to incorporate an exception into a rule on the occasion of a particular case. When this occurs, the rule loses its definitive character for the case. The incorporation of an exception can

---

[53] On the concept of prima facie character, see principally, even if unclear at many points, A. Ross, *The Right and the Good* (Oxford, 1930), 19 ff., 28 ff., as well as K. Baier, *The Moral Point of View* (Ithaca, NY and London, 1958), 102 ff. and R. M. Hare, *Moral Thinking* (Oxford, 1981), 27 ff., 38 ff., which refers to Ross. J. Searle, 'Prima Facie Obligations', in J. Raz (ed.), *Practical Reasoning* (Oxford, 1978), 84 ff., proposes abandoning the term 'prima facie' and its counterparts, preferring to distinguish instead between 'what one has an obligation to do', and 'what one ought to do all things considered' (ibid., 88 f.). The only interesting point here is that for Searle as well there are two uses of 'ought', one that is 'all things considered' and one that is *not*. One has to object to Searle that there are certain problems associated with the latter idea. Abandoning the term 'prima facie' would only be advisable if one wanted to do without terminological markers altogether. For an interesting attempt to reconstruct prima facie character by way of deontic logic, see J. Hintikka, 'Some Main Problems of Deontic Logic', in R. Hilpinen (ed.), *Deontic Logic: Introductory and Systematic Readings* (Dordrecht, 1970), 67 ff.

[54] Dworkin, *Taking Rights Seriously*, 24, 26.

be based on some principle. But contrary to what Dworkin says,[55] the exceptions incorporated into rules on the basis of principles are unquantifiable in theory as well.[56] One can never be sure that in some new case a new exception should not be created. It is of course possible to conceive of a legal system which prohibits the limiting of rules by the incorporation of exceptions. But as the many cases of so-called teleological reduction show, the German legal system does not contain such a prohibition, at least not for all areas of law.[57] Rules for which this prohibition does not apply lose their strictly definitive character. But the prima facie character which rules acquire on losing their strictly definitive nature is of a fundamentally different type from that of principles. A principle is trumped when some competing principle has a greater weight in the case to be decided. By contrast, a rule is not automatically trumped when the competing principle is of greater weight than its own underlying principle on the facts of the case. Here, there are other principles which also need trumping, such as the one that rules passed by an authority acting within its jurisdiction are to be followed, and the principle that one should not depart from established practice without good reason. Such principles can be called '*formal* principles'. The more weight that is given to formal principles within a legal system, the stronger is the prima facie character of its rules.[58] It is only when such principles are completely deprived of any weight that the rules would no longer apply as rules. Only then would rules and principles have the same prima facie character.

The fact that weakening the definitive character of rules does not give them the same prima facie character as principles is only one side of the coin. The other side is that strengthening the prima facie character of principles does not give them the same prima facie character as rules either. The prima facie character of principles can be strengthened by creating a burden of argumentation in favour of certain principles or types of principle. The decision concerning fitness to stand trial showed that both norms guaranteeing individual constitutional rights and norms requiring the pursuit of common interests can be seen as principles. One could create a burden of argumentation in favour of the first type and to the detriment of the second type of principle, in other words a burden of argumentation in favour of individual and to the detriment of collective interests. This is roughly what

---

[55] Dworkin, *Taking Rights Seriously*, 25.

[56] Alexy, 'Zum Begriff des Rechtsprinzips', 68 ff.

[57] See e.g. BGHZ 24, 153; 59, 236. For an overview, see H. Brandenburg, *Die teleologische Reduktion* (Göttingen, 1983).

[58] In this connection one can introduce the ideas of the hardness and softness of a legal system. A legal system is harder, the stronger the prima facie character of its rules is, and the more it is regulated by rules within it. To show that the debate about the necessary degree of hardness of a legal system is no new theme, see O. Behrends, 'Institutionelles und prinzipielles Denken im römischen Privatrecht', *Zeitschrift der Savigny-Stiftung für Rechtsgeschichte, Romanistische Abteilung*, 95 (1978), 187 ff.

Schlink has in mind when he says that constitutional rights are 'rules concerning the burden of argumentation'.[59] Whether the assumption of such rules concerning the burden of argumentation is justified is not in issue here. The point is simply that the assumption of burdens of argumentation in favour of certain principles does not give them the same prima facie character as rules. Even a burden of argumentation does not relieve us of the need to establish conditions of precedence in any given case. It merely has the consequence that where reasons are equally strong, or in cases of doubt, one principle takes precedence over the other. A burden of argumentation does strengthen the prima facie character of a principle, but the prima facie character of a rule resting on authoritative creation or long-standing acceptance is something quite different and much stronger.

Thus the proposition that rules and principles differ from each other in their prima facie character should be maintained in spite of some necessary modifications.

5. RULES AND PRINCIPLES AS REASONS

The discussion so far has shown that rules and principles are different types of reason. Principles are always *prima facie reasons* and rules are *definitive reasons*, so long as no exception is to be read into them. But saying that rules and principles are definitive and prima facie reasons does not tell us what they are reasons *for*. They could be reasons for actions or reasons for norms, and as reasons for norms they could be reasons for universal (abstract-general) norms or reasons for individual norms (concrete legal ought-judgments).[60] Raz takes the view that norms are reasons for actions.[61] By contrast, the position taken here is that rules and principles are reasons for norms. The gap between the two views is actually smaller than might seem, since if rules and principles are reasons for norms they are indirectly reasons for actions. The view adopted here is simply a jurisprudential one. The study of law concerns propositions about what is required, forbidden, and allowed, and the judge has to make decisions in precisely these terms. The semantic conception of a norm is designed to replicate this approach. By treating rules and principles as reasons for norms, basic relations are kept to entities of one category, which makes matters—and particularly logical analysis—easier.

One of the possible criteria for distinguishing rules from principles considered above suggested that principles were reasons for rules and only reasons for rules. If this were correct, principles could not be direct reasons for concrete ought-judgments. The view that principles are reasons for rules

---

[59] Schlink, *Abwägung im Verfassungsrecht*, 195.
[60] On these distinctions, see above at 46 fn. 11.
[61] J. Raz, *Practical Reason and Norms* (London, 1975), 15, 58.

and rules reasons for concrete ought-judgments (individual norms) is at first sight rather plausible. But on closer examination it does not work. Rules can also be reasons for rules and principles can be reasons for concrete ought-judgments. Someone who adopts the norm that one should never injure another's self-esteem as a norm of personal conduct without exception has adopted a rule. This rule can be the reason for a further rule: never speak to another person about their failures. On the other hand, principles can be reasons for decisions, that is, for concrete ought-judgments. Thus in the decision concerning the fitness to stand trial, the principle of the preservation of life was a reason for the impermissibility of conducting the trial. Having said that, the characterization of principles as reasons for rules makes a good point. It reflects the different character of rules and principles as reasons for concrete ought-judgments. If a rule is a reason for making a concrete ought-judgment, which is the case when it is valid, applicable, and without relevant exception, then it is a *definitive reason*. If the content of the concrete ought-judgment is that an individual has a certain right, then that right is a *definitive right*. By contrast, principles can only ever be *prima facie reasons*. In and of themselves they can only create prima facie rights. Thus in the Lebach case, ZDF only had a *prima facie right* to broadcast. Decisions about rights presuppose the identification of definitive rights. The route from the principle, that is, the prima facie right, to the definitive right runs by way of the relation of preference. But establishing a preference relation is, according to the Law of Competing Principles, to create a rule. We can therefore say that whenever a principle turns out to be the dominant reason for a concrete ought-judgment, then that principle is a reason for a rule, which in turn is the definitive reason for the judgment. Principles in themselves are never definitive reasons. Esser is probably making this point when he states that 'a principle is not itself a "recommendation" but the reason, criterion and justification for a recommendation'[62] and what Kant means when he says that 'a subject may have, in a rule he prescribes to himself, two grounds of obligation (*rationes obligandi*), one or other of which is not sufficient to put him under obligation (*rationes obligandi non obligantes*), so that one of them is not a duty'.[63]

6. GENERALITY AND PRINCIPLES

It is fairly easy to justify the relative correctness of the criterion of generality. Principles are on the whole relatively general, because they have not yet been related to the possibilities of the factual and normative world. When they are related to the boundaries of the factual and normative world, they produce a *differentiated rule system*. The idea of a principle-dependent

---

[62] Esser, *Grundsatz und Norm*, 51.
[63] I. Kant, *The Metaphysics of Morals*, trans. M. Gregor (Cambridge, 1991), 50.

differentiated rule system will become significant when we dicuss objections to the supposedly arbitrary nature of balancing. That the criterion of generality is only relatively accurate can be seen in the existence of norms of a high degree of generality which are not principles. The normative proposition, 'an act may only be punished if its criminal nature was established by law before it was committed' (art. 103(2) Basic Law, sect. 1 Criminal Code) may give rise to a whole host of problems of interpretation, and in interpreting it, one may reveal a latent underlying principle, but it is actually a rule, since what it requires is something that is either satisfied or not as the case may be. The fact that this norm is often called a 'principle' makes it an example of those cases in which the theory defended here departs from ordinary linguistic usage.

The reasons for many other characteristics of principles are obvious. As reasons for sometimes highly technical rules, their evaluative content is more obviously apparent; as the main reasons for innumerable rules, principles have greater substantive significance for the legal system; their relation to the idea of law arises from a model of justification that moves from the general to the particular; and the fact that they are often characterized as 'evolved' rather than 'created' lies in the fact that they need not be expressly enacted, but can be derived from a tradition of detailed norm-creation and judicial decision-taking which are often the expression of a widespread understanding of what the law ought to be.

7. THREE OBJECTIONS TO PRINCIPLES

Quite independently of their applicability to a theory of constitutional rights, three objections can be made to the idea of principles propounded here. The first argues that there can be conflicts of principle which are resolved by declaring one of the principles invalid. The second objection suggests that there are absolute principles which can never be placed in a relation of preference with any other principle, and the third states that the concept of a principle is too broad and is thus useless, because it embraces all possible interests, needs, and so on which could be balanced against each other.

7.1 The Invalidity of Principles

It cannot be denied that there are principles which, were they to emerge within a given legal system, would be declared invalid on their first encounter with other principles. One example is the principle of racial segregation. German constitutional law excludes this principle. There is not a single case in which it takes precedence and several in which it is overridden; for as long as the principles of current constitutional law remain unchanged, this principle will be overridden in every case, which is to say that it is not a valid principle. If it came to a competition of principles, this

would be resolved in the same way as a conflict of rules. One could therefore conclude that the theory of competing principles outlined above does
not apply. But this would miss the point. To explain why this is the case, let
the ideas of a conflict of rules and competing principles be grouped together
under a single broad concept of norm inconsistency. The real point is that
there are two categorically different types of norm inconsistency. The first
type concerns membership in a legal system, that is, validity. The conflict of
rules is the key example of this type of inconsistency. The principle of racial
segregation shows that the question of validity can also be put in the case
of principles, even if this is rare. The question of validity is always
concerned with what is to be located inside and outside the legal system.

  The other sort of norm inconsistency takes place within the legal system.
Norm inconsistencies of this type are always competing principles and
competing principles are always found inside a legal system. This makes it
clear that the idea of competing principles presupposes the validity of those
principles. The reference to the possibility of classifying principles as invalid
therefore does not affect the theory of competing principles, but only points
up one of its presuppositions.

7.2 Absolute Principles

The problem of the invalidity of principles is concerned with extremely
weak principles, that is, with principles which in no case take precedence
over other principles. Absolute principles are extremely strong principles,
that is, principles which in no case are preceded by other principles. If there
are any absolute principles, then the definition of a principle must be
emended, because if a given principle always takes precedence over any
other, including the principle that enacted rules are to be followed, then its
realization would know no legal limits. There would only be the limits of
the factually possible, and the theory of competing principles would be
inapplicable.

  It is quite easy to argue against the validity of any absolute principles in
a legal system containing constitutional rights. Principles can be related
either to collective interests or to individual rights. If there is an absolute
principle relating to a collective interest, constitutional rights norms can set
no limit to it. For as far as the absolute principle reaches, there are no
constitutional rights. If the absolute principle guarantees individual rights,
then its legal illimitability leads to the conclusion that when the right it
protects of one person conflicts with the similar rights of other individuals,
the latter must give way, which is inconsistent. Thus absolute principles are
either incompatible with constitutional rights or can only apply where the
rights they create benefit just one person.

  One could take the view that the Basic Law contains at least one absolute
principle by pointing to article 1(1)(1): 'human dignity is inviolable'. It is
true that article 1(1)(1) Basic Law gives an impression of absoluteness.

However, the reason for this impression does not lie in the fact that this constitutional provision enacts an absolute principle, but firstly in the fact that the human dignity norm is treated partly as a rule and partly as a principle, and secondly in the fact that there is a very large set of conditions of precedence for the principle of human dignity together with a strong degree of certainty that when they are satisfied it takes precedence over other competing principles. The area defined by such conditions, that is, the area protected by the rules corresponding to these conditions, is what the Federal Constitutional Court calls, 'the absolutely protected core area of private autonomy'.[64]

The character of the human dignity norm as a rule can be seen in those cases in which the norm is relevant and in which it is not considered whether it takes precedence over other norms or not, but simply whether it has been breached or not. Given the open-texture of the human dignity norm, there is of course a further discretion in answering this question. The comments of the Federal Constitutional Court in the telephone tapping case are apposite: 'as regards the principle of the inviolability of human dignity laid down in article 1 Basic Law . . . it all depends on establishing the circumstances under which human dignity might be violated. Clearly this cannot be stated in general terms, but only in the light of the concrete case.'[65] By using the idea of 'despicable treatment'[66] in their judgment, the Court opens up a wide discretion in establishing the circumstances of violation. In establishing the circumstances, there is always the possibility of balancing interests. Indeed, the Court uses this possibility as shown by statements such as the one asserting that human dignity is not at any rate violated 'if the exclusion of judicial oversight is not motivated by a failure to respect or an undervaluing of the human person, but by the necessity to maintain the secrecy of certain measures to protect the democratic order and the security of the state'.[67] This can be understood to mean that when secrecy is necessary, and if other conditions such as legal oversight by bodies constituted by representative assemblies are satisfied, the principle of state protection takes precedence over the principle of human dignity as regards the exclusion of legal remedies in cases of telephone tapping. The fact that reason and counter-reason are set in relation to each other shows

---

[64] BVerfGE 34, 238 (245). It is interesting how the Court in this case defines the relationship of the concept of an absolutely protected area to the concept of balancing: 'even outweighing principles of the general interest cannot justify an infringement of the absolutely protected core area of private self-determination; balancing in accordance with the principle of proportionality does not take place'. This sentence gives rise to problems of interpretation. Is it to be understood that the principle of human dignity takes precedence even in those cases when *from the perspective of constitutional law* a competing principle has greater weight? That would be illogical. To avoid this illogicality, the phrase 'outweighing principles of the general interest' must be understood to refer to interests which outweigh from some perspective which is not that of constitutional law. But then one can simply balance from the perspective of constitutional law and find the principle of human dignity more weighty.

[65] BVerfGE 30, 1 (25).   [66] BVerfGE 30, 1 (26).   [67] BVerfGE 30, 1 (27).

that were the conditions listed to be unsatisfied, the same measure in question would become impermissible. The principle of human dignity would take precedence over state security. This point can be made more generally: if human dignity takes *precedence* at the level of principle, then it has been *breached* at the level of rule.

Balancing the principle of human dignity against other principles in order to establish the content of the rule of human dignity can be seen particularly clearly in the life imprisonment case, in which it was stated that 'human dignity is also not infringed if the completion of the sentence is rendered necessary by the continued danger represented by the prisoner, and if on this basis early release is inappropriate'.[68] These words establish that the protection of 'civil society' in the circumstances stated takes precedence over the principle of human dignity. In other circumstances, the preference could be reversed.

There are thus two human dignity norms, a human dignity rule and a human dignity principle. The preference relation between the human dignity principle and other competing principles determines the content of the human dignity rule. The principle is not absolute, but the rule is, which in view of its semantic open-texture stands in need of no limitation on the grounds of any conceivable relation of preference.[69] The human dignity principle can be realized to different degrees. The fact that under certain circumstances it clearly takes precedence over other principles does not make it absolute, but merely means that the constitutional reasons for giving precedence to human dignity in those circumstances can scarcely be questioned. But such a thesis about the core significance of a right exists for other constitutional rights as well. This does not affect their character as principles. We can therefore say that the principle of human dignity is not an absolute principle. The impression of absoluteness arises from the fact that there are two human dignity norms, a human dignity rule and a human dignity principle, along with the fact that there is a whole host of conditions under which we can say with a high degree of certainty that the human dignity principle takes precedence.

---

[68] BVerfGE 45, 187 (242).

[69] The advantage of this way of putting it is that on one hand no limiting clause needs to be read into the human dignity norm of the constitution, but that on the other hand the human dignity principle can still be balanced with other constitutional principles. The danger identified by Kloepfer, that 'a human dignity enforceable against every other constitutional interest under every possible circumstances ... will in the final analysis [reduce] the guarantee of human dignity to a defence against apocalyptic brutalities' (M. Kloepfer, 'Grundrechtstatbestand und Grundrechtsschranken in der Rechtsprechung des Bundesverfassungsgerichts—dargestellt am Beispiel der Menschenwürde', in C. Starck (ed.), *Bundesverfassungsgericht und Grundgesetz: Festgabe aus Anlaß des 25jährigen Bestehens des Bundesverfassungsgerichts*, ii (Tübingen, 1976), 411) can thus be avoided, without adopting an unwritten limiting clause in the preconditions of the human dignity norm, as Kloepfer seems to prefer. The possibility of this construction is a result of the semantic open-texture of the concept of human dignity.

7.3 The Breadth of Principles

Principles can be related both to individual rights and to collective interests. Thus in the Lebach Judgment there were two opposing principles of which one was a prima facie right to privacy and the other a prima facie right to free media reporting.[70] In the Fitness to Stand Trial Judgment the rights to life and bodily integrity competed with the principle of maintaining a functioning criminal justice system[71]—a principle which serves a collective interest. The case-law of the Federal Constitutional Court offers a wide variety of examples of collective interests as the subject-matter of principles. They range from public health,[72] the provision of energy,[73] securing the food-chain[74] and the combating of unemployment,[75] through to securing the internal structure of the armed forces,[76] the security of the Federal Republic of Germany,[77] and protecting the free democratic order.[78] That a principle relates to such collective interests means that it requires the creation or maintenance of states of affairs which satisfy certain criteria, broader than the enforcement or satisfaction of individual rights, to the greatest extent legally and factually possible.[79]

---

[70] BVerfGE 35, 202 (219). See also BVerfGE 30, 173 (195).

[71] BVerfGE 51, 324 (345).   [72] BVerfGE 7, 377 (414 f.).

[73] BVerfGE 30, 292 (317).   [74] BVerfGE 39, 210 (227).

[75] BVerfGE 21, 245 (251).   [76] BVerfGE 28, 243 (261).

[77] BVerfGE 28, 175 (186).

[78] BVerfGE 30, 1 (26 f.). For many further references, see H. Schneider, *Die Güterabwägung des Bundesverfassungsgerichts bei Grundrechtskonflikten* (Baden-Baden, 1979), 133 ff.

[79] This definition shows that the distinction between individual rights and collective goods is not as simple as it might at first sight seem. Four different relations between individual rights and collective goods can be identified, which can be combined with each other in many different ways. (1) An individual right is an exclusive means to a collective good. Such a relation is assumed, for example, by those who consider the right to property exclusively as a means to the creation of economic productivity. A collision between this right and the collective good is excluded, because if the right loses its character as a means or even hinders productivity, there is no longer any reason for the right. If all individual rights were only means to collective goods, then there could no longer be any collisions between individual rights and collective goods. Rights as means to collective interests would in this sense have no force of their own. (2) A collective good is the exclusive means to certain rights. Those who say that the guaranteeing of a functioning criminal justice system simply secures the protection of individual rights are assuming such a relation. From this perspective a competition of individual rights with the principle of guaranteeing a functioning criminal justice system is in reality a competition of individual rights (or the principles which grant them). If all collective goods were simply means to rights, then there would only be competing rights. (3) A collective good is a state of affairs in which the norms granting individual rights apply or are satisfied. If this were true for all collective goods, talk of collective goods would be redundant. (4) Between individual rights and collective goods there is neither the means–end relation of (1) or (2), nor the identity relation (3). If individual rights have no absolute character as against collective goods, then under the conditions of (4), competitions between individual rights and collective goods are collisions between categorically different objects. Relations of the fourth type can exist alongside relations of the first to third type. Which of the relations applies depends on arguments about the content and character of individual rights and collective goods. Both arguments that individual rights are not simply means to collective goods and that there are collective goods

Dworkin's understanding of a principle is narrower than this. According to him, principles are only those norms which can be offered as reasons for individual rights. Norms which relate to collective interests, he calls 'policies'.[80] Without doubt, the distinction between individual rights and collective interests is important. But it is neither necessary nor desirable to tie the concept of a principle to that of an individual right. The common logical characteristics of both types of principle, which Dworkin alludes to with his 'principle in the generic sense',[81] and which become patently obvious when principles compete, make a wider concept of principle appear more suitable. The distinction which Dworkin wants to draw can be made within that wider concept if one wishes—and that point holds for other possible distinctions as well.

8. PRINCIPLES AND PROPORTIONALITY

It has already been hinted that there is a connection between the theory of principles and the principle of proportionality. This connection is as close as it could possibly be. The nature of principles implies the principle of proportionality and vice versa. That the nature of principles implies the principle of proportionality means that the principle of proportionality with its three sub-principles[82] of suitability, necessity (use of the least intrusive means), and proportionality in its narrow sense (that is, the balancing requirement) logically follows from the nature of principles; it can be deduced from them. The Federal Constitutional Court has stated in rather obscure terms that the principle of proportionality emerges 'basically from the nature of constitutional rights themselves'.[83] What follows will try to demonstrate that this is true in the strongest possible sense whenever constitutional rights are principles.[84]

---

independent of individual rights can be well grounded. The first argument can be based on the dignity and autonomy of the individual, that is, it can be justified along Kantian lines, while the second argument can be justified by the fact that not all state activity has to be concerned with rights. It can also be concerned with what is useful, pleasant, or desirable. This is sufficient to justify us in talking both of individual rights and also of collective goods.

[80] Dworkin, *Taking Rights Seriously*, 82, 90.

[81] ibid. 23.

[82] On the three sub-principles of the principle of proportionality, see, with extensive references, L. Hirschberg, *Der Grundsatz der Verhältnismäßigkeit* (Göttingen, 1981), 2, 50 ff., 75 ff.; See also R. Wendt, 'Der Garantiegehalt der Grundrechte und das Übermaßverbot', AöR 104 (1979), 415 ff.; E. Grabitz, 'Der Grundsatz der Verhältnismäßigkeit in der Rechtsprechung des Bundesverfassungsgerichts', AöR 98 (1973), 571 ff.; M. Gentz, 'Zur Verhältnismäßigkeit von Grundrechtseingriffen', NJW 1968, 1601 ff.; P. Lerche, *Übermaß und Verfassungsrecht* (Cologne, Berlin, Munich, and Bonn, 1961), 19 ff.; K. Stern, *Das Staatsrecht der Bundesrepublik Deutschland*, i (Munich, 1977), 674; F. E. Schnapp, 'Die Verhältnismäßigkeit des Grundrechtseingriffs', JuS 1983, 851.

[83] BVerfGE 19, 342 (348 f.); 65, 1 (44).

[84] The principle of proportionality is not actually a principle in the sense defined here. Suitability, necessity, and proportionality in the narrow sense (balance) are not balanced

Principles are optimization requirements relative to what is legally *and* factually possible. The *principle of proportionality in its narrow sense*, that is, the requirement of balancing, derives from its relation to the *legally* possible. If a constitutional rights norm which is a principle competes with another principle, then the legal possibilities for realizing that norm depend on the competing principle. To reach a decision, one needs to engage in a balancing exercise as required by the Law of Competing Principles.[85] Since the application of valid principles, if indeed they are applicable, is required, and since their application in a case of competing principles requires a balancing exercise, the character of constitutional rights norms as principles implies that when they compete with other principles, a balancing exercise becomes necessary. But this means that the principle of proportionality in its narrow sense can be deduced from the character of constitutional rights norms as principles.

The principle of proportionality in its narrow sense follows from the fact that principles are optimization requirements relative to what is legally possible. The principles of necessity and suitability follow from the nature of principles as optimization requirements relative to what is *factually* possible.

In order to demonstrate that the principle of *necessity* derives from the nature of principles, we will use here the simplest possible form of an examination of necessity. The fact that more complex forms give rise to difficulties says nothing about logical deduction but about the limits of the process.[86] The simplest form possible is characterized by the fact that only

---

against other things. They do not take precedence in one situation and not in another. Rather, the question is whether the sub-principles are satisfied or not, and their non-satisfaction leads to illegality. Thus the three sub-principles are actually rules. See on this, G. Haverkate, *Rechtsfragen des Leistungsstaats* (Tübingen, 1983), 11, who speaks of a 'legal maxim under which subsumption is possible'.

[85] See above at 50 ff.

[86] The simplest set of facts possible arises when there are only two legal subjects, namely the state and a citizen, and two relevant principles. If more than two principles are relevant, then the following situation can arise: M_1 and M_2 are two equally suitable means to end E, the pursuit of which is required by P_1, or is identical to P_1. M_2 hinders the realization of P_2 to a smaller degree than M_1, but M_1 hinders the realization of P_3 to a smaller extent than M_2. In this case the principle of necessity allows no choice to be made between the three resulting possibilities: (1) M_1 is chosen, thus preferring P_3 to P_2 and realizing P_1; (2) M_2 is chosen, thus preferring P_2 to P_3 and realizing P_1; (3) neither M_1 nor M_2 is chosen, thus preferring P_2 and P_3 together over P_1. In order to justify the choice of one of these possibilities, say the first, one has to show that it is justified to prefer the non-hindering of P_3 by M_2 together with the realization of P_1 over the hindering of P_2 by M_1. But this is none other than the justification of a conditional relation of preference between P_2 on the one side and P_1 and P_3 on the other, that is, a balancing exercise.

The problems which can arise when more people are involved are similar. Let M_1 and M_2 be once again two equally good means to the principle P_1 pursued by the state. M_1 hinders the prima facie right of x protected by P_2 to a lesser extent than M_2. M_2 hinders the prima facie right of y protected by P_2 or a further principle P_3 to a lesser extent than M_1. In this case as well, the principle of necessity admits of no decision.

two principles and two legal subjects (state/individual) are in play. It has the following structure: either the state justifies pursuing end E by reference to principle P_1, or indeed the two are identical. There are at least two means, M_1 and M_2, which are both equally suitable in bringing about or promoting E. M_2 affects less intrusively, or indeed not at all, the realization of what a constitutional rights norm in the form of a principle, P_2, requires. Under these circumstances, it is irrelevant, as far as P_1 is concerned, whether M_1 or M_2 is chosen. P_1 does not prefer M_1 over M_2 or vice versa. However, it is not irrelevant as far as P_2 is concerned. As a principle, P_2 requires optimizing relative to what is both legally and factually possible. Relative to what is factually possible, P_2 can be satisfied to a greater extent by the choice of M_2 over M_1. From the perspective of optimization relative to what is factually possible, and assuming the validity of both P_1 and P_2, M_2 is permitted and M_1 prohibited. This applies to any conceivable principles, ends, and means. Thus the principle of necessity, which the Federal Constitutional Court among other things characterizes as the requirement, 'that the end cannot equally well be achieved by the use of other means less burdensome to the individual'[87] derives from the nature of constitutional rights norms as principles.

The interconnection between legal and factual possibility can also be clarified with the help of this the simplest type of case. If both M_1 and M_2 hinder the realization of P_2, which is generally likely to be the case if one is examining the necessity of a state measure, and if M_2 does this to a smaller extent than M_1, then M_1 and M_2 together do not exhaust the scope of factual possibility for the realization of P_2, even if one assumes that M_1 and M_2 are the only suitable means for attaining the end E required by P_1. From the point of view of the factually possible, a greater level of realization of P_2 is possible if neither M_1 nor M_2 is adopted. The principle of necessity only enables us to distinguish M_1 from M_2. The question whether any of the alternatives should be chosen at all is not a question of the factually possible, that is, of necessity, but a question of what is legally possible, that is, one of balancing P_1 with P_2 (proportionality in its narrow sense). Thus the principle of necessity, if even the least intrusive means affects the realization of P_2, is always to be considered before the principle of proportionality in its narrow sense, that is, the balancing requirement.

Given what has just been said, the deduction of the principle of *suitability* is no longer problematic. If M_1 is not suitable for the furtherance or

---

The problems of the application of the principle of necessity even to the simplest set of facts are to be distinguished from the problems of complex sets of facts. These problems include above all the question of the extent to which the legislature and administrative bodies are to be granted a prognostic discretion in assessing necessity and establishing alternative means. (On these problems, see with numerous further references Hirschberg, *Der Grundsatz der Verhältnismäßigkeit*, 50 ff.).

[87] BVerfGE 38, 281 (302).

attainment of the end E required by P_1 or identical with it, then M_1 is not required by P_1; it is irrelevant for P_1 whether M_1 is adopted or not. If under these circumstances M_1 hinders the realization of P_2, then M_1 is prohibited by the need to optimize P_2 as far as is factually possible. This applies for all principles, ends, and means. Thus the principle of suitability also derives from the principled nature of constitutional rights norms.[88]

This process of deduction provides a justification for the principle of proportionality out of constitutional rights norms, to the extent that they are principles. It can be called the 'justification from constitutional rights'. This is not intended to exclude other possible justifications based on the Rule of Law,[89] adjudicative practice or the concept of justice.[90] [91] To the extent that these work, they are welcome support for the justification from constitutional rights.

II. THREE MODELS

1. The Model of Pure Principles

The discussion up to this point has demonstrated that the Federal Constitutional Court treats constitutional rights norms, at least in some cases, as principles. The connection between constitutional rights norms as principles and decision-related constitutional rights rules can be clarified with the help of the Law of Competing Principles: the conditions under which one principle takes precedence over another constitute the conditions of a rule which requires the legal consequences of the principle taking precedence.

These observations suggest a simple model of constitutional rights norms. Under this model, there are two types of constitutional rights norms, rules and principles. Directly enacted guarantees found in the constitutional rights provisions are to be understood as principles. Rules

---

[88] Grabitz, 'Der Grundsatz der Verhältnismäßigkeit in der Rechtsprechung des Bundesverfassungsgerichts', 586, comes close to deducing the principle of proportionality as set out here: 'if one understands the principle underlying liberty rights positively as the *greatest possible* opportunity for personal self-development guaranteed to the individual on account of the constitution, every "excessive" regulation thwarts the maximization of opportunities, and is thus constitutionally illegitimate'.

[89] On this strand of justification, see e.g. BVerfGE 23, 127 (133); 38, 348 (368).

[90] See on this H. Schneider, 'Zur Verhältnismäßgkeits-Kontrolle insbesondere bei Gesetzen', in C. Starck (ed.), *Bundesverfassungsgericht und Grundgesetz*, ii (Tübingen, 1976), 393 f.; Wendt, 'Der Garantiegehalt der Grundrechte und das Übermaßverbot', 416. R. v. Krauss, *Der Grundsatz der Verhältnismäßigkeit* (Hamburg, 1955), 41, speaks of the 'natural right in a timeless sense of the individual to be protected from burdens to the extent that they exceed the degree necessary'.

[91] For an account of the various attempts to justify the principle of proportionality, see P. Wittig, 'Zum Standort des Verhältnismäßigkeitsgrundsatzes im System des Grundgesetzes', DÖV 1968, 818 ff.

derive from the establishment of conditions of precedence as the result of balancing exercises. Since in such a model the rules are totally dependent on the principles, this model can be called the model of pure principles.

E. von Hippel has proposed a model which corresponds to this. According to von Hippel, constitutional rights norms are '(mere) principles [which] indicate that certain interests in freedom (faith, opinion, profession, property etc.), in short the idea of individual autonomy, are to be given special weight in the structuring of society and the resolution of conflicts. However, this is not intended to exclude the consideration of other perspectives.'[92] 'The result of this general indication, which often admittedly makes a clear decision entirely possible, on any particular case, can only be established after a careful analysis of the situation at hand with an appropriate weighing of all the relevant interests.'[93] The idea that the problem of the limits of constitutional rights might be solved by the limiting and reserving provisions found in the Constitution is, according to him, an 'illusion'.[94] On the contrary, one should proceed from the following maxim: 'a constitutional rights norm applies only to the extent that the interest in freedom it protects is not opposed by any more important interest'.[95] The application of this maxim presupposes an 'evaluation of the relevant interests'.[96] In 'balancing the interests', the 'facts of the individual case' are very important.[97]

The objections to such a model of pure principles should be obvious. The most immediate is that it does not take the text of the Constitution seriously. This objection refers above all to the fact that the model of pure principles undermines the differentiated approach of the Basic Law to the limitation of rights. The makers of the Basic Law expressly avoided general clauses limiting rights and chose instead to modify the individual guarantees of constitutional rights with a wide variety of limitations.[98] While the Federal Constitutional Court treats constitutional rights norms as principles, it also stresses the significance of this point when it speaks of a 'system of limitations which is carefully fashioned according to the nature of each

---

[92] Hippel, *Grenzen und Wesensgehalt der Grundrechte*, 15 f.   [93] ibid. 18.
[94] ibid. 22.   [95] ibid. 25 f., 30.
[96] ibid. 32.   [97] ibid. 34.
[98] Article 21(3) and (4) of the Herrenchiemsee draft (1948) still contained the provisions, '(3) To the extent that their content does not otherwise provide, constitutional rights are to be understood in the context of the general legal order. (4) A limitation of constitutional rights is only permissible by statute and on condition that public security, morals or health makes it absolutely necessary.' As regards the removal of the general clauses, H. v. Mangoldt explained in the eighth sitting of the Basic Principles Committee of the Parliamentary Council of 7 October 1948 that the committee 'considered this statement about the validity of constitutional rights in the context of the general legal order to be dangerous from the outset and have thus attempted to concretize it in the context of individual constitutional rights, so that it can be omitted as a general clause. Similarly, article 21(4)(1) of the Herrenchiemsee draft is also made redundant by the concretization of individual constitutional rights, and thus a stronger protection of constitutional rights has been achieved' (JöR NF (1951), p. 177).

individual constitutional right'.[99] To the extent that the model of pure principles fails to take these provisions seriously, the objection can be made that it contradicts the text of the Constitution.[100] It replaces the obligation to uphold the Constitution with a balancing exercise and misunderstands the character of the Basic Law as a 'rigid Constitution' having 'normative clarity and unambiguity'.[101]

There can be no doubt that this objection to the model of pure principles makes an important point. However, its understanding of the obligation to follow the Constitution, and whether in specific cases one can depart from the literal meaning of the text, can be questioned. It is at any rate unquestionable that one must start with the text of the Constitution, and that if it is permissible to depart from it, this can only be for special reasons. Even if it is true that the makers of the Constitution created a 'chaos of limitations' rather than a 'system of limitations',[102] this does not deprive the provisions of legal force.

The question is what consequences should be drawn from valid objections to the model of pure principles. There are two possibilities. One could replace the model of pure principles with a model of pure rules, or one could also try to construct a combined model.

2. THE MODEL OF PURE RULES

From the perspective of respect for the constitutional text, legal certainty, and predictability, the model of pure rules is without doubt the most attractive option. While accepting that constitutional rights norms may need elaboration, the model of pure rules sees them as applicable without any balancing exercise, and in this sense as *balancing-free* norms. Of course, within the model of pure rules one is still left with the complicated task of interpreting the provisions concerning constitutional rights, perhaps with the 'old and proven rules of legal interpretation',[103] but one can do without the procedure of balancing, hampered as it is with so much uncertainty. These potential advantages provide reason enough to consider the acceptability of this model. The question can be put in respect of three types of constitutional right: those without reservation, those with simple reservations, and those with qualified reservations. This does not embrace all types of constitutional provision, but it does cover three of such great importance that if the model of pure rules fails to account for these it will be generally unacceptable.

---

[99] BVerfGE 32, 54 (75).

[100] See T. Wülfing, *Grundrechtliche Gesetzesvorbehalte und Grundrechtsschranken* (Berlin, 1981), 21.

[101] F. Müller, *Die Positivität der Grundrechte* (Berlin, 1969), 17 ff.

[102] On the chaos-of-limitations thesis, see K. A. Bettermann, *Grenzen der Grundrechte* (Berlin, 1968), 3.

[103] Forsthoff, *Zur Problematik der Verfassungsauslegung*, 34.

2.1 Constitutional Rights Guaranteed without Reservation

If one is governed simply by textual indicators of limitless guarantees, then freedom of religion, freedom of artistic expression, and the right of conscientious objection are limitless. Nevertheless, there is widespread agreement that not everything that can somehow be brought within the scope of a right guaranteed without limits is actually constitutionally protected. One could take the view that this fact alone would be sufficient to reject the model of pure rules. But this would only apply for an extreme variant of the model which holds strictly to the text of the constitutional provisions and to nothing else. A model of pure rules need not be as rigid as that. It could try to achieve non-protection by *implied* limiting clauses or by implied narrowing of the initial scope of the right. The details of the form of such 'immanent'[104] limitations can be left open here.[105] The interesting point at the moment is whether the criteria one uses for establishing the scope of constitutional protection in the case of limitlessly guaranteed constitutional rights can be formulated *without using any balancing test.*

A textbook example of one criterion which *incorporates a balancing test* is the formula expressed by the Federal Constitutional Court in its 1970 decision concerning conscientious objection,[106] and which since then has in various guises formed the basis for its case-law on the limitation of limitlessly guaranteed constitutional rights.[107] This formula, which is significant evidence for the fact that the Federal Constitutional Court understands constitutional rights at least to an extent as principles, goes like this:

> only conflicting constitutional rights of third parties and other legal values of constitutional status are capable, with due respect for the unity of the constitution and the entire order of values it upholds, of limiting limitless constitutional rights in certain circumstances. The conflicts arising in such situations can only be resolved by establishing which constitutional provision is of greater weight for the concrete issue at hand. . . . The weaker norm may only be overridden to the extent that appears logically and systemically necessary; whatever happens, its fundamental substantive value must be respected.[108]

The question is whether there are any acceptable alternatives to such formulae, free from the need to engage in balancing exercises.

Dürig's theory of immanent non-disrupting limitations is paradigmatic for theories which at first sight appear to do without balancing, and thus correspond to a model of pure rules. Following Maunz[109] he finds them in

---

[104] For a comprehensive account and critique of theories of so-called immanent constitutional rights limitations, see H. van Nieuwland, 'Darstellung und Kritik der Theorien der immanenten Grundrechtsschranken', diss. (Göttingen, 1981).
[105] See on this below at 181 ff.   [106] BVerfGE 28, 243.
[107] See e.g. BVerfGE 30, 173 (193 ff.); 32, 98 (108); 33, 23 (29); 41, 29 (50); 44, 37 (50); 49, 24 (56).
[108] BVerfGE 28, 243 (261).
[109] T. Maunz, *Deutsches Staatsrecht*, 23rd edn. (Munich, 1980), 123.

the threefold limitation of article 2(1) Basic Law, understood not merely as a defensive right but as a rule of interpretation for all constitutional rights.[110] The 'three basic non-disrupting limitations'[111] are, first, a 'logically immanent limitation' based on the 'rights of others', secondly, a 'socially immanent limitation' based on the 'constitutional order', and, thirdly, an 'ethically immanent limitation'[112] based on the 'law of morals'. The derivation of these limitations does not concern us here.[113] The only relevant question is whether the three suggested by Dürig are truly free from any need to engage in balancing.

The logically immanent limitation relates to the legal rights of others, and in particular to private law rights. It is easy to see that this cannot be free from balancing. If it were, constitutional rights norms could be limited by any and every private law norm protecting private rights. It is significant that when Dürig refers to the Lüth Judgment, a classic case of balancing interests, he comments that this could lead to 'real problems concerning the balancing of values' for judges in civil cases 'who are not indifferent towards the order of values established by constitutional rights'. Balancing is unavoidable, if 'all are equally beneficiaries of constitutional rights'.[114]

Things are rather more complicated in the case of 'socially immanent limitations'. Dürig includes in these among other things, a 'limitation based on the prohibitions of the criminal law'.[115] In order to prevent the legislature from limiting constitutional rights at will through criminal prohibitions, he has to restrict immediately the idea of criminal prohibitions. He does this by restricting it to rules concerning 'substantive criminal injustice' and which thus relate to 'obvious social disturbance'.[116] But by building in such qualifications, the 'constitutional limitation of criminal law prohibitions' loses the clarity necessary for the model of pure rules. The question of substantive criminal injustice is controversial, and different people have different ideas as to what is 'obvious' when dealing with constitutional rights. Of course there are many crimes which one can be certain are never constitutionally permitted—the right of resistance in article 20(4) Basic Law aside. Murder is an obvious example. But there are others, such as in quasi-criminal law, which according to Dürig are 'as a rule' 'obvious non-disturbance limitations', where one can well ask whether they can legitimately limit constitutional rights.[117] To answer this question by referring to what is 'obvious' is to give a rationally uncontrollable answer and to run into constitutional intuitionism.

In easy cases one might well be happy talking in terms of substantive criminal injustice. But even in such cases one can ask why this excludes

---

[110] G. Dürig, in T. Maunz and G. Dürig *et al.*, *Grundgesetz Kommentar*, 5th edn. (Munich, 1983), art. 2(1), para. 72.

[111] ibid. para. 70.   [112] ibid. para. 73 ff.

[113] See, rejecting this, BVerfGE 30, 173 (192 f.).   [114] *Grundgesetz* para. 13, fn. 1.

[115] ibid. para. 75 f.   [116] ibid. para. 76.   [117] ibid. para. 79.

constitutional protection. The answer is that what is protected by the criminal law, such as human life, is from a constitutional perspective more important than what is protected by the constitutional rights norm being limited. The criterion of substantive criminal injustice is thus better seen as a generalization of a large number of situations in which the criminal law correctly prohibits something which limitlessly formulated constitutional rights norms prima facie permit. The weakness of such a generalization shows itself in those cases where it is questionable whether the criminal rule imposing a sanction really should override the constitutional prima facie permission or not. The decisive question can only be whether the criminal law prohibition, or its underlying reason, is more important from the perspective of constitutional law than the permission guaranteed by the constitutional right. Dürig's comment, that 'cases are conceivable in which the penalizing of certain forms of behaviour is questionable in the light of constitutional rights'[118] points in this direction. In such controversial cases, the criterion of substantive criminal injustice loses its definitive character, or it becomes the expression of the outcome of a balancing exercise. It loses its definitive character once one accepts the possibility that some action may be substantively criminally wrongful *only to such a small extent* that it no longer justifiably limits a constitutional right. It becomes the *expression of the outcome of a balancing exercise* whenever one maintains the possibility of justifying a limit to a constitutional right by reference to substantively criminal behaviour, but then determines that question by whether the criminal law in question protects something so important that the limitation of the constitutional right is justified. In both cases one ends up engaging in a balancing exercise, and this is unavoidable, since there is no other rational way in which the reason for the limitation can be put in relation to the constitutional right. An isolated analysis of the reason for the limitation alone can lead to some useful insights, but it cannot give a well-grounded answer to the question whether it is important enough to limit something equally important, that is, a constitutional right.

The points which have been made with respect to Dürig's criterion of substantive criminal injustice can be generalized. While we can formulate criteria to cover a large number of cases which appear free from the need to engage in balancing exercises, these criteria are simply the expression of underlying relations of precedence between the constitutional right and the reason for limiting it. If the relation of precedence is certain, the criterion appears self-evident. And if the criterion is self-evident, at any rate extensive consideration of preferences is unnecessary to justify the decision in the case. It can indeed confuse the issue. But unlike concrete relations of precedence, abstract limiting clauses often lead to borderline cases on the grounds of their open-texture and the range of constitutional legal rela-

---

[118] *Grundgesetz* para. 76.

tions. In such borderline cases, the balancing exercise resumes its rightful role. Clauses that are free from balancing can serve a useful function as rules of thumb, but their justification depends on an underlying balance of interests. The moments doubts arise, the balancing exercise becomes indispensible. Criteria that do without balancing are thus always categories of outcome which rest on a preceding balance of interests and which at best summarize those outcomes rather too broadly. A direct, intuitive access to such criteria does not satisfy the requirements of rational justification and collapses in borderline cases. The intuitive impression of their correctness or self-evident nature in a large number of cases depends upon the obviousness of the weighting of the opposing principles.

As far as the 'ethically immanent limitation' of the moral law is concerned, it is only necessary to make the point that whatever one understands its content to be, it can never be totally immune from balancing. This is because on one hand the constitutional rights to be limited have themselves a moral content, and because on the other hand the moral law, if it is to be legally relevant, must address the relationship between individual persons and between the individual and the collectivity. This in turn means that balancing is unavoidable in applying it to concrete cases.

The points which have been made in respect of Dürig's limitation clauses can be equally applied to attempts to solve the problem of limitlessly guaranteed constitutional rights by controlling the scope of their protection. An example of such an attempt is Müller's theory of the subject-specific action-type. This theory, which addresses the relationship between the scope of a constitutional right and limitation clauses in general will have to be discussed in detail at a later stage,[119] so it will be sufficient here to consider one of Müller's examples. It concerns the case of an artist who is painting in the middle of a crossroads. According to Müller, a ban on doing this does not infringe the constitutional right to artistic freedom, because it does not regulate a 'protected constitutional-right-specific action-type'.[120] What is decisive is that an 'equally valuable, alternative and specific possibility [remain] open'.[121] It is assumed that it makes no great difference—either subjectively as far as the artist is concerned, or objectively as far as the work of art is concerned—whether the painting takes place on the crossroads or on a stretch of grass nearby. Given that assumption, Müller's criterion has a significant impact. However, it is easy to see that it cannot function without balancing. Suppose that the crossroads is closed[122] such that painting on the crossroads disturbs nobody and affects no public interest. In such circumstances, forcing the painting onto the stretch of grass is in the circumstances unjustified, because there is no adequate reason for it. The

---

[119] Below at 202 ff.
[120] Müller, *Die Positivität der Grundrechte*, 64.   [121] ibid. 101.
[122] See on this J. Schwabe, *Probleme der Grundrechtsdogmatik* (Darmstadt, 1977), 160.

alternatives are equal. However, if one wants to draw a distinction between painting on a busy crossroads and one that is closed, the existence of an equally acceptable alternative cannot be the distinguishing criterion. The distinguishing criterion is the obstruction and endangering of traffic. This and the constitutional right to artistic freedom have to be set in relation to each other. The existence of alternatives can play an important role in the balancing exercise which becomes necessary, because where there is a viable alternative, the infringement of a constitutional right is less serious than where there is none. But the criterion of alternativity cannot replace the balancing exercise.

2.2 Constitutional Rights with Simple Reservations

Taken literally, limitlessly guaranteed constitutional rights norms protect too much. The problem with constitutional rights norms with simple limitations is that, taken literally, they seem to guarantee too little. Thus according to the actual words of constitutional provisions such as freedom of the person guaranteed by article 2(2)(2) Basic Law (that is, freedom of physical movement),[123] under the limiting rule of article 2(2)(3) it can be limited by the legislature down to its essential core, with only the need to respect the procedural requirements of article 19(1). If one takes the text literally, constitutional rights with simple limitations become meaningless beyond their essential core, at any rate as against the legislature.[124] This cannot be right, as the obligation of the legislature to respect constitutional rights in article 1(3) Basic Law shows. To the extent that a legislature can limit a constitutional right at will, it is not bound by it.

The potential meaninglessness can be prevented either by extending the guarantee of the essential core to cover every infringement of a right, or by introducing an additional unwritten criterion for the area of protection outside the essential core which limits the competence of the legislature to limit rights. The guarantee of an essential core is extended to all constitutional infringements by so-called relative theories of the essential core. According to these, a limitation of a constitutional right touches the essential core whenever it is disproportionate,[125] that is, if it is unsuitable, unnecessary, or disproportionate in the narrow sense, that is, if it 'does not take appropriate account of the weight and significance of the constititutional right'.[126] But this basically turns control of the legislative competence to limit constitutional rights into a matter of balancing.[127] If, on the other

---

[123] BVerfGE 35, 185 (190).

[124] On the concept of the meaninglessness of constitutional rights, see R. Thoma, 'Grundrechte und Polizeigewalt', in H. Triepel (ed.), *Festgabe für die Preußische Oberverwaltungsgericht* (Berlin, 1925), 195.

[125] K. Hesse, *Grundzüge des Verfassungsrechts* (Heidelberg, 1984) para. 332 ff.

[126] ibid. para. 318.

[127] See above at 66 ff. On the relationship between balancing and the essential core in relative theories of the essential core, see P. Häberle, *Die Wesensgehaltgarantie des Art. 19 Abs. 2*

hand, one adopts a so-called absolute,[128] and hence narrower, approach to the essential core, then the question of a criterion to be satisfied by limitations outside of that core remains. But once again, this can only be the test of proportionality. Just as in the case of limitless constitutional rights, criteria which avoid balancing can resolve a number of easy cases; the appearance of controversial cases makes it obvious that these criteria are the expression of a certain order of preference between principles. The long-standing case-law of the Federal Constitutional Court, which requires the satisfaction of the principles of suitability, necessity, and proportionality for every limitation of a constitutional right corresponds to the theoretical insights of the model of principles.[129] The impossibility of a solution to the problem of rights with simple limiting clauses confirms the accuracy of the insight and the judicial practice. Thus the pure model of rules also fails to account for constitutional rights with simple limitations.

2.3 Constitutional Rights with Qualified Reservations

Finally, the model of pure rules also proves to be inadequate where one might have thought it would have the greatest chance of success, in the case of constitutional rights with qualified limiting clauses. Not every state action within the scope of the inviolability of the home is justified simply because it is the means to one of the ends listed in article 13(3) Basic Law, and because it satisfies the other formal requirements. Beyond that, state action must be necessary and proportionate. Severe shortage in the housing market can easily be classified as an 'accommodation crisis' for the purposes of article 13(3) Basic Law. In the case of a measure which does not limit the inviolability of the home particularly seriously and which is suitable and necessary to deal with an accommodation crisis, there is no need to engage in detail in a balancing exercise between the significance of removing the crisis and breaching the constitutional right. In such clear cases, by introducing the concept of an accommodation crisis, the makers of the Constitution took a directly applicable decision as to the order of preference. The matter is different where there is a shortage of housing, but not too serious a shortage, and where the question arises whether its removal justifies a very intensive breach of the inviolability of the home. The attempt to solve this case rationally without engaging in a balancing exercise by subsuming it under the concept of an accommodation crisis has to fail. The question is not whether the shortage of accommodation is

---

Grundgesetz, 3rd edn. (Heidelberg, 1983), 58 ff.; Hippel, *Grenzen und Wesensgehalt der Grundrechte*, 47.

[128] The extent to which so-called absolute guarantees of an essential core can really be absolute, that is, the extent to which they can do without balancing, will have to be considered below at 192 ff.

[129] See e.g. BVerfGE 19, 330 (337); 21, 150 (155); 26, 215 (228); 27, 211 (219); 30, 292 (316).

correctly called an accommodation crisis, but whether as an accommodation crisis it justifies limiting the right. It is entirely possible that someone might classify it as an accommodation crisis requiring urgent state intervention, but not as one which justifies limiting constitutional rights. Given this possibility, the concept of an accommodation crisis can only be used in all cases as a definitive criterion, if it is understood as 'accommodation crisis for the purposes of article 13(3) Basic Law' which exists by definition whenever the accommodation crisis is such as to justify limiting the constitutional right. But this means that the concept of an accommodation crisis becomes a term for the result of a balancing exercise. This makes the link between concepts even in qualified limiting clauses to the balancing exercise obvious. The Federal Constitutional Court expresses this when, in the context of interpreting article 13(3), it stated that, 'the limits of the exercise of constitutional rights acceptable under the Rule of Law are to be fixed having respect for the basic presumption of freedom and the constitutional principles of proportionality and reasonableness'.[130]

The difficulties to which the model of pure rules can lead in the case of qualified limitation clauses, and how these difficulties can be avoided by having regard for principles, are exemplified by the fast cleaning service case.[131] In this case, the Federal Constitutional Court had to decide whether rights of entry and investigation under trade legislation for the purposes of economic regulation breached article 13 Basic Law.

The Court chose to approach the matter as if it were subsuming facts under rules. In the first step it included the rooms of fast cleaning services within the concept of living accommodation, in doing which, as it pointed out, the literal meaning of article 13(1) 'was not decisive'.[132] This expansive reading of the scope of protection led to difficulties when it came to the limitations. The goal of economic regulation cannot be found in the list of legitimate purposes for intervention in article 13(3). Thus in order to make access to and regulation of places of work permissible, the court stated that to the extent that they were permissible, they were not 'infringements or limitations'.[133] The Court had some doubts about this construction, which contradicts the basic concepts of constitutional rights doctrine—since action within the scope of right remains so however well justified it might be—as can be seen by their description of it as an 'uninhibited perspective' which the drafting constitutional council was supposed to have shared, and by their call for a 'reformulation of the constitutional text'.[134]

From the perspective of a theory of principles, it is possible to reconstruct this case such that the extension of protection to the rooms of shops and factories does not lead to such problems when it comes to limitations.

---

[130] BVerfGE 32, 54 (72).   [131] BVerfGE 32, 54.   [132] BVerfGE 32, 54 (72).
[133] BVerfGE 32, 54 (76): 'rights of entry and observation which are no longer to be qualified as "infringements or limitations" '.
[134] BVerfGE 32, 54 (76).

The starting point is that the provision of article 13(1) Basic Law, 'the home is inviolable' is an expression of a principle of protection for the spatial context of individual personal development. In this connection, the Court mentions the 'protective purpose' of the constitutional right.[135] If one follows the Court in including 'uninterrupted work' as one element of individual personal development, then 'it is only logical to give the spatial context within which that work takes place a correspondingly effective legal protection'.[136] Under the reconstruction preferred here, this means that fast cleaning services do not enjoy the protection of article 13 Basic Law because they fall within the meaning of its terms, but because they are embraced by its underlying principle. This principle leads to an expansion of the scope beyond its literal meaning. The limitations are not designed for such an expansive reading. The reasons justifying limitations are designed for acts affecting the home properly so called. So long as one is only concerned with that, the text and the weight of the relevant principles roughly correspond. But this is not true in the case of shops and factories. As the Court rightly points out, 'the interests of others and of the general public' have greater weight against the principle of protection for the spatial private sphere.[137] In the light of this weighting, the Court lists a whole row of conditions for the permissibility of investigation and access for the regulation of trade and industry. For example, they include a limitation on the normal times of business.[138] This condition can be expressed in terms of a rule, which in accordance with the Law of Competing Principles[139] expresses the balance of competing principles. This rule is not a refining of the literal meaning of article 13 Basic Law, but is derived from that provision because it rests on the principle enacted in it. In this way, first, one does not contravene the literal meaning of article 13. Fast cleaning services are not, contrary to linguistic usage, characterized as 'homes'. And, secondly, there can be no question of violating the literal meaning of the limiting clause in article 13(3). The literal meaning of that clause is only to be related to the literal meaning of the scope of protection. To the extent that the scope of protection is given a more extensive reading, in that a further rule protecting constitutional rights is adopted on the basis of the underlying principle alongside the literal rule, then the restriction of that rule is not bound to the literal meaning of the limiting clause either. This relates only to the literal meaning of the scope of protection. In this way, by adopting the theory of principles, one can create just the level of constitutional protection desired by the Court without creating problems in the reasoning.

---

[135] BVerfGE 32, 54 (70).
[136] BVerfGE 32, 54 (71).
[137] BVerfGE 32, 54 (75 f.).
[138] BVerfGE 32, 54 (77).
[139] See above at 53 f.

3. The Model of Rules and Principles

The model of pure rules fails in the case of all three types of constitutional norm considered. We can therefore safely assume that it is also inadequate in the case of other types of norm contained in the Basic Law. The model of pure principles was rejected because it does not take the provisions of the Basic Law seriously. Where two pure forms are unacceptable, one should consider a mixed or combined form. The model of rules and principles is such a combined model, and it consists of a level of principles interconnected with a level of rules.

3.1 The Level of Principles

All the principles relevant to constitutional adjudication under the Basic Law belong to the level of principles. A principle is relevant to the adjudication of constitutional rights under the Basic Law when it can *correctly* be cited for or against a decision. If it may correctly be cited, then it is valid. The question of which principles apply in this sense can of course be controversial. But for obvious reasons much less use is made of the possibility of disputing validity than of disputing the abstract or concrete weight of principles. A dispute about the abstract weight of a principle would be, for example, a discussion about the maxim, *'in dubio pro libertate'*, which is taken to express a basic preference in favour of those principles which are directed towards individual legal liberties.[140] Disputes about the concrete weight or precedence of principles take place in the context of disagreements about the correct solution of individual cases.

The principles relevant to constitutional adjudication do not simply include those related to individual rights, that is, prima facie constitutional rights, but also those relating to collective interests and which can be used above all as reasons against prima facie constitutional rights, sometimes also as reasons for them. The ground of existence of principles guaranteeing prima facie constitutional rights can be relatively easily stated. Wherever a constitutional provision protects a subjective right, at least one such principle can be derived from it. The question is harder to answer in the case of principles protecting collective interests. Some can be straightforwardly derived from the limitation clauses, others according to an institutional interpretation of constitutional rights as part of their scope of protection.[141] Still other principles such as the principles of the social state[142] and democracy[143] can be

---

[140] See below at 384 f.

[141] See e.g. BVerfGE 20, 162 (176), 'free press'; BVerfGE 35, 79 (120), ' the functionality of the institution of "free science" as such'.

[142] On the social state principle as a ground of limitations, see BVerfGE 8, 274 (329), 'the social state principle, which determines and limits the content of freedom of contract as well', and also BVerfGE 21, 87 (91).

[143] One case in which the principle of democracy was used as a principle relating to a collec-

derived from constitutional provisions which are not constitutional rights provisions, without this causing any particular difficulty. By contrast, the derivation of principles such as that of military defence from jurisdictional norms of the Constitution is not unproblematic,[144] since the mere fact that something lies within the jurisdiction of the Federation says little about its weight with respect to other constitutional rights. The jurisdiction of the Regions—one thinks of education or police law—can be just as, or even more, important.

The derivation of principles from provisions of the Basic Law is above all else significant for the question of their constitutional status. But some principles are relevant to constitutional rights even though their content cannot be derived from any constitutional provision. Many limitation clauses empower the legislature to decide for itself which principles it will be governed by, that is, they permit the legislature to limit constitutional rights according to principles which from the perspective of the Constitution do not need to be maintained. One example is the principle of the 'maintenance and support of the manual crafts'.[145] Principles such as this one, which express so-called 'relative public interests',[146] owe their constitutional relevance partly to the fact that the legislature has appropriated them within the competence granted by the limiting clauses of constitutional rights. To this extent, one could say that they are procedurally derived from constitutional rights provisions. This does not mean that the only relevant characteristic of such principles is their formal derivation. The issue of their substantive weight, which has to be demonstrated in the course of constitutional reasoning, remains indispensable.[147] This leads to the problem whether such a principle, which has to be demonstrated in the course of constitutional reasoning to be sufficiently weighty to override another constitutional principle, must not itself have constitutional status. To solve this problem we can distinguish between constitutional status of first and second degree. A principle has first degree constitutional status when it is capable of limiting a limitlessly protected constitutional right. It has second degree status if it can only limit a constitutional right when combined with a jurisdictional norm enacted in a limiting provision. In

---

tive interest to strengthen a constitutional right—albeit at the cost of a competing constitutional right—was the Lüth Judgment, BVerfGE 7, 198 (208, 212).

[144] BVerfGE 28, 243 (261).

[145] BVerfGE 13, 97 (110).

[146] On the distinction between absolute, 'i.e. generally recognised public interests independent of the current politics of society (such as public health)' and relative public interests, which flow from the 'specific economic, social and political ideas and goals of the legislature', see BVerfGE 13, 97 (107 ff.).

[147] The sentence in which the Federal Constitutional Court summarizes its discussion of the substantive weight of the principles of the maintenance and support of the manual crafts is typical: 'if the legislature were able with reason to consider maintaining and caring for a high level of performance of the manual trades to be a particularly important public good . . .' (BVerfGE 13, 97 (113)).

other words, in the case of principles of second degree constitutional status, the substantive and jurisdictional or procedural aspects combine in mutually supportive fashion to justify limiting a constitutional right. The fact that the substantive component of the principle legitimizes its second degree constitutional status can by definition not be shown by its direct derivation from a constitutional provision, but has to be based on constitutional reasoning. Thus second degree constitutional status is a much less certain matter than the already uncertain first degree constitutional status. When 'constitutional status' is used in what follows, only first degree status is meant.

The distinction between substantive and procedural derivation is, as such, not connected with the distinction between two structurally different types of principle. Substantive principles with the same structure can be either substantively or procedurally derived. But it does gesture towards a distinction between two fundamental types of principle which is of wide-ranging significance, namely the distinction between *substantive* or *material* and *formal* or *procedural* principles. A formal or procedural principle is, for example, the principle which says that the democratic legislature shall take decisions which are significant for society as a whole. This procedural principle, together with a substantive principle serving some secondary public interest, can be balanced against a constitutional principle guaranteeing an individual right. Furthermore, that formal principle is the reason for the many instances of discretion which the Federal Constitutional Court allows the legislature. To the extent that granting discretion results in less protection for constitutional rights than would otherwise be the case, then that principle can rightly be called an independent ground of limitation.

This short and by no means exhaustive glance at the level of principles shows that a great variety of things are brought together. But more important than a reference to variety is its undecided nature. There is a lot of room in the spacious world of principles. It can be described as the world of the ideal Ought.[148] The moment one steps from the spacious world of the ideal to the narrow world of the definitive, or real, Ought, one finds competing principles, or to use other common expressions, tensions, conflicts, and antinomies.[149] Decisions about the relative weight of competing principles, that is, decisions about relations of preference, are unavoidable.

3.2 The Level of Rules

Constitutional rights provisions can be seen not only as the enactment of, and hence decisions in favour of, certain principles, but also as the expres-

---

[148] On this concept, which will only be used cautiously here on account of the ease with which it can be misunderstood, see Alexy, 'Zum Begriff des Rechtsprinzips', 79 ff.

[149] See e.g. N. Achterberg, 'Antinomien verfassungsgestaltender Grundentscheidungen', *Der Staat*, 8 (1969), 159 ff.

sion of an attempt to take decisions in the light of the requirements of competing principles. At this point we move to the level of rules, and in this way the provisions acquire a double aspect. On one hand they enact principles; on the other—to the extent that they show differentiated expressions of their scope and limits—they contain decisions relative to the requirements of competing principles. Of course, the decisions they contain are incomplete. In no way do they make decision-taking free from balancing exercises possible in every case. Different expressions of constitutional rights show great variation in their degree of precision. Compare, for example, the expression of the freedom of artistic expression with the inviolability of the home.

Whenever a constitutional rights provision makes some sort of decision relative to the requirements of competing principles, then it has not merely enacted a *principle*, it has also enacted a *rule*. If the rule is not applicable without some balancing test, then it is an incomplete rule. To the extent that it is incomplete in this sense, constitutional adjudication must fall back on the level of principle with all its uncertainty. But this does not alter the fact that the decisions, to the extent that they apply, are to be taken seriously. The requirement to take seriously the decisions made in constitutional rights provisions, that is, the text of the Constitution, is one part of the postulate of the binding nature of the Constitution. It is only one part of it, because both the rules enacted in constitutional provisions and the principles enacted are constitutional norms. This raises the issue of the relative status of the two levels. And the answer can only be that from the perspective of the binding nature of the Constitution, the level of rules takes precedence. Of course, the level of principles is also the result of positive enactment, that is, the result of a decision. But a decision in favour of competing principles leaves much undecided, for a collection of principles can accommodate a variety of decisions concerning concrete relations of preference. To the extent that decisions have been made at the level of rules, more has been established than by the mere decision for certain principles. But to be bound by the Constitution means to be bound to the decisions of the constitution makers. So decisions made at the level of rules take precedence over other alternative decisions which the level of principles merely makes possible. Of course, the question is how strong this precedence is. The case-law of the Federal Constitutional Court shows that it does not assume that preference for text-based decisions is totally unquestionable. A good example of this is the Pharmacists Judgment. According to the text of article 12(1)(1) Basic Law, the freedom to choose a profession is, by contrast to the freedom to exercise a profession, subject to no limitations. The persuasive argument of the Court that 'it would not correspond to real life and it would have legally implausible consequences if one refused the legislature outright *every* possible act within the scope of freedom to choose a profession'[150] can be understood to mean that there are conditions under which competing principles are so much weightier than the freedom to choose a profession that a departure from the literal meaning of the Constitution is justified. In other words, this is a case which does not correspond to the precedence of the level of rules over the level of principles as defined by the text of constitutional provisions. So the relation of precedence between the two levels is not strict. Rather, the rule of precedence is that the level of rules takes precedence over the level of principles unless the reasons for taking a decision contrary to that which has been made at the level of rules are so strong that they override the principle of commitment to the text of the Constitution. The question of the relative strength of the reasons is the subject-matter of constitutional argumentation.[151]

3.3 The Double Aspect of Constitutional Rights Norms

The fact that constitutional rights provisions enact two types of norm, that is, rules and principles, establishes the double aspect of constitutional *provisions*. This does not mean that constitutional rights *norms* share the same characteristic. To start with they are either (generally incomplete) rules *or* principles. However, constitutional rights norms do have a double aspect when they combine both levels. Such a combination of both levels arises through the incorporation in a constitutional rights norm of a principled, and hence to-be-balanced, limitation clause. The form of such clauses can be seen, first, in the example of artistic freedom. The constitutional rights provision can be given the form:

(1)   Art is free.

We can proceed from the basis that 'article 5(3)(1) Basic Law guarantees freedom of artistic activity in a broad sense', as does the Federal Constitutional Court.[152] This means among other things[153] that prima facie every regulation of behaviour belonging to the artistic sphere is prohibited. Thus:

(2)   State regulation of activity belonging to the artistic sphere is prohibited.

If one understood this as a complete rule, one would have a limitless right, which, in view of the fact that there are cases in which other principles take precedence over artistic freedom, cannot be correct. So a limitation clause which takes account of this fact has to be introduced. If one creates such a clause on the basis of the formula developed by the Federal Constitutional Court in volume 28 of its decisions,[154] the norm will take the following form:

---

[150] BVerfGE 7, 377 (401).   [151] See on this below at 369 ff.
[152] BVerfGE 30, 173 (191).
[153] What else it might mean does not interest us here.   [154] BVerfGE 28, 243 (261).

(3) State regulation of activity belonging to the artistic sphere is prohibited, unless it is necessary to satisfy competing principles of constitutional status (whether protecting the constitutional rights of others or collective interests) which in the circumstances of the case take precedence over the principle of artistic freedom.[155]

The interpolated clause requires, first, that the competing principles, call them $P_2, \ldots P_n$, have *constitutional status*, secondly that state intervention is *necessary* to satisfy $P_2, \ldots P_n$ (which includes its *suitability*), and thirdly, that $P_2, \ldots P_n$ under the circumstances of the case (C) *take precedence* over the principle of artistic freedom, which can be called P_1, in short that $(P_2, \ldots P_n \, P \, P_1) \, C$ applies. It is apparent that this clause, including the requirement from the apparently limitless protection of artistic liberty that the competing principles have constitutional status, is none other than the three parts of the principle of proportionality. If we call the conditions for the satisfaction of the entire clause 'L', state regulation of any form of activity within the scope of artistic liberty 'S', and the legal consequence of the constitutional prohibition of the state intervention in question 'Q', then the most general form of a constitutional rights norm equipped with a limitation clause is:

(4) S and not $L \to Q$

In two respects this norm has entirely the character of a rule. It is applicable without needing to be balanced by any other norm, and cases can be subsumed under it.[156] Whatever falls within the scope of the norm but does not satisfy the requirements of the limitation clause is prohibited. But it does not have the character of a rule when the limitation clause refers explicitly to competing principles. Norms of this form can be called double aspect constitutional rights norms.

Such norms always arise whenever one tries to expand into applicable rules what has been directly enacted in the constitutional rights provisions with the help of clauses referring to competing principles. So for example, what is enacted by article 2(2)(2) and 2(2)(3) Basic Law can be expanded into the following form:

(5) Infringements by the state of the freedom of the person are prohibited, if they are not carried out on the basis of law or if they are not necessary to satisfy such competing principles, which under the circumstances take precedence over the principle of the freedom of the person.

The fact that the competing principles do not need to pass the filter of

---

[155] According to the absolute theory of an essential core, a further core-related limitation clause would be necessary. But theories of an essential core will only first be considered below. For now, it should therefore be left open whether a clause relating to the guarantee of an essential core should be added.

[156] On the logical form of subsuming under such a norm, see Koch and Rüßmann, *Juristische Begründungslehre*, 101 ff.

constitutional status derives from the decision of the constitution makers expressed in article 2(2)(3) Basic Law for an unqualified limitation clause.

Norms containing qualified limitations also need expanding to build in the principle of proportionality and hence part of the level of principles. Their difference lies in the fact that the set of competing principles is limited at the level of rules. Article 13(3) Basic Law provides an example of this limitation.

The details can be refined and made more precise.[157] For now, this is not necessary. What needed demonstrating has been demonstrated. It is inadequate to conceive of constitutional rights norms either purely as rules or purely as principles. An adequate model derives both rules and principles from the provisions of the Constitution. Both are combined in the double aspect constitutional rights norm.

One fundamental objection remains. It can be argued that the theory of principles is intrinsically flawed. It leads to the balancing of competing interests and hence to unbearable uncertainty. In this respect it is related to the theory of constitutional values. Everything which can be said of the latter applies to the former. This objection must now be considered in depth.

III. THEORIES OF PRINCIPLES AND VALUES

1. PRINCIPLES AND VALUES

Two considerations indicate that principles and values are related to each other. Just as one can speak of competing principles and a balance between principles, so also one can speak of competing values and a balance between values. In addition, the gradated satisfaction of principles corresponds to the gradated realization of values. Accordingly, statements of the Federal Constitutional Court about values can be reformulated in terms of principles and vice versa without loss of meaning. Instead of stating that 'freedom of the press carries with it the possibility of coming into conflict with other values upheld by the Basic Law',[158] the Court could have stated in its Spiegel Judgment that freedom of the press carries with it the possibility of competing with other principles enacted in the Basic Law,[159] and in its 1973 decision about the length of investigative detention, instead of

---

[157] See e.g. the attempts to refine this by R. Rubel, *Planungsermessen* (Frankfurt a. M., 1982), 91 ff.

[158] BVerfGE 20, 162 (176).

[159] That this is not a remote alternative can be seen from the fact that later in its reasoning, the Court speaks on one hand of 'the principle of press freedom', and on the other hand, of the 'surely no less important constitutional principle of the unconditional duty of all state organs, institutions and citizens to defend the existence and security of the state and its order of liberty' (BVerfGE 20, 162 (218 f.)).

talking about a conflict of principles,[160] it could have talked about competition between different values.

1.1 Deontological, Axiological, and Anthropological Concepts

However, in spite of these obvious similarities there is a significant difference. This can be seen most clearly by adopting von Wright's division of practical concepts. According to von Wright, the concepts of practical reason fall into three groups, the deontological, the axiological, and the anthropological.[161] Examples of *deontological* concepts are the command, the prohibition, the permission, and the right to something. As will be shown below, these concepts have a common derivation from a single basic deontological concept, that of the command or the Ought. *Axiological* concepts are characterized by their derivation from a different single basic concept, that of the Good. The variety of axiological concepts derives from the variety of criteria by which something may be judged good. Axiological concepts are being used whenever something is described as beautiful, effective, reliable, valuable, democratic, socially just, liberal, or consistent with the Rule of Law. By contrast, the concepts of will, interest, need, decision, and action are all examples of *anthropological* concepts.[162] These groups of concepts cover the field of basic disputes both in practical philosophy and in jurisprudence. Think for example of the dispute over the deontological or teleological nature of ethics, which is in the main a dispute about the primacy of the concept of the Ought or the Good.[163] Think also of the

---

[160] BVerfGE 36, 264 (270).

[161] G. H. v. Wright, *The Logic of Preference* (Edinburgh, 1963), 7; id., *The Varieties of Goodness* (London, 1963), 6 f. Von Wright's terminology varies. Occasionally he uses two terms. Thus instead of 'anthropological' he also speaks of 'psychological', instead of 'deontological' 'normative', and instead of 'axiological' he uses 'value concepts'. On the threefold division, see also Raz, *Practical Reason and Norms*, 11 f.

[162] The characterization of what is to be balanced by way of anthropological expressions seems to be more common than by way of deontological or axiological expressions. Thus the two decisions mentioned in the text above include the following anthropological expressions: 'desires', 'needs', 'interests', and 'goals' (BVerfGE 36, 264 (269 f.); 20, 162 (176 ff.)). A further term is 'concern' (BVerfGE 35, 79 (122)). Of course, as names for the objects of legal balancing, in no way can these expressions refer to purely anthropological concepts. The expression 'interest' would refer to a purely anthropological concept if it identified what somebody really wanted. Somebody really wanting something is neither a necessary nor a sufficient condition for taking account of an interest in balancing, even if it can be a reason among others for doing so. In order for it to be taken account of, it has to be an interest which is to be considered, or is valuable, from the perspective of the law. Thus when anthropological expressions are used to identify the objects of legal balancing, they stand for concepts betraying a deontological or axiological dimension. In this context, they are always replaceable with deontological or axiological expressions. The same applies for the identification of something as a 'legal good', which stands for a concept composed of deontological and/or axiological and/or anthropological elements. On this concept, see in place of many K. Amelung, *Rechtsgüterschutz und Schutz der Gesellschaft* (Frankfurt a. M., 1972) as well as M. Marx, *Zur Definition des Begriffs, 'Rechtsgut'* (Cologne, Berlin, Bonn, and Munich, 1972).

[163] See on this e.g. Wright, *The Varieties of Goodness*, 156 f.; M. Scheler, *Formalism in Ethics and Non-formal Ethics of Values*, trans. M. S. Frings and R. L. Funk (Evanston, Ill.,

development from analytical through interest-based to value-based jurisprudence which can be represented as the consequence of adopting in turn the primacy of deontological, anthropological, and axiological concepts.

Taking this threefold division into account, the significant difference between principles and values is easy to see. Principles are requirements of a particular nature, namely optimization requirements. As such they belong to the deontological realm. By contrast, values are located on the axiological plane. However, this does little more than identify crudely the nature of values. In order to identify their relation to principles more precisely, a deeper analysis is necessary.

1.2 On the Concept of Value

The idea of values is used in a great many different ways in ordinary speech, in philosophy, and in the technical language of various other disciplines.[164] It is not necessary to describe the different usages at this point, or to go into the various attempts to classify and theorize values.[165] The comparison of values with principles can be based on a few general and basic structural characteristics of values. These become apparent in a basic distinction in usage: the difference between the idea that something *has* value and that something *is* a value.[166]

1.2.1 Classificatory, Comparative, and Metric Value-Judgments

If someone says of something that it has value, they are making a *value-judgment*[167] and are engaging in *evaluation*.[168] Value-judgments, along

1973), 163 ff; N. Hartmann, *Ethics*, trans. S. Coit, vol. i (London, 1932), 81 f; E. Husserl, *Logical Investigations*, trans. J. N. Findlay (London, 1970), 81 ff.

[164] See on this e.g. W. K. Frankena, 'Value and Valuation', in P. Edwards (ed.), *The Encyclopedia of Philosophy*, ii (New York and London, 1967), 229 ff.

[165] Apart from the work of Scheler, Hartmann, and von Wright mentioned already, see on this e.g. C. v. Ehrenfels, *System der Werttheorie*, 2 vols. (Leipzig, 1897/8); R. B. Perry, *General Theory of Value* (New York, 1926); V. Kraft, *Die Grundlagen einer wissenschaftlichen Wertlehre*, 2nd edn. (Vienna, 1951); R. Lautmann, *Wert und Norm: Begriffsanalysen für die Soziologie*, 2nd edn. (Opladen, 1971); M. Rokeach, *The Nature of Human Values* (New York, 1973); E. Laszlo and J. B. Wilbur (eds.), *Value Theory in Philosophy and Social Science* (New York, London, and Paris, 1973).

[166] On this distinction see Kraft, *Die Grundlagen einer wissenschaftlichen Wertlehre*, 10 f.; R. B. Perry, *Realms of Value*, (Cambridge, Mass., 1954), 1 f.

[167] The counterpart to a value-judgment, which is to be located on the axiological level (prototype: 'x is good'), is a judgment of obligation to be located on the deontological level (prototype: 'x ought to be done'). On the concepts of value-judgments and judgments of obligation, see P. Edwards, *The Logic of Moral Discourse* (New York and London, 1955), 141; W. K. Frankena, *Ethics* (Englewood Cliffs, NJ, 1963), 9 f.; R. Alexy, *A Theory of Legal Argumentation*, trans. R. Adler and N. MacCormick (Oxford, 1989), 59 ff.

[168] The word, 'evaluation', is ambiguous. Assume that x expresses the value-judgment, 'φ is good'. Three things could be called the evaluation: (1) that which the sentence expressed by x means, namely that φ is good (semantic concept of evaluation); (2) the speech act which x performs in expressing the sentence in question (pragmatic concept of evaluation); (3) the

with the concepts of value they include, can be divided into three groups: classificatory, comparative, and metric.[169] A *classificatory* value-judgment is made when, for example, someone identifies a particular constitution as good or bad.[170] The function of classificatory value-judgments is to divide the subject-matter being evaluated into things which have a positive and things which have a negative value, and, if the criteria being adopted permit, into things which have neutral value.[171] *Comparative* value-judgments allow one to make differentiated evaluations. This is what is being used when one says of two objects that one is better than the other, or that they are both of equal value. Comparative evaluative statements such as 'constitution X is better than constitution Y' or 'both constitutions are equally good' express judgments of preference and indifference respectively. The most precise form of evaluation is offered by *metric* value-judgments which allocate a number to the object being evaluated which is indicative of its value. A classic example of metric evaluation is the evaluation of a piece of property in terms of a sum of money.[172] Thus classificatory value concepts enable us to say that something has positive, negative, or neutral value, comparative value concepts enable us to say of two objects that one is better than the other or that they are equally valuable, and metric value concepts enable us to say that something has a specific value. All these cases involve judgments that something *has* a value. But what does it mean for something to *be* a value? The key to answering this is the distinction between the object and the criterion of evaluation.

1.2.2 Values as the Criteria of Evaluation

All sorts of things can be the *object* of evaluation, among other things, natural objects, artefacts, ideas, experiences, actions, and states of affairs. The *criteria* of evaluation can also be highly diverse. A car can be evaluated, among other things, according to its speed, safety, comfort, price, economy, and beauty. The criteria of evaluation can compete with each other: take for

psychic event which generally precedes or accompanies the expression of a value-judgment, and the content of which is expressed by the value-judgment (psychological concept of evaluation). Here, we will use the semantic concept of evaluation.

[169] See on this F. v. Kutschera, *Einführung in die Logik der Normen, Werte und Entscheidungen* (Freiburg and Munich, 1973), 85 ff.

[170] On classification according to evaluative criteria, see J. O. Urmson, 'Einstufen', in G. Grewendorf and G. Meggle (eds.), *Seminar: Sprache und Ethik* (Frankfurt a. M., 1974), 140 ff.

[171] The concept of neutrality is to be distinguished from that of indifference. According to the criterion of tastiness, meals can be divided into those with positive, negative, and neutral values. Meals which taste neither good nor bad have a neutral value. But not everything which tastes neither good nor bad can be given a neutral value according to the criterion of tastiness. A poem, to which this criterion is inapplicable, cannot be given any value at all. It is indifferent as regards that criterion. See on this, and with alternative terminology, Weinberger and Weinberger, *Logik, Semantik, Hermeneutik*, 151.

[172] On the metric concept of value, see Kutschera, *Einführung in die Logik der Normen, Werte und Entscheidungen*, 87 ff.

example speed and economy. Since they compete, they have to be brought into relation with each other in order to establish an *overall evaluation* of any given car. In the Spiegel Judgment mentioned already, the objects of evaluation were, among other things, states of legal regulation. They were judged principally against two criteria, freedom of the press and national security. One of the states of legal regulation to be evaluated was 'a right of the press to maintain the confidentiality of their sources even in situations in which the matter being investigated is a crime of intentional treason and the editor is suspected of this crime with his sources of information as accomplices'.[173] If one simply adopted the criterion of press freedom, this state of affairs would be evaluated as 'good'; if one proceeds on the basis of national security it is 'bad'. The two criteria compete. In order to achieve an overall evaluation they must be brought into relation with each other.

Neither the car nor the state of legal regulation can be said to be a value. As objects of evaluation they have a value, and indeed a different value depending on the criterion one adopts. It is not the objects but the *criteria of evaluation* which can be called 'values'. This corresponds both to systematic considerations and to normal usage. So it is overblown, but not wrong, to say that one car satisfies the value of safety to a higher degree than another; what one cannot say is that one car *is* a higher value than another. In the more detached legal context it is normal to say that a certain state of regulation respects the value of press freedom to a higher degree than another.

Evaluations can be based on a single criterion of evaluation or on several. A person who says that a car is good and bases this judgment only on the fact that it is safe is engaging in evaluation on only one criterion. The criterion of safety can be satisfied by cars to varying extents. This opens up the possibility of several different classifications under one criterion. For example, one could classify as good all cars which in comparison with other cars are relatively safe, or all cars attaining a certain level of safety not determined by what has hitherto been realized, or, in the strictest type of evaluation, only those cars which offer the maximum safety conceivable. Evaluations according to just one criterion can have fanatical tendencies.

Generally, evaluations take place according to several criteria which must be balanced with each other, because they compete with each other. The evaluation 'good' is thus the expression of an overall evaluation. The application of evaluative criteria which have to be balanced against each other corresponds to the application of *principles*. In what follows only those criteria for evaluations which can be balanced against each other will be termed '*evaluative criteria*'. Their counterpart are criteria which, like *rules*, are applicable without balancing. These will be called '*evaluative rules*'. One type of evaluative rule is presupposed by classification accord-

---

[173] BVerfGE 20, 162 (219).

ing to one criterion just considered. It has the form: whenever a car attains safety level s, then it is good. According to this evaluative rule, the satisfaction of an evaluative criterion to a *certain degree* is an adequate ground for definitively considering it 'good'. Generally, evaluative rules contain several preconditions. They then take the following form: if x displays characteristics $F_1, \ldots F_n$, then x is good. Such evaluative rules are applicable in the same way as rules as defined above.[174] Thus the structural distinction between rules and principles can also be found on the axiological plane. Evaluative criteria correspond to principles, evaluative rules to rules. If we add to the terminological apparatus the idea that only evaluative criteria are to be called values and if we use 'norm' as the most basic concept, we end up with the following scheme:

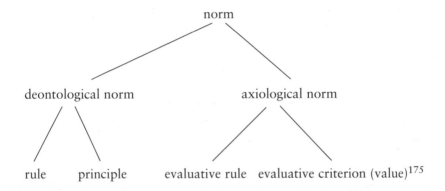

It is easy to show that metric value judgments are also based on evaluative criteria. The level of safety of a car can be expressed on a scale from 0–1. Someone who says that a car has a safety value of 0.7 can engage in metric evaluation according to the criterion or value of safety. In constitutional law, metrication is of little or no use. If we wanted to solve the problem of balancing press freedom with national security by way of metrication we would have to give the alternatives comparable and thus calculable numbers. Let it be said right away that such metrication is not possible in constitutional law.

---

[174] Together with further premises, concrete value-judgments can be deduced from them, see R. M. Hare, *The Language of Morals* (London, Oxford, and New York, 1952), 145 f.; Alexy, *A Theory of Legal Argumentation*, 67 f.

[175] The subject-matter of this diagram is in part identified by other expressions, in part the expressions used here are used differently, and in part the distinctions drawn here are not drawn at all. In the light of this conceptual variation, it cannot be claimed that the diagram reproduces the dominant linguistic usage. The terms chosen can only be seen as an attempt to give objects which need distinguishing on systematic grounds names which correspond as far as possible to current usage.

Of all three types, it is comparative value-judgments which have the most significance for constitutional law. The relation between them and evaluative criteria leads to the determination of the relation between principles and values. According to the evaluative criterion of press freedom, state of affairs S_1, in which more press freedom is realized than in state of affairs S_2, is better than S_2.[176] The greater extent need not be expressed in *figures*. S_1 might realize press freedom to a greater extent than S_2 because S_1 is characterized by *circumstances* not present in S_2. Thus for example S_1, in which editorial confidentiality is absolutely protected, is to be adjudged better according to the evaluative criterion of press freedom than a state of affairs S_2, in which this is not the case. According to the evaluative criterion of national security, the opposite may hold. Since neither of the evaluative criteria can be abandoned, and since a metrication of the calculation is not possible, the only thing left is balancing. But this means that a state of affairs which according to the evaluative criterion of press freedom is better or the best, is only prima facie better or best. The definitively better or best state of affairs can only be determined as the result of an overall evaluation which has regard to all valid criteria of evaluation.

1.3 The Difference between Principles and Values

That last point corresponds fully with the model of principles. The difference between principles and values is reduced to just one point. What under a system of values is prima facie the best, is under a system of principles what prima facie ought to be; and what under a system of values is definitively the best, is under a system of principles what definitively ought to be. Principles and values are only distinguished by their respective deontological and axiological characters.

Law is concerned with what ought to be. This counts in favour of the model of principles. But on the other hand it is not difficult to move from the idea that a certain solution is the best, constitutionally speaking, to the idea that it is required by the constitution. The moment one accepts that such transitions are possible, it is entirely acceptable for legal reasoning to proceed from a model of values instead of a model of principles. However,

---

[176] Statements such as 'the more press freedom there is, the better it is' express the evaluative criterion or the value of press freedom, if one understands them in the following sense: 'if there is more press freedom in state S_1 than there is in state S_2, then S_1 is better than S_2 in respect of press freedom'; generally on such statements, see G. Otte, 'Komparative Sätze im Recht', *Jahrbuch für Rechtssoziologie und Rechtstheorie*, 2 (1972), 301 ff. One could consider understanding these statements as expressions of rules for evaluation. But the concept of a rule will only be used here for norms leading to definitive outcomes. The statements just cited only make a prima facie evaluation possible. What they express should therefore not be called a rule. On the definition of values as rules, see (with further references) A. Podlech, 'Wertungen und Werte im Recht', AöR 95 (1970), 195 f. ('rules of preference'), and W. Kirsch, *Einführung in die Theorie der Entscheidungsprozesse*, ii, 2nd edn. (Wiesbaden, 1977), 121 ('a type of decision-rule').

the model of principles has the advantage that it expresses the obligatory nature of law clearly. In addition, the concept of a principle gives rise to fewer misconceptions. Both of these points are important enough for us to prefer the model of principles.

2. OBJECTIONS TO THEORIES OF PRINCIPLES AND VALUES

Apart from the fact that one operates in the deontological field (the realm of the Ought) and the other in the axiological field (the realm of the Good), principles and values have basically the same conceptual structure. This means that objections raised to a theory of constitutional rights as values apply equally to a theory of constitutional rights as principles.

Value theories of constitutional rights were already being propounded at the time of the Weimar Imperial Constitution. One of the most influential of the relevant authors was Rudolf Smend. According to a well-known formulation of Smend's, the 'substantive meaning of a Bill of Rights' lies in its attempt to create a 'substantive set with a certain degree of closure, that is, a system of values or interests, or a cultural system'.[177] Value-theory assumptions and modes of speech have entered constitutional case-law under the Basic Law. This reached a climax in the Lüth Judgment. The Federal Constitutional Court, even in this judgment, proceeded from the assumption that 'constitutional rights are in the first instance designed to protect the freedom of the individual from infringements by public bodies', that is, that they are 'defensive rights of the citizen against the state'.[178] But it then continued,

it is equally true that the Basic Law, which does not consider itself a value-neutral system . . . has established an objective order of values in its constitutional rights catalogue . . . This order of values, which is centred on the dignity of the freely developing person within society, must be seen as a fundamental constitutional decision for all areas of law.[179]

In the course of the judgment, the order of values is further described as a '*ranked* order of values' between which 'balancing exercises' are necessary.[180] And with this, the central concepts of a theory of values expressed

---

[177] R. Smend, 'Verfassung und Verfassungsrecht' (1928), in id., *Staatsrechtliche Abhandlungen*, 2nd edn. (Berlin, 1968), 264. Reference should also be made to A. Hensel, *Grundrechte und politische Weltanschauung* (Tübingen, 1931), 10: 'thus the content of any given legal system is the realization of a constitutionally established system of political values'. See also H. Gerber, *Die weltanschaulichen Grundlagen des Staates* (Stuttgart, 1930), 13 ff.; G. Leibholz, *Das Wesen der Repräsentation und der Gestaltwandel der Demokratie im 20. Jahrhundert*, 3rd edn. (Berlin, 1966), 46 ff.; G. Holstein, 'Von den Aufgaben und Zielen heutiger Staatsrechtswissenschaft', AöR 50 (1926), 29 ff.; E. Kaufmann, 'Die Gleichheit vor dem Gesetz im Sinne des Art. 109 der Reichsverfassung', in VVDStRL 3 (1927), 3 ff.
[178] BVerfGE 7, 198 (204).　　　　　[179] BVerfGE 7, 198 (205).
[180] BVerfGE 7, 198 (215).

in innumerable decisions of the Court have been identified: value, order of values, ranked order of values, value-system, and balancing.[181]

The evaluation of such a value theory of constitutional rights ranges from radical rejection to enthusiastic acceptance. Forsthoff expresses a rejecting position most sharply. According to him, the theory of values leads to the 'dissolution of conceptual clarity in speech'[182] and a 'loss, not only of rationality, but also of intellectual status',[183] to the 'dissolution of the constitution as law' and to the elimination of the freedom contained in the constitutional rights.[184] The American constitutional lawyer, Kommers, has more recently expressed himself equally opposed to a 'conception of constitutional law rooted in a system of values'. According to him, 'the genius of German constitutional thought lies in the fact that such a system is displayed in the hierarchical order of values of the Federal Constitutional Court'.[185] Objections to the theory of values can be grouped into three: philosophical, methodological, and doctrinal.

2.1 Philosophical Objections

Philosophical objections are above all concerned with the *objectivity* of the order of values. The concept of an objective order of values has received its most original and extensive exposition at the hands of Max Scheler.

According to Scheler, values are not simply valid, they have their own order of existence, the 'being of values'.[186] Scheler thinks that he can thereby characterize values as facts ('independent facts of the moral life').[187] The evaluative proposition, '*A* is good' is supposed to correspond to a moral fact in the same way that the descriptive proposition, '*A* is green' corresponds to an empirical fact. 'The sole difference here lies in the *contents* of the predicates.'[188] Correspondence with facts is what makes both propositions true.[189]

Knowledge of values is supposed to be acquired through a distinctive epistemological capacity, which Scheler describes in the following terms:

---

[181] For an account of the case-law of the Federal Constitutional Court, see H. Goerlich, *Wertordnung und Grundgesetz* (Baden-Baden, 1973), 29 ff.; Schneider, *Die Güterabwägung des Bundesverfassungsgerichts*, 43 ff.; W. Schreckenberger, *Rhetorische Semiotik* (Freiburg and Munich, 1978), 191 ff. Of the many proponents of a value theory under the Basic Law only Dürig, in Maunz and Dürig, *Grundgesetz*, art. 1 abs. 1 para. 1 ff., is mentioned here.

[182] E. Forsthoff, *Der Staat der Industriegesellschaft*, 2nd edn. (Munich, 1971), 69.

[183] id., 'Zur heutigen Situation der Verfassungslehre', in H. Barion, E.-W. Böckenförde, E. Forsthoff, and W. Weber (eds.), *Epirrhosis, Festgabe für C. Schmitt* (Berlin, 1968), 209.

[184] id., 'Die Umbildung des Verfassungsgesetzes', in Barion *et al.*, *Epirrhosis*, 47.

[185] D. P. Kommers, 'Der Gleichheitssatz: Neuere Entwicklungen und Probleme im Verfassungsrecht der USA und der Bundesrepublik Deutschland', in C. Link (ed.), *Der Gleichheitssatz im modernen Verfassungsstaat, Symposion zum 80. Geburtstag von G. Leibholz* (Baden-Baden, 1982), 50.

[186] Scheler, *Formalism in Ethics and Non-formal Ethics of Values*, 187.

[187] ibid. 163, 183, 187.   [188] ibid. 183.   [189] ibid. 188.

the actual seat of the entire value-a priori (including the moral a priori) is the *value-cognition* or *value-intuition* that comes to the fore in feeling, basically in love and hate, as well as the 'moral cognition' of the interconnections of values, that is, their 'being-higher' and 'being-lower'. This cognition occurs in *special* functions and acts which are *toto caelo* different from all perception and thinking. These functions and acts supply the only possible *access* to the world of values.[190]

A theory which assumes, first, that there are 'value-qualities . . . that . . . constitute a special domain of *objectivities*'[191] and, secondly, that these objects are accessible by a form of direct perception which is neither empirical nor analytical, but which can best be described as a matter of insight or experience of self-evidence, is intuitionistic.[192] The strongest argument against intuitionism is that different people under the same optimal conditions of evidentiality for the perception of evaluative judgments (such as lack of emotion and mental clarity) can come up with no definitive criterion for true and false, or reliable and unreliable evidence.[193] In the absence of such a criterion, intuitionism turns into subjectivism. This epistemological argument has consequences for the ontological thesis of the existence of values. The fact that something cannot be perceived with intersubjective certainty is no argument against its existence, but it is an argument against building an intellectual argument on its existence.

These objections justify a rejection of intuitionistic value theories, but not of value theories *per se*. Intuitionistic value theories such as Scheler's are only one variety in the spectrum of value theories. The strong, easily criticizable, assumptions of the real existence and evidential nature of values are in no way necessarily part of the concept of value. The fact that the Federal Constitutional Court talks in terms of values, an order of values, and a system of values does not mean that it shares these assumptions.[194] Since there are no necessary reasons for adopting these assumptions, it is more appropriate to interpret the value-based theses of the Court according to a weaker and less objectionable account of values. Such an account could include the assumption that values are criteria of evaluation which, like norms generally, are either valid or invalid. Their validity, along with the evaluations they make possible, is not the object of some sort of evidence, but a matter of justification. The form of justification depends on the type of validity one is concerned with: legal, social, or ethical. What follows

---

[190] ibid. 68.   [191] ibid. 15.

[192] On intuitionism, see with further references Alexy, *A Theory of Legal Argumentation*, 37 ff.

[193] See P. F. Strawson, 'Ethical Intuitionism', *Philosophy*, 24 (1949), 27; A. Podlech, 'Wertungen und Werte im Recht', 205; id., 'Recht und Moral', *Rechtstheorie*, 3 (1972), 135.

[194] This occurs for example in the case of H. Harnischfeger, *Die Rechtsprechung des Bundesverfassungsgerichts zu den Grundrechten* (Hamburg, 1966), 233 f. Critical of this, see E. Stein, 'Werte und Wertewandel in der Gesetzesanwendung des öffentlichen Rechts', in J. Esser and E. Stein, *Werte und Wertewandel in der Gesetzesanwendung* (Frankfurt a. M., 1966), 40 ff.

presupposes such a theory of values, purified from all questionable onto-logical and epistemological assumptions. The philosophical objections noted here do not apply to such a theory.

2.2 Methodological Objections

The methodological objections are more serious. In referring to values and an order of values, the Federal Constitutional Court is accused of aban-doning the requirements of rational justification.[195] By appealing to the concept of an order of values, every possible decision can be justified; talk about values destroys the transparency of judicial decision-taking[196] and leads to an ' "arcanum" of constitutional interpretation'.[197] Decisions about competing principles and how to balance them are made on some other basis, masked with an 'appearance of rationality' with the 'real reasoning removed'. 'From a practical point of view', appeal to an order of values and the balancing of values is a 'formula for disguising judicial or interpretive decisionism'.[198]

Methodological arguments against the theory of values tend to be directed against two ideas, against the idea of an order of values in the sense of a ranked order of values, and against the idea of balancing values. The objections to the idea of a ranked order of values are almost entirely justi-fied; those against the idea of balancing can be addressed in the context of the model of principles being developed here.

2.2.1 The Concept of a Ranked Order of Values

Those who talk in terms of a ranked order of values have to start by iden-tifying which values should be ordered according to their rank. We are concerned here with values relevant to decisions about constitutional rights. Talk about a ranked order of values is only concerned with these values. There we have the first problem. How can this set of values be defined? It has already been pointed out that such a definition is difficult particularly in the context of limiting clauses. One can argue about which values are constitutionally relevant and which not. The possibility of such disputes makes the creation of an order of values containing all and only those values relevant to constitutional rights—that is, a *complete and closed* order of values—rather difficult. A complete and closed order of values can be reached relatively easily at a higher level of generality. A few ideas such as dignity, liberty, equality, and the protection and welfare of the commu-nity cover just about everything that needs considering when balancing

---

[195] See e.g. Goerlich, *Wertordnung und Grundgesetz*, 64.
[196] ibid. 133, 189.   [197] ibid. 140, 134, 189.
[198] E.-W. Böckenförde, 'Grundrechtstheorie und Grundrechtsinterpretation', 1534; similarly E. Forsthoff, 'Zur heutigen Situation einer Verfassungslehre', 190 ff.; E. Denninger, *Staatsrecht*, ii (Reinbek, 1979), 184; U. K. Preuß, *Die Internalisierung des Subjekts* (Frankfurt a. M., 1979), 151 ff.

constitutional principles. Those who try to establish a ranked order of values at this sort of level have few problems identifying the elements to be ranked. But it does not stand much chance of being an informative system. The chances increase as one moves to a more concrete level, but at the same time the problems of identifying the elements to be ranked increase. It is already doubtful enough whether a single person could completely identify all the more concrete values which in their view would be relevant for constitutional justification and decision. A complete catalogue commanding universal assent would be well-nigh impossible. This fact alone lands the idea of a ranked order of values in difficulties. If a complete catalogue cannot be drawn up, something has to be ranked which is only incompletely known.

Even harder than the problem of identifying what is to be ranked is the ranking itself. This is possible in two ways, cardinal and ordinal ranking. A *cardinal* ranking is one in which the values are given numbers on a scale which express their rank or weight. So one could try to express the rank of a set of values on a scale from 0 to 1. *Ordinal* ranking is less demanding; it simply requires that given any two values a relation of higher value (preference) or equal value (indifference) can be established.[199] It should be plain that an abstract order of constitutional values, whether cardinal or ordinal, is unacceptable.

Take a case like the one in the Lebach Judgment in which two values (principles) were relevant, the protection of privacy and freedom of television media reporting.[200] Consider, first, the task of reaching some sort of conclusion about the ranking of these values on a cardinal scale. On such a scale, the two values can be ordered in two different ways. They can be given the same number (equal rank) or a different number (rank). If they are given the same number, then the cardinal ordering does not help us any further. If they are given different values, say that the right to privacy is given 0.8 and freedom of media coverage 0.4, then the case is decided. The ordering of numbers expresses the idea that the protection of privacy has double the value of the freedom of media reporting.[201] But if one proceeds simply on the basis of such an *abstract* ranking, the protection of privacy will always take precedence over media freedom. Such an abstract ranking would not only contradict the correct conclusion of the Federal Constitutional Court that neither of the values takes precedence in the abstract,[202] it would also have fatal consequences. If the protection of

---

[199] On the concepts of cardinal and ordinal ranking, see G. Gäfgen, *Theorie der wirtschaftlichen Entscheidung*, 3rd edn. (Tübingen, 1974), 150 ff.

[200] BVerfGE 35, 202 (219 ff.).

[201] Steiner's thesis that 'it is difficult to assign any meaning to such a statement' has something going for it (see J. M. Steiner, 'Judicial Discretion and the Concept of Law', CLJ 35 (1976), 153).

[202] BVerfGE 35, 202 (225).

privacy were to take precedence over media freedom in *every* case, the most trivial form of protection for privacy would justify the most serious breaches of press freedom. This would usher in what Carl Schmitt called, after Hartmann,[203] the 'tyranny of values': 'the logic of values demands that the highest price is never too high for the highest value and must be paid'.[204]

One can well ask whether this has anything to do with 'the logic of values'. The consequence arises not from the concept of a value (or principle) but from a certain flawed conception of the relation between competing values (principles) which is inconsistent with the understanding of principles as defined above, which itself includes a reference to the requirements of competing principles. If an absolute relation of precedence is adopted between two values, in cases of conflict, they behave like rules.

What is true for abstract cardinal scales is also true for abstract ordinal scales. Where values are equally ranked there is no result, where they are ranked differently the same applies as for cardinal scales.

This consequence can be avoided in the case of cardinal scales by factoring the intensity of realization into the values as well as their rank.[205] Suppose that privacy (P_1) and press freedom (P_2) are in competition with each other. P_1 is given the abstract ranking of 0.8, P_2 of 0.4. The question is, which is to be preferred, a prohibition on the broadcast (R_1) or a permission (R_2). The intensity of realization of both alternatives is expressed in the following table:

	P_1 (privacy) = 0.8	P_2 (media freedom) = 0.4
R_1 (prohibition)	0.4	0.3
R_2 (permission)	0.3	0.9

The broadcasting ban only contributes a small additional amount to the realization of privacy (0.4 as against 0.3), while the loss of press freedom is considerable (0.3 as against 0.9). The alternative to be selected can now be calculated by a simple operation. The abstract ranked value is to be multiplied by the intensity of realization and the results added for each alternative.[206] For R_1 this means 0.32 (0.4 x 0.8) + 0.12 (0.3 x 0.4) = 0.44, while for R_2 0.24 (0.3 x 0.8) + 0.36 (0.9 x 0.4) = 0.6. R_2 has the higher total value

---

[203] Hartmann, *Ethics*, ii, 421 ff.

[204] C. Schmitt, 'Die Tyrannei der Werte', in *Säkularisation und Utopie, Festschrift für E. Forsthoff* (Stuttgart, Berlin, Cologne, and Mainz, 1967), 60.

[205] See Schlink, *Abwägung im Verfassungsrecht*, 131 ff.

[206] On this procedure, see K. Haag, *Rationale Strafzumessung* (Cologne and Berlin, 1970), 45 ff.; Schlink, *Abwägung im Verfassungsrecht*, 132 f.

and is therefore to be chosen, even though R_1 is required by the principle ranked higher from an abstract point of view. The 'tyranny of values' has been destroyed. However, all this is in reality no solution. Once the figures have been established, the outcome is easy enough to determine. The problem is with establishing the figures. It is already questionable whether individual values or principles can be given abstract rankings at all. But at any rate an intersubjectively persuasive allocation of figures to intensity of realization is impossible. One cannot produce a firm answer on the basis of reliable quantification; rather the outcome—however it is determined—can only be *illustrated* numerically. Thus the idea of a ranked order of values on a cardinal scale collapses at the problems of the metrication of the weights and intensity of realization of values or principles.[207]

It is no way out to assume the equal ranking of all values or principles and then deal only with cardinal intensities of realization. This merely pushes the problem back to the insoluble question of the metrication of intensities of realization.

In general we can say that an order of values or principles which determines constitutional adjudication in a way that is intersubjectively binding does not exist.[208] But the impossibility of such a 'hard' ordering says nothing about the possibility of 'soft' orderings, and certainly nothing about the technique of balancing interests. Soft orderings can be created in two ways: (1) through prima facie preferences in favour of particular values or principles or (2) through a network of concrete preference decisions. Soft orderings of constitutional values by way of prima facie preferences arise, for example, when one establishes a burden of argumentation in favour of individual liberty, or equality, or certain collective interests. A soft ordering of a network of concrete preference decisions has been created by the case-law

---

[207] See Schlink, *Abwägung im Verfassungsrecht*, 134 f.

[208] The possibility discussed by Schlink in depth of solving the problem of the order of values by way of welfare economics, which permits one to draw conclusions about social utility (collective preferences or collective conceptions of value) on the basis of individual utility (individual preferences or individual conceptions of value) only needs mentioning in passing (see Schlink, *Abwägung im Verfassungsrecht*, 154 ff.). Such an approach presupposes that what applies as a matter of constitutional law can be equated to social utility in the form of a function of individual utilities. While such an equation would have both individualistic and democratic tendencies, as Schlink emphasizes, it would nevertheless bind constitutional law totally to existing widespread conceptions of value. But the mere fact that a particular conception of value is widespread does not mean that it is valid as a matter of constitutional law. Apart from this problem, such an approach runs up against the difficulty of aggregating individual utilities into social utility. If the individual utilities to be aggregated are measured on a cardinal scale, virtually insuperable difficulties of measurement and comparison arise, at any rate in respect of constitutional questions (see ibid., 166 f.). While these difficulties can be avoided by the use of ordinal scales, the aggregation then runs up against Arrow's impossibility thesis. On this, see K. J. Arrow, *Social Choice and Individual Values*, 2nd edn. (New York, London, and Sydney, 1963); R. D. Luce and H. Raiffa, *Games and Decisions* (New York, London, and Sydney, 1957), 327 ff.; Podlech, *Gehalt und Funktionen des allgemeinen verfassungsrechtlichen Gleichheitssatzes* 274 ff.; Schlink, *Abwägung im Verfassungsrecht*, 180 ff.

of the Federal Constitutional Court. Both of these types of ordering are closely tied up with the question of balancing, which must now be considered in more detail.

2.2.2 *The Idea of Balancing*

The objection is repeatedly made to the idea of balancing that it does not represent a method subject to rational control. Values and principles do not determine their own application, and so balancing remains within the discretion of the one carrying it out. The moment balancing cuts in, the control of norms and legal method ends. This creates the space for judicial subjectivism and decisionism. These objections are correct to the extent that they mean that balancing is not a procedure leading in every case to a precise and unavoidable outcome. They are incorrect if this is taken to mean that balancing is a non-rational or irrational procedure.

It has already been suggested that competing principles are to be resolved by the determination of a conditional relation of precedence. The example was used of the Lebach Judgment in which the Federal Constitutional Court resolved the clash between privacy (P_1) and press freedom (P_2) by giving P_1 preference in cases of a 'repeat television report of a serious criminal act, no longer covered by the interest in up-to-date information' and which 'endangers the resocialization of the criminal'.[209] In other words it created a preferential statement of the form:

(1) $(P_1 \mathbf{P} P_2) C_2$

And according to the Law of Competing Principles,[210] this produces the rule:

(2) $C_2 \rightarrow Q$

which under the conditions C_2 requires the legal consequence (Q) of P_1.

2.2.2.1 Models of Decision-Taking versus Justification

If balancing consisted merely in the creation of such preferential statements, and thus establishing a consequential rule for the case, then it would indeed not amount to a rational procedure. Establishing the conditional preference would be entirely intuitive. The one doing the balancing could follow his own personal presuppositions, and it would be impossible to speak in terms of a correct or false balancing of interests.

However, such a *decision-taking* model of balancing can be countered with a *justification* model. In both cases the outcome of the balancing exercise is a conditional preferential statement. In the decision-taking model, the determination of the statement of preference is the outcome of a rationally uncontrollable mental process. By contrast, the justification model distinguishes between the mental process which leads to the determination

---

[209] BVerfGE 35, 202 (237).   [210] See above at 53 f.

of the statement of preference and its justification.[211] This distinction permits us to relate the requirement that the balancing be rational to the justification of the statement of preference and to say: a balancing of principles is rational when the preferential statement to which it leads can be rationally justified. So the problem of the rationality of balancing principles leads to the question of the rationality of establishing statements which determine conditional preferential statements between competing values or principles.

2.2.2.2 The Justification of Non-balanced Statements of Conditional Preference

Conditional statements of preference give rise via the Law of Competing Principles to rules which require the consequences of the principle taking precedence whenever the conditions are satisfied. The justification of preferential statements is thus similar to the justification of relatively concrete rules derived from constitutional rights provisions. To justify these one can use all the arguments available in constitutional argumentation generally. Having said that, linguistic arguments are excluded if they have already been used to establish the fact that certain constitutional provisions are in competition with each other. But then one can always use the other standard canons of interpretation, doctrinal considerations, precedent, general practical and empirical arguments, as well as specific types of legal argument.[212] So to justify any given conditional preferential statement, and thus to justify its corresponding rule, one could refer to the intention of the constitution makers, to the negative consequences of an alternative statement of preference, to doctrinal consensus, and to earlier decisions. When this happens, the justification of statements of conditional preference is no different from the justification of semantic rules for making vague concepts more precise. The difference is further weakened when one remembers that balancing regularly takes place in the context of normal statutory interpretation as well. Think of the case in which a narrow interpretation of a statutory term leads to weak protection for constitutional rights and a broad interpretation to strong protection. It only needs pointing out that in view of the great variety of possible arguments in favour of preferential statements, the suggestion that one should simply consider the consequences[213] is an unjustified restriction.

2.2.2.3 The Justification of Balanced Principles

What has just been said as regards legal argumentation in general does not

---

[211] This corresponds to the oft-cited distinction between the process of discovery and the process of justification; see e.g. R. A. Wasserstrom, *The Judicial Decision* (Stanford Calif. and London, 1961), 27.

[212] See on this Alexy, *A Theory of Legal Argumentation*, 231 ff.

[213] See e.g. Schlink, *Abwägung im Verfassungsrecht*, 181, 192, 199; Podlech, 'Wertungen und Werte im Recht', 208.

address the specific nature of the justification of preferential statements. If these were the only arguments, one could consider doing without the preferential statement and base justification simply on the consequential rule.

The fact that there are arguments unique to problems of balancing principles can be seen in statements of the Federal Constitutional Court such as the following: 'The right of the individual to freedom becomes that much stronger the more his right freely to choose a profession is under threat; the protection of the public interest becomes that much more urgent, the greater the disadvantages and dangers to the community arising from an unrestricted exercise of profession.'[214] 'The more that statutory intervention affects the basic expressions of human freedom of action, the more carefully the reasons justifying it must be weighed against the citizen's basic right to freedom.'[215] 'Furthermore . . . the balancing necessary must take account on one hand of the breach of privacy caused by a broadcast of the nature in question and on the other the concrete interest served by the broadcast and to satisfy which the broadcast is designed.'[216] These expressions[217] point to a constitutive rule for balancing exercises undertaken by the Federal Constitutional Court which goes like this:

(A)   The greater the degree of non-satisfaction of, or detriment to, one principle, the greater must be the importance of satisfying the other.[218]

This rule expresses a law for balancing all types of principle, and it can be called the *Law of Balancing*. According to the Law of Balancing, the permissible level of non-satisfaction of, or detriment to, one principle depends on the importance of satisfying the other. In defining principles, the clause 'relative to the legally possible' puts what the principle in question requires into relation with what competing principles require. The Law of Balancing states what this relation amounts to. It makes it clear that the weight of principles can never be determined independently or absolutely, but that one can only ever speak of relative weight.[219]

The idea behind the Law of Balancing can be illustrated by the use of

---

[214] BVerfGE 7, 377 (404 f.).

[215] BVerfGE 20, 150 (159); see also BVerfGE 17, 306 (314).

[216] BVerfGE 35, 202 (226).

[217] See also BVerfGE 41, 251 (264), where the Court speaks of 'an overall balancing between the seriousness of the infringement and the weight and urgency of its justifying reasons'.

[218] For a somewhat different formulation, see R. Alexy, 'Die logische Analyse juristischer Entscheidungen', ARSP, Beiheft NF 14 (1980), 206. Further specification of this rule can be dispensed with here. It is presupposed that the principles in question compete with each other, that is, that one principle can only be satisfied at the cost of another. Competition only arises in respect of the resolution of cases. Thus what is generally being put into relationship is the infringement of one principle by a certain solution to a certain case and the importance of satisfying the other principle in the same case.

[219] See B. Barry, *Political Argument* (London and New York, 1965), 7.

indifference curves,[220] as they are used in economics. An indifference curve is a means of representing a relation of substitution between interests. Assume that x is in favour both of press freedom and national security, and that he is prepared to accept a certain increase in press freedom for a certain loss of national security and vice versa. The states of affairs which x will consider equally acceptable or indifferently can then be represented by points on a curve.

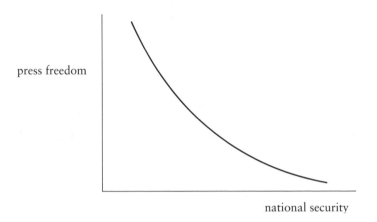

Such indifference curves correspond to the law of diminishing marginal utility.[221] As press freedom diminishes, so even greater gains in national security are necessary to balance any further loss of press freedom, and vice versa.

Indifference curves like this do not correspond directly to the Law of Balancing. The Law of Balancing focuses firstly on the *importance* of satisfying certain principles and then formulates a requirement. By contrast, the curve on the graph merely describes substitutions about which x is indifferent. The importance of press freedom relative to national security *for x* is expressed by the curve. The fact that national security is more important to y than to x can be expressed as shown on page 104.

In constitutional balancing, the question is not how important somebody thinks press freedom and national security are, but how important they *actually* are. One could try to represent the relation of substitution adopted by the Federal Constitutional Court by an indifference curve, but from the perspective of the technique of balancing we are concerned with a rule

---

[220] On the idea of indifference curves, see in place of many T. Scitovsky, *Welfare and Competition* (London, 1952), 30 ff. On the use of indifference curves in practical philosophy, see Barry, *Political Argument*, 4 ff.; J. Rawls, *A Theory of Justice*, 37 ff. Schlink has attempted to make an indifference approach fruitful in the case of constitutional law, see Schlink, *Abwägung im Verfassungsrecht*, 168 ff., 179 ff.

[221] See on this Barry, *Political Argument*, 6 ff.; Schlink, *Abwägung im Verfassungsrecht*, 168.

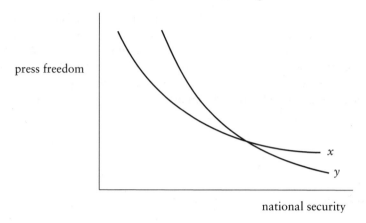

which states how one ought to balance principles. The Law of Balancing is to be understood as a rule requiring the determination of correct indifference curves. It is located on a meta-level to the indifference curves illustrated so far. At this meta-level we can represent the following *second-level indifference curve.*

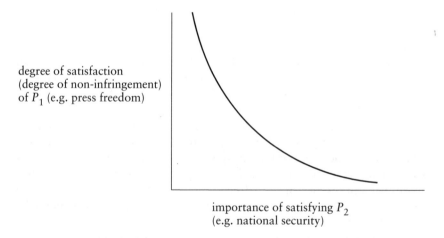

This curve has the interesting characteristic that even people whose views are represented by different indifference curves at the first level must agree with it. Once x and y accept that both principles are ranked equally in the abstract, they cannot deny that a smaller degree of satisfaction, or a greater infringement of press freedom, is only permissible in favour of national security when the relative degree of importance of national security is very high. Precisely when the relative degree of importance of national security is very high is a matter of disagreement between them, which expresses itself in different indifference curves at the first level.

Indifference curves illuminate the idea lying behind the Law of Balancing, but they do not offer a definitive decision-taking procedure.[222] First-level curves simply represent different weightings; their correctness is determined by the Law of Balancing, which corresponds to the second-level curve, according to the degree of importance of satisfying one principle and satisfaction/non-satisfaction (non-infringement/infringement) of the other. But these ideas cannot be metricated in a way which leads to an intersubjectively binding calculation of the result.

Having said that, the Law of Balancing is not valueless. It identifies what is significant in balancing exercises, namely the degree or intensity of non-satisfaction of, or detriment to, one principle versus the importance of satisfying the other. Those who say that a very intensive infringement can only be justified by a very important satisfaction of an opposing principle are not saying when a very intensive infringement and a very important satisfaction are present. But they are saying what has to be shown in order to justify the conditional preferential statement which is to result from the balancing exercise, namely statements about degrees of infringement and importance. The arguments which can be used to justify such statements have nothing to do with balancing. One can rely on every possible type of legal argument. The Lebach Judgment provides us with a good example of the justification of statements about degrees of infringement and importance. The argument that the broadcast in question amounted to a very serious[223] breach of privacy was supported by reference to the extent[224] of broadcasts, the impact of the documentary form,[225] the high degree of plausibility that television broadcasts have in the eyes of the public,[226] the threat to resocialization caused by

---

[222] We are only concerned here with balancing in the sense of the weighing of principles, that is, with what is required by the principle of proportionality in the narrow sense. As was shown above, the question of the necessity of infringements of principles, which concerns the factual possibility of their realization, is to be distinguished from the weighing of principles, which concerns the legal possibility of their realization. In the context of indifference approaches, the structure of necessity can be represented by way of Pareto-optimality. According to this criterion, situation *A* is to be preferred to situation *B*, 'if in moving from B to A, none of the participants are placed in a worse position, and at least one in a better position' (W. Kirsch, *Einführung in die Theorie der Entscheidungsprozesse*, iii, 2nd edn. (Wiesbaden, 1977), 77). The connection between this criterion and the principle of necessity is obvious. For a reconstruction of necessity by way of Pareto-optimality, see Schlink, *Abwägung im Verfassungsrecht*, 181 ff.

[223] An example of the justification of a statement about a very minimal degree of infringement can be found in the Co-determination Judgment. In the context of considering the constitutional right to freedom of profession of companies within the industries covered by co-determination law, it was stated, 'the influence of workers cooperating in the supervisory board on the management of the business is in principle not decisive; rather, the right of final decision belongs to the members of the board selected by the shareholders of the company as those running the business. To the extent that decisions of representative bodies are dependent on those of the supervisory board, they can in principle be traced back to members of the company. *Accordingly*, there is a limitation of *minimal intensity*' (BVerfGE 50, 290 (365); emphasis added).

[224] BVerfGE 35, 202 (227).   [225] BVerfGE 35, 202 (228).
[226] BVerfGE 35, 202 (229).

this and other aspects of the broadcast,[227] and the additional infringement involved in the broadcast of the matter some time after the immediate report.[228] As far as the importance of satisfying media freedom was concerned, to start with, many reasons for the importance of up-to-date reports of serious crimes were listed. Against this background, the repeat report in question was qualified as insufficiently important to justify the intensity of the infringement.[229]

The reasons put forward by the Court are understandable. And it is easy to see without further analysis that a great variety of things can be found in them, such as references to facts (extent of broadcasting) and empirical regularities (causation of a threat to resocialization) as well as normative judgments (characterization of resocialization as urgently required by article 1(1) together with article 2(1) Basic Law). Such a set of reasons including evaluations is entirely typical of judicial reasoning. It is equally necessary for determinations within the scope of vague concepts, in other words in the field of classical interpretation. The point that values play a role in balancing exercises does not of itself represent an objection to the rational justification of balancing decisions, unless one is prepared to say that legal argument is always non-rational or irrational the moment one enters the arena of non-authoritatively binding predetermined evaluations. However, not only would such a view have the consequence that a large part of what jurisprudence has always considered its task would have to be characterized as non-rational or irrational, but good reasons for questioning its underlying thesis of the unjustifiability of value-judgments and judgments of obligation can also be made.[230] It is not the fact that non-binding predetermined values play a role in the decision, but the extent to which they play a role, which could be raised as an argument against rationality. In response to this, one has to say, first, that there are many instances of balancing which as regards their evaluative content raise fewer difficulties than some instances of interpretation. Secondly, this argument on its own is not adequate to show that balancing exercises display less rationality than interpretation. At any rate, the argument is not capable of revealing the irrationality or non-rationality of balancing.

The model of justification described here avoids a whole range of difficulties associated with the idea of balancing. It makes it clear that balancing is not a process whereby one interest is 'rashly' realized at the cost of another.[231] Under this model, balancing is hardly an abstract or superficial procedure. Its outcome is a conditional preferential statement, which according to the Law of Competing Principles results in a differentiated rule

---

[227] BVerfGE 35, 202 (236 f.).
[228] BVerfGE 35, 202 (234)   [229] ibid.
[230] See on this Alexy, *A Theory of Legal Argumentation*, 33 ff.
[231] See Hesse, *Grundzüge des Verfassungsrechts*, para. 72.

for decision. The very idea of a principle means that balancing is not a matter of all or nothing but a requirement to optimize. To this extent the model outlined here corresponds to the requirement of 'practical consistency'.[232] The objection that there is no standard by which the balancing can be decided[233] and that the principle of balancing interests is a 'null formula' fails.[234] Of course, the *Law of Balancing* as such does not give us a standard by which cases can be definitively decided, but the *balancing model as a whole* does provide us with a criterion because it ties the Law of Balancing to the general theory of rational legal argumentation. The Law of Balancing tells us what it is that has to be rationally justified. So it does not say nothing and it is not a null formula. The repeated objection of irrationalism has been dealt with already.[235] The thesis that the approach leads to 'decisions on the facts' is at best misleading.[236] To the extent that decisions involving the balancing of principles are judicial decisions, then they are generally designed to resolve individual cases. But under the Law of Competing Principles, balancing always forms the basis of a rule. Balancing on the facts of a case and universalizability are thus not irreconcilable. They are tied together in the model of balancing developed here.[237] The objection that balancing interests is only a matter of pure rhetoric also fails.[238] One principle is set against another, which has the consequences as formulated in the Law of Competing Principles and the Law of Balancing.

The model of balancing not only avoids the problems just cited, it also has advantages over alternative models without being hampered by their difficulties. This can be seen from the example of Müller's alternative to balancing interests, the analysis of the normative field.[239] Müller highlights the role of empirical arguments (real data) in the context of constitutional rights reasoning. He also argues for a differentiated 'doctrine of normative fields' for individual constitutional rights.[240] Both requirements are satisfied by the model of balancing. In the context of justifying statements concerning the intensity of infringement and the importance of satisfying competing principles, empirical arguments which are sensitive to the distinctive characteristics of the subject-matter as well as possible consequences of the decision are fully relevant. In justifying a certain balance of

---

[232] ibid.

[233] C. v. Pestalozza, 'Kritische Bemerkungen zu Methoden und Prinzipien der Grundrechtsauslegung in der Bundesrepublik Deutschland', *Der Staat*, 2 (1963), 447; Müller, *Die Positivität der Grundrechte*, 18; id., *Juristische Methodik*, 2nd edn. (Berlin, 1976), 53.

[234] Pestalozza, 'Kritische Bemerkungen', 448.

[235] See e.g. Müller, *Juristische Methodik*, 54.   [236] ibid.

[237] On universalizability as a basic requirement of practical reason, see Alexy, *A Theory of Legal Argumentation*, 65 ff., 188 ff., 222; on the construction of rules as a requirement of constitutional law, see BVerfGE 66, 116 (138).

[238] F. Müller, *Normstruktur und Normativität* (Berlin, 1966), 209.

[239] Müller, *Juristische Methodik*, 49, 117 ff.

[240] See id., *Die Positivität der Grundrechte*, 87.

interests, empirical arguments apply as they do for legal reasoning generally.[241] The fact that balancing leads to differentiated doctrines for different constitutional rights is demonstrated by the Law of Competing Principles. Where principles compete, a conditional relation of precedence is to be determined. This corresponds to a rule with a relatively high degree of precision. Through the balancing exercises undertaken by the judiciary and the consensus of proposed balancings of interests put forward by the academic community, over time a network of relatively concrete rules derived from constitutional rights provisions develops, which is an important foundation and a central element of legal doctrine.

Thus the model of balancing proposed here can on one hand satisfy the legitimate requirement to respect factual circumstances and empirical regularities and produce a detailed doctrine of constitutional rights. On the other hand it can avoid the difficulties associated with the idea of analysing the normative field. These difficulties arise from the ambivalent status of elements of the normative field in Müller's account. As has already been observed,[242] these could be purely empirical arguments, or empirical arguments together with evaluative judgments. If the normative field covers purely empirical arguments, then analysis is inadequate to answer constitutional rights questions. Questions of constitutional rights are normative questions, and normative statements do not follow from empirical propositions alone. But if the components of the normative field are a mixture of empirical and evaluative elements, the question of where these evaluative elements come from and how they are to be controlled arises. This question becomes all the more pressing when Müller himself insists that a 'jurisprudence without decision or evaluation [would be] neither practical nor true to life'.[243] Certain of Müller's formulations in which he equates the 'structure of the normative field' to the 'nature of the regulated areas of daily life'[244] seem to indicate a certain relation between his conception of the analysis of normative fields and the theory of the intrinsic nature of things [*Natur der Sache*].[245] But this is not an adequate answer to the problems of

---

[241] See on this Alexy, *A Theory of Legal Argumentation*, 232 ff.   [242] At 42.
[243] Müller, *Juristische Methodik*, 134.   [244] ibid. 40.
[245] See also id., *Die Positivität der Grundrechte*, 28 (fn. 59), where there is talk of the 'material characteristic of the constitutional rights normative field' as a 'special version of the "nature of things" '. The close relation of the concepts of the normative field and the nature of things is noted by Larenz (K. Larenz, *Methodenlehre der Rechtswissenschaft*, 4th edn., 323); see on this as well, H. Ryffel, 'Review of M. Kriele, "Theorie der Rechtsgewinnung" (Berlin, 1967) and F. Müller, "Normstruktur und Normativität" (Berlin 1966)' DVBl 1971, 84. Müller himself rejects the equation of his theory with traditional conceptions of the nature of things (id., *Juristische Methodik*, 34 f., 86; id., 'Thesen zur Struktur von Rechtsnormen', ARSP 61 (1970), 498). In spite of this rejection, his attempt to replace the 'things' with the normative field and the 'nature' by its 'basic structure selectively ascertained from the perspective of the normative programme' (id., *Juristische Methodik*, 88) is subject to the same objections as theories of the nature of things simply from the fact that concrete constitutional ought-judgments do not follow in all cases of doubt from directly enacted constitutional rights norms (the

evaluation. The model of balancing based on a theory of principles is capable of supplying just such an answer because it ties the formal structure of balancing to a theory of legal reasoning, which includes a general theory of practical reason.[246]

2.3 Doctrinal Objections

The doctrinal objections are easier to deal with than the methodological ones. One such suggests that a value-theory of constitutional rights leads to the destruction of constitutional liberty in the liberal sense. The 'freedom of the legal subject is replaced by the objectivity of a value',[247] it results in a substantial alignment of constitutional liberty[248] towards a 'commitment' to values.[249] This view would only be correct if freedom and value were opposed to each other. But this is not the case. Rather, legal liberty—this is all we are concerned with at the moment—is one value among many. Legal liberty consists—as will be shown in more detail below[250]—in the legal permission to do and not to do as one pleases. It is limited by every single prohibitive and mandatory norm. The more that is commanded and forbidden, the smaller is the scope of legal liberty. The principle of legal liberty requires a state of legal regulation in which as little as possible is commanded and forbidden. Its maximal fulfilment is the state of affairs in which nothing is legally commanded or forbidden, that is, in which everything is legally permitted. Of course, it is easy to see that such a state of affars is hardly desirable. Controversy arises when the question is what and how much to forbid or command. This dispute is a dispute about the optimum degree of satisfaction of the principle of legal liberty in the light of competing principles. These principles can be very differently weighted. The scale extends from radically liberal theories, which only give competing principles greater weight in a few extreme situations, to radically illiberal theories which adopt an alternative weighting and permit a legal command or prohibition for almost every type of action. This should make it clear that the principle or value-based theory of constitutional rights is neutral as far as legal liberty is concerned. While a low weighting of the principle of legal liberty can lead to its being outweighed, alternative weightings can lead to its outweighing other principles.

That alone does not deal with all the doctrinal objections to a principle-theory of constitutional rights. One can accept that the liberal objection is misplaced while still maintaining one based on the Rule of Law. Treating

---

normative programme) and empirical statements about what is to be constitutionally regulated. For an analysis and critique of such theories, see R. Dreier, *Zum Begriff der 'Natur der Sache'* (Berlin, 1965).

[246] See on this below at 369 ff.
[247] Forsthoff, 'Zur heutigen Situation einer Verfassungslehre', 190.
[248] Böckenförde, 'Grundrechtstheorie und Grundrechtsinterpretation', 1533.
[249] Goerlich, *Wertordnung und Grundgesetz*, 37.   [250] 144 ff.

constitutional rights norms as principles creates the possibility of turning quite different balancing outcomes into constitutional requirements. 'Thus' so one could agree with Forsthoff, 'one turns constitutional rights into a manipulative possibility of over-, under- and revaluing and transforms the basic decisions of the constitution makers into a total empowerment of the constitutional interpreter. The result is the destabilizing of the Constitution. . .'.[251] This objection combines two aspects. The first is that a theory of principles does not take the binding nature of the Constitution seriously. The second is that it leads to interpretative arbitrariness and constitutional instability.

As far as the binding nature of the Constitution is concerned, the objection would only work if the model of pure rules secured a higher level of obligatoriness than the mixed rule/principle model. But the model of pure rules has been shown to be inadequate. It became clear that in the case of constitutional rights with simple limitation clauses it leads from difficulties identifying the essential core to meaninglessness and the collapse of obligatoriness. Expansion from the level of rules to the level of principles is necessary precisely to secure the binding nature of constitutional rights. Forsthoff's reference to respect for the 'basic decisions of the constitution makers' implies not so much opposition to the theory of principles itself but to the possibility of a theory of principles of a certain content. A basic decision of the constitution makers can hardly be anything other than a decision in favour of a certain principle or principles. But if this is correct, then the objection based on the binding nature of the Constitution ceases to be an objection to the structure of a theory of principles. It becomes an objection to a certain weighting of principles and thus to a plea for a certain substantive conception of constitutional rights, as against which the theory of principles as a structure of reasoning is neutral.

The final objection concerns legal certainty. Once again one has to refer to the lack of acceptable alternatives which guarantee a higher level of certainty than the rule/principle model. But this is only one side of the issue. The other is that the character of constitutional rights as principles implies the permanent possibility of more extensive protection, but that this is reconcilable with an adequate level of legal certainty. The combined model of rules and principles does contain a level of rules.[252] It will be shown below[253] that the certainty created by the level of rules rests not only on the respect required for the literal meaning and the intention of the constitution makers, but also fundamentally on the precedential force of decisions of the Federal Constitutional Court.

---

[251] Forsthoff, 'Zur heutigen Situation einer Verfassungslehre', 190.

[252] This means that in the rule/principle model, deduction is not displaced by balancing. Rather, it combines both. For two types of combination, see on one hand Alexy, 'Die logische Analyse juristischer Entscheidungen', 195 ff., and on the other hand H.-J. Koch and H. Rüßmann, *Juristische Begründungslehre*, 97 ff.   [253] 373 ff.

4

Constitutional Rights as Subjective Rights

I. ON THE CURRENT DEBATE ABOUT SUBJECTIVE RIGHTS

The debate about subjective rights has not been able to reach agreement, in spite of its considerable duration and intensive, and extensive, efforts.[1] As Kelsen bemoaned, one important reason for this could be the 'failure to ask precise and correct questions'. 'People refused to consider exactly what the concept of a subjective right was supposed to do for jurists; people were not clear enough in their minds about the question it was supposed to answer.'[2] Current debate about subjective rights covers a great variety of matters as well. Three types of question can be asked: normative, empirical, and analytical.

1. SUBJECTIVE RIGHTS AND NORMATIVE QUESTIONS

As far as normative questions are concerned, we can distinguish ethical questions from legal-doctrinal questions and their corresponding answers.

When asked in isolation from any given legal system, the question of why individuals have rights and which rights they have is an *ethical* one. One classic answer to that question is the Kantian one, whereby the 'only original right' of every human being, 'by virtue of their humanity',[3] by which Kant means the attribute of human beings as rational,[4] is 'freedom (independence from being constrained by another's choice), insofar as it can co-exist with the freedom of every other in accordance with a universal law'. Larenz offers a further example of an answer to the same question:

---

[1] Kelsen's conclusion in 1911, that 'it would certainly be no exaggeration were one to maintain that of all the basic juridical concepts, it is precisely that of the subjective right which is most discussed in the theoretical literature' (H. Kelsen, *Hauptprobleme der Staatsrechtslehre entwickelt aus der Lehre vom Rechtssatz* (Tübingen, 1911), 568) while it is not more applicable to the current literature, is none the less not far out. As will become apparent in the following discussion, the concept of a subjective right certainly belongs to the set of the most discussed concepts in the theoretical literature.

[2] Kelsen, *Hauptprobleme der Staatsrechtslehre*, 618.

[3] I. Kant, *The Metaphysics of Morals*, trans. M. Gregor (Cambridge, 1991) 63.

[4] id., *The Moral Law (Groundwork of the Metaphysics of Morals)*, trans. H. J. Paton (London, 1948), 107 ff.

'We perceived the basic legal relation to be the right of each person to be respected as a person by every other, and simultaneously his duty towards every other is likewise to respect him as a person. The "right" of a person is what is rightly his as a person, and which the other is therefore obliged, or bound, to grant or respect.'[5]

It has been suggested above that the doctrine of constitutional rights, in common with all legal doctrine, is a three-dimensional discipline, and that one of the three dimensions is normative.[6] The substance of ethical questions can therefore also play a part in constitutional rights doctrine. The difference between ethical and legal questions lies in the fact that in the case of the latter we are concerned with validity within a legal system, whereas the former is independent of any system.

Legal-doctrinal questions ask whether a legal subject has particular subjective rights within a legal system. Here we are only interested in two situations in which this question can arise. In the first situation there is no doubt that norm N, if it applies in x's case, grants him a subjective right; the doubt is whether it is applicable in x's case, that is, whether it gives him a subjective right in the circumstances at hand. Answering this question is a standard problem of interpretation. Problems associated with the concept of a subjective right are irrelevant. The second type of situation is characterized by the absence of doubt that norm N is applicable to x's case; the doubt is whether N grants any sort of subjective right. The classic example of this situation is Ihering's example of a protectionist import duty. 'The law which introduces a protectionist import duty in the interest of certain industries is to the *advantage* of workers in those industries, it *supports* them and *protects* them in their work, and yet it does not grant them any *rights*. All there is, is a *reflex-effect*, a relationship which bears great similarity to a right, but which must therefore be distinguished all the more carefully from it.'[7]

The question of when a legal norm grants subjective rights is of practical significance above all from a procedural perspective. For example, according to sections 42(2) and 113(1) Rules of the Administrative Court, it is a condition for the admissibility (and success) of a complaint that the complainant can allege (and substantiate) an infringement of his subjective rights.[8] The only point to be made here is that the question of whether a

---

[5] K. Larenz, *Allgemeiner Teil des Deutschen Bürgerlichen Rechts*, 1st edn. (Munich, 1967), 60.

[6] 6 ff.

[7] R. v. Ihering, *Geist des römischen Rechts auf den verschiedenen Stufen seiner Entwicklung*, part 3, 5th edn. (Leipzig, 1906), 351. On this case, see O. Bachof, 'Reflexwirkungen und subjektive Rechte im öffentlichen Recht', in O. Bachof, M. Drath, O. Gönnenwein, and E. Walz, *Gedächtnisschrift für W. Jellinek* (Munich, 1955), 288; H. L. A. Hart, 'Bentham on Legal Rights', in A. W. B. Simpson (ed.), *Oxford Essays in Jurisprudence*, second series (Oxford, 1973), 189.

[8] On the discussion about subjective rights in administrative law, see e.g. O. Bachof, 'Reflexwirkungen und subjektive Rechte im öffentlichen Recht', 287 ff.; H. H. Rupp, *Grundfragen der heutigen Verwaltungsrechtslehre* (Tübingen, 1965), 246 ff.; W. Henke, *Das*

norm grants a subjective right or not is a normative question. It arises whenever the text of a norm leaves this question open, which is, for example, the case when a norm N obliges the state to undertake act ϕ, but it does not make clear whether x has a right to this act as against the state. Further assumptions are necessary if it is to be held that x has such a right. These could lie in a purposive interpretation of the norm, as in the protective norm theory of the Federal Administrative Court.[9] But this takes us into an area in which we are no longer deducing results from what is authoritatively predetermined, but have to engage in independent evaluative judgments.[10] Normative propositions that go beyond what is written have to be justified.

2. Subjective Rights and Empirical Questions

The idea of an empirical question covers a great variety of matters. This applies to empirical questions regarding subjective rights as well. For example, we can identify statements about the historical development of subjective rights,[11] about the history of the concept of a subjective right,[12] and about the social function of subjective rights,[13] in particular perhaps about their 'specific function for the organization and legitimation of relationships of authority'.[14]

Given what has already been said about the three-dimensionality of the study of law,[15] we need not waste many words on the significance of empirical questions for a legal theory of subjective rights. They are particularly apparent in the context of historical and purposive arguments. Facts such as the fact that a certain subjective right R was granted at time t_1 to address a certain undesirable state of affairs S, and that R successfully dealt with this state of affairs, and assuming that R is also still suitable at the current moment in time t_2 to avoid S, which is still considered undesirable, together amount to a strong argument for the maintenance of R.[16] Again, the fact that a certain subjective right R when interpreted according to I, leads to a

---

subjektive öffentliche Recht (Tübingen, 1968); M. Zuleeg, 'Hat das subjektive öffentliche Recht noch eine Daseinsberechtigung?' DVBl 1976, 510 ff.

[9] See e.g. BVerwGE 1, 83; 27, 29 (32); 28, 268 (270); 32, 173 (175); 41, 58 (63); 52, 122 (128); see also BVerfGE 27, 297 (307).

[10] See R. Alexy, *A Theory of Legal Argumentation*, trans. R. Adler and N. MacCormick (Oxford, 1989), 240 ff.

[11] M. Weber (ed. G. Roth and C. Wittich), *Economy and Society* (Berkeley, 1968), 666 ff.

[12] H. Coing, 'Zur Geschichte des Begriffs "subjektives Recht" ', in id., *Zur Geschichte des Privatrechtssystems* (Frankfurt a. M., 1962), 29 ff.

[13] N. Luhmann, 'Zur Funktion der "subjektiven Rechte" ', in *Die Funktion des Rechts in der modernen Gesellschaft, Jahrbuch für Rechtssoziologie und Rechtstheorie*, 1 (1970), 321 ff.; J. Schapp, *Das subjektive Recht im Prozeß der Rechtsgewinnung* (Berlin, 1977), 14.

[14] U. K. Preuß, *Die Internalisierung des Subjekts* (Frankfurt a M., 1979), 30.

[15] 6 ff.

[16] On such historical arguments, see Alexy, *A Theory of Legal Argumentation*, 239.

particular consequence C or has social function F, assuming that C or F are desirable, amounts to a strong argument for interpreting R according to I. The examples could be multiplied. But every example would show that empirical propositions about the history, social consequences, or functions of subjective rights *alone* have no consequences for legal-doctrinal disputes. In order to be relevant, they must be coupled with normative statements.

3. SUBJECTIVE RIGHTS AND ANALYTICAL QUESTIONS

3.1 Norm and Position

A theory of the structure of constitutional rights is mainly concerned with analytical questions. In the analytical treatment of constitutional rights, the distinction between norm and position is of fundamental significance.[17] A norm is what is expressed by a normative statement.[18] The statement,

(1)   'Every person has the right freely to express . . . their opinions . . .' (art. 5(1)(1) Basic Law)

expresses a universal norm.[19] Since there can be no doubt that this norm grants a subjective right against the state, the following individual norm can be formulated on its basis:

(2)   x has the right, as against the state, to express his opinions freely.

If the statement applies, that is, the norm expressed in (2) applies, then x is in the legal position as against the state, which is exactly constituted by x's having a right as against the state to express his opinions freely. This position can be expressed by the same statement which expresses the corresponding norm. If the individual norm granting x a right to G as against y is valid, then x finds himself in the legal position of having a right to G as against y. And if the legal position of x is that he has a right to G as against y, then the individual norm that x has a right to G against y must be valid. Under these circumstances, we can well ask what the point of talking about legal positions is; it seems superfluous.

The answer is that it is necessary for certain perspectives, namely when one has to consider the *normative characteristics* of persons and acts, and *normative relations* between persons, and between persons and acts. Norms can be seen quite generally as qualities of persons and acts. Thus it can be said that a norm which prohibits x from ϕ-ing, gives to x the legal characteristic of being one of those prohibited from ϕ-ing. This legal characteristic, which can be expressed by the complex predicate, 'one of those prohibited from ϕ-ing', is the position in which x is put by the norm. If the

---

[17] On the use of the expression 'position' by the Federal Constitutional Court, see BVerfGE 45, 63 (76); 53, 30 (58).
[18] See above at 21 f.
[19] On this concept, see above at 46 fn. 11.

only legal positions were of this nature, then the language of positions would indeed be useless. But it gets interesting when one is no longer simply considering characteristics but relations expressed in double predicates such as, 'has a right to G as against . . .' or triple predicates such as '. . . has a right to . . . as against . . .'. In what follows, it will be suggested that it is useful to think of subjective rights as such positions and relations.

3.2 A Three-Stage Model of Subjective Rights

If by subjective rights one understands legal positions and relations in the sense identified, then we can distinguish between (*a*) justifications for subjective rights, (*b*) subjective rights as legal positions and relations, and (*c*) the legal enforcement of subjective rights. Failure to distinguish these three matters is a major cause of the unending controversy about the concept of subjective rights, and above all of the dispute between various versions of the interest and will theories of rights.[20]

The points around which the debate about the nature of rights revolves were expressed by Ihering with insurpassable force. 'The concept of a right is constituted by two aspects, a *substantive* aspect, which is concerned with practical purpose, namely the use, advantage or gain guaranteed by the right, and a *formal* aspect, which is a means of achieving that purpose, namely legal *protection* or the *cause of action*.'[21] While the purpose was

---

[20] These theories found classic expression at the hands of Windscheid and Ihering. According to Windscheid, a subjective right was 'a power or mastery of the will granted by the legal system' (B. Windscheid, *Lehrbuch des Pandektenrechts*, 9th edn., ed. T. Kipp (Frankfurt a M., 1906), 156), while according to Ihering, subjective rights are 'legally protected interests' (Ihering, *Geist des römischen Rechts*, part 3, 339). The discussion of these theories has led to numerous so-called combination theories (see on this e.g. L. Enneccerus and H. C. Nipperdey, *Allgemeiner Teil des Bürgerlichen Rechts*, i, 15th edn. (Tübingen, 1959), 428 f.: 'a subjective right is conceptually a legal power, granted to the individual for the purpose of providing a means to the satisfaction of human interests', and G. Jellinek, *System der subjektiven öffentlichen Rechte*, 2nd edn. (Tübingen, 1905), 44: 'thus a subjective right is a human power of the will recognized and protected by the legal system and directed towards some good or interest'). On the dispute between these positions, see in place of many Kelsen, *Hauptprobleme der Staatsrechtslehre*, 572 ff.; Bachof, 'Reflexwirkungen und subjektive Rechte im öffentlichen Recht', 291 ff.; L. Raiser, 'Der Stand der Lehre vom subjektiven Recht im Deutschen Zivilrecht', JZ 1961, 465; F. Kasper, *Das subjektive recht—Begriffsbildung und Bedeutungsmehrheit* (Karlsruhe, 1967), 49 ff.; J. Aicher, *Das Eigentum als subjektives Recht: Zugleich ein Beitrag zur Theorie des subjektiven Rechts* (Berlin, 1975), 24 ff.

In the English-speaking world, the controversy between Ihering and Windscheid is paralleled by the positions of Bentham (benefit theory) and Austin (will theory); see on one hand J. Bentham (ed. J. H. Burns and H. L. A. Hart), *An Introduction to the Principles of Morals and Legislation* (London, 1970), 206 (and on this, Hart, 'Bentham on Legal Rights', 177) and on the other hand J. Austin, *Lectures on Jurisprudence*, i, 4th edn. (London, 1873), 410. In more recent times the dispute between the will and interest theories has flared up once again. On the side of the will theory stands Hart ('Bentham on Legal Rights', 183 ff.) and on the side of the interest theory stand MacCormick and Lyons (N. MacCormick, 'Rights in Legislation', in P. M. S. Hacker and J. Raz (eds.), *Law, Morality and Society, Essays in Honour of H. L. A. Hart*, (Oxford, 1977), 189 ff.; D. Lyons, 'Rights, Claimants and Beneficiaries', Am Phil Q 6 (1969), 173 ff.).

[21] Ihering, *Geist des römischen Rechts*, part 3, 339.

central for Ihering, the will theory sees the control of the right-holder over the position granted him by the norm, a control expressed among other things in the ability to bring an action, as central. He can sue; he need not. What he does depends on his free choice, his will.[22]

Statements about the purpose of rights, as indeed statements about the purpose of norms in general, are statements about the reasons, or grounds, for rights or norms. Under Ihering's scheme, two types of statement have to be distinguished: statements about the reasons for rights, and statements about their protection or enforcement. A typical statement of reasons goes, 'these rights exist . . . to serve the interests, needs and purposes of trade'.[23] Such general statements of reasons correspond to concrete *statements of reasons* such as,

(1)   G is a 'need unavoidably linked to the animal nature of human beings'.[24]

which can be advanced as an argument for the thesis that x has a right to G.[25] A *statement about protection* would be:

(2) x can seek redress for the infringement of his right to G by bringing an action.

But neither statements of reasons nor statements about enforcement are, in themselves, identical in meaning to *statements about rights* such as,

(3) x has a right to G.

So what is the relationship of these statements to each other? This is one of the central problems for a theory of subjective rights.

The relationship between statements of reasons (1) and statements of rights (3) is relatively easy to determine. It is a justificatory relationship. The reason for a right is *one* thing, the right which is based upon this reason is another. A complete analysis, which aims, as Ihering puts it, to 'consider the inside of a right, its essence',[26] must consider both aspects. But this does not stop us making the logical structure of a right the object of investigation as a first step in our analysis; on the contrary, this is indispensable, because asking the reason for something presupposes knowledge of the thing to be justified.

The relationship between statements about rights such as (3) 'x has a right to G' and statements about enforcement such as (2) 'x can seek redress for the infringement of his right G by bringing an action' is not as easy to

---

[22] See on this Hart, 'Bentham on Legal Rights', 196 ff. The aspect of free choice is not restricted to the cause of action, that is, the enforcement of the right, but can be related to the disposition over the right itself; see on this e.g. B. Windscheid, *Lehrbuch des Pandektenrechts*, i, 156. If this aspect is considered constitutive of subjective rights, then considerable difficulties arise in the case of inalienable rights: see on this MacCormick, 'Rights in Legislation', 195 ff.

[23] Ihering, *Geist des römischen Rechts*, part 3, 338.   [24] ibid. 333 f.

[25] Whether this argument works can be left open at this point.

[26] Ihering, *Geist des römischen Rechts*, part 3, 328.

determine. Statements about enforcement also express legal positions, namely the legal capacity (power or competence[27]) to enforce a right. This position can also be called a right. So we are concerned with the relationship between two positions or rights. The much discussed problem of this relationship arises from the high degree of plausibility with which one can assert that one can only really speak of a subjective right where there is a legal capacity of enforcement. Writers such as Kelsen define the subjective right in its technical or specific sense precisely by referring to such a capacity: 'the right in the specific sense of the word is the legal power to enforce [*geltend machen*] an existing duty'.[28] This definition makes do with the concept of a legal power (legal capacity or competence) together with the concept of a duty to fulfilling or enforcing which the legal power relates. Does this mean that talk of a position characterized by x's having a right to G as against y, and hence the use of statements such as 'x has a right to G as against y', is otiose?

This possibility is to be rejected for two reasons. The first reason is a consideration of usefulness. The adoption of statements of rights is still possible and useful, even if one assumes that subjective rights only exist when there is a corresponding capacity of enforcement. The possibility of using statements of the form 'x has a right to G as against y' is not excluded, but its permissibility is limited to cases in which there is a legal capacity of enforcement. The usefulness of adopting such statements is already made apparent in that otherwise straightforward situations of the legal capacity of enforcement and infringements of duties would have to be expressed in complex terms. So, even if Kelsen's definition of a right is to be followed, we would still be justified in conducting significant portions of legal debate with the help of statements about rights. In addition to this technical reason, there is a systemic one. It does not seem necessary to limit the use of rights-language to cases of legal capacity of enforcement, perhaps by bringing a legal action. We are free to define rights in this way, but such a stipulative definition does not reflect existing linguistic usage,[29] nor is it fruitful for our understanding of legal systems. The fact that it does not reflect linguistic usage can be seen, for example, by the existence of norms such as article 19(4) Basic Law, which guarantees a legal remedy to everyone whose rights have been infringed by a public body. If the capacity to enforce a right were already implicit in the concept of a right, this norm would be unnecessary.[30] Norms such as this one suggest that it might be

---

[27] On these concepts, see below at 149 ff.

[28] H. Kelsen, *General Theory of Norms*, trans. M. Hartney (Oxford, 1991), 324; see also at 136 f.; id., *Pure Theory of Law*, trans. M. Knight (Berkeley, 1967), 134 ff.

[29] See on this e.g. E. R. Bierling, *Zur Kritik der juristischen Grundbegriffe*, part 2 (Gotha, 1883), 62 f.

[30] The inclusion of a power to bring an action within the concept of a subjective right under § 42(2) Rules of the Administrative Court, according to which appealing to a breach of a

better to see rights as reasons for the legal capacity to enforce them, which after the basic relationship between statements of reasons for rights and statements of rights would lead to a second basic relationship between statements of rights and statements about their protection.[31] But a deeper problem concerning the structure of the legal system lies beneath this. Does a legal system consist simply of that which is capable of judicial enforcement, or can it also include positions not capable of judicial enforcement, perhaps because their enforcement is incompatible with the role they play in the legal system, or because although their enforceability is not recognized, they can still be required from the perspective of the legal system. This question cannot be pursued here.[32] Even without answering it, we can say that a stipulative definition is inadequate.[33]

Combining the technical with the systemic reasons, there is much in favour of seeing the level of statements about rights as central for legal doctrine.

3.3 The Variety of Subjective Rights

The most important analytical contribution to the debate about subjective rights lies in the analysis and classification of legal positions which are called 'rights' generally and in legal language. In this area one can think of examples such as the distinction between absolute and relative rights of authority on one hand and formative rights on the other,[34] Jellinek's suggested distinction between negative, positive, and active status rights,[35] and Kelsen's distinction between reflex rights, subjective rights in the technical sense, positive official permissions, political rights, basic rights, and liberty rights.[36] One can also include in this area classifications such as Windscheid's between cases in which the will of the right-holder 'is determinative of the command issued by the legal system' and cases in which it is 'determinative of the creation of rights, or for their destruction or alter-

---

subjective right is a *precondition* of the right to bring an action, gives rise to similar problems (see on this Henke, *Das subjektive öffentliche Recht*, 2 f.).

[31] On the latter, see MacCormick, 'Rights in Legislation', 204.

[32] The answer to this question depends on whether the concept of a valid legal system includes the requirement that what it requires can be upheld by acts of force provided for by the system. The *fact* that this is true of the great majority of legal systems does not itself justify the conclusion that this is required by the *concept* of a valid legal norm. The fact that in every legal system there have to be norms protected by state sanctions (see H. L. A. Hart, *The Concept of Law* (Oxford, 1961), 195, 212) does not mean that in every legal system every legal norm must be protected by sanctions either.

[33] On the fact that one cannot conclude that a right does not exist simply because it is inadequately enforceable, see G. Leibholz, *Die Gleichheit vor dem Gesetz*, 2nd edn. (Munich and Berlin, 1959), 236: '. . . only it is incorrect to seek to conclude that these rights do not exist simply because state law gives these subjective rights no, or inadequate, protection'.

[34] H. Lehmann, *Allgemeiner Teil des Bürgerlichen Gesetzbuches*, 13th edn. (Berlin, 1962), 75 ff.

[35] Jellinek, *System der subjektiven öffentlichen Rechte*, 87, 95 ff.

[36] Kelsen, *Pure Theory of Law*, 125 ff.

ation',[37] and definitions such as Bucher's: 'a subjective right is a law-making power granted by the legal system to the right-holder'.[38]

Even these few examples point out the great variety in what has been called a 'subjective right'. They also give rise to the suspicion that the various positions lumped together under this concept could be more complex than the classifications, distinctions, and definitions allow. This would explain the difficulties which the concept of a right has raised—and still raises—for analysis.

The investigations of Lindahl are instructive in this respect.[39] Traditional theories are characterized by the attempt to conceptualize actually existing legal positions by using ordinary language or technical legal language in a more or less direct grasp of the legal system. Lindahl's theory is fundamentally different. He attempts to set out all possible coherent normative positions.[40] In order to do this, he considers the possible combinations of two operators, a deontic operator (Shall operator) and an act operator (Do operator).[41] Both operators are incorporated into a system of basic logic. In this way Lindahl derives seven basic types of one-agent legal positions,[42] thirty-five types of normative relation between two subjects, which relate to acts which can be carried out by each legal subject separately (individualistic two-agent types),[43] and 127 types of normative relation between two subjects, which relate to acts requiring coordination between the subjects (collectivistic two-agent types).[44] On this basis, Lindahl proposes a reworking of normative positions in the field identified by terms such as 'legal capacity', 'legal power', 'competence', and 'legal ability', which gives rise to such a large number of possibilities,[45] that Lindahl seeks to separate the useful from the useless by way of non-logical 'rules of feasability'.[46]

Lindahl's analyses do not constitute an objection to conceptual clarification in the traditional mould. On the contrary, from the point of view of usefulness, the great variety of logically possible combinations makes it seem appropriate to develop concepts which, without going into every conceivable distinction, allow one to conceptualize the domain of subjective rights economically and adequately. At the same time, such analyses show that even a simple model, such as will be presented here, cannot do without a glance at logical structures.

---

[37] Windscheid, *Lehrbuch des Pandektenrechts*, i, 156.

[38] E. Bucher, *Das subjektive Recht als Normsetzungsbefugnis* (Tübingen, 1965), 55.

[39] L. Lindahl, *Position and Change* (Dordrecht, 1977).

[40] Lindahl bases himself in this respect mainly on the work of Kanger, see S. Kanger, 'New Foundations for Ethical Theory', in R. Hilpinen (ed.), *Deontic Logic: Introductory and Systematic Readings* (Dordrecht, 1970), 36 ff.; S. Kanger and H. Kanger, 'Rights and Parliamentarism', *Theoria*, 32 (1966), 85 ff.

[41] Lindahl, *Position and Change*, 84.   [42] ibid. 92.

[43] ibid. 128 f.   [44] ibid. 162 ff.

[45] 2^7 one-agent legal positions, 2^{35} individualistic two-agent types, and 2^{127} collectivistic two-agent types, see ibid. 218.   [46] ibid. 225 ff.

The variety of what has been called 'a right' leads to a terminological difficulty. Should the expression 'right', which in its degree of ambiguity and vagueness is hard to beat, be reserved for a small number of legal positions, or should it be used in as all-embracing a sense as possible? The first route carries with it a danger of fruitless dispute about what is correctly called a 'right'. An insight into the structure of different positions is far more important than this dispute. It therefore seems better to use the expression 'a right' in reliance on current usage as a general term for a set of quite distinctive legal positions, and then to make the necessary distinctions and terminological identifications within the context of this term.

II. A SYSTEM OF BASIC LEGAL POSITIONS

The basis of an analytical theory of rights is a threefold division into (1) rights to something, (2) liberties, and (3) powers.[47]

1. RIGHTS TO SOMETHING[48]

1.1 The Basic Structure of Rights to Something

The most general form of a statement of a right to something is

(1) x has a right to G as against y.

This statement makes it clear that a right to something can be understood as a three-point relation, of which the first element is the beneficiary or *holder* of a right (x), the second is the *addressee* of the right (y), and the third is the subject-matter or *object* of the right (G).[49] This three-point rela-

---

[47] This division is linked to Bentham's distinction between 'rights to services', 'liberties', and 'powers' (J. Bentham (ed. H. L. A. Hart), *Of Laws in General* (London, 1970), 57 f., 82 ff., 98, 119, 173 ff.) as well as to Bierling's distinction between 'legal claim', 'simple legal permission', and 'legal ability' (Bierling, *Zur Kritik der juristischen Grundbegriffe*, part 2, 42 ff.).

[48] The expression 'rights to something' may well seem rather wooden. Possible alternatives are the expressions '(subjective) right' and 'claim'. But liberties and powers are also subjective rights. So this term is hardly suited for the identification of positions which are to be clearly distinguished from liberties and powers. The expression 'claim' [*Anspruch*] is more suitable. The concept of a right to something shares a relational character with the claim. Both rights to something and claims are always directed towards another person, and the object in both cases is always either an act or an omission. Nevertheless, we shall do without a technical application of the concept of a claim. This concept is burdened with numerous controversies, which are of no interest in the current context (see e.g. Enneccerus and Nipperdey, *Allgemeiner Teil des Bürgerlichen Rechts*, ii, 15th edn. (Tübingen, 1960), 1363 ff.). If one ignores the controversy surrounding the concept of a claim, which turns for example on issues such as actuality, the certainty of the other party and enforceability, then rights to something could of course be called claims. Apart from that it only needs pointing out that talk of rights to something loses its unusual character when we are concerned with the formulation of specific rights. 'x has a right to G as against y' is from a linguistic perspective to be understood in the same way as the sentence, 'x has a claim to G against y'.

[49] On the three-point nature of this relation, see A. R. Anderson, 'Logic, Norms and Roles', *Ratio*, 4 (1962), 42.

tionship will be expressed by 'R'. The most general form of a statement of a right to something can thus be expressed

(2) $RxyG$

This scheme can give rise to a great variety of rights, depending on what x, y, and G stand for. Whether x refers to a natural person, or a public body, whether y is the state or a private individual, whether G is a positive act or an omission, are all highly significant from the perspective of a doctrine of constitutional rights. Here we need only consider the structure of the subject-matter of a right to something.

The subject-matter of a right to something is always an *act* of an addressee. This is a consequence of the three-point structure of the right between a holder, an addressee, and a subject-matter. If the subject-matter were not an act of the addressee, there would be no point including him in the relation.

The link to an act, along with the three-point structure, is not always directly expressed by individual constitutional rights provisions. One example is article 2(2)(1) Basic Law:

(3)   'Every person has the right to life . . .'.

If one were to consider only the literal meaning of this provision, one might think that the right it guarantees is only a two-point relation between a right-holder and an object, which in this case is a certain state of affairs for the right-holder, namely his being alive. Such a right would correspond to what in classical terminology is called a '*ius in rem*' and can be contrasted with a '*ius in personam*'. There can be no doubt that for reasons of simplicity it is often better to speak of rights in the sense of relations between a legal subject and an object. But, as Kant rightly pointed out,[50] and as has since then been regularly demonstrated,[51] talk of such relations is nevertheless nothing other than an abbreviation for a complex of rights to something, liberties and/or powers.[52] Thus, according to the Federal Constitutional Court, article 2(2)(1) Basic Law grants not only '*negatively* a right to life' which 'in particular [excludes] state-sponsored murder',[53] but is also *positively* a right that the state act 'protectively and supportively towards this life', which principally means that it must 'guard against unlawful infringements by others'.[54] Both rights have the $RxyG$ structure and relate to acts of the addressee:

---

[50] Kant, *The Metaphysics of Morals*, 69, 82, 93.

[51] See e.g. Kelsen, *Pure Theory of Law*, 130 ff.

[52] More recently, A. M. Honoré, 'Rights of Exclusion and Immunities against Divesting', Tul L Rev 34 (1960), 453 ff., and J. Raz, *The Concept of a Legal System* (Oxford, 1970), 180, have spoken out against the view that the *ius in rem* is a complex of rights to something, liberties and/or powers. For a critique of these views with compelling arguments, see Lindahl, *Position and Change*, 34 ff.

[53] BVerfGE 1, 97 (105).

[54] BVerfGE 46, 160 (164). This decision does not speak in terms of a right to the protection

(4) x has a right as against the state that it not kill him.
(5) x has a right as against the state, that it protect his life from unlawful infringements by third parties.

The rights listed are distinguished exclusively by their subject-matter. The object of one right (4) is a negative act (omission), the object of the other (5) is a positive act.[55] The distinction between negative and positive acts is a main criterion for the division of rights according to their subject-matter. In the context of rights against the state, which will be dealt with in more detail below, rights to negative acts correspond to what are generally called 'defensive rights'. By contrast, as will be shown below,[56] rights to positive acts only correspond partially to what are called 'entitlements'.

1.1.1 *Rights to Negative Acts (Defensive Rights)*

Rights of the citizen against the state to negative acts can be divided into three groups. The first group consists of rights that the state should not prevent or hinder certain *acts* of the right-holder. The second group consists of rights that the state should not adversely affect certain *characteristics* or *situations* of the right-holder. The third group consists of rights that the state should not remove certain *legal positions* of the right-holder.

1.1.1.1 Rights to the Non-obstruction of Acts

Examples of acts of a constitutional right-holder which could be interfered with are: walking along a street, professing a faith, expressing an opinion, creating a work of art, educating children, assembling on a street, and opting for a career. The difference between preventing and interfering with such acts can be stated as follows: an act of x's is *prevented* by y when y brings about a state of affairs, which makes it impossible as a matter of fact for x to do the act. So y prevents x's walking along a street by putting him in prison, and he prevents x's educating his children himself by taking them away from him. y *interferes* with x's acts, when y creates a state of affairs which could discourage x from undertaking the act. If one defines the concepts of prevention and interference in this way, then raising the standards of entry into a particular profession such that x can only satisfy them with great effort and personal sacrifice does not prevent him from entering the profession, but it interferes with his entering. By contrast, there is a quite different alternative conception of prevention, where one focuses not on the situation of x, but on the success of y in interfering with the act. On

---

of life, but only of a protective state duty. It will be shown below at 301 ff. that constitutional protective duties correspond to subjective rights, at any rate where there are no problems concerning the identity of the right-holder as there were in the termination of pregnancy case (BVerfGE 31, 1 (41)).

[55] On the concept of the negative act or omission, see in place of many G. H. v. Wright, *Norm and Action* (London, 1963), 45 ff.
[56] 294 ff.

this account, *y* is said to have prevented the act when his interference leads to *x*'s not carrying out the act. A further distinction is possible. From the perspective of the factually impossible, a legal prohibition is not a prevention but only an interference. *x* could take the risk of breaking the law into account and perform the act anyway. If, by contrast, one presupposes the legal obedience of *x*, the legal prohibition does not simply interefere with the act, it prevents it.

In addition to the concepts of prevention and interference, there are various internal distinctions. There are many *types* of prevention and interference, and interferences can have different *degrees* of severity. The last point is the reason why the borderline between prevention and interference is fluid—this is, of course, no argument against the distinction itself. If one is looking for some term to cover both prevention and interference, the idea of *obstruction* is appropriate.[57] The idea of obstruction will be used whenever further distinctions are irrelevant.

The state can have an influence on acts in a way other than that already described: it can make them *legally impossible*. Rights that this should not happen are to be distinguished from rights to non-obstruction. An act can only be made legally impossible when it is a *legal act*. Legal acts are acts which would not exist in the absence of constitutive legal norms. So, without the norms of contract law, there could be no *legal* act of formation of contract; without the norms of company law, no formation of a company *in law*, without the law of marriage, no *legal* act of marriage, without procedural law no bringing of a *legal* action, and without electoral law, no *legal* act of voting.[58] The constitutive nature of the enabling norms turn these acts into *institutional acts*.[59] Institutional legal acts become impossible when their constitutive legal norms are repealed. There is a *conceptual connection* between the repeal of such norms and the impossibility of an institutional act. Of course, institutional legal acts can be interfered with as well as made legally impossible. Where this occurs, there is a *factual connection* between the act of obstruction and its success. The legal act or institutional legal act of marriage is made legally impossible by abolishing the norms of marriage law. However, a particular act of marriage by *x* is only interfered with if it has the consequence that *x* is dismissed from public service. The range of possible obstructions of legal acts is very broad. The bringing of a legal action is interfered with when it is coupled with court fees that are too high, and the act of voting is interfered with when the

---

[57] See e.g. Bühler's formulation, according to which constitutional rights which are 'rights to omission . . . [are] claims against the state that it refrain from obstructing certain activities of the individual' (O. Bühler, *Die subjektiven öffentlichen Rechte und ihr Schutz in der deutschen Verwaltungsrechtsprechung* (Berlin, Stuttgart, and Leipzig, 1914), 63).

[58] Without their constitutive *legal* norms, these acts would only be possible as *social* acts.

[59] See on this J. R. Searle, *Speech Acts* (Cambridge, 1969), 33 ff.; N. MacCormick, 'Law as Institutional Fact', LQR 90 (1974), 105 ff.

voting stations are so placed that they are hard to reach from certain voting districts, and the possibility of a postal vote is excluded.

If a legal act is made legally impossible by the repeal of its constitutive norms, the individual is deprived of a legal position, namely the capacity or competence to change the legal state of affairs.[60] Rights that this should not happen therefore fall into the third group of rights to negative acts, that is, in the group of rights that the state should not destroy certain legal positions of the right-holder. The first group only encompasses rights that the state not obstruct acts of the right-holder of whatever sort, that is, that it not prevent or interfere with those acts in some way.

The statement of such a right can be given the following standard form:

(6) x has the right as against the state, that it should not obstruct x in ϕ-ing.[61]

1.1.1.2 Rights to the Non-affecting of Characteristics and Situations

The second group of rights to omissions on the part of the state is constituted by the requirement that the state should not try to *affect* certain characteristics or situations of the right-holder. As examples of characteristics which could be influenced, one could name those of living and being healthy, an example of a situation is the inviolability of the home.[62] [63] A statement of such a right can be given the following standard form:

(7) x has a right as against the state that it should not disturb characteristic A (or situation B).[64]

---

[60] See on this below at 149 ff.

[61] If one symbolizes the state by 's', and takes 'ϕx' to mean 'x performs act ϕ', then by using the sign '$\sim$' for negation one can represent this statement in the following way:

(6') $Rxs (\sim \text{obstruct } s (\phi x))$.

[62] Instead of characteristics and situations, people often talk in terms of interests, for example, the interest in life. There is nothing particularly wrong with this way of putting it; it is just rather misleading. That x lives does not mean that there are two things, x and something else, the interest, between which there is a relation of having. Rather, it means that x is granted a certain characteristic, namely that of living. See in this sense Jellinek, *System der subjektiven öffentliche Rechte*, 83, fn. 1: 'Life, health, liberty, dignity etc. are not themselves objects which humans have, but characteristics which define their concrete existence'.

[63] An explicitly situation-related, and not act-related, interpretation of art. 13 Basic Law can be found in BVerfGE 7, 230 (238). Merten places such rights as 'defensive' or 'protective rights' in opposition to 'action rights', by which he understands rights to the non-obstruction of acts (D. Merten, 'Handlungsgrundrechte als Verhaltensgarantien', VerwArch 73 (1982), 103). This terminology does not seem entirely happy. Rights to the non-obstruction of acts can also be called 'defensive rights', and this is often the case. It is therefore more appropriate to draw the distinction between situation-related and act-related rights within the concept of the defensive right.

[64] If one lets 'Sx' stand for both 'x has characteristic A' and 'x finds himself in situation B', then the structure of this statement can be represented in the following way:

(7') $Rxs (\sim \text{disrupt } s (Sx))$.

1.1.1.3 Rights to the Non-removal of Legal Positions

The third group of rights to omissions on the part of the state is constituted by the right that the state should not remove certain legal positions of the right-holder. The prototype of a complex legal position is that of the property-owner. The Federal Constitutional Court has correctly commented that, 'in order for [property] to be workable in legal life, it must *necessarily* be legally structured'.[65] This structuring occurs through legal norms which define the legal institution of property. Among these defining norms are those concerning the start and end of one's position as owner, as well as norms setting out the legal consequences of this position.[66] The state could remove 'concrete subjective legal positions'[67] or 'concrete property rights'[68] which are components of the legal institution of property required by its norms (such as conveyance and inheritance), or it could remove norms relating to property itself. If the latter occurs, then abstract legal positions such as the legal possibility or competence to acquire or convey ownership of specific objects, or the possibility or competence to carry out certain legal acts on the basis of one's ownership,[69] will be removed. A good example of the removal of an abstract legal position would be when the acquisition of agricultural or forested land is made dependent on state approval, and thus in some circumstances made impossible.[70] The constitutional guarantee of the legal institution of property is personalized to the extent that individual rights of non-removal of abstract legal positions exist in connection with the start, the end, and the consequences of one's position as an owner.

The removal of positions is not only present in institutional contexts such as property. If the transmission of certain opinions is prohibited, then a legal position of *A*, which consists of his being allowed to express his opinions, is removed. Such a prohibition can thus be seen from two aspects, in the obstruction of an act and in the removal of a position. In the case of

---

[65] BVerfGE 58, 300 (330) (emphasis added).

[66] See N. MacCormick, 'Law as Institutional Fact', 106 f.

[67] BVerfGE 52, 1 (27).   [68] BVerfGE 58, 300 (331).

[69] An example of this is the power of owners of rented accommodation to increase the rent; on the constitutional protection of this power, see BVerfGE 37, 132 (139 ff.).

[70] On such a case, see BVerfGE 21, 73. The Federal Constitutional Court expressly left it open in this decision whether 'the right to acquire agricultural and forested land' is protected by art. 14(1)(1) Basic Law, and resolved the case on the basis of art. 2(1) Basic Law (BVerfGE 21, 73 (76 f., 79, 86 f.)). On this question, see in place of many M. Kloepfer, *Grundrechte als Entstehungssicherung und Bestandsschutz* (Munich, 1970), 37 ff., who gives significant arguments for considering the 'location of the liberty to acquire property under art. 14 basic Law' to be 'constitutionally required' (ibid. 48; O. Kimminich, in *Bonner Kommentar* (Drittarbeitung), art. 14 GG, para. 88, is in agreement; against this view, see P. Wittig, 'Der Erwerb von Eigentum und das Grundgesetz', NJW 1967, 2185 ff.). It should be pointed out that we are only talking here of the legal and not the factual possibility of acquiring property, that is, not of 'the chances and possibilities of earning money' (see on this BVerfGE 30, 292 (335)). If the latter were relevant, we would be concerned—in the context of rights to omissions—with the obstruction of acts and influencing of situations which could occur in parallel to the removal of legal positions.

acts which are not legal acts, the factual obstruction is the decisive perspective.

Once again, it is appropriate to reduce these situations to a general form:

(8) x has a right as against the state, that it should not remove x's legal position LP.[71]

The existence of a legal position means that a corresponding (individual or general) norm applies. Thus the right of the citizen against the state that it should not remove a legal position of the citizen, is a right that the state should not repeal certain norms.[72]

1.1.2 Rights to Positive Acts

Rights of the citizen against the state to positive acts on the part of the state can be divided into two groups: those having factual acts as their object, and those having normative acts as their object.

A right to a positive *factual* act is, say, the right of an owner of a private school to a state subsidy,[73] the right to an existential minimum,[74] or the 'claim of the individual citizen to the creation of university places'.[75] That the satisfaction of such rights will be carried out by law does not change the nature of the rights as rights to a factual act. The legal form in which the right is satisfied is quite irrelevant. The only decisive question is whether the owner of the private school has got sufficient means after the subsidy has been granted, whether the poor person has enough to live on, and whether the aspiring student has a university place. The irrelevance of the legal form of the state intervention for the satisfaction of the right[76] is the criterion for distinguishing between positive factual and positive normative acts.

Rights to positive *normative* state acts are rights that the state create certain legal norms. If one assumes that the foetus benefits from constitutional rights protection, which has been hitherto unresolved by the Federal

[71] If one takes 'LPx' to mean 'x is in the legal position LP', then the structure of this sentence can be represented as follows:

(8′) Rxs (~ remove s (LPx)).

[72] In the case of norms such as those defining the legal institution of property, this leads to interesting problems as regards the positive or negative character of state acts to which the right relates. x has a right to the non-removal of a norm N, if x has the right that N apply. If x has a right that N apply, then the positive or negative character of his right depends entirely on whether N already applies or not. If one treats not only norm-enacting and norm-repealing acts, but also maintaining-in-force, as acts of the legislature, then rights to non-removal, which are rights to negative acts, will always correspond to rights to maintain in force, which are rights to positive acts. This problem will play a further part below in the discussion of normative state performance (319 ff.).

[73] BVerwGE 27, 360 (362 ff.).

[74] G. Dürig, in T. Maunz and G. Dürig *et al.*, *Grundgesetz Kommentar*, 5th edn. (Munich, 1983), art. 1, para. 43 f.

[75] BVerfGE 33, 303 (333).

[76] The irrelevance as regards the satisfaction of the right does not mean that it is irrelevant for the satisfaction of other norms.

Constitutional Court,[77] then the right of the foetus to protection under the criminal law is such a right. Another example is the right of a beneficiary of the constitutional right to academic freedom to 'such state measures, including organizational ones, which are indispensible for the protection of his contitutionally guaranteed liberty'.[78]

When people speak of 'performance rights', they generally mean rights to positive factual acts. Such rights to factual performance, which could in principle be carried out by private individuals, should be termed '*performance rights, or entitlements, in the narrow sense*'. But one could refer to normative performance as well as factual performance, so rights to positive normative acts could also be called performance rights. They will be called '*performance rights, or entitlements, in the wide sense*'.[79] An example of a right to a normative performance would be the right to the creation of a certain form of participation in an organization, such as a university. The fact that the object of this right is a power which can be located in the active civic status is no objection to calling the right *to* such a power a right to a positive normative performance. The positive normative performance consists in the granting of a power to participate.

A great variety of things fall under the concepts of rights to a factual as well a normative performance. At present, we are only concerned with the basic structure:

(9) x has a right as against the state that it should undertake the positive factual act ϕ_f.

(10) x has a right as against the state that it should undertake the positive normative act ϕ_n.[80]

We can now draw up a table of rights to something as against the state (s) (see page 128):

1.2 On the Logic of Rights to Something

We have hitherto been concerned with distinguishing rights to something in accordance with their subject-matter. It is just as important for the doctrine of constitutional rights to determine the relationship between the concept of a right and the concepts of duty and liberty. A consideration of basic elements of deontic logic is therefore in order.

---

[77] BVerfGE 39, 1 (41). While the more recent abortion decision shows a noticeable tendency to subjectify the position of the foetus (BVerfGE 88, 203 (225)) the correct interpretation of the judgment in this respect is still uncertain.

[78] BVerfGE 35, 79 (116).

[79] See on this below at 294 ff.

[80] If one takes $\phi_f s$ to stand for 'the state undertakes positive factual act ϕ_f' and $\phi_n s$ for 'the state undertakes positive normative act ϕ_n', then the structure of these statements can be represented in the following way:

(9') $Rxs\ (\phi_f s)$;
(10') $Rxs\ (\phi_n s)$.

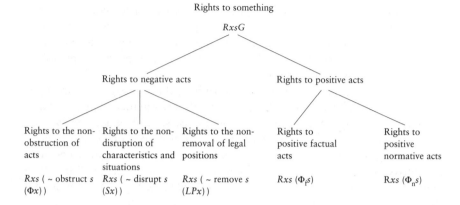

Rights to something

$RxsG$

Rights to negative acts   Rights to positive acts

Rights to the non-obstruction of acts	Rights to the non-disruption of characteristics and situations	Rights to the non-removal of legal positions	Rights to positive factual acts	Rights to positive normative acts
Rxs ($\sim$ obstruct s (Φx))	Rxs ($\sim$ disrupt s (Sx))	Rxs ($\sim$ remove s (LPx))	Rxs ($\Phi_f s$)	Rxs ($\Phi_n s$)

1.2.1 The Basic Deontic Modes

Deontic logic[81] is the logic of deontic concepts and statements.[82] The basic deontic concepts are those of the command, the prohibition, and the permission. Deontic statements are statements constructed with the help of these concepts. Examples are:

(1) x is commanded to express his opinion.
(2) x is prohibited from expressing his opinion.
(3) x is permitted to express his opinion.

The counterpart of a deontic statement is an expressive statement. If one considers these in the form:

(4) x expresses his opinion.

then a structural comparison is difficult. But if that statement is put in the form

(5)   It is the case that x expresses his opinion.

---

[81] Instead of the now current expression, 'deontic logic', which derives from the Greek '*to deon*' ('that which ought to be', one could use the expressions, 'the logic of ought', or 'normative logic'. The term 'deontic' was first used by Mally (E. Mally, 'Grundgesetze des Sollens: Elemente der Logic des Willens' (Graz, 1926), reprinted in E. Mally, *Logische Schriften* (Dordrecht, 1971), 227–324, 232). On the history of deontic logic, see G. Kalinowski, *Einführung in die Normenlogik* (Frankfurt a. M., 1973), 15 ff.

[82] One of the most important stimuli in the establishment of deontic logic as a special discipline within logic was the 1951 article by G. H. v. Wright, 'Deontic Logic', (Mind 60 (1951), 1–15, reprinted in id., *Logical Studies* (London, 1977), 58–74). Further important work at this time was carried out by O. Becker, *Untersuchungen über den Modalkalkül* (Meisenheim and Glan, 1952), G. Kalinowski, 'Théorie des propositions normatives', in *Studia Logica*, 1 (1953), 147–82 and O. Weinberger, 'Úvahy o logice normativních vět', in *Filosofický časopsis*, ČSAV 4 (1956), 918–26. Worth mentioning among their older predecessors are above all Leibniz (G. W. Leibniz, 'Elementa Juris Naturalis' (1671), manuscript draft B (Hanover), manuscript final version C (Hanover) reprinted in id., *Sämtliche Schriften und Briefe*, ed. Prussian Academy of Science, series 6, vol. 1 (Darmstadt, 1930), 465 ff, 480 ff.) and Bentham (*An Introduction to the Principles of Morals and Legislation* (1789), 299 f.; id., *Of Laws in General*, 15). On the more recent discussion, see R. Hilpinen (ed.), *Deontic Logic: Introductory and Systematic Readings* (Dordrecht, 1971); H. Lenk (ed.), *Normenlogik* (Pullach, 1974); R. Stuhlmann-Laeisz, *Das Sein-Sollen-Problem* (Stuttgart and Bad Cannstatt, 1983), 54 ff.

it becomes apparent that deontic and expressive statements have the same descriptive content (. . . that x expresses his opinion) but that they differ in their mode.[83] The same descriptive content, Wittgenstein calls them 'proposition-radicals',[84] Hare 'phrastics',[85] appears in (5) in descriptive mode and in (1) to (3) in various deontic modes. Deontic concepts are thus to be understood as *deontic modes*.[86] If one symbolizes the radical by 'p' and the deontic modes by the *deontic operators* O (commanding operator), F (prohibiting operator), and P (permitting operator), then one can represent the statements (1) to (3) as:

(6) Op

(7) Fp

(8) $Pp.$[87]

The three deontic operators can be defined in relationship to each other. That one is commanded to express one's opinion (Op) means that one is not permitted not to express one's opinion. That last idea can be expressed with the help of the negation sign '~'[88] as '$\sim P \sim p$'. Thus it is the case that,

(9) $Op =_{df} \sim P \sim p.$

Command and permission can thus be defined in each other's terms. The same applies to the relationship between permission and prohibition. That one is forbidden to express one's opinion means that it is not permitted to do it:

(10) $Fp =_{df} \sim Pp.$

The mutual definability of the basic deontic concepts makes it clear that they are not all necessary. One of them—any one of them—would suffice.

As far as the theory of constitutional rights is concerned, the permission is of particular interest. If one follows the definitions above, which themselves follow the standard system of deontic logic,[89] a permission is the negation of a prohibition:

---

[83] See on this E. Stenius, *Wittgensteins Traktat* (Frankfurt a. M., 1969), 206 ff.

[84] L. Wittgenstein, *Philosophical Investigations*, trans. G. E. M. Anscombe, 2nd edn. (Oxford, 1958), 11.

[85] R. M. Hare, 'Meaning and Speech Acts', in id., *Practical Inferences* (London and Basingstoke, 1971), 90; see on this Alexy, *A Theory of Legal Argumentation*, 62 ff. A. Ross, *Directives and Norms* (London, 1968), 9 ff., 34 ff., uses the term, 'topic'.

[86] On the structural parallels between the deontic modes and those of general modal logic (necessity/impossibility/possibility), see G. H. v. Wright, *An Essay in Deontic Logic and the General Theory of Action* (Amsterdam, 1968), 13 f., as well as, foundationally, G. W. Leibniz, 'Elementa Juris Naturalis', 466: 'omnes ergo Modalium complicationes et transpositiones et oppositiones, ab Aristotele aliisque in Logicis demonstratae ad haec nostra Iuris Modalia non inutiliter transferri possunt'.

[87] 'Op' is not infrequently interpreted as the combination of a deontic operator and a proposition (p); see e.g. M. Herberger and D. Simon, *Wissenschaftstheorie für Juristen* (Frankfurt a. M., 1980), 183. Here, 'p' stands for the proposition-radical.

[88] On negation, see W. V. O. Quine, *Methods of Logic*, 2nd edn. (London, 1962), 1 f.

[89] See on this the account by D. Føllesdal and R. Hilpinen, 'Deontic Logic: An Introduction', in Hilpinen (ed.), *Deontic Logic: Introductory and Systematic Readings*, 13 ff.

(11) $Pp =_{df} \sim Fp$.

That one is permitted to express one's opinion means that one is not forbidden from doing so. This understanding of permission is relatively weak. What is permitted in the sense of not forbidden can be commanded. Someone who takes the view that one has a duty to exercise one's rights is gesturing towards a similar combination of permission and command. What this concept of permission does not include is the idea of an absence of command as well as prohibition. The construction of this position can be represented in the so-called deontic quadrate:

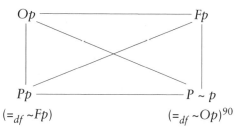

Permission appears twice in this, once as the negation of a prohibition (Pp) and once as the negation of a command ($P\sim p$). 'Pp' can be understood as the permission to do something and '$P\sim p$' as the permission not to do something. The former can be called a positive permission, the latter a negative permission. The conjunction of positive and negative permission creates a combined position of 'liberty' and can be symbolized by 'Lp'.[91] By using the conjunctive sign '$\wedge$' for 'and',[92] we can create the following definition:

(12) $Lp =_{df} Pp \wedge P\sim p$.

The complete liberty plays an important part in discussions about freedom. What has so far been established in connection with basic deontic concepts can be represented in the following scheme:

---

[90] Between the deontic statements of this scheme, the following relations obtain: Op and Fp are *contraries*. They are logically incompatible, but one does not follow from the negation of the other. Op and $P\sim p$ as well as Fp and Pp are *contradictories*, that is the one follows from the negation of the other. Op and Pp as well as Fp and $P\sim p$ are *subalternates*, that is, the second follows from the first in each case. Pp and $P\sim p$ are *subcontrary*, that is, Pp and $P\sim p$ are logically compatible. On the corresponding relationships within the quadrate of predicatory logic, see G. Frege, *Conceptual Notation*, trans. T. W. Bynum (Oxford, 1972), 135.

[91] Adomeit uses the expression 'liberation' for the negative permission expressed by '$P\sim p$' (K. Adomeit, *Rechtstheorie für Studenten*, 2nd edn. (Heidelberg and Hamburg, 1981), 42 f.). Herberger and Simon use the expression in the same way as here, although they use the sign 'l' (M. Herberger and D. Simon, *Wissenschaftsthoerie für Juristen* (Frankfurt a. M., 1980), 184 f.).

[92] On the conjunction, see Quine, *Methods of Logic*, 2.

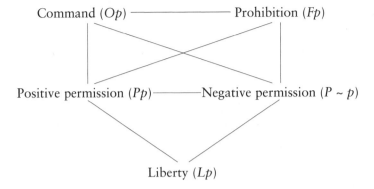

Command (Op) ———————— Prohibition (Fp)

Positive permission (Pp) ———— Negative permission $(P \sim p)$

Liberty (Lp)

1.2.2 *Rights to Something as Legal Relations*

In order to analyse the concept of a right to something and its relationship to other concepts on the basis of the deontic modes, a fundamental modification is necessary within the theory of subjective rights: its *relational character* has to be accounted for.

It has been established that a right to something is a three-point relation between a right-holder (x), an addressee (y) and a subject-matter (G). The key to analysing the correspondence of right and duty is that the three-point relationship of right is logically equivalent[93] to a three-point relationship of duty or command. From:

(1) x has a right as against y that y help him

there follows:

(2) y is obligated to x to help him

and vice versa.

Statement (2) expresses a *relational obligation*. By contrast, a non-relational obligation is expressed by:

(3) y is obligated to help x.

The existence of this duty does not mean that x has a right to help from y. It could be that nobody, or that some third party, has the right. One can express the non-relational obligation by

(4) OG[94]

---

[93] On the concept of logical equivalence, see R. Carnap, *Meaning and Necessity*, 2nd edn. (Chicago and London, 1956), 11.

[94] 'G' thus stands for the proposition-radical, 'that y help x'. (4) expresses y's obligation in a non-person-related way. A person-related way is created if one writes,

(4') OyG

'O' in (4') is a two-point operator referring to the relation between a legal subject and an act, but not to the relation between two different legal subjects. It should therefore only be called 'personal' and not 'relational'. The use of personal operators is redundant in the case of commands to act, if the subject of the act is the subject of the obligation.

By contrast, the relational obligation expressed in (2) has this form:

(5) $OyxG$

'O' in this formula is a *three-point operator* expressing a *relational* deontic mode.[95] That

(6) $RxyG$

is equivalent to (5) expresses the idea that statements about rights to something and statements of relational obligation are the same thing, one described from x's perspective, one from y's.

Statements of non-relational obligations such as (4) are statements that *do without* a relational aspect. They are not to be confused with statements about obligations to everybody. The latter do not lack a relational aspect; they contain it in its strongest form. One can call the obligations they express 'absolute relational obligations'.

The modern debate about legal relations was significantly promoted and influenced by the work of W. N. Hohfeld in a two-part piece appearing in 1913 and 1917, '(Some) Fundamental Legal Conceptions as Applied in Judicial Reasoning'.[96][97] According to Hohfeld there are eight 'strictly legal relations . . . sui generis'.[98] He called these 'right', 'duty', 'no-right', 'privilege', 'power', 'liability', 'disability', and 'immunity'. The first four concern the field of rights to something, the last four the field of powers. At this point we are only concerned with the first four.

---

[95] On the concept and logic of relational modes, see R. Hilpinen, 'An Analysis of Relativised Modalities', in J. W. Davis, D. J. Hockney, and W. K. Wilson (eds.), *Philosophical Logic*, (Dordrecht, 1969), 181 ff.

[96] W. N. Hohfeld, 'Some Fundamental Legal Conceptions as Applied in Judicial Reasoning', Yale LJ 23 (1913/14), 16 ff.; id., 'Fundamental Legal Conceptions as Applied in Judicial Reasoning', Yale LJ 26 (1916/17), 710 ff.; reprinted in id., *Fundamental Legal Conceptions as Applied in Judicial Reasoning and Other Legal Essays* (New Haven, 1923), 23 ff., 65 ff. Many of Hohfeld's insights were foreshadowed in the work of Bentham, in particular in his work *Of Laws in General*, which he completed in 1782 (see H. L. A. Hart, 'Bentham's "Of Laws in General" ', in *Rechtstheorie*, 2 (1971), 57). However this work was first published in 1945 under the title, 'The Limits of Jurisprudence Defined' (ed. C. W. Everett, New York, 1945). In one important respect Bentham is more advanced than Hohfeld: he bases his analysis on a system of deontic logic, which in many respects can be seen as a precursor to modern systems (see Hart, 'Bentham's "Of Laws in General" ', 60 ff.; Lindahl, *Position and Change*, 4 ff.). Nevertheless, the choice of Hohfeld's analysis as a starting-point is justified not simply by the fact that his work has been able to have far greater influence on the discussion to this point, but also because his work surpasses Bentham's in simplicity and clarity, and that while it does not explicitly use the standard system of deontic logic, it implicitly presupposes it, which makes it an ideal basis for further investigation.

[97] From the extensive literature on Hohfeld, see A. L. Corbin, 'Legal Analysis and Terminology', Yale LJ 29 (1919), 163 ff.; M. Moritz, *Über Hohfelds System der juridischen Grundbegriffe* (Lund and Copenhagen 1960); A. Ross, *On Law and Justice* (London, 1958), 161 ff.; id., *Directives and Norms*, 118 ff.; D. J. Hislop, 'The Hohfeldian System of Fundamental Legal Conceptions', ARSP 53 (1967), 53 ff.; J. Stone, *Legal System and Lawyers' Reasonings* (London, 1964), 136 ff.; J. Schmidt, *Aktionsberechtigung und Vermögensberechtigung* (Cologne, Berlin, Bonn, and Munich, 1969), 32 ff.

[98] Hohfeld, 'Some Fundamental Legal Conceptions', 36.

The expressions 'right', 'duty', 'no-right', and 'privilege' stand in Hohfeld's system for legal relations between two legal subjects. Here we are going to take rights as three-point relations between a right-holder, an addressee, and a subject-matter. But this does not make Hohfeld's scheme inapplicable, because instead of the relation

(7) . . . has as against . . . a right to . . .

which corresponds to a rights-statement of the form

(8) $RxyG$

one can always consider the relation

(9) . . . has a right to G as against . . .

which corresponds to the rights-statement of the form

(10) $R_G xy$

and vice versa.

The heart of Hohfeld's theory is his thesis about the logical connections between jural relations. Hohfeld's theory can be seen as a theory about the logical relations of legal relations. The logical relations in the field of rights to something can be represented according to Hohfeld by the following scheme:

I.

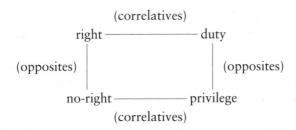

For purposes of clarification, an example has been inserted into the scheme as follows (shown on page 134):

The logical connections between these four positions are easy to spot. The no-right is a *negation* of a right, and the privilege is a *negation* of a duty.[99] Hohfeld terms these relations 'jural *opposites*'.

---

[99] ibid. 39: 'a given privilege is the mere negation of a duty'. It is significant that at times Hohfeld speaks of 'non-duty' instead of 'privilege' (ibid. 48, fn. 59). There is controversy over whether privilege and no-right are relations at all, since they are concerned with something negative. The point is denied among others by A. Kokourek, 'Non-legal-content Relations', Ill LQ 4 (1922), 234; id., *Jural Relations*, 2nd edn. (Indianapolis, 1928), 91 ff.; and Moritz, *Über Hohfelds System der juridischen Grundbegriffe*, 84. That they are relations is accepted by G. W. Goble, 'Affirmative and Negative Legal Relations', Ill LQ 4 (1922), 94 ff.; id., 'Negative Legal Relations Re-examined', Ill LQ 5 (1922), 37 f. It can be that x is permitted by the state

I′.

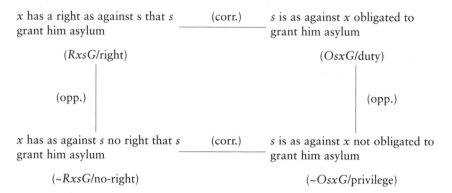

x has a right as against s that s grant him asylum	(corr.)	s is as against x obligated to grant him asylum
(*RxsG*/right)		(*OsxG*/duty)
(opp.)		(opp.)
x has as against s no right that s grant him asylum	(corr.)	s is as against x not obligated to grant him asylum
(~*RxsG*/no-right)		(~*OsxG*/privilege)

Similarly straightforward is the second type of relationship in Hohfeld's square between the jural correlatives, namely between right and duty, and between no-right and privilege. To explain this relation we can make use of the possibility mentioned above of treating rights as two-point relations. For '*RxyG*' there is 'R_Gxy' and for '*OyxG* there is 'O_Gyx'. [Note that in *RxyG*, G is a variable; by contrast in R_Gxy, G together with R makes up the complex two-point predicate R_G. The equivalent point can be made with respect to *OyxG* and O_Gyx.] It is easy to see that the correlativity of the relations R_G and O_G consists in none other than that O_G is the *converse* relation to R_G.[100] If x has a right as against y then y has a corresponding duty to x, and vice versa. The relation expressed by R_G is the converse of the relation expressed by O_G just as the teacher–pupil relationship is the converse of the pupil–teacher relationship. If x is the teacher of y then y is x's pupil, and vice versa. This corresponds to what Hohfeld says: 'if X has a right against Y that he shall stay off the former's land, the correlative (and equivalent) is that Y is under a duty toward X to stay off the place'.[101]

The most interesting part of Hohfeld's scheme is what he calls a 'privilege'. A privilege is, to use Hohfeld's own words, 'the mere negation of a duty', which was expressed above as '~*OyxG*'. In discussing the basic deon-

---

to carry out some act φ, but is forbidden to do so in relation to some third party. In this situation it is appropriate to speak of two legal relations in which x stands, and of which one— the one with the state—is the complement, or the negation, of the relation of duty. This, together with the fact that there are no disadvantages associated with accepting such relations, justify us in treating the result of a negation of a relation as a relation, which furthermore corresponds to the general logic of relations, according to which 'the negation (or complement) of a relation R (R′) . . . [is] the relation which exists between x and y when xRy does not apply' (G. Patzig, 'Artikel: Relation', in H. Krings, H. M. Baumgartner, and C. Wild (eds.), *Handbuch philosophischer Grundbegriffe*, iv (Munich, 1973), 1229).

[100] On the concept of the converse, see Patzig, 'Artikel: Relation', 1229; A. Tarski, *Einführung in die mathematische Logik*, 2nd edn. (Göttingen, 1966), 102.
[101] Hohfeld, 'Some Fundamental Legal Conceptions' 38.

tic modes, it became clear that the negation of a command to do something is equivalent to the *permission* not to do it, that is, that

(11) $\sim\!Op \leftrightarrow P\!\sim\!p.$[102]

This rule can be applied to three-point operators

(12) $\sim\!OxyG \leftrightarrow Pxy\!\sim\!G.$[103]

An example is:

(13)   Precisely when x is not obligated by the state to join an association, is x permitted as against the state not to join an association.

So Hohfeld's scheme can be represented in the following way:

II.

$$
\begin{array}{ccc}
RxyG & \leftrightarrow & OyxG \\[1ex]
\sim & & \sim \\[1ex]
\sim\!RxyG & \leftrightarrow & Pyx\!\sim\!G
\end{array}
$$

---

[102] Hohfeld's privilege is thus none other than a permission. As a term for a bare permission, the word 'privilege' is confusing. See on this G. Williams, 'The Concept of Legal Liberty', in R. S. Summers (ed.), *Essays in Legal Philosophy* (Oxford, 1968), 124 f.

[103] Anderson has objected to the Hohfeldian equivalence of the negation of duty with privilege on the grounds that while the latter presupposes the former, the former does not presuppose the latter. As an example, he points out that just because x is under no duty to see to it that y's lawn is not mowed, it does not follow that x is permitted to mow y's lawn (A. R. Anderson, 'Logic, Norms and Roles', *Ratio*, 4 (1962), 44 f., 48). It is true that the permission proposed in the example does not follow from the preceding statement about the negation of a duty. This lies in the fact that the objects of the duty and the permission are quite different. To demonstrate this, let the clause, 'see to it that' be replaced by the act-operator '*Do*' (see on this Lindahl, *Position and Change*, 65 ff.). Let 'p' stand for the object of *this* operator. The first statement thus has the form $\sim\!OxDo\!\sim\!p$, the second, the form $PxDop$. $\sim\!OxDo\!\sim\!p$ is, as Anderson also accepts, equivalent to $Px\!\sim\!Do\!\sim\!p$. $PxDop$ would follow from $Px\!\sim\!Do\!\sim\!p$, if $\sim\!Do\!\sim\!p$ and Dop were the same. The fact that $\sim\!Do\!\sim\!p$ and Dop are not the same can easily be seen from the fact that one cannot not see to it that one's friend does not drink at the same time as seeing to it that he drinks. One can do the former by doing nothing. This makes it clear that the problem raised by Anderson is a problem of the logic of action. So long as one takes care that the objects of rights, duties, and permissions are only negated in their entirety (externally) in the transformations of Hohfeld's scheme, and that no negations are introduced into the act-descriptions (internal negation), then the transformations do not give rise to any difficulty. If x is not commanded to see to it that y's lawn is not mowed, then x is permitted not to see to it that y's lawn is not mowed, and if x is not commanded to see to it that y's lawn is mowed, then x is permitted not to see to it that y's lawn is mowed. This solution avoids Anderson's problem, but it does show that the logic of Hohfeld's scheme does not grasp the structure of legal objects except by way of very crude external negation. However, since a logic of action which makes this grasp possible is not necessary here, the limitation can be accepted. In addition, doing without it is a small price to pay, because introducing the logic of action would only refine, not alter, the model. For such refined models, see Kanger and Kanger, 'Rights and Parliamentarism', 87 ff.; Lindahl, *Position and Change*, 66 ff.

When one puts it like this, a distinctive disordering becomes apparent. This is not so much that a new sign appears, the three-point permissive operator, but rather that the subject-matter of the permission appears in negated form (~G).[104] This indicates a basic incompleteness about the scheme. It is not only an omission that may be permitted, but also an act. A corresponding incompleteness can also be identified in each of the other three relations in Hohfeld's scheme. Removing this incompleteness does not destroy Hohfeld's scheme; rather, it leads to the following double scheme, which demonstrates the fruitfulness of Hohfeld's approach.[105] The act or omission in this scheme is always an act or omission on the part of *y*.

III.

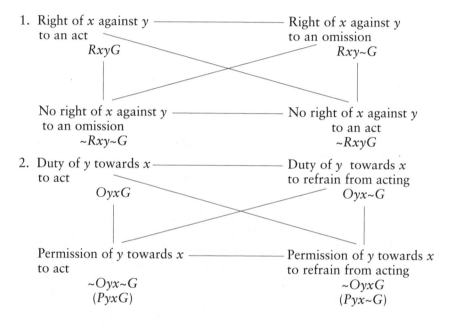

The relationships *within* each half-scheme correspond to the relationships in the deontic logic quadrate above,[106] the relationship *between* the two half-schemes is that the position in one is equivalent to the corresponding

[104] This matches precisely Hohfeld's explanation of his point 'that a given privilege is a mere negation of a duty'. '[W]hat is meant, of course, is a duty having a content or tenor precisely *opposite* to that of the privilege in question' (Hohfeld, 'Some Fundamental Legal Conceptions', 39).
[105] See on this F. B. Fitch, 'A Revision of Hohfeld's Theory of Legal Concepts', *Logique et Analyse*, 10 (1967), 270 ff.
[106] See above at 130.

position in the other, because it relates to the converse relation.[107] The two half-schemes can thus be called each other's converse.[108]

The double scheme can be seen as an elaboration of the concept of a right to something into an elementary, but for practical purposes, adequately complex logical system.[109] Like all analytical insights, the lessons to be drawn from it, such as that the negation of a right of x as

[107] Hohfeld expresses the view that his relations are 'strictly fundamental legal relations . . . sui generis' ('Some Fundamental Legal Conception', 36). As the scheme shows, this cannot mean that they are mutually indefinable.

[108] And so the correctness of the reduction thesis, which asserts that one can make do with just *one* deontic mode (see Ross, *Directives and Norms*, 117 f.) has been made out as regards rights to something. Since all positions in the rights half-scheme are equivalent to positions in the duty half-scheme, and since all positions in the duty half-scheme can be expressed by way of the three-point commanding operator, all statements about rights to something can be transformed into statements about relational obligations formulated by way of the three-point deontic commanding operator. Admittedly, this only shows the possibility of a reduction to the three-point operator. The question is how this relates to the one-point operator of the standard system. This depends on the interpretation of statements containing one-point operators. A weak and a strong interpretation are possible. According to the weak interpretation, to focus solely on the two most important statements, OG and PG are simply abstractions from $OxyG$ and $PxyG$ in respect of their relational aspect. On this interpretation, it can be said that OG is implied by $OxyG$ and PG by $PxyG$. According to the strong interpretation, OG and PG say that G, for example, x's φ-ing, is commanded or permitted as the case may be by the legal system as a whole. On this interpretation, $OxyG$ implies OG, but $PxyG$ does not imply PG. If x is legally obligated to y to φ ($OxyG$), then it is required in the relevant legal system that x φ. But if it is not required in the relevant legal system that x φ, then nor can x be obligated to do this as against y. It is no objection to the implication of OG from $OxyG$ that there may be mutually incompatible relational obligations. If x is obligated to y to φ at the same time as being obligated to z to ~φ, which means that both $OxyG$ and Oxz~G apply, then it can be accepted that both OG and O~G apply on the strong interpretation, and that the legal system as a whole contains an inconsistency. If the inconsistency between the relational obligations is resolved, so also is that between the non-relational ones. Matters are not so straightforward in the case of the relationship between the relational permission ($PxyG$) and the non-relational permission (PG). That x is permitted as against y to φ does not mean that the legal system as a whole permits x to φ. The legal system as a whole prohibits x from φ-ing, if x is obligated to z not to φ (Oxz~G). Someone who breaches a prohibition in one relation breaks the law. Someone who makes use of a permission in one relation need not be doing something permitted by the legal system as a whole. If there is at least one legal subject against whom x is legally obligated to φ, then the legal system as a whole contains a requirement that x φ (OG). By contrast, x is only permitted to φ by the legal system as a whole (PG), if x is permitted to do this in all relations.

The connections between relational and non-relational deontic modalities are thus complex. All the same, it is clear that relational modes cannot be replaced by non-relational ones, and in this sense reduced to them. However, everything that can be said by way of non-relational modes can be said by way of relational ones. This makes the correctness of the reduction thesis plain. Reduction to one deontic mode is possible, but this mode needs internal differentiation (relating), which differentiation none the less requires no additional normative concepts. As far as rights to something are concerned this shows that there is what can be called a 'unity of the Ought'.

[109] Significantly more complex structures can be arrived at by further analysing the object of a right, rather than simply referring to 'G'. This is the route taken by Kanger and Kanger and Lindahl, who base their analyses not simply on the logic of deontic modes, but on a combination of this with the logic of action (see Kanger and Kanger, 'Rights and Parliamentarism', 87 ff.; Lindahl, *Position and Change*, 66 ff.; the simple model presented here will suffice for present purposes.

against *y* to an omission on *y*'s part is equivalent to a permission for *y* as against *x* to carry out some act, do not lead to decisions in hard cases. For this, the appeal to values and empirical knowledge is generally unavoidable. But it constitutes the necessary basis of a rational, maximally clear, legal argument. This is particularly true for the second group of basic legal positions, the liberties. A significant part of the discussion has already been established by our consideration of Hohfeld's concept of a privilege, which is itself derived from the idea of permission.

2. LIBERTIES

2.1 On the Concept of Liberty

The concept of liberty is simultaneously one of the most fundamental of practical concepts and one of the most obscure. Its applications seem almost unlimited. Almost everything that from some perspective can be considered good or desirable has been associated with it.[110] This is as true for philosophical dispute as it is for political polemic. Aldous Huxley expressed the point trenchantly in his *Eyeless in Gaza*: 'Freedom's a marvellous name. That's why you're so anxious to make use of it. You think that if you call imprisonment true freedom, people will be attracted to the prison. And the worst of it is, you're quite right.'[111] The *emotive connotations* of the word could hardly be characterized more pointedly. Someone who describes something as 'free' is not in general merely describing it, but is expressing a positive evaluation and stimulating his audience to share this evaluation.[112] This relatively constant positive emotive connotation can be combined with various descriptive components. This opens up the possibility of persuasive definition.[113] If someone wants to persuade another to perform some act, they can try to do it by suggesting that freedom consists in the doing of it. This may well be one reason why debate about the concept of liberty is so interminable and its usage so arbitrary.

A discussion of everything that has and will be associated with the expression 'liberty' would expand into an all-embracing legal, social, and moral philosophy. Here we are concerned with basic legal positions. In connection with this, one particular concept of liberty stands out, the idea of *legal liberty*. The concept of legal liberty can be discussed in two ways. One could see it as a particular expression of a more general concept of

---

[110] I. Berlin, 'Two Concepts of Liberty', in id., *Four Essays on Liberty* (Oxford, 1969), 121, speaks of 'more than two hundred senses of this protean word recorded by historians of ideas'.

[111] A. Huxley, *Eyeless in Gaza* (London, 1955), 123.

[112] See C. L. Stevenson, *Ethics and Language* (New Haven and London, 1944), 20 ff., 206 ff.

[113] id., 'Persuasive Definitions', *Mind*, 47 (1938), 331 ff. See, already, T. Hobbes, *Leviathan* (Oxford, 1960), 140: 'it is an easy thing, for men to be deceived, by the specious name of liberty'.

liberty, but one could also derive it directly from its constituent basis, the idea of legal permission.

The first route can only be taken by asking what liberty *in and of itself* really is—which as suggested would expand into a demanding project in the philosophy of liberty—but it can also be taken by considering the logical *structure* of the concept of liberty. This is less demanding, the chance of a successful answer is greater, and it will form the foundation for answering more extensive questions. The question of the structure of liberty can be given a negative answer to start with. Liberty is not an object in the same way as a hat is. Of course, one can speak of the liberty that someone *has*, in the same way as one can speak of the hat they have. But having in the case of liberty does not consist of a relation of possession between a person and an object. It would therefore seem appropriate to think of liberty as a quality which can be associated with persons, objects, and societies. But this is too crude and superficial. Someone who says that somebody else is free is saying that certain obstacles, limitations, and resistance do not exist for that person.[114] So liberty could be conceived as a two-point relation between a person and an obstacle to liberty. Even this is not yet adequate. Assume that state *s* wants to prevent *x* from visiting *y* abroad. *s* could do this by prohibiting the visit; but it could also do this by refusing a passport, refusing to permit the sale of aircraft tickets, threatening to terminate employment if the visit goes ahead, or by requiring participation in a military exercise. In all these cases the loss of liberty varies considerably. A statement of the form, '*x* is not free to visit *y*' does not comprehend all the distinctions. Even statements such as '*x* is not free to buy an aircraft ticket' do not fully describe the situation. A complete description must contain reference to three elements: the person lacking liberty, the obstacle to their liberty, and that which the obstacle makes difficult or impossible. This indicates that we should think of an *individual* liberty of a person as a three-point relation,[115] the *liberty of a person* as the sum of their individual liberties, and the *liberty of a society* as the sum of the liberties of its members.

This understanding is heavily dependent on persons as holders of liberties. But other things can also be described as 'free', such as acts or the will. This does not represent a serious objection to the personalized conception of liberty, since statements about the liberty of acts and wills can easily be derived from statements about the liberty of persons. Freedom of action

---

[114] The absence of obstacles, limitations, and resistance makes up the core of the concept of liberty; see the classic formulation of Hobbes, *Leviathan*, 136: 'Liberty, or Freedom, signifieth, properly, the absence of opposition'. The question is what is to be identified as opposition, and what the opposition relates to.

[115] See on this G. C. MacCallum, 'Negative and Positive Freedom', *Philosophical Review*, 76 (1967), 314 ff., and following him, J. Rawls, *A Theory of Justice* (Cambridge, Mass., 1971), 201 ff.

and freedom of the will are abstractions from the freedom of the individual person.[116] The basis of the concept of liberty is thus a three-point relation between a liberty-holder, a liberty-obstacle, and a liberty-object.

If one takes this as a starting-point, there is an important division depending on whether the object of liberty is a *choice of actions* or simply an *act*. In the case of a single act (however abstract that might be), the one for whose benefit the liberty exists will want to do what is necessary or rational. Examples of such concepts of *positive* liberty are the philosophical definitions of Spinoza, 'that thing is called free which exists from the necessity of its nature alone, and is determined to act by itself alone',[117] Kant, 'the positive concept of freedom is that of the capacity of pure reason to be of itself practical. But this is not possible except by the subjection of the maxim of every action to the condition of its qualifying as universal law',[118] and Hegel: 'the rational, as the substance of things, is necessary, and we are free in so far as we recognise it as law and follow it as the substance of our own being'.[119] Even concepts of liberty tied to a single act[120] include the idea of an obstacle to liberty. These obstacles could be unclear thoughts, affections, sensual desires, or false consciousness. So positive liberty can also be represented as a three-point relation.[121]

---

[116] Hobbes, *Leviathan*, 137; MacCallum, 'Negative and Positive Freedom', 315 f.

[117] B. de Spinoza, 'Ethics', in *Collected Works*, trans. and ed. E. Curley (Princeton, 1985), 409 (I, def. 7).

[118] Kant, *The Metaphysics of Morals*, 42 f.

[119] G. W. F. Hegel, *Lectures on the Philosophy of History*, trans. H. B. Nisbet (Cambridge, 1975), 97.

[120] In the context of constitutional rights, a concept of positive liberty which relates to correct action, and not to a choice of actions performable at will, has been maintained for example by W. Hamel, *Die Bedeutung der Grundrechte im sozialen Rechtsstaat* (Berlin, 1957), 8: 'Liberty consists—generally speaking—in recognising the will of the Creator, and is thus the constitutive ground of existence for human beings in all areas of life', and H. Krüger, 'Der Wesensgehalt der Grundrechte', in J. Seifert and H. Krüger, *Die Einschränkung der Grundrechte* (Hanover, 1976), 53: 'It is obvious that a liberty which has no purpose, in particular no shared purpose, ceases to be liberty, at any rate if by this concept one means something—and any other meaning is barely conceivable—valuable and not valueless'.

[121] In the case of the positive conception of liberty there is a special relationship between the obstacle to liberty and the object of liberty, which is the necessary, or rational, in short, the correct, act. If the obstruction is removed, there is no other possibility than that of undertaking the correct act; it has become necessary. This relationship can be extended to the liberty-holder. If the liberty-holder is freed from the obstacle to liberty and is in this sense a free or rational person, then he will necessarily undertake the correct act. Together with the further point that a person freed from obstacles to liberty is autonomous, in charge of himself, it follows that an autonomous person does exactly one thing, namely what is correct. Berlin has pointed out that when this conception is made the basis of a political theory, then it can have despotic consequences (Berlin, 'Two Concepts of Liberty', pp. xxxvii, 131 f.; see also C. Link, *Herrschaftsordnung und bürgerliche Freiheit* (Vienna, Cologne, and Graz, 1979), 155). Political force can be represented as the removal of obstacles to liberty and thus as liberation to do what the individual would do were he rational, in short, as liberation. Admittedly, this is no logical consequence of the positive conception of liberty, but the result of an undifferentiated transfer into the field of law and politics. The Kantian philosophy of law shows that such a transfer is not necessary. See further C. B. Macpherson, 'Berlins Teilung der Freiheit',

Here we are concerned with legal liberty. As will shortly be explained, the object of a legal liberty has to be a choice of actions. When the object of liberty is a choice of actions, one can speak of '*negative* liberty'. A person is free in the negative sense to the extent that their choice of actions is not limited. What the negatively free person ought to do or will do is not a concern of negative liberty, which is only concerned with the *possibilities* of doing something.[122] The broader concept of liberty, of which legal liberty is a particular expression, is thus a three-point relation whose third element is a *choice of actions*. On this basis, a statement about liberty has the following form:

(1)   *x* is free (or not free) from *y*, to do or not to do *z*,[123]

or it can be restated in this form:[124] '*x*' stands for the liberty-holder, '*y*' for the obstacle to liberty, and '*z*' for the act doing or not doing which is the object of the liberty.

According to what has been said, the only difference between positive and negative liberty lies in their object. In the case of positive liberty, the object is a single act, whereas in the case of negative liberty it is a choice of actions. These concepts of positive and negative liberty do not correspond in every respect with normal usage. The concept of negative liberty is broader than usual, while the concept of positive liberty is narrower. The example of foreign travel used above makes this clear. The object of liberty is the choice of actions: to travel abroad or not. From the great variety of obstacles that could be put in *x*'s way, only two are of interest. The journey could be legally prohibited, but he might also not be able to afford it. In the first situation there is a loss of legal liberty, in the second a loss of economic liberty. Both are treated here as expressions of negative liberty. By contrast, widespread ordinary usage would suggest that only legal liberty is negative liberty, and if economic liberty is a matter of liberty at all, then it is positive liberty. The common distinction is not without justification. In order for *x* to escape from his economic bondage to a situation of economic liberty, he must receive or acquire something. If the transformation from economic

in id., *Demokratietheorie* (Munich, 1977), 178 ff.; C. Taylor, 'What's Wrong with Negative Liberty?', in A. Ryan (ed.), *The Idea of Freedom: Essays in Honour of Isaiah Berlin* (Oxford, New York, Toronto, and Melbourne, 1979), 175 ff.

[122] See I. Berlin, *Four Essays on Liberty*, 'Introduction', p. xlii: 'The freedom of which I speak is opportunity for action, rather than action itself'.

[123] The relation underlying this statement is not to be confused with the three-point relation of von Freytag Löringhoff. According to him, the liberty relation has the following form: 'X is free from the lower obligation Y by the higher obligation Z' (B. v. Freytag Löringhoff, 'Die logische Struktur des Begriffs Freiheit', in J. Simon (ed.), *Freiheit* (Freiburg and Munich, 1977), 43). This version expresses the substantive assumption that 'one can only release oneself from obligations by accepting new ones, higher in the order of values' (ibid. 42). This assumption is not shared here. The liberty relation presupposed here is neutral not only as regards the question of 'whereby', but also as regards the question of 'for what purpose', which introduces an element of duty into the concept of liberty.

bondage to economic liberty is to be legally guaranteed by the state, he must be given a suitable entitlement as against the state, that is, a right to a *positive* act on the part of the state. By contrast, ensuring a situation of legal liberty only requires a *negative* act, or omission, on the part of the state. Securing legal liberty only requires defensive rights, not entitlements. It cannot be denied that this distinction is very important; the question is how the conceptual structure should respond to it. Both the broader conception of liberty outlined above and the common narrower one just given can claim the title of 'negative' on traditional grounds; in both cases the distinction between positive and negative liberty is of fundamental significance. It therefore seems appropriate to refer to '*negative liberty in the wide sense*' and '*negative liberty in the narrow sense*'. Negative liberty in the narrow sense is the liberal conception of liberty. A negative liberty in the narrow sense is always a negative liberty in the wide sense, but not the other way round.

A negative liberty in the narrow sense derives from the three-point relation of liberty when the object of liberty is a choice of actions and the obstacle to liberty is the act of another, above all the state. That different liberties derive from inserting different contents in x, y and z shows the fruitfulness of the three-point relation of liberty. On this basis it is possible to bring some order into the confusion of conceptions of liberty, because it becomes possible to create an extensive classification based on the different contents for the liberty-holder x, the obstacle y, and the object z. Just two examples: if one puts economic deprivation into y, then one gets a concept of liberty that we could call a 'socio-economic conception of liberty'.[125] This socio-economic conception is quite different from the liberal-economic

---

[124] On the restatement of statements about liberty in statements of this form, see G. C. MacCallum, 'Negative and Positive Freedom', 315 ff.

[125] There can be no doubt that a situation of economic want can obstruct x in respect of a choice of actions. But one can doubt whether this justifies us in describing x as 'unfree'. On this point, three comments: (1) Constitutional rights norms are supposed to secure liberty. If one calls the absence of situations of economic want 'freedom', then it seems to follow that constitutional rights norms should secure this as well, that is, they should be interpreted accordingly. Someone who wants to avoid the conclusion of this crudely sketched argument could maintain that one should not speak of freedom or unfreedom in situations of economic want. But this is in no way necessary. One can also avoid the problem by being more precise about exactly what sort of freedom it is that constitutional rights norms secure. (2) In numerous contexts, the concept of freedom is associated with a positive emotive connotation. Every attempt to establish the meaning of freedom therefore runs the risk of being suspected of persuasive definition, in an attempt to win assent without argument for a certain evaluation. But this does not exclude the possibility of a specifically non-evaluative use of the concept of liberty. If x does not have enough money to buy a bigger car, then x is in a certain respect economically unfree, but one does not have to deprecate the fact. If one describes x as regards the purchase of a car as 'economically unfree', refraining from any evaluation, one is using the expression purely analytically or classificatorily. Such a use is possible and suitable if a grasp of the structure of what is to be evaluated is to precede the evaluation. (3) The absence of certain situations of want is often not described as freedom but as the condition for the exercise or value of freedom (see I. Berlin, *Four Essays on Liberty*, pp. xlvi, liii f.; Rawls, *A Theory of Justice*, 204 f.; H. H. Klein, *Die Grundrechte im demokratischen Staat* (Stuttgart, Berlin,

conception which arises when one puts acts of others, in particular the state, into y and choices of economic action into z. If one puts obstacles to political debate in y and choices of political action in z, then one gets a democratic conception of negative liberty.[126] These examples should be sufficient to show that by putting different components into the three-point relation we could build up a table of all possible liberties. The usefulness of such a table in the conceptually confused area of liberty is beyond question. It is false to assume that such a table of conceptual clarification presupposes some evaluative judgment. On the contrary, different positions on the table of liberties can be positively and negatively evaluated. Some can be derived from constitutional rights norms, or the Basic Law as a whole, some not. Relationships of precedence can be established between different positions, and not least it becomes possible to analyse the logical and empirical connections between different positions on a conceptually secure basis.

In what follows we are only concerned with one position on the table, legal liberty. As an example, we can use the following liberty, which in the form of the relational statement is:

(2) x is free from legal prohibitions to express his opinion or not.

This statement is equivalent to

(3) x is legally permitted to express his opinion, and he is legally permitted not to express his opinion.

Statement (3) expresses the idea of legal liberty most simply and clearly. The reworking of (2) into (3) is possible because there is an analytical connection between the obstacle to liberty and the object of liberty. The legal prohibition is a prohibition of the object of liberty. In the case of non-legal liberties the matter is more complicated, because here there is only an empirical connection between the obstacle and the object. It is a distinctive feature of legal liberty that it is possible to analyse its structure directly on the basis of the idea of permission, rather than merely on the basis of the general three-point relation of liberty.

In connection with, and in distinction from, the concept of legal liberty,

---

Cologne, and Mainz, 1974), 50). These terms express a preference for a certain conception of liberty, namely liberty in the narrowly negative or liberal sense. Even someone who wants to maintain this preference can none the less say, when he wants to use the concept of liberty analytically rather than evaluatively, that economic liberty is the condition for the exercise or value of liberal liberty.

[126] As a sub-category of negative liberty, the democratic conception of liberty is a concept of *possibility*. This can be contrasted with a democratic conception of liberty as *actuality*. According to this, democratic liberty does not simply exist when there are no obstacles to political participation, but only when such participation actually takes place. Such an actualized conception of democratic liberty is a variant of the positive conception of liberty. An example of democratic liberty as actualized liberty can be found in U. Scheuner, 'Pressefreiheit', VVDStRL 22 (1965), 20: 'Liberty [is] . . . not simply defensiveness and flight into a state free sphere without responsibility, but lively participation in the whole, joint influence and joint responsibility'.

Constitutional Rights as Subjective Rights

one can identify a concept of *factual* liberty, which for legal analysis is particularly important as a counter-concept to legal liberty:

(4)   As regards a legally unrestricted choice of alternatives, *x* is factually free to the extent that he has the possibility in fact of doing or not doing what is permitted.

2.2 Legal Liberties

The connection between legal liberty and permission in the sense of an absence of command and prohibition has often been variously described. In Hobbes's words, 'In cases where the sovereign has prescribed no rule, there the subject hath the liberty to do, or forbear, according to his own discretion'.[127] Bentham put it, that as long as the legislator 'hath neither commanded nor prohibited any act ... all acts therefore are free: all persons as against the law are at liberty'.[128] In Jellinek, we can read, 'if one examines this liberty from its legal side, then we can see that it is identical with acts of the subject which for the state are *legally irrelevant*'.[129] On closer investigation, it will become apparent that in spite of these similarities, very different positions can be called legal liberty. In order to see this, we need to distinguish between *protected* and *unprotected* legal liberties.[130]

2.2.1 Unprotected Liberties
Unprotected liberties can be derived straightforwardly from permissions in the sense used above. What is permitted is an act or an omission. If legal liberty is a negative liberty in the sense explained above, then it cannot relate just to one or the other.[131] The permission to manifest one's faith, which can co-exist with the command to do so, constitutes on its own a legal liberty as little as the prohibition on doing this. A legal liberty to manifest one's faith only and always arises when it is permitted both to do it and not to do it.[132] The unprotected legal liberty, reducible entirely to permissions, can thus be defined as a conjunction of a legal permission to do something with a legal permission not to do that same thing. This conjunction was symbolized as 'Lp' above.[133] If one uses 'G' instead of 'p' to make the comparison with the right to something ($RxyG$) easier, and assuming that 'P' stands for a legal permission, the definition of the unprotected legal liberty takes the following form:

[127] Hobbes, *Leviathan*, 143.   [128] Bentham, *Of Laws in General*, 253.
[129] Jellinek, *System der subjektiven öffentlichen Rechte*, 104.
[130] Bentham distinguishes between 'naked' and 'vested' liberties (J. Bentham, in *The Works of Jeremy Bentham*, ed. J. Bowring, facsimile of the edition 1835–43, vol. iii, (New York, 1962), 218). This distinction comes close to the one used here between protected and unprotected liberties.
[131] Williams, 'The Concept of Legal Liberty', 132 f., uses a narrower concept of legal liberty, in which legal liberty is simply the negation of a prohibition and is thus compatible with a command.
[132] See BVerfGE 12, 1 (4).   [133] See 134 above.

(1) $LG =_{df} PG \wedge P{\sim}G$.

The negation of an unprotected liberty is the *non-liberty*. By using the disjunction sign '$\vee$' for 'or' it can be defined thus:

(2) ${\sim}LG =_{df} O{\sim}G \vee OG$.

A legal subject x is legally unfree as regards a certain act (${\sim}LG$), if the omitting of the act ($O{\sim}G$), or the performance of it (OG), is legally commanded.

2.2.1.1 Person/Object-Absolute and Person/Object-Relative Unprotected Liberties

'L' in (1) is a non-relational (one-point) operator. But liberties can be relational. x can be free as against the state to ϕ, but not as against a third party, and vice versa. In order to express the idea that one legal subject is in a position of unprotected liberty as against another legal subject, one has to use a three-point operator, just as with the right to something.

(3) $LxyG =_{df} PxyG \wedge Pxy{\sim}G$.

Statement (3) expresses an unprotected liberty as against only one legal subject such as the state or a private individual. A counterpart to this is the unprotected liberty as against all legal subjects. This liberty is a bundle of exactly as many relations of liberty as there are legal subjects in the legal system. It can be called a 'person-absolute unprotected liberty'.[134] By contrast, the person-relative unprotected liberty does not exist against everybody, but as against some or at least one legal subject(s).

The counterpart to person-absolute and person-relative liberty is object-absolute and object-relative liberty. x has an object-absolute liberty as against y if x is permitted as against y to do or refrain from doing everything; he has an object-relative liberty if he is permitted to do or refrain from doing at least one thing as against y. If every person is person-absolutely and object-absolutely free, the normative situation assumed by Hobbes in the state of nature obtains.[135]

2.2.1.2 Unprotected Liberty as the Mere Negation of Ought

The definition of unprotected liberty (LG) by the combination of a permission to do and a permission to refrain from doing ($PG \wedge P{\sim}G$) makes it clear that the unprotected liberty is a mere conjunction of positive and negative permission. These permissions are none other than the negations of corresponding commands (OG) and prohibitions ($O{\sim}G$). Instead of defining LG as '$PG \wedge P{\sim}G$', one could equally well write '${\sim}O{\sim}G \wedge {\sim}OG$'. This shows two things. First, it shows that the introduction of the concept of unprotected liberty does

---

[134] The person-absolute unprotected liberty can be symbolized with the aid of the universal quantifier '(y)' (for all y it is the case that . . .; see on this Quine, *Methods of Logic*, 83 ff.) as follows: $(y)LxyG$.

[135] Hobbes, *Leviathan*, 85.

not require a new category to the Ought in the sense of command. From a logical perspective, unprotected liberties are simply a certain combination of negations of Oughts. This is not to take any position on the question of whether within a norm system the idea of liberty is primary, which is then limited by the Ought, or whether the Ought is primary, which only creates liberty by the introduction of non-commands and non-prohibitions. The neutrality of the concept of unprotected liberty as against this question results from the fact that it makes no difference for the concept of negative liberty whether one sees liberty as the negation of Ought, or Ought as a negation of liberty. Secondly, the possibility of defining LG as '$\sim O{\sim}G \wedge \sim OG$' also shows that the unprotected liberty implies no right to be unhindered in the realization of this freedom.[136] Such a right is a right to something and is fundamentally different from a combination of permissions. Where such a right is added, the unprotected liberty turns into a protected one.

2.2.1.3 Constitutional Permissive Norms

An unprotected liberty exists when both an act and its omission are permitted. Characterizing an act as permitted can take place on two grounds. It can take place on the basis of an explicitly enacted permissive norm, but it can also be based on the absence within the legal system of any commanding or prohibiting norms covering the act, or its omission, in question.[137]

---

[136] See on this Hohfeld, 'Some Fundamental Legal Conceptions', 43, as well as Bierling, *Zur Kritik der juristischen Grundbegriffe*, part 2, 324: 'I would even go so far as to maintain that mere '*may*' or permissibility *never* correlates to a special, specific, corresponding *duty*, but rather that wherever this appears to be the case, there is never merely a permission but also at the same time a claim-right'.

[137] In this case the qualification is based on the maxim, 'what is not prohibited is permitted' ($\sim O{\sim}p \rightarrow Pp$ or $\sim Op \rightarrow P{\sim}p$). The maxim seems trivial, but if one looks at the discussion of it, one gets exactly the opposite impression (see e.g. Wright, *Norm and Action*, 85 ff.; id., *An Essay in Deontic Logic and the General Theory of Action*, 82 ff.; C. E. Alchourrón and E. Bulygin, *Normative Systems* (Vienna and New York, 1971), 119 ff.; Kelsen, *General Theory of Norms*, 101; Raz, *The Concept of a Legal System*, 170 ff.). One of the problems which has always given rise to doubts about the maxim, 'what is not prohibited is permitted', is that of the openness of legal systems. As C. and O. Weinberger, *Logik, Semantik, Hermeneutik* (Munich, 1979), 116, put it: 'Only if it is presupposed that the normative system is closed, i.e. that in this system only that is obligatory which is expressly established as obligatory, does the principle, "whatever is not prohibited is permitted" apply'. This is only true on the presupposition that 'what is not prohibited is permitted' is to be interpreted as 'what is not expressly prohibited is permitted'. But such an interpretation is neither necessary nor appropriate. It seems much more appropriate to understand the statement, 'what is not prohibited is permitted' in the following way: 'what is not expressly or impliedly prohibited is permitted'. On this interpretation it applies even to normative systems which are open as regards the degree of expressivity. It makes the point that in a consistent normative system, an act is always to be qualified either as prohibited or as permitted. Retrospective normative qualifications give rise to further problems. But even here one can say that every act can only ever be qualified by *one* consistent legal system S at time t_1 as either prohibited or permitted. Someone who considers retrospective normative qualifications to be possible can say that ϕ-ing was permitted until t_1 by S, and from t_1 onwards was prohibited by S, but he cannot say that the act was qualified at *one* point in time by the *same* legal system as *both* prohibited *and* permitted. In other words, he must accept that $\sim(O{\sim}p \wedge Pp)$, whereby it follows that $\sim O{\sim}p \rightarrow Pp$.

The first situation can be called an *explicit* permission, the second an *implicit* permission. To the extent that constitutional rights norms permit something, they can be called *explicit* permissive norms.

The concept of a permissive norm has long given rise to difficulties. Kant gave the problem its classical formulation:

> An action that is neither commanded nor prohibited is merely permitted, since there is no law limiting one's freedom (one's authorization) with regard to it and so too no duty . . . The question can be raised whether . . . there must be permissive laws (*lex permissiva*) in addition to laws that command and prohibit (*lex praeceptiva*, *lex mandati*, *lex prohibitiva*, *lex vetiti*) in order to account for someone's being free to do or not to do something as he pleases.[138]

Thon gives a clear answer to this question. According to him, permissive norms are 'completely pointless and futile'.[139] The legal system creates 'law simply by passing commands and prohibitions'.[140] Permissions are none other than the absence of prohibitions. Laws consist entirely of commands and prohibitions which protect the carrying out of acts neither commanded nor prohibited.[141] In the context of constitutional rights norms, the thesis of the superfluity of permissive norms is objectionable. Constitutional permissive norms are norms with constitutional status, that is, norms of the highest level. Prohibiting and commanding norms of a lower level, which prohibit or command what they permit, *contradict* them and are therefore unconstitutional. In the context of the hierarchical construction of the legal system, constitutional permissive norms have the supremely important function of setting the 'Ought-limits'[142] to lower levels. This function cannot be fulfilled by the mere absence of commanding and permissive norms. It can be fulfilled by norms protecting permissions, that is, through norms which prohibit the state from prohibiting or commanding certain acts, and through negative jurisdictional norms which remove from the state the competence to prohibit or require certain acts. But such permission-protecting norms do not allow one to talk of a contradiction between prohibiting and commanding norms of a lower level and a constitutional permissive norm. One can only talk in terms of a legislative breach of a prohibiting norm addressed to it, or a transgression of jurisdictional limits. But why should one want to

---

[138] Kant, *The Metaphysics of Morals*, 49

[139] A. Thon, *Rechtsnorm und subjektives Recht* (Weimar, 1878), 292. The view of Raz, *The Concept of a Legal System*, 172 ff., is related. Raz only accepts the existence of permissive norms when they represent exceptions to commanding or prohibiting norms. See also H. Nawiasky, *Allgemeine Rechtslehre*, 2nd edn. (Einsiedeln, Zürich, and Cologne, 1948), 109, who considers permissive norms as legally insignificant.

[140] Thon, *Rechtsnorm and Subjectives Recht* 288.

[141] As far as constitutional rights are concerned, this view is maintained by Schwabe: 'Permission is, as has been mentioned, the purpose and object protected by the claim to desist, but it is no independent normative category. As a consequence, it cannot be part of a subjective constitutional right' (J. Schwabe, *Probleme der Grundrechtsdogmatik* (Darmstadt, 1977), 46).   [142] Weinberger and Weinberger, *Logik, Semantik, Hermeneutik*, 115.

avoid thinking in terms of contradictions between prohibiting and commanding norms of a lower level and constitutional permissive norms? A practical argument can be added to this theoretical one. From the perspective of the beneficiary of constitutional rights, constitutional rights norms represent norms which guarantee permissions. Thus general understanding and current linguistic usage supports a perspective which includes the existence of constitutional permissive norms. This is, of course, not an overriding argument from a certain doctrinal construction, but combined with the theoretical points already made, it is sufficient justification for treating talk of constitutional permissive norms as neither meaningless nor unnecessary.

2.2.2 *Protected Liberties*

The position of unprotected legal liberty, consisting merely of the permission to do something and the permission to refrain from doing it, includes as such no security by way of protective norms and rights. In the case of unprotected legal liberties of constitutional status, this does not mean there is no protection at all. As we have seen, norms of a lower status which command or prohibit what is permitted in the constitution are unconstitutional. But the constitutional protection of liberty is not limited to this. It consists of a bundle of rights to something and other objective norms which together secure to the constitutional right-holder the possibility of carrying out the act permitted. Where a liberty is combined with such rights or norms it becomes a *protected liberty*.

2.2.2.1 The Basic Structure of Protection

The structure of the protection of liberty is most easily seen in interchangeable relationships. Both dealer x and dealer y are free to win z as a customer. Neither has the right against the other that he should not obstruct his efforts to win over z, perhaps by making a better offer. However, they are not unprotected in the exercise of their liberty. y is not allowed to obstruct x by killing or injuring him, or by adopting anti-competitive practices. In this connection, Hart speaks of a 'protective perimeter' which surrounds every liberty to a greater or lesser extent in every legal system.[143] Such a protective perimeter should be distinguished from a *substantively equivalent* protection of a liberty. Protection is substantively equivalent if x has a right as against y that y should not obstruct him in winning z as a customer. Liberties that are only protected by a protective perimeter are *indirectly* protected liberties. Liberties protected by a substantively equivalent protection are *directly* protected liberties. Both indirect and direct protection can be achieved by norms granting subjective rights (*subjective* protection) and by norms not granting subjective rights (*objective* protection). There are thus four basic types of protected liberty.

---

[143] Hart, 'Bentham on Legal Rights', 180 ff.

2.2.2.2 On the Protection of Constitutional Liberties

Every constitutional liberty is a liberty at least in relation to the state. Every constitutional liberty held in relation to the state is directly and subjectively protected by at least one substantively equivalent right that the state should not prevent the liberty-holder from doing what he is constitutionally free to do. If one combines liberty and protection into the concept of protected liberty, this type of protected liberty consists of the combination of an unprotected liberty and a right to the non-obstruction of acts.[144] The right of non-obstruction is a right to a negative act. Rights to negative acts correlate to prohibitions of these acts. Protection through prohibitions can be called 'negative protection'. When constitutional rights are treated as defensive rights, then generally what is meant is that they are constitutional liberty-protecting rights to omissions on the part of the state. These rights are combined with the *power* to challenge their infringement before the courts. When these three positions come togther: a legal *liberty*, a *right* against the state to non-obstruction, and a *power* to challenge infringements before the courts, one has a completely constituted negative liberty right against the state.

Positive protection of liberty against the state arises from the combination of liberty with a right to a positive act. The idea of positive protection is hardly problematic when one is concerned with things like the protection from third parties by the norms of criminal law. Problems arise in the case of entitlements such as state subsidies. There is a certain structural correspondence in that both cases concern making what is *legally* possible for the right-holder *factually* possible as well. This structural correspondence permits us, in spite of general linguistic usage, to call the combination of a liberty with an entitlement in its narrow sense ensuring the factual appropriation of the liberty, a protection of liberty. The question of whether and to what extent the Basic Law contains positive protections of this nature will for the moment be left entirely open.[145]

3. POWERS

3.1 Terminological Issues

Rights to something and liberties only represent one part of the normative positions called 'rights'. A third, no less important, group are those posi-

---

[144] The structure of this type of protected liberty can be represented by:

(1) $Lxs\phi x \wedge Rxs$ (~hinder $s(\phi x/\text{~}\phi x)$).

This is to be read as:

(2) x is at liberty to ϕ in relation to the state s, and x has as against the state a right that it not hinder him in respect of the choice of action to ϕ or not to ϕ.

[145] See on this below at 334 ff.

tions identified with expressions such as 'force', 'legal power' [*Rechtsmacht*],[146] 'power',[147] 'competence'[148] [*Kompetenz*],[149] 'authorization',[150] 'capacity',[151] 'formative right',[152] and 'legal ability'.[153] All positions belonging to this group will be called powers, since the other terms are less appropriate. 'Force' and 'legal force' are too closely associated with something factual, 'authorization' is too closely related to permission, formative rights are only one type of power, and while 'legal ability' is accurate, it is too long-winded.[154]

3.2 Power and Permission

There are public law powers as well as private law powers.[155] The formation of a contract and the act of marriage involve the exercise of powers, but then so do the enactment of a law and taking an administrative decision.[156] The common element of these cases lies in the alteration of the legal state of affairs by certain acts of the power-holder(s). Altering a legal situation by an act can be described in two ways. It can be described as the creation of individual or general *norms*,[157] which would not apply in the

---

[146] Kelsen, *General Theory of Norms*, 102.

[147] Bentham, *Of Laws in General*, 80 ff.; Hohfeld, 'Some Fundamental Legal Conceptions', 36.

[148] Ross, *Directives and Norms*, 119; Wright, *Norm and Action*, 192.

[149] Kelsen, *Pure Theory of Law*, 148 f.

[150] Kelsen, *Pure Theory of Law*, 145 ff.

[151] Adomeit, *Rechtstheorie für Studenten*, 49; Moritz, *Über Hohfelds System der juridischen Grundbegriffe*, 85.

[152] K. Adomeit, *Gestaltungsrechte, Rechtsgeschäfte, Ansprüche* (Berlin, 1969), 7 ff.

[153] A. Brinz, *Lehrbuch der Pandekten*, i, 2nd edn. (Erlangen, 1873), 211; Bierling, *Zur Kritik der juristischen Grundbegriffe*, part 2, 50; Jellinek, *System der subjektiven öffentlichen Rechte*, 48.

[154] One disadvantage of the term power [*Kompetenz*] is that it can easily be confused with the organizational idea of competence [*Zuständigkeit*]. This latter term is defined by Wolff in the following way: 'Organizational implementation competence to act in a matter to be undertaken is thus the *obligation* and *entitlement* based upon organizational regulations and legal acts to deal with certain matters concerning an organizational entity in what are usually specific ways and forms' (H. J. Wolff and O. Bachof, *Verwaltungsrecht II*, 4th edn. (Munich, 1976), 15 (emphasis added)). He distinguishes 'competences narrowly so called' from this concept of competence, which consist of capacities based upon authorizations. As an example he gives the authorization to make dispositions and regulations (ibid.). Wolff's distinction is not entirely clear, and this is particularly true of his use of entitlement. However, it can be said that the concept of a power used here more or less corresponds to Wolff's competence narrowly so called. By contrast, his organizational competence in a matter to be undertaken is something which is made up mostly of commands and permissions to fulfil tasks, as well as prohibitions on other organizational entities on undertaking the same tasks. Wolff uses 'competence' on its own for neither idea, but for the 'object of the obligation to undertake a matter, in other words, the task to be undertaken' (ibid.). This attempt at definition by an author as concerned as he is with precision makes clear just how slippery the idea of power is. We will only get a secure grasp of it by resorting to an analysis of basic legal concepts.

[155] An account which is still interesting today can be found in A. Brinz, *Lehrbuch der Pandekten*, 130 ff.

[156] See on this Hart, *The Concept of Law*, 27 ff.; Ross, *Directives and Norms*, 130 ff.

[157] Thus Kelsen, *General Theory of Norms*, 54.

absence of the act. It can also be described as an alteration of the legal *position* of the legal persons subject to the norms.[158]

The concept of power must be clearly distinguished from the concept of permission.[159] While an act carried out in appropriation of a power is generally also permitted,[160] an act which merely makes use of a permission is not thereby an appropriation of a power, which is obvious from the fact that there are many permitted acts which do not alter the legal situation.[161] The difference between permissions and powers can also been seen in their negations. The negation of a permission is a prohibition; the negation of a power is a disability.[162]

A permission itself has no effect on the actual capacity to act, which is fully independent. It is entirely possible to smoke or not to smoke independently of whether one or the other is permitted or forbidden. It is, of course, generally true that people prefer to smoke when it is permitted and not forbidden in combination with legal sanctions. But when a person smokes in spite of the prohibition, the act is identical to smoking when it is permitted, but for the fact that the act is forbidden. Matters are quite different in the case of powers. As Jellinek puts it, powers add

something to the actual physical capacity of the individual, which by nature it does

[158] See Lindahl, *Position and Change*, 193, who speaks appropriately of 'the "dynamics" of the theory of legal positions'.

[159] See on this, Brinz, *Lehrbuch der Pandekten*, 211; Hohfeld, 'Some Fundamental Legal Conceptions', 58. Attempts to explain the concept of power by way of the concept of permission can be found in Wright, *Norm and Action*, 192 f.; Lindahl, *Position and Change*, 212 ff. See also Kelsen, *Hauptprobleme der Staatsrechtslehre*, 639: ' "Can" and "may" are thus conceptually combined'.

[160] But it can also be prohibited. This is at any rate the case in the context of a relative prohibition, that is, an obligation towards other legal persons not to undertake the act in question (see on this Bierling, *Zur Kritik der juristischen Grundbegriffe*, part 2, 50). By contrast, the relationship between power and absolute prohibition is more complex. It is usually appropriate to take the corresponding power away from those affected by a general prohibition. But this need not happen. Thus the Federal Supreme Court has treated a contract for a certain medicine as valid, even though the sale of the medicine breached the Pharmaceuticals Act (BGH NJW 68, 2286). The last clause of § 134 Civil Code also presupposes that a power and a prohibition on implementing it can co-exist: 'A legal transaction which breaches a statutory prohibition is void, unless the statute states to the contrary'. A classic example of the simultaneous co-existence of prohibition and power was the marriage ban on cohabitees (§ 4(2) of Law no. 16 of the Control Council—the Marriage Act—of 20 February 1946 (ABlKR p. 77), on which the Federal Constitutional Court commented, 'marriage conducted in breach of the prohibition is valid ab initio' (BVerfGE 36, 146 (148, 160)).

[161] This is particularly clear in the case of non-prohibited acts which would amount to the appropriation of powers were they carried out by other persons or under other circumstances. See Bierling, *Zur Kritik der juristischen Grundbegriffe*, part 2, 54: 'While it is certainly true that according to our laws contracts concluded by minors do not bind them, even if the minor intends to create legal relations, it is just as true that they are not forbidden to conclude contracts, take out loans and promise repayment, that such a promise would not be illegal'. Jellinek, *System der subjektiven öffentlichen Rechte*, 47, makes the same point: 'It would not be correct to say that a person lacking capacity *may* not make a contract, rather, he *cannot* make a contract; whatever it is that he does does not result in a contract'.

[162] See Adomeit, *Rechtstheorie für Studenten*, 49.

not possess ... The individual can engage in whatever sexual relationships he pleases, it will only become marriage under the conditions laid down by objective law. He can give whatever directions in the event of his death he pleases, but they will only constitute a will on the basis of the relevant legal rules. At this point natural liberty is limited. For all provisions which concern the validity of legal acts and legal transactions create a *legal ability* expressly granted by the legal system. This ability stands in sharp contrast to permissibility.[163]

3.3 Power and Factual Ability

The criterion of alteration of the legal situation is suitable for distinguishing power from permission, but it is unsuitable for distinguishing factual ability from power. Not every act which alters legal positions can be seen as the exercise of a power. When *x* acts tortiously towards *y*, then he alters both his own and *y*'s position. From this point on, *x* is obligated to *y* to pay him compensation, and *y* has a corresponding right as against *x*. Nevertheless, engaging in tortious activity cannot be seen as the exercise of a power.[164]

3.4 Exercises of Powers as Institutional Acts

Thus a central problem for the concept of a power is how one distinguishes between acts in the exercise of powers and acts which while not in the exercise of powers, still alter the legal situation. The answer is that acts in the exercise of powers are *institutional acts*. Institutional acts are those which cannot be performed merely on the basis of natural abilities, but which presuppose constitutive rules.[165] The classic example of constitutive rules are the rules of chess. Without these rules one could move figures around a board, but one could not carry out 'a move' or a speak of 'checkmate'. Promising is just the same. Without the constitutive rules of promising, expressions such as 'I promise you that . . .' could be interpreted as information about intention or predictions of future behaviour, but not as

---

[163] Jellinek, *System der subjektiven öffentlichen Rechte*, 47.

[164] See Bierling, *Zur Kritik der juristischen Grundbegriffe*, part 2, 50. Hohfeld's attempt to define the concept of power by way of the concept of 'volitional control' is to be rejected for the same reasons (see Hohfeld, 'Some Fundamental Legal Conceptions', 51). When Hislop states, 'A has the legal power by assaulting B of creating a *claim* to damages in B, but this *power* is coupled with the duty not to use it' (Hislop, 'The Hohfeldian System of Fundamental Legal Conceptions', 64), then he is using the concept of power in the sense of factual ability to bring about legal consequences, not in the sense used here. Attempts to define the concept of power with the concept of factual ability in the context of a formal system can be found for example in F. B. Fitch, 'A Revision of Hohfeld's Theory of Legal Concepts', 273 ff. See also Moritz, *Über Hohfelds System der juridischen Grundbegriffe*, 102, who also speaks of 'capacity' in the sense of power in the context of tortious acts.

[165] See on this Searle, *Speech Acts*, 33 ff.; J. L. Austin, 'Performative Utterances', in id., *Philosophical Papers*, 2nd edn., (London, Oxford, and New York, 1970), 233 ff.; Ross, *Directives and Norms*, 53 ff.; N. MacCormick, 'Law as Institutional Fact', 105 ff., who speaks of 'institutional facts' instead of institutional acts. J. L. Austin, *How to do things with Words* (London, Oxford, and New York, 1962), 19, uses the term 'conventional acts'.

promises. The counterpart of constitutive rules, which make certain acts possible in the first place, are regulative rules which relate to acts independently possible.[166]

The same is true for the law. Interpreting the behaviour of two people as the formation of a contract, or the behaviour of a group of people as law-making, presupposes the existence of rules turning observable natural or social acts into legal acts.[167] These constitutive legal rules will be called here 'competence norms'.[168] *Competence norms* are to be contrasted with *behavioural norms*. Competence norms make legal acts possible and create the ability to change legal positions by legal acts. Behavioural norms create no alternatives for action which would be impossible without them; they only qualify acts by creating obligations, rights to something, and liberties.

There have been many attempts to derive competence norms from behavioural norms or the legal modality of competence from permissions, commands, and prohibitions. These attempts can be grouped into two. The first group embraces attempts to treat the legal consequences of not following competence norms—generally the voidness or voidability of norms created—as a sanction, so that following of the competence norm can then be seen as commanded in avoidance of the sanction. This perspective, which may be appropriate enough in certain circumstances, cannot grasp the constitutive character of competence norms. In the case of norms of behaviour as regulative rules there is some behaviour which can exist independently from the norm, which is then characterized by the norm as commanded, prohibited, or permitted, and a sanction may be attached. This behaviour, which is independent of the norm's existence, would not have the characteristic of being commanded, prohibited, or permitted in the absence of the norm, and in many cases it would not carry a term such as 'grievous bodily harm' or 'extortion', which are used to link it to legal consequences. But where the norm applies, it is no different from what it would be were the norm not to apply, but for the fact that it would not be characterized as commanded, prohibited, or permitted and carry certain special terms such as 'grievous bodily harm' or 'extortion'. Competence norms are quite different because of their constitutive character. Without the rules of legislation, it would be possible to carry out the physical act of

---

[166] Searle, *Speech Acts*, 33. Even such acts can be described by reference to a rule. This occurs, for example, whenever a certain act is described as 'murder'. This act is exactly what it is even without § 211 Criminal Code; its characterization as murder is simply one of several possible general ways of describing natural acts which has been chosen in order to turn it into a prohibited act by the enactment of a norm and to attach legal consequences to it.

[167] See on this Ross, *Directives and Norms*, 56 f.

[168] Another equally suitable expression would be 'authorization norms'; see Adomeit, *Rechtstheorie für Studenten*, 48 ff. Competence norms can be further sub-divided into norms which establish who has competence (competence-subject norms), norms which regulate the procedure for the exercise of competence (procedural competence norms), and norms which determine the object of competence (substantive competence norms); (see on this Ross, *Directives and Norms*, 130).

raising hands in a gathering of people, it would even be possible to interpret this as an expression of collective will, but it could not be an act of lawmaking.[169] The difference between norms of behaviour and competence norms becomes particularly apparent when they are not followed. Not following a competence norm does not lead to illegality, but to the voidness or vitiation of the act. If some behaviour in non-conformity with a competence norm is also classified as illegal, then this presupposes some norm of behaviour requiring the correct appropriation of the power.

The second group of reductive attempts is more significant. This includes all attempts to treat natural or social facts which constitute the means of exercising the power as preconditions for the validity of behavioural norms. Ross puts it like this: 'Norms of competence are logically reducible to norms of conduct in this way: norms of competence make it obligatory to act according to the norms of conduct which have been created according to the procedure laid down in them'.[170] This reduction can be carried through,[171] but at the price of an important aspect of legal systems.[172] The legal position of the power-holder is not identified. But this position is of central significance, at least for developed legal systems.[173] Neither the hierarchical structure of the legal system nor private law autonomy can be adequately represented in a model limited to the outworking of chains of preconditions for commands, prohibitions, and permissions. Without the concept of power or its equivalent, the position of the citizen (for example) could only be described as the addressee of (relational and non-relational) commands, prohibitions, and permissions, and not as a private legislator.[174] His private competence to shape the law would only be understandable as a factual ability to release certain legal consequences by some sort of behaviour. And at that point whatever it is that distinguishes a legal power from the ability to release legal consequences by way of tortious acts has disappeared from sight.

The reductive thesis is justified in a different respect. The normative content of a power is identical with the class of its possible (relational and non-relational) commands, prohibitions, and permissions.[175] Just as the introduction of the relational modes does not affect the unity of the Ought,

---

[169] For a further elaboration of this argument, see Hart, *The Concept of Law*, 34 f.

[170] Ross, *Directives and Norms*, 118.

[171] Hart's objections to reductive attempts in the second group rest to a large extent on the fact that 'law without sanction is perfectly conceivable' (Hart, *The Concept of Law*, 38). This objection does not apply to the version considered here, which does without the concept of sanction.

[172] See Adomeit, *Gestaltungsrechte, Rechtsgeschäfte, Ansprüche*, 19.

[173] Hart calls the introduction of law-making and adjudicative powers a 'step forward as important to society as the invention of the wheel' (Hart, *The Concept of Law*, 41).

[174] See ibid. 40.

[175] The commands, prohibitions, and permissions possible under a power C_1 include not only those directly possible, but also those made indirectly possible. A command is indirectly possible under C_1 if a further power C_2 can be based on C_1 and if the command is possible under C_2. The chain of sub-competences is in principle unlimited.

but merely qualifies the Ought as a relational Ought, so also the introduction of the concept of power changes nothing in this respect. The concept of Ought is simply further qualified as *potential* Ought.

3.5 Powers, Liabilities, Disabilities, and Immunities

A power is a legal position created by a competence norm. At this point we are only concerned with the position that one legal subject x has when he can affect the legal position of another subject y without the acts of other legal subjects being necessary.[176] The fact that x can affect the legal position of y means that through his own act, x can create a legal position for y which y would not have had in identical circumstances but for x's act. The position of x can be described in the following way:

(1) x has a power as against y to create a legal position LP for y.

If one calls the three-point competence operator C in correspondence to the three-point right-relation, and LPy as a statement of y's position, then (1) can be written:

(2) $Cxy\,(LPy)$.

LP can stand for any legal positions, for simple non-relational obligations (OyG), for rights to something $(RyzG)$, or for liberties $(LyzG)$, even for powers of a lower status $(C'yz\,(LPz)\,)$.

As in the case of rights to something, so also converse relations can be stated for powers. The converse relation to a power will be called a *liability*.[177] If x has a power over y to alter y's position, then y finds himself in a position of liability as regards this position, and vice versa. If one takes S to be the relation of liability, then:

(3) $Cxy\,(LPy) \leftrightarrow Syx\,(LPy)$.

Two further positions can be created by negating '$Cxy\,(LPy)$' and '$Syx\,(LPy)$':

(4) $\sim Cxy\,(LPy)$

stands for the statement that x has no power over y with respect to LPy. This position can be called a *disability*.

(5) $\sim Syx\,(LPy)$

stands for a statement that y does not find himself in a position of liability as against x with respect to LPy. This position can be called *immunity*. The four positions can be put in the following Hohfeldian scheme of powers:

---

[176] The main example of a power which needs the act of another legal subject for its appropriation is the power to conclude a contract.

[177] See on this Ross, *Directives and Norms*, 119, 132. The Hohfeldian term 'liability' (see Hohfeld, 'Some Fundamental Legal Conceptions', 36) is used here in place of the German, '*Subjektion*'.

IV.

$$Cxy(LPy) \qquad \leftrightarrow \qquad Sxy(LPy)$$
$$\text{(power)} \qquad\qquad\qquad \text{(liability)}$$

$$\sim \qquad\qquad\qquad\qquad\qquad \sim$$

$$\sim Cxy(LPy) \qquad \leftrightarrow \qquad Syx(LPy)$$
$$\text{(disability)} \qquad\qquad\qquad \text{(immunity)}[178]$$

3.6 Constitutional Rights and Powers

The concept of a power is indispensable in grasping the structure of constitutional rights. This is as true for the powers of the citizen as it is for the powers of the state.

3.6.1 Powers of the Citizen

There can be no doubt that there are powers of the citizen which enjoy constitutional protection. The legislature would breach constitutional norms if it tried to remove the power to marry, to form associations, to acquire property, and to write wills. But that does not tell us much about the role of powers in the context of constitutional positions. To appreciate them more precisely, they need to be related to rights to something and to liberties. A 1969 decision of the Federal Constitutional Court concerning the law regulating trade in real property is instructive.[179] This law limited the power to dispose of and acquire agricultural and forested land *at will*. While the Court had left open in an earlier decision whether the power to acquire property—it spoke then of freedom of acquisition—is protected by article 14(1) Basic Law,[180] in this decision it brought the power to *dispose* of property within the protection of article 14, which had the consequence that the removal of certain powers, such as the power to dispose of agricultural and forested land at will, needed justification. At this point it is only significant that a prima facie constitutional right[181] to a power was being assumed. This right has the same structure as that of the right to the non-removal of a position discussed above. What is interesting is the way the Court justified this right to a power: 'This capacity is an elementary component of freedom of action in the system of property. A ban on disposing of property is thus one of the most serious infringements of the freedom

---

[178] See Hohfeld, 'Some Fundamental Legal Conceptions', 36, 50 ff. The German equivalents for Hohfeld's terms are '*Kompetenz*' (power), '*Subjektion*' (liability), '*Nicht-Kompetenz*' (disability), and '*Nicht-Subjektion*' (immunity). Ross adopts terminology closer to the German, using 'competence', 'subjection', 'disability', and 'immunity' respectively; see Ross, *Directives and Norms*, 119. Hohfeld's more familiar terms have been symbolized with 'C' (for competence/power) and 'S' (for subjection/liability) to avoid confusion with permissions and liberties respectively.

[179] BVerfGE 26, 215.   [180] BVerfGE 21, 73 (76 f.).

[181] On the concept of a prima facie constitutional right, see above at 60, 80.

of the citizen in this area.'[182] Directly before this, the Court states that article 14(1)(1) Basic Law guarantees private property as a legal institution: 'this guarantee secures a basic set of norms, which constitute property in the sense of this constitutional rights provision'. At this point the right to a power gets linked both to the concept of an institution-guarantee and to the concept of liberty.

The idea of an institution-guarantee was established by Martin Wolff,[183] extended by Carl Schmitt,[184] and adopted by the Federal Constitutional Court.[185] Its doctrinal core is a prohibition addressed to the legislature on removing or fundamentally changing certain private law institutions. Private law institutions are complexes of norms, consisting for the most part of powers. The institution-guarantee is thus in the first instance a prohibition addressed to the legislature on removing certain powers of the citizen. If this prohibition does not correspond to any right of the citizen, then the protection is (merely) *objective*. The idea of an institution-guarantee is limited to the claim that there is such objective protection. If the prohibition correlates to rights of the citizen, then the protection is (also) *subjective*. In that the Federal Constitutional Court assumes that article 14(1) Basic Law grants a prima facie right to the non-removal of a power to dispose of property, it has subjectified the protection of the legal institution to some extent. Precisely how far the protection of private law legal institutions should be subjectified by the recognition of rights to powers will be discussed properly below.[186]

The more individualistic a normative theory of constitutional rights is, the more rights to powers it will adopt. The reason for this lies in the relationship between liberty and power. As has been noted, the Court expresses this in the decision referred to as follows: 'this capacity is also an elementary component of freedom of action in the system of property'.[187] Jellinek's thesis, that legal powers 'add something to the freedom of action of the individual, which he does not by nature have'[188] has already been noted. This expresses the central point for the relationship between liberty and power. By granting powers, the freedom of action of the individual is increased. Expanding the powers of the individual means (assuming that the appropriation of the power is neither commanded nor prohibited) increasing his legal liberty. The non-granting or removal of a power is thus an obstacle to liberty, and a particularly effective one too. As a matter of

---

182 BVerfGE 26, 215 (222).

183 M. Wolff, 'Reichsverfassung und Eigentum', in *Festgabe für W. Kahl* (Tübingen, 1923), 5 f.

184 C. Schmitt, 'Freiheitsrechte und institutionelle Garantien der Reichsverfassung', in id., *Verfassungsrechtliche Aufsätze aus den Jahren* 1924–1954 (Berlin, 1973), 160 ff.

185 See e.g. BVerfGE 6, 55 (72).   186 324 ff.

187 BVerfGE 26, 215 (222).

188 Jellinek, *System der subjektiven öffentlichen Rechte*, 47.

conceptual necessity, it destroys the object of liberty (carrying out the legal act or not). The legal liberty to carry out a legal act necessarily presupposes the power to do so.

The relationship between power and legal liberty is interesting in one further respect. Although the legal system is passive as regards the appropriation of legal liberty, that is, as regards a choice to do or refrain from doing, it is active in granting a power; it creates a choice of actions. The granting of powers whether in private law (acquisition of property) or public law (voting) is only one of three ways in which the legal system can actively increase the freedom of action, and hence the negative liberty, of the individual. The two other ways are by the enactment of protective norms, in particular those of the criminal law, which ensure that third parties do not obstruct the realization of choices of action, and the granting of entitlements in the narrow sense, which are designed to secure the factual possibility of realizing alternative courses of action. In that the law actively creates liberties, so also it always causes—directly or indirectly—losses of liberty. The appropriation of powers leads to the imposition of duties, no-rights, and liabilities. Criminal norms which protect liberty take away the legal liberty to do what they forbid, and the fulfilment of social entitlements requires the state to take away the necessary means for their fulfilment from others, which limits their factual freedom of action. But all this does not alter the fact that actively created liberties are liberties; it only raises the question of the *correct* distribution of liberties.

3.6.2 *Powers of the State*

The counterpart to the powers of the citizen are those of the state or its organs. At this point, constitutional rights norms as negative competence norms become relevant.[189] A negative competence norm is one which limits a positive competence norm.[190] One could say that negative competence

---

[189] On the classification of constitutional rights norms as negative competence norms, see e.g. H. Ehmke, *Wirtschaft und Verfassung* (Karlsruhe, 1961), 29 ff.; id., 'Prinzipien der Verfassungsinterpretation', VVDStRL 20 (1963), 89 ff.; K. Hesse, *Grundzüge des Verfassungsrechts der Bundesrepublik Deutschland*, 14th edn. (Heidelberg, 1984), para. 291; F. Müller, *Die Einheit der Verfassung* (Berlin, 1979), 142; Schwabe, *Probleme der Grundrechtsdogmatik*, 291; P. Häberle, 'Grundrechte im Leistungsstaat', VVDStRL 30 (1972), 135; E.-W. Böckenförde, 'Grundrechtstheorie und Grundrechtsinterpretation', NJW 1974, 1530.
[190] The sort of problems that calling constitutional rights norms negative competence norms can give rise to are demonstrated in the following comment made by Goerlich: 'For constitutional rights as liberties are original capacities, powers by contrast are derived capacities of democratic or federal ordering. If they were "negative competence norms" then constitutional rights would no longer be first and foremost liberties, but only subjective rights to a bounded capacity, like powers they would only be described negatively, not on the basis of their substance' (H. Goerlich, *Grundrechte als Verfahrensgarantien* (Baden-Baden, 1981), 20). But why should constitutional rights (norms) as negative competence norms only be (protect) 'subjective rights to a bounded capacity'? As negative competence norms they limit the competence of the state. To the extent that they do this, they place the constitutional right-holder in a position of immunity (see above at 155). This position is anything but a 'bounded capacity'.

norms create exceptions to positive competence norms. In this way they put the state in the position of disability and the citizen in the position of immunity. It is questionable whether it is necessary to talk of such positions and thus of negative competence norms. Whenever the citizen finds himself in a position of constitutional immunity as against the state, he always has a right as against the state that the state should not become active in the area of immunity defined by the constitutional rights norms. However, it is not only possible and harmless to talk about negative competence norms and hence immunities and disabilities, it is also positively useful. Otherwise the flaws of legislative acts within the area of immunity could only be incompletely explained. One would have to treat them first of all as prohibitions. The flaw would have to be characterized as the consequence not of a crossing of jurisdictional boundaries but as a breach of prohibition. If one accepts the existence of both prohibitive norms and negative competence norms, it is easy to explain why the first can be characterized as prohibited and the second as flawed.

III. THE COMPLETE CONSTITUTIONAL RIGHT

Hitherto we have been concerned with individual constitutional rights positions. But when people speak of a constitutional right such as the right to life or freedom of speech, they do not generally refer to single positions but to the complete constitutional right. But what is a complete constitutional right? The simplest answer is that a complete constitutional right is a bundle of constitutional rights positions. That leaves us with the question of what it is that draws these positions together into a single constitutional right. Again, the simplest answer is their derivation from a single constitutional rights provision. Legal positions always correspond to norms which create them. The *collection* of a bundle of positions into one constitutional right corresponds to the *derivation* of a bundle of norms from one constitutional provision. But as will be seen, this only captures one aspect of the entire picture of a complete constitutional right.

In order to see the complete picture, we need to cast a glance at another example. Because of the variety of positions it concerns, a good example is the decision concerning the Interim Act for comprehensive university education in Lower Saxony,[191] considered already when discussing the problem of derivation. As far as the citizen is concerned, three very different positions

---

Rather it is characterized by the fact that the occupant of the position is not subject to commands and prohibitions within the scope of the negative competence norm, that is, that he is free.

[191] BVerfGE 35, 79. See on this A. Sattler, 'Die Pflicht des Gesetzgebers zum Erlaß von Vorschriften über die Organisation der Hochschulen', in H. Schneider and V. Götz (eds.), *Festschrift für W. Weber* (Berlin, 1974), 325 ff.

were considered: a *legal liberty* to act in the field of academic life,[192] a right
against the state that it should not obstruct acts within the field of academic life,[193] that is, a *right to an omission* on the part of the state in protection of this legal liberty (defensive right), and a *right to positive act*s on the
part of the state to protect the legal liberty. That last position plays a central
role in the judgment. The Court expresses it in the following words: 'The
value-judgment of Article 5(3) Basic Law gives to the individual constitutional right-holder a right to such state measures, including organizational
ones, which are indispensable in protecting his constitutionally secured
sphere of liberty, because it is they that make free academic activity possible in the first place.'[194] This statement combines the formulation of the
right with its justification. Here we are only interested in the right itself.
What is remarkable is how the acts of the state which make up its content
are described. The description places the state action in a means–end relationship.[195] The constitutional right-holder gets a right to those acts of the
state 'which are indispensable in protecting his constitutionally secured
sphere of liberty'. It can hardly be more clearly stated that we are concerned
with the positive subjective protection[196] of liberty.

As far as the state is concerned, the Court formulates at an abstract level
the requirement that 'the beneficiaries of constitutional rights under article
5(3) Basic Law are to be granted as much liberty in their academic activities by suitably free university structures as is possible having regard to the
functions of a university and the needs of the various beneficiaries of constitutional rights active within it'.[197] This requirement expresses the *principled nature* of the constitutional rights norm. In concretizing this right into
positive acts one has to formulate relatively specific *definitive duties*. So the
first requirement to be formulated is to take account of the special position
of university teachers in organizing academic liberty.[198] This is further
concretized into a measured influence on teaching and an exclusive influence on research.[199] At the level directly related to the case, prohibitions
relating to the majorities and procedures for decision as well as the composition of groups are formulated.[200] Such prohibitions, such as that a university teacher in an appeal committee cannot be rejected simply on the basis
of a minority vote,[201] clearly have the character of rules.

These few examples are sufficient to make clear how broad and multifaceted what is brought together under the concept of a complete constitutional right is. The norms and positions can be divided according to three
perspectives: (1) according to the type of position within the system of basic

[192] BVerfGE 35, 79 (112 f.).   [193] ibid.   [194] BVerfGE 35, 79 (116).
[195] The Court speaks explicitly of a 'causal connection between organizational norms . . .
and interferences with the free exercise of research and teaching' (BVerfGE 35, 79 (120)).
[196] See above at 149 f.   [197] BVerfGE 35, 79 (123 f.).
[198] BVerfGE 35, 79 (126 f.).   [199] BVerfGE 35, 79 (131 f.).
[200] BVerfGE 35, 79 (139 f.).   [201] BVerfGE 35, 79 (145).

constitutional positions, (2) according to their degree of generality, and (3) according to whether they are rules or principles, or whether they are definitive or prima facie positions. Quite different relations can exist between these norms and positions. Three relations which go beyond mere co-existence in a bundle of positions can easily be distinguished: a relation of precision, a means–end relation, and a balancing-relation. An example of a relation of *precision* is that between the legal liberty to do anything, 'which in its content and form can be regarded as a serious and structured attempt to attain to truth' and the freedom to choose which questions to ask and basic methodological principles.[202] The *means–end* relation has already been referred to briefly. It often plays a decisive role in norms concerning organization and procedure. Majorities have nothing as such to do with research activity, but they can have an impact on research activity. To use another example: the abandoning of references in state examinations has, as such, nothing to do with the choice and exercise of the profession of the candidate, but it can have an effect upon it.[203] A lot of the discussion about constitutional rights as procedural guarantees[204] is concerned with locating procedural positions in the complete constitutional right by way of a means–end relation. The most interesting is the relationship of *balancing*. This can play a part in the context of a relation of precision in justifying the establishment of meaning and in the context of means–end relations in identifying and excluding ends and excluding means. But it can also apply outside of these relations. The relation of balancing exists in the relation between a prima facie position and a definitive position in accordance with the Law of Competing Principles. In order to move from one to the other, the prima facie position must be put into relationship with other prima facie positions as well as with principles that relate not to legal positions of the individual but to collective interests. The Federal Constitutional Court expresses this in the judgment already referred to in the following words: 'However, the duty of the state to realize whatever degree of academic freedom is attainable runs up against natural limits arising from the combination of the concerns of many constitutional right-holders and from the regard to be had for other important public interests'.[205]

If one accepts that the degree of generality is no reason for or against the inclusion of a certain position in the complete constitutional right, there are four things the complete constitutional right could refer to: (1) a bundle of definitive positions, (2) a bundle of definitive positions together with the relations between them, (3) a bundle of definitive and prima facie positions, and (4) a bundle of definitive and prima facie positions including the relations between them. It was suggested above that constitutional rights have

---

[202] BVerfGE 35, 79 (113).   [203] See BVerfGE 52, 380 (388 ff.).
[204] See with numerous further references, Goerlich, *Grundrechte als Verfahrensgarantien*.
[205] BVerfGE 35, 79 (122).

a double aspect, which among other things means that constitutional rights provisions are to be treated as containing rules as well as principles.[206] This means that the bundle of positions constituting the complete constitutional right includes both definitive and prima facie positions. Adding in the relations between them is not only possible and without adverse consequences, it is necessary if we want to create a theoretically interesting concept of the complete constitutional right, that is, a concept which has more content than a mere summation of positions. A complete constitutional right is thus a bundle of definitive and prima facie positions, related to each other in the three ways indicated and derived from a constitutional rights provision.

Such a complete constitutional right is fundamentally different from a constitutional right consisting solely of a combination of definitive positions. The latter would have a static character, whereas the former is dynamic. One is the end-result of a process of argumentation and decision which is to be located outside the constitutional right itself, the other includes claims going beyond what is certain, competes with other constitutional rights and principles serving collective interests, and in this way is necessarily bound up with its normative environment. In addition it includes the reasons for its own definitive positions. In one, the value-judgment which the Federal Constitutional Court refers to[207] is included in the form of principles, in the other, it is something external.

So the complete constitutional right is a highly complex, but not impenetrable, object. It is made up of elements with a well-defined structure, the individual positions of the citizen and the state, along with the clearly definable relations between these positions, relations of precision, of means to ends, and of balancing. This does not mean that there will be no controversy about what is to be included in a complete constitutional right. The controversy about what belongs to a complete constitutional right is paralleled by the controversy about which norms are to be derived from constitutional provisions as constitutional rights norms. One can derive very different concrete requirements on the basis of the requirement as formulated by the Federal Constitutional Court that the state must make available not only organizational but also the personnel and financial means for 'free academic enterprise'.[208] One can be even more radical and dispute the suggestion that such requirements are derived from article 5(3)(1) Basic Law at all, maintaining that the state is permitted, but not required, to worry about functioning academic institutions; it could leave the fostering of academic life entirely to private initiative, which it is only prevented from interfering with. This should make it clear that all problems of constitutional interpretation can be located in the context of the question of what belongs to a complete constitutional right.

---

[206] See above at 84 ff.   [207] BVerfGE 35, 79 (114, 116).
[208] BVerfGE 35, 79 (115).

5

Constitutional Rights and Legal Status

I. JELLINEK'S THEORY OF LEGAL STATUS

As the last example that was discussed shows, a complete constitutional right is a bundle of positions with a variety of contents and structures. Such concrete total positions should be distinguished from abstract total positions. The paradigm of an abstract total position is Georg Jellinek's theory of legal status. It is not merely its historical role as an example of great juridical theoretical and conceptual construction which justifies an examination of it. It still has current relevance as a basis for the categorization of constitutional rights.[1] As will be shown, significant parts of it are among the most reliable insights in the field of constitutional rights, which surely counts for something in such a controversial field. The vitality of Jellinek's status theory can be seen in attempts such as Häberle's to, as he puts it, 'place its late-absolutist head on democratic feet'[2] as well as in the construction of alternative or supplementary statuses, such as Denninger's *status constituens*,[3] Hesse's constitutional and general civic statuses,[4] Häberle's *status activus processualis*,[5] and Grabitz's *status libertatis*.[6]

Jellinek identifies four statuses, the *passive* status (*status subjectionis*), the *negative* status (*status libertatis*), the *positive* status (*status civitatis*), and the *active* status, or status of active citizenship.[7]

Exactly what a status is, is described by Jellinek in different ways. His

---

[1] See in place of many F. Klein, in H. v. Mangoldt and F. Klein, *Das Bonner Grundgesetz*, i, *Vorbemerkung* A II 3 (58 ff.); W. Schmitt Glaeser, *Mißbrauch und Verwirkung von Grundrechten im politischen Meinungskampf* (Bad Homburg, Berlin, and Zürich, 1968), 83 ff.; J. Schwabe, *Probleme der Grundrechtsdogmatik* (Darmstadt, 1977), 10 ff., 201 ff., 278 ff.; C. Starck, 'Die Grundrechte des Grundgesetzes', JuS 1981, 239 ff.

[2] P. Häberle, 'Grundrechte im Leistungsstaat', VVDStRL 30 (1972), 80.

[3] E. Denninger, *Polizei in der freiheitlichen Demokratie* (Frankfurt a. M., 1968), 33 ff.; id., *Staatsrecht*, (Reinbek, 1973), 28 ff.

[4] K. Hesse, *Grundzüge des Verfassungsrechts* (Heidelberg, 1984), para. 280.

[5] Häberle, *Grundrechte im Leistungsstaat*, 52, 81.

[6] E. Grabitz, *Freiheit und Verfassungsrecht* (Tübingen, 1976), 245.

[7] G. Jellinek, *System der subjektiven öffentlichen Rechte*, 2nd edn. (Tübingen, 1905), 86 f.; see also id., *Allgemeine Staatslehre*, 7th reissue of the 3rd edn. (1914) (Bad Homburg, 1960), 418 ff.

characterization of it as 'a relationship to the state which qualifies the individual'[8] is of central importance. A status is some sort of *relation* between the individual and the state. In that the relation *qualifies the individual*, it is to be seen as a state of affairs,[9] rather than a right.[10] This is because, as Jellinek puts it, status is concerned with what the person 'is' legally, rather than with what he 'has'.[11] What Jellinek means by 'is' and 'has' can be seen from his examples. Granting a person the right to vote and the unconditional right to acquire property affects his status and so also his legal existence,[12] but the acquisition of a particular piece of land only affects what he 'has'. However, these general descriptions are rather obscure. The idea of status is better clarified in the context of a fourfold division into the four 'status relationships'.[13]

1. THE PASSIVE STATUS

The passive status (*status subjectionis*) can be dealt with quite quickly. This expresses the role of the individual as 'subjected to the state . . . in the sphere of individual duty'.[14] This can be read in two ways. On the first reading, the fact that *x* finds himself in a passive status means simply that there are *some sort of* state commands or prohibitions applying to *x*, or that there are *some sort of* commands or prohibitions which could apply to *x*, that is, that the state has the power to issue commands and prohibitions applying to *x*. This is none other than *x*'s finding himself in a position of liability as against the state, in the sense used above.[15] On the second reading, the passive status of a person consists in the *entirety* or class of commands and prohibitions placed upon him by the state, or which the state has the power to place upon him. On the first account, the status does not change when individual applicable commands and prohibitions change, or when the power of the state to create them changes. The passive status would only cease to exist when there are no longer any applicable commands or prohibitions and when the state no longer has any power to create them. By contrast, on the second account every change of command or prohibition, or the state's power to create them, results in a change of status.

Comments of Jellinek's such as 'the relation between the individual and the state . . . [remains] quite unaffected by whatever content one chooses to

---

[8] id., *System der subjektiven öffentlichen Rechte*, 83: 'From a theoretical perspective, personality is a relationship to the state which qualifies the individual. Legally, it is therefore a state of affairs, a status.' On p. 118, Jellinek speaks of 'a relation between the individual and the state enhanced to the level of existence'. This corresponds to Wolff's characterization as 'the essential qualification of a person' (H. J. Wolff and O. Bachof, *Verwaltungsrecht I*, 9th edn. (Munich, 1975), para. 32 IV *a*).

[9] ibid. 83.   [10] ibid. 83 f.   [11] ibid. 84.   [12] ibid.
[13] ibid. 86.   [14] ibid.   [15] 155.

put into it',[16] and 'the substance of a status can thus never be defined'[17] indicate that the first interpretation was what he meant.

There is none the less a connection between the first and second interpretations. If x is not subject to at least one state command or prohibition, or if the state does not have the power to impose at least one particular command or prohibition on x, then x is not in a passive status. x's being in a passive status simply means that he finds himself in certain legal positions describable by way of the modes of command, prohibition, and power, or its converse, liability. Exactly what is commanded and prohibited can vary as much as the subject-matter of the power or liability. In other words, we have to distinguish between the content of a status and the status as such. The *content* of x's passive status can always be described by a bundle of positions as stated. By contrast, x's passive *status* as such is whatever it is that stays constant when the number or content of positions constituting the bundle change. The concept of the passive status is thus an *abstraction* of certain positions which are fully describable in terms of the normative modes referred to. In this sense it is reducible to the normative modes.[18]

[16] ibid. 118.

[17] ibid.

[18] According to Wolff, status is 'a concept of potential rights and duties' (Wolff and Bachof, *Verwaltungsrecht I*, para. 32 IV *a*; previous editions: 'essence'), the passive status is the 'essence [*Inbegriff*] of all potential duties of the private individual towards towards the state' (ibid., para. 32 IV *c* 1). The expression 'potential duty' is ambiguous. In its widest meaning it stands for every conceivable duty which could be imposed on the individual. It can hardly be assumed that Wolff is using the term in this sense. The passive status would then be the class of all possible duties. One ends up with a narrower meaning if by 'potential duties' one understands the class of all duties which the state can impose on the subject on the grounds of its *powers* within a certain legal system. Since in discussing the potential character of the duties, Wolff does not talk in terms of powers and liabilities, but states rather that they are realized 'in various forms according to varying social situations' (ibid., para. 32 IV *a*), a third possible meaning comes into play, namely that potential duties are *conditional* or hypothetical duties of (for the most part) relatively general character. Thus the owner of any piece of property has the conditional or hypothetical duty to remove any threat to public safety or public order which might arise from it. As a conditional duty, this duty applies to him even when the property is in an acceptable condition. The conditional duty becomes unconditional or categorical if a situation arises in which some danger flows from the property. Whether Wolff's definition of the passive status on one of these interpretations of the concept of potential duty reflects Jellinek's intentions depends on what he means by 'essence'. If by this he means a totality in the sense of a class, which would correspond to normal usage, then this does not match Jellinek's sense. The passive status is neither the *class* of conditional, nor unconditional, nor potential relative to state powers, nor merely conceivable, duties, but an *abstraction* of all classes of duty. If by 'essence' Wolff understands such an abstraction, which while not as close to the normal meaning of the word is still possible, then his definition only reflects Jellinek's intentions if it is related not only to potential duties in the third sense, but also to potential duties in the second sense and to unconditional duties. In short, Wolff's definition of passive status corresponds to the one given in the text above if 'essence' is understood to mean abstraction and the concept of potential duties is taken to include potential duties in both the second and third senses as well as unconditional duties.

2. The Negative Status

The idea of the passive status is relatively unproblematic. The same cannot be said of the negative status. One central problem concerning the structure of this status can be put like this: is the negative status constituted entirely by unprotected legal liberties in the sense used above,[19] or does it also include protection by way of rights of non-interference? When writers refer to the negative status, they are generally referring to defensive rights, that is, to rights to omissions as against the state. But this is inconsistent with Jellinek's own discussion.

Jellinek explains the idea of negative status in the following oft-cited words: 'Thus the member of the state acquires a status in which he is master, a sphere free from the state in which the right to govern is denied. It is the individual sphere of freedom, the *negative status* (status libertatis), in which purely individual purposes are satisfied by the free act of the individual.'[20] So the negative status is an individual sphere of freedom. But for Jellinek, the individual sphere of freedom is the class of 'legally irrelevant acts of the individual, as far as the state is concerned'.[21] Actions are legally irrelevant as far as the state is concerned if they are 'not capable of releasing a legally relevant effect'[22] at least as regards the relationship between the individual and the state. As examples of legally irrelevant acts, Jellinek cites the publication of a magazine, the enjoyment of one's own wine, and walking on one's own estate. Of course, the publication of a magazine could be tied to the conclusion of a contract, but this act only has significance as against third parties. Its legal irrelevance as far as the state is concerned remains unaffected.

What Jellinek calls 'legal irrelevance'[23] is simply freedom as explained above, which as legal freedom is the same thing as unprotected legal liberty.[24] An act is free when it is neither commanded nor prohibited, that is, when both doing it and not doing it are permitted. Jellinek actually wants to use the words 'permit' and 'may' in quite another context, applying them to legally relevant acts in a relationship of equality, that is, citizen to citizen.[25] We do not need to go into the many difficulties this gives rise to.[26] In the

---

[19] 144 ff.   [20] Jellinek, *System der subjektiven öffentlichen Rechte*, 87.
[21] ibid. 104.   [22] ibid. 46.
[23] Instead of legal irrelevance, Jellinek also speaks of 'legally indifferent' acts (ibid. 46).
[24] Thus Jellinek's *legal* irrelevance is not to be equated with *factual* irrelevance. If it is both permitted that one take part in political life as well as that one refrain from doing so, then participation in political life is legally irrelevant to the state in Jellinek's sense. In fact, for a democratic state it is highly relevant whether there are at least some citizens who take part in political life. But factual relevance does not give rise to legal relevance in Jellinek's sense. Of course, factually relevant acts can be turned into legally relevant ones. If this occurs by way of interpretation, then factual relevance can be put forward as an argument for legal relevance.
[25] ibid. 46, 49.
[26] See on these H. Kelsen, *Hauptprobleme der Staatsrechtslehre* (Tübingen, 1911), 632 ff.

context of removing a prohibition he is prepared to speak of a permission which is 'purely negative',[27] and the idea that legally irrelevant acts are neither commanded or prohibited is true in his system as well. So there is no reason to reject the point that Jellinek's mode of irrelevance is the same as liberty as expounded above.

The fact that Jellinek's negative status consists entirely of freedoms, that is, of unprotected legal liberties, is confirmed by his comments as regards their protection by rights of non-interference as against the state, in other words by what are generally called defensive rights. According to Jellinek, the negative status is 'protected by the individual's claim to recognition, and by the prohibition on state officials disturbing it, that is, the prohibition on any command or force without statutory basis'.[28] But this claim belongs 'like any other claim to specific state behaviour, to the *positive status* of the individual'.[29] It will be shown that Jellinek's location of the right to non-interference in the positive status is not unproblematic. It has the consequence that defensive rights have a distinctively homeless character in his system.

Once one assumes that the negative status only consists of unprotected legal liberties, it can be defined easily in parallel to the passive status. As with the passive status, one can distinguish within the negative status between the entirety of an individual's unprotected legal liberties and that which stays constant when he has differing liberties. The idea of a negative status is an abstraction like the passive status, only an abstraction of certain unprotected legal liberties. So once again we can distinguish the negative status as such and its content. The content can change, the negative status itself stays the same. This ties in with Jellinek's point that it is only a matter of 'freedom in the singular', and that 'the individual circumstances derived from the laws which recognize and enact freedom . . . is substantially singular for all cases'.[30]

The content of the negative status of an individual x at time t_1 consists of the entirety or class of all (unprotected legal) liberties which x has at time t_1 in relation to the state. The class of these unprotected legal liberties can be called 'x's *scope of freedom* at time t_1 in relation to the state'. Instead of 'scope of freedom' one could say, along with Jellinek, 'sphere of freedom' or 'area of freedom'.[31]

Jellinek's comments on the relationship between the negative and passive statuses are instructive and confirm earlier discussions. According to Jellinek, 'subjection and freedom from subjection' are the two mutually exclusive possibilities the state has in regulating its relationship to its subjects.[32] This points out that the passive and negative statuses are

---

[27] Jellinek, *System der subjektiven öffentliche Rechte*, 46.   [28] ibid. 105.
[29] ibid. (emphasis added).   [30] ibid. 104.   [31] ibid. 87, 104.
[32] ibid. 104.

contradictories. All actions which are neither commanded nor prohibited to
the individual belong to his sphere of freedom. All actions which are either
commanded or prohibited can be said to belong to his *sphere of duty*. Just
as the sphere of freedom is the content of the negative status, so the sphere
of duty is the content of the passive status.[33] Every negation of a freedom
belonging to the content of the negative status leads to an equivalent
command or prohibition in the passive status. Every negation of a
command or prohibition belonging to the content of the sphere of duty
leads to an equivalent freedom in the negative status, assuming that no new
command or prohibition has been enacted.[34] Every increase of the legal
sphere of duty is (logically) a reduction in the legal sphere of freedom, and
vice versa. The fact that Jellinek sees the content of the passive and negative statuses as mutually exclusive possibilities on the same level is a further
argument for treating the negative status as embracing only unprotected
legal liberties.

Jellinek's views on the relationship between status and rights are problematic. Jellinek says that subjective public law rights[35] *result from*, are
based upon,[36] are *connected to*,[37] *spring from*,[38] are *created by*,[39] statuses.
If someone says that the negative status creates a right to non-obstruction,
they could mean two things. They could mean that the right follows logically from the status, but they could also mean that some weaker sort of
relation exists between the two. The first would be false, because as has
been shown above, unprotected freedoms cannot give rise to rights to
anything, and thus also not to rights that the beneficiary should not be
obstructed. So the relation must be a non-logical one. A non-logical relation
could be established by the purpose of the freedom. If the individual is to
be guaranteed a sphere of freedom in as secure a fashion as possible, it is
necessary to protect him by granting him rights of non-obstruction and
non-removal.

Thus the connection between negative status and its protection is
supported by substantive considerations. What these substantive consider-

[33] More precisely, one could distinguish between the spheres of actual and potential duty.
The sphere of potential duty is constituted by the class of commands and prohibitions which
the legislature has the power to enact. A corresponding distinction can be drawn in the case of
the sphere of liberty.
[34] This clause is necessary, since a prohibition could be enacted in place of a command, and
this would exclude the creation of a legal liberty. It is hardly worth mentioning the requirement that the content of the passive status must be internally consistent. If it were to include
both a command to perform and a prohibition on performing the same act, the negation of
either the command or the prohibition would lead to a removal of the inconsistency, but not
to liberty.
[35] Jellinek often talks of claims [*Ansprüche*] rather than rights. By this, he means concrete
and actual rights, such as the right of an owner against an actual trespasser that he refrain
from trespass (ibid. 54 f.). Under the terminology adopted here, this is a right to something.
[36] ibid. 86.   [37] ibid. 84.   [38] ibid. 106.
[39] ibid. 106. Similarly also Wolff, in Wolff and Bachof, *Verwaltungsrecht I,* para. 32 IV *a.*

ations connect together are positions within Jellinek's system which are, from a formal point of view, quite different—positions belonging to the negative and positive statuses. This does not count against the system; it simply highlights the fact that it is rather crude and that it needs grounding in a theory of basic legal positions.[40]

3. THE POSITIVE STATUS

It was said of the passive and negative statuses that they stand in contradiction to each other, just as command and prohibition do to liberty. Jellinek's comment about the positive status being an 'equal counterpart to the negative'[41] seems to point to an equally close relationship. In order to establish what he meant by this, we need to look at his understanding of the positive status, the *status civitatis*.

The individual is placed in such a status whenever the state 'recognizes his legal capacity to use state power and institutions for his own purposes, that is, to grant the individual positive claim-rights'.[42] It is not clear what this means. It becomes clearer when Jellinek says that the state grants the individual 'civic status' by (1) 'granting him claims to its activity' and (2) 'making available legal means to realize this'.[43] Jellinek describes rights which the individual can enforce though some legal procedure as 'formal positive legal claims [*Ansprüche*]'.[44] The fact that the individual has such claims against the state means first that he has *rights to something* as

---

[40] The reconstruction undertaken here differs at significant points from Rupp's version, which is one of the most interesting developments of Jellinek's status theory. Rupp's discussion is limited to the negative and positive statuses. As far as the negative status is concerned, Rupp emphasizes, as does Jellinek, that this is to be strictly distinguished from subjective rights: 'a status is in reality only a state of affairs outlined in statute by a bundle of normative "duties of respect" on the part of the Administration' (H. H. Rupp, *Grundfragen der heutigen Verwaltungsrechtslehre* (Tübingen, 1965), 162). With this, negative status is not defined as in the text above as an abstraction of freedoms or unprotected legal liberties, and there is no concept of protection by way of rights to non-obstruction. Rather, Rupp agrees with Jellinek that the status can 'give rise' to subjective rights (ibid.). But departing from Jellinek he makes it clear that such rights do not flow from the status alone (ibid. 172). On the contrary, if this is to happen, a further 'substantive administrative basic norm' giving rise to these rights is necessary (ibid. 250, 251, 253). As the comments in the text above show, this argument can in principle be accepted. What cannot be accepted is Rupp's definition of this basic norm. According to Rupp, it does not lead to rights to omissions, such as Jellinek's right to non-obstruction, but purely to claim-rights of reaction which arise when the status is infringed (ibid. 164). According to Rupp, such reaction claim-rights are the only possible relevant subjective rights (ibid. 164 f.). By reaction claim-rights he means rights to remove the infringement (ibid. 254 ff.). There can be no objection to the idea that infringements of status give rise to reaction claim-rights. But what is not obvious is why only these should be called 'subjective rights'. There are no difficulties associated with treating liberties of the negative status as protected by subjective rights to non-obstruction, and where these rights are infringed, which is always simultaneously an infringement of the corresponding state duty, adopting a claim-right to remove the infringement as a secondary subjective right.

[41] Jellinek, *System der subjektiven öffentlichen Rechte*, 121.

[42] ibid. 87.   [43] ibid. 114.   [44] ibid. 70.

against the state, and secondly that he has the *power* to enforce them. According to Jellinek, the existence of such a power is a necessary condition of the individual's occupying the positive status.[45] The formula by which Jellinek pulls together 'all the formally recognized individualized legal claims which arise from the positive status'—the 'legally protected capacity to demand positive performance from the state'[46]—is to be read in this double sense.[47]

The aspect of power and other refinements aside, the heart of the positive status is the right of the citizen as against the state, to certain actions by the state. This is what Jellinek is getting at with his 'equal counterpart to the negative'. The right of x against the state to some state action ϕ correlates to the duty of the state to x to perform ϕ. Just as a dispute about the content of the negative status of x will turn on whether x is required to do or refrain from ϕ'-ing, or whether he is at liberty in respect of ϕ', so a dispute about the content of the positive status is concerned with whether the state is required to do or refrain from ϕ-ing, or whether the state is at liberty in respect of ϕ. In other words, one is 'determining the freedom of the state'.[48] Talk of equal counterpart points to the idea that the extent of the positive status of the citizen corresponds to what one could call the 'passive status of the state', as well as to the idea that everything in the state–citizen relationship which does not belong to the positive status of the citizen belongs to what can be called the 'negative status of the state'.[49]

As with the passive and the negative statuses, so also the positive status

---

[45] See ibid. 115 f.

[46] ibid. 121.

[47] In reality, matters are more complex than this. Jellinek distinguishes three main types of claim within the positive status, the claim to legal protection, the claim to the satisfaction of interests, and the claim that regard should be had for interests (ibid. 124 ff., 128 ff., 130 ff., 132). The claim to legal protection serves on one hand the protection of private law positions and on the other hand 'the protection of public law claims arising from public status relationships' (ibid. 126). According to Jellinek, the claim to legal protection consists 'every time of the legally guaranteed capacity to enforce public law norms for reasons of individual interest' (ibid. 127). This is to be seen as a power. At the same time, there are several formulations which indicate an interpretation of the claim to legal protection as a right against the state to something. So Jellinek speaks of 'a claim against the state itself that it carry out judicial acts at the request of the individual' (ibid. 127). Thus even in the field of legal protection there is a duplication. The consequence of this for formal public law claims can be shown from the example of the claim to the satisfaction of interests, and in particular the right 'of admission to places of higher education' (ibid. 129). To amount to a formal claim-right this right must be connected with a claim to legal protection. If one adopts this connection, the following threefold structure emerges: (i) a right against the state to attend a place of higher education, (ii) a power to pursue this right by way of legal action, and (iii) a right against the state that it process properly the legal proceedings commenced under the power. Jellinek's claim to legal protection in the case of private law positions is to be read such that the first element arising from the connection with a claim to legal protection is not a right against the state but a right against a private individual.

[48] ibid. 121.

[49] Both are represented in the equivalences discussed above: $RxyG \leftrightarrow OyxG$ and $\bar{R}xyG \leftrightarrow \bar{\ } OyxG$.

is not identical to the rights 'springing from it'.[50] [51] But if the positive status does not consist of certain rights to something, then as with the statuses already considered, it can only consist of what stays the same as the enforceable rights to something against the state change. If the positive status is such an abstraction, one can hardly talk about rights 'springing from it'.[52]

In discussing the negative status, it was pointed out that Jellinek included a 'claim of non-interference against state officials'[53] as 'belonging to the positive status of the individual, like any other claim to specific state action'.[54] This claim is a right against the state to a non-action, or omission. However, locating such a right in the positive status, which is consistent with Jellinek's definition of the negative status, contradicts his statement that the rights forming the content of the positive status presuppose 'a *positive act* on the part of the state'.[55] Omitting to obstruct the individual's freedom could be described as an 'act', but hardly as a 'positive act'. If one were to take these words seriously, then the right to non-obstruction, which corresponds to what is generally known as a defensive right, would not be located in any status. One would have to conclude that one of the most important constitutional rights positions has no place in Jellinek's system. This can only be avoided by locating it as part of the negative or the positive status.

The problem is that both solutions have undesirable consequences. If one puts the right to non-obstruction in the negative status, this fundamentally changes its character. The architecture of Jellinek's system starts collapsing. If one puts it in the positive status, the fundamentally important distinction in constitutional doctrine between rights to negative and positive acts of the state is no longer expressed. Locating defensive rights in the positive status contradicts the widespread and not unjustified terminology of standard constitutional doctrine. This dilemma is a consequence of the crude nature of Jellinek's system. The solution is to refine the negative and positive statuses in the light of basic legal positions into narrow and broad senses. The *negative* status in the *narrow* sense—Jellinek's own sense—consists exclusively of unprotected legal liberties. The negative status in the *broad* sense, going beyond Jellinek's system, includes the rights to non-actions by the state to protect the negative status in the narrow sense (defensive rights). The *positive* status in the *broad* sense embraces both rights to positive

---

[50] ibid. 124, 121, 128.   [51] ibid. 118.

[52] Rupp takes the view that Jellinek's thesis that subjective rights arise from the statuses 'only actually applies in the case of the status negativus or libertatis' (Rupp, *Grundfragen der heutigen Verwaltungsrechtslehre*, 265). It has already been shown that the 'arising' or 'springing' of rights from the negative status is really the *addition* of rights to something onto unprotected liberties. If one rejects this, then there is a really significant difference between the positive and negative status. Positive status rights are not added to something, but constitute in their entirety the content of the positive status.

[53] ibid. 111.   [54] ibid. 105.   [55] ibid. 121 (emphasis added).

actions as well as rights to negative actions, but the positive status in the *narrow* sense only includes rights to positive actions. The systematic consequences of this division for Jellinek's system are simple to grasp. Rights which are added to the negative status in its narrow sense to expand it to the broad sense (defensive rights) are a sub-division of positive status rights in the wide sense.

The practical objection which can be made to this solution is that it complicates constitutional discourse. Whenever one speaks of positive or negative status, one has to make clear whether one is referring to narrow or wide senses, and qualifications such as these are not self-explanatory. But this objection can easily be dismissed. In normal constitutional argument, the context generally makes clear what is meant by negative and positive status. Generally, negative status is meant in its wide sense, and positive in its narrow sense. They can be used in this way without qualification, as they will be from now on. Whenever doubt arises, this can quickly be dispelled by reference back to the basic positions, which form the basis of the distinctions drawn here. When we are concerned with difficult constitutional issues involving the theory of statuses itself, then the distinctions just drawn are absolutely necessary.

4. THE ACTIVE STATUS

What the relationship between the command or prohibition applicable to the individual is to the passive status, what freedom is to the negative status, and what the right to something is to the positive status, so is legal power to the active status or status of active citizenship.[56] In order to grant the individual such a status he must be given 'a capacity beyond that of his natural liberty'[57] such as the right to vote.[58] A detailed discussion of the formal structure of this status can be dispensed with here. The possibility of reconstructing it, so far as constitutional rights are concerned, with the help of the juridical mode of power is obvious, and the general problem of the separation of status from the rights 'springing from it' has already been adequately referred to.

By contrast to the formal structure of the active status, which can be adequately characterized by using the idea of power, its substantive content needs some comment. Not every power within the legal system is to be counted part of the active status. If this were true, the power to conclude a contract would be included. According to Jellinek, only those powers of 'participation in the state',[59] which serve the 'process of state decision-taking',[60] belong to the active status. This introduces a substantive element into the purely formally constructed status theory, which gives rise to prob-

---

[56] See on this above at 149 ff.   [57] ibid. 138.   [58] ibid. 159 ff.
[59] ibid. 137.   [60] ibid. 136.

lems of boundaries. It is easy enough to say that the power to conclude a contract does not belong to the active status and there can be little doubt that the right to vote is the prototype of an active status power. But alongside such clear cases there are plenty of doubtful ones. Thus the power to bring an action before the administrative courts is a power within the citizen–state relationship, but under Jellinek's criterion of participation within the state, it is doubtful whether it belongs to the active status. At this point we see once again the relatively crude character of Jellinek's theory, and the necessity of expanding and correcting it by way of the more precise theory of basic legal positions.

Of particular significance for the active status is its connection with positions within the other statuses. Positions within the active status are always associated with positions of some other status, because the appropriation of a power is always either commanded or prohibited (passive status) or left free (negative status). According to Jellinek, the individual is incorporated within the active status when his sphere 'is not limited by duty, but expanded by the capacity to act legally'.[61] This should not be understood to mean that the active and passive statuses are incompatible with each other. Even those who are under an obligation to vote are given the power or the 'capacity to become active for the state'.[62] They are incorporated 'as members of the state organization'; they are 'active for the state'.[63] As a rule, the realization of the powers that make up the content of the active status are 'left free to the individual'.[64] In these cases, the active status is combined with the negative status. Finally, the active and positive statuses can be combined, as in the right to the power or capacity to vote. When Jellinek refers to a 'legal claim to a position within a public body'[65] this is what he is referring to.

II. ON THE CRITIQUE OF JELLINEK'S STATUS THEORY

Jellinek's status theory is, in spite of its many obscurities and some faults, one of the greatest examples of analytical construction in the field of constitutional rights. The central concepts of this theory—the four statuses—are abstractions of elementary positions. This explains both its strengths and its weaknesses. Its weaknesses lie in the fact that the relationships between the elementary positions and the statuses, as well as between the different elementary positions, are not always clear. However, these weaknesses can be removed by grounding the theory in an account of basic legal positions. If the latter is itelf in turn based on a theory of basic deontic modes, we end up with a system of perfect clarity, which enables a high degree of necessary

[61] ibid. 139.　[62] ibid. 87.　[63] ibid. 139.　[64] ibid.
[65] ibid. 140.

analytical insight into constitutional rights. It can also be pointed out that the theory has a certain conceptual beauty.

This evaluation of the formal or analytical part of Jellinek's theory does not extend to the substantive content which Jellinek ties it to. One can raise objections most of all to Jellinek's thoughts on the content of the negative status (in what follows, understood in its narrow sense). Its content is determined by what the individual is neither required nor forbidden to do. According to Jellinek, it is up to the legislature to decide this, since 'all these freedoms are only recognized within the boundaries of the law'.[66] The content of the negative status thus lies at the disposal of the legislature. Consistently with this view, Jellinek limits the negative status to the right of the citizen against the state that 'it should not engage in any *illegal* activity'. 'All freedom is simply freedom from unlawful force.'[67]

These comments on the content of the negative status contradict applicable constitutional law, which binds the legislature to constitutional rights norms. They could not be maintained in the context of the Basic Law. This does not mean that the concept of negative status has become dispensable. In considering the idea of unprotected legal liberty, it was pointed out that constitutional rights norms are to be understood, among other things, as permissive norms.[68] On this basis, we can build up a concept of negative *constitutional* status. The content of the negative constitutional status of *x* consists of everything that *x* is free to do on the basis of constitutional permissive norms. The negative constitutional status can be infringed by the legislature, say by enacting prohibiting norms in contradiction to a constitutional permissive norm. The problem of the content of the negative status can thus be resolved by introducing the idea of negative constitutional status.[69]

Fundamental objections are often made to Jellinek's status theory on the ground of its formal nature. Hesse complains that his negative status is 'purely formal', that the person benefiting from it is 'not the human being or citizen of real life', and the freedom guaranteed is 'unrelated to specific concrete relationships in real life'. By contrast, constitutional rights norms contain a 'substantive guarantee and foundation', and so Jellinek's formal statuses should be replaced with a 'material legal status', which is based upon and guaranteed by the constitutional rights of the Basic Law.[70]

---

[66] ibid. 103.   [67] ibid. (emphasis added).
[68] 146.
[69] See H. H. Rupp, 'Grundrechtlicher Freiheitsstatus und ungesetzlicher Zwang', DÖV 1974, 194, who emphasizes that Jellinek's arguments concerning the content of the negative status do not stand in the way of an application of this concept in the field of constitutional rights: 'Nothing stands in the way of understanding the specific constitutional status of liberty as individual freedom from *unconstitutional* force'.
[70] K. Hesse, *Grundzüge des Verfassungsrechts der Bundesrepublik Deutschland*, 14th edn. (Heidelberg, 1984), para. 280 f.

Häberle[71] objects that Jellinek's status theory removes from constitutional rights an 'active civic moment'. The individual statuses appear 'in a spatial manner of thinking in isolation and starkly next to each other'. They make it impossible to express the point that the protection of constitutional rights turns their 'beneficiaries factually and socially into active state citizens'. What Smend defines as the 'point of a constitution', 'to order living human beings into common political body' gets lost.[72] Preuß—to mention a third perspective—locates his criticism of Jellinek's status theory[73] in a more basic criticism of the category of subjective right. One of his basic assumptions is that 'social relations of human beings . . . do not admit of being organized into a system of allocated individually-controlled spheres of life. The current order of highly interdependent and organizationally-mediated social relationships requires a set of legal categories which capture this social medium and overcome the idea of individually controlled spheres of life.'[74] The concept of a subjective right, and thus also Jellinek's status theory, cannot do this.[75] Preuß recommends instead an understanding of 'constitutionally guaranteed freedoms, not as subjective rights, but as organizational norms of social freedom', a 'conception of constitutional rights as guarantees of concrete liberty in society'.[76]

These comments, which could be increased by many more in similar vein, contain the most important headings of a general critique of the formal nature of Jellinek's status theory. It goes: formalism, abstraction, spatialization, isolated individual, obsolete. The counterparts are: reality, concrete, mediation, common life/society, current. This list makes it clear that we are dealing with an old opposition between formal and substantive theories. By qualifying the problem this way, it means that the basic dispute about (formal) status theory is not a matter of true and false, but of relevance and irrelevance. If legal norms regulate the relationship of the individual to the state, then this can only happen by commanding or prohibiting the individual or the state from doing certain things, or granting them liberty, and by giving the individual certain entitlements and powers. If this occurs, then abstractions from classes of commands and

---

[71] P. Häberle, *Die Wesensgehaltgarantie des Artikel 19 Abs. 2 Grundesetze*, 3rd edn. (Heidelberg, 1983), 18 f.; see also E. Denninger, *Rechtsperson und Solidarität* (Frankfurt and Berlin, 1967), 294; W. Krebs, *Vorbehalt des Gesetzes und Grundrechte* (Berlin, 1975), 64.

[72] R. Smend, 'Bürger und Bourgeois im deutschen Staatsrecht', in id., *Staatsrechtliche Abhandlungen und andere Aufsätze*, 2nd edn. (Berlin, 1968), 320, fn. 15.

[73] U. K. Preuß, *Die Internalisierung des Subjekts* (Frankfurt a. M., 1979), 23, 119, 131, 136.

[74] ibid. 28.

[75] See Preuß's critique of Rupp's version of the status theory, ibid. 198 f.

[76] ibid. 193. See also 165 f.: 'In this day and age the fact that the "classic" liberal dimension of constitutional rights—the status libertatis in Jellinek's status theory—is not exhausted by its function of limiting state power needs no justification. It is now well-established that the liberty rights of the Basic Law presuppose social fields of organized liberty, even if there is admittedly no agreement over the consequences of this fact.'

prohibitions, liberties, entitlements, and powers are also possible. But in that case we can speak of four different statuses. The qualification of the legal position of the citizen performed by this process has a purely *analytical* character. This has nothing to say—and makes no assumptions—about the substantive *normative* question of how the legal positions are to be fleshed out. And the same applies to the *empirical* question of what it means for the individual and society that the citizen has a certain status.

Constitutional rights norms grant the citizen a status with a particular content, among other things, a negative constitutional status. To this extent, Hesse's suggestion of a 'substantive legal status' is valid. But it does not follow from this that formal status theory is objectionable. The complete legal position of the citizen can be viewed from both formal and substantive perspectives. When Häberle says that status theory does not comprehend the real social situation of the active citizen, in which constitutional rights norms are supposed to place the individual, he is right. But first, this is not its point, and, secondly, it does not prevent one from doing this. The content of status theory is the formal structure of the complete legal position of the citizen. The fact that some understanding of this is useful even in the context of the problems raised by Häberle can be seen by the fact that we need to consider not only the necessary content of constitutional rights norms, so that the individual can be put into the position of an active citizen, but also what form these norms are to have for this purpose. For example, are liberties and powers of the citizen adequate, or are civic duties, or duties of the state to ensure certain factual conditions, also necessary? Clarity about such questions is a necessary precondition for a rational discussion about theses such as Häberle's. The same applies for Preuß's conception of constitutional rights norms as 'organizational norms of social freedom'. If these organizational norms are legal norms, they must express commands, prohibitions, liberties, entitlements, and powers. Preuß confirms this when he admits that within the organizational norms that create social freedom, 'naturally one can find individual entitlements'.[77] On the whole he does not appear to be criticizing the concept of a subjective right as a juridical mode, but rather subjective rights of a certain content and the theories underlying them. This becomes apparent when he admits that the 'problem about subjective rights lies . . . not in their function in allocating individual interests and powers' but in an individualizing and subjectivizing of collective interests.[78] In short, the problem is one of content.

There can be no doubt that the problem of content highlighted by these writers is a very significant one for a 'three-dimensional' theory of constitutional rights.[79] But this does not imply, either from an intellectual or from

---

[77] Preuß, *Die Internalisierung des Subjekts*, 193.   [78] ibid. 200.
[79] On the three-dimensionality of constitutional rights theory, see above at 6 ff.

a practical perspective, that an analytical status theory is less important or not important at all. As an attempt to understand complicated structures it has an intellectual justification quite apart from any practical use. Its practical usefulness is demonstrated by the many obscurities and contradictions which experience shows that theories in the complex field of constitutional rights cannot avoid, if they abandon the formal to focus solely on the substantive.

The criticism of 'spatial thought processes'[80] seems to go further than mere formality. According to Rupp, 'thinking in spatial categories is the enemy of all academic legal attempts to conceive of law as a social phenomenon'.[81] In the context of our discussion of status theory, the idea of a sphere of freedom was explicitly included. A sphere of freedom is none other than a class of specific liberties. So long as one understands the idea of a sphere of freedom in this sense, it is not only harmless, it is indispensable. Relating to classes of objects is an unavoidable element of thought and speech. One could criticize the use of the expression, 'sphere'. But its use as a mark of certain classes is possible and normal. In general contexts one can refer to 'scope for action' and in philosophical connections to the 'realm of the possible'. So it is not just harmless, it is also appropriate for the Federal Constitutional Court to refer to a 'legally free sphere',[82] a 'legal sphere',[83] and a 'sphere of freedom'.[84]

---

[80] Häberle, *Die Wesensgehaltguarantie*, 18.
[81] Rupp, *Grundfragen der heutigen Verwaltungsrechtslehre*, 258, fn. 425; see also E. v. Hippel, *Grenzen und Wesensgehalt der Grundrechte* (Berlin, 1965), 19.
[82] BVerfGE 32, 98 (106).   [83] BVerfGE 33, 23 (28).   [84] BVerfGE 35, 79 (112).

6

The Limits of Constitutional Rights

I. THE CONCEPT AND TYPES OF CONSTITUTIONAL RIGHTS LIMIT

At first sight, the concept of a limited right seems familiar and unproblematic. The idea that rights have limits and that they can be limited seems to be an obvious—almost trivial—point, reflected most clearly when the Basic Law speaks of limits (arts. 5(2); 14(1)(2) [*Schranken*]) and limitations (arts. 8(2), 10(2), 13(3), 104(1) [*Beschränkungen*] and arts. 11(2), 17a(1) and (2), 19(1) [*Einschränkungen*]). It is not the concept of a limit to a constitutional right which is problematic, but rather identifying permissible content and extent, along with the way to distinguish limitation from other things such as regulation, outworking, and concretization.

1. THE LOGICAL POSSIBILITY OF LIMITS

As often with basic concepts, the first impression of simplicity is misleading, and among those who have helped to destroy it, Friedrich Klein should be mentioned. Klein objects to the view connected with the 'term "limits", which prioritizes a "natural" perspective [that] . . . constitutional rights—as something permanent because they are prior to the state or because they are constitutionally guaranteed—are limited (relativised)'. Such a relationship between the enactment and limitation of constitutional rights provisions simply cannot exist, he argues, 'according to the laws of pure logic'. 'According to the laws of pure logic [there are] no limits to constitutional rights provisions, but only definitions of those provisions.'[1] The question is whether Klein is right.

The concept of a limit to a right seems to presuppose that there are two things—a right and its limit—between which there is a certain special type of relation, namely a relation of limitation. If the relation between a right and its limit is to be thought of in this way, then there is first the *right in*

---

[1] F. Klein, in H. v. Mangoldt and F. Klein, *Das Bonner Grundgesetz*, i, 5th edn. (Berlin and Frankfurt, 1957), *Vorbemerkung* B XV 1 *b* (122).

itself, which is not limited, and secondly there is what is left over once the limit has been applied, that is, the *right as limited*. This view is called the '*external theory*', often with negative overtones.[2] The external theory can accept that rights in legal systems appear mostly or exclusively as limited rights, but it must insist that they are also conceivable without limits. So according to the external theory there is no necessary relationship between the concept of a right and the concept of a limit. The relationship arises first with the requirement external to the right itself to reconcile it with the rights of other individuals or with other individual rights and collective interests.

The so-called '*internal theory*' paints quite a different picture.[3] According to this approach, there are not two things, a right and its limit, but simply one, a right which has a certain content. The idea of a limit is replaced by that of extent.[4] Doubts about the extent of rights are not doubts about how far they can be limited, but doubts about their content. If instead of the 'extent' of a right one wants to talk about its 'limits', then the term 'immanent limits' can be used.

The dispute between the internal and the external theories is not merely a dispute about conceptual and formal matters. There are significant connections between a given theory of limits and general normative assumptions. Someone who maintains an individualistic theory of state and society will tend towards the external theory, and someone who is more concerned about the role of members of society in a common life will tend towards the internal theory. It is not possible to establish more than this general tendency without engaging in more precise analysis of the relation between a right and its limits.

Which of the external and internal theories is correct depends primarily upon whether constitutional rights norms are seen as rules or principles, that is, whether they give rise to definitive or prima facie positions. If one assumes that they give rise to definitive positions, then the external theory can be disproved; if one assumes that they give rise to prima facie positions, then the internal theory must go.

A simple case can be used to demonstrate the way in which the external theory can be refuted, and Klein's thesis of the logical impossibility of

---

[2] See W. Siebert, 'Vom Wesen des Rechtsmißbrauchs', in G. Dahm *et al.*, *Grundlagen der neuen Rechtswissenschaft* (Berlin, 1935), 195.

[3] On this, see above all W. Siebert, *Verwirkung und Unzulässigkeit der Rechtsausübung* (Marburg, 1934), 85 ff.; id., *Vom Wesen des Rechtsmißbrauchs*, 195, 200 ff. Siebert refers to Gierke's 'germanic view . . . that every right has its own immanent limits' (O. v. Gierke, *Die soziale Aufgabe des Privatrechts* (Berlin, 1889), 20; see also id., *Deutsches Privatrecht*, ii (Leipzig, 1905), 358). K. Larenz, 'Rechtsperson und subjektives Recht', in G. Dahm *et al.*, *Grundlagen der neuen Rechtswissenschaft* (Berlin, 1935), 230 ff. is among those who follow Siebert. Häberle has attempted to evaluate the internal theory in the context of constitutional rights (P. Häberle, *Die Wesensgehaltgarantie*, 3rd edn. (Heidelberg, 1983), 179 f.).

[4] See Häberle, *Die Wesensgehaltgarantie*, 126.

constitutional rights limits confirmed, if one proceeds exclusively on the basis of *definitive positions*. The case concerned a constitutional complaint against the imposition of a fine on motorcycle riders who failed to wear a crash helmet.[5] The requirement to wear a crash helmet limits general legal liberty by removing the specific legal liberty of motorcycle riders to choose whether to wear a crash helmet or not. The Federal Constitutional Court therefore speaks appropriately of 'limiting . . . freedom of action'.[6] But has a constitutional right been limited? The only possible candidates are positions under article 2(1) Basic Law. As has been shown above,[7] combining the scope and limiting clause of a right results in an *abstract definitive* position. The abstract definitive position relevant here is the right of the individual that his general freedom of action should not be limited by norms which are not part of the constitutional order, that is, which are not procedurally and substantively compatible with the Constitution.[8] We can assume, along with the Federal Constitutional Court, that the norm in question is fully compatible with the Constitution. This means that the abstract definitive right in article 2(1) Basic Law cannot be concretized into a right against the state that this particular norm should not be passed. If one assumes that there is only this abstract definitive right, then such a concrete right does not exist. But if it does not exist, then the norm in question cannot limit any right under article 2(1) Basic Law. Nor would there be a limitation if the norm were not compatible (procedurally or substantively) with the Constitution. Then it would simply infringe the abstract right and be unconstitutional. The infringement of a constitutional right is something quite different from its limitation. This shows that if one proceeds exclusively on the basis of definitive positions, it is not possible for rights under article 2(1) Basic Law to be limited. The point can be generalized: when the outcome is that it is definitively permissible to command or prohibit some act ϕ, then there is, in the outcome, no definitive right freely to choose ϕ. Norms which prevent one from doing what one has no right to do cannot limit rights. However, if there is, in the outcome, a definitive right to liberty in respect of ϕ, then norms which command or prohibit ϕ do not limit that right, they infringe it.[9]

If one wanted to maintain the assumption that constitutional rights are only definitive positions, it could be argued that it is not constitutional rights which can be limited, but only constitutional liberties. This suggestion would only make sense by distinguishing between general legal liberty and constitutionally protected liberty, because it is trivially true that general

---

[5] BVerfGE 59, 275.   [6] BVerfGE 59, 275 (279).
[7] 85 f.
[8] BVerfGE 59, 275 (278); with reference to BVerfGE 6, 32 (37 ff.).
[9] For a similar argument, see K. Brinkmann, *Grundrechts-Kommentar* (Bonn, 1967), Art. 1 III a ß, Art. 19 I 1 b; J. Schwabe, *Probleme der Grundrechtsdogmatik* (Darmstadt, 1977), 64 ff.

legal liberty, which consists solely of the absence of legal commands and prohibitions,[10] can be limited. A constitutional liberty arises when a choice of action is kept free *by a constitutional rights norm*. But even here a distinction must be drawn between definitive and prima facie positions. If one sticks with definitive positions, as assumed, then the suggestion that constitutional liberties can be limited does not apply. There is no definitive constitutional liberty to wear a crash helmet, that is, no constitutional permission to wear a helmet or not. So there is no constitutional liberty to be limited by the duty to wear a helmet. What can be, and is, limited, is general legal liberty. General legal liberty could be called the 'interest protected' by article 2(1) Basic Law. By proceeding on the basis of definitive positions, one comes to the conclusion that constitutional rights can never be limited, but constitutionally protected interests can be.

By contrast, one reaches quite a different conclusion, if what is to be limited is understood not as a definitive but as a prima facie position, as in the theory of principles. A principle is to be derived from article 2(1) Basic Law requiring as great a degree of freedom of action as possible. The prima facie constitutional right corresponding to this principle is something over-extensive which can be limited. This over-extensive principle is neither something outside the legal system, perhaps a natural right, liberty, or state of affairs, nor is it something of lower status to the Constitution. Rather it belongs to the norms of the Constitution. By proceeding on the basis of the model of principles, it is not simply an interest protected by a constitutional rights norm, but a guaranteed prima facie right which is being limited. Within the model of principles, talk of limits to constitutional rights is justified.[11] The external theory applies, and Klein's objections do not.

2. The Concept of a Constitutional Rights Limit

Now that it is clear that we can speak in terms of 'limits to constitutional rights' and what we mean by that, we have to ask what limits actually are. The things that are limitable are constitutionally protected interests (liberties, states of affairs, ordinary legal positions) and prima facie positions protected by constitutional rights. There are close connections between these two types of object. Constitutional principles require a maximally extensive protection of interests, such as the greatest protection possible for general freedom of action, bodily integrity, or an owner's power of alienation. The limitation of a protected interest is thus always a limitation of a prima facie position established by a constitutional principle. So the following straightforward answer can be given to the question of what constitutional rights

---

[10] See above at 144.

[11] Since it is the case that talk of constitutional rights limits is only appropriate in the model of principles, those who adopt this manner of speech must either be speaking purely metaphorically, or they must presuppose the model of principles.

limits are: constitutional rights limits are norms limiting prima facie constitutional rights positions. This answer is rather circular, because in defining
limits it uses the idea of limiting. But it does take us a little further, because
it tells us that constitutional rights limits are norms. So we can now ask
what it is that turns a norm into a constitutional rights limit.

We can start with a general point. A norm can only limit a constitutional
right if it is itself constitutional. If it were unconstitutional, then its enactment might be an infringement of a right, but it cannot set limits. This
establishes a first characteristic: norms are only limits to constitutional
rights if they are *compatible with the constitution*.

In solving the problem of what turns norms compatible with the constitution into constitutional rights limits, we have to distinguish between
different types of norm. The distinction between competence norms establishing norm-enacting powers of the state on one hand, and commands and
prohibitions addressed to the citizen on the other, is particularly important.
Competence norms, which are the most important in limiting constitutional
rights, can be found in the constitutional statutory reservations. These
empower the legislature to set limits to rights; the power of the legislature
thus corresponds to a liability of the right-holder.[12] Indirect powers are to
be distinguished from the direct powers found in statutory reservations to
constitutional rights provisions. Indirect powers arise, for example, when
the legislature empowers an administrative body to pass delegated legislation or administrative acts. All types of competence norm do not *limit*
constitutional rights but only establish their *limitability*. So statutory reservations are as such not limitations of constitutional rights; they simply
establish the *legal possibility* of limiting rights, which is apparent from the
fact that a power to set limits can exist without being used. We can therefore say that at whatever level competence norms establishing the power to
enact norms appear within the legal system, they are not limits to constitutional rights. One must accept that from the perspective of the constitutional right-holder, powers to set limits to rights are, in one sense,
restrictive. The extent of the power of the state organ correlates to the
extent of subordination to norms created under the power. But powers to
set limits are only restrictive because it is limits that the norms empower the
state to enact. Their limiting nature is thus merely potential and indirect,
and based on the nature of the norms which may be enacted under the
power.[13]

A moment ago, a contrast was drawn between competence norms which

---

[12] See above at 155, where the relationship between power and liability was represented by
the equivalence $Cxy\ (LPy) \leftrightarrow Syx\ (LPy)$.

[13] P. Lerche, *Übermaß und Verfassungsrecht* (Cologne, Berlin, Munich, and Bonn, 1961),
106 describes authorizing statutes as 'infringing norms' as well. This is correct to the extent
that the power to set limits, which is always also a power to infringe rights, *potentially and
indirectly* limits or infringes in the sense described above.

grant powers to the state to set limits to rights, and commanding and
prohibiting norms addressed to the citizen. It is not actually only commanding and prohibiting norms which are relevant, but also norms which limit
the powers of the citizen. But what is about to be said in respect of
commanding and prohibiting norms can in principle be applied to other
norms as well. Only commanding and prohibiting norms will be considered
here. The distinction between rules and principles is fundamentally important in this context. Let us consider first rules which set limits. A (constitutionally compatible) *rule* limits a constitutional right when, if it is
applicable, a definitive no-liberty or no-right of the same content applies in
place of a constitutional prima facie liberty or right.[14] Some examples will
explain what this means. So long as there is no command that motorcycle
riders should wear crash helmets, the individual constitutional right-holder
has, on the basis of the principle of general freedom of action, a prima facie
constitutional liberty to wear or not to wear a crash helmet as a motorcycle rider. The moment the command applies validly, he finds himself in a
position of definitive no-liberty to wear or not to wear a crash helmet as a
motorcycle rider. The rule which obligates a motorcycle rider to wear a
helmet is a constitutional rights limit because in place of a prima facie
liberty, a definitive no-liberty with the same content as the rule applies.

As an example of the relationship between a limiting rule and a definitive no-right, we can turn to section 17(2) Trade Regulations, which 'authorizes' the representative of the local trade association to enter places of
work to examine and investigate matters, and which explicitly treats this as
limiting the constitutional right of the inviolability of the home.[15] If one
joins the Federal Constitutional Court in extending the protection of article
13 Basic Law to places of work, then the constitutional principle of the inviolability of the home grants to each individual a prima facie right that his
place of work shall not be entered by a representative of the local trade
association. This prima facie right to an omission corresponds to a prima
facie prohibition on entering places of work addressed to the representative.[16] In that section 17(2) Trade Regulations permits ('authorizes') the
entry, the prima facie prohibition is replaced by definitive permission. This
definitive permission is equivalent to a definitive no-right to non-entry by
the representative.[17] The prima facie right is thus replaced by a definitive
no-right of identical content. So the rule of section 17(2) is a constitutional
rights limit.

Until now, the idea of a constitutional rights limit has only been defined
with respect to rules. *Principles* can also be constitutional rights limits.

[14] On the concepts of no-liberty and no-right, see above at 134, 145.
[15] See on this BVerfGE 32, 54.
[16] On the equivalence of rights to negative acts (Rxy^-G) and (relational) prohibitions
(Oyx^-G) see above at ??.
[17] On the equivalence: $PyxG \leftrightarrow {^-Rxy^-G}$, see above at 136.

When the Federal Constitutional Court says that 'conflicting constitutional rights of third parties and other legal values with constitutional status' can limit constitutional rights,[18] it is referring to limits in the form of principles. Limiting principles on their own are not capable of putting the individual in specific, definitively limited, positions (no-liberties, no-rights). In order to reach a definitive limitation one needs to balance the relevant constitutional principle with its limiting principle(s). One could take the view that it is not principles which are limits to constitutional rights, but the rules which emerge as the result of balancing under the Law of Competing Principles.[19] In a certain way this view would put principles in a similar position to competence norms as only potentially creative of limits. But there is a serious argument against doing this. Countervailing principles limit the legal possibilities for realizing constitutional principles as a matter of substance. If the countervailing principles did not apply, or if they did not have constitutional status, then the possibilities for realization would be greater. The problem is not their nature as limiting, but establishing the extent to which they definitively limit other principles.

So principles are also to be included among the norms which can limit constitutional rights. A principle is a constitutional rights limit if there are cases in which it is a reason that in place of a prima facie constitutional liberty or right, a definitive no-liberty or no-right with the same content applies.

This definition of the concept of a constitutional rights limit as applied to both rules and principles has a relatively technical character. We cannot do without this if we want to draw a clear distinction between norms which do and do not set limits. But the desire for a definition closer to normal usage lingers on. Many different restatements are possible on the basis of the definition given here. Here is one which extends beyond commanding and prohibiting limiting norms to all limiting norms: constitutional rights limits are norms which limit the realization of constitutional rights principles. What it means to limit a constitutional rights principle is shown paradigmatically in the case of commanding and prohibiting norms.

3. TYPES OF LIMIT

Proposals for classifying types of limit are many and various. The variety results in part from different purposes of division, in part it rests on obscurities in the basic concepts, in particular in that of the limit itself. Two different formal purposes can easily be distinguished. The first seeks to represent possible distinctions *within* the class of limits. A prominent example is the highly detailed classification of Friedrich Klein, constructed on

---

[18] BVerfGE 28, 243 (261).   [19] See above at 53 f.

the basis of a distinction between guaranteeing and reserving limits.[20] The second purpose seeks to distinguish *between* limiting norms and other sorts of norm in the field of constitutional rights, be they outworking, content-determining, or regulating norms. The example to note here is Lerche's distinction between restricting, clarifying, typifying, abuse-protecting, and conflict-resolving norms.[21] But in spite of many efforts, which have led to numerous valuable insights, it cannot be said that there is a single satisfying system of limits. One reason for this may be that for a long time people have avoided developing a structure-theoretical foundation for the theory of limits. What follows attempts to derive a meaningful division for an analytical theory of constitutional rights, based on the distinction between rules and pinciples as well as the basic legal modes, which have already formed the basis of our definition of a constitutional rights limit. For now, we are only concerned with distinctions within the class of limits. The problem of distinguishing limits from other types of norm in the field of constitutional rights will be dealt with later on.

3.1 Constitutionally Immediate Limits

As rights with constitutional status, constitutional rights can only be limited by or on the basis of norms likewise with constitutional status. Constitutional limits are thus either norms of constitutional status or norms below constitutional status, power to create which has been granted by the constitution. Limits with constitutional status are *constitutionally immediate*; limits with a lower status are *constitutionally mediate*. Apart from this distinction, to understand the system of limits of the Basic Law, the distinction between *limit* and *limiting clause* is essential. The concept of a limit belongs to the rights-perspective; the concept of a limiting clause belongs to the norm-perspective. A limiting clause is part of the complete constitutional norm which states how what is prima facie guaranteed by the constitutional right is or may be limited. Limiting clauses may be *written* or *unwritten*. Let us consider first written clauses containing constitutionally immediate limits.

In some cases, it is unclear whether these clauses are really limiting clauses or part of the scope of the right. The classic example is the qualification 'peaceably and without weapons' in the right to freedom of assembly (article 8(1) Basic Law). The view that such clauses 'are not limitations of constitutional rights, but constitutionally immediate descriptions of the material extent of the guarantee contained in a constitutional provision' is widespread.[22] If one relies simply on the formulation in the constitutional

---

[20] Klein, in Mangoldt and Klein, *Das Bonner Grundgesetz*, i, *Vorbemerkung* B XV 2, 3.

[21] Lerche, *Übermaß und Verfassungsrecht*, 106 ff.

[22] F. E. Schnapp, 'Grenzen der Grundrechte', JuS 1978, 730; K. Hesse, *Grundzüge des Verfassungsrechts*, 14th edn. (Heidelberg, 1984), para. 310, speaks in this context of 'constitutional rights immanent limits'.

right, each term could be treated either as the expression of part of the right, or as the expression of a limit. On the first account, peacefulness and the absence of weapons are conditions for the switching on of constitutional protection; on the second account, the clause formulates negative conditions (not unpeaceful or with weapons) for the exclusion of constitutional protection. This makes it clear that a decision about whether a clause is a limit is not possible on the basis of the text alone. A decision could effectively be taken by adopting the thesis that all limitations within the constitution are not limits properly so called, but rather descriptions of the extent of what is protected. This would mean that there are no constitutionally immediate limits. All constitutionally immediate limits would be descriptions of the extent of protection, just as the internal theory suggests, and could in this sense be described as immanent. But such a view is not required on conceptual grounds, and its consequences are not desirable. The phrase, 'peaceably and without weapons' , can be seen as the abbreviated formulation of a rule which turns the prima facie right based on the principle of freedom of assembly into a definitive no-right. This corresponds exactly to the definition of a limit given above. The rule expressed in the clause limits the realization of a constitutional principle. Its unusualness consists of the fact that it was the constitution-makers themselves who formulated the definitive limit. To this extent, the provision has the character of a rule. But behind the rule, the level of principle retains its significance. When it is clear that an assembly is not peaceable, then it no longer enjoys the protection of article 8 Basic Law.[23] Where there is doubt, in order to establish whether an assembly is or is not peaceable, it becomes necessary to interpret the concept of peace. In the context of this interpretation, it becomes essential to balance the constitutional principle of freedom of assembly with the countervailing principles which led the constitution-makers to enact the constitutionally immediate limiting clause. This should make it clear that the clause is none other than a decision of the constitution-makers in favour of certain reasons against constitutional protection. But reasons against constitutional protection, however they are expressed as a matter of detail, belong to the sphere of limits. If we were to dispense with this way of looking at the matter, there would be the danger that the interplay of reason and counter-reason would be replaced by more or less intuitive interpretations.

The problem that the clause 'peaceably and without weapons' creates in terms of its character as a limiting clause comes about mainly because it appears as part of a sentence which guarantees the constitutional right. Similar problems arise in the case of phrases such as 'all Germans' (e.g. art.

---

[23] This outcome could only be prevented by introducing an unwritten excepting clause into the written limiting clause, that is, by an interpretation contrary to the literal meaning of the text.

8(1) Basic Law), 'armed' (art. 4(3)(1) Basic Law) and 'generally accessible sources' (art. 5(1)(1) Basic Law). On the basis of what has been said, these clauses should be seen as expressions of constitutionally immediate definitive limits. There are fewer problems of identification if the clause appears in a sentence of its own. Thus the prohibition in article 9(2) Basic Law on associations which are 'directed against . . . good international relations' can quite obviously be seen to be a constitutionally immediate definitive limit.

It is difficult to know how to classify clauses which, while not containing an express power to limit rights, nevertheless refer to norms which are at least in part of lower status than the Constitution. The example of article 2(1) Basic Law is instructive. The rights of others can only be a constitutionally immediate limit in so far as those rights have constitutional status. Rights without constitutional status, the existence of which depends on decisions of the legislature to create, maintain, or remove them, cannot be constitutionally immediate limits. The same applies for the constitutional order. According to the interpretation of the Federal Constitutional Court, the constitutional order consists of every norm of constitutional status as well as 'every legal norm which is procedurally and substantively compatible with the Constitution'.[24] Only norms of constitutional status can be consitutionally immediate norms. In so far as the phrase 'constitutional order' permits the right to be limited by norms of lower status, it is a statutory reservation clause: it empowers the legislature to enact constitutionally mediate limits. The third part of the threefold limit in article 2(1) Basic Law, public morals, refers to non-legal norms.[25] The limitation of a constitutional right by reference to public morals does not presuppose any interpolation of norms of lower than constitutional status. Any reference to the competence of the legislature, which is the distinguishing mark of constitutionally mediate limits, is lacking. So the non-legal norms embraced by the idea of public morals can be treated as constitutionally immediate.

Clauses which refer to specific legal norms without constitutional status give rise to particular problems. Examples are the prohibition of associations 'whose purposes or activity contravene the criminal law' (art. 9(2) Basic Law), and the 'requirements of the general law', the 'legal provisions for the protection of young persons' as well as the 'right of personal dignity' by which the rights in article 5(1) Basic Law are limited in article 5(2). If these norms are at the disposition of the legislature, that is, if the legislature is equally free to maintain, repeal, or amend them, then they are constitutionally mediate and the clauses should be treated as statutory reservations creating legislative powers to set limits. Matters start getting problematic if

[24] BVerfGE 59, 275 (278); 6, 32 (41).
[25] See on this C. Starck, 'Das "Sittengesetz" als Schranke der freien Entfaltung der Persönlichkeit', in G. Leibholz *et al.*, *Menschenwürde und freiheitliche Rechtsordnung, Festschrift für W. Geiger* (Tübingen, 1974), 259 ff., with further references.

one assumes that the Constitution requires the continued existence of at least some limiting norms of the type listed. We can assume without further argument that the legislature would be acting unconstitutionally if it were to repeal the entire law concerning personal dignity. Does this mean that those norms protecting personal dignity, which according to the Constitution must continue to apply, represent constitutionally immediate limits? The answer is no. If the legislature repeals the norms protecting personal dignity required by the Constitution, then these norms no longer apply.[26] What applies is the constitutionally based command to the legislature to protect personal dignity to the degree required, as well as the corresponding rights to protection. The power to set limits granted to the legislature by the phrase 'the law of personal dignity' is thus a power combined with a constitutional duty of protection. This does not stop it being a power, and thus does not undermine the constitutionally mediate nature of the norms which the legislature has to enact, or refrain from repealing, in order to exercise its power dutifully.

So far, we have been concerned with written limiting clauses enacting constitutionally immediate limits. The classic example of an *unwritten* limiting clause is the formula of the Federal Constitutional Court whereby, 'having due regard for the unity of the Constitution and the entire order of values protected by it, conflicting constitutional rights of third parties and other legal values of constitutional status . . . are capable, in exceptional circumstances, of limiting unqualified constitutional rights'.[27] This formula refers to limiting principles, namely principles of constitutional rights (conflicting constitutional rights of third parties) and other principles of constitutional status (other legal values . . .).

One could object that assuming the existence of constitutionally immediate limits by way of principles has the consequence that every state organ can restrict constitutional rights merely on the basis of constitutional principles, without statutory empowerment. But this is not the case, since constitutional rights provisions give rise not only to *substantive* positions but also to *formal/procedural* ones. This distinction corresponds to that of Schwabe between substantive and modal aspects of constitutional protection. The modal aspect relates to 'the manner of affecting a protected interest'.[28] By 'manner' Schwabe means the formal conditions for the activity of the three powers in the field of constitutional rights. These include, among other things, the maintenance of the constitutional division of jurisdiction, executive empowerment by way of sufficiently precise norms, and the

---

[26] In a similar situation, the Federal Constitutional Court has resorted to an order under sect. 35 Statute of the Federal Constitutional Court (BVerfGE 39, 1 (2 f., 68)); see on this J. Ipsen, *Rechtsfolgen der Verfassungswidrigkeit von Norm und Einzelakt* (Baden-Baden, 1980), 241 ff.

[27] BVerfGE 28, 243 (261).

[28] J. Schwabe, *Probleme der Grundrechtsdogmatik*, 23.

observance of procedural requirements. An example of a procedural constitutional rights position is the right derived by the Federal Constitutional Court from article 12(1) Basic Law, that the regulating authority should not regulate the exercise of a profession without sufficient statutory authority.[29] Procedural constitutional rights positions, which are most significant in connection with statutory reservations to constitutional rights,[30] mean that more weighty countervailing constitutional principles do not automatically justify every state action within the protected area of a right. So, for example, the executive must still base its action on a constitutionally mediate limit such as a statute, even if countervailing constitutional principles functioning as immediate limits justify action within the protected area of a right as a matter of substance.

3.2 Constitutionally Mediate Limits

Constitutionally mediate limits are limits which the Constitution empowers somebody to set. The clearest expression of the power to set constitutionally mediate limits can be found in the express reservation clauses. Express reservation clauses are provisions, or parts of provisions, which explicitly empower another to act within the protected area of, or to limit, a right (arts. 2(2)(3); 8(2); 10(2); 11(2); 13(2) and (3), 17*a* Basic Law). A further distinction between simple and qualified reservations can be drawn depending on whether the power to set limits is granted absolutely (e.g. art. 2(2)(3) Basic Law) or subject to some substantive limitation (e.g. art. 11(2) Basic Law).[31] Previous discussions have shown that the power to set limits does not only exist where it is expressly granted. Wherever ordinary law is referred to as a limit, then a power to enact limits has been created. Examples are article 2(1)(2nd clause), article 5(2) and article 9(2) Basic Law. When such provisions refer to ordinary law, they can be called 'implied reservation clauses'.

The main problem of reservations is the problem of their extent. Here we can distinguish between formal and substantive aspects. The formal aspect concerns the power to set limits, its form and procedure. Here we are only interested in the substantive aspect, and that only in so far as it concerns the

---

[29] BVerfGE 53, 1(15 f.).

[30] See on this W. Krebs, *Vorbehalt des Gesetzes und Grundrechte* (Berlin, 1975), 102 ff., 110 ff.; T. Wülfing, *Grundrechtliche Gesetzesvorbehalte und Grundrechtsschranken* (Berlin, 1981), 36 ff.

[31] The classification of art. 8(2) Basic Law is problematic. At times it is treated as a simple reservation (thus, for example, Wülfing, *Grundrechtliche Gesetzesvorbehalte und Grundrechtsschranken*, 27) and at times, a qualified reservation (thus R. Zippelius, in T. Maunz and R. Zippelius, *Deutsches Staatsrecht*, 24th edn. (Munich, 1982), 150). If one focuses on freedom of assembly as such, then it contains a qualified reservation, since it only permits a limitation on the condition that the assembly takes place in the open. If one focuses on freedom of assembly in the open, then it contains a simple reservation. Since the constitutional rights principle is the reference point for the concept of a limit, the first perspective is preferable.

power of the legislature. This is controlled not only by the conditions set
out in qualified reservation clauses and by the inalienable core of the right
in question (assuming one accepts the doctrine of an absolute inalienable
core),[32] but also by the principle of proportionality and thus by the requirement to balance interests.[33] By connecting competence and balancing in this
way one avoids placing constitutional rights entirely at the disposal of the
legislature, at least outside the protected area of the inalienable core, which
would be incompatible with the binding nature of constitutional rights. But
this gives rise to a new problem, which can be put briefly like this: the
danger of too weak a subjection to constitutional rights is replaced by too
strong a one. The danger of too strong a subjection can be stated most
clearly by way of the thesis that statutory reservations only give the legislature the competence to enact what is the outcome of a balancing of relevant
principles. If this is so, then all permissible constitutionally mediate limits
would merely reproduce constitutionally immediate limits; they would
never have a constitutive character, merely a declaratory one. To the extent
that even in the case of constitutionally immediate limits, the detail is to be
clarified by the legislature, the difference between immediate and mediate
limits would completely disappear. Legislation under statutory reservations
would simply be the interpretation of already existing constitutional limits.
As Häberle puts it, 'all permissible constitutional rights limits [would be]
immanent to them'.[34] Statutory reservations would not create a power to
set limits, but a power to interpret, and the reason for granting the legislature such a power would lie simply in the scope for interpretative discretion.[35]

One important weakness of the interpretation theory of statutory reservations is that there are many cases in which the legislature can decide
whether to set limits or not. Here one can distinguish between two types of
situation. In the first situation, it is not clear whether some limit *L* is
permissible in view of the weight of countervailing principles. In these
circumstances, the competence of the legislature is a competence to establish the authoritative interpretation. The second type of situation arises
when it is clear that some limit *L* is permissible in the light of the relevant
principles, but the legislature is free to set that limit or not. The existence
of this sort of case would only be excluded if every permissible limit were
also required. This cannot be assumed to be true. There are cases in which

---

[32] On this, see immediately below at 192 ff.

[33] See above at 66 ff.

[34] Häberle, *Die Wesensgehaltgarantie*, 126; Krebs, *Vorbehalt des Gesetzes und Grundrechte*, 115, follows Häberle.

[35] See Krebs, *Vorbehalt des Gesetzes und Grundrechte*, 116. Contrary to the view of W.
Knies, *Schranken der Kunstfreiheit als verfassungsrechtliches Problem* (Munich, 1967), 102,
the interpretation approach does not necessarily have the consequence that the legislature
would in principle be deprived of the right to set limits. The power of interpretation could be
granted to the legislature.

the legislature is allowed to be more generous in favour of individual rights and at the cost of collective interests than it has to be. An example is the manual trades decision in which the Federal Constitutional Court, on one hand, declared the certification of competence requirement to be compatible with the Basic Law, but on the other hand left it open to the legislature, 'to leave the protection and maintenance of standards of service and the skill of the occupant of a manual trade to the free interaction of economic forces'.[36] Both types of situation can be said to concern a constitutive legislative power to set limits, the first case in so far as the legislature is given authority over competing interpretations, the second case because the statutory reservation permits the legislature to realize more of the constitutional right than countervailing principles of the Constitution require. There is thus a constitutive legislative power to set limits to constitutional rights.

This shows that statutory reservations do not simply empower the legislature to establish what already exists. There is still the question of whether it also permits it to engage in what Bachof calls a 'real limitation of liberty', that is 'to set the limits to freedom with constitutive effect further than they are drawn directly by the Constitution itself'.[37] When the legislature decides for L in the context of the first type of situation above, it is deciding for a limit which is interpretatively possible given the weight of the various countervailing principles. In this type of case, one cannot say that it is going beyond the limits directly drawn by the Constitution, only that it is going beyond what an alternative interpretation sees as a limit directly drawn by the Constitution. The second type of situation is the exact opposite of Bachof's 'genuine limitation'. The legislature does not go as far as the limits permitted in the Constitution. It therefore seems that neither of the two types of situation serves Bachof's purposes, and that there is a third type of situation defined by the fact that the legislature is setting a limit which goes beyond what is permissible given the weight of the various countervailing principles. But a limitation of a constitutional principle that goes beyond what the balance of countervailing principles permits is impermissible.

This rejection of the theory of genuine limitations only works because of a failure to differentiate on the side of the countervailing principles. If one differentiates, then the theory can be seen to be making a good point. It was suggested above that when balancing principles, not only substantive but also formal principles need considering.[38] So in balancing principles, as well as the substantive principle of professional freedom and the substantive

---

[36] BVerfGE 13, 97 (113 f.).

[37] O. Bachof, 'Freiheit des Berufs', in K. Bettermann, H. C. Nipperdey, and U. Scheuner (eds.), *Die Grundrechte*, vol. 3.1 (Berlin, 1958), 208; see also T. Maunz, *Deutsches Staatsrecht*, 23rd edn. (Munich, 1980), 123, who speaks of the power 'to infringe the actual content of the constitutional right itself'.

[38] 58, 82.

principle of professional self-regulation, the formal principle of decision-taking by the democratically legitimated legislature can also play a role. This formal principle relating to the decision-taking competence of the legislature is the reason for a constitutive limit-setting competence of the legislature, even if it is one which is controlled by substantive principles. To the extent that the theory of genuine limitations is referring to this, it is correct.

4. ON THE GUARANTEE OF AN INALIENABLE CORE AS A LIMIT TO LIMITS

We have been thinking about the limits of constitutional rights. The principled nature of constitutional rights gives rise not only to the idea that constitutional rights are limited and limitable in the light of countervailing principles, but also that their limiting and limitability is itself limited. A limitation of a constitutional right is only permissible if principles competing with the principle underlying the right have greater weight in the circumstances of the case.[39] One could say that the constitutional right as such limits its own limiting and limitability. Article 19(2) Basic Law seems to set another limit to the limiting of constitutional rights by prohibiting action in the core of each right. The interpretation of this provision is controversial. Many nuances aside, the various interpretations can be ordered according to two pairs of ideas, first, whether the guarantee of an inalienable core relates to *subjective* positions or an *objective* state of constitutional rights law, and, secondly, whether the guarantee is *absolute* or *relative*. The debate about the inalienable core cannot be reproduced here;[40] we are simply concerned to see what consequences the theory of principles has for it.

In one of its earlier decisions, the Federal Constitutional Court left open the question of whether article 19(2) is to be interpreted subjectively or objectively. 'It need not be decided whether article 19(2) prohibits the withdrawal of a constitutional right without remainder in the individual case, or whether it is only intended to prevent the destruction of the essential core as such, for example by practical loss of the guarantee granted to everyone and generally rooted in the Basic Law.'[41] But in decisions following this one, it has consistently related the guarantee of the essential core to indi-

---

[39] For the detail of this, see above at 101 ff.

[40] See on this the accounts of T. Maunz, in T. Maunz and G. Dürig *et al.*, *Grundgesetz Kommentar*, 5th edn. (Munich, 1983), Art. 19; H. Jäckel, *Grundrechtsgeltung und Grundrechtssicherung* (Berlin, 1967), 49 ff.; J. Chlosta, *Der Wesensgehalt der Eigentumsgewährleistung* (Berlin, 1975), 39 ff.; L. Schneider, *Der Schutz des Wesensgehalts von Grundrechten nach Art. 19 Abs. 2 GG* (Berlin, 1983).

[41] BVerfGE 2, 266 (285).

vidual positions.[42] This is correct. Constitutional rights are—as has still to
be shown—primarily positions of the individual. If the Basic Law includes
something claiming to be so significant as a prohibition on affecting the
essential core of constitutional rights, then this must at least apply to individual positions.

An objective interpretation, such as that of Friedrich Klein, according to
which article 19(2) Basic Law prevents 'the applicability of a constitutional
rights provision from being so reduced that it becomes meaningless for all
individuals, or for a large part of them, or for life in society generally'[43] can
be adopted alongside the subjective interpretation, but it cannot replace it.
The fact that problems concerning the guarantee of an essential core are
easier to resolve in the context of an objective theory rather than in the
context of a subjective theory is not a good enough reason for rejecting the
subjective theory. The character of constitutional rights as rights of individuals counts towards adopting a subjective theory at least alongside an
objective one.[44]

Subjective guarantees of an essential core can be absolute or relative.
According to the relative theory,[45] the essential core is what is left over after
the balancing test has been carried out. Limitations which correspond to the
principle of proportionality do not infringe the essential core, even if they
leave nothing left of the constitutional right in an individual case. This
reduces the guarantee of an essential core to the principle of proportionality. Since this applies anyway, this would mean that article 19(2) Basic Law
simply has declaratory effect. According to the absolute theory,[46] there is,
by contrast, a core to each right which cannot be limited under any circumstances.

Numerous statements of the Federal Constitutional Court indicate that
it takes an absolute position. So in the decision concerning secret tape
recording of conversations, 'even overwhelmingly important public interests cannot justify a limitation of the absolutely protected essential core of

---

[42] See BVerfGE 6, 32 (41); 7, 377 (411); 13, 97 (122); 15, 126 (144); 16, 194 (201); 21, 92
(93); 22, 180 (219); 27, 344 (352); 30, 1 (24); 31, 58 (69); 32, 373 (379); 34, 238 (245); 45,
187 (242, 270 f.).
[43] Mangoldt and Klein, *Das Bonner Grundgesetz*, i, Art. 19 *Anmerkung* V 2 a. Further
proponents of the objective theory are E. R. Huber, 'Der Streit um das Wirtschafts verfassungsrecht', DÖV 1956, 142 f.; H. Peters, 'Elternrecht, Erziehung, Bildung und Schule', in
K. A. Bettermann, H. C. Nipperdey, and U. Scheuner (eds.), *Die Grundrechte*, vol. 4.1 (Berlin,
1960), 383; Jäckel, *Grundrechtsgeltung und Grundrechtssicherung*, 49 ff.; S. Hendrichs, Art.
19, para. 23 ff. in I v. Münch (ed.), *Grundgesetz-Kommentar*, i, 2nd edn. (Munich, 1981).
[44] For a combination of subjective and objective theories, see Hesse, *Grundzüge des
Verfassungsrechts*, para. 332 ff.
[45] See Häberle, *Die Wesensgehaltgarantie*, 58 ff.; E. v. Hippel, *Grenzen und Wesensgehalt
der Grundrechte* (Berlin, 1965), 47 ff.; Hesse, *Grundzüge des Verfassungsrechts*, para. 332 f.;
BGH, DVBl. 1953, 371; BGHSt 4, 375 at 377.
[46] See H. Krüger, 'Der Wesensgehalt der Grundrechte i. S. des Art. 19 GG', DÖV 1955, 597
ff.; J. P. Müller, *Elemente einer schweizerischen Grundrechtstheorie* (Berne, 1982), 152 ff.

private life; balancing under the principle of proportionality is not in issue'.[47] In other decisions it talks of an 'absolute limit, crossing which would infringe the essential core of this constitutional right',[48] an 'outermost limit',[49] and 'final untouchable areas'.[50] However, there are also decisions which can only be interpreted as supporting a relative theory. In its judgment on welfare and social support for young people,[51] the Court had to consider provisions of the Federal Social Welfare Law, which required certain people to be maintained in state institutions if they were particularly weak-willed, or uncontrolled in their natural desires, or neglected, or in risk of neglect, and who could only be helped in the context of such an institution. In the view of the Court, these provisions touch the essential core of article 2(2)(2) Basic Law. In justifying this conclusion, it states first of all that, 'freedom of the person . . . is such an important legal interest, that it may only be restricted for particularly good reasons'. Then it suggests that particularly good reasons are the protection of the general public and the protection of the individual concerned. At this point it is interesting that it includes within these reasons the maintenance within closed institutions of dangerous mentally ill patients and others deprived of legal capacity for reasons of mental disability—these are classic instances of hard cases under the absolute theory. The third stage of the argument establishes that the case at hand does not concern either the protection of the general public or the individual, but the improvement of the individual.[52] The fourth stage of the argument formulates the outcome: 'since the purpose of improving the well-being of an adult does not count as a sufficiently important reason for removing their personal liberty' the constitutional right of personal liberty is affected in its essential core.[53] This argument follows the Law of Balancing and thus the third part of the principle of proportionality, proportionality in its narrow sense. An intensive restriction is only justified by weighty reasons. Here there was an intensive restriction, but no sufficiently weighty reason for it, so the restriction was not justified. The prohibition on limiting the essential core, as the Court understands it in this decision, adds nothing at all.[54] If the Court had maintained the absolute theory, it would have to have proceeded on the basis of some fixed understanding. Such an understanding could be a right not to be detained permanently or for a long period of time in a state institution. But it does not adopt such a position. Rather it allows the situation covered by the essen-

---

[47] BVerfGE 34, 238 (245).   [48] BVerfGE 16, 194 (201).
[49] BVerfGE 31, 58 (69).
[50] BVerfGE 6, 32 (41); see also BVerfGE 32, 373 (379).
[51] BVerfGE 22, 180.   [52] BVerfGE 22, 180 (219).
[53] BVerfGE 22, 180 (220).
[54] After establishing a breach of art. 19(2) Basic Law, the court went on to establish a breach of the principle of proportionality (BVerfGE 22, 180 (220)). It could have started with this principle straight away.

tial core to depend on the relevant reasons against protection. This is precisely the approach of the relative theory.[55]

The decision just discussed is inconsistent with the statement in the decision about secret tape recordings of conversations, which contains a clear adoption of the absolute theory. In the discussion of absolute principles above,[56] the point has already been made that that statement is either inconsistent or it adds nothing to the absolute theory. Even weighty public interests cannot justify a restriction of the absolutely protected essential core of private life.[57] When from the *perspective of constitutional law*, the public interest has greater weight than the protection of private life, then it necessarily takes priority. If it takes priority from some other perspective, it cannot outweigh the level of protection required by the constitution, irrespective of whether one presupposes an absolute or a relative theory. In short, what this means is that an absolute guarantee of an essential core cannot say that outweighing reasons do not outweigh, but only that there are no outweighing reasons.

The absolute theory goes too far in saying that there are legal positions such that no possible legal reason can ever restrict them. To the extent that this is true, it rests on the relative theory. It has been suggested above[58] that the more a principle is restricted, the more resistant it gets. The strength of the countervailing principles has to grow disproportionately. This corresponds to the law of diminishing marginal utility as represented by indifference curves. There are thus conditions under which one can say with a very high degree of certainty that no countervailing principle will take priority. These conditions define the 'essential core of private life'.[59] But the absoluteness of its protection remains a matter of the relation between different principles. A set of circumstances under which competing principles do take precedence after all cannot be ruled out. However, the certainty of protection is so high that under ordinary circumstances we can talk about absolute protection. But the relativized basis of this protection must not be lost from sight. The extent of 'absolute' protection depends on the balance of principles. The impression that the core can be identified directly without balancing interests, or known intuitively, derives from the certainty

---

[55] An informative conjunction of the guarantee of an essental core with the principle of proportionality can also be found in the decision concerning the service of divorce papers. Service is characterized as an infringement of the spouse's personality rights. Then the Court states, 'without her agreement, it is only permissible if justified by the principle of proportionality. If this is not the case, the measure breaches article 2(1) Basic Law in connection with articles 1(1) and 19(2)' (BVerfGE 27, 344 (352)).

[56] See above at 62.   [57] BVerfGE 34, 238 (245).

[58] 102 ff.

[59] See Häberle, *Die Wesensgehaltgarantie*, 64: 'What is described as the inviolable "core" of freedom of action, or freedom of contract, is that area in which there are without question no legitimate legal interests capable of limiting constitutional rights which are of equal or higher value'.

with which we are able to relate principles in the case. The conviction that there must be rights which even in the most extreme circumstances are not outweighed—only such rights are genuinely absolute rights[60]—may be held by any individual who is free to sacrifice himself for certain principles, but it cannot be maintained as a matter of constitutional law.

The result is that the guarantee of an essential core contained in article 19(2) Basic Law does not contain any further control on the limitability of constitutional rights beyond that already contained in the principle of proportionality. Since it is equivalent to one part of the principle of proportionality, there is yet another reason for supposing that that principle applies as a matter of constitutional law.

II. THE SCOPE AND LIMITS OF CONSTITUTIONAL RIGHTS

Until now we have been considering the limits of constitutional rights, that is, that which leads to a restriction of constitutional protection, and in this sense represents the negative side of a constitutional rights norm. Now we have to consider the positive side of constitutional guarantees. Here we are concerned with two ideas, the scope of a constitutional right and its area of protection. First of all, we have to consider the relationship between the ideas of scope and protected area; then it will be necessary to justify a broad conception of scope or protected area.

1. THE PROTECTED AREA AND SCOPE OF RIGHTS

The concepts of the protected area [*Schutzbereich*][61] and scope [*Tatbestand*] are to be differently defined depending on the type of constitutional norm in question. However, at times they have their form in common, as here, when they are used as counterparts to the concept of a limit. They relate to what is prima facie covered by a constitutional right, that is, covered without considering any limit.[62] At this point we are only concerned with these concepts in the context of constitutional permissive norms and norms which protect defensive rights. The structure of constitu-

---

[60] On the problem of the existence of absolute rights, see A. Gewirth, 'Are there any Absolute Rights?', Phil Q 31 (1981), 1 ff.; J. Levinson, 'Gewirth on Absolute Rights', Phil Q 32 (1982), 73 ff.; A. Gewirth, 'There are Absolute Rights', Phil Q 32 (1982), 348 ff.

[61] Instead of protected area [*Schutzbereich*], talk is also of 'area of validity' [*Geltungsbereich*] (see e.g. J. P. Müller, *Elemente einer schweizerischen Grundrechtstheorie*, 89 ff.) and 'normative field' [*Normbereich*] (see above also F. Müller, *Juristische Methodik* 2nd edn. (Berlin, 1976), 117 ff.). Sometimes these expressions are used synonymously; sometimes not.

[62] Schwabe, *Probleme der Grundrechtsdogmatik*, 152, speaks in this context of an 'area of potential constitutional rights protection'.

tional norms requiring positive state intervention, along with the peculiarities of the general right to equality, will be considered later.[63]

The ideas of scope and protected area cause the least difficulty in the case of constitutional *permissive norms*.[64] The constitutional norm permitting one to proselytize[65] can be given the following form:

(1)   If an act is one of proselytism, then its performance is prima facie constitutionally permitted.[66]

The scope of this norm is proselytism; its protected area covers all acts which instantiate this behaviour. Scope and protected area are completely congruent; whatever falls within the scope of the right lies within its protected area. There is a further congruence: one can call the proselytizing the 'protected interest' of this norm.

The connection is not so straightforward in the case of norms guaranteeing defensive rights. Defensive rights are *rights to omissions* on the part of the addressee. They were divided above into rights of non-interference with acts of the beneficiary (e.g. non-obstruction of the choice of profession), rights of non-affecting of characteristics and states of affairs (e.g. non-interference with the spatial private sphere), and rights of non-removal of basic legal positions (e.g. non-removal of certain aspects of ownership).[67] One can reduce the ideas used in formulating these rights down to two: the idea of a protected interest and the idea of an infringement. Protected interests are the actions, characteristics, states of affairs, and simple legal positions which may not be obstructed, interfered with, or removed. The concept of *infringement* is a general term covering obstruction, interference, and removal.[68] Thus rights to omissions are rights that certain protected interests should not be infringed. As has been shown already,[69] the right that something should not be infringed correlates to a duty not to infringe the interest in question.

---

[63]   286 f., fn. 91; 308 ff., 345 ff.   [64]   See on this above at 146 ff.

[65]   See BVerfGE 12, 1 (4).

[66]   Koch takes the view that to the extent that constitutional rights norms permit the right-holder to do something they enact unconditional permissions (H.-J. Koch and H. Rüßmann, *Juristische Begründungslehre* (Munich, 1982), 20). This is correct to the extent that a norm such as (1) can easily be reformulated as an unconditional permissive norm: (1') Everyone is prima facie permitted to proselytize. However, every unconditional permissive norm can be conditionalized. Conditionalizations of unconditional permissive norms are simplest when acts are quantified. The following scheme then applies: (1″) $(x) (Fx \rightarrow PVx)$. 'x' is an act-variable concerning act-individuals, '(x)' is the universal quantifier. (For all x, it is the case that . . .), '$\rightarrow$' is the sign for the conditional (whenever, . . . then), 'F' is an act-predicate, 'P' the permissive operator, and 'V' an act-operator. (1″) is thus to be read in the following way: for all acts x it is the case that, if x has characteristic F, then it is permitted to carry out x. The advantage of such a conditionalizing is that one ends up with a clearly defined set of scopes. On the concept of the act-individual, see D. Davidson, 'The Logical Form of Action Sentences', in N. Rescher (ed.), *The Logic of Decision and Action* (Pittsburgh, 1967), 84 ff. On the concept of an act-operator, see L. Lindahl, *Position and Change* (Dordrecht, 1977), 50 ff.

[67]   122 ff.

[68]   On these concepts, see above at 122 ff.   [69]   134, 136.

It is possible to give norms guaranteeing omissions a formulation by which only the protected interest appears in the if-clause. As an example,

(2)   If an act is a choice of profession, then there is a prima facie right that it should not be infringed.

The formulation of the corresponding duty is

(3)   If an act is a choice of profession, then infringements are prima facie prohibited.

The advantage of putting it like this is that one ends up with a very simple statement of the scope of the norm. The scope of the norm simply describes the protected interest—in the example, the constitutionally protected actions. This description is also that of the protected area. In this formulation, the scope and the protected area of norms guaranteeing constitutional liberties and defensive rights coincide. On this approach, the scope can be called a '*protected interest scope*'.

However, this construction is not advisable. The concept of scope loses its character as counterpart to the concept of limit. Such a relationship between the two concepts would only arise if in satisfying the scope a prima facie right or prima facie prohibition becomes, in the absence of a limitation, a definitive right or prohibition. By choosing a protected interest scope, the dualism of scope and limit is replaced by a triad of scope, infringement, and limit. Closer examination shows that this is none other than a dissection of the scope into two elements. Statement (3) can be reformulated:

(4)   If a measure restricts choice of profession, then it is prima facie prohibited.

Statement (4) can itself be written:

(5)   If an act ϕ of a constitutional right-holder is a choice of profession, and if some measure M infringes ϕ, then M is prima facie prohibited.

This may sound rather wooden, but it makes the structure clear. Now, there is no objection to this threefold structure (scope, infringement, and limit) for examining a constitutional right. On the contrary it forms the basis of (5). But this is not an adequate reason for formulating the scope of a norm solely in terms of the interest it protects. The idea of the scope of a right as a counterpart to its limits has the function of completely stating the substantive prerequisites for the existence of a prima facie right. Unlike simple liberties, in the case of norms guaranteeing defensive rights, this can only be achieved by bringing together two elements: the interest protected and the infringement. Such a set of conditions can be called a '*protected interest/infringement scope*'.

That it is right to incorporate the infringement into the statement of the scope of a norm is also supported by the fact that the extent of prima facie protection depends equally on the extent of the interest protected and the extent of what counts as an infringement. The decision of the Federal Constitutional Court on rights to enter and investigate places of work makes this connection clear. The Court first adopts an extremely wide interpretation of the word 'home', such that places of industry and business are included,[70] but then interprets the idea of an infringement so narrowly, that entry and investigation for the purposes of regulating trade are not covered. So, in spite of a wide reading of the abstract interest protected, it ends up with a narrow understanding of the scope of the right.

If one adopts protected interest/infringement scopes in the case of defensive rights, this gives rise to problems as regards the material correspondence between the scope of a norm and its protected area. The usual talk of infringements in the protected area of a right presupposes a conception of protected area which corresponds to the interest protected. There is no congruence between this conception of protected area and a conception of scope which incorporates the idea of infringements. To achieve substantive congruence, one has to contrast the protected area relating only to a protected interest (call this protected area in the narrow sense) with protected area in the wide sense. Everything which is prima facie prohibited falls within the protected area in the wide sense. Both conceptions of protected area have their justification. Since we are concerned here with the relationship between the scope of a norm and its limits, we shall generally use the concept of protected area in its wide sense.

The construction of protected interest/infringement scopes depends on connections between the idea of an infringement, the interest protected, the limit, and definitive and prima facie prohibitions (or rights), which can be expressed in the following two laws ('*Laws of Infringement*') and clarified by their counterparts.

(I)　　All measures which infringe a constitutionally protected interest are prima facie constitutionally prohibited.

(II)　　All measures which infringe a constitutionally protected interest and are not justified by some limit, are definitively constitutionally prohibited.

(I′)　　All measures which are not prima facie constitutionally prohibited are not infringements of a constitutionally protected interest.

(II″)　　All measures which are not definitively constitutionally prohibited are either not infringements of a constitutionally protected interest, or they are justified by a limit.[71]

---

[70] BVerfGE 32, 54 (68 ff.).

[71] It is easy to see that (I′) follows logically from (I), and that (II′) follows logically from (II), since, in brief, $\neg F \rightarrow \neg E$ follows from E (infringement) $\rightarrow F$ (prohibition). It is an interesting question, as far as the concept of infringement is concerned, whether '(III) All measures which are prima facie constitutionally prohibited are infringements of a constitutional rights protected interest' is valid. This question will not be pursued here.

These laws make it clear that the ideas of a protected interest and an infringement need not be systematically the first stage of a constitutional rights examination. One can conclude that there is a prima facie prohibition from an infringement of a protected interest (I), but one can also conclude that there is no infringement of a protected interest from the non-existence of a prima facie prohibition (I'). The first route is preferable when it is clear that something is an infringement. But in cases where it is unclear if something is a infringement—such cases are mostly discussed under the heading of 'factual infringements'[72]—the other route is preferable. The question of whether something is constitutionally prohibited is then answered directly by reference to the relevant principles. When in connection with private law norm-purpose-theory[73] it is suggested that the existence of an infringement should be determined not by characteristics of infringements such as directness and finality, but according to the purpose of the constitutional rights norms,[74] then it is precisely this latter type of reasoning which is being proposed.

2. NARROW AND WIDE THEORIES OF SCOPE

The legal consequences of a norm are released when all its conditions are satisfied. One could adopt a definition of the scope of a constitutional rights norm which embraces all the conditions requisite for a definitive constitutional consequence. This conception of scope is a wide one. Within this conception, one must distinguish a narrower one, which is what has been called the 'scope' until now, from the limiting clause. In what follows, 'scope' is to be understood in its narrow sense.

In order for the definitive constitutional consequences (definitive protection of constitutional rights) to be released, the scope must be satisfied and limiting clause not be satisfied; if they are not to be released, then either the measure does not fall within the scope of the right, or the limiting clause is satisfied. This simple point is the logical basis for two quite different types of constitutional justification, that of the *wide* and *narrow* theories of scope.

If there is a question whether a certain action is constitutionally

---

[72] See H.-U. Gallwas, *Faktische Beeinträchtigungen im Bereich der Grundrechte* (Berlin, 1970); U. Ramsauer, *Die faktischen Beeinträchtigungen des Eigentums*, (Berlin, 1980); Schwabe, *Probleme der Grundrechtsdogmatik*, 176 ff.; A. Bleckmann, *Allgemeine Grundrechtslehren* (Cologne and Berlin, 1979), 230 ff.

[73] See e.g. E. v. Caemmerer, *Das Problem des Kausalzusammenhangs im Privatrecht* (Freiburg, 1956); J. G. Wolf, *Der Normzweck im Deliktsrecht* (Göttingen, 1962); H. Stoll, *Kausalzusammenhang und Normzweck im Deliktrecht* (Tübingen, 1968); E. Deutsch, *Haftungsrecht* (Cologne, Berlin, Bonn, and Munich, 1976), 234 ff.; J. Esser and E. Schmidt, *Schuldrecht*, vol. 1.2, 5th edn. (Heidelberg and Karlsruhe, 1976), 184 ff.

[74] U. Ramsauer, 'Die Bestimmung des Schutzbereichs von Grundrechten nach dem Normzweck', in VerwArch 72 (1981), 99 ff.; J. P. Müller, *Elemente einer schweizerischen Grundrechtstheorie*, 90.

protected then there are two possible answers, either protected or not protected. Because of the division between scope and limits, this gives rise to four possible forms of justification, which can be represented in the following scheme:

(1) Scope (+), Limit (+): not protected
(2) Scope (+), Limit (−): protected
(3) Scope (−), Limit (+): not protected
(4) Scope (−), Limit (−): not protected.

In the first case, the act in question falls within the scope of the norm, but is covered by the limiting clause and so is not protected; in the second case the act falls within the scope of the norm and is not covered by the limiting clause and so it is protected, and so on. It is clear that in order to justify constitutional protection, there is only one possible form of argument, but to reject protection there are three. These three are *equivalent in outcome*. Those who maintain a *wide* conception of scope will typically opt for arguments of type (1); those who adopt a *narrow* conception of scope will opt for (3) or (4). The third type contains a double justification: the act does not fall within the scope of a right and if it did it would be covered by a limiting clause.

The common observation that the wider the scope is drawn, the wider the limits must be drawn[75] refers to the relationship between (1) and (4), assuming, of course, that the same result is to be reached regardless of how broadly scope is defined. Someone who wants to achieve a high level of constitutional protection can do this by adopting a wide definition of scope and a narrow definition of limits. A wide set of scopes is not necessarily tied to a wide set of limitations. Whether it is to be so tied is a normative question.

Thus we have to distinguish between a wide theory of scope which is simply a theory of the *structure* of rights, and a wide theory which is a results-oriented *normative* theory. But since the conceptualization of a problem influences its outcome, even a wide theory of scope as a purely structural theory has some normative significance.

As has already been indicated above, a wide structural theory of scope will be adopted here. In order to justify this, we need to consider critically two versions of a narrow scope theory: Friedrich Müller's theory of material extent, and Rüfner's theory of scope-limitations on the basis of general laws.

---

[75] See W. Berg, *Konkurrenzen schrankendivergenter Freiheitsrechte im Grundrechtsabschnitt des Grundgesetzes* (Berlin and Frankfurt, 1968), 42; U. Scheuner, 'Die Funktion der Grundrechte im Sozialstaat', DöV 1971, 508; M. Kloepfer, *Grundrechte als Entstehenssicherung und Bestandsschutz* (Munich, 1970), 44.

202   *The Limits of Constitutional Rights*

2.1 Narrow Scope Theories

2.1.1 *Müller's Theory of Material Extent*

Müller's theory of the scope of constitutional rights is based upon his theory of norms which has already been summarized and criticized above.[76] But the rejection of his theory of norms does not automatically exclude his thesis about what is constitutionally protected and in this sense belongs to the scope of constitutional rights. Müller's answer to this question must now be considered in detail.

According to Müller, 'no constitutional right is guaranteed without limit'.[77] This is supposed to follow 'from the single truly immanent limit, based on its legal quality'.[78] This 'reservation of the legal quality of constitutional rights' is explained by Müller on the basis of their location in the constitutional legal order, and the impossibility of their illimitability which this is supposed to give rise to:

As rights they are based in the Constitution. Thus one must maintain the material-systemic perspective of their belonging to the constitutional legal order, from which the impossibility of illimitability 'in all directions' results, as an indispensable element of each constitutional theory, or, if one can put it like this, as an unwritten element of every constitutional rights normative programme. One can call this reservation the reservation of the legal quality of constitutional rights.[79]

Müller does not intend this 'reservation of legal quality' to mean that all constitutional rights norms either have an explicit limiting clause or must be equipped with an unwritten one. In fact he rejects this suggestion sharply.[80] Rather, he wants to say that '*each* constitutional right is already materially limited in what it guarantees on account of its legal quality'.[81] 'According to the basic conception of a norm, in setting the margins of substantive constitutional protection' it is a matter 'not of unwritten amendments, but of the written normative content, that is, the *material normative extent* of the *normative field* expressed, indicated or clearly presupposed by the words of the constitutional provision'.[82] 'Determining the margins' and 'determining the content' are thus 'substantively saying the same thing'.[83] 'The primary doctrinal question is thus not, how may a constitutional right be limited, but, how far does it extend, given the *analysis of its normative field* and its combination with a validity content developed on the basis of the constitutional normative programme.'[84]

---

[76] 38 ff.
[77] F. Müller, *Die Positivität der Grundrechte* (Berlin, 1969), 41.
[78] ibid.   [79] ibid. 44.
[80] ibid. 40, 50. This may well be the reason why Müller himself rejects the expression 'reservation' [*Vorbehalt*] in his formulation 'reservation of legal quality' as 'unnecessary and confusing' (ibid. 67).
[81] ibid. 32.   [82] ibid. (emphasis added).
[83] ibid. 32 f.   [84] ibid. 87 (emphasis added)

Consistently with Müller's general theory of norms, the decisive consideration for the 'material extent of a constitutional right'[85] is thus the normative field. The quotations make it clear that the idea of a normative field plays two roles, the one as setting the scope ('material-normative extent of the normative field'), the other as a source of arguments (by analysis of the normative field). Here we are only interested in the first role,[86] which is the role the normative field plays in the type of situation envisaged by Müller when he says of painting in the middle of a road junction, that it does not 'belong' to the normative field of article 5(3)(1) Basic Law.[87]

All this should have made it clear that Müller's theory of material extent is a narrow conception of scope. This only becomes completely clear in Müller's theory of the 'content-specific modes of exercise'. Only 'content-specific',[88] 'specific',[89] 'constitutional rights specific',[90] protected or 'materially' belonging[91] but not 'unspecific modes of exercising constitutional rights'[92] belong to the normative field. The central concept of 'specific' used in these phrases is defined by Müller in the following way: 'a form of exercise of rights is specific when it does not demonstrably lack a material connection with the structure of the constitutional normative field (to be developed in advance as a matter of doctrine)'.[93] So whether a mode of exercise is specific to a constitutional right or not depends upon its satisfying the criterion 'connected with the structure of the normative field'. Müller keeps the requirements of this connectivity relatively high. It is present if the mode of exercise 'falls in the area of what is *structurally* necessary or essential for the substantively-defined normative field'.[94] Müller offers a straightforward test to determine whether this is the case or not. A mode of action is not specific if it is *exchangeable*, if an 'equally valuable, alternative ... specific possibility within the normative field'[95] remains open to the one prevented from engaging in the 'unspecific' mode of exercise. This exchangeability test corresponds to a distinction between exercising constitutional rights and 'accidental "by chance" circumstances of an exercise of constitutional rights'.[96] [97]

---

[85] ibid. 20. The phrase is taken from BVerfGE 12, 45 (53).
[86] On the second, see above at 39 ff.
[87] F. Müller, *Freiheit der Kunst als Problem der Grundrechtsdogmatik* (Berlin, 1969), 59.
[88] id., *Die Positivität der Grundrechte*, 74; see also 93, 98.
[89] ibid. 73.   [90] ibid. 64.   [91] ibid. 74.   [92] ibid. 88.
[93] ibid. 100.   [94] ibid. 99.   [95] ibid. 101.   [96] ibid. 96.
[97] Müller attempts to flesh out these highly formal criteria with further ones. This occurs primarily in his theory of the *typical*. According to this, in determining the 'materially specific normative field ... [one should proceed] first of all from typical forms of exercise and states of affairs' (ibid. 98). However, the typical is 'not limited to the conventional or normal' (ibid. 98; id., *Freiheit der Kunst*, 64), since 'it is precisely the atypical, individual, new and spontaneous which can be materially specifically protected' (id., *Die Positivität der Grundrechte*, 99). But if the atypical can fall within the scope of a right, then although the concept of the typical can be a criterion for inclusion, it cannot be one for exclusion from protection.

A second criterion, which looks to the *purpose* of constitutional protection, is interesting.

What Müller means by this can be seen from his examples. His example of an artist who wants to paint on a busy road junction is instructive.[98] Müller's solution goes as follows: painting as such is protected by article 5(3)(1) Basic Law. However, the aspect of the act, 'on a road junction' is not. A law that prohibits painting on road junctions therefore does not limit any 'right-specific protected form of action',[99] it does not restrict any 'specific possibility of action'[100] within the normative field. It is directed against 'an act which falls within the surroundings of artistic licence, . . . but not within its normative field'.[101] Such a law would not be, or would not permit, an infringement and would not need a statutory reservation.[102] The same would 'apply in the case of a ban on preaching, or a ban on political speech, on the . . . road junction',[103] or for a 'musician who improvises his piece for the trumpet in the middle of the night on the streets or in rented accommodation with thin walls'.[104]

The weaknesses of this construction become apparent if one tries to subsume the cases under article 5(3)(1) Basic Law. There can be no doubt that whatever else this provision protects, artistic expressions are permitted. If one follows the text of the article, which guarantees artistic freedom without limitation or limitability, then it seems correct to start by deriving the following permissive norm from it:[105]

(1)   If an act is an artistic expression, then its performance is permitted.[106]

If one starts with this norm, the decisive question, so far as the scope of the right is concerned, is whether painting on a road junction is an artistic expression or not. The answer is simple: it is an artistic expression, but it is also at the same time something else, namely a disruption and threat to road traffic. This second characteristic is a reason for prohibiting the act, but what is forbidden remains an artistic expression. But this means that painting on the road junction falls within the scope of the permissive norm, and

---

This includes 'the reasons arising from historical experience, political conviction and legal insight as to why the constitutional right is guaranteed' in what is '*structurally* necessary, or essential, for the materially specific normative field' (ibid.). The purposes of constitutional rights can only be used to define scopes if they themselves are defined in such a way that individual scopes making the determination of controversial cases of exclusion possible can be assigned to them. But this must be doubted, and not simply for the reason that the allocation of purposes to norms seems generally problematic (see on this R. Alexy, 'Teleologische Auslegung und Gesetzesbindung', in *Sprache und Recht, Loccumer Protokolle*, 31 (1980), 143 ff.), but above all because the purposes to be allocated to constitutional rights provisions generally have the character of principles.

[98] ibid. 64, 73; id., *Freiheit der Kunst*, 56 f.
[99] id., *Die Positivität der Grundrechte*, 64; id., *Freiheit der Kunst*, 56, 65.
[100] id., *Die Positivität der Grundrechte*, 73.
[101] id., *Freiheit der Kunst*, 59; see also 124.
[102] id., *Die Positivität der Grundrechte*, 64.
[103] id., *Freiheit der Kunst*, 60.   [104] ibid. 124.
[105] On the concept of derivation, see above at 33 ff.
[106] On the logical structure of permissive norms such as (1), see above at 197 f., fn. 66.

if it is to be prohibited, the norm must be changed. It cannot have the content as expressed in (1).

One can well ask what Müller's theory of content-specific modes has to say about this simple way of putting things. The idea that 'unspecific modes of constitutional rights exercise'[107] do not belong to the area of normative protection means that acts which have the characteristics set out in the scope of constitutional permissive norms do not enjoy constitutional protection if they have further characteristics which are to be classified as unspecific modes of exercise. This simply means that an exception for unspecific modes has to be inserted into the permissive norm stated above:

(2)   If an act is an artistic expression and does not demonstrate the characteristic of being an unspecific mode of exercise, then its performance is permitted.

If one wants to alter the norm in this way and at the same time maintain that it is not an unwritten limiting clause which is being created, then one has to maintain that an exception is not a limit, but part of the scope. This thesis is unsustainable on both substantive and formal grounds.

It is unsustainable on substantive grounds because the criterion of specificity along with that of exchangeability is not suitable to distinguish between what is constitutionally protected and what is not protected. Would painting on the road junction also be an untypical mode of exercise, and thus excluded from constitutional protection, even if the junction were out of action, and the painting would disturb nobody, that is, if there were no rational ground for excluding constitutional protection?[108] If one could justify exclusion from the road junction under these circumstances as well, by saying that being there was not typical for painting, and that the location is exchangeable, then every act could be prohibited whenever there is a possibility of carrying it out in a different place, at another time, or in some other way. This would remove from the constitutional right-holder the right to decide for himself in what way he is going to make use of his constitutional liberty. But this right is an important constitutional position.[109]

---

[107] Müller, *Die Positivität der Grundrechte*, 88.

[108] See Schwabe, *Probleme der Grundrechtsdogmatik*, 160.

[109] The right to determine for oneself the manner in which a constitutional right is exercised is not to be confused with a clearly non-existent right of constitutional right-holders to define the scopes of constitutional rights norms for themselves (see on this J. Isensee, *Wer definiert die Freiheitsrechte?* (Heidelberg and Karlsruhe, 1980), 10 ff.). As a prima facie right, each right extends as far as its scope, and as a definitive right to the extent that the situation is not covered by limits. The fact that one can decide for oneself *in the context of* the scope does not mean that one can decide *on* the scope. On the right to determine the manner of exercise of constitutional rights for oneself, see W. Schmitt Glaeser, 'Die Freiheit der Forschung', *Wissenschaftsrecht, Wissenschaftsverwaltung, Wissenschaftsförderung*, 7 (1974), 119. In reference to the freedom of research, he emphasizes that the constitutional right-holder is to decide what is necessary for research.

The formal ground is directly connected with this. If it is not the untypical nature and exchangeability which excludes protection in the case of the road junction artist, then it must be something else. What it is, is easy to see. It is the rights of others and collective interests such as security and smoothness of traffic flow. This reveals that Müller's criterion, even if it leads to the right outcome in a case, does so only because relevant limiting reasons lie behind the decision. But if this is so, the rationality of legal argumentation requires us to state these reasons. But this means that a limiting clause based on permissible limiting reasons must be inserted into the permissive norm. Since artistic freedom is guaranteed without limit, this limiting clause can only be derived from norms of equal constitutional status. Such a clause can easily be formulated on the basis of the case-law of the Federal Constitutional Court concerning the limitation of constitutional rights guaranteed without statutory reservation.[110] [111] If one adds such a clause into the permissive norm, it looks like this:

(3)   If an act is an artistic expression, then its performance is permitted, unless principles of constitutional status, which under the circumstances take precedence over the principle of artistic freedom, require its prohibition.[112]

With this, the norm together with its limiting clause makes explicit reference to the interplay of reason and counter-reason, which Müller's criteria mask without rendering superfluous. In order to see the interplay in operation and to start justifying the establishment of definitive limits in a rational way it is important to keep the scope of protection broad to start with. Müller's version of narrow scopes of constitutional rights should be rejected.

2.1.2 *Limiting the Scope on the Basis of General Laws*
A second group of narrow scope theories is made up of those views which remove from the protected area everything which is covered by general laws. The generality of laws can mean many things.[113] Here we are only interested in two types of generality, what Smend calls 'material' and 'objective' generality.[114]

According to Smend, who derived the distinction in the context of his interpretation of article 118 Weimar Imperial Constitution (freedom of

---

[110] See e.g. BVerfGE 28, 243 (261); 30, 173 (193).

[111] See above at 84, 188.

[112] Schwabe, *Probleme der Grundrechtsdogmatik*, 163, proposes a clause with a similar content, which adds the general limitation, 'in individual cases, artistic freedom must give way to more valuable legal interests' to 'the constitutional guarantee of free art'.

[113] See C. Starck, *Der Gesetzesbegriff des Grundgesetzes* (Baden-Baden, 1970), 49 ff.

[114] R. Smend, 'Das Recht der freien Meinungsäußerung', in id., *Staatsrechtliche Abhandlungen*, 2nd edn. (Berlin, 1968), 96 ff. On this distinction, see with comprehensive references E. Schwark, *Der Begriff der 'Allgemeinen Gesetze' in Artikel 5 Absatz 2 des Grundgesetzes* (Berlin, 1970).

expression), laws are *materially* general, 'if they take priority over article 118 because the social interest they protect is more important than freedom of expression'.[115] Häberle, who extends the theory of material generality to all constitutional rights, similarly terms 'general' all those 'laws which are seen by the Constitution as of equal or higher value than the relevant constitutional right'.[116] Both expressions make it clear that material generality is a matter of precedence and balancing of interests. But this means that the theory of material generality cannot be a theory of narrow scope. In order to get to the point of balancing, the act to be evaluated has to be covered by a constitutional right in the first place. It has to be prima facie protected. But this means that it falls within the protected area. The idea of material generality is the outcome born of balancing. It is the result of balancing reasons for definitive constitutional protection on the side of the scope of the constitutional right with reasons against on the side of the limits.

By contrast, the idea of *objective* generality can lead to a narrow scope theory. According to Smend, a law is objectively general if it does not contain 'legal limitations specifically on freedom of expression'.[117] To make it clear that this is a different idea from that of material generality, it can also be called 'formal generality'.[118] The idea of objective or formal generality can lead to a narrow scope theory, because it is possible to reach definitive exclusion of constitutional protection without engaging in a balancing of interests. Many variants of definitive exclusion of constitutional protection on the grounds of (objective or formal) generality have been proposed.[119] One particularly well developed one, which is explicitly presented as a narrow theory of protected area and scope, is that of Rüfner.

Rüfner starts by establishing that 'the unlimited protection of freedom, proof even against statute, is as little the intention of the Basic Law as it is of any democratic Constitution under the Rule of Law'.[120] One can agree with that without further ado. The question is, how the limitation is to be conceived. Rüfner's conception consists of connecting the idea of general laws and the general legal system with that of protected area. Appealing to a constitutional right should not guarantee 'any exemption from the *legal system in general*'; on the contrary, 'general laws are to be observed even in the exercise of constitutional rights'.[121] This does not mean that 'a general

---

[115] Smend, 'Das Recht der freien Meinungsäußerung', 97 f.

[116] Häberle, *Die Wesensgehaltgarantie*, 32.

[117] Smend, 'Das Recht der freien Meinungsäußerung', 96.

[118] See R. Scholz, *Die Koalitionsfreiheit als Verfassungsproblem* (Munich, 1971), 335 ff.

[119] See Bachof, 'Freiheit des Berufs', 195 f.; K. A. Bettermann, *Grenzen der Grundrechte* (Berlin, 1968), 26 ff.; U. Scheuner, 'Die Funktion der Grundrechte im Sozialstaat', 510 f.; P. Selmer, 'Generelle Norm und individueller Grundrechtsschutz', DÖV 1972, 558; U. Schwäble, *Das Grundrecht der Versammlungsfreiheit* (Berlin, 1975), 176 ff.; H. Ridder, *Die soziale Ordnung des Grundgesetzes* (Opladen, 1975), 78.

[120] W. Rüfner, 'Grundrechtskonflikte', in C. Starck (ed.), *Bundesverfassungsgericht und Grundgesetz*, ii (Tübingen, 1976), 456. [121] ibid. 457.

statutory reservation is being postulated for all constitutional rights'.[122] General laws, which Rüfner defines as 'having no connection with the exercise of the right in question', do not 'infringe the protected area of the—limited!—constitutional right'. This is decisive for his conception. They concern 'activity outside the area of protection'. The general legal order begins where the substantive limit of the constitutional right ends. Thus general laws do not set additional limits to constitutional rights.[123] Balancing is thus supposed to be neither necessary nor appropriate:[124] 'The important and difficult task of the interpreter in such cases is merely to determine correctly the protected area of the constitutional right.'[125]

So the concepts of protected area and general laws relate to two aspects of the same matter. If a law does not restrict the area protected by a particular constitutional right, then it is general so far as that right is concerned, and if it is general in respect of a particular constitutional right then it does not restrict the area of protection. Thus one can argue from the area of protection to generality and from generality to the area of protection. When Rüfner says that one has to '*identify* the area protected by individual rights'[126] he is expressing a certain preference for arguing from the area of protection to generality. The question is how to carry out this identification. Rüfner offers the following test, 'one has to imagine that the right opposed to the (supposed) exercise of constitutional rights were not to be found in the Constitution and could not be supported from it. Could one then seriously maintain . . . that a funeral procession could not be prohibited on account of a risk of infection? To put these questions is to reply in the negative.'[127]

The weaknesses of this criterion become apparent if one expands the thought experiment. Assume that avoiding the risk of infection is not only not in the Basic Law, and not based upon the Basic Law, but that it is also not a proper reason for the prohibition, quite independently of the Basic Law. The procession would then be a religious exercise with nothing counting against its being constitutionally protected. In these circumstances there is no doubt that it would fall within the area of constitutional protection. This makes it clear that when it is excluded from the area of protection on account of the risk of infection, this occurs *because of a reason counting*

---

[122] Rüfner, 'Grundrechtskonflikte', 457.

[123] ibid. 458.

[124] This is only supposed to be different in the context of art. 5(2) Basic Law. The statutory reservation in favour of general laws has a double function. On one hand it expresses the general principle that acts outside the protected area of the right are limited by general laws; on the other hand it opens up the possibility of limitations within the protected area of art. 5(1). Balancing is only permissible in the case of the latter. Rüfner thus abandons his earlier view that balancing might be necessary in the case of every general law (cf. id., 'Überschneidungen und gegenseitige Ergänzungen der Grundrechte', *Der Staat*, 7 (1968), 57 f. with id., 'Grundrechtskonflikte', 457, fn. 16).

[125] ibid. 458.   [126] ibid. 460 (emphasis added).   [127] ibid. 460 f.

against constitutional protection. But if there is constitutional protection in
the absence of such a counter-reason, then that counter-reason must have
characteristics justifying its restriction of the constitutional protection
which would otherwise apply. It has such characteristics if it satisfies the
requirements of a clause such as that of the Federal Constitutional Court on
the infringement of constitutional rights guaranteed without statutory
reservation. But it lacks such characteristics if it is not equally as important
as the principle counting for constitutional protection.

These straightforward considerations do not just remove the foundation
of Rüfner's approach, they create serious problems for narrow conceptions
of scope generally, because they show that constitutional protection always
depends on a relationship between a reason for constitutional protection
and some relevant contrary reason. It does not depend on some independently identifiable characteristics of the protected area, a set of associated
objects of protection, or general laws. There is just one way out of this difficulty for narrow theories of scope. They can accept that denying the satisfaction of scope or protected area is concerned with an interplay of reason
and counter-reason, but not with balancing. In cases of excluded protection, the superiority of the counter-reason is so great, that a balancing of
interests becomes quite unnecessary. The artist who steals his materials and
homicide on the stage are obvious examples.[128] But not all cases which
Rüfner argues are beyond the scope of rights are as clear as these. It cannot
be doubted that a funeral procession can be prohibited in a case of serious
risk of infection. But should even a relatively low risk of infection exclude
the constitutional right to exercise one's religion? Acts of religious persecution could no longer be countered by an appeal to constitutional rights in
cases of minimal risk of infection, which can often arise. The narrow
conception of scope is too crude to cope with such situations. It can adopt
an exclusion of constitutional protection in cases of high risk of infection,
and definitively accept constitutional protection where there is no risk of
infection, but for the legally interesting intermediate cases, in which it is
necessary to balance the relevant interests, it either gives no answer, or leads
to contradictions, or to overly complicated constructions. It becomes
contradictory when it makes the exclusion of protection depend on balancing, because the whole point of the theory is to limit the protected area
without balancing. It becomes overly complicated when it accepts that the
protected area is limited where the counter-reason is obviously stronger, but
reverts to balancing for cases of doubt. By contrast, the solution adopted by
a wide conception of the scope of rights is consistent and simple. If there is
a reason for constitutional protection, then the matter falls within the scope
of the relevant right, however strong the contrary reasons are. This does not
mean that a wide-ranging balancing exercise is necessary in every case. It

[128] ibid. 460.

does mean that even clear cases of constitutional non-protection are the result of balancing principles, that the *possibility* of balancing is kept open in all cases, and that it cannot be replaced by 'self-evidence' of any sort.

2.2 A Wide Conception of Scope

The weakness of both of the narrow conceptions of scope considered above is that they treat the definitive exclusion of constitutional protection not as the result of an interplay of reason and counter-reason, and that means not as the result of balancing principles, but at least in a series of cases, as the result of the application of criteria apparently independent of balancing. It can be shown that when these criteria lead to correct outcomes, then they are the result of appropriate balancing. This can be generalized. Constitutional judgments are only correct if they correspond to the outcome of an appropriate balancing of principles. If they are justified without balancing, then their correctness depends on whether the outcome can also be justified by an appropriate balancing of principles.

This conclusion demands a wide conception of scope. A wide conception of scope is one in which everything which the relevant constitutional principle suggests should be protected falls within the scope of protection. The form of inclusion within the protected area or scope can vary. A wide conception of scope consists of a bundle of rules which relate to diverse forms of inclusion. Here, we can consider just two of the most important:

(1) Everything which has at least one characteristic, which—viewed in isolation—would suffice to bring the matter within the scope of the relevant right, does so, regardless of what other characteristics it has.

Examples here would be the ones already discussed of painting on a road junction and the funeral procession carrying a risk of infection.

(2) Within the semantic leeway of the concepts defining the scope, wide interpretations are to be adopted.[129]

A good example here is the concept of the press. A whole series of authors propose narrow interpretations at this point. So, it is suggested, 'the press only embraces the publication of news and opinions of a politico-cultural and philosophical orientation as well as other reporting of information in newspapers and magazines'.[130] By contrast, the Federal Constitutional Court has adopted a wide interpretation, 'the concept of "the press" is to be interpreted widely and by formal criteria; it cannot be made dependent upon an evaluation of individual publications, by whatever criteria. The

---

[129] On the concept of semantic leeway, see R. Alexy, 'Die logische Analyse juristischer Entscheidungen', ARSP, Beiheft NF 14 (1980), 186 ff.

[130] Mangoldt and Klein, *Das Bonner Grundgesetz*, i, Art. 5 *Anmerkung* VI 3. For other narrow interpretations, see H. Krüger, 'Der Wesensgehalt der Grundrechte' in J. Seifert and H. Krüger, *Die Einschränkung der Grundrechte* (Hanover, 1976), 58; Hesse, *Grundzüge des Verfassungsrechts*, para. 394.

freedom of the press is not limited to the "serious" press.'[131] What is interesting is the consequences which the Court draws from this on the side of the limitations. The wide interpretation does not mean that constitutional protection is granted 'to the same extent to every publisher in every legal context and for every content'. Rather, in 'balancing press freedom with other constitutionally protected interests', the particular characteristics of the publication in question can be taken into account.[132] This fully corresponds to a wide conception of scope.

It was pointed out above that in the case of protected interest/infringement conceptions of scope, the extent of the scope not only depends on the breadth of the interests protected, but also relates to the form of infringement.[133] Thus rule (2) requires a broad understanding of infringement as well. An example of a decision which satisfies this requirement is the judgment concerning shops' closing hours in which the Federal Constitutional Court treats the rules addressed to shopkeepers concerning hours of business as an obstruction of the customer's shopping, and thus an infringement of his general freedom of action.[134] [135]

Wide conceptions of scope have been subject to many criticisms. The first group of objections relates to a dilemma. It is suggested that a wide conception of scope either gives too much constitutional protection, which leads to a disabling of the legislature[136] and an endangering of other legal interests,[137] or, in order to attain to an appropriate level of constitutional protection, it does not take seriously its obligation to the text of the Constitution.[138] In addition it is dishonest because it takes by way of limitation what it has guaranteed within the scope.[139]

These objections can indeed be based on the fact that a wide conception of scope has to exclude more with its limitations than a narrow one. This is practically significant above all in the case of constitutional rights guaranteed without statutory reservation. A narrow conception of scope has the advantage that it can totally, or mostly, do without unwritten limiting clauses. But it has to pay a high price for this. It has to find some way of excluding acts which fall within the literal meaning of the scope of constitutional rights.

---

[131] BVerfGE 34, 269 (283).   [132] ibid.

[133] 199.   [134] BVerfGE 13, 230 (232 f.).

[135] As has already been noted, the discussion of the wide theory of scope is limited here to defensive rights. The scope of norms guaranteeing equality rights will be discussed below. That norms which grant rights to positive acts can also be divided into scope and limiting clause is made clear by the 'reservation of the possible, in the sense of what the individual can reasonably demand of society', which the Federal Constitutional Court contrasts with an (undetermined) 'individual claim of the citizen to the creation of university places' (BVerfGE 33, 303 (333)). The moment a division into scope and limits is adopted for entitlements as well, the question of a narrow or wide theory of scope necessarily arises.

[136] Rüfner, 'Grundrechtskonflikte', 456.

[137] Isensee, *Wer definiert die Freiheitsrechte?* 30.

[138] Rüfner, 'Grundrechtskonflikte'.

[139] Isensee, *Wer definiert die Freiheitsrechte?*, 31.

Even where there is a risk of infection, a funeral procession remains an exercise of religion, and painting in places which endangers or hinders others
remains an expression of artistic talent. The argument that the text of the
Constitution is not being taken seriously applies equally well to the narrow
conception. Contrary to the literal meaning, it takes what falls within the
scope away from it. The question is only which is to be preferred, a relax-
ation of the literal meaning on the side of the scope or on the side of the
limitations. At least the latter has the chance of orientating itself by a clause
such as that proposed by the Federal Constitutional Court on the limitation
of constitutional rights without statutory reservation.

   In answering this question, the problem of dishonesty becomes relevant.
In considering this, it is important to remember that it is a problem which
concerns not just rights without statutory reservation but all constitutional
rights. The style of enacting constitutional rights has repeatedly given rise
to critical comment. Fechner speaks of a 'deeply disturbing questionability'
and a 'half-light of constitutional rights', which becomes particularly
apparent when a first paragraph 'creates the illusion of unlimited applicability, which on further reading disappoints'.[140] In his report on the
Constitution of the French Republic, Marx called it a 'trick of granting full
liberty, of laying down the finest principles, and leaving their application,
les détails, to be decided by subsequent laws'.[141] At the start of his investigation of statutory reservations, W. Jellinek asked what the use was 'of the
first sentence of a constitutional right ceremoniously enacting a right, when
a second sentence permits limitations by statute'.[142] If we wanted to remove
totally the problem raised by these quotations, we would have to replace
the catalogue of constitutional rights with an all-embracing system of
concrete rules. This would require an exercise of codification which one
suspects would exceed even that of the Civil Code. Such an approach,
which would actually make constitutional rights cease to be what they are,
is of course not the only solution to the problem of dishonesty. The uncertainty which would result if one could only have regard to the literal meaning of the limiting clauses can be reduced by a continuous and rational
constitutional jurisprudence oriented towards the principle of proportionality. Where this happens, one cannot talk seriously any more of half-light,
tricks, uselessness, and hypocrisy. From this point it is only a small step
further to the recognition that the objection of dishonesty does not apply to
a wide conception of scope. On the contrary, a citizen who is interested in
the form of argument and justification as well as the decision itself will find
it more honest and more persuasive if the refusal to extend the protection

---

[140] E. Fechner, *Die soziologische Grenze der Grundrechte* (Tübingen, 1954), 1 ff.
[141] K. Marx, 'The Constitution of the French Republic adopted on 4 November 1848', in K.
Marx and F. Engels, *Works*, x, (London, 1978), 567.
[142] W. Jellinek, 'Grundrechte und Gesetzesvorbehalt', *Deutsche Rechts-Zeitschrift*, 1 (1946),
4.

of constitutional rights is justified by appeal to the constitutional rights of others or to competing public interests which the Constitution requires to be respected, than if he is told that his behaviour is not materially specific, or that it is covered by general laws, or that it is excluded from protection for some other reason which takes it outside the scope.

A second group of objections must be taken more seriously. The wider the scope is conceived, the greater the number of cases in which constitutional rights norms are relevant, and the greater the number of competing principles. Against this, the accusation of a 'constitutional rights-ification of the entire law' has been made, an 'expansion of constitutional rights' which carries with it the danger of stretching the capacity of the Federal Constitutional Court beyond its limits.[143]

It has already been pointed out that a wide conception of scope does not necessarily lead to a greater degree of definitive constitutional protection. What a narrow conception excludes from the scope can, at least in general, fall within the limitations under a wide conception. But the expansion thesis makes a good point, although what is being expanded is not necessarily definitive but prima facie protection. This means that the number of cases is increased in which the outcome is the result of balancing reasons for protection on the side of the scope with reasons against protection on the side of the limitations. The question is whether this is a bad thing.

Many reasons for a negative evaluation can be given. The first is that practically every case becomes a matter of constitutional rights, which leads to an unnecessary and confusing displacement of ordinary legal reasoning with constitutional reasoning. This objection can be met by distinguishing actual from potential constitutional rights cases. A *potential* constitutional rights case is a case in which constitutional rights arguments can be made, but in which they are quite superfluous, because there is no doubt about the constitutionality of the ordinary legal solution. An *actual* constitutional rights case is distinguished by the fact that doubts about constitutional protection or non-protection are appropriate, so that constitutional arguments are necessary. If it was always clear that a case was either actually or only potentially a constitutional rights case, a narrow conception of scope would have something going for it. In potential constitutional rights cases, the matter would be excluded from the scope of the right, while the resolution of actual ones would take account of the limits. But there is no clear boundary between actual and potential constitutional rights cases. Rather, there is a scale of degrees of certainty from the absolute certainty that there is or is no constitutional protection down to total uncertainty. And the existence of various degrees of uncertainty is only one side of the problem. There is a personal aspect as well: different people will put different cases at different points on the scale of certainty/uncertainty. In the light of this,

---

[143] C. Starck, 'Die Grundrechte des Grundgesetzes', 245 f.

every narrow conception of scope is in a difficult situation. It is plausible enough in cases in which everyone—or at least every reasonably well-informed person—is completely certain that there is no constitutional protection, but it becomes problematic in those cases where some do not share the sense of certainty. The proponents of an exclusion of constitutional protection can try to persuade their opponents by appealing to the intention of the legislature, tradition, the materially non-specific character of the exercise of constitutional rights, or similar arguments. All this can happen within the context of a narrow conception of scope. But if this is not sufficiently persuasive, the only rational way forward is to focus on the reasons based on the rights of others or common interests which counter-balance the substantive reasons put forward by those wishing to extend constitutional protection. Once this interplay of reason and counter-reason begins, we have entered the arena of a wide conception of scope, which accepts constitutional protection in principle, even given the existence of easily outweighed reasons for constitutional protection. This means that the narrow conception of scope only works well where there is no doubt about non-protection. But a legal theory that does not help, or does not help much, in cases of doubt is not much use.

By contrast, a wide conception of scope has significant advantages. It can treat unambiguous cases of constitutional non-protection as merely potential constitutional rights cases, in which a constitutional rights argument is conceivable, but quite unnecessary. This avoids the danger of displacing ordinary legal reasoning with constitutional reasoning. On the other hand, the moment doubts about constitutional protection or non-protection arise, the wide conception treats it as an actual constitutional rights case, which opens the way for a substantive constitutional argument based on the principle of proportionality. This avoids the danger of suppressing constitutional reasoning by ordinary legal reasoning.

The wide conception of scope leads to a *model of two domains*. The first domain is that of potential constitutional rights cases, the second that of actual ones. Whenever a constitutional principle is relevant, then, no matter how surely the principle is outweighed by competing principles, the case is at least a potential constitutional rights case. An example is the prohibition on theft. The individual's general freedom of action is limited by this. General freedom of action is, as the principle of freedom of action, prima facie constitutionally protected.[144] In the case of theft, the principle is without doubt correctly outweighed by competing principles. So it is simply a potential constitutional rights case. But a potential constitutional rights case is still a constitutional rights case. Thus the legal system takes on the char-

---

[144] On the fact that 'the command, "thou shalt not steal" restricts me in the use I can make of my liberty', see H. H. Klein, *Die Grundrechte im demokratischen Staat*, 2nd edn. (Stuttgart, Berlin, Cologne and Mainz, 1974), 89, fn. 59.

acter of a comprehensive system of resolutions of constitutional rights conflicts. The majority of legal norms can be assigned to the domain of merely potential constitutional rights cases. The domain of potential constitutional rights cases makes up the substrate of the domain of real constitutional problems and argument, which is the domain of actual constitutional rights cases. This domain, which embraces all that is uncertain and controversial, rests on that in which the mass of indubitable and agreed cases fall. The most important point about the two-domain model is that belonging to one of the two domains is not something fixed for all time. One situation can, through the raising of doubts, leave the domain of the indubitable, that is, that of potential constitutional rights cases, and doubtful cases can, through a process of decision, argument, and/or practice, return from the domain of actual constitutional rights cases to the potential. The possibility of movement is open in both directions. No case may be prevented by a narrow conception of scope from becoming an actual constitutional rights case.

The plausibility of this model can be questioned, particularly in cases like that of theft. Starck speaks of a 'grotesque conception, destructive of legal sensibility, of a constitutional right to kill, to steal and to defame' and argues for exclusions from the scope of rights.[145] This objection cannot simply be met with the answer that a wide conception of scope is only concerned with the form of argument, and that there is agreement about the outcome, for Starck says at another point that he is 'not concerned about the outcome, but about the route to the outcome'.[146] However, one has to ask whether legal sensibility can really be destroyed by the legal construction of potential cases, that is, through forms of justification which in daily legal life are not necessary. This still applies when the construction of appropriate justifications in the cases named (murder, theft, defamation) can hardly be exceeded in their certainty. The impression of grotesqueness is above all a result of the ambiguity of the term 'constitutional right'. There is no question of a definitive right to steal and so on. A wide conception of scope simply accepts a prima facie right to do and to refrain from doing as one pleases. This right is limited, among other things, by the prohibition on theft. Such a construction may be unnecessary in the case of theft, but it is not grotesque. Its sense lies in its being the logical end of a scale of degrees of certainty in the setting of limits to rights. Why should legal constructions, if they lead to the most rational conclusions by the most rational way, not depart somewhat from immediately intuitive conceptions and follow their own rules?

Closely related to these objections is the one which says that a wide conception of scope leads to an increase in the number of constitutional

---

[145] C. Starck, 'Die Grundrechte des Grundgesetzes', JuS 1981, 245 f.
[146] C. Starck, 'Noch einmal: Die Grundrechte des Grundgesetzes', JuS 1981, 644.

rights conflicts and competition between rights.[147] This cannot be denied. It must also be accepted that the resolution of competing and conflicting principles has until now caused great difficulties for constitutional rights doctrine. In the final analysis, all proposed resolutions involve questions of evaluation. But evaluative decisions also lie behind narrow conceptions of scope. In the light of this, one can question whether the increase in the number of conflicts, which only becomes significant in actual constitutional rights cases, is something negative. Is it not rather the case that the restriction of the number of conflicts is to be negatively evaluated, on the grounds of the requirement that one should consider all relevant perspectives on a case? That this requirement does not lead to an overburdening of the parties is ensured by a contrary requirement of rationality, which says that what is not in doubt or controversial need not be justified. These requirements are better satisfied by a wide conception of scope on the two-domain model than by a narrow one.

There remains a jurisdictional objection. A wide conception of scope hits the jurisdictional objection when it leads to an unacceptable 'growth in the jurisdiction of the Constitutional Court', whether as against the legislature or as against other specialist courts.[148] But such a consequence is not a necessary part of the wide conception of scope. One can even question whether it leads to a growth in the number of actions before the Federal Constitutional Court. Someone who brings an action is interested in definitive constitutional protection, not in the doctrinal conclusion that his act falls within the scope of a constitutional right but that it is also covered by a limitation. If a constitutional complaint is brought on the basis of a one-sided consideration of the scope alone, the application can be rejected by the judicial committee for lack of sufficient chance of success (sect. 93a(3) Federal Constitutional Court Act). The senate's decision to accept a case (sect. 93a(4)) is a further filter. If the rejection of the application is reasoned, then a reference to the limits is just as persuasive as the case not falling within the scope of a right. If the constitutional complaint is accepted, the wide conception does not only not necessarily lead to extra-jurisdictional decisions, it does not even get close to them. As has already been shown, procedural principles, that is, those that take account of jurisdictional matters, are included in the competing principles. Exceeding or not exceeding jurisdiction depends not on the form of reasoning, but on the

---

[147] On the concepts of constitutional rights conflicts and competition, as well as for some proposed solutions, see W. Berg, *Konkurrenzen schrankendivergenter Freiheitsrechte im Grundrechtsabschnitt des Grundgesetzes* (Berlin and Frankfurt, 1968), 49 ff.; M. Lepa, 'Grundrechtskonflikte', DVBl 1972, 161 ff.; H. Blaesing, *Grundrechtskollisionen*, Diss. (Bochum, 1974); P. Schwacke, *Grundrechtliche Spannungslagen* (Stuttgart, Berlin, Cologne, and Mainz, 1975); Rüfner, 'Grundrechtskonflikte', 453 ff.; H. Bethge, *Zur Problematik von Grundrechtskollisionen* (Munich, 1977), L. H. Fohmann, *Konkurrenzen und Kollisionen im Verfassungsrecht* (Berlin, 1978); Schwabe, *Probleme der Grundrechtsdogmatik*, 304 ff.
[148] See Starck, 'Die Grundrechte des Grundgesetzes', 246.

weight of the relevant principles, and thus on the content of the reasoning. A narrow conception of scope may, in some situations, end up excluding extra-jurisdictional decisions by way of the substantive elements implicated in narrow conceptions of scope. But a high price has to be paid for getting this to work in any other than trivial cases in which wide and narrow conceptions lead to the same outcome. One has to take account of the danger that substantive constitutional protection is not even considered in cases where it could be relevant. Jurisdictional considerations must not give one element too great a weight, namely the non-interference with decisions of the legislature and the specialist courts. Substantive constitutional rights protection is just as important.[149] The wide conception of scope offers better chances than the narrow one of optimizing both elements, of reaching the right answers from both substantive and jurisdictional perspectives.

III. LIMITATION AND OUTWORKING

Not every norm of the ordinary law which concerns the same subject-matter as a constitutional right limits this right. Section 1922(1) Civil Code, 'on the death of a person, their entire property is transferred to one or more other persons', does not limit the constitutional guarantee of succession. This raises the question of how to distinguish between limiting and non-limiting norms in the field of constitutional rights. This question is very important from a practical point of view; norms which do not limit a constitutional right do not need justifying as limits.

Ordinary legal norms in the field of constitutional rights may be classified in various ways. One example is Lerche's division, already mentioned, between restricting, clarifying, typifying, abuse-protecting, and conflict-resolving norms.[150] However enlightening such distinctions may be, the one between *limiting* and *non-limiting* norms remains fundamental in the light of the practical implications just noted.

A non-limiting norm *in the field* of constitutional rights is a norm which has something to do with what the constitutional rights cover. In common with a widespread terminological use, it can be said to *outwork [ausgestalten]* the right.[151] Norms which do not have anything to do with a constitutional right neither limit it nor outwork it. The question is what is differentiated by limitation and outworking.

The discussion about the distinction between limitation and outworking tends to look for a point of departure in the constitutional rights provisions, which say that something can be 'regulated' on the basis of statute, or that it can be regulated or determined by statute (e.g. arts. 4(3)(2), 12(1)(2),

---

[149] See below at 366 ff.   [150] Lerche, *Übermaß und Verfassungsrecht*, 106 ff.
[151] Häberle, *Die Wesensgehaltgarantie*, 180 ff.; K. Hesse, *Grundzüge des Verfassungsrechts*, para. 303 ff.

12*a*(2)(3), 14(1)(2), 38(3), 104(2)(4) Basic Law). But it goes beyond an interpretation of these formulations. Häberle goes the furthest. According to him, all constitutional rights are 'capable and in need' not only of limitation, but also of 'statutory outworking'.[152] Not only does Häberle extend the idea of outworking to all constitutional rights, he also adopts a very wide understanding of outworking. Outworking is concerned with the 'goal of the Constitution, the realization of constitutional rights in social life'. To reach this goal, the Constitution needs 'legislation as the "medium" and means to social realization'.[153] The legislature acting in pursuit of this goal has to undertake 'creative outworkings'[154] and make "constitutive contributions" to the content of the liberty-rights'.[155] Even the process of legislating for criminal law is an instance of outworking: 'Where the legislature in the field of criminal law acts in such a way that it secures the constitutional rights of one against the same rights of another, it is moulding constitutional rights as a whole, quite apart from the fact that it is also determining the content of the individual's rights'.[156] From here it is only a small step to extend the idea of outworking to the area of limitation as well: 'The legislature, which limits constitutional rights in the interests of equal or higher-ranking legal interests, does not thereby abandon the idea of outworking. It is not only constitutional rights, but also their limits which form the subject-matter of the outworking activity of the legislature.'[157]

There would be no objection to such a wide conception of outworking, if it were simply to be used as a general term for the limiting and non-limiting role of the legislature. But if it is still (also) to be used as a parallel to limitation, then there are grounds for objecting. If something limits a constitutional right, it remains a limit, even if from some other perspective it also outworks the right.

The problems in theories of outworking are mainly the result of obscurities which arise from the many different ways in which the idea of outworking is used. Here we can distinguish between two different uses. In the first use, outworking refers to the entire set of norms associated with a

---

[152] Häberle, *Die Wesensgehaltgarantie*, 181.   [153] ibid. 184.   [154] ibid. 186
[154] ibid. 186.
[155] ibid. 187. According to Häberle, the 'constitutive contributions' of the legislature to the content of constitutional rights does not prevent its being bound by them. This gives rise to conceptual problems. The legislature cannot be bound to the content which it will constitutively provide in the process of enacting norms. The obligation must arise in respect of something else. One candidate could be constitutional principles. But the circumstances of constitutive norm-creation are defined by the relevant principles not necessarily establishing just one rule; if they did, only one 'provision of content' by the legislature would be permitted, and this would no longer be constitutive. But if several rules are equally compatible with the principles, they cannot determine the choice between them. So the legislature has a discretion in that it can constitutively select one rule without obligation. The constitutive and the obligatory thus relate to two quite different things: the constitutive to a discretion and the obligation to its limits.
[156] ibid. 189.   [157] ibid. 190 f.

constitutional right. This is what Häberle has in mind when he states that the legislature in the field of criminal law, 'in that it secures the constitutional rights of one against the equivalent rights of another . . . [outworks] constitutional rights as a whole'.[158] It is clear that this sort of outworking includes limitations. A criminal prohibition displaces the legal liberty to do what has just been prohibited. The prohibition on duress removes x's liberty to engage in duress. This is not affected by the fact that a prohibition addressed to everybody at the same time protects x's general freedom of action,[159] in that it protects x from being coerced by his fellow citizens. Criminal prohibitions are still limits on constitutional rights, even if every reasonable person agrees with them, indeed, even if there is a constitutional right that the state should protect the freedom of the individual by passing criminal laws protecting him from his fellow citizens.[160] In short, the fact that a limiting norm is reasonable and required for constitutional reasons to protect liberty does not stop it being a limiting norm.

The second usage treats the idea of outworking as a counterpart to limitation. One could say that this use represents the narrow and proper sense of outworking. As a counterpart to limitation, the idea of outworking cannot extend to commanding and prohibiting norms, but only to powers,[161] because commanding and prohibiting norms have by definition a limiting character.[162] The standard examples of formative powers are the norms of private law institutions. Constitutional guarantees such as marriage, property, and inheritance presuppose private law norms.[163] Without the norms of property law, the constitutional guarantee of property would be meaningless. It is the great contribution of the idea of an institution-guarantee to make this plain.[164] The private law norms necessary for constitutional guarantees not only do not limit the constitutional rights of the individual, they positively express them. A legislature which repealed the laws of marriage would not only infringe an objective guarantee of the legal institution of marriage, it would also breach a subjective right of the individual to get and to remain legally married.

---

[158] ibid. 189. Scholz may also be referring to the first usage when he characterizes ' "constitutionally compatible" law-making as the substantive outworking (formation) of general freedom of action' (R. Scholz, 'Das Grundrecht der freien Entfaltung der Persönlichkeit in der Rechtsprechung des Bundesverfassungsgerichts', AöR 100 (1975), 100).

[159] On the concept of the protection of a liberty, see above at 148 ff.

[160] See Klein, *Die Grundrechte im demokratischen Staat*, 57, who emphasizes that 'norms do not lose their character as limitations simply because and to the extent that they create the conditions for the real usefulness of individual liberty'.

[161] On the concept of a power, see above at 149 ff.

[162] We are concerned here with the limiting and non-limiting (outworking) character of norms. If one relates the concept of outworking to positions, further distinctions can be drawn. Thus the prohibition of duress outworks the protection of legal liberty, but it also infringes legal liberty. The former occurs through the latter.

[163] See e.g. BVerfGE 24, 367 (389); 36, 146 (161); 58, 300 (330).

[164] Klein speaks correctly of 'conceptually necessary associated institution-guarantees' (Mangoldt and Klein, *Das Bonner Grundgesetz*, i, *Vorbemerkung* A VI 3 d).

Classifying private law powers as formative norms in the narrow and proper sense is certainly connected with a whole host of problems. The first is that the exercise of private law powers leads to rights and duties, that is, to commands and prohibitions, and thus to limitations of general legal liberty. The distinctiveness of these limitations of general legal liberty is that they depend directly upon legally unconstrained acts of the individual. The question of whether and to what extent limitations of general legal liberty of this nature are to be seen as limitations of a constitutional right leads to the problem of the so-called third party or horizontal effect of constitutional rights. This problem will be dealt with below.[165] At this point it is only important to establish that the legislative creation of private law powers *as such* has no limiting character.

A second problem arises from the fact that private law powers can be differently expressed. The legislature can give the private law subject more or less powers. It can repeal exisiting powers and refuse to create possible but non-existing powers. The question is whether all these activities are a matter of outworking, or whether some of them could amount to a limitation of rights. An example would be the repeal of the so-called power of 'alteration-termination' whereby a former power of owners of rented accommodation was removed.[166] Does this simply outwork the position of the owner, or does it limit it? It is easy to argue that it is a limitation, if one takes the relevant subject-matter to be the entire ordinary legal position of the owner as it existed before the change in the law. But this does not help us, because we are concerned with the limitation of constitutional rights positions. Whether the power of alteration-termination belongs to the constitutionally protected position of the owner is precisely the question. If the removal of this power is a limitation and not merely a matter of outworking, then something constitutional must be found which has been limited. The obvious candidate is the constitutional principle of private property.[167] The constitutional principle of private property, like all principles, requires a maximally high level of realization.[168]

A maximally high level of realization of the constitutional principle of private property includes a maximally high level of private enjoyment and powers of disposal. But excluding the power of alteration-termination realizes a smaller degree of this than keeping it. By excluding it, the constitutional principle is a little bit more restricted. This means that the prima facie right corresponding to this principle has been limited. So in the light of the

---

[165] 354 ff.; see also 304 ff.

[166] See on this BVerfGE 37, 132 (139 ff.).

[167] Some decisions speak explicitly of examining norms of ordinary legal institutions against the standard of constitutional principles, as for example in the decision concerning the prohibition of marriage of cohabitees, in which it was stated that 'the individual regulations of the civil law are to be judged against art. 6(1) Basic Law as a higher law and a guiding norm itself containing the basic principles' (BVerfGE 36, 146 (162)).

[168] See above at 47 f.

theory of principles one can talk about a limitation of the constitutional right to property, in need of justification.

The 1974 decision of the Federal Constitutional Court on the right to terminate contracts for the lease of accommodation[169] should be interpreted in just this way. The Court starts from a conflict of principles. It states that the legislature 'in the context of private law according to article 14(1)(2) Basic Law . . . must take equal account of both dialectically related elements of the Basic Law of constitutionally guaranteed liberty and the requirement of a socially fair order of property. It must bring the interests of all parties which are worthy of protection into a fair balance and a balanced relationship.'[170] This is a clear description of a conflict of principles. It is said of the 'removal of the so-called alteration-termination' that 'to a certain extent [it] *limits* the landlord's freedom of action' but that 'in the light of the high significance of the home to the individual and the family it is *justified* by article 14(2) Basic Law'.[171] This expresses the result of a balancing process which leads to a limitation. Admittedly, the Court talks in terms of a limitation of general freedom of action and not the constitutional right to property. But the limitation of freedom of action occurred through a removal of a private law power,[172] to which the principle of private property gave a prima facie right.[173] The removal of the alteration-termination is thus to be seen not as mere outworking but as a limitation.[174]

What has just been said can be generalized. Whenever the removal of a power hinders the realization of a constitutional principle it is not mere outworking, it is limitation, and as such it needs justifying.

The criterion of non-obstruction of the realization of a constitutional principle can be used in all cases to separate outworking from limitation. Thus the Federal Constitutional Court allows the enactment of a formal registration procedure for conscientious objectors to be covered by article

---

[169] BVerfGE 37, 132.   [170] BVerfGE 37, 132 (140).

[171] BVerfGE 37, 132 (141) (emphasis added).

[172] On the connection between liberties and powers, see above at 157.

[173] On the structure of such rights, see above at 125 ff.

[174] The Federal Constitutional Court classifies the provisions of the Water Supply Act which fell for consideration in the water drainage case (BVerfGE 58, 300) as a regulation of the content and limits of property for the purposes of art. 14(1)(2) Basic Law, whereby the accent lies at times more on determining content, at times on setting limits (BVerfGE 58, 300 (332 ff.)). The object and extent of protection guaranteed by art. 14(1)(1) are supposed to result from this regulation among others (BVerfGE 58, 300 (336)). One could take the view that the concept of limitation developed above is inconsistent with this. But this is not the case. That the Court proceeds on the basis of a limitation in the sense defined here is shown by its justification of the norms in question against the requirements of constitutional rights, which include a consideration of proportionality (BVerfGE 58, 300 (338 f.)). The key point of the decision is that the (by definition) unlimited prima facie right is not the reference point for expropriation, but rather a right already permissibly and definitively limited by constitutionally compatible statutes (BVerfGE 58, 300 (336)). This does not contradict the concept of limitation portrayed here; rather, it presupposes it.

4(3)(2) Basic Law, but not the limiting of its legal effect to the time period after it is in force. This limitation is dealt with in the context of balancing the constitutional principles it restricts with the other competing constitutional principles relevant to the case.[175]

The criterion of non-obstruction of the realization of constitutional principles implies that wherever a balancing of interests under the principle of proportionality is necessary (actual constitutional rights case) or possible (potential constitutional rights case), it is not a matter of outworking, but of limitation. The balancing which the Federal Constitutional Court has undertaken in its case-law on the freedom of choice and exercise of profession[176] shows that it considers the regulatory power of article 12(1)(3) Basic Law not as a power to outwork, but as a power to limit rights.

Only such a narrow conception of outworking, which matches a correspondingly wide conception of limitation, satisfies the requirements of the rationality of constitutional justification. What can be characterized as outworking does not need further justification. Keeping the field of what needs to be, and can be, justified wide open by a narrow conception of outworking does not guarantee that only permissible limitations will take place, but it does guarantee that no limitation is exempt from the need for justification, which is a significant safeguard that only permissible limitations will be enacted.

---

[175] BVerfGE 28, 243 (260 f.).
[176] See above all BVerfGE 7, 377 (399 ff.).

7

The General Right to Liberty

The constitutional law of the Federal Republic of Germany not only guarantees rights to specific liberties, such as freedom of expression and freedom of profession, along with rights against certain forms of discrimination, such as that on the grounds of sex or race, but it also grants a general right to liberty and a general right to equality. Thus two of the most controversial objects of political philosophy are turned directly into objects of positive law. It is hardly surprising that this has led to a whole series of doctrinal questions. The purpose of this and the following chapter is to show what the theory of constitutional rights and constitutional rights norms has to offer by way of a solution to some of the problems raised. First of all, we must consider the general right to liberty.

I. THE CONCEPT OF A GENERAL RIGHT TO LIBERTY

In one of its most important early decisions, the Elfes Judgment,[1] the Federal Constitutional Court interpreted the right to free development of personality protected in article 2(1) Basic Law as a right to general freedom of action, and it has maintained this position, albeit with various doctrinal refinements, ever since.[2] It has thereby clearly rejected those attempts which, by criticizing this approach as an empty formula,[3] seek to control the scope or limits of the right in article 2(1) Basic Law either by reducing the scope of the right, or by modifying the entire character of the provision. Examples of such attempts are on one hand *objective* interpretations, which deny to article 2(1) Basic Law the character of a norm directly granting a subjective right,[4] and on the other hand *narrow* theories which limit the

---

[1] BVerfGE 6, 32.
[2] From more recent times, see BVerfGE 59, 275 (278).
[3] See E. Grabitz, *Freiheit und Verfassungsrecht* (Tübingen, 1976), 113. H. C. Nipperdey, 'Freie Entfaltung der Persönlichkeit', in K. A. Bettermann and H. C. Nipperdey (eds.), *Die Grundrechte*, vol. 4.2 (Berlin, 1962), 789 speaks of the problem of 'delimiting two general clauses'.
[4] See F. Klein in H. v. Mangoldt and F. Klein, *Das Bonner Grundgesetz*, i, 5th edn. (Berlin and Frankfurt, 1957), *Anmerkung* III 5 *a*, *b* to art. 2; D. Haas, 'Freie Entfaltung der Persönlichkeit', DÖV 1954, 70 f.; H. Wehrhahn, 'Systematische Vorfragen einer Auslegung des Art. 2 Abs 1 des Grundgesetzes', AöR 82 (1957), 250 ff.; W. Wertenbruch, 'Der Grundrechtsbegriff und Art. 2 Abs. 1 GG', DVBl 1958, 481 ff.; These theories are all subject

scope of the right. The most extreme form of the latter type is Peters's theory of the essential core of personality, according to which article 2(1) Basic Law only protects 'expressions of true human nature as understood in western culture'.[5] [6] In contrast to all this, the Federal Constitutional Court, which from its first decisions has never called into question the subjective nature of article 2(1) Basic Law,[7] and which has interpreted the free development of personality as 'human freedom of action in the widest possible sense',[8] has taken the bull by the horns and adopted an extremely wide and subjective interpretation: a general right to liberty.[9]

The thesis that article 2(1) Basic Law contains 'a free-standing constitutional right, guaranteeing general human freedom of action'[10] has far-reaching consequences. General freedom of action is the liberty to do or not to do as one pleases. The idea that this liberty is protected by article 2(1) means two things. First, it means that everyone is *permitted* to do as they please (permissive norm), assuming that limitations do not apply. Secondly, it means (absent relevant limitations) that everyone has a *right* against the state that it should not hinder acts and omissions, that is, that it should not infringe this right (a rights-norm). The scope of article 2(1) Basic Law is thus very widely drawn. It embraces all actions of all constitutional right-holders (permissive norm) and all interferences by the state in actions of those right-holders (rights-norm).

---

to the overriding objection that the Basic Law itself identifies art. 2(1) as a norm guaranteeing constitutional rights by the words, 'the following constitutional rights' in art. 1(3).

[5] H. Peters, 'Die freie Entfaltung der Persönlichkeit als Verfassungsziel', in D. S. Constantopoulos and H. Wehberg (eds.), *Festschrift für R. Laun* (Hamburg, 1953), 673; id., *Das Recht auf freie Entfaltung der Persönlichkeit in der höchstrichterlichen Rechtsprechung* (Cologne and Opladen, 1963). For a critique of this view, see H.-U. Evers, 'Zur Auslegung von Art. 2 Abs. 1 des Grundgesetzes, insbesondere zur Persönlichkeitskerntheorie', AöR 90 (1965), 94 f., who makes the telling objection that Peters's theory attempts to legalize a certain philosophical anthropology which from the perspective of the Basic Law one is not required to adopt at the cost of other views of human nature also compatible with the Constitution. Thus also Nipperdey, 'Freie Entfaltung der Persönlichkeit', 771 ff.

Theories such as Hesse's, who sees in art. 2(1) the 'guaranteeing of a narrow personal sphere of life, albeit not one limited to purely intellectual and moral development' (K. Hesse, *Grundzüge des Verfassungsrechts der Bundesrepublik Deutschland*, 14th edn. (Heidelberg, 1984), para. 428), are not subject to this objection. Nevertheless, one has to respond along with Starck to such philosophically neutral variants of the narrow interpretation, that in defining the 'sphere of life, they open the door to *uncontrolled* limitations of liberty', because their justification as a limit to a right becomes unnecessary (C. Starck, 'Das "Sittengesetz" als Schranke der freien Entfaltung der Persönlichkeit', in G. Leibholz et al., *Menschenwürde und freiheitliche Rechtsordnung* (Tübingen, 1974), 261).

[6] For an account and critique of various attempts to resolve this, see J. Müller, *Auswirkungen der unterschiedlichen Auffassungen zum Rechtscharakter des Art. 2 Abs. 1 GG und zu dessen Schranken* (Hamburg, 1972).

[7] BVerfGE 1, 7 (8); 1, 246 (273).

[8] BVerfGE 6, 32 (36).

[9] When the Federal Constitutional Court speaks occasionally of a 'general statement of liberty' (BVerfGE 13, 21 (26)), then it is referring to a norm which guarantees the general right to liberty.

[10] BVerfGE 6, 32 (36).

Even this is not the widest possible interpretation. The permissive and rights-norms relate only to *actions* of constitutional right-holders. Along with the Federal Constitutional Court we can extend the general right to liberty even further by including not only the protection of actions, but also states of affairs[11] and legal positions[12] of constitutional right-holders.[13] The right would then protect not only what the individual 'does', but also what he factually and legally 'is'. Only then is the general right to liberty a truly exhaustive general right to freedom from interference.

One can justify the inclusion of protecting states of affairs and legal positions by the fact that interferences with the state of a right-holder's affairs or his legal position always have an indirect effect on his freedom of action. So, for example, affecting the state of unconstrained communication by making secret recordings[14] or removing the legal position of membership in an advisory council[15] impacts on the possibilities for action of the individual concerned. From this perspective, the general right to liberty protects freedom of action both directly and indirectly (via the protection of states of affairs and legal positions). By contrast, if the right of general freedom of action were limited to the direct protection of actions, this would only cover one part of general liberty. The only point here is to bear this distinction in mind.

Such a wide scope as that of the general right to liberty requires a correspondingly wide conception of the limiting clause.[16] It was thus only logical that the Federal Constitutional Court should have adopted the widest limitation possible under the Basic Law with its formula of 'every legal norm procedurally and substantively compatible with the Constitution'.[17] The combination of such an extremely wide scope and extremely wide limiting clause has major procedural consequences: 'Everyone can allege by way of constitutional complaint that a law limiting his freedom of action does not belong to the constitutional order because it infringes (either procedurally or substantively) individual provisions of the Constitution or general constitutional principles and thus that it infringes his constitutional right under article 2(1) Basic Law'.[18]

The idea of a general right to liberty which has just been outlined was, and still is, subject to many objections. These objections are in part objec-

---

[11] See BVerfGE 34, 238 (246): uninhibited communication. The protection of states of affairs is above all the subject-matter of various expressions of the general right to personality, see BVerfGE 54, 148 (153 f.).

[12] See BVerfGE 51, 77 (89): legal position of an advisory council member.

[13] The trio of acts, states of affairs, and legal positions can be combined in the disadvantage-formula of the Federal Constitutional Court; see BVerfGE 9, 83 (88); 19, 206 (215); 29, 402 (408). On the distinction between act-related, situation-related, and position-related rights, see above at 122 ff.

[14] BVerfGE 34, 238 (246).   [15] BVerfGE 51, 77 (89).

[16] See above at 201.   [17] BVerfGE 6, 32 (38).

[18] BVerfGE 6, 32 (41).

tions to the case-law of the Federal Constitutional Court—it is sometimes said that the Court does not follow its interpretation consistently, but increasingly abandons a formal definition for a substantive one.[19] It will be argued here that a general right to liberty leads to more advantages than disadvantages, and that the decisions of the Federal Constitutional Court which appear inconsistent at first sight can be interpreted consistently with such a general right.

II. A FORMAL–MATERIAL CONCEPTION OF THE GENERAL RIGHT TO LIBERTY

One of the most important objections to the idea of a general right to liberty is that such a right is without content, lacking substance,[20] and thus offers no standard for the evaluation of permissible limitations of liberty.[21] It is a 'right to liberty without any liberty-content'.[22] What the right guarantees is not the result of the 'substance of freedom' but emerges only as a result of the permissible 'limits to legal interferences with liberty'.[23] Instead of freedom of action, one should really only speak of freedom from interference.[24] The general right to liberty thus becomes a constitutional right to the constitutionality of all state action. So the 'basic principle of the Rule of Law' becomes a constitutional right.[25] This has far-reaching and undesirable consequences for constitutional procedure, as Ehmke points out in the following words: 'Every law that limits general freedom of action—and which law does not do this?—can now be challenged by way of constitutional complaint by alleging that it infringes *any* provision of the constitution. This consequence seems to me directly to contradict the sense of section 90 Federal Constitutional Court Act.'[26]

1. THE NO-CONTENT OBJECTION

These objections tie substantive and procedural aspects closely together. Let us consider first the substantive aspect. The question here is whether interpreting article 2(1) Basic Law as a general right to liberty really leads to its

[19] Thus R. Scholz, 'Das Grundrecht der freien Entfaltung der Persönlichkeit in der Rechtsprechung des Bundesverfassungsgerichts', AöR 100 (1975), 89 ff.
[20] W. Schmidt, 'Die Freiheit vor dem Gesetz', AöR 91 (1966), 47, 49.
[21] Grabitz, *Freiheit und Verfassungsrecht*, 76, 120, 124, 248.
[22] W. Schmidt, 'Die Freiheit vor dem Gesetz', 48.
[23] ibid. 49.   [24] ibid.
[25] H. Ehmke, 'Prinzipien der Verfassungsinterpretation', VVDStRL 20 (1963), 84. Cf. the following formulation of the Federal Constitutional Court, 'this constitutional right prohibits infringements by the state which are not in accordance with the Rule of Law' (BVerfGE 42, 20 (27)).
[26] Ehmke, 'Prinzipien der Verfassungsinterpretation', 84 f.

having no content. This can usefully be put in terms of two theses concerning the absence of scope and the absence of substance. The no-scope thesis alleges that the idea of a general right to liberty produces a constitutional norm without scope. The no-substance thesis suggests that the idea of a general right to liberty makes any obligation of the legislature 'as regards the liberty-element' impossible to sustain.[27]

1.1 The No-Scope Thesis

The idea that the general right to liberty is without scope identifies an important structural characteristic, but this characteristic is not objectionable. If one interprets article 2(1) Basic Law as a general right to liberty, the following norm can be derived from it:

(1)   Every action (act or omission) is permitted, unless forbidden by a procedurally and substantively constitutional legal norm.

This norm can be reformulated as follows:

(2)   If A is an action (act or omission) and it is not forbidden by a legal norm procedurally and substantively compatible with the constitution, then the doing of A is permitted.

In its *external* form this norm corresponds exactly to every other constitutional permissive norm, the protasis of which is divided into a statement of scope (S) and limiting clause (L) and whose apodosis is the legal consequence (Q):

(3) S and not $L \rightarrow Q$.[28]

The differences concern the internal form of S. In the case of specific constitutional permissive norms, S stands for a certain characteristic action, such as an expression of opinion, or of artistic endeavour, or a religious activity; in the case of the general constitutional permissive norm, S stands simply for the characteristic of being an action. One could say that the inclusion of the characteristic of being an action in a permissive norm is superfluous, since what else could be permitted other than actions? Permissive norms presuppose that one is concerned with actions and these do not need to be expressed as part of their content. This is correct, but it does not mean that the right has no scope. Even obvious prerequisites for a legal consequence can be expressed as elements of the scope. In most cases this is superfluous and hence pointless. In the case of the general right to liberty it is useful and not superfluous. By identifying the characteristic of being an action, the range of what is prima facie protected is explicitly expressed and with all desirable clarity. This is precisely the function of the

---

[27] Grabitz, *Freiheit und Verfassungsrecht*, 248. See also W. Schmidt, 'Die Freiheit vor dem Gesetz', 47; H. Schulz-Schaeffer, *Der Freiheitssatz des Art. 2 Abs. 1 Grundgesetz* (Berlin, 1971), 28.

[28] See on this above at 85.

statement of scope in a constitutional rights norm divided into scope and limitation. The only possible objection is the breadth of this scope, but this concerns its content and not its suitability as a means of describing what is prima facie protected, that is, its suitability as a scope. The same point applies to the scope of the rights-norm which protects the permissive norm.

1.2 The No-Substance Thesis

The objection that the general right to liberty has no content cannot be based on the idea that the right has no scope. The question is whether the thesis that the right has no substance leads to this conclusion. The general right to liberty is supposed to be without substance because general freedom of action, that is, the freedom to do or not to do as one pleases, cannot be a criterion or standard for what limits may be set and what not,[29] which means that general freedom of action is defined solely by reference to its limits. The correctness of this thesis must be challenged, and in order to do this we should consider briefly two relatively diverse decisions of the Federal Constitutional Court: its judgment on the law of public collections,[30] and its decision concerning the prohibition on feeding pigeons.[31]

The question in the Law of Collections Judgment[32] was whether public collections could be subjected to a repressive prohibition coupled with a scheme of permission. The court starts by establishing that collecting is an activity covered by the right of general freedom of action, and that a repressive prohibition with a scheme of permission would limit this.[33] In order for this limitation to be permissible the Court requires it to be consistent with the principle of proportionality.[34] In doing this, it proceeds on the basis of a requirement of balancing already set out in the Passengers Judgment:[35] 'The more the statute interferes with elementary expressions of human freedom of action, the more carefully should the reasons put forward for it be balanced with the constitutional claim of the citizen to liberty'.[36] Apart from the idea of carefulness, this requirement corresponds to the Law of Balancing set out above,[37] which in the case of increasing degrees of interference requires an increasingly important satisfaction of competing principles.[38]

---

[29] Grabitz, *Freiheit und Verfassungsrecht*, 120, 248; W. Schmidt, 'Die Freiheit vor dem Gesetz', 51.

[30] BVerfGE 20, 150.   [31] BVerfGE 54, 143.

[32] See on this H. H. Rupp, 'Das Urteil des Bundesverfassungsgerichts zum Sammlungsgesetz—eine Wende in der Grundrechtsinterpretation des Art. 2 Abs. 1 GG?' NJW 1966, 2037 ff.

[33] BVerfGE 20, 150 (154).   [34] BVerfGE 20, 150 (155).

[35] BVerfGE 17, 306 (314).   [36] BVerfGE 20, 150 (159).

[37] At 102.

[38] By including the aspect of carefulness, the Court's requirement of balancing contains additional subjective or procedural elements alongside the objectively formulated Law of Balancing. But there can be no doubt that it includes the Law of Balancing. A balancing process which gave precedence to competing principles in the face of a high degree of inter-

Not all decisions concerned with limiting the general right to liberty express the need to balance interests so explicitly. This says nothing about the application of the Law of Balancing. Often the fact that the Court is following it is only indicated by occasional comments. An example of this is the decision concerning the prohibition on the feeding of pigeons which mentions on one hand, 'the extremely minor interference with the freedom of expressing one's love for animals' and on the other, 'overriding public interests' which justify the interference.[39]

Both these decisions, along with many others,[40] show that, in examining the infringement of the general right to liberty, the Court applies the principle of proportionality, whose third element, proportionality in its narrow sense, is identical to the Law of Balancing.[41] But if it is possible to balance something with the general right to liberty, the latter cannot be without substance, because you cannot balance something with something else which has no substance. From the fact that the Federal Constitutional Court engages in balancing exercises with the general right to liberty, we can conclude that it cannot be without substance.

A proponent of the no-substance thesis would reply that this argument does not hold, because its premiss is false. The Court is not in fact balancing the general right to liberty, even if it claims to be doing so. The content of what is being balanced on the side of liberty is really a set of substantive principles, which are surreptitiously being introduced. This is exposed by the requirement of balancing stated in the Law of Collections Judgment quoted above. The court did not say, 'the more the statute interferes with human freedom of action', but 'the more the statute interferes with *elementary expressions* of human freedom of action'.[42] This exposes the fact that it is not freedom of action in itself, but rather freedoms *judged* to be elementary which are being weighed.

This objection leads to the question of the 'balanceability' of general freedom of action. And this question is tied up with that of its appropriateness as the content of a principle. The idea that the individual should, within the constraints of what is legally and factually possible, be granted a maximally high degree of freedom to do or not to do as he pleases, seems at first sight, at least from a logical perspective,[43] to be an unproblematic

---

ference and a low level of importance could never be called careful. B. Schlink, *Abwägung im Verfassungsrecht* (Berlin, 1976), 72, takes the view that the formulation of the Federal Constitutional Court 'pushes a procedural aspect into the foregound'. But this is too strong an interpretation. Only one procedural aspect (the aspect of carefulness) is mentioned, which is so obvious that it needs no specific mention in most cases of balancing.

[39] BVerfGE 54, 143 (147).

[40] See e.g. BVerfGE 10, 354 (364, 369); 13, 230 (235); 15, 235 (243); 17, 306 (314); 18, 315 (327); 19, 93 (96); 59, 275 (278).

[41] See on this above at 66 f., 102.   [42] Emphasis added.

[43] Only this perspective interests us here. The principle of general freedom of action serves negative liberty in the narrow, liberal sense (see on this above at 142). It is obvious that not

requirement. However, closer analysis reveals difficulties. To discuss these requires us to be clear about the content of the principle corresponding to the general right to liberty.

In discussing the concept of liberty above,[44] the liberty to do and not to do as one pleases, that is, the liberty to choose between alternative courses of action, was described as 'negative liberty in its wide sense'. A person can be described as negatively free to the extent that the alternative courses of action open to him are not limited by obstacles to action. Obstacles to action could be further differentiated. To the extent that they are positive acts of others, in particular the state, we are concerned with negative liberty in its narrow sense or liberal liberty. Negative liberty exists in its narrow liberal sense when positive acts obstructing liberty are not carried out. The most precisely defined case of liberal liberty is legal liberty. A legal liberty exists when one is both permitted to do something and also permitted not to do it. This is exactly the case when one is neither commanded nor prohibited from doing something.[45]

Negative liberty in its wide sense extends beyond this. It includes liberal liberty but extends beyond this to embrace things such as socio-economic liberty which exists to the extent that the economic deprivation of the individual does not prevent him from realizing alternative courses of action.[46]

The principle the viability of which is to be examined here concerns negative liberty in its narrow sense, or liberal liberty. Its aim is to achieve a maximally high degree of legal liberty. This principle will be called the 'principle of negative freedom of *action*'. In the light of the character of the general right to liberty as related not only to action but also to states and positions, this principle can be associated with two others; one that requires a maximally high degree of non-interference with states of affairs, and one which requires the maximum non-removal of legal positions of the constitutional right-holder. These three principles can be subsumed under a single overarching one, the *'principle of negative liberty'*.[47] What follows concerns primarily the most simple sub-principle of this principle, the prin-

only formal but also substantive objections can be made to the principle of negative liberty in the narrow, liberal sense. For example, someone who takes the view that liberty makes one unhappy and a lack of liberty happy can object to the principle of negative liberty on the grounds that happiness is all that counts. But this is an objection to the validity of the principle, not an objection to the possibility of general freedom of action being the subject-matter of a principle.

[44] 138 ff.   [45] See above at 144 ff.   [46] See above at 141 f.
[47] The principle of negative liberty differs fundamentally in content and structure from Grabitz's 'constitutional principle of liberty'. Grabitz's constitutional principle of liberty embraces a bundle of liberties (negative, real, social, democratic, and political liberty; see Grabitz, *Freiheit und Verfassungsrecht*, 243 ff.). Since it includes just about everything which can conflict under the name of liberty it does not express a principle in the strict sense of the word, but rather an ideal which combines everything falling within the concept of liberty into a just and rational harmony.

ciple of legal liberty which requires that alternative courses of action be affected to the smallest degree possible by commands and prohibitions.

One way in which the principle of negative liberty is indistinguishable from other principles is easy to spot. Everything which affects the realization of this principle can be subjected to an examination of its suitability and its necessity. Problems arise when it comes to examining proportionality in its narrow sense, that is, when it comes to balancing. The Law of Balancing requires increasing intensity of interference with liberty to be matched by an increasing weight of reasons justifying the interference. But what is meant by the intensity of an interference with negative liberty? Does negative liberty give us a basis for thinking in terms of degrees of intensity of interference at all? Is not the prohibition on feeding pigeons and attending a religious service from the perspective of negative liberty simply the same thing, namely a limitation of negative liberty? How should one determine the degree of intensity? Is, for example, somebody more intensively affected by the ban on feeding pigeons than by a ban on attending a religious service, because in the absence of both prohibitions he would feed pigeons more often than go to church, and thus *more* actions are affected? But then is not the erection of numerous traffic lights a more intensive limitation (that is, one in need of stronger justification) than closing down churches, which altogether will affect far fewer acts?[48] And if one is not going to proceed on the basis of the number of actions, on what basis then? Are not evaluative standards necessary that have nothing to do with negative liberty? And if this is the case, does that not mean that it is those evaluative standards which are in truth the subject-matter of balancing. So is not the principle of negative liberty superfluous in balancing exercises simply because it is unbalanceable?

These questions make clear the sort of arguments which can be put forward for the no-substance thesis. But closer examination shows that ultimately they fail. To start with, it is to an extent possible to establish intensity of interferences with the realization of the principle of negative liberty without recourse to other substantive principles. The other point is that even if it is not possible to establish the degree of intensity without such principles, it does not follow that negative liberty plays no role at all. It may play a role in connection with other principles.

Examples of cases in which the degree of intensity can be established without the application of further standards are easy to find. Thus the intensity of interference increases with the prohibition of the following series of actions: feeding pigeons in the market-place, feeding pigeons in town, feeding animals in town, approaching animals at all. Each subsequent interference includes

---

[48] See C. Taylor, 'What's Wrong with Negative Liberty?' in A. Ryan (ed.), *The Idea of Freedom, Essays in Honour of Isaiah Berlin* (Oxford, New York, Toronto, and Melbourne, 1979), 183.

the previous one and more. Such a criterion of extent permits us to say that a repressive prohibition is a more intensive interference than a preventative one, a prohibition on travelling abroad is more intensive than a prohibition on travelling to one country, and a long-lasting prohibition is more intensive than a short one.

It could be objected that such comparative judgments of intensity do not get us very far. And there is certainly some truth in that. The degree of intensity 'in itself' cannot be established in this way. But it does represent some progress, because it shows that there is such a thing as degrees of intensity of interference with negative liberty. We can go on to say that the prohibition of a certain type of action in all its forms is a truly intensive interference. The Federal Constitutional Court correctly characterized the feeding of pigeons in the streets and public places of Mönchengladbach as an 'extremely limited interference with the freedom of expressing a love for animals'.[49] A general prohibition of every sort of expression of love for animals, being a wider interference with the freedom of expressing one's love for animals, would be a more intensive interference with negative liberty.

2. THE COMBINATION OF FORMAL AND MATERIAL PRINCIPLES

Which of a prohibition on feeding pigeons or attending church is the more intensive interference admittedly cannot be decided on the basis of what has so far been established. This requires further content-based criteria. In this example, we could try to find such a criterion in the positive legal guaranteeing of religious liberty. If this is to be avoided, then the most general positive legal criterion for content-based criteria is provided by the human dignity norm. It is in this sense that the Federal Constitutional Court has stated, 'in determining the content and extent of the constitutional right found in article 2(1) Basic Law, one must have regard to the fact that according to the constitutional rights norm of article 1(1) Basic Law, human dignity is inviolable, and demands respect and protection from all state power'.[50]

One could take the view that this abandons a conception of a general right to negative liberty, replacing it with a substantive conception of freedom oriented towards human dignity. In the place of the general freedom to do and not to do as one pleases, there are specific positively evaluated freedoms. That this is not the case is shown by a glance at the relationship between negative liberty and human dignity. This relationship can be described in the following way: Negative liberty is a necessary but not a sufficient condition of human dignity. Recourse to human dignity cannot therefore ever lead to a replacement of the 'formal' principle of negative

---

[49] BVerfGE 54, 143 (147).   [50] BVerfGE 34, 238 (245); 32, 373 (379).

liberty with substantive principles required by the human dignity norm. Just because something else is necessary for human dignity does not mean that what is already necessary becomes unnecessary and replaceable. Reference to the human dignity norm thus cannot lead to the replacement of the principle of negative liberty with substantive principles derived from human dignity, rather it can only lead to a *supplementing* of that principle. These suggestions must be considered more closely and justified.

It has been pointed out above[51] that at least one norm having the character of a principle may be derived from article 1(1) Basic Law, namely the principle of human dignity. The principle of human dignity is as ill defined as the concept of human dignity. Apart from general formulae such as the idea that human beings must not be made into mere objects,[52] the concept of human dignity can be expressed by way of a bundle of more concrete conditions which must hold (or which may not hold) if human dignity is to be protected. It is easy to reach agreement on some conditions: human dignity is not guaranteed where the individual is degraded, branded, persecuted, or outlawed.[53] Other conditions are more controversial, such as whether the long-term unemployment of a person willing to work, or the lack of certain material goods, infringes human dignity. It is simply a fact that different people will define human dignity according to different bundles of conditions. On the other hand, it is plain that the various bundles will not be totally different from each other. Many sets of conditions diverge in some respects but correspond in others, and often the differences only lie in the weight to be ascribed to individual conditions within the bundle. In addition, general formulae, such as the object-formula above, command a high level of consensus.[54] This allows us to speak of a single concept and varying conceptions of human dignity.[55] The different conceptions are hard to classify—there are no clear boundaries, only what Wittgenstein called 'family resemblances': 'a complicated network of similarities, overlapping and criss-crossing: sometimes overall similarities, sometimes similarities of detail'.[56]

The Federal Constitutional Court summarizes its conception in its human-nature-formula.[57] According to this, the human dignity norm is

---

[51] 63 f.

[52] See BVerfGE 27, 1 (6); 28, 389 (391); 45, 187 (228); 50, 125 (133); 50, 166 (175); 50, 205 (215).   [53] BVerfGE 1, 97 (104).

[54] On the difficulties in applying this formula in the individual case, see BVerfGE 30, 1 (25 f.).

[55] On the distinction between concept and conceptions, see J. Rawls, *A Theory of Justice* (Cambridge, Mass., 1971), 5; R. Dworkin, *Taking Rights Seriously*, 2nd edn. (London, 1978), 134 ff. For an account of different conceptions of human dignity, see B. Giese, *Das Würde-Konzept* (Berlin, 1975), 3 ff.

[56] L. Wittgenstein, *Philosophical Investigations*, trans. G. E. M. Anscombe, 2nd edn. (Oxford, 1958), 32 (§§ 66, 67).

[57] See on this in place of many R. Dreier, 'Das Menschenbild im Recht', in W. Böhme (ed.), *Was halten wir für Recht?*, Herrenalber Texte, 29 (1981), 87 ff.; W. Geiger, *Das Menschenbild des Grundgesetzes*, in Böhme, *Was Walten wir für Recht?* 9 ff.

'based on an understanding of the human being as an intellectual and moral creature capable of freely determining and developing itself. The Basic Law conceives of this freedom not as that of an isolated and autonomous individual, but as that of an individual related and bound to society.'[58] The significant point is that liberty plays a central role in this formula, and that it is asserted that if it were to play no role, one would not be dealing with a conception of dignity any more.[59] Of course, in view of the ambiguity of the concept of liberty, this does not help us very much. But to clarify this, it must emphasized that we are dealing with the securing of human dignity through law. A positive internal liberty, such as that which consists in following the moral law out of pure duty,[60] cannot be meant here. The formula has got to refer to the external liberty[61] which obtains when the individual is not hindered in his choice of different alternatives by external pressure, for in no other sense can one speak in a *legal* context of 'independence of the person'[62] and a 'responsible personality'.[63] Such a freedom always basically includes negative legal liberty. We can say that without negative legal liberty there would be no human dignity in any legally significant sense.[64]

It is no objection to this connecting of human dignity with negative liberty that the freedom which the Federal Constitutional Court associates with human dignity is not unlimited, but is that of an 'individual related and bound to society'.[65] The meaning of this is explained by the Court in the following words: 'the individual must submit himself to those limits on his freedom of action which the legislature sets in order to maintain and support social co-existence within the limits of what is generally acceptable according to the relevant subject-matter, and so long as the independence of the person remains guaranteed'.[66] This formulation, which clearly points to the principle of proportionality, is not just saying that liberty can be limited, but that it can only be limited for sufficient reasons. But this is exactly the content of the principle of negative liberty, which as a *principle* does not give a definitive permission to do and not to do as one pleases, but only to

---

[58] BVerfGE 45, 187 (227); see also BVerfGE 4, 7 (15 f.); 27, 1 (7); 30, 173 (193); 32, 98 (108); 33, 303 (334); 45, 187 (227); 50, 166 (175); 50, 290 (353).

[59] On the connection between dignity and liberty, see G. Dürig, 'Der Grundrechtssatz von der Menschenwürde', AöR 81 (1956), 125; K. Stern, 'Menschenwürde als Wurzel der Menschen-und der Grundrechte', in N. Achterberg, W. Krawietz, and D. Wyduckel (eds.) *Recht und Staat im sozialen Wandel, Festschrift für H. U. Scupin*, (Berlin, 1983), 632; E. Benda, 'Die Menschenwürde', in E. Benda, W. Maihofer, and H.-J. Vogel, *Handbuch des Verfassungsrechts* (Berlin and New York, 1983), 112. See also I. Kant, *The Moral Law (Groundwork of the Metaphysics of Morals)*, trans. H. J. Paton (London, 1948), 97: 'autonomy is therefore the ground of the dignity of human nature and of every rational creature'.

[60] Kant, *The Moral Law (Groundwork of the Metaphysics of Morals)*, 107 ff.

[61] On the distinction between internal and external liberty, see I. Kant, *Metaphysics of Morals*, trans. M. Gregor (Cambridge, 1991), 42, 186, 199, 207.

[62] BVerfGE 4, 7 (16).   [63] BVerfGE 45, 187 (228).

[64] It should be pointed out that this sentence only expresses a necessary, not a sufficient, condition.

[65] BVerfGE 45, 187 (227).   [66] BVerfGE 4, 7 (16).

do and not to do as one pleases in so far as reasons (the rights of others and collective interests) are not sufficient to justify a limitation of liberty. The principle of negative liberty is quite capable of taking full account of the social interdependence of the individual.

There is, of course, still the peculiarity that the principle of negative liberty requires an adequate ground for every limitation of liberty—even trivial ones—and one could take the view that to this extent it has nothing to do with human dignity. To see that this view is incorrect, one only has to reflect on what it would mean if no adequate ground were necessary for trivial infringements of liberty. It would mean that in these cases, arbitrary restrictions would be permissible. In small matters, the individual could be subjected to all sorts of irrational harassment. But then the arbitrary limitation of freedom would contradict human dignity even in small matters, quite apart from the fact that there is considerable variation of opinion as to what counts as 'small' or 'trivial'.[67] The principle of negative liberty is supported to its full extent by the principle of human dignity.

The principle of negative liberty expresses only one of the conditions for protecting human dignity. Alongside the formal principle of negative liberty, other substantive principles must be subsumed under the principle of human dignity, principles which relate to the substantive conditions on which the satisfaction of the human dignity guarantee depends. These substantive principles include, among others, those which protect the innermost aspect of human beings, and those which grant to the individual a prima facie right to self-representation before fellow human beings. Substantive aspects expressed by such material principles take their place *alongside* the formal aspect of negative liberty, and do not supplant it, because negative liberty as such is an independent ground of constitutional protection. It is an independent ground of constitutional protection because it is a *value in itself*. In the words of Isaiah Berlin, 'to be free to choose, and not to be chosen for, is an inalienable ingredient in what makes human beings human'.[68] If two situations are identical in every respect, save that

[67] Good examples of 'trivial cases' are provided by those concerned with feeding birds. Ehmke, and following him, W. Schmidt, have held up a (supposed) constitutional right to feed sparrows as an absurd and laughable consequence of a right to general freedom of action (H. Ehmke, *Wirtschaft und Verfassung* (Karlsruhe, 1961), 58; W. Schmidt, 'Die Freiheit vor dem Gesetz', 81). It is an irony of the history of constitutional interpretation that almost twenty years later, the Federal Constitutional Court held that the feeding of pigeons was prima facie constitutionally protected (BVerfGE 54, 143). The Federal Constitutional Court got it right. It is certainly not appropriate to consider the feeding of pigeons as exceptionally worthy of protection. But nor is it right to see it as totally unworthy of protection. There may well be human beings for whom such activity is very important, indeed more important than religious acts. Doubtless, importance from a constitutional perspective does not follow from subjective importance, but subjective importance is significant as far as the Constitution is concerned in so far as the respect for individual decisions and forms of life it requires imposes at least the obligation that these are not interfered with without good reason.

[68] I. Berlin, *Four Essays on Liberty*, (London, Oxford, and New York, 1969), p. lx.

in the first there is an element of negative liberty not present in the second, then the first situation is better than the second.

Thus the principle of human dignity is capable both of supporting and explicating the principle of negative liberty. This is possible because the principle of human dignity has to be made more precise by a bundle of sub-principles, which apart from the formal principle of negative liberty include numerous substantive principles which in the balancing process appear alongside negative liberty and can determine its weight. When in what follows it is more simply stated that the principle of human dignity appears alongside negative liberty in the balancing process, it is this relationship which is being referred to.

The conception of a general right to liberty set out here can be called a *'formal–material conception'*. It is formal, in that it proceeds on the basis of negative liberty and treats this as a value in itself. It is substantive in that in cases of conflict, the weight of the principle of negative liberty in the concrete case is determined with reference to other principles, which by contrast to negative liberty have a substantive character.

III. SPHERES OF PROTECTION AND IMPLIED LIBERTIES

The formal–material conception can avoid opposing a 'formal (substantively empty) concept of freedom (general freedom of action)' with a 'material (substantive or evaluatively-closed) concept of freedom (inviolable core of rights)' in the sense of a 'bifurcated interpretation of article 2(1) Basic Law'.[69] On the contrary, it allows us to combine what are at first sight divergent facets of the case-law of the Federal Constitutional Court[70] into a consistent and logical whole. In order to do this successfully, it must be able to explain two things: the theory of spheres of protection along with the related theory of implied liberties, and the consequences which arise from adopting a general right to freedom of action and freedom from interference. The first set of problems will be dealt with next; the second set will follow in the context of a discussion of further objections to a general right to liberty.

1. SPHERE THEORY

The theory of spheres of protection can be found already in the Elfes Judgment, in which the Court spoke of a 'final inviolable field of human freedom'.[71] It represented the guarantee of general freedom of action as an

---

[69] See Scholz, 'Das Grundrecht der freien Entfaltung der Persönlichkeit', 91.

[70] It is characteristic that the pigeon-feeding decision directly follows the Eppler Judgment in the official reports (see BVerfGE 54, 143; 54, 148).

[71] BVerfGE 6, 32 (41).

extension of protection beyond this field: 'By "free development of the personality", the Basic Law cannot have meant only development within this central core of personality'.[72] The distinction between spheres of differing degrees of protection indicated here has been expanded by the Court in subsequent cases.[73] It is possible to identify three spheres of decreasing intensity of protection: the *innermost sphere* ('final inviolable field of human freedom',[74] 'innermost field (of intimacy)',[75] 'inviolable sphere of intimacy',[76] 'absolutely protected core area of private life'),[77] the *broader sphere of privacy*, which embraces private life to the extent that it is not already covered by the innermost sphere,[78] and the *social sphere*, which includes everything which is not already covered by the private sphere.[79]

To the extent that sphere theory is relevant and useful, it can be seen as the result of balancing the principle of negative liberty *together* with further principles against competing principles. One could take the view that this cannot be the case with the *innermost sphere*, because its extent has nothing to do with balancing. But this is incorrect. If one defines the innermost sphere as that sphere in which the individual does *not* 'affect others by his existence or behaviour, and thus disturb the personal sphere of fellow human beings or the requirements of life in community with others'[80] then the innermost sphere is by definition that sphere in which the principles pointing towards protection are always conclusive, since competing principles, which always relate either to the rights of others or to common interests, are not relevant. The statement of the Federal Constitutional Court, 'balancing according to the principle of proportionality does not take place'[81] points to this conception of the innermost sphere in a trivial way, because there is nothing which could be weighed against the principles counting towards protection. However, even this case can be seen as an application of the Law of Balancing, in fact the most extreme case conceivable. It must be doubted whether such a conception of the innermost sphere has any practical application. One can well ask whether there is any aspect of a person's existence or behaviour which does not have some impact on the sphere of others or the requirements of life in community with others. Quite apart from the answer to this question, we can say that if there are such cases, they will be cases over which there can be no serious dispute, for who would want to hinder something that affects neither himself, nor

---

[72] BVerfGE 6, 32 (36) (emphasis added).

[73] See on this D. Rohlf, *Der grundrechtliche Schutz der Privatsphäre* (Berlin, 1980), 70 ff.

[74] BVerfGE 6, 32 (41); similarly BVerfGE 27, 1 (6); 27, 344 (350); 32, 373 (379); 34, 238 (245).   [75] BVerfGE 27, 1 (8).

[76] BVerfGE 32, 373 (379).   [77] BVerfGE 34, 238 (245).

[78] See BVerfGE 27, 1 (7 f.); 27, 344 (351); 32, 373 (379); 33, 367 (376); 34, 238 (246); 35, 202 (220).

[79] On this threefold division, see Scholz, 'Das Grundrecht der freien Entfaltung der Persönlichkeit', 92, 266 ff., 273 ff.

[80] BVerfGE 35, 202 (220).   [81] BVerfGE 34, 238 (245).

others, nor the needs of society in some respect? If talk of an 'inviolable area of private life' is to have any practical significance at all, then it must be based on a stronger conception of the innermost sphere. One would have a stronger conception, if certain situations and forms of individual behaviour are to be protected in every case, even when the rights of others or the needs of society can be put forward as arguments against protection. But such a conception would be the result of a balancing process, which under certain circumstances (certain forms of behaviour or situations of the individual) leads to an absolute precedence for the principle of negative liberty together with that of human dignity against all other conceivable competing principles. It has already been pointed out that absolute precedence even relative to certain circumstances is not unproblematic, because it assumes that no further circumstances could arise which from the perspective of constitutional law might give the competing principles an overriding weight after all.[82] But this does not affect the fact that there are circumstances under which the outcome of the balancing process is so certain, that we can speak of highly secure *rules* protecting an innermost area.[83] The Federal Constitutional Court is quite at liberty to apply these rules without engaging in balancing. But this does not alter the fact that such rules are the outcome of a balancing process, and that in cases of doubt, whether in the context of clarifying, restricting, or extending the rules,[84] recourse must be had once again to balancing the relevant principles.

In the case of the *broader private sphere*, the Federal Constitutional Court emphasizes the necessity of a 'strict regard for the requirement of proportionality'.[85] One could take the view that this means that the principle of proportionality applies less strictly in the social sphere than in the private sphere. But this cannot be the case. Legal validity is a matter of all-or-nothing, and the fact that the Court undertakes examinations of proportionality in the social sphere shows that it considers the proportionality principle valid for this area too. The requirement of strict application of proportionality can only mean that particularly weighty reasons are necessary to justify limitations in the private sphere. This is half-true and half-false, and the latter half makes the weaknesses of sphere theory plain. It can hardly be denied that a very intrusive interference in the social sphere requires more weighty reasons than a very trivial one in the private sphere. In addition, it is often hard to decide whether a case belongs to the wider

---

[82] 195 f.

[83] These rules follow from the establishment of relations of precedence under the Law of Competing Principles set out above, see 53 f.

[84] On the concepts of clarifying, reducing and extending, see A. Aarnio, R. Alexy and A. Peczenik, 'The Foundation of Legal Reasoning', in A. Aarnio and D. N. MacCormick (eds.), *Legal Reasoning*, i (Aldershot, 1992), 252 ff.; R. Alexy, 'Zum Begriff des Rechtsprinzips', *Rechtstheorie*, Beiheft 1 (1979), 68 f.

[85] BVerfGE 32, 373 (379); 33, 367 (377); 34, 205 (209); 34, 238 (246); 35, 35 (39); 35, 202 (232).

private sphere or the social sphere. The shift from what is most private to what is certainly not is gradual. It is thus not possible to identify two classes, one benefiting from a stronger protection of constitutional rights, the other from a weaker. Rather, we must differentiate according to the degree of interference and the degree of privacy. What the distinction between private and social spheres does correctly identify is that constitutional protection is stronger, the more weight those privacy-protecting principles appearing alongside the principle of general freedom of action have in the case at hand.

Sphere theory is thus an extremely crude description[86] of different degrees of constitutional protection under different circumstances. To the extent that it applies, it simply expresses the point that the stronger the principle of negative liberty in connection with other principles, in particular human dignity, the greater the protection of freedom. In the area of the innermost sphere, the weightings are so certain that they can be formulated in terms of relatively general rules. Apart from this, it boils down to balancing exercises, with the principle of negative liberty, along with associated principles, on the side of freedom. This exactly fits the formal–material conception.

2. IMPLIED LIBERTIES

The theory of implied liberties[87] rests in part on sphere theory, but in part extends beyond this. In order to discuss it we need to clarify what it means, and this is best done by drawing three distinctions.

The first distinction concerns whether the interest protected by the implied liberty is an *action* or a *state* of the right-holder. Actions would be emigration,[88] collecting,[89] feeding pigeons,[90] and so on. In the case of actions, we can formulate a permissive norm, for example x is permitted to collect. Examples of states of affairs are the maintenance of a state of confidentiality[91] and the existence of conditions under which the individual 'can develop and preserve his individuality'.[92] States of affairs do not give rise to permissive norms but to prohibitions addressed to those bound by constitutional rights, corresponding to substantively identical rights for the right-holders. For example, y is forbidden to violate x's sphere of confidentiality; x has as against y the right that y shall not infringe his sphere of confidentiality.[93]

---

[86] The criticism of D. Merten, 'Das Recht auf freie Entfaltung der Persönlichkeit', JuS 1976, 349, that a 'rigid division into spheres . . . [seems] artificial and impractical' can be assented to, simply on account of the crudeness of the division. J. Schwabe, *Probleme der Grundrechtsdogmatik* (Darmstadt, 1977), 314 ff.; E. Schwan, 'Datenschutz, Vorbehalt des Gesetzes und Freiheitsgrundrechte', VerwArch 66 (1975), 147 ff. are also critical of sphere theory.

[87] On this term, see BVerfGE 54, 148 (153).   [88] BVerfGE 6, 32.

[89] BVerfGE 20, 150.   [90] BVerfGE 54, 143.

[91] BVerfGE 27, 1 (7 f.).   [92] BVerfGE 35, 202 (220).

[93] More precisely, even if more awkwardly, x has as against y a right that y shall not alter

The second distinction is between *abstract* and *concrete* implied liberties. 'The constitutionally protected general right to personality'[94] is a highly abstract right, a more concrete one is 'the right to control the representation of one's person',[95] and a highly concrete right is the right that 'a repeat television report of a serious criminal act, no longer covered by the interest in current affairs' should not be broadcast 'if it endangers the resocialization of the offender'.[96]

The third and final distinction relates to the difference between *prima facie* and *definitive* positions. The right to travel abroad is a prima facie position. Emigration is covered by article 2(1) Basic Law, but could be subject to its limitations.[97] Permitting people travelling by car in response to a public advertisement to take a sum of money not exceeding the cost of the travel is a definitive position.[98]

2.1 Act-Related Rights

On the basis of these three distinctions, it is possible to draw up an exhaustive table of positions derivable from article 2(1) Basic Law.[99] Calling some of them 'implied liberties' requires a whole series of decisions which in the final analysis are to be made as a matter of convenience.

This problem is particularly obvious in the case of rights related to actions. If all actions are covered by article 2(1) Basic Law, then each specific action, such as emigration, collecting, and feeding pigeons is also covered. When the Federal Constitutional Court states that the freedom to emigrate is an 'expression' of general freedom of action,[100] this cannot mean anything more than that the concept of action includes the concept of emigration. Taking the relation of inclusion as the basis for implied liberties in the case of prima facie rights related to actions has unacceptable consequences. There would then be as many implied rights as there are act-descriptions, of which there are an infinite number. The concept of an implied right would then lose its point in the case of prima facie positions related to actions. This can be countered by introducing two restrictions.

---

the state of affairs in which *x* finds himself whereby certain facts known only to *x* and the persons entrusted with them by *x*, become known to *y* or third parties even though *x* does not wish this to happen. If *y* wants to achieve the revelation of the facts by commanding *x* to reveal them, then a permission not to carry out the act of revelation becomes relevant alongside the right to non-interference with a state of affairs. Rights to the non-interference with a state of affairs are often described with the help of the concept of toleration. If *x* has no right to non-interference, then he must tolerate the corresponding interference. If *x* has a right to non-interference, he need not tolerate the corresponding interference.

[94] BVerfGE 54, 148 (153).   [95] BVerfGE 35, 202 (220).
[96] BVerfGE 35, 202 (237).   [97] See BVerfGE 6, 32 (42 ff.).
[98] BVerfGE 17, 306 (313 ff.). When this position is decribed as definitive, this does not mean that it cannot be changed, perhaps by way of limitation in the light of new sets of facts. This would result in a new definitive position.
[99] On the concept of derivation, see above at 35 ff.   [100] BVerfGE 6, 32 (42).

The first says that only relatively general act-descriptions[101] may be the subject-matter of implied liberties. Thus one could correctly speak of an implied liberty to emigrate, but not an implied liberty to emigrate in an unusual suit of clothes. If someone is prohibited from emigrating in an unusual suit of clothes, he would not be able to appeal to a concrete implied liberty to emigrate in an unusual suit of clothes, but rather he should appeal to two relatively abstract implied rights: the right to emigrate and the right to dress as one pleases. The second limitation states that actions prohibited by norms the constitutionality of which is not in question must be excluded from the set of implied prima facie liberties. The prima facie protection which even these actions enjoy under the wide understanding of the scope of liberty is not achieved by a (specific) implied liberty but by the general right to liberty. In this way it is possible to create a limited and useful conception of implied act-related prima facie liberties. The rights embraced by this conception of implied liberties correspond structurally to the express liberty rights contained in the constitution.

2.2 Situation-Related Rights

Rights related to states of affairs are more complicated than those related to actions. An example of such a right at a very high level of abstraction is the 'constitutionally guaranteed general right to personality' the function of which is to 'guarantee the narrow personal sphere of life and the maintenance of its basic conditions'.[102] The hallmark of the general right to personality recognized by the Federal Constitutional Court is its location in both article 1(1) Basic Law as well as article 2(1). It is supposed to be protected by 'article 2(1) taken in conjunction with article 1(1) Basic Law'. In spite of this connection, the right remains derivative to article 2(1) Basic Law, which alongside the ' "active" element' (where the object of the right is an action) protects what can be called a passive element of the development of personality (where the object of the right is an aspect of existence),[103] in that it guarantees a 'right of respect for the guaranteed area'. This corresponds fully with the formal–material theory according to which the principle of negative liberty combines with other principles as a principle relating to states of affairs as well.

The close connection between sphere theory and the general right to personality is obvious. The general right to personality can be seen as an element of sphere theory raised to the level of rights. It is given definition by deriving from it a bundle of more concrete rights. The objects of these more concrete rights can be described as the 'interests protected by the general right to personality', which the Federal Constitutional Court, in

[101] On the concept of generality, see above at 46, fn. 11.
[102] BVerfGE 54, 148 (153).   [103] ibid.

summarizing its case-law, listed in the Eppler Judgment.[104] According to this list, the rights derived from the abstract general right to personality include: the right to spheres of privacy, confidentiality, and intimacy,[105] the right of personal reputation, the right to control the representation of one's own person,[106] the right to one's own picture and spoken word,[107] 'the right, under certain circumstances, to be free from having certain expressions attributed to oneself',[108] and the right not to be affected in one's 'self-defined social role'.[109] Most recently, the Court has added the right to informational self-determination to the list.[110] The particularization of the general right to personality by these more concrete rights is an entirely typical process for the particularization of general clauses.[111]

The fact that, and the way in which, these concrete personality rights are dependent upon balancing as the formal–material conception insists, is shown by the Tape Recording Judgment,[112] which concerned the constitutionally protected right to one's own words. Secret tape recordings, which intrude upon the 'absolutely inviolable area of private life', are supposed to be totally prohibited. The Court grants quite openly, that the question of what belongs to the absolutely inviolable area 'can only be described in the abstract with great difficulty' and can only be decided 'from case to case, having regard to all the circumstances'.[113] This suggests that the 'absolutely inviolable area' is actually a bundle of concrete definitive protected positions, which are the relatively certain outcomes of balancing exercises. The need to balance interests is emphasized in the case of the outer area of personality rights. The Court speaks of 'tensions' between the right to free development of the personality and the need to maintain an effective system of justice. The resolution of these tensions lies in 'establishing on the facts of the concrete case which of these two principles has the greater weight'.[114] The right to one's own words could hardly be more clearly treated as a prima facie right in the sense of the theory of principles. The scope of the norm protecting such a right is thus structurally identical to that of norms guaranteeing explicit written constitutional rights.

Implied liberties relevant to freedom of action and non-interference with the situation and position of a constitutional right-holder are thus not something qualitatively different and opposed to the general right to liberty; rather they are forms of the same thing, only qualified in two respects. They

---

[104] BVerfGE 54, 148 (154).
[105] With reference to BVerfGE 27, 1 (6); 27, 344 (350 f.); 32, 372 (379); 34, 238 (245 f.); 47, 46 (73); 49, 286 (298).
[106] With reference to BVerfGE 35, 202 (220).
[107] With reference to BVerfGE 34, 238 (246).
[108] With reference to BVerfGE 34, 269 (282 f.).
[109] BVerfGE 54, 148 (155 f.); 54, 208 (217).   [110] BVerfGE 65, 1 (41 f.).
[111] See F. Wieacker, *Zur rechtstheoretischen Präzisierung des § 242 BGB* (Tübingen, 1956).
[112] BVerfGE 34, 238.   [113] BVerfGE 34, 238 (248).
[114] BVerfGE 34, 238 (249).

are qualified firstly by the fact that they are more precisely defined in their scope and more specialized. Secondly, they have undergone judicial definition and clarification. They rest on norms of judge-made law, developed in the context and on the basis of the general right to liberty. This gives them a certain independence and similarity to the explicit specific liberty rights. There is thus the same relationship between the general right to liberty and implied liberties as there is between the general right to liberty and express liberties. Express liberties are the reactions of the constitution-makers to certain threats to liberty experienced as particularly pressing. In an analogous way, implied liberties can be seen as the reaction of constitutional jurisprudence to new threats to liberty seen as particularly pressing. In this sense, article 2(1) Basic Law is the written source of unwritten liberties. But this does not mean, as W. Schmidt suggests, that article 2(1) 'only becomes a constitutional right when connected with the new area of protected liberty'.[115] The formal–material conception shows that a general right to liberty is possible to construct and practically applicable. As particular rights, implied liberties can never guarantee an exhaustive protection of liberty. Since such is constitutionally required, it is also required that negative liberty should not only be protected by implied liberty rights. Where these are not applicable, the general right to liberty must be applied directly. In addition, it maintains its significance as the positive legal basis of implied liberties.

IV. PROBLEMS WITH THE GENERAL RIGHT TO LIBERTY

According to the formal–material conception, the general right to liberty embraces a spectrum characterized by a variation in the weight of the supporting principle of human dignity. One end of the spectrum covers cases in which one can talk about a final inviolable area, because the supporting principle has the greatest conceivable weight. As the weight of the supporting principle decreases, so one comes across those cases criticized as 'merely formal' freedom of action and freedom from interference. Since the formal–material conception includes the whole spectrum of rights to general freedom of action and freedom from interference, even in its most formal expressions, it stands and falls with the acceptance of such a right. The acceptability of such a right is challenged on many grounds. The most important objection, the argument from lack of substance, has already been answered. We must now consider four further objections.

---

[115] W. Schmidt, 'Die Freiheit vor dem Gesetz', 83.

1. THE GENERAL RIGHT TO LIBERTY AND SELECTED
GUARANTEES

The historical objection is easy to counter. The historical objection argues that constitutional rights arise 'out of historically specific situations of demand for securing rights, or out of situations of pressing danger' and that they are thus to be understood as 'specific guarantees of a quite particular area of protection',[116] or, as it is often put, as 'selected guarantees'. This is supposed to be incompatible with a general right to liberty. There can be no doubt that many valid arguments can be made for the thesis that individual constitutional rights are the reaction to specific dangers. But this is only one side of the matter. Alongside this 'concrete' line of tradition, there is an 'abstract' aspect. Evidence of this can be found in article 4 of the *Déclaration des droits de l'homme et du citoyen* of 1789, 'Liberty is the power to do anything which does not harm another; hence the only limits to the exercise of each man's natural rights are those which secure to other members of society the enjoyment of the same rights' and Kant's maxim, 'Freedom (independence from being constrained by another's choice), insofar as it can coexist with the freedom of every other in accordance with a universal law, is the only original right belonging to every man by virtue of his humanity'.[117] The thesis that from a historical perspective, constitutional rights are only to be treated as selected guarantees can only be accepted with some reservations. A second historical argument directed against the historical objection is Dürig's *tabula rasa* argument, which refers to the 'historical experience of an apocalyptic historical tabula rasa, to which the Basic Law makes an *historical answer*', and which accuses the theory of selected guarantees of being 'totally a-historical'.[118] This argument can be supported by reference to the legislative history of article 2(1) Basic Law.[119]

---

[116] U. Scheuner, 'Die Funktion der Grundrechte im Sozialstaat', DöV 1971, 509; see also id., 'Pressefreiheit', VVDStRL 22 (1965), 37; Ehmke, 'Prinzipien der Verfassungsinterpretation', 82; Hesse, *Grundzüge des Verfassungsrechts*, para. 428; W. Rüfner, *Grundrechtskonflikte*, in C. Starck (ed.), *Bundesverfassungsgericht und Grundgesetz* (Tübingen, 1976), 456; F. Müller, *Die Positivität der Grundrechte* (Berlin, 1969), 41 ff.; 87 ff.; C. Graf v. Pestalozza, 'Kritische Bemerkungen zu Methoden und Prinzipien der Grundrechtsauslegung in der Bundesrepublik Deutschland', *Der Staat*, 2 (1963), 437; W. Schmidt, 'Die Freiheit vor dem Gesetz', 84; Scholz, 'Das Grundrecht der freien Entfaltung der Persönlichkeit', 82 f.
[117] Kant, *Metaphysics of Morals*, 63.
[118] G. Dürig, in T. Maunz and G. Dürig *et al.*, *Grundgesetz Kommentar*, 5th edn. (Munich, 1983), art. 3 abs. 1, para. 251, fn. 1.
[119] JöR, NF 1 (1951), 54 ff.; BVerfGE 6, 32 (38 ff.). D. Suhr, *Entfaltung der Menschen durch die Menschen* (Berlin, 1976), 52, rightly refers to the fact that contrary to the statement of the Federal Constitutional Court, the original version did not say, 'each person may do or refrain from doing as he pleases' (BVerfGE 6, 32 (36)). However, the original versions do not deviate markedly from this. The only significant difference is that the original versions contained a limiting clause. See e.g. art. 2(2) of the Chiemsee-Draft: 'Everyone has the liberty to do what is not harmful to others within the limits of the legal order and public morals' (JöR, NF 1 (1951), 54).

In addition to the historical arguments against the historical objection, there is a systemic consideration. Even if there were only the concrete line of tradition, and even if the makers of the Basic Law did not want to provide the possibility of new answers implied by the general right to liberty, we would not necessarily be required to interpret the catalogue of constitutional rights always according to the concrete line of tradition. Neither jurisprudence nor case-law are prevented from grounding historically developed concrete norms in more general ones.[120] On the contrary, this is an important part of jurisprudence, and such an approach is at least useful for case-law. The question can only be whether the assumption of a general right to liberty is capable of rational constitutional justification. In view of the ambiguity of the tradition and the relatively clear legislative history, the historical objection hardly places an obstacle in the way of such justification.

2. THE GENERAL RIGHT TO LIBERTY AND THE SYSTEM OF CONSTITUTIONAL RIGHTS

The second objection is systemic. It is raised when the general right to liberty is allied to the idea of an 'axiomatically closed system', which is then rejected.[121] The main object of this critique is Dürig's 'system of values and claims', in which the general right to liberty plays a central role.[122] So in order to discuss this objection it is worthwhile looking briefly at Dürig's system.

Dürig's system of values and claims can be seen as a three-stage model of constitutional rights. The first stage contains the 'highest principle of the constitution', that of human dignity.[123] On the second stage there is on one hand the general right to liberty as the 'principal liberty-right'[124] and on the other hand the general right to equality as the 'principal equality-right'.[125] The third stage contains specific rights to liberty and equality. These specific rights are substantive particularizations of the general rights to liberty and equality.[126] The relationship of the principal to the specific rights is that of *lex generalis* to *lex specialis*.[127] The entire system is described by Dürig as 'closed'.[128]

This temptingly simple model, which is clearly derived from the Elfes

---

[120] See H.-U. Gallwas, *Faktische Beeinträchtigungen im Bereich der Grundrechte* (Berlin, 1970) 57.

[121] Scholz, 'Das Grundrecht der freien Entfaltung der Persönlichkeit', 82 f.; id., *Die Koalitionsfreiheit als Verfassungsproblem* (Munich, 1971), 91 f. See also Scheuner, 'Pressefreiheit', 38 f.; Ehmke, 'Prinzipien der Verfassungsinterpretation', 82.

[122] Dürig, in Maunz and Dürig, *Grundgesetz Kommentar*, art. 1 para. 6 ff.

[123] ibid. art. 1 para. 14.

[124] ibid. art. 1 para. 11.

[125] ibid. art. 1 para. 12; art. 3 paras. 248 ff.

[126] ibid. art. 1 para. 10.

[127] ibid. art. 2 para. 6.

[128] ibid. art. 3 para. 254.

Judgment,[129] is subject to a whole series of questions and objections. It is doubtful whether it is truly inclusive and in this sense whether it is also really closed. There are at least some constitutional entitlements, such as the right to an existential minimum[130] and the right of a mother to protection and support (article 6(4) Basic Law). These rights can hardly be seen as particularizations of either principal constitutional right.[131] If this is correct, then Dürig's system does not include all constitutional rights, and it is therefore not closed. Of course, this is not an argument against the general right to liberty. It is quite possible, as will be shown below, to expand Dürig's whole system. Furthermore, the partial system represented by the general right to liberty would still be of great doctrinal interest, even if it could not be located within a complete, all-inclusive system of rights.

There are no persuasive objections to the partial system which can be constructed on the basis of a concept of general liberty. Objections could be directed either to the relationship between the first and second stages or to the relationship between the second and third stages. As has already been shown,[132] there is a twofold relationship between the first and second stages, that is, between the concept of human dignity and the general right to liberty, a particularizing relation and an expanding relation. Here we are only interested in the particularizing relation. The principle of negative liberty particularizes the principle of human dignity, in that it expresses one aspect of this more inclusive principle. Such a relation is always in addition a reason-giving relation, because a more inclusive perspective can always be put forward as a reason for one element of it. Someone who cites the principle of human dignity as a reason for the principle of negative liberty is not simply deducing one from another. Rather, he is following a particularization which conforms to the following deductive scheme:

(1)	It is required that human dignity be respected and protected.
(2)	If the principle of negative liberty were not to apply, human dignity would not be respected and protected.
(3)	It is required that the principle of negative liberty apply.

The principle of negative liberty, and thus the general right to liberty, do not simply follow from the human dignity norm; rather, they only follow from such a norm in conjunction with the particularizing premise (2), which is not deducible from the norm itself. One can dispute whether the principle of negative liberty is a necessary condition for the respecting and protecting of human dignity by the legal system. Where the dispute arises, the second

---

[129] See BVerfGE 6, 32 (37, 40 f.). For a few disagreements, see G. Dürig, 'Anmerkung zum Elfes-Urteil', JZ 1957, 169 ff.
[130] See BVerfGE 45, 187 (228) as well as below at 343 ff.
[131] See K. Löw, 'Ist die Würde des Menschen im Grundgesetz eine Anspruchsgrundlage?' DÖV 1958, 520.
[132] 233 ff.

premiss has to be defended by way of substantive argument. This is typical of the construction of juridical systems and legal argument, and it is entirely unproblematic. It shows that the construction of systems is possible, and how, without reducing the process to a matter of simple deduction. Once one accepts that many other particularizing principles can appear alongside (2) ((2) only contains a necessary condition), and that the particularization represented by (2) occurs by way of a principle which can come into conflict with other particularizing principles, the objection of an axiomatically closed system, at least as regards the relation between the first and second stages, loses all force.

In the present connection, the relation between the second and third stages, that is, between the general right to liberty and specific liberties, is more important. Dürig stresses that his thesis that 'specific liberties are only expressions of the general right to liberty . . . is not to be understood as a matter of mere logical derivation from a more general proposition'.[133] In order to understand what this might mean, we have to consider what would follow if the Basic Law only contained the general right to liberty and no specific rights. Everything currently protected by specific liberties would be protected by the general right to liberty. To this extent there is a logical relation of inclusion. By definition, the scope of the general right to liberty includes the scopes of all specific liberties. From the fact that one is prima facie permitted to do and not to do as one pleases, it follows that one is prima facie permitted to express or not to express one's opinion, to choose or reject a certain career and so on. But this relation of inclusion in respect of the scope of the right exhausts the logical relationship between the second and third stages. The specific characteristics of the third stage neither follow logically from the general right to liberty, nor are they incompatible with it. Rather they represent, as against the general right to liberty, additional clarifications on the part of the constitution-makers. Thus the inviolability of the home with its qualified statutory reservation, and artistic freedom guaranteed without reservation, are more strongly protected than they would be if there were only the general right to liberty, and there would be less of a difference in the relative strength of the freedom of movement of German citizens and aliens, if Germans, like aliens, could only appeal to article 2(1) Basic Law in freedom of movement cases.[134] Not only does it not follow from the idea of a general right to liberty that its limits are carried over to all constitutional rights, but such a transfer would also contradict the requirement to take the text and the decisions of the Constitution seriously. The differences between degrees of protection are significantly reduced in practice by the fact that considerations of proportionality apply in the context of article 2(1) Basic Law, by the fact that written limiting clauses are in

---

[133] Dürig, in Maunz and Dürig, *Grundgesetz Kommentar*, art. 1 para. 11.
[134] See BVerfGE 35, 382 (399).

considerable need of interpretation, and by the possibility of relying on unwritten limiting clauses in the absence of written ones,[135] but the differences still remain. It does make a difference when in limiting the effect of a constitutional right one has to argue against the literal meaning of the relevant provision, or whether the literal meaning covers the most extensive limitation possible, that is, is subject only to the principle of proportionality. Consistently with the thesis of the double aspect of constitutional rights as containing both rules and principles,[136] specific liberties contain, as against the general right to liberty, additional clarifications in the form of rules. There is as little a deductive relationship between these clarifications and the general right to liberty as there is in the case of concrete decisions taken directly under the general right. The clarifications are the outcome of balancing principles and thus also of evaluative judgments.[137]

In the light of all this, it is not correct to talk of a deductive system, and it is only possible in a limited sense to talk of a closed system. The system is closed to the extent that it contains an all-inclusive prima facie protection of the general right to liberty (in the narrow sense). It is open to the extent that the general right to liberty is itself open to the possibility of new definitive rights and new implied rights. Both aspects are benign. The systemic objection to the general right to liberty is in this respect quite incorrect as well.

3. The General Right to Liberty and the 'Isolated Individual'

The third objection is a substantive one. According to this, the general right to liberty is the expression of a mistaken conception of the individual and his relationship to state and society. As a right to general freedom of action and freedom from interference, the general right to liberty corresponds to a view of humanity which the Basic Law is supposed to have superseded, namely that of 'an isolated, sovereign individual', rather than that of a 'person related and bound to society'[138] which is supposed to be the view of the Basic Law.[139] Freedom is 'misunderstood as the release from every obligation'.[140] It fails to recognize that 'the material and social state under the Rule of Law . . . is not simply an "interfering" state, potentially limiting civil liberties [but rather] a productive and care-taking state securing and creating freedom'.[141]

---

[135] See above at 188.   [136] See above at 84 ff.

[137] If in 1949 only a general right to liberty had been enacted and no specific ones, all clarifications would have had to have been made by the judiciary. It is an interesting, but insoluble, question, whether and to what extent the concrete constitutional rights rules established by precedent would have departed from the ones valid today.

[138] See BVerfGE 4, 7 (15 f.).

[139] See P. Häberle, *Die Wesensgehaltgarantie des Art. 19 Abs. 2 Grundgesetz*, 3rd edn. (Heidelberg, 1983), 227, 150 ff.   [140] Scheuner, 'Pressefreiheit', 37, fn. 110.

[141] Scholz, 'Das Grundrecht der freien Entfaltung der Persönlichkeit', 97.

The objection is directed principally towards two characteristics of the general right to liberty, first, against the fact that its scope is unlimited, and secondly, that it is a negative right in the sense explained. It is true that the general right to liberty has these characteristics; it is not true that it leads to the consequences feared.

The fact that the scope of liberty is unlimited and without boundaries[142] tells us very little in the light of its limiting clause. As far as the individual is concerned, what matters is what is definitively protected, and what is definitively protected is certainly not unlimited. It is the outcome of balancing contradictory principles, and there are many such principles. It is the weight given to them which is decisive. One can accept the idea of a general right to liberty and still generally give those principles which protect collective interests a greater weight, so that in practice very little definitive negative liberty remains. This shows the high degree of neutrality that the general right to liberty has in respect of different substantive theories about the relative importance of individual rights and collective interests. However, the neutrality of the general right to liberty ceases at a certain point. Interferences with negative liberty are interferences with a certain type of freedom and, as such, are in need of justification.

Against the insight that interferences with negative liberty, however well justified they may be, indeed, even if they are necessary to protect other liberties, are still interferences with a certain type of liberty and thus in need of justification, there is the thesis of the ' "interrelationship" of law and liberty', which emphasizes the 'significance of law and legislation for creating and maintaining freedom'.[143] Such views fail to differentiate carefully enough in the context of the concept of liberty. There is hardly any other concept in greater need of careful differentiation than liberty. The example of duress used above makes this point clear.[144] The prohibition on duress removes from everyone the legal liberty to engage in coercion, and thus limits their negative liberty. At the same time it increases everyone's negative liberty, because in private relationships it leads to the fact that the individual is far less subject to duress in choosing from a variety of courses of action than he would be if the prohibition on duress did not apply. A state of affairs in which freedom from duress by fellow citizens obtains is for all sorts of obvious reasons better than one in which one has the freedom to coerce fellow citizens. The first state of affairs can thus be called the 'freer', and that there is 'more freedom' in it. But this does not alter the fact that the increase in freedom has been brought about by the introduction of a legal no-liberty. To doubt this is to refuse to call things by their proper name

---

[142] For a critique of the 'lack of boundaries of subjective rights', which applies most fully to the general right to liberty, see U. K. Preuß, *Die Internalisierung des Subjekts* (Frankfurt a. M., 1979), 37.

[143] Häberle, *Die Wesensgehaltgarantie*, 152.

[144] 219.

and simply leads to conceptual obscurity. This might not be particularly damaging in a clear case such as the prohibition of duress. There can be no doubt that one should exchange the freedom to coerce for the freedom not to be coerced. But in cases in which the exchange is not so clear, the dangers of conceptual obscurity should not be underestimated. There is the danger that limitations of freedom are no longer recognized and justified as such, simply because they are introduced to secure or create more highly valued freedoms of the same or other constitutional right-holders.

In spite of its simplicity, the example of duress shows that there are many different liberties which have to be brought into relationship with each other in order to reach a justifiable '*overall state of liberty*'. It seems entirely misguided only to extend the concept of liberty to what ends up being protected in this overall state. It fails to recognize that the creation and maintenance of an overall state of liberty requires a certain sacrifice of liberty. The justification of the overall state of liberty presupposes the justification of the sacrifices to liberty connected with it. If sacrifices of liberty are not recognized as such, one can no longer talk in terms of their justification.

It is a trivial point that the overall state of liberty, which is none other than the correct or just state of society, is not simply a matter of maximizing negative legal liberty in the sense of an absence of commands and prohibitions. There can be no overall state of liberty without freedom from interference by legal persons of equal status (negative liberty in relations of equal status), without the legal power to participate in collective decision-taking (negative democratic liberty), without the absence of a certain degree of economic deprivation (negative social freedom), and also without the power to participate in the political community with one's own opinions and on one's own responsibility (positive democratic liberty).[145] In addition, the conditions of its existence are not simply a matter of individual rights, powers, and actions, but also the result of numerous characteristics of the organization of state and society, from the separation of powers to the pluralistic structure of the media. But just as it is certain that negative liberty alone cannot create an overall state of liberty, so it is also certain that without it, an overall state of affairs could never be given the positive predicate 'free'. A state of affairs in which there is no negative liberty at all, that is, in which every conceivable action is either commanded or prohibited, is for conceptual reasons problematic enough.[146] At any rate, it would not be

---

[145] On the classification of liberties, see above at 140 ff.

[146] This state of affairs cannot be created by making every concrete act the subject-matter of a norm. This would presuppose that a complete list of all conceivable acts could be created, which is impossible. So this state of affairs can only be achieved through norms of a higher degree of generality. The norms, 'what is not commanded is prohibited' and, 'what is not prohibited is commanded' have to be excluded from consideration. If an act ϕ is currently neither commanded nor prohibited, that is, if neither its performance (ϕ) nor its non-performance ($\sim\phi$) is currently commanded, or if neither its non-performance ($\sim\phi$) nor its performance

a state of freedom. But this point is only a first step in recognizing the significance of negative liberty for freedom. A state of freedom does not simply require that there are any old negative liberties. It presupposes that the liberty of the individual, along with the situation in which he finds himself, and the legal rights that he has, are only interfered with when there are justifying reasons for the interference. This is exactly what the general right to liberty requires, and it is thus a necessary component of the overall state of liberty.

In this way the general right to liberty brings into the overall state of liberty both something of the freedom of the state of nature as well as a securing of the status quo. This has nothing to do with the idea of an isolated individual. The Law of Balancing locates the general right to liberty in the overall state of liberty in such a way that it can take account of the 'person related and bound to society' without any difficulty. It can also secure the conditions of freedom which even under modern circumstances are necessary to secure the 'independence of the person'.[147]

4. THE GENERAL RIGHT TO LIBERTY AND OTHER CONSTITUTIONAL NORMS

A fourth objection must be taken rather more seriously. This argues that the extremely wide scope of the general right to liberty, which embraces not only every action, but also every situation and legal position of the constitutional right-holder,[148] along with its limiting clause, which not only *always*, but only *ever* permits an interference when this is formally and substantively compatible with the constitution,[149] leads to a constitutional

---

(ϕ) is currently prohibited, then the first of the norms in question leads to ϕ and $\sim\phi$ being simultaneously prohibited, and the second norm to ϕ and $\sim\phi$ being simultaneously commanded. So both norms lead to a contradiction. This contradiction could easily be resolved by a norm such as 'it is commanded (or, for that matter, prohibited) that one do what one is neither commanded to do nor commanded to refrain from doing'. Such a norm would remove many liberties, but it would also be of no use in the case of commands which could be fulfilled in more than one way. In addition, one can well ask whether the state of affairs created by it makes sense. It is also questionable whether all liberties can be removed by a teleological norm of the form, 'whatever achieves E better than any other alternative is commanded', or through a deontological norm of the form, 'what is intrinsically the best is always commanded'. There is some support for the hypothesis that for every end, as for every set of ends, there are end-neutral alternative courses of action, and that there are acts of which it is true that neither performance nor their non-performance is intrinsically better. In short, it is probable that there is no consistent and sensible system of norms in which there are no liberties.

[147] BVerfGE 4, 7 (15 f.).

[148] The breadth of the scope becomes particularly apparent when the Federal Constitutional Court uses its disadvantage-formula; see BVerfGE 29, 402 (408), which speaks of a 'constitutional right of the citizen, only to be burdened with a disadvantage on the basis of provisions which are formally and substantively compatible with the constitution'. See also BVerfGE 9, 83 (88); 19, 206 (215); 42, 20 (27).

[149] See BVerfGE 6, 32 (41); 42, 20 (27).

right to the constitutionality of all state action.[150] Such a constitutional right results in the 'subjectifying of objective legal constitutional principles'[151] and leads procedurally to an unsustainable expansion of the scope of the constitutional complaint.[152]

4.1 Jurisdictional Norms

The problems associated with this objection are revealed sharply by those cases in which an infringement of a constitutional right under article 2(1) Basic Law is alleged on the grounds that the state has breached a jurisdictional norm. The decision in the case of the Engineers' Law is instructive.[153] The Federal Constitutional Court based its finding of a breach of constitutional rights solely on the fact that the proposed regulation of the professional designation 'engineer' did not fall within the jurisdiction of the federal legislature, but within that of the Regions. One can well ask what this has to do with the constitutional right to general freedom of action. Why should a norm which would not infringe the general right to liberty, were it passed by the legislature of a Region, do so when passed by the federal legislature?

The first point to make in answering this question is that the 'examination of formal interference'[154] is no speciality of the general right to liberty. The Federal Constitutional Court does it in the context of specific constitutional rights as well.[155] The real question is therefore why constitutional rights provisions are taken to embrace formal positions as well as substantive ones, that is, positions directed to ensuring that procedural requirements and requirements of form, along with formal elements of the Rule of Law such as the requirement of certainty, are maintained. There are two possible answers. According to the first, which we can call the '*Rule of Law thesis*', formal positions are the expression of a subjective right to the consistency of all state action with the Rule of Law.[156] In so far as a specific constitutional right is affected, it is combined with this subjective right; in so far as no specific right is affected, the right is guaranteed by article 2(1) Basic Law. Protection does not depend on any internal connection with the relevant constitutional right. Rather, the right to the Rule of Law rests on its own reason, namely the obligation of the state arising from the Rule of Law to uphold the norms of the constitution, which are subjectivized in that

---

[150] See in place of many W. Schmidt, 'Die Freiheit vor dem Gesetz', 68.

[151] Scholz, 'Das Grundrecht auf freie Entfaltung der Persönlichkeit', 84.

[152] See ibid. 84 f., with further references.   [153] BVerfGE 26, 246.

[154] On this expression, see W. Schmidt, 'Die Freiheit vor dem Gesetz', 66.

[155] See BVerfGE 13, 181 (190); 13, 237 (239); 14, 105 (116); 15, 226 (231); 24, 367 (385); 32, 319 (326); 34, 139 (146); 40, 371 (378); 53, 1 (15).

[156] When von Münch says (in I. v. Münch, *Grundgesetz-Kommentar*, i, 2nd edn. (Munich, 1981), para. 23 on art. 2) that the formal position is 'in truth better [located] in the Rule of Law principle than in art. 2(1)', but that it is to be derived from art. 2(1), because otherwise there would be a 'questionable gap in the Rule of Law', he comes at least close to this answer.

whenever the non-fulfilment of this obligation results in a disadvantage for the individual, then this person has suffered a breach of constitutional rights, or at any rate a breach of the general right to liberty. The second answer tries to find a connection between substantive and formal positions. According to this argument, a breach of a jurisdictional norm is thereby also a breach of a constitutional right, because jurisdictional norms of the Constitution, along with other procedural and formal norms of the organizational part of the Basic Law, have among their many functions that of protecting individual liberty.[157] This view can be called the '*protected liberty thesis*'. The Rule of Law thesis and the protected liberty thesis lead in most cases to identical outcomes, since the set of constitutional norms which have some degree of protective function towards whatever liberty is affected is very large. But in spite of a far-reaching identity of outcome, it is not totally irrelevant which thesis one adopts. The protected liberty thesis justifies one in treating formal positions as constitutional rights positions. This justification rests on the 'primary significance' of constitutional rights as individual positions,[158] and can argue that without formal positions, there would be a gap in the constitutional protection of liberty. Associated with this is a second point. The protected liberty thesis can require that the constitutional norms which are to be examined in the context of an alleged breach of constitutional rights have a protective function *vis-à-vis* the individual liberty in question. The formula in the Elfes Judgment must therefore be restricted. The necessary condition for the non-infringement of a liberty right is not that every constitutional norm must be followed, but only that those norms which have the function of protecting the particular liberty in the particular case must be followed. It will be seen that this limitation is not without consequences when it comes to the infringement of constitutional rights of third parties.

However, the point for now is that the protected liberty thesis does not lead to any limitation in the examination of formal constitutional norms, because one must proceed on the basis that all these norms have a protective function. The objection that the constitutional complaint procedure is expanded to a system of general norm control thus still applies. However, it is not justified. For examinations of formal breaches are equally concerned with individual constitutional rights. It is therefore inappropriate to speak pejoratively in terms of 'overflowing'; rather, we are dealing with a constitutionally required elaboration of the scope of the constitutional complaint. The maxim applies that in principle procedural law follows substance, and not substantive law procedure. In addition, the obvious objective aspect of the examination of formal infringement does not

---

[157] See J. Schwabe, 'Mißdeutungen um das "Elfes-Urteil" des BVerfG und ihre Folgen', DÖV 1973, 623.
[158] See BVerfGE 50, 290 (337).

contradict the purpose of the constitutional complaint. As the Federal Constitutional Court correctly emphasizes, the constitutional complaint has a 'double function'. It is first, 'an extraordinary remedy, granting the citizen the right to defend his constitutional rights', but it has also 'the function of upholding objective constitutional law, and serving its interpretation and development'.[159] The decisive point with both functions, so far as admissibility is concerned, is the link to a 'subjective constitutional right', because 'the Basic Law knows no public interest action'.[160] But the connection with a substantive subjective constitutional right is exactly what turns formal positions into constitutional rights positions under the protected liberty thesis.

4.2 Constitutional Rights Norms

The forgoing is concerned with formal constitutionality; the requirement of *substantive* constitutionality, which the Court places alongside formal constitutionality[161] gives rise to quite a different set of problems. The problems of formal constitutionality are well illustrated by the case of jurisdictional norms; the problems of substantive constitutionality by the case of constitutional rights norms. Every constitutional rights norm is a substantive constitutional norm. If one takes the requirement of substantive constitutionality literally, then every restriction of negative liberty is a breach of article 2(1) Basic Law if it breaches some other constitutional rights norm.

The first problem is that this is circular. Article 2(1) Basic Law is itself a substantive constitutional rights norm, so article 2(1) has to be examined in the light of article 2(1) etc. The same problem arises in the case of specific constitutional rights, because consistency with formal and substantive requirements of the Constitution is required when they are interfered with as well. So the constitutional right to property is infringed if the constitutional right to property is infringed, and this infringement in turn would depend on the infringement of the right to property *ad infinitum*. But the solution to this circularity is as obvious as its existence. The Federal Constitutional Court expresses it when it states that the constitutional order which the interference must satisfy encompasses the constitutional norms *'apart from* article 2(1) Basic Law',[162] and when in the context of article 14 Basic Law it does not require consistency with all, but with *all outstanding*,[163] or *all other*,[164] substantive constitutional norms.

Steiger objects that the problem of circularity in the case of article 2(1) Basic Law cannot be resolved in this way. Liberty is part of human dignity, and this must be included in any examination of substantive consistency

[159] BVerfGE 33, 247 (258 f.).   [160] BVerfGE 45, 63 (74 f.).
[161] BVerfGE 6, 32 (41).
[162] BVerfGE 17, 306 (313); 9, 137 (146) (emphasis added).
[163] BVerfGE 21, 150 (155); 34, 139 (146) (emphasis added).
[164] BVerfGE 26, 215 (222) (emphasis added).

with the constitutional order.[165] But the formal–material conception of the general right to liberty is capable of solving this problem. According to this conception, the human dignity norm and the negative liberty norm are not considered in separate stages. Rather, the weight of the reasons counting for constitutional protection arises from the conjunction of the principle of negative liberty with the principle of human dignity (more precisely, the substantive sub-principles of the principle of human dignity). Both principles *together* are to be balanced against the principles justifying interference. But if the substantive sub-principles of the principle of human dignity are not to be examined at a stage before the formal sub-principle of negative liberty, then it is not true that the principle of negative liberty, as a sub-principle of human dignity, has to be examined before the principle of negative liberty. This way of looking at things corresponds to the approach of the Federal Constitutional Court when in cases in which human dignity has particular weight in the context of article 2(1) Basic Law it does not say that there is a breach of the constitutional right in article 2(1) Basic Law because of an infringement of article 1(1) Basic Law, but rather that there is a breach of the constitutional right arising from article 2(1) Basic Law in connection with article 1(1) Basic Law.

The problem of circularity which arises when the constitutional right of a certain subject has to be examined in the context of exactly the same right can thus be resolved. But this does not resolve the problem of the examination of *other* constitutional rights in the context of the right under examination. The objection is repeatedly raised that if all constitutional rights norms belong to the constitutional order, then every breach of constitutional rights has to be considered in the context of article 2(1) Basic Law.[166] Each examination of a breach of constitutional rights could start and finish with article 2(1) Basic Law, and all constitutional complaints could be founded on article 2(1).[167] Indeed, there are decisions of the Federal Constitutional Court which support such an idea. In a decision concerned with the law regulating trade in real property, the Court examines article 14 in the context of article 2(1) Basic Law,[168] and in another decision concerned with the law of adoption, it states that article 2(1) Basic Law is, among other things, not breached, *because* constitutional rights have not been infringed.[169]

As regards the problem of the examination of other constitutional rights

---

[165] H. Steiger, 'Institutionalisierung der Freiheit?', in H. Schelsky (ed.), *Zur Theorie der Institution*, (Düsseldorf, 1970), 97.

[166] See W. Schmidt, 'Die Freiheit vor dem Gesetz', 50, 52; Scholz, 'Das Grundrecht der freien Entfaltung der Persönlichkeit', 286.

[167] P. Lerche, *Übermaß und Verfassungsrecht* (Cologne, Berlin, Munich, and Bonn, 1961), 299, fn. 158.

[168] BVerfGE 21, 73 (79, 87).

[169] BVerfGE 24, 220 (235); see also BVerfGE 10, 354 (363).

in the context of article 2(1) Basic Law, we must distinguish between whether we are dealing with other constitutional rights of the same subject, or with constitutional rights (including article 2(1) Basic Law) of others. If we are dealing with other constitutional rights of the same subject, we must distinguish further between liberties and other rights which are not liberties.

Where there are other liberties of the same subject at play, then the problem of nested examinations of constitutional rights can be dealt with by reference to the subsidiarity of article 2(1) Basic Law as against other specific liberties.[170] Whatever falls within the scope of a specific liberty is no longer to be considered under article 2(1) Basic Law because of the subsidiarity rule. Thus the problem of nested constitutional rights can no longer arise. This is by no means a merely technical solution. The subsidiarity rule makes a substantive point. The scope of the general right to liberty embraces the scopes of all the specific liberty rights. If there were no specific liberties, then article 2(1) Basic Law would protect what specific liberties protect, albeit with differing levels of intensity. Specific liberties are the expression of decisions by the Constitution in the field of the principle of negative liberty. They accent certain aspects of that principle. As the theory of the double aspect of constitutional rights norms as rules and principles shows,[171] these accents have the character of rules. If the specific liberties of the same subject were to be considered in the context of the general right to liberty, then to start with, the principle of negative liberty would be balanced twice over, which makes no sense, and then there would also be the danger that decisions of the Constitution having the character of rules would be overridden.

What has been said applies equally to implied specific liberties, where these are sufficiently well-fixed in the case-law to be treated in the same way as express liberties. This is the case in particular for the general right to personality and the more concrete rights derived from it.[172] Because of its guaranteed place in the case-law, the general right to personality is to be treated as *lex specialis*, and thus considered before, not in the context of, an examination of the general right to liberty. Its relationship to express specific liberties corresponds to that between express specific liberties.

The matter is more complex in the case of other constitutional rights of the same subject, which are not liberties, above all the general right to equality. An examination of an interference with liberty does not include a consideration of equality and vice versa. State action can restrict liberty, but not equality, because all are restricted equally in their liberty, and it can be a breach of equality but not liberty, where different forms of treatment taken individually do not infringe liberty, but where in comparison with each other they are discriminatory. At any rate, this is true if one does not

---

[170] See BVerfGE 32, 98 (107).   [171] 84 ff.
[172] See above at 24 f.

interpret the general principle of equality as a ban on arbitrary treatment independently of comparisons, which turns every breach of liberty into a breach of equality on the ground of arbitrariness, and if one does not assume that the right to equality is an element of the right to liberty. Thus the idea of subsidiarity alone does not prevent a consideration of article 3 Basic Law either in the context of article 2(1) Basic Law or of the other liberties. But against doing this there are arguments based both on positive law and on usefulness. The fact that the constitution-makers enacted a general right to equality means that they decided that the citizen should have the possibility of appealing to this right as an independent constitutional right. Unless there are good reasons for not doing so, it should therefore be examined independently, and not in the context of article 2(1) Basic Law or any other liberty. There are no good reasons for not doing so, because while it is possible, it is not necessary to do this. Thus the concept of the constitutional order in the context of article 2(1) Basic Law can be limited such that constitutional equality rights of the same subject are in general not included.[173] Such a limitation is useful, because it is useful to consider different relevant aspects in turn, and not in the context of a global examination.

The only remaining problem is that of considering the constitutional rights of others in the context of article 2(1) Basic Law. The judgment in the case of the shops closing hours law[174] is instructive in this respect. The Court considered the constitutional complaints of customers against what were in their view too early closing times for shops in the context of article 2(1) Basic Law. It would have been appropriate to consider a shops closing hours law in the context of article 12(1) Basic Law. There can be no doubt that article 12(1) Basic Law belongs to the constitutional order. Thus the Court could have asked whether the general right to liberty is infringed because the shops closing law breached the constitutional order on the grounds of its infringing the constitutional rights of shop owners to freedom of trade and profession. Such an approach would have meant that the breach of some constitutional right of some person would amount to a sufficient condition for considering the infringement of some other person's general right to liberty, so long as the relevant act hinders the latter in some way. But the Federal Constitutional Court did not do this. Rather, after considering formal constitutionality on the basis of jurisdictional norms, it went on to consider the proportionality of the measure under article 2(1) Basic Law.[175] This is correct if there are sufficient reasons for treating

---

[173] We are only concerned here with the constitutional *right* to equality. Whether the general principle of equality contains a separable *objective* component, which is to be considered in the context of art. 2(1) Basic Law, can be left open. Such an examination would not touch the problem of whether art. 2(1) makes the examination of other constitutional *rights* unnecessary.

[174] BVerfGE 13, 230. See on this and in relation to the current discussion, E. Hesse, *Die Bindung des Gesetzgebers an das Grundrecht des Art. 2(1) GG* (Berlin, 1968), 121 f.

[175] BVerfGE 13, 203 (234 ff.).

jurisdictional norms differently from the constitutional rights of third parties in the context of article 2(1) Basic Law. There is such a reason. Jurisdictional norms, even if only in an abstract way, have a protective function *relative to* the liberty of the individual. By contrast, the shopkeeper's constitutional right of freedom of trade only has a protective function *relative to* the shopkeeper, not *relative to* the freedom of the customer to shop. There are, of course, connections. If a shops closing law is declared void for breach of the freedom of trade of shopkeepers, then the freedom of customers to shop increases accordingly. But this connection is not of such a nature that it justifies concluding on the basis of a breach of the freedom to trade that there has been a breach of the freedom to shop. As a rule, both aspects will operate in parallel, because if there are insufficient reasons for limiting the freedom to trade, there are also likely to be insufficient reasons for limiting the freedom to shop. But this need not be the case. One can imagine cases in which the legislature's reasons are not an adequate justification for limiting freedom of trade but are for limiting freedom to shop and vice versa. It could be that a prohibition on the operators of petrol stations from selling products outside of normal opening hours which have no direct connection with the technical operation of vehicles could breach the right to freedom of trade, perhaps because it makes some petrol stations uneconomic, but would not breach the customer's right to shop, because the goods can easily be obtained during normal opening hours, in other words because they are far less severely affected. If in such cases the breach of one person's constitutional rights were considered sufficient to ground the breach of another person's constitutional rights, one person would be participating in the protection granted to another outside of the scope of his own substantive constitutional position. This would have the procedural consequence that somebody unaffected as a matter of substance could bring an action in respect of another who is substantively affected, even if the latter does not wish to bring the action.

The solution consists in relativizing the concept of incompatibility with constitutional rights. Illegality within one legal relation[176] does not necessarily give rise to illegality within another. It cannot be objected to such relativizing that each breach of constitutional rights adversely affects the overall state of constitutional rights. The individual is granted certain constitutional rights relevant to himself, not a constitutional right to an unaffected overall state of constitutional affairs, which would include a constitutional right to the non-infringement of the constitutional rights of others. If some state action is an unjustified interference with y's constitutional right and is also an interference with x's rights, it is not a breach of x's constitutional rights because it infringes y's rights, but only because it is unjustifiable in the context of x's rights.

---

[176] On the concept of a legal relation, see above at 131 ff.

This conclusion cannot be overturned by reference to the protective character of *y*'s constitutional liberty for *x*. Of course, *y*'s constitutional rights have a protective *effect* for *x*'s rights, because if *y*'s rights are breached in a way which is also a breach of *x*'s, the declaration of invalidity as regards the norm infringing *y*'s rights also means the removal of the infringement of *x*'s rights. Protective effect is however not the same thing as protective character. The prerequisite for this is that *y*'s constitutional right should have the *purpose* of protecting *x*. Of course, constitutional rights also have the purpose of securing an overall state of liberty from which all benefit. In this respect they do have a connection with the situation of other subjects. But they do not have the purpose of creating individual constitutional positions for other subjects. *Their own* constitutional rights have this purpose. In this respect there is a fundamental difference between jurisdictional norms and the constitutional rights of others which justifies us in not considering them in the context of a constitutional rights case, as the Federal Constitutional Court refrained from doing in the shops closing hours case.

To summarize what has been said in the matter of nested constitutional rights, it has been established that neither the infringement of other constitutional rights, nor the infringement of the rights of others should be considered in the context of article 2(1) Basic Law. The concept of the constitutional order for the purposes of article 2(1) Basic Law is to be amended by a clause excluding nested constitutional rights. This states that only those constitutional norms which have a character protective of the general liberty of the plaintiff should be considered.[177] This clause expresses a substantive limitation on the rights derived from article 2(1). It is thus not merely of technical but also of material significance.

---

[177] This does not prevent the Federal Constitutional Court from emphasizing the function of the constitutional complaint as a 'specific means for the protection of objective constitutional law' (BVerfGE 33, 247 (259); 45, 63 (74)) and adopting a constitutional complaint based on art. 2(1) Basic Law in order to consider the constitutional rights of others as well. But the plaintiff has *no right* to this, and the question of the breach of *his* right under art. 2(1) does not depend on the outcome of this examination. The Court may also have regard for other objective-legal aspects of other constitutional rights norms in the context of considering art. 2(1), if these have a liberty-protecting tendency in relation to the individual liberty in question.

8

The General Right to Equality

I. EQUALITY IN THE APPLICATION AND CREATION OF LAW

As with liberty rights so also with equality rights there is a distinction between the general right to equality and specific equality rights. Specific equality rights are to found, for example, in articles 3(2) and (3), 6(5), 33(1) to (3), 38(1), and 136(1) and (2) Weimar Imperial Constitution as incorporated by article 140 Basic Law. The general right to equality can be found in article 3(1) Basic Law. Here, we are only concerned with the latter.

Article 3(1) Basic Law, 'everyone is equal before the law', uses the traditional phrase, 'before the law'.[1] As its literal meaning suggests, this phrase was understood for a long time exclusively in terms of a requirement of equality in the application of law.[2] The requirement of equality in application can by definition only apply to bodies that apply the law, not to the legislature itself.[3] Anschütz expressed the point of this in the following brief terms, 'laws should be executed without regard for persons'.[4] The requirement of equality in application has a complicated structure at the level of detail, for example, in cases where vague, ambiguous, or evaluatively open

---

[1] Cf. art. 3 of the Declaration of the Rights of Man and the Citizen of the 1773 French Constitution; Preamble to the Constitution of the Kingdom of Bavaria of 26 May 1818; art. 6 of the Constitution of Belgium of 7 Feb. 1831; art. 37(3), Paulskirchen Constitution; art. 4 of the Prussian Constitution of 31 Jan. 1850; art. 109(1) Weimar Imperial Constitution. On the history of this formula, see H. P. Ipsen, 'Gleichheit', in F. L. Neumann, H. C. Nipperdey, and U. Scheuner (eds.), *Die Grundrechte*, ii (Berlin, 1954), 115 f.; K. Schweiger, 'Zur Geschichte und Bewertung des Wilkürverbots', in *Verfassung und Verfassungsrechtsprechung, Festschrift zum 25-jährigen Bestehen des BayVGH* (Munich, 1972), 57 ff.

[2] See G. Anschütz, *Die Verfassung des Deutschen Reiches*, 14th edn. (Berlin, 1933), art. 109, *Anmerkung* 1, 2 (522 ff.); J. Hatschek, *Deutsches und Preußisches Staatsrecht*, i, 2nd edn. (Berlin, 1930), 243; R. Thoma, 'Die juristische Bedeutung der grundrechtlichen Sätze der deutschen Reichsverfassung im allgemeinen', in H. C. Nipperdey (ed.), *Die Grundrechte und Grundpflichtender Reichsverfassung*, i (Berlin, 1929), 23; id., 'Ungleichheit und Gleichheit im Bonner Grundgesetz', DVBl 1951, 457 ff.

[3] C. Schmitt, *Unabhängigkeit der Richter, Gleichheit vor dem Gesetz und Gewährleistung des Privateigentums nach der Weimarer Verfassung* (Berlin and Leipzig, 1926), 22 f. commented that equality before the law presupposes that the law is applicable to more than one person, that is, that it is not an individual norm or single command. This gives rise to a requirement addressed to the legislature to engage in a practice of universal norm enactment. However, this requirement is not part of the command to respect equality in the application of law, which is addressed to organs of law enforcement, but a requirement that one formal aspect of equality in the creation of law should apply.

[4] Anschütz, *Die Verfassung des deutschen Reiches*, art. 109, *Anmerkung* 1 (523).

concepts need clarification, or where the exercise of discretion requires the adoption of rules sensitive to the facts of cases.[5] However, at root it is straightforward. It simply requires that every legal norm be applied to every case falling within its ambit, and to no case not falling within its ambit, which is tantamount to saying that legal norms must be followed.[6] That legal norms are to be followed is expressed by the norms themselves, in that they incorporate ought-statements. So the requirement of equality in the application of law only requires what applies anyway whenever there are valid legal norms.[7] It strengthens the obligation of bodies applying the law to follow the norms created by the legislature, without imposing any requirements on the content of these norms, that is, without binding the legislature itself. The legislature can discriminate as much as it pleases; so long as its discriminatory norms are followed in all cases, the requirement of equality in the application of law is satisfied.

There are decisive arguments against limiting the meaning of article 3(1) Basic Law merely to the requirement of equality in the application of law. Article 3(1) would be a constitutional rights provision incapable of binding the legislature both in theory and hence also in practice. To start with, this would contradict article 1(3) Basic Law which obligates all three powers, that is, including the legislature, to observe 'the following constitutional rights'. Secondly, it would contradict the intentions of the makers of the Constitution, who at one stage expressly stated that the legislature was bound by the principle of equality,[8] and only later abandoned that formulation because it was unnecessary in the light of article 1(3). Thirdly, it would contradict the idea of constitutional rights, which express a certain degree of mistrust towards the legislature,[9] subjecting statutes enacted by it to constitutional review whenever rationally possible. It will be argued below that rational control on the basis of the principle of equality is indeed possible.

For these reasons the Federal Constitutional Court has assumed as a matter of course from its very first decisions that the principle of equality binds the legislature. Article 3(1) has been interpreted not only as a requirement of equality in the application of law, but also in the creation of law.[10] In important respects it was able to rely on work done during the time of

[5] See R. Alexy, *A Theory of Legal Argumentation*, trans. R. Adler and N. MacCormick (Oxford, 1989), 221 ff.; H.-J. Koch and H. Rüßmann, *Juristische Begründungslehre* (Munich, 1982), 113 f.; 236 ff.

[6] See C. Perelman, *The Idea of Justice and the Problem of Argument*, trans. J. Petrie (London, 1963), 38: 'Equality of treatment is merely a logical consequence of the fact of keeping to the rule'.

[7] See H. Kelsen, *Pure Theory of Law*, trans. M. Knight (Berkeley, 1967), 141 f.

[8] See JöR 1 (1951), 66 ff. See on this C. Starck, 'Die Anwendung des Gleichheitssatzes', in C. Link (ed.), *Der Gleichheitssatz im modernen Verfassungsstaat* (Baden-Baden, 1982), 52 f.

[9] See J.-H. Ely, *Democracy and Distrust*, (Cambridge, Mass. and London, 1980).

[10] See BVerfGE 1, 14 (52), and standing case-law.

the Weimar Republic,[11] above all by Leibholz.[12] Apart from a few dissenters,[13] the case-law of the Court in its basic outline has met with agreement or simple acceptance. It will form the principal object of investigation in the following discussion of the structure of the general right to equality.

II. THE STRUCTURE OF THE REQUIREMENT OF EQUALITY IN THE CREATION OF LAW

The requirement of equality in the creation of law demands that everyone should be treated equally by the legislature. What does this mean?

It is easier to say what it cannot mean. It cannot mean either that the legislature should put everyone in the same legal position, or that it has the responsibility to ensure that everyone has the same personal characteristics or lives under the same material circumstances. The legislature is not only permitted to impose military service only on adults, punishments on criminals, taxes according to the level of income, social welfare for the needy, and honours for the worthy citizen, it must do this if it is not to act inappropriately (military service for children), pointlessly (punishments for everyone), or unjustly (poll tax).[14] The equality of all with respect to all legal positions would not only lead to inappropriate, pointless, and unjust laws, it would also undermine the basis for the exercise of powers. Each voter would also have to be a candidate, and each master a servant; every vendor would not only have the right to the purchase price, but also the duty to pay it. It is just as obvious that the principle of equality cannot require the identity of all personal characteristics and material circumstances in which the individual finds himself. Differences of health, intelligence, and beauty can perhaps be somewhat reduced and compensated for, but their removal runs up against natural boundaries. Furthermore, the creation of an identity between all people in all respects, even if it were possible, would not be desirable. The identity of all in all respects would

---

[11] See H. Triepel, *Goldbilanzenverordnung und Vorzugsaktien* (Berlin and Leipzig, 1924), 26 ff.; E. Kaufmann, 'Die Gleichheit vor dem Gesetz im Sinne des Art. 109 der Reichsverfassung', VVDStRL 3 (1927), 2 ff.; H. Aldag, *Die Gleichheit vor dem Gesetz in der Reichsverfassung* (Berlin, 1925), 51 ff.; G. Holstein, 'Von Aufgaben und Zielen heutiger Staatsrechtswissenschaft', AöR 50 (1926), 3 ff.

[12] G. Leibholz, *Die Gleichheit vor dem Gesetz* (1925), 2nd edn. (Munich and Berlin, 1959).

[13] See N. Luhmann, *Grundrechte als Institution*, 2nd edn. (Berlin, 1974), 167 ff.; E. Forsthoff, *Der Staat der Industriegesellschaft*, 2nd edn. (Munich, 1971), 134 ff.; E. Eyermann, 'Gleichheitssatz, Wurzel des Willkürverbots?' in *Verfassung und Verfassungsrechtsprechung, Festschrift zum 25-jährigen Bestehen des BayVGH*, (Munich, 1972), 45 ff.; Schweiger, 'Zur Geschichte und Bewertung des Willkürverbots', 55 ff.

[14] See H. Kelsen, 'Das Problem der Gerechtigkeit', in id., *Reine Rechtslehre*, 2nd edn. (Vienna, 1960), 391; A. Podlech, *Gehalt und Funktionen des allgemeinen verfassungsrechtlichen Gleichheitssatzes* (Berlin, 1971), 44 f.; Ipsen, 'Gleichheit', 141.

have the consequence that everybody would want to do the same things, and if everybody were to do the same things, only a very limited level of intellectual, cultural, and economic life would be attainable.

So the general principle of equality, when addressed to the legislature, cannot require that each person should be treated in exactly the same way, and it cannot require that everyone should be the same in every respect. On the other hand, nor can it permit every differentiation and distinction whatever the content. The question is, how one can find a middle way between these two extremes. One way in is the classic formula, 'treat the same similarly and differences differently',[15] which with many modifications and clarifications forms the backbone of the case-law of the Federal Constitutional Court on article 3(1). The formula, 'treat the same similarly and differences differently' can be understood in two quite different ways. The first interpretation limits it to a requirement of universalizable decision-taking.[16] As far as the legislature is concerned, this means that the norms created must take the form of universal conditional norms, that is, the form, 'for all X, if X has characteristics C_1, C_2, . . ., C_n, then it is required that X have legal consequence Q'.

Norms of this form treat all X similarly, because all X, being similar in respect of their sharing characteristics C_1, C_2, . . ., C_n, have the same legal consequence. There can be no doubt that such a requirement, which corresponds to Hare's principle of universalizability[17] and Perelman's principle of formal justice,[18] is a basic requirement of practical reason,[19] which applies equally well to the legislature as to those who apply the law. There can also be little doubt that this requirement does not get us very far. It says nothing about which characteristics of which individuals are to be treated in which way.[20] If the general principle of equality were to be limited to a requirement of universalizable decision-taking, the legislature could enact all sorts of discriminatory measures without breaching it, so long as they took the form of universal norms, which is always possible. On this account, Nazi laws relating to Jews would not have fallen foul of the requirement to 'treat the same similarly'.[21]

---

[15] See Plato, *Laws*, trans. T. J. Saunders (London, 1970), VI 757; Aristotle, *Politics*, III. 9 (1280a): 'For example, justice is thought by them to be, and is, equality—not, however, for all, but only for equals. And inequality is thought to be, and is, justice; neither is this for all, but only for unequals' (in J. Barnes (ed.), *The Complete Works* (Princeton, 1984), 2031; id., *Nichomachean Ethics*, V 3 (1131a).

[16] For such an interpretation, see Kelsen, 'Das Problem der Gerechtigkeit', 392 ff.

[17] See R. M. Hare, *Freedom and Reason* (Oxford, 1963), 30 ff.

[18] See Perelman, *The Idea of Justice and the Problem of Argument*, 40.

[19] Alexy, *A Theory of Legal Argumentation*, 65 ff.

[20] See Starck, 'Die Anwendung des Gleichheitssatzes', 58 f.; O. Weinberger, 'Gleichheitspostulate', in id., *Logische Analyse in der Jurisprudenz* (Berlin, 1979), 152.

[21] If one reads the statement, 'treat the same similarly and differences differently' as a requirement of universalizable decision-taking, the second half of the statement gives rise to problems. Whenever both x and y have committed fraud, then according to § 263(1) Criminal

A substantive limitation of the legislature will only be attained if we understand the formula, 'treat the same similarly and differences differently', not as a requirement for the logical form of norms, but as a requirement for their content, that is, not in the sense of formal equality but of substantive equality. The problems of such an interpretation are, as the Federal Constitutional Court has pointedly put it,[22] that no two human individuals or two sets of circumstances are ever exactly the same.[23] The similarity and difference of human beings and situations is always similarity and difference in respect of certain characteristics. Judgments of similarity, which establish similarity in respect of certain characteristics, are judgments about three-point relations:[24] x is similar to y in respect of characteristic C (characteristics C_1, C_2, . . ., C_n). Since they only relate to some and not all characteristics of the pair to be compared, such judgments are judgments about partial factual similarity. They are true to the extent that x and y actually have characteristic C (characteristics C_1, C_2, . . ., C_n). The same applies for judgments of difference.

Judgments about partial factual similarity do not yet tell us if similar or different treatment is required. Partial factual similarity is compatible with different treatment, partial factual difference compatible with similar treatment. The fact that both x and y are sailors does not stop us punishing x for theft, but not y. The fact that x is a sailor and y a bank clerk does not stop us punishing both for theft. The words 'same' and 'different' in the formula 'treat the same similarly and differences differently' must refer to something other than partial factual similarity and difference in any respect. Since there are no two human individuals and human situations which are not factually the same in part and factually different in part, everything would have to be treated simultaneously similarly and differently if the formula referred to partial factual similarity and difference in any respect.

Since there is no similarity or difference in all respects (universal factual

---

Code—other criminal law norms apart—they are both to be treated equally in that both are to be punished with imprisonment for up to five years or a fine. In this sense it is true that the same are to be treated similarly. It is also true that if x has committed fraud and y not, they are to be treated differently in respect of § 263(1) Criminal Code. To this extent it is true that differences are to be treated differently. But it is not true that y must always be treated differently from x, when unlike x he has committed no fraud, that is, when he is different from x in respect of § 263(1). y may have committed no fraud, but he may have been in receipt of stolen goods, which just like fraud is to be punished with imprisonment for up to five years or a fine. In respect of norms which express a sufficient, but not a necessary condition for a legal consequence, only the phrase, 'treat the same similarly' and not, 'treat differences differently' applies in the interpretation as a requirement of universalizable decision-taking (see Weinberger, 'Gleichheitspostulate', 150).

[22] See BVerfGE 6, 273 (280); 13, 181 (202); 13, 225 (228); 50, 57 (77); 50, 177 (186); 53, 164 (178).

[23] This point is sufficient for now. On the logical and epistemological problems of equality and identity, see Weinberger, 'Gleichheitspostulate', 147 ff.; K. Hesse, 'Der Gleichheitsgrundsatz im Staatsrecht', AöR 77 (1951/2), 172 ff.

[24] See Podlech, *Gehalt und Funktionen*, 30 f.

similarity/difference) between human individuals and situations, and since partial factual similarity (or difference) in some respects does not work as a condition for the application of the principle, the formula can only refer to one thing: evaluative similarity and difference. If a differentiated legal system is to be possible, evaluative similarity (or difference) must be modified in two ways. It must be an evaluative similarity relative to partial factual similarities (or differences), because were it to refer to an evaluative similarity of the individual as a whole, it would not be able to justify differentiated treatment. Secondly, it must be an evaluative similarity relative to certain actions, because if it were not, one could not explain why two people who are to be treated the same way in one respect are not to be treated the same way in all respects. In addition to these two modifications, which are the conditions of the possibility of differentiated treatment, there is a third, which is reference to a criterion of evaluation allowing one to say what is evaluatively similar and different. The proposition, 'treat the same similarly and differences differently' does not contain such a criterion; but its application presupposes it. Substantive equality thus leads necessarily to the question of correct evaluation, and thus also to the question of correct, rational, or just law-making. This exposes the main problem of the general principle of equality. It can be put in the form of two closely connected questions, namely, first, to what extent are the value-judgments which are necessary in the context of the principle of equality subject to rational justification, and secondly, who within the legal system—legislature or constitutional court—should have the final and authoritative say over such value-judgments? These questions indicate the problems which any interpretation of article 3(1) Basic Law as binding on the legislature have to address.

III. THE FORMULAE OF THE FEDERAL CONSTITUTIONAL COURT

The Federal Constitutional Court tries to resolve the problems of evaluation necessarily associated with the general principle of substantive equality by using the concept of arbitrariness. There are two strands of interpretation in the case-law of the Court on arbitrariness. The first strand maintains that in applying the general principle of equality, there must always be a pair of objects for comparison. The second strand, to which the Second Senate tends, reduces the general principle of equality to a general ban on arbitrary treatment, in which comparative pairs no longer play any necessary part.[25] As Geiger has shown,[26] there are strong arguments

[25] See BVerfGE 42, 64 (74 ff.); 57, 39 (42). Leibholz, *Die Gleichheit vor dem Gesetz*, 72, clearly tends in this direction.
[26] BVerfGE 42, 79 ff. (dissenting judgment). See also the contributions of W. Geiger on one hand and G. Leibholz on the other to the discussion in C. Link (ed.), *Der Gleichheitssatz im modernen Verfassungsstaat* (Baden-Baden, 1982), 100 ff., 105 ff.

against reducing the principle of equality to a general ban on arbitrary treatment. An examination of equality would no longer be what it claims to be. The fact that one should consider arbitrariness in the context of equality does not mean that the principle of equality also requires one to test for arbitrariness independently from difference. To derive a general prohibition on arbitrariness from article 3(1) unrelated to comparative pairs might be required if there were no other way of carrying out such examinations of arbitrariness. But there can be no question of this. The arbitrary treatment of a constitutional right-holder by the state, perhaps one 'which is no longer comprehensible on a proper understanding of the guiding ideas of the Basic Law',[27] in the absence of any comparator, always breaches some other constitutional right, at any rate article 2(1) Basic Law. Against a general investigation of arbitrariness, and in favour of connecting arbitrariness to particular constitutional rights provisions, there is the fact that a general investigation of arbitrariness would lead to an impenetrable muddle of reasoning, in which the material content of constitutional rights would play a significant, but barely comprehensible, role. So the application of the general principle of equality must be strictly limited to the identification of comparators.

The Federal Constitutional Court relates its investigation of arbitrariness in part directly to the classic formula, 'treat the same similarly and differences differently', but predominantly to two formulations which amend the classic formulation by adding the words, 'substantially' or 'arbitrarily'. Let us consider first the formulations in respect of the 'same' part of the test. According to these, the legislature is prevented from treating,

(1)   'the same differently'[28]
(2)   'substantially the same differently'[29]
(3)   'substantially the same arbitrarily differently'[30]

The question is whether these different formulations express different norms.

Similarity in the sense of the first formulation is evaluative similarity. Substantial similarity, which is what the second formulation refers to, is also evaluative similarity. The legal consequence which the second formulation attaches to substantial similarity is the prohibition of differential treatment. But this prohibition can only relate to evaluative similarity, by whatever standard the evaluation is made. Evaluative similarity and substantial similarity for the purposes of the second formulation amount to the same thing. The first and second formulae express the same idea in different ways.

---

[27] BVerfGE 42, 64 (74).   [28] See BVerfGE 3, 58 (135); 9, 124 (129); 42, 64 (72).
[29] See BVerfGE 1, 14 (52); 21, 6 (9); 21, 227 (234); 45, 376 (386).
[30] See BVerfGE 4, 144 (155); 22, 254 (263); 42, 64 (72); 49, 148 (165); 50, 177 (186); 51, 295 (300); 55, 114 (128); 57, 250 (271); 61, 138 (147).

The relationship between the second and the third formulation is problematic. The third formulation can be understood in two ways. The first
interpretation takes it literally. Accordingly, substantial similarity still does
not require similarity of treatment. Two situations can be substantially the
same without there being a requirement to treat them the same way. The
proposition that what is substantially the same should be treated similarly
does not apply. What is forbidden is not every differential treatment of
substantially the same situations, but only arbitrary differential treatment
of substantially the same situations. So substantial similarity in the third
formulation either means something different from what it means in the
second, or the two formulations contradict each other. According to this
first interpretation, the test of equality should proceed in three stages. The
first stage would require one to establish differential treatment as well as a
partial factual similarity which could serve as the basis for a consideration
of inequality. The second stage would consider whether the partial factual
similarity could be counted as substantial. Finally, the third stage would
consider whether the differential treatment of what is substantially the same
was arbitrary. The second possible interpretation reaches a quite different
result. It does not take the formula, 'what is substantially the same may not
arbitrarily be treated differently' literally. It treats the expression 'arbitrary'
in this formulation as redundant, which means that the third formulation
corresponds to the second and first. This means that the test of equality
takes place in two stages. The first stage establishes a difference of treatment and a partial similarity which can form the basis of the examination.
The second stage considers whether the partial similarity is substantial, that
is, whether there is evaluative similarity in the sense used above.

In establishing which of these interpretations is the correct one, the first
point to consider is that the Federal Constitutional Court, even when it
adopts the second formulation, that is, the one without reference to arbitrariness, still makes the breach of the principle of equality dependent on
the arbitrary nature of the treatment. The following sentence keeps on
appearing like a golden thread throughout the Court's equality case-law:
'The principle of equality is breached, when a persuasive and reasonable
ground, arising from the nature of the subject-matter or some other material circumstance, cannot be given for the legal differentiation or similarity
of treatment, in short, when the provision can only be called arbitrary'.[31]
For the moment, we need only consider the part of this sentence which says
that the principle of equality is breached when the difference of treatment
is arbitrary. This means that the arbitrary nature of the treatment is both a
necessary and a sufficient condition for its breaching the principle of equality.[32] The principle of equality is breached if and only if the difference of

---

[31] BVerfGE 1, 14 (52); standing case-law, see e.g. BVerfGE 60, 101 (108).
[32] Occasionally, one comes across formulations which speak of arbitrariness as a necessary

treatment is arbitrary. On the other hand, it is also true, if one proceeds on the basis of the second formulation, that the principle of equality is breached if and only if what is substantially the same is treated differently. This gives rise to the following proposition:

(4)   Substantial equality arises whenever a difference of treatment would be arbitrary.

The idea of substantial equality in the second formulation can be defined by way of the idea of arbitrariness of differential treatment.

Also within the context of the third formulation, 'what is substantially the same may not arbitrarily be treated differently', one must suppose that an arbitrary difference of treatment is both a necessary and a sufficient condition for a breach of the principle. But this leads to problems in respect of the idea of substantial similarity. If no element of the third formulation is to be redundant, this concept must be defined in such a way that substantial similarity does not already indicate a requirement of similar treatment. This means that the idea of substance cannot be defined as it is in the second formulation by way of the idea of arbitrariness. This leaves the question of what substantial similarity could be, which unlike the second formulation cannot be equated to non-arbitrary difference of treatment. There are three possibilities: substantial similarity could be (1) partial factual similarity, (2) relevant similarity, and (3) evaluative similarity in an ideal sense. None of these possibilities is acceptable.

Interpreting substantial equality as partial factual similarity would have the consequence that every correspondence in every respect would have to be called substantial, which would make the qualifier, 'substantial', in the third formulation redundant. It would give rise to the following fourth formulation alongside the existing three:

(5)   What is the same may not be arbitrarily treated differently.

Since 'what is the same' in this formulation relates to partial factual similarity, and since everything which falls to be legally evaluated corresponds to everything else in some respect, that is, since the first half of this formulation is always satisfied, it is possible to reduce this formulation to the proposition that every arbitrary difference of treatment is prohibited. But as we have seen above, this proposition can be used to define substantial similarity in the context of the second formulation. The third formulation would thereby lose its character as a competing formulation on the same level as the second one. If the third formulation is one about which one can meaningfully ask whether it is to be preferred to the second, then some definition of substantial similarity must be found which on one hand is stronger than partial factual similarity, but on the other is weaker than substantial

---

condition for a breach of equality. However, these formulations should *not* be understood to mean that arbitrariness is *only* one necessary condition for a breach.

similarity as defined by way of the concept of arbitrariness. The candidates for such an interpretation are relevant similarity and evaluative similarity in an ideal sense.

Relevant similarities could be all those partial factual similarities which make a consideration of arbitrariness worthwhile. The idea of relevant similarity is attractive, because it promises to limit the limitless field of comparative possibilities. The problem is that it cannot fulfil this promise in a rational way. On what criterion should those partial factual similarities be excluded for which a consideration of arbitrariness is not worthwhile? The criterion will only boil down to the fact that it is certain that there is no arbitrary treatment. Whether this is the case can only be decided on the basis of the criterion of arbitrariness itself. It makes no sense to adopt a criterion to be applied before considering arbitrariness, which, itself orientated towards the question of arbitrariness, is supposed to exclude a consideration of arbitrariness. For practical reasons such a filter is also not necessary, because if it is clear that a differentiation is not arbitrary, there is no reason to use a criterion of relevance to free oneself from the necessity of saying that the differentiation is not arbitrary. It is simpler in such cases to say it straight out.

This leaves only the interpretation of substantial similarity as evaluative similarity in an ideal sense. The Federal Constitutional Court repeatedly emphasizes that in the area of equal treatment, the legislature has a 'very wide discretion'. It is 'not the concern of the Federal Constitutional Court to consider whether the most just or appropriate rules have been adopted, but simply whether the outermost limits [set by the concept of arbitrariness, R.A.] have been respected'.[33] On the basis of this statement, which is obviously influenced by the desire to limit the competence of the Court to consider issues of equality, one can distinguish strong and weak versions of the principle of equality. The strong version relates to the ideal, that is, the most just and appropriate solution. According to this, two cases are always substantially the same and to be treated similarly, when their similar treatment satisfies requirements of justice or appropriateness to a greater extent than treating them differently. If the Federal Constitutional Court were to proceed on this basis, there would be no discretion left to the legislature. Since there is no certain knowledge of what is most just and appropriate, its function would be limited to taking those decisions which the Court considers most just and appropriate. It hardly needs demonstrating that this cannot be the meaning of the principle of equality.

So the only possibility is a weak version of the principle of equality, which is only concerned with maintaining the limits of legislative discretion set by the concept of arbitrariness, and which is thus not concerned with evaluative similarity in an ideal sense, but only evaluative similarity in a

---

[33] See e.g. BVerfGE 17, 319 (330). Leibholz's distinction between incorrectness and arbitrariness amounts to the same thing, see Leibholz, *Die Gleichheit vor dem Gesetz*, 76 f.

limited sense. But then it would be unnecessary and pointless to precede the investigation of arbitrariness with an investigation of evaluative similarity in an ideal sense, in order then to ask whether deviations from it are arbitary or not. It would be unnecessary, because the result of the investigation into arbitrariness does not depend on the result of the investigation into evaluative similarity in an ideal sense, and pointless because it would have the consequence that the Federal Constitutional Court would unnecessarily have to do something which stretches its competence.

This means that the concept of substantial similarity in the third formulation is to be understood in the same way as in the second. In both statements, the idea of substantial similarity can be defined by way of the arbitrariness of differential treatment. And this means that the expression 'arbitrary' in the formula, 'what is substantially the same may not arbitrarily be treated differently' is redundant. All three formulae say the same thing. The best way of expressing this is by way of the second formula, 'what is substantially the same may not be treated differently'. If one defines 'substantial similarity' in this formulation by way of the arbitrariness of different treatment as we did in (4), the formulation is equivalent to

(6)   Arbitrary differences of treatment are prohibited.

The question is how this formula, which expresses the necessarily weak version of the principle of equality, is to be understood.

IV. SIMILAR AND DIFFERENTIAL TREATMENT

1. THE REQUIREMENT OF SIMILAR TREATMENT

According to the ongoing case-law of the Federal Constitutional Court, arbitrary differentiation is to be found 'whenever a persuasive and reasonable ground, arising from the nature of the subject-matter or some other material circumstance, cannot be given for the legal differentiation'.[34] So a differentiation is arbitrary and thus prohibited when a certain sort of reason cannot be given for it. The qualification of this reason can be described in many different ways. In the quotation just cited it is described as reasonable, or arising from the nature of the subject-matter, or in some other way materially apparent. Other formulations require that the irrelevance of the reason for the differentiation should not be 'evident',[35] yet another simply requires that the reason be 'justified'.[36] Behind all these formulations is the requirement of 'a perspective guided by considerations of justice'.[37]

---

[34] BVerfGE 1, 14 (52); similarly, e.g., BVerfGE 12, 341 (348); 20, 31 (33); 30, 409 (413); 44, 70 (90); 51, 1 (23); 60, 101 (108).
[35] See e.g. BVerfGE 12, 326 (333).   [36] See e.g. BVerfGE 38, 154 (167).
[37] See e.g. BVerfGE 9, 334 (337) and standing case-law.

All this points to the fact that there must be an adequate reason for the differentiation, which is sufficient to justify it, and that the qualification of a reason as adequate is a problem of evaluation. Only the first point is of interest for the moment. The fact that the permissibility of differentiations depends upon the existence of an adequate reason, sufficient to justify it, means that if such a reason is absent, similar treatment is required. This can be put in terms of the following proposition, which is a clarification of the weak version of the general principle of equality defended above.

(7)   If there is no adequate reason for permitting an instance of differential treatment, then similar treatment is required.[38]

There is no adequate reason for permitting a differentiation when all possible reasons are considered inadequate. In such a case, attempts to justify permitting the differentiation fail.[39] Thus, as has often been pointed out,[40] the general principle of equality establishes a burden of argumentation in respect of differential treatment.[41]

2. The Requirement of Differential Treatment

The second half of the sentence, 'treat the same similarly and differences differently' is a test-case for this proposition as well as a means of expounding it. The symmetry of the formulation would seem to suggest that the requirement of differential treatment should be expressed by way of a differential treatment norm structurally identical to the similar treatment norm.

(8)   If there is no adequate reason for permitting an instance of similar treatment, then differential treatment is required.

---

[38] For a version of this statement which does without the element of permissibility, see Podlech, *Gehalt und Funktionen*, 77.

[39] The concept of an adequate reason is thus related to the success of a justification process which is dependent on whether all reasons worth considering are judged adequate or not. This means that the presence of an adequate reason is to be determined in the context of a rational legal discourse. Even when legal discourses are rational, they do not always lead to precisely one answer, and even if they do lead to precisely one answer at one point in time, they can still lead to a different answer at another point in time (see R. Alexy, 'Die Idee einer prozeduralen Theorie der juristischen Argumentation', *Rechtstheorie*, Beiheft 2 (1981), 180 ff.). The presence or existence of an adequate reason for differentiation is thus not to be understood as presence or existence *per se*, but as presence or existence for concrete, but rational, discourse partners.

[40] See e.g. Luhmann, *Grundrechte als Institution*, 169 ff.; Podlech, *Gehalt und Funktionen*, 85 ff.; Starck, 'Die Anwendung des Gleichheitssatzes', 61; M. Gubelt, in I. v. Münch (ed.), *Grundgesetz-Kommentar*, i, 2nd edn. (Munich, 1981), art. 3, para. 26.

[41] On the burden of argumentation in respect of differential treatment as a general requirement of rationality, see M. G. Singer, *Generalization in Ethics* (New York, 1961), 31; J. Rawls, 'Justice as Fairness', in *The Philosophical Review*, 67 (1958), 166; Alexy, *A Theory of Legal Argumentation*, 195.

But this would have the consequence of establishing a burden of argumentation both for similar and differential treatment, which would remove any benefit given to similar treatment, and, as Podlech has remarked, would simply amount to the requirement that 'the legal regulation be thus and not different'.[42] The principle of equality would simply become the requirement to justify norms, and it would lose any tendency towards equality. As a result, Podlech proposes dropping the second half of the formula, thus turning article 3(1) Basic Law into a similar treatment norm, and not a differential treatment norm.[43]

Such a radical solution would only be advisable if it were unavoidable, which it is not. It is possible to have not only a tendency towards equality but also both similar treatment and differential treatment norms. However, in order to do this, the differential treatment norm must have a different structure from the similar treatment norm (7). Instead, it must have the following form:

(9)   If there is an adequate reason for requiring differential treatment, then differential treatment is required.[44]

---

[42] Podlech, *Gehalt und Funktionen*, 57.

[43] ibid.

[44] A comparison of the similar and differential treatment norms ((7) and (9)) shows that their protases differ in two respects. The first difference consists in the fact that the protasis of (7) speaks of the *non-existence*, while the protasis of (9) speaks of the *existence*, of an adequate reason. The second difference consists in the fact that the protasis of (7) speaks of the *permissibility*, while the protasis of (9) speaks of the *requirement*, of differential treatment. It is easy to see that the three protases presented in the text do not exhaust all the alternatives. If one assumes that the negation of similar treatment is differential treatment, and that the negation of differential treatment is similar treatment (~sim. ↔ diff.; ~diff. ↔ sim.), there are eight possible protases of similar and differential treatment norms:

(1)   There is no adequate reason for permitting differential treatment
(2)   There is no adequate reason for permitting similar treatment
(3)   There is no adequate reason for commanding similar treatment
(4)   There is no adequate reason for prohibiting similar treatment
(5)   There is an adequate reason for permitting differential treatment
(6)   There is an adequate reason for permitting equal treatment
(7)   There is an adequate reason for commanding equal treatment
(8)   There is an adequate reason for prohibiting equal treatment

A more extensive analysis of the principle of equality than is undertaken here would trace the logical connections between these statements, as well as their connection with all conceivable legal consequences. It is left open at this point whether the eight protases fully describe the field to be analysed. For those who do not accept that the existence (non-existence) of an adequate reason for p is the same as the existence (non-existence) of an adequate reason against ~p, the number of protases to be analysed rises to sixteen. For those who do not accept that similar and differential treatment are contradictory, but think they are simply contraries, the number rises to thirty-two. However many protases one starts with, each can be associated with at least four legal consequences: permission (P), permission not (P~), command (~P~), prohibition (~P) on treating similarly. Many of the combinations can be quickly rejected. But often the decision is not easy, and often the logical relations between the various equality norms are not easy to identify. This is one explanation for the difficulties of analysing the principle of equality.

This formulation differs from the one in (7) in that it demands the success of the justification for differential treatment as a condition of the same,[45] while the similar treatment norm simply requires all the attempts to justify the permissibility of differential treatment to have failed.[46] It is this asymmetry which maintains the burden of argumentation in favour of similar treatment.

The asymmetry between similar and differential treatment norms has the consequence that the general principle of equality is indeed a principle of *equality*, which prima facie requires similar treatment and only permits differential treatment if this can be justified by competing reasons.

V. THE PRINCIPLE OF EQUALITY AND EVALUATION

The interpretation of the principle of equality as a burden of argumentation rule might be able to structure the problem of evaluation, but it cannot resolve it. The question of what counts as an adequate reason for permitting or requiring difference of treatment cannot be answered by the principle of equality as such. This requires further, and evaluative, considerations.[47] It is precisely this point which is relied on by fundamental criticisms of attempts to subject the legislature to the general principle of equality. It is argued that such a subjection leads to the constitutional court imposing its conception of correct, reasonable, and just law-making on the legislature itself, which amounts to a 'displacement of competence to the benefit of the judiciary and at the cost of the legislature in breach of the constitutional system'.[48] However, this objection, which is aimed at preventing the Federal Constitutional Court from becoming a court of pure justice with unlimited jurisdiction by way of the principle of equality, can be answered.

The first point to make is that the general principle of equality is *lex generalis* to various specific equality norms.[49] This leads to a considerable reduction of the problem. The 'substantive equality judgments'[50] expressed in specific norms such as article 3(2) and (3) Basic Law make it unnecessary

---

[45] See e.g. BVerfGE 37, 38 (46).

[46] Thus the scope of the similar treatment norm corresponds to the first combination in the table set out in fn. 44; the scope of the differential treatment norm corresponds to the eighth combination. This presupposes that prohibiting similar treatment is the same as commanding differential treatment (O~sim. ↔ O diff.).

[47] R. Zippelius, *Wertungsprobleme im System der Grundrechte* (Munich, 1962), 33 ff.

[48] Ipsen, 'Gleichheit', 181. See also 156 ff., 178 ff as well as W. Zeidler, 'Die Aktualität des Gleichheitssatzes nach dem BGG', DÖV 1952, 5 f.; F. Klein, 'Zum Begriff und zur Grenze der 'Ungleichheit und Gleichheit im Bonner Grundgesetz', DVBl31 1951, 459; W. Böckenförde, *Der allgemeine Gleichheitssatz und die Aufgabe des Richters* (Berlin, 1957), 88 f.

[49] See e.g. G. Dürig, in T. Maunz and G. Dürig *et al.*, *Grundgesetz Kommentar*, 5th edn. (Munich, 1983), art. 3 para. 248.

[50] See Ipsen, 'Gleichheit', 156.

274 The General Right to Equality

in the many cases covered by them to solve the evaluative problem in the context of the general principle of equality.

Furthermore, the general principle of equality, as interpreted in the weak sense defended here, leaves the legislature with a wide discretion. The argument that it puts the Court in the place of the legislature must be coupled with considerable caveats. The discretion of the legislature, repeatedly emphasized by the Federal Constitutional Court,[51] arises from two elements, the structure of the similar and differential treatment norms, and the concept of arbitrariness.

Where there are adequate reasons for differential treatment under (7), similar treatment is not required. But under these circumstances nor is differential treatment, since according to (9) this presupposes not merely adequate reasons for permitting it, but adequate reasons for requiring it. If there are cases in which there are adequate reasons for permitting differential treatment, but not for requiring it, then neither similar nor differential treatment is required, which means that both are permitted, which means that the legislature has a discretion.

Ensuring that there are cases in which there are adequate reasons for permitting but not requiring differential treatment is the function of interpreting the idea of an adequate reason by using the idea of arbitrariness. A reason is adequate for permitting differential treatment, if differential treatment on the basis of this reason is not arbitrary. Arbitrariness is, as Leibholz points out, a strengthened form of incorrectness.[52] An instance of differential treatment is not only not arbitrary if it is the best or most just solution, but already if there are only plausible reasons for it. The fact that there is a difference between a plausible reason and the best reason is shown by the Court's willingness to hold that the better argument is against differential treatment but still to accept that there are plausible grounds for it. A plausible reason for permitting differential treatment is, however, not an adequate reason for requiring it. So, the fact that an instance of differential treatment is not arbitary does not mean that similar treatment would be arbitrary. All this does not tell us at what point the legislature has a discretion; it simply establishes that there is a discretion.

So it cannot be argued against subjecting the legislature to the principle of equality that it leads to an uncontrolled jurisdiction on the part of the Federal Constitutional Court to impose its values without limit on the legislature. All that can be said is that the general principle of equality gives the Court a certain jurisdiction to set limits to the competence of the legislature. This means that some value-judgments of the Court take precedence over those of the legislature, but this is unobjectionable.

Every control of a legislature by a constitutional court means that to a

[51] See e.g. BVerfGE 9, 334 (337); 57, 107 (115).
[52] Leibholz, *Die Gleichheit vor dem Gesetz*, 76 f.: 'quantitative difference'.

certain extent evaluative judgments by the court will take precedence over those of the legislature. In many cases, the requirements of constitutional norms do not follow logically from the text of the constitution alone, nor can they necessarily be established by way of canons of interpretation and other relevant legal data. The maxim that every interpretation of the constitution incorporates the evaluative judgment of the interpreter is as trivial as it is basic. Unless one wants to give up constitutional adjudication altogether along with legislative subordination to the principle of equality, it is no use appealing to the fact that its application presupposes evaluative judgments to establish that the Court's jurisdiction is being unjustifiably extended. What one has to demonstrate is that the application of the general principle of equality incorporates such a high degree of subjective, uncontrollable evaluative judgments, that as regards its application to the legislature it must be treated differently from other constitutional rights norms.[53] But there is no basis for this. Fundamental problems of evaluation need resolving in the application of all constitutional rights norms. In interpreting these as well, the Court has the possibility of ensuring that the discretion granted to the legislature by the Basic Law is not unjustifiably limited.

Of course, one could attempt to reduce the danger that the constitutional court might unjustifiably limit the competence of the legislature further still by removing the reviewable subordination of the legislature to certain constitutional rights norms such as article 3(1) Basic Law. But the price for doing this is too high. Not all possible discrimination is covered by specific equality norms by a long way. The possibility can never be ruled out that a parliamentary majority may discriminate in a way not covered by specific equality norms and which from the perspective of constitutional law is illegal. Not extending constitutional protection to such discrimination would be justified if judgments about their constitutional permissibility or impermissibility were necessarily purely subjective. But this is not the case. Even without going into the theory of rational legal justification,[54] one can say that there is a whole range of possibilities for rationally justifying constitutional judgments of equality and inequality.[55] Consider the possibility, for instance, of relating the necessary value-judgments to other constitutional norms (systematic arguments)[56] and the ever-increasing possibilities of argument on the basis of precedent, along with the use of ideas such as systemic justice.[57]

---

[53] In this sense, see e.g. Ipsen, 'Gleichheit', 178.
[54] See on this Alexy, *A Theory of Legal Argumentation*, 221 ff.
[55] Generally on the reliability of constitutional rights justification, see below at 369 ff.
[56] See on this Starck, 'Die Anwendung des Gleichheitssatzes', 64 ff.
[57] See C. Degenhart, *Systemgerechtigkeit und Selbstbindung des Gesetzgebers als Verfassungspostulat* (Munich, 1976).

VI. LEGAL AND FACTUAL EQUALITY

Until this point we have been concerned primarily with the preconditions for commanding, prohibiting, or permitting similar and differential treatment. The question of what counts as similar and differential treatment has hardly been considered. There are many reasons for turning to this problem, because it leads to the question of whether the formula 'treat the same similarly and differences differently' imposes obligations on the state to achieve factual equality or not.

1. THE CONCEPTS OF LEGAL AND FACTUAL EQUALITY

The concepts of similar and differential treatment are ambiguous in a very basic way. They can be related both to acts and consequences. The act-related meaning is concerned merely with the evaluation of state action itself. By contrast, the consequence-related meaning is concerned with the factual consequences of state action. The case-law of the Federal Constitutional Court on legal aid is useful in clarifying this distinction. An early decision was concerned with whether the refusal of legal aid for a certain legal procedure in spite of a requirement for legal representation breached article 3(1) Basic Law.[58] According to the act-related version of the idea of treatment, both the well-off and the poor were treated similarly, because the advantages of legal aid were denied to both. We can say, in common with a widespread usage, that both groups were legally treated equally. But in the consequence-related version of treatment, well-off and poor were not treated similarly but differently, because the non-granting of legal aid prevented the poor, but not the well-off, from 'pursuing their legal remedies, merely because they cannot afford to do so'.[59] Again, in common with widespread usage, we can say that they were *in fact* treated unequally. On the basis of the factually differential treatment, the Federal Constitutional Court held that the requirement to 'treat the same similarly' had been breached, and justified this in a way which was entirely consistent with what has been said above, by holding that no adequate reason justified the (factually) differential treatment.[60] The distinction between legal and factual similarity and difference can be considerably refined, but what has been said will suffice for present purposes.

2. THE PRINCIPLES OF LEGAL AND FACTUAL EQUALITY

That legal aid decision, which was followed by many others[61] and which is structurally similar to decisions concerning the equality of opportunity of

---

[58] BVerfGE 2, 336.   [59] BVerfGE 2, 336 (340).   [60] ibid
[61] See the references in BVerfGE 56, 139 (143 ff.).

political parties,[62] reveals a basic problem for the interpretation of the general principle of equality as a requirement to promote factual equality. The Federal Constitutional Court puts it like this: 'to support some groups means treating others differently'.[63] Those who want to create factual equality must reckon with legal inequality.[64] On the other hand, the variety of human beings in fact means that legal equality always leaves some factual inequalities unaffected, and indeed often strengthens them.[65] If one derives from article 3(1) both a principle of legal equality and a principle of factual equality, then in the context of the principle of equality alone, one has created a fundamental conflict. What is equal treatment according to one principle is unequal treatment according to the other, and vice versa. If one combines both principles into a super-principle of equality, then we can say that this wide principle contains an equality-paradox. Those who want to work with such a wide principle not only have to deal with the much-disputed problem of the relationship between liberty and equality,[66] they also have to resolve a significant proportion of the problems raised by equality within the context of that principle alone.

The paradox of equality could easily be avoided if one could dispense entirely with either of the principles of legal or factual equality. Doing without the principle of legal equality has to be excluded on the basis of existing constitutional law, because there can be no doubt that it is part of currently valid law. If there are any doubts about this, they can be laid to rest by a glance at the case-law of the Federal Constitutional Court. In addition to

---

[62] See e.g. BVerfGE 8, 51 (64 ff.).   [63] BVerfGE 12, 354 (367).

[64] More precisely: legally differential treatment in the act-related sense.

[65] See Hesse, 'Der Gleichheitsgrundsatz im Staatsrecht', 180. The proposition that legal equality always leaves some factual inequalities in place, and often reinforces them, on account of the factual variety of human beings is consistent with the proposition that legal equality can bring about factual equality, that is, that the creation of legal equality can have factual equality as its consequence. As in all judgments of equality, one must not lose sight of the connection with individual persons and individual aspects of equality. Thus the repeal of class privileges led to an increase in factual equality in respect of some persons and some aspects. At the same time, the creation of civic equality has left factual inequalities in respect of some persons and some aspects in place, and has often reinforced them.

[66] A consideration of this much discussed problem will be avoided here. Comments on the general rights to liberty and equality, as well as the discussion of the theory of principles and modalities, point the way to a possible solution: one has to distinguish carefully between various conceivable liberty and equality norms, and the legal positions and factual situations in which members of society are placed by these norms. The outcome of such an analysis is that 'liberty' and 'equality' are to be understood in part as things necessarily connected, in part as things in conflict, and in part as things simply compatible with each other. From the unending literature, which has emphasized the complexity of the subject-matter, reference will only be made here to the contributions of D. D. Raphael ('Tensions between the Goals of Equality and Freedom'), R. Walter ('Das Spannungsverhältnis der sozialen Ziele Freiheit und Gleichheit'), S. S. Nagel ('Issues regarding Tensions between Goals of Equality and Freedom'), and O. Weinberger ('Gleichheit und Freiheit: Komplementäre oder widerstreitende Ideale'), all in G. Dorsey (ed.), *Equality and Freedom*, ii (New York and Leiden, 1977), 543 ff., 583 ff., 603 ff., 641 ff., and M. Kriele, *Befreiung und politische Aufklärung* (Freiburg, Basel, and Vienna, 1980), 57 ff.

this precedential argument, there are general practical ones. Legal equality is a value in itself. Given two states of affairs identical in every respect except that in the first there is an instance of legal inequality absent in the second, the second is preferable. In this respect there is a certain parallelism between legal equality and negative liberty. Another point is that, as has been suggested above,[67] the burden of argumentation for differential treatment is a basic requirement of practical reason. At the very least, this requirement applies for differential treatment in the act-related sense. Finally, there is what is only superficially a purely pragmatic argument. Since the principle of legal equality only considers the act of treatment itself and not the many consequences of the act, it is far easier to apply, and with more confidence, than factual equality. A father who gives his two children the same type of ball fully satisfies act-related equality without much thought and with certainty. Whether he thereby brings about a degree of consequence-related equality is by contrast very uncertain and difficult to judge. If one child is pleased with the gift and the other disappointed, then there is no consequence-related equality, at least in respect of equal pleasure. Now the criterion of equal pleasure is one of the most unsure criteria of factual equality. But it reveals a key problem with the promotion of factual equality, which is that the decision-taker can only partially oversee and control the process of promoting equality. In the light of all this, it should be clear that the principle of legal equality cannot simply be abandoned in favour of a principle of factual equality.

3. ON THE ROLE OF THE PRINCIPLE OF FACTUAL EQUALITY

If we want to avoid a conflict of principles within article 3(1) Basic Law, the only alternative is to abandon the idea that the principle of factual equality is a legally binding and fully enforceable subjective right arising from article 3(1). To do this, the principle need not be excluded from the legal system entirely. It could be treated as an unenforceable norm which nevertheless binds the legislature, either derived from article 3(1) or from the social state clause of article 20(1) Basic Law. Even on this interpretation it can still have some connection with subjective rights, not as a norm giving rise to subjective rights, but as one which justifies the limitation of other rights. But these are secondary matters. The first question is whether the principle of factual equality derived from article 3(1) Basic Law can or must be abandoned as a principle which essentially gives rise to subjective rights and which can be enforced by a constitutional court.

Opinions are divided on this point,[68] and the case-law of the Federal

[67] 270 ff.

[68] For a rejection of an interpretation of art. 3(1) Basic Law as (in addition) a principle of factual equality, see Starck, 'Die Anwendung des Gleichheitssatzes', 55 ff., 67 ff.; Podlech, *Gehalt und Funktionen*, 200 ff.; V. Götz, *Recht der Wirtschaftssubventionen* (Munich and

Constitutional Court is ambiguous. On one hand, it has been said that the principle of equality does not require the legislature to 'enact laws preventing different situations which correspond to existing inequalities from resulting in different legal consequences'.[69] On the other hand, it has been said in the context of article 3(1) Basic Law, that 'the legislature may not simply satisfy itself by accepting pre-existing factual differences; if they are incompatible with the requirements of justice, they must be removed'.[70] That second quotation can be understood in the same way as the sentence often cited from the German Communist Party Judgment, which holds that the social state principle requires, 'equality to be progressively realized to the extent rationally required'.[71]

Scholler has remarked that the 'particularization of the principle of equality . . . is dependent on one's concept and view of the state'.[72] But concepts and views of the state are always more or less developed legal and political philosophies. So one might as well say, as Dreier does, that one's choice of interpretation of the principle of equality depends on one's legal and political philosophy.[73] This is actually true in the case of every constitutional rights provision, but it is more significant in the case of the principle of equality, because the questions in legal and political philosophy associated with equality are particularly controversial. It is not only the correct content of the requirements of equality which is controversial, but also whether questions of equality are amenable to rationally justifiable answers at all, or whether the dispute about equality is not rather a non-rational conflict of ideologies and world-views. So it seems as if the question of whether article 3(1) Basic Law is to be taken as including a principle of factual equality can only be adequately answered in the context of a thoroughgoing legal, political, and epistemological discussion.

However, to follow this conclusion, and to engage in a discussion of basic normative and epistemological questions, would be premature. It would ignore one possible solution which requires much less effort, and which has a much greater chance of success than a direct engagement with fundamental issues: the solution of a doctrinal analysis based on the theory of norms. Such an analysis shows that there is a solution which takes

Berlin, 1966), 263; more or less clearly in favour, by contrast, Hesse, 'Der Gleichheitsgrundsatz im Staatsrecht', 180 ff., 213 ff.; id., contribution to discussion in Link, *Der Gleichheitssatz im modernen Verfassungsstaat* 78; H. F. Zacher, 'Soziale Gleichheit', AöR 93 (1968), 341 ff.; H. Scholler, *Die Interpretation des Gleichheitssatzes als Willkürverbot oder als Gebot der Chancengleichhei*, (Berlin, 1969), 14 ff.; P. Häberle, contribution to discussion in Link, *Der Gleichheitssatz im modernen Verfassungsstaat*, 84, 105.

[69] BVerfGE 9, 237 (244) (emphasis added); see also BVerfGE 4, 193 (203).
[70] BVerfGE 3, 58 (158).   [71] BVerfGE 5, 85 (206).
[72] Scholler, *Die Interpretation des Gleichheitssatzes*, 13.
[73] R. Dreier, 'Zur Problematik und Situation der Verfassungsinterpretation', in id., *Recht—Moral—Ideologie* (Frankfurt a. M., 1981), 114. Dreier makes this point in connection with the choice of theories of interpretation.

account both of legal and factual equality, and which at the same time leaves space for a wide spectrum of views about the relative weight of the two principles. It will be seen that this model is sufficient to resolve the relevant problems. First the model will be explained; then certain objections to deriving a principle of factual equality from article 3(1) Basic Law will be discussed.

The basis of the model is the classic statement, 'treat the same similarly, and differences differently'. As explained above, the first half is to be expanded into the similar treatment norm:

(7)   If there is no adequate reason for permitting differential treatment, then similar treatment is required,

and the second half into the differential treatment norm:

(9)   If there is an adequate reason for requiring differential treatment, then differential treatment is required.[74]

The decisive step is to understand the idea of treatment in both cases in the act-related sense. Thus both norms apply directly only to legal equality. Taken together they express a basic preference for legal equality. The second step in our model is to take account of the principle of factual equality within the concept of an adequate reason in both norms. It can be an adequate reason for permitting differential treatment, and even an adequate reason for requiring differential treatment. In the first case, it is the reason for a definitive no-right[75] to a certain instance of legal similarity of treatment, and in the second case it is the reason for a definitive right to a certain instance of legal difference of treatment, which serves the promotion of factual equality. The first case is familiar. Here, the principle of factual equality plays the role of a justified limit to the general right to legal equality—often in the name of the 'social state principle'.[76] The second case is more interesting. Here, the principle of factual equality plays the role of a reason for a right to a certain instance of legal difference, in particular a legal difference that serves the promotion of factual equality. It gives rise to a subjective right to the promotion of an element of factual equality.

That last point is the critical one. In order to evaluate it properly, it is absolutely essential to remember what it means for factual equality to be the subject-matter of a principle. As has been pointed out,[77] principles are not definitive but prima facie reasons. In a concrete case they can be trumped by competing principles. The principle of factual equality is only an adequate reason for a definitive subjective right to an instance of legal difference of treatment serving the promotion of factual equality if it trumps all other relevant competing principles. A whole range of competing principles will need

---

[74] See above at 270 ff.
[75] On the concept of a no-right, see above at 132 ff.
[76] See e.g. BVerfGE 29, 402 (412).
[77] 57 ff.

consideration. One which is always relevant is legal equality, because each legal difference of treatment in pursuit of factual equality is by definition a limitation of the realization of the principle of legal equality.[78] Furthermore, those principles concerned with the division of competence between constitutional court and legislature will also always be relevant. In accepting the existence of a right to factual equality, a constitutional court severely limits the discretion of the legislature, not simply because it no longer has the freedom to grant the right in question or not, but because the existence of such rights regularly implies a requirement on the legislature to provide significant financial means, which removes the possibility of funding many other projects instead. The formal principle of the discretion of the democratically legitimated legislature in structuring society is thus the second main counter-principle to the principle of factual equality. In addition to these two, which are always relevant, there are many other principles which can compete with factual equality, not least those relating to negative liberties. This should make it clear that including the principle of factual equality as a potentially adequate ground for requiring a certain instance of legal difference, which promotes factual equality, implies neither that legal equality and negative liberty are unjustifiably suppressed by factual equality nor that the competence to structure the social order gets transferred from the legislature to the court to an impermissible extent. Rather, a model has been created which allows us to include factual equality within article 3(1) Basic Law, and thus to treat that provision as the expression of a broad concept of equality, without prejudging the issue of the correct conception of equality. The norm-theoretical and methodological key to all this is the theory of principles.

One could object to this model on the grounds that it is practically irrelevant and just an intellectual exercise, since the competing principles, above all the freedom of the legislature in structuring society, are so strong in all conceivable cases, that the case for a definitive concrete right to the promotion of factual equality recognized by the Federal Constitutional Court directly on the basis of article 3(1) always fails. This would show that the principle of factual equality could not be derived from article 3(1) as a constitutional rights principle in the full sense of the word, because in order to be such, it must be capable, in at least one case, of giving rise to a definitive concrete right.

This objection is based mainly on formal principles. The main argument against directly derived, that is, original,[79] rights to factual equality is that

---

[78] The Federal Constitutional Court has this conflict in mind when it states that 'even the social state principle does not authorize every form of social engineering, which would destroy the requirement of equality' (BVerfGE 12, 354 (367)).

[79] The counterpart to original rights to factual equality are derivative rights, which are associated with a prior guaranteeing act of the state (see W. Martens, 'Grundrechte im Leistungsstaat', VVDStRL 30 (1972), 21 ff.). In the case of derivative rights, the only question which arises is one of legal equality.

the idea of factual equality is far too uncertain a basis for the judicial recognition of concrete rights.[80] The court would be drawn into non-justiciable questions of social policy and it would thereby necessarily exceed its jurisdiction. Interference with the competence of the legislature would be that much more serious if the case-law on factual equality interfered not only with the legal discretion but also directly with the financial discretion of the legislature.

There is something in these arguments. The concept of factual equality is particularly open to interpretation. This is because judgments of factual equality and inequality can be based on a great variety of criteria. Examples include money, education, political influence, capacity for self-determination, fostering of talents, social recognition, chances of entry into different social spheres, self-respect, the realization of life plans, and contentment.[81] It is clear that there are numerous incompatible theories of factual equality. But every theory of factual equality is, among other things, a programme for the distribution of socially distributable goods. It is not only methodological reasons which make it impossible to derive just one programme of distribution from the Basic Law; there are also ones stemming from the constitutional system. Issues of distribution are a central subject-matter of dispute between the parties competing for a parliamentary majority. This makes it impossible for a constitution which has opted for parliamentary democracy to be based upon one all-inclusive basic theory of factual equality, to which any distributive decision of Parliament could either only correspond or not as the case may be.

But this only addresses one side of the argument. The other side is that we are concerned with the existence of rights, and that the mere fact that their recognition is uncertain, and that their enforcement by a constitutional court excludes a certain discretion on the part of the legislature, is not a sufficient argument against their existence. It is precisely the point of constitutional rights not to leave certain individual positions at the mercy of the legislature; they are meant to limit the discretion of the legislature, and it is characteristic of constitutional rights that their precise content can be controversial. If one takes the view that it is not impossible to resolve this controversy by rational means, and if one is not going to let the parliamentary majority determine the scope of its own discretion, which would contravene the maxim that no one should be a judge in his own cause, then

---

[80] See Starck, 'Die Anwendung des Gleichheitssatzes', 68; Podlech, *Gehalt und Funktionen*, 202 ff.

[81] On a more abstract level, these criteria can be divided into 'equality of welfare' and 'equality of resources', as Dworkin suggests. The first would obtain if resources (such as money) were so distributed that no redistribution would achieve a higher degree of equal welfare (e.g. contentment). The second would obtain if resources were so distributed that no redistribution would achieve a higher degree of equality of resources (R. Dworkin, 'What is Equality?' in *Philosophy and Public Affairs*, 10 (1981), 186 ff.).

the only alternative is to let the constitutional court decide.[82] So the real question is this: do the special features of factual equality, the particularly high degree of uncertainty in its application (variety of theories of distribution), and the particularly severe limitation of legislative discretion (financial means), give to the principle of the freedom of the legislature to structure society such weight, that the adoption of a concrete right to factual equality under the control of the constitutional court must necessarily be excluded? This way of putting the question itself makes it clear that it is not a matter of the constitutional court imposing its theory of distribution on the legislature. Rather, it is a question of whether the freedom of the legislature to structure society can in some cases be limited from the perspective of factual equality. At this point, it is important to recall the asymmetry between legal and factual equality in the model of the general principle of equality. There is a burden of argumentation in favour of legal equality; there is none in favour of factual equality. A differentiation in pursuit of factual equality is only required, if sufficient reasons can be put forward for such a requirement.

Examples of cases in which the principle of factual equality takes priority over competing principles can be found in the decisions of the constitutional court concerning legal aid discussed above. One could object that these cases do not tell us much, because they display peculiarities which make a generalization impossible. It has been pointed out that in these cases the guarantee of access to the courts in article 19(4) Basic Law is an additional guiding concern,[83] and that questions of equality here are capable of judicial determination, unlike other cases of factual equality.[84] It has been pointed out above that one of the main problems with factual equality is the respect in which factual equality should be achieved. That the principle of access to justice in the legal aid cases is combined with the principle of factual equality means that the respect in which factual equality should be achieved has been determined. But this does not stop the legal aid cases being cases of factual equality, and it tells us nothing about whether the constitution might not in other respects require the promotion of factual equality as well. It is, of course, true that the legal aid cases were relatively strightforward, which is what turns them into relatively certain cases of the

[82] See R. Dworkin, *Taking Rights Seriously*, 2nd edn. (London, 1978), 140 ff., as well as Zacher, 'Soziale Gleichheit', 359, who emphasizes in connection with the principle of equality the 'classic function of constitutional rights in a democracy' of the protection of minorities. Similarly also H. P. Schneider, contribution to discussion in Link, *Der Gleichheitssatz im modernen Verfassungsstaat*, 86 f.

[83] Starck, 'Die Anwendung des Gleichheitssatzes', 68, n. 84. Starck suggests quite generally that the principle of equality should be substantively determined with the help of the 'prohibitions and commands to differentiate directly or indirectly expressed in the Basic Law' (ibid. 64). One can agree with this. The problem is the extent to which sufficiently precise standards can be extracted from the Basic Law for this purpose with adequate certainty.

[84] Podlech, *Gehalt und Funktionen*, 220 ff.

priority of the principle of factual equality. But this does not exclude that principle's application in other cases either. All this tells us that the legal aid cases may not be very suitable as an inductive basis for other situations, but that they must still be seen as instances of the application of the principle of factual equality and that their special features do not exclude the application of the principle in other cases.

Like all negatives, the thesis that there are no further cases in which the principle of factual equality takes precedence over all other principles is hard to prove. The argument that in the light of the present state of legislation there is no situation in which the Federal Constitutional Court would need to find an original right to factual equality is insufficient, because the state of legislation can change, and the Constitution does not just apply to the present. Since it is not possible to consider all possible cases, the thesis that there are no further cases can only be considered a presumption which will be rebutted the moment a case arises in which the principle of factual equality is relevant and takes precedence.

It is possible that the case of the existential minimum is such a case.[85] What belongs to the constitutionally guaranteed existential minimum can hardly be determined without comparisons. The absolute existential minimum can, as a glance at history and other countries shows, be extremely low. What the Basic Law is concerned with is the relative existential minimum, relative, that is, to the conditions currently obtaining in Germany. Simply to accept whatever level the legislature has adopted is to abandon any attempt to determine a constitutional standard for what it is the legislature has to adopt. In such cases, the concept of human dignity hardly provides us with a rationally controllable standard at a constitutional level, but the principle of factual equality does. It requires an orientation towards the current real standard of living, but may be outweighed by other competing principles. Of course, this turns the whole question into one of balancing principles, but there is nothing odd about this in the context of constitutional rights, and, in addition, balancing can be carried out in a rational way. The principle of equality, which includes factual equality, is capable of giving rise to concrete definitive rights to the promotion of factual equality in cases concerning the existential minimum.[86]

It could be objected that this example shows precisely that factual equality is better located within the social state principle rather than the general principle of equality. It is true that the principle of factual equality can also be seen as a sub-principle of the social state principle. But the decisive point is that the social state clause, unlike the equality principle, is not a constitutional rights provision. If factual equality were derived from the social

---

[85] See on this, from an entitlement perspective, below at 290 f.

[86] Only the principle of factual equality is to be considered at this point. The discussion of social constitutional rights will show that this principle can work together with the principle of factual liberty; see below at 340, 343.

state principle alone, there would no longer be the possibility of constitutional rights-based argument or any concrete subjective right, however limited, to factual equality. As has been shown, there is no cause to abandon this possibility. Quite the contrary.

If one adopts the model suggested here, then it is possible on one hand to respect the division of competence between legislature and judiciary presupposed by the Basic Law along with the many principles which conflict with factual equality (in particular legal equality and negative liberty), and on the other hand to protect a concrete definitive right to the promotion of certain instances of factual equality in cases in which the principle of factual equality is so important that it outweighs all other competing principles. All this leads to a model which is coherent, relatively straightforward, and which remains open to a wide range of evaluative judgments.

VII. THE STRUCTURE OF EQUALITY RIGHTS AS SUBJECTIVE RIGHTS

According to Leibholz, subjective rights which arise from the general principle of equality are, like defensive rights, rights to omissions, that is, 'rights to the non-performance of illegal disruptions of legal equality'.[87] The general principle of equality thus has a negative character.[88] It is easy to object to this mirroring of equality and liberty rights by pointing out that the principle of equality includes rights which have to be treated as belonging to the positive status. An example is the decision on housing support for welfare recipients.[89] This gives rise to the need to consider the structure of subjective rights to equality.

There are three types of right which can arise from the general principle of equality: abstract definitive equality rights, concrete definitive equality rights, and abstract prima facie equality rights.

There are two abstract definitive equality rights: the right to be treated similarly, if there is no adequate reason for permitting differential treatment, and the right to be treated differentially, if there is an adequate reason for requiring this. Both rights correspond to the similar and differential treatment norms derived above:[90]

(7) If there is no adequate reason for permitting differential treatment, then similar treatment is required;

---

[87] Leibholz, *Die Gleichheit vor dem Gesetz*, 235.
[88] ibid. 118.
[89] BVerfGE 27, 220 (230).
[90] 270, 272.

(9)   If there is an adequate reason for requiring differential treatment, then differential treatment is required.[91]

In detail, these abstract rights lead to a great variety of concrete rights. Nevertheless, they can always be formulated in terms of defensive rights. The first corresponds to a state duty to refrain from certain instances of differential treatment, the second corresponds to a state duty to refrain from certain instances of similar treatment. Leibholz's mirroring thesis applies to these, but only to these, formulations. But a closer examination of what exactly lies behind these formulations forces us to abandon his thesis.

This is clearest in the case of concrete definitive equality rights. The right to 'refrain from differential treatment' can embrace concrete equality rights

---

[91] The formulation of these norms does not show a distinction between scope (in the narrow sense) and limiting clause. The question is whether a construction is possible which does this. Only the similar treatment norm (7) will be considered here. To get to a norm which distinguishes between scope (S) and limiting clause (L) as positive and negative conditions of the legal consequence Q, that is, which follows the scheme $S \wedge \sim L \rightarrow Q$, the following reformulation of (7) seems appropriate: if a state measure M is a differential treatment, and if there is no adequate reason for permitting differential treatment, then the carrying out of M is prohibited. The scope of this norm is extremely wide. It embraces every legal differentiation, and thus nearly every state measure. But this is no disadvantage. If the general principle of equality is to be a standard against which all state activity can be measured with reference to all comparative pairs, this width, which corresponds to the scope of the general right to liberty (see above at 226 ff.) and which matches the wide theory of scope (see above at 210 ff.) is unavoidable. The heart of the limiting clause is the concept of an adequate reason. A great variety of arguments can be given to show that something has the characteristic of being an adequate reason for a differentiation or not. These arguments can be structured within the framework of the model of principles, which implies the principle of proportionality, as shown above (66 ff.). That differentiation D is a means for reaching end E is a reason for D. To qualify this as an inadequate reason, it can be shown (1) that D is not suitable for reaching E, (2) that D is not necessary for reaching E, or (3) that while D is suitable and necessary for reaching E, and that while reaching E serves the realization of principle P_1, which collides with legal equality, the principles $P_2, \ldots, P_n$ in respect of D and E, which include the principle of legal equality, take precedence over principle P_1 (proportionality in the narrow sense). The principle of legislative discretion must be taken account of in this balancing exercise.

Problems of the application of the similar treatment norm in the context of the limiting clause are to be resolved according to this construction. Kloepfer has proposed a quite different construction. According to this, the scope does not consist simply of differential treatment, but differential treatment of what is substantially the same. The limiting clause comprises a reservation in favour of legislative discretion. Thus the prohibition on arbitrariness together with the principle of proportionality are located in a limit-limiting clause (M. Kloepfer, *Gleichheit als Verfassungsfrage* (Berlin, 1980), 54 ff.). There are some objections to this construction. The first problem is the use of the concept of *substantial* equality in the scope. As was shown above, substantial equality can only be sensibly understood as evaluative equality. But evaluative equality always requires similar treatment, so that limits and the limits to limits become superfluous. It also seems inappropriate to relate the limit simply to the formal principle of legislative discretion. Legislative discretion as such is never an adequate reason for differentiation. A reason based on a substantive principle must always be added to the formal principle of legislative discretion. Substantive aspects should therefore not be removed from the limiting clause and placed in a limit-limiting clause. Rather, they should appear in the limiting clause. The 'impenetrable mess of subsuming' which Kloepfer fears (ibid. 56) can be avoided if, as has been shown above, one structures the arguments for and against the existence of an adequate reason.

pertaining to the negative, the positive, and also the active status. If someone is affected by a prohibition which discriminates against him, then he
might have a concrete definitive right based on the principle of equality that
the state refrain from the interference. In other words, a negative status
right.[92] In this case, 'refraining from discrimination' is a negative act. By
contrast, if someone fails to receive a benefit in a discriminatory way, then
he might have a concrete definitive right based on the principle of equality
to the benefit. In other words, he has a positive status right.[93] In this case
'refraining from discrimination' amounts to a positive act. And if someone
is discriminated against by being denied a power to participate in the
process of state decision-taking, then he might have a concrete right based
on the principle of equality within the active status. The fact that the victim
of discrimination only 'might have' these rights is a consequence of the fact
that a breach of the abstract right to equality can often be remedied in many
different ways. The choice between not carrying out the discriminatory
interference or extending it to all substantially identical legal persons, of
which the first alternative is an omission and the second a positive act, is
one example. It is not necessary here to consider where rights to the performance of one of these alternatives are to be located within the status
theory.[94] It is sufficient to establish that the case-law of the Federal
Constitutional Court shows that there are at least some cases in which the
general principle of equality gives rise to rights which are not part of the
negative status.

The picture becomes even clearer if one considers abstract prima facie
rights, of which there are two, just as with abstract definitive rights. The
first corresponds to the principle of legal equality, the second to the principle of factual equality. The prima facie right to legal equality can be seen as
a prima facie right to the omission of differential treatment; by contrast, the
prima facie right to factual equality is a prima facie right to positive acts of
the state.

Many more clarifications and distinctions are possible. These brief
comments should be sufficient to make the point: it is not good enough to
interpret article 3(1) Basic Law in the sense of a negative status right.
Rather, this constitutional provision contains a bundle of subjective rights
which have great structural variety. It is only this bundle of rights which
defines the complete constitutional right in article 3(1).[95]

---

[92] See e.g. BVerfGE 21, 292 (301 ff.).
[93] See e.g. BVerfGE 27, 220 (230).
[94] See on this M. Sachs, 'Zur dogmatischen Struktur der Gleichheitsrechte als
Abwehrrechte', DÖV 1984, 414 ff.
[95] On the concept of a complete constitutional right, see above at 159 ff.

9

Rights to Positive State Action (Entitlements in the Wide Sense)

I. BASIC TERMS AND CONCEPTS

According to the classic liberal understanding,[1] constitutional rights 'are designed in the first instance to secure a sphere of liberty for the individual from interferences by public power; they are defensive rights of the citizen against the state'.[2] Defensive rights of the citizen against the state are rights to *negative* actions (omissions) on the part of the state.[3] They belong to the citizen's negative status, and indeed to the negative status in its wide sense.[4] Their counterparts are rights to *positive* state action, which belong to the positive status, and to the positive status in its narrow sense.[5] If one adopts a wide understanding of the notion of entitlement, all rights to positive state action can be called entitlements in the wide sense. The question of whether and to what extent norms guaranteeing entitlements in the wide sense can be derived from constitutional rights provisions[6] is one of the most controversial questions of more recent constitutional doctrine. So-called social constitutional rights, that is, rights such as those to welfare, work, accommodation, and education, have been particularly hotly disputed. It will be seen that while these rights are an important part of all 'entitlements', they do not occupy the whole field of potential entitlements.

1. CONSTITUTIONAL TEXT AND LEGISLATIVE HISTORY

The Basic Law is very cautious in formulating entitlements. To this extent it is significantly different from a whole series of regional constitutions, which alongside the classic defensive rights guarantee rights such as the right to work,[7] to accommodation,[8] to minimum support in case

---

[1] See on this C. Schmitt, *Verfassungslehre*, 5th edn. (Berlin, 1970), 163 ff.
[2] BVerfGE 7, 198 (204).   [3] See above at 122 ff.
[4] On this qualification, see above at 171.   [5] See above at 171.
[6] On the concept of derivation, see above at 35 ff.
[7] Art. 166 Constitution of Bavaria; art. 12 Constitution of Berlin; art. 8 Constitution of Bremen, art. 28 Constitution of Hesse; art. 24 Constitution of Northrhine-Westphalia; art. 53 Constitution of Rhineland-Palatinate; art. 45 Constitution of Saarland.
[8] Art. 106 Constitution of Bavaria; art. 19 Constitution of Berlin; art. 14 Constitution of Bremen.

of need,[9] to education,[10] and to participation.[11] [12] It also differs from the constitutions of many other states.[13] If one is guided solely by the text of the Basic Law, the only express formulation of a social constitutional right in the sense of a *subjective* entitlement is the right of mothers to the protection and support of society (art. 6(4) Basic Law).[14] An interpretation of the constitutional rights of the Basic Law which wants to find subjective entitlements guaranteed at constitutional level is thus forced to derive the appropriate norms from provisions which do not expressly guarantee the subjective entitlements one is looking for.

The fact that the constitution-makers deliberately refrained from incorporating norms protecting subjective entitlements[15] is of course only one side of the matter. The other is that the Basic Law contains a whole row of *objectively* expressed starting-points for an entitlements-oriented interpretation. The most obvious provisions are the 'duty of all state power to protect' human dignity (art. 1(1)(2) Basic Law) and the social state clause (art. 20(1) and 28(1)(1) Basic Law). It is also worth mentioning the guarantee of protection for marriage and the family (art. 6(1) Basic Law) as well as the constitutional mandate to bring about the equal status of illegitimate children (art. 6(5) Basic Law). But the existence of these provisions, like the existence of the general principle of equality, which can justify the recognition of derivative entitlements, and which can be understood in the sense of a principle of factual equality capable of giving rise to completely new entitlements,[16] should not detract from the fact that as regards its *text* and *legislative history*, the Basic Law is primarily oriented towards defensive rights in the traditional civic-Rule of Law conception.

---

[9] Art. 168 Constitution of Bavaria; art. 14 Constitution of Berlin; art. 58 Constitution of Bremen; art. 28 Constitution of Hesse.

[10] Art. 11 Constitution of Baden-Württemberg; art. 128 Constitution of Bavaria; art. 27 Constitution of Bremen; art. 8 Constitution of Northrhine-Westphalia.

[11] Art. 175 Constitution of Bavaria; art. 17 Constitution of Berlin; art. 47 Constitution of Bremen, art. 37 Constitution of Hesse; art. 26 Constitution of Northrhine-Westphalia; art. 67 Constitution of Rhineland-Palatinate.

[12] See on this H. F. Zacher, *Sozialpolitik und Menschenrechte in der Bundesrepublik Deutschland* (Munich and Vienna, 1968), 11 ff.

[13] Catalogues of rights to positive state acts can be found both in the constitutions of western industrialized states (see the Constitution of the Republic of Italy of 27 Dec. 1947), in the constitutions of socialist states (see the Constitution of the GDR of 6 Apr. 1968), and in the constitutions of Third World states (see the Indian Constitution of 26 Nov. 1949, reprinted in JöR NF 4 (1955), 183–254).

[14] See BVerfGE 55, 154 (157 f.).

[15] See JöR NF 1 (1951), 54 ff., 94; H. v. Mangoldt, 'Grundrechte und Grundsatzfragen des Bonner Grundgesetzes', AöR 75 (1949), 275 f.; W. Weber, 'Die verfassungsrechtlichen Grenzen sozialstaatlicher Forderungen', *Der Staat*, 4 (1965), 411 ff.

[16] See above at 279 ff.

2. THE CASE-LAW OF THE FEDERAL CONSTITUTIONAL COURT

This has not hindered the debate about entitlements under the Basic Law, and the discussion has received a significant boost from the case-law of the Federal Constitutional Court. The significant decisions as regards the issue of subjective entitlements have been above all those decisions in which there is talk not only of objective state obligations, but of more extensive subjective rights to positive state action. Three decisions in particular are worth considering: the Welfare Judgment of 1951, the first Numerus-Clausus Judgment, and the case concerning the interim statute for comprehensive higher education in Lower Saxony.

The Court expressed itself both cautiously and ambiguously in the Welfare Judgment. To start with, the Court stated that article 1(1) Basic Law did not impose an obligation on the state to protect the individual from material want, and that article 2(2)(1) did not give the individual any right to suitable state provision. However, the court went on to emphasize that this did not mean that 'the individual had no constitutional right to welfare whatsoever'. The duty of the legislature to 'realize the social state' would not generally give rise to any subjective rights, but if 'the legislature arbitrarily, that is, without relevant ground, failed to respect this duty, then it was possible that the individual might have a corresponding claim, enforceable by way of the constitutional complaint procedure'.[17] In a 1975 decision, the court went a significant step further. There, it stated that 'there can be no doubt that support for those in need is one of the unquestionable duties of the social state. This necessarily includes social help for those fellow citizens who are hampered in their personal and social development by physical or mental weakness and who are not capable of looking after themselves. The state community must secure for them at least the basic conditions for a dignified existence.'[18] If one puts both decisions together, there can hardly be any doubt that the Federal Constitutional Court presupposes the existence of a constitutional right to an existential minimum. In this respect it is in line with the long-standing case-law of the Federal Adminstrative Court[19] and the overwhelming majority of academic opinion.[20] One can therefore say that there is at least one unwritten social constitutional right, interpretatively derived from constitutional rights

---

[17] BVerfGE 1, 97 (104 f.).   [18] BVerfGE 40, 121 (133).
[19] BVerwGE 1, 159 (161 f.); 5, 27 (31); 27, 58 (63); 52, 339 (346).
[20] See e.g. G. Dürig, 'Der Grundrechtssatz von der Menschenwürde', AöR 81 (1956), 131 f.; id., in T. Maunz and G. Dürig, *Kommentar Grundgesetz*, art. 1 abs. 1 para. 43 f., art. 2 abs. 2 para. 27; J. M. Wintrich, *Zur Problematik der Grundrechte* (Cologne and Opladen, 1957); C. Starck, 'Staatliche Organisation und staatliche Finanzierung als Hilfen zur Grundrechtsverwirklichungen?', in C. Starck (ed.), *Festgabe aus Anlaß des 25jährigen Bestehens des Bundesverfassungsgerichts*, ii (Tübingen, 1976), 522; R. Breuer, 'Grundrechte als Anspruchsnormen', in O. Bachof, L. Heigh and K. Redeker (eds.), *Verwaltungsrecht zwischen Freiheit, Teilhabe und Bindung* (Munich, 1978), 95 ff.

provisions. It has been stated that 'it would be a waste of time to engage in doctrinal dispute on the basis of this example alone'.[21] If this means that the right to an existential minimum is doctrinally uninteresting, then we must disagree. It is hardly a matter of course that a subjective right to an existential minimum should be overwhelmingly supported in the case-law and academic opinion under a constitution which does not expressly contain such a right. But it is none the less true that it would be a mistake to suppose without further argument that further entitlements exist on the basis of this alone. The fact that there is one entitlement which can correctly be derived from constitutional rights provisions means that the thesis that constitutional rights provisions contain no entitlements is false. But it does not follow from this alone that any further entitlements may also be correctly derived.

With the second example, the first Numerus-Clausus Judgment, we enter a highly controversial domain.[22] In this case the Court distinguished between two rights, a right to 'participation' (as it put it) in existing educational establishments, and a right to the creation of new university places. To start with, only the first needed to be considered. The Court based this right on the principle of equality in connection with article 12(1) Basic Law and the social state principle, along with the fact that the state has assumed 'a factual monopoly which cannot be relinquished at will' on education for academic careers, which 'in turn is a necessary condition for the realization of constitutional rights'.[23] The first important point for the theory of constitutional entitlements is that among the three provisions on which the court relies, article 12(1) expresses a liberty right, and must be taken to express a liberty right in order for the reasoning to work. Without reference to the freedom to choose one's university and career, an important justifying element for the requirement of the exhaustive exploitation of existing student capacity would be missing.[24] The principle of equality on its own, at any rate as understood as prohibiting arbitrary treatment, is compatible with a lower level of exploitation of capacity.[25] The right to a free choice of

---

[21] H. H. Klein, *Die Grundrechte im demokratischen Staat*, 2nd edn. (Stuttgart, Berlin, Cologne, and Mainz, 1974), 90 (fn. 73), with reference to Dürig, in Maunz and Dürig, *Grundgesetz Kommentar*, art. 2 abs. 2 para. 26.

[22] See the literature collected by the Federal Constitutional Court itself in BVerfGE 43, 291 as well as F. Ossenbühl, 'Die Interpretation der Grundrechte in der Rechtsprechung des Bundesverfassungsgerichts', NJW 1976, 2104 f.; Breuer, 'Grundrechte als Anspruchsnormen', 112; G. F. Schuppert, *Funktionell-rechtliche Grenzen der Verfassungsinterpretation* (Königstein/Ts., 1980), 10 ff. [23] BVerfGE 33, 303 (331 f.).

[24] BVerfGE 33, 303 (338); emphasizing this point, BVerfGE 43, 291 (326).

[25] See on this in more detail, Breuer, 'Grundrechte als Anspruchsnormen', 115 ff.; Schuppert, *Funktionell-rechtliche Grenzen der Verfassungsinterpretation*, 25. The view that recourse to the general principle of equality would have sufficed (see E. Friesenhahn, 'Der Wandel des Grundrechtsverständnisses', in *Verhandlungen des fünfzigsten Deutschen Juristentages* (Hamburg, 1974), G32; Ossenbühl, 'Die Interpretation der Grundrechte in der Rechtsprechung des Bundesverfassungsgerichts', 2104) cannot be followed.

university and career thus has decisive weight against arguments in favour of differential treatment, such as arguments based on the efficacy of education. As regards the social state principle, one has to question whether it grants a right to an education appropriate for an academic career, either of itself or in combination with the principle of equality. The fact that the Court makes use of a liberty right in its reasoning is significant, because this use presupposes that it cannot be interpreted exclusively as a defensive right. If it were only such, it would contribute nothing to the argument. It can only play a part in the reasoning, if it is extended to 'the necessary preconditions for the realization' of liberties,[26] that is, if it is read as a guarantee of an element of factual freedom, which the court justifies, among other ways, with the following words: 'the liberty right would be valueless without the factual preconditions for taking advantage of it'.[27] These words open up a new dimension in the justification of derivative rights.

As regards the right to participate in existing educational possibilities, the consequences are relatively minor. The matter gets interesting when it concerns a right to the creation of new university places. In its judgment of 8 February 1977,[28] the court distinguished more clearly than it had done in its first Numerus-Clausus Judgment between an abstract 'constitutionally guaranteed right of the citizen who fulfils the individual entry requirements to enter the university degree programme of their choice', which is 'subject to the limits of the possible, in the sense of what the individual can reasonably demand from society',[29] and a concrete 'enforceable individual claim of the citizen to the expansion of existing educational capacity'.[30] In terms of the theory of principles, the first right is a prima facie right which only becomes definitive if conflicting reasons do not require some other outcome.[31] The Court expresses this well when it states that each qualified citizen '*in principle*', that is, without regard to specific legal and factual possibilities, has a right of entry to the degree programme of their choice.[32] By contrast, the second right is a *definitive* right. The Court explicitly leaves open 'whether and under which conditions' the prima facie right 'may happen' to become a definitive right.[33] But in that it asserts the existence of a prima facie right and refuses to exclude the possibility of a definitive right, it opens the door to the derivation of entitlements in exemplary fashion.

The subjective right to state organizational measures derived from article 5(3) Basic Law in the University Judgment has quite another character.

The basic value-judgment of article 5(3) gives the individual constitutional rightholder a right to such state measures, including organizational ones, which are an

---

[26] BVerfGE 33, 303 (337).   [27] BVerfGE 33, 303 (331).
[28] BVerfGE 43, 291.
[29] BVerfGE 43, 291; first referred to in BVerfGE 33, 303 (333).
[30] BVerfGE 43, 291 (315); 33, 303 (333).
[31] See above at 60.   [32] BVerfGE 43, 291 (315).
[33] BVerfGE 43, 291 (315, 325); 33, 303 (333).

indispensable precondition for the protection of his constitutionally secured sphere of freedom, because they are what makes free academic activity possible in the first place. If this were not so, the basic norm which expresses this value-judgment would largely be robbed of its protective effect. This power of the individual constitutional right-holder to force the state to observe the value-oriented basic norm, is part of the content of the individual constitutional right, the effectiveness of which is thereby strengthened.[34]

The right to state organizational measures is a right to the creation of certain legal norms. This introduces a new aspect into the realm of entitlements: the right to a normative performance.[35]

3. THE NATURE OF THE DISPUTE ABOUT ENTITLEMENTS

The three decisions which have just been considered in no way exhaust the relevant statements of the Federal Constitutional Court. But even these make it clear that the case-law provides much richer points of contact for the dispute about entitlements in the Basic Law, than do its text or legislative history. If one is to locate the Court as a participant in the dispute, one can say that it adopts a middle position in a spectrum of views which extends from near total denial, 'constitutional rights [cannot] simultaneously be both claims to state action and their negation'[36] to extensive support, 'in a highly complex industrial society, constitutional rights are rights of participation or they are nothing'.[37]

The dispute about entitlements is characterized by fundamental disagreements about the nature and function of the state, of law, and of the Constitution, including constitutional rights,[38] as well as over the assessment of the current state of society. Since it has implications for issues of distibution, its 'high degree of political controversy'[39] is obvious. In hardly any other field is the connection between juridical outcome and general practical or political evaluation so obvious; in hardly any other is it so stubbornly disputed. It is significant that people speak in this situation, whether critically or supportively, of a 'shift in the conception of constitutional rights'[40] and that there are calls to 'de-demonize, de-ideologize and

---

[34] BVerfGE 35, 79 (116). For a critique of the recognition of such a subjective right, see above all the dissenting judgment of Judges Simon and Rupp–v. Brüneck, BVerfGE 35, 148 (155).

[35] See above at 126 f.

[36] Klein, *Die Grundrechte im demokratischen Staat*, 65.

[37] H. Willke, *Stand und Kritik der neueren Grundrechtstheorie* (Berlin, 1975), 216.

[38] See P. Badura, 'Das Prinzip der sozialen Grundrechte und seine Verwirklichung im Recht der Bundesrepublik Deutschland', *Der Staat*, 14 (1975), 17.

[39] See W. Schmidt, 'Soziale Grundrechte im Verfassungsrecht der Bundesrepublik Deutschland', *Der Staat*, Beiheft 5 (1981), 12.

[40] See in place of many Friesenhahn, 'Der Wandel des Grundrechtsverständnisses', G1 ff.; P. Saladin, *Grundrechte im Wandel*, 2nd edn. (Berne, 1975); H. H. Rupp, 'Vom Wandel der Grundrechte', AöR 101 (1976), 161 ff.

de-emotionalize the concept of social constitutional rights'.[41] A second additional characteristic of the dispute is that a resolution is hampered not only by basic substantive differences of opinion, but by fundamental conceptual and doctrinal obscurities, expressed, among other things, by the terminological confusion which is often bemoaned in this field.

The reflections which follow address the conceptual/terminological problems by proposing a threefold division of entitlements. As regards the existence and content of entitlements, they proceed on the basis of a single, if only formal, guiding idea. Both elements will now be introduced.

4. The Concept and Division of Entitlements

As has already been pointed out, the concept of an entitlement will be broadly understood here. Every right to a positive action on the part of the state is an entitlement. The concept of an entitlement is thus the exact counterpart to that of a defensive right, which includes every right to a non-action, or an omission, on the part of the state.

The range of positive state actions which can be the object of an entitlement stretches from the protection of citizens from other citizens by the criminal law, through the enactment of organizational and procedural norms, to the provision of money and other goods. This concept of an entitlement is broader than usual.[42] Normally, the expression 'entitlement' is tied to a conception of a right to something which the right-holder could obtain from private individuals had he the financial means to do so, and were there sufficient offers on the market. However, there are two important reasons for extending the concept of an entitlement beyond such rights to factual performance to rights to normative performance[43] such as protection by the norms of the criminal law or the enactment of organizational and procedural norms.[44]

The first reason is that in the case of the many so-called social constitutional rights, which are sometimes treated as typical entitlements, one is dealing with bundles of legal positions relating in part to factual, in part to normative, performance. This is particularly clear in the case of the much-

---

[41] L. Wildhaber, 'Soziale Grundrechte', in P. Saladin and L. Wildhaber (eds.), *Der Staat als Aufgabe, Gedenkschrift für M. Imboden* (Basle and Stuttgart, 1972), 390.

[42] This does not mean that the broader conception is never used. Thus R. Scholz, for example, speaks of 'a state performance in the form of authoritative engagement against third party citizens as (potential) infringers' (in 'Nichtraucher contra Raucher', in JuS 1976, 234). For a proposal for a correspondingly broad conception of entitlement in administrative law, see E. Becker, 'Verwaltung und Verwaltungsrechtsprechung', in VVDStRL 14 (1956), 109; G. Beinhardt, 'Das Recht der öffentlichen Sicherheit und Ordnung in seinem Verhältnis zur Eingriffs-und Leistungsverwaltung', in DVBl 1961, 612 f.

[43] On the concepts of factual and normative performance, see above at 126 f.

[44] In the final analysis, the issue is one of usefulness, as it is with all terminological questions; see H. J. Wolff and O. Bachof, *Verwaltungsrecht III*, 4th edn. (Munich, 1978), 181.

discussed environmental constitutional right,[45] which is not infrequently classified as a social constitutional right, or is at least placed in their proximity.[46] Closer analysis shows that such a right, regardless of whether it is introduced into the catalogue of constitutional rights by amendment or by the interpretation of existing provisions, has a totally different structure from that of, say, the right to welfare, which is basically a pure right to factual performance and no more. An environmental constitutional right corresponds rather to what has been called above a 'complete constitutional right'.[47] It consists of a bundle of extremely varied positions. The person who proposes enacting an environmental constitutional right, or interpreting existing provisions in this way, could be incorporating in this bundle of positions, among other things, a right that the state refrain from certain interferences with the environment (defensive right), a right that the state protect the right-holder from environmentally damaging acts of third parties (protective right), a right that the state allow the right-holder to participate in environmentally relevant decisions (procedural right), and a right that the state undertake certain environmentally enhancing measures (factual performance right).[48] Furthermore, these proposed or asserted positions could be prima facie rights or definitive rights. The same applies for other rights considered under the term 'social constitutional rights'. It is entirely typical for Brunner to speak of 'the right to work, with its various special rights such as free choice of profession, the right to a job, just wages, suitable working conditions, the protection of certain groups of persons (women, children), holidays, unemployment benefit, the rights to form trade unions and to strike, and the right of co-determination'.[49] Even when one excludes defensive rights from this list, what remains is structurally highly varied. In order to be able to grasp this variety and set it systematically in relation to defensive rights, a broad concept of entitlement is advisable.

The second reason for a broad concept of entitlement is that rights to positive actions share certain problems not associated with rights to negative actions, or at least not to the same extent. Rights to negative actions set limits to the purposes the state may pursue. But they say nothing about those purposes. Rights to positive action impose upon the state, to some extent, the purposes to be pursued. Thus all rights to positive state action

---

[45] See on this in place of many D. Rauschning, 'Staatsaufgabe Umweltschutz', VVDStRL 38 (1980), 167 ff. with further references.

[46] See e.g. G. Brunner, *Die Problematik der sozialen Grundrechte* (Tübingen, 1971), 12; Wildhaber, 'Soziale Grundrechte', 375; H. H. Klein, 'Ein Grundrecht auf saubere Umwelt?' in H. Schneider and V. Götz (eds.), *Festschrift für W. Weber* (Berlin, 1974), 654 f.; Badura, 'Das Prinzip der sozialen Grundrechte', 23.

[47] 159 ff.

[48] On the richly differentiated structure of a right to environmental protection, see H. Steiger, *Mensch und Umwelt* (Berlin, 1975), 40 ff.

[49] Brunner, *Die Problematik der sozialen Grundrechte*, 11.

raise the problem of whether and to what extent the state's pursuit of certain purposes can and should be tied to the constitutional subjective rights of the citizen. Under a constitution which subjects the enforcement of constitutional rights to the broad control of a constitutional court, this is at root a problem of the division of competence between the constitutional court on one hand and the legislature on the other. The fact that all rights to positive state action share this problem is a decisive reason for grouping them all together under a single concept of 'entitlements'. Rights to factual performance, that is, rights to actions that private individuals could undertake, are thus only one type of entitlement. Where it is relevant, we can talk in terms of *'entitlements in the narrow sense'* and *'entitlements in the wide sense'*.

Entitlements (in the wide sense) can be divided into three groups: (1) rights to protection, (2) rights to organization and procedure, and (3) entitlements in the narrow sense. A discussion and refinement of this division will be undertaken in the context of discussing the individual groups.

Rights of this nature are only constitutional entitlements if they are *subjective* rights protected at *constitutional* level. As such they can be distinguished both from subjective rights not protected at constitutional level, and from norms which do not grant subjective rights, and which can in that sense be called 'objective'. Again, subjective non-constitutional rights could be rights guaranteed by other legal norms of lower status, or moral rights resting on norms of morality. Norms that do not give rise to rights could be constitutional, simply legal, or moral. The discussion of entitlements, and in particular social constitutional rights, gives cause to emphasize these distinctions. They are frequently blurred at the cost of clarity and watertight argumentation. Emphasizing these distinctions does not mean that there are no connections. Precisely because the connections are close, it is important to make the differences as clear as possible. The connections consist above all in the fact that moral argument for the general content of constitutional rights norms is at any rate not excluded, that it is possible interpretatively to derive what have been hitherto constitutionally unrecognized moral rights from constitutional provisions, and from the fact that every objective norm which benefits a legal subject is a potential candidate for subjectification.

As subjective rights, all entitlements are three-point relations between a constitutional right-holder, the state and a positive act by the state. If right-holder x has the right against the state s that it carry out positive act ϕ, then the state has *relative* to x the duty to ϕ.[50] Whenever such a constitutional relation between a right-holder and the state exists, then the right-holder has the power to enforce the right before the courts. This is true as a matter of express constitutional law in article 19(4) Basic Law. This enforceability,

---

[50] On the equivalence of $RxsG$ and $OsxG$, see above at 131 ff.

which Wolff calls 'perfect',[51] takes into account the fact that entitlements, just like defensive rights, can have prima facie, or principled, character. The right to do or not to do as one pleases is no less valid and enforceable because the definitive outcome for the individual is to a large extent that he cannot do or not do as he pleases. Rather, as a prima facie right it is a right which is necessarily limitable.

If one adds limiting clauses to the norms granting prima facie rights, they become norms which, while in need of concretization, largely through the balancing of principles, guarantee definitive rights.[52] If action falls within the scope of the right and the limiting clause is not satisfied, the right-holder has a definitive right. The nature of a norm as a principle and perfect enforceability are thus compatible. This applies as much to entitlements as it does to defensive rights.

5. THE GUIDING IDEA

Many and various are the arguments which can be put forward for and against the derivation of entitlements from constitutional rights provisions. It would seem appropriate to discuss them in the context of a guiding perspective. A suitable guiding perspective or idea would seem to be the general formal concept of constitutional rights, which can be put like this: constitutional rights are positions which are so important that the decision to protect them cannot be left to simple parliamentary majorities. This statement is in need of much greater precision. One can be noted at once. We are concerned with the constitutional rights of the Basic Law, that is, we are concerned with positions which from the perspective of constitutional law are so important that the decision to protect them cannot be left to simple parliamentary majorities. Thus the following definition applies: the constitutional rights of the Basic Law are positions which from the perspective of constitutional law are so important that the decision to protect them cannot be left to simple parliamentary majorities.

The formal concept of constitutional rights expresses a central problem with constitutional rights in a democratic state. Constitutional rights norms, such as those of the Basic Law which bind the legislature, establish what the democratically legitimated legislature may not and must decide. From the legislature's perspective, they consist of prohibitions and commands, limiting its freedom, and furthermore they are negative competence norms, limiting its competence.[53] To this extent there is necessarily a conflict between the principle of democracy and constitutional rights.[54] The fact that on the other hand a whole series of constitutional rights (e.g. the

---

[51] H. J. Wolff and O. Bachof, *Verwaltungsrecht I*, 9th edn. (Munich, 1974), § 40 (295).
[52] See above at 85.   [53] See above at 158 f.
[54] See BVerfGE 56, 54 (81).

right to vote, freedom of expression) are required by the principle of democracy does not remove this conflict; it only shows that the principle of democracy can be divided into several sub-principles which can conflict with each other. As an aside, it should be noted that this is the theoretical basis of the so-called paradox of democracy,[55] which relates to the old problem of the democratic removal of democracy. The necessary conflict between the principle of democracy and constitutional rights implies that the problem of the division of competence between the directly democratically legitimated and accountable (in the sense of removable) parliamentary legislature and the merely indirectly democratically legitimated and tenured constitutional court is an unavoidable and permanent problem. Ely was right when he described its solution as a 'tricky task'.[56]

The formal concept of a constitutional right takes account of these conflicts and problems of competence. The importance which a position must have from the perspective of constitutional law in order for it to be treated as a constitutional right is not an intrinsic importance, but an importance relative to the principles which count for and against characterizing a certain position as a constitutional one. These principles always include at least one constitutional rights principle which tends towards constitutional securing of the position and one principle of democracy which tends towards keeping the competence of the democratically legitimated legislature as wide as possible. If everything important to the individual in public life were constitutionally secured, the legislature would only have what is unimportant left to decide. But the principle of democracy requires that the legislature have important issues to decide. The fact that entitlements are important—which is not disputed by those who refuse to grant them constitutional status either—is in itself not an adequate reason for giving them constitutional status. The question is whether and to what extent they are so important from the perspective of constitutional law that decisions about them cannot be left to a parliamentary majority.

It should be noted that this concept of a constitutional right is purely formal. It can be adopted by proponents of quite different substantive conceptions. Someone who accepts it and rejects entirely the idea of constitutional entitlements presupposes that they are not so important that they cannot be left to the decision of the majority. Someone who accepts the definition and broadly accepts the existence of constitutional entitlements must be making the opposite assumption.

It could be objected that this does not tell us very much, because a conception based on 'importance' alone is inadequate. It does not depend merely on relative importance but beyond that, and decisively, on the real

[55] See on this K. R. Popper, *The Open Society and its Enemies*, i, 5th edn. (London, 1966), 123 f.; H. Steinberger, *Konzeption und Grenzen freiheitlicher Demokratie* (Berlin, Heidelberg, and New York, 1974), 196 ff.

[56] J. H. Ely, *Democracy and Distrust* (Cambridge, Mass. and London, 1980), 7 f.

necessity for constitutional anchoring. Liberties are always in danger, and thus their constitutional securing as perfectly enforceable rights is necessary. By contrast the democratic industrial state is characterized by a tendency to ever-increasing state support. Entitlements are anything but endangered. However important they are, there is no necessity to secure them at constitutional level. The weakness of this argument lies in the fact that the satisfying of a right tells us nothing about its existence. Even a constitutional right which is satisfied in every situation and every respect is still of systemic importance. If we want to paint a complete picture of constitutional rights we cannot leave out something simply because it is widely respected. Since the satisfaction of one constitutional right often costs a partial non-satisfaction of others, the satisfied constitutional right retains its significance as a constitutional reason justifying the non-satisfaction of others. But the most important point is that the satisfaction of a right in the past and present is no reason for assuming that it will be satisfied in the future. If there is no constitutional right, the legislature has some freedom and competence which it would not have if the right existed. Since no one knows what any future legislature, or the circumstances it will operate under, will be like, no one can tell whether it will not make use of that freedom and competence differently from in the past or present and in a way disadvantageous to the individual.

Just as superficial and quick to disprove is the objection that the concept of importance in the definition proposed is entirely vague. This is no weakness in the definition but a condition of its suitability as a guiding idea. The formal concept can and must be coupled to a substantive conception.

The concept which has just been introduced is an all-embracing *formal* basic concept. It can be paralleled by an extensive *substantive* basic concept. The Basic Law defines this broad substantive basic concept by the idea of human dignity.[57] It hardly needs pointing out that concrete constitutional propositions cannot be derived either from the formal or the substantive basic concepts alone, or from either simply combined with each other. Expanding both concepts is the function of substantial constitutional argumentation. Here, we are only interested in the significance of the formal basic concept. It consists in the fact that every substantive conception of entitlements includes an answer to the question whether the entitlements under consideration are so important from the perspective of constitutional law that they should not be left to the disposal of simple majorities, or whether they are not so important. The substantive basic concept becomes relevant in the context of this question.

The formal concept underlies all constitutional rights. It is of particular importance for entitlements because of their controversial character. The

---

[57] Mention need only be made from the case-law of BVerfGE 5, 85 (204) and from the literature of Dürig, 'Der Grundrechtssatz von der Menschenwürde', 119.

following general proposition about entitlements can be formulated on its basis:

(E)   On the basis of constitutional rights norms, each person has those entitlements which from the perspective of constitutional law are so important, that their granting or denial cannot be left to simple parliamentary majorities.

This proposition expresses a *general entitlement*.

II. PROTECTIVE RIGHTS

1. ON THE CONCEPT OF PROTECTIVE RIGHTS

By 'protective rights' is meant those constitutional rights which a right-holder has against the state that it protect him from interferences by third parties. Protective rights can have a great variety of objects. The spectrum extends from homicide of the most primitive form to protection from the dangers of the peaceful use of atomic energy. It is not just life and health that are potentially protected interests, but everything worthy of constitutional protection, such as dignity, freedom, the family, and property. The possible forms of protection are no less varied. For example, they include protection through the norms of the criminal law, through the law of tort, through procedural law, through administrative acts, and through factual action. The common element underlying all this variety is that protective rights are subjective constitutional rights against the state to positive factual or normative acts concerned with delimiting the spheres of equally ranked legal persons, along with the enforceability and enforcement of this delimitation. Securing the enforceability and enforcement of this delimitation is a classic function of the legal system. Kant's well-known dictum, that 'right is therefore the sum of the conditions under which the choice of one can be united with the choice of another in accordance with a universal law of freedom'[58] points to this function. Protective rights are thus constitutional rights that the state structure and maintain the legal system as it affects the interrelationship of equally ranked legal subjects in a certain way.

A discussion of protective rights has to consider three closely connected issues: their existence, their structure, and their justiciability. The problems are most apparent when protective rights are addressed to the legislature. Such rights will therefore be in the forefront of our discussion.

---

[58]   I. Kant, *The Metaphysics of Morals*, trans. M. Gregor (Cambridge, 1991), 56.

2. The Existence of Protective Rights

The problem of the existence of protective rights has substantive and structural aspects. The substantive aspect concerns the question of what is to be protected and how. Giving answers to this question is the function of individual constitutional rights doctrine. Here, we are mainly interested in the structural aspect. As regards the problem of existence it can be divided into two questions. The first is whether there are subjective rights to protection, or only norms which require the state to protect individuals, without giving those individuals rights. So this question is the well-known problem of *subjective* right or (merely) *objective* norm. The second question is whether protective rights, if they exist, really differ at all from classic defensive rights. This question is concerned with the distinction between *defensive* right and *protective* right.

2.1 Subjective Right or (Merely) Objective Norm?

As regards the alternative of subjective right or merely objective norm, the case-law of the Federal Constitutional Court is not entirely clear. The Court prefers objective formulations and constructions. In its judgment on abortion it leaves the constitutional status of the foetus as a right-holder open and opts for an objective rather than a subjective solution.[59] The Schleyer Judgment talks simply in terms of state duties and not of rights of the individual to protection.[60] The Kalkar Judgment distinguishes between constitutional rights and 'objective legal protective duties derivable from the constitutional rights system'.[61] This phrase was repeated in the Müllheim–Kärlich Judgment, which saw itself as a development of the Limitation/Schleyer/Kalkar line of cases.[62] But the clear objective tendency in these judgments is only one side of the matter. In the context of balancing competing principles in the Abortion Judgment, the Court speaks of the 'right of the unborn child'.[63] The Schleyer Judgment distinguishes between a 'protective duty *towards* the individual' and a duty 'towards all citizens'.[64] If one understands the former to be a relational obligation,[65] which seems to be correct, then the duty of the state corresponds to the right of the individual.[66] The thesis put forward in the Kalkar Judgment that the constitutional guarantee of rights can give rise to protective duties, 'which require legal regulations to be structured in such a way as to limit the danger of constitutional rights infringements'[67] is in great need of interpretation. With these

---

[59] BVerfGE 39, 1 (41 ff.).   [60] BVerfGE 46, 160 (164 f.).
[61] BVerfGE 49, 89 (140).
[62] BVerfGE 53, 30 (57). See also BVerfGE 56, 54 (73).
[63] BVerfGE 39, 1 (50).   [64] BVerfGE 46, 160 (165) (emphasis added).
[65] On this concept, see above at 131.
[66] This correspondence is a result of the law, $RxyG \leftrightarrow OyxG$.
[67] BVerfGE 49, 89 (142).

words, the Court seems to be presupposing the possibility of infringements of constitutional rights by equally ranked third parties. But this possibility would only arise if there were constitutional relations between equally ranked persons, consisting in the fact that equally ranked persons are addressees of constitutional rights, which is a very strong and problematic version of horizontal effect.[68] A much weaker and thus less problematic thesis is the argument that the individual has a constitutional right against the state to protection from third parties. One could then speak in terms of a breach of constitutional rights by the state for failing to fulfil its protective duty to a sufficient extent. This would imply a subjectification of the protective duty. This is unavoidable in the Müllheim–Kärlich Judgment, because this was commenced by way of constitutional complaint, which has to allege an infringement of rights. If one wants to avoid the highly artificial and doctrinally suspect construction of considering the breach of the duty to protect life and health under article 2(2) Basic Law in the context of a breach of the constitutional order under article 2(1), then the only alternative is to derive a protective right corresponding to the duty from article 2(2).

The examples make it clear that in spite of its objectivist tendency, the case-law of the Federal Constitutional Court contains significant material for a subjective interpretation.[69] The question is whether there are better reasons for the derivation of subjective rights to protection than not. In answering this question it is instructive to consider some cases in which the existence of a protective duty is not in doubt; the only uncertainty surrounds its subjectification. Such an example, correctly described by the dissenting judges in the Abortion Judgment as 'academic',[70] is the protection of the individual by the state from murder and manslaughter. There can be no doubt that the state is obligated to protect the individual from murder and manslaughter. Furthermore, there can hardly be any doubt that the state is obligated to do this by way of criminal prohibitions and sanctions. The question is whether the individual has a subjective constitutional right to this, and how such a right is to be justified. There are two possible doctrinal arguments. The first points to the obligation of the state set out in article 1(1)(2) Basic Law to protect human dignity, and transfers that protective requirement to the subsequent constitutional rights.[71] The advantage of this route is that it rests directly on the constitutional text. Its disadvantage is

---

[68] On the problem of horizontal effect, see below at 354 ff.

[69] In relation to the case-law of the Federal Constitutional Court, one can therefore say that the question of the subjectifying of protective duties is an open one. For a discussion of this problem in the literature, see E. Schmidt-Assmann, 'Anwendungsprobleme des Art. 2 Abs. 2 GG im Immissionsschutzrecht', AöR 106 (1981), 214 ff.; J. Isensee, *Das Grundrecht auf Sicherheit* (Berlin and New York, 1983).

[70] BVerfGE 39, 1 (78).

[71] See Dürig, 'Der Grundrechtssatz der Menschenwürde', 118 ff.; id., in Maunz and Dürig, *Grundgesetz Kommentar*, art. 1 abs. 1 para. 16; art. 1 abs. 3 para. 102.

that it faces the dilemma either of expanding the concept of human dignity so widely that it can embrace everything worth protecting, which carries with it the often-asserted danger of trivializing human dignity, or of abandoning its embrace of things worth protecting. The second only uses the human dignity argument supportively, and rests directly on individual human rights. This route, which is preferred by the Federal Constitutional Court,[72] presupposes that constitutional rights are more than defensive rights against state interference. The court refers to the 'objective-legal content'[73] of constitutional rights, and to the 'objective order of values' which constitutional rights embody.[74] Admittedly, this says nothing about the question which concerns us here, whether there are subjective rights which correspond to objective protective duties. However, the concept of an order of values gives us a way into its answer. It has already been suggested that a theory of values purified of untenable assumptions can be recast as a theory of principles.[75] It is possible to derive the principle of the protection of life from article 2(2)(1) Basic Law. Just like any other principle, this principle requires that it should be realized to the greatest extent factually and legally possible. In general, it is true that the recognition of subjective rights implies a higher degree of realization than the enactment of mere objective requirements.[76] A merely objective prohibition of interference is less than an equivalent subjective defensive right. The subjectification of protective duties can thus be defended by way of the principled nature of constitutional rights. Now this does not say anything about the definitive content of protective rights. That all depends, as it does with all principle-based rights, on what is factually and legally possible. Just as with other constitutional rights positions, so also with protective rights, we must distinguish clearly between prima facie and definitive positions.

It is only the subjectification of constitutional rights which will satisfy the 'original and ongoing point of constitutional rights' as individual rights.[77] Unlike social constitutional rights, or entitlements in the narrow sense, protective rights fit comfortably within the traditional liberal understanding of constitutional rights.[78] Indeed, their justification within the context of classic social contract models of the state, which have recently undergone a vigorous renaissance,[79] is practically unavoidable. The far-reaching abandonment of rights to effective self-defence required by the

---

[72] BVerfGE 39, 1 (41); 46, 160 (164); 49, 89 (141); 53, 30 (57).
[73] BVerfGE 53, 30 (57).   [74] BVerfGE 39, 1 (41).   [75] 86 ff.
[76] See M. D. Bayles, 'Courts vs. Legislatures as protectors of Human Rights', Lecture before the 11th World Congress of the International Association of Legal and Social Philosophy (Helsinki, 1983 (appearing in the proceedings of the Congress).
[77] BVerfGE 50, 290 (337).
[78] See J. Isensee, 'Verfassung ohne soziale Grundrechte', *Der Staat*, 19 (1980), 374.
[79] See the two main works, J. Rawls, *A Theory of Justice* (Cambridge, Mass., 1971); R. Nozick, *Anarchy, State, and Utopia* (New York, 1974).

(hypothetical)[80] transfer from a state of nature to a state of government can only be rationally justified if the individual receives effective state protection in return. The fact that this idea is no mere hypothesis, but has a 'Sitz im Leben', can be seen from the fact that where the state lacks the will or the ability to satisfy rights to protection, private protective associations regularly form with the purpose of enforcing individual rights. Locating protective rights within the individualistic liberal tradition does not mean that there are no problems associated with them which are more extensive than those brought about by defensive rights directed towards negative actions of the state. On the contrary, as rights to positive state action, protective rights share a whole series of difficulties with social constitutional rights, entitlements in the narrow sense. But it will be seen that these problems are no reason for doing without protective rights. The similarity of the difficulties also shows that the chasm which is supposed to separate rights in the liberal tradition from social rights is not as deep as one might think at first sight.

2.2 Defence and Protection

Rights to protection and defensive rights are placed in opposition to each other, because the former are rights to positive state action and the latter rights to negative state action. The correctness of this opposition can be doubted. Thus Dürig has stated that 'the positive action of "*protecting*" is defensive state activity and not positive *structuring*'.[81] This is correct to the extent that protective rights are concerned with defence. But this is all that defensive rights and protective rights have in common. The former are rights against the state that it refrain from interfering, the latter are rights against the state that it take care that third parties refrain from interfering. The difference between the duty to refrain from interfering and the duty to take care that third parties refrain from interfering is so fundamental and consequential, that it prohibits any weakening of the distinction, at least for doctrinal purposes. Thus at most, the reference to defensive character can be taken to refer to the location of protective rights within the liberal tradition, but not to placing them within the class of state-aimed defensive rights. Dürig cannot be followed in his assertion that defensive rights do not lead to positive structuring. In that the legislature undertakes the delimitation of individual spheres of freedom required by protective rights, it structures an important part of the legal system and thus also a significant part of social life.

Schwabe challenges the opposition of defensive rights and protective rights in a much more radical way.[82] According to Schwabe, the acceptance of protective duties and thus also protective rights is largely[83] unnecessary

---

[80] On the epistemological status of social contract theory, see Nozick, *Anarchy, State, and Utopia*, 6 ff.

[81] Dürig, in Maunz and Dürig, *Grundgesetz Kommentar*, art. 1 abs. 1 para. 3.

[82] J. Schwabe, *Probleme der Grundrechtsdogmatik* (Darmstadt, 1977), 213 ff.

[83] For a limited acceptance of protective duties, see ibid. 215 f.

and misleading. Their role can be much more easily and appropriately maintained in the context of the 'negatory function' of constitutional rights.[84] The reasoning is of beguiling simplicity. When the state fails to prohibit third parties from interfering with constitutional interests such as life or health, then it *permits* them. But state permissions correspond to *duties of toleration*. Whenever the state shields private action by legal regulation, judicial decision, or executive action it *participates* in the breaching process, for which it is therefore *accountable*.[85] The problem of protection against private parties thus becomes a problem of defence against privately sponsored, but in the final analysis state, interferences.[86] The permission, the duty to tolerate, as well as its judicial and extra-judicial implementation, is thus to be assessed by the standards of constitutional rights as defensive rights. No place is left, a few exceptions apart, for duties of protection and thus also protective rights.

The decisive move in this theory is the assignment of private interferences to the state.[87] This assignment, which turns private interference into state interference basically rests on three points: (1) state permission, (2) associated duties of toleration, and (3) state enforcement of the duty of toleration. But none of these reasons is a suitable one for preferring the defensive to the protective construction.

The mere fact that some action is not prohibited and is thus permitted means neither that the state participates in its performance, nor that the state is responsible for its performance. If this were so, the state would have to be treated as participating in every non-prohibited human action. It would be responsible for every non-prohibited human action, including, for example, private invitations to dinner. This cannot seriously be what Schwabe's theory of state responsibility means.[88] What could be meant is that the state carries a certain sort of responsibility for certain acts of one

[84] ibid. 219; see also id., *Die sogenannte Drittwirkung der Grundrechte* (Munich, 1971), 140, 145, 154, as well as id., 'Grundrechtlich begründete Pflichten des Staates zum Schutz gegen staatliche Bau-und Anlagegenehmigungen?' NVwZ 1983, 523 ff.; critically on this, R. Alexy, 'Das Gebot der Rücksichtnahme im baurechtlichen Nachbarschutz', DÖV 1984, 958.
[85] Schwabe, *Probleme der Grundrechtsdogmatik*, 213 ff.
[86] id., *Die sogenannte Drittwirkung der Grundrechte*, 149.
[87] The Federal Constitutional Court is at times ambiguous. Thus in the Mülheim–Kärlich Judgment it speaks both of a protective duty and of the state's 'own joint responsibility' (BVerfGE 53, 30 (58, 61)). But since it cannot be proceeding both on the basis of a defensive right and a protective right, it has to be interpreted in accordance with the latter.
[88] The thesis that the state is responsible for all non-prohibited human acts presupposes universal state liability for everything that human beings permissibly do. The allocation of responsibility on the basis of such a universal liability is not an impossible construction. The state would then be liable for the private invitation to dinner discussed in the text, but its failure to prohibit it would not amount to an interference with constitutional rights, or at least the interference would be justified. The problem with this construction lies in the substantive justification of universal state liability. The only significant point here is that the liability and responsibility of the state cannot be justified on the grounds of the state's *participation* in the invitation, simply by failing to prohibit it. If the invitation is to be related to the state in some

citizen towards another. The acts for which it is responsible are private interferences with constitutional interests such as life, liberty, and property. The responsibility which the state has can only consist in a duty to prevent third parties from interfering with constitutional interests. But this makes the *duty* to prevent interferences the crux of the argument.

By contrast, a mere permission tells us nothing about participation and responsibility. Nor is mere impact on a constitutional interest adequate. A third party can endanger the state of a marriage as much as he pleases, but this still does not involve state participation in his action, even if it is legally permissible. The decisive issue is always the existence of a state duty of protection and its corresponding right. Non-prohibition or permission on the part of the state might be a breach of protective rights within the positive status. But it is not an interference with a defensive right.[89]

Nor do duties of toleration succeed in bypassing protective rights. The concept of a duty of toleration is one of a number of notoriously obscure concepts in general legal theory. Schwabe himself comments in passing that it would be better to avoid it.[90] In the case of duties to tolerate interferences by private individuals, one must distinguish between two levels. The first level is that of the pure no-right. A non-smoker x has as against the smoker y a no-right that y refrain from smoking ($\sim G$), whenever y is permitted to smoke (G) in relation to x.[91] As regards this relational permission and the no-right what has just been said in connection with permissions generally applies. It does not follow that the state is responsible for y's smoking as an interference with x's constitutional rights from the mere fact that y is not prohibited from smoking in relation to x and that x is in a position of no-right as against y as regards refraining from smoking. The mere fact that the state leaves x in a position of a no-right as against y in respect of refraining from smoking does not mean that it has interfered with x's right against the state to bodily integrity. Rather, it might be the case that the state infringes x's right against the state that it protect him from interferences by third parties, in that it burdens him with the position of a no-right. The fact that x's no-right is a sufficient reason for a civil court to reject x's action for an injunction against y adds nothing to the argument. The rejection of an application, although it is a state act, cannot be an infringement of a state-aimed defensive right, but only an infringement of a state-aimed entitlement in the form of a protective right, which the state has failed to fulfil.

way, this can only come about by way of a universal state *duty*. But this turns the whole issue once again into a matter of protective duties and rights. What then is the point of the complex defensive right construction?

[89] See D. Rauschning, 'Staatsaufgabe Umweltschutz', VVDStRL 38 (1980), 184 with further references.

[90] Schwabe, *Probleme der Grundrechtsdogmatik*, 16.

[91] See above 136: $\sim Rxy\sim G \leftrightarrow PyxG$.

The second level of the duty to tolerate is no different. This second level consists of the prohibitions and rights which protect the permission (freedom) of the interfering private individual.[92] The freedom of *y* to smoke is protected as against *x*, as indeed against all other private individuals, by the fact that *x* is not allowed to do certain things to prevent *y* from smoking. *x* is not allowed to injure, coerce, or defame *y*. These protections are not intrinsically related to smoking, but protect all legal liberty as a 'protective perimeter'.[93] So the question is whether the state can be held responsible for the use made of legal liberty against other private individuals because it protects liberty generally in this way. The answer again is no. The state is not accountable for private acts just because it protects the legal permission to engage in them. If that were so, the state would be accountable for innumerable acts. Rather it is the case that *because* the state by the general legal protection of liberty has removed many possibilities of self-defence from the victims of adverse acts of fellow-citizens, it also has the constitutional *duty* to grant protection to an appropriate extent. So in respect of the duty to tolerate, the protective duty/right route is preferable to that of defensive rights.

The third aspect, state enforcement of the duty to tolerate, makes no difference either. Assume that a non-smoker has violently prevented a smoker from smoking and has thus committed a criminal offence. As a result he is sentenced to a term of imprisonment. There is no doubt that in implementing this sanction the state is interfering with the constitutional right to the freedom of the person, which becomes relevant as a defensive right against the state sanction. Even if one assumes that smoking is generally capable of interfering with bodily integrity, it does not follow that the state is simultaneously interfering with the constitutional defensive right of the non-smoker to bodily integrity. The state may bring about a situation in which the non-smoker is only left with the choice of putting up with the smoking or committing a criminal offence. But what has to be put up with is still a private act.[94] Of course, this does not mean that a non-smoker may not be injured by the state in his constitutional right to bodily integrity. But the injury does not consist in the state's participation in the act of smoking, thus breaching the *defensive* constitutional right to bodily integrity, but only rather in the fact that the state in regulating the relationship between smokers and non-smokers has breached the constitutional right of the non-smoker in the form of a *protective* right.

One could take the view that the effort which has gone into distinguishing defensive and protective rights is not worthwhile. This impression is misleading, as the following consideration of the structure of protective rights shows.

---

[92] On the concept of protection, see above at 148 ff. [93] See above at 148.
[94] See A. Bleckmann, *Allgemeine Grundrechtslehren* (Cologne and Berlin, 1979), 142.

3. Structure and Justiciability of Protective Rights

It has been regularly pointed out that the justiciability of rights to negative actions (defensive rights) gives rise to fewer problems than rights to positive actions (entitlements). An important reason for this lies in a simple but fundamental structural distinction. Defensive rights are prohibitions on destroying, adversely affecting, and so on, directed to the addressee. Entitlements are commands to protect, support, and so on.[95] When there is a *prohibition* on destroying or adversely affecting something, then *every* act which represents or brings about destruction or an adverse effect is prohibited.[96] By contrast, if there is a *command* to protect or support something, then *not every* act which represents or brings about protection or support is required.[97] The prohibition on killing implies, at least prima facie, the prohibition of every act of killing, whereas the command to rescue does not imply a command to carry out every possible act of rescuing. If it is possible to save a drowning man by swimming to him, or by throwing him a life-ring, or by sending out a boat, then in no way are all three acts simultaneously required. What is required is rather that *either* the first, *or* the second, *or* the third act be performed. But this means that the addressee of the command to rescue the drowning man, in the absence of other limiting reasons, has a *discretion* as to which method he will choose to satisfy the command. And it is that word 'discretion' which is decisive for the issue of the justiciability of rights to positive acts.

One might be tempted to see the reason for the distinction just drawn in the fact that rights to positive acts, unlike the rights to negative acts, are concerned with means–end relations. But this is not an adequate explanation. Just as a protective right requires the adoption of at least one *means* of protection, so defensive rights exclude the adoption of any *means* of destruction or adverse effect. The reason for the difference lies deeper. It consists in the fact that refraining from each individual destructive or adverse act is a necessary condition, and only refraining from all destructive and adverse acts is a sufficient condition, for satisfying the prohibition on destruction and adverse effect and thus for satisfying the defensive right,

---

[95] See above at 126 f.

[96] In the language of rights: if there is a right that something should not be destroyed or interfered with, then there is a right that each act which represents or brings about destruction or interference be not performed. On the basis of the deontic law $O\ (p \wedge q) \leftrightarrow Op \wedge Oq$ (see on this D. Føllesdal and R. Hilpinen, 'Deontic Logic: An Introduction', in R. Hilpinen (ed.), *Deontic Logic: Introductory and Systematic Readings* (Dordrecht, 1971), 13), it is irrelevant whether one understands this as one right that acts x_1, x_2, . . . be omitted, or whether one understands it as a right that x_1 be omitted, a right that x_2 be omitted, etc.

[97] These propositions are very general formulations capable, and in need of, further qualification. In particular, as the immediately following examples show, it is necessary to distinguish prima facie and definitive prohibitions and commands. Thus a prima facie prohibition on destroying something is only a prima facie prohibition of each act of destruction.

while the satisfaction of commands to protect or support, as indeed generally for the satisfaction of entitlements, requires only the adoption of one suitable protective or supporting act. Where several protective or supporting acts are suitable, no single one is necessary to satisfy the command to protect or support. It is only necessary that one be adopted. Only if there is only one suitable protective or supportive act does this become necessary to satisfy the entitlement. In this case the structure of the entitlement would match that of defensive rights.

This distinction is to be found in the case-law of the Federal Constitutional Court in that the Court on one hand says *that* the state has a protective duty, but on the other hand emphasizes that the decision *how* this duty is to be fulfilled, 'in the first instance', 'to a large extent', or 'in principle' is a matter for the legislature.[98] Thus to start with, the Schleyer Judgment states, 'article 2(2)(1) in connection with article 1(1)(2) Basic Law obligates the state to protect every human life. This protective duty is comprehensive.' Then there follows, 'how the state organs are to fulfil their duty effectively to protect life is *in principle* to be decided by them on their own responsibility. They are to decide which protective measures are appropriate and required to ensure a real protection of life.'[99] If one ignores for the moment the phrase 'in principle', which indicates a more extensive obligation, then in respect of the obligation of the legislature the two quotations give rise to two propositions: (1) the state must adopt an effective means; (2) if there is only one effective means, the state must adopt this one. This latter point is made in the Schleyer Judgment in the following way: The 'freedom to choose the means of protecting life can in certain circumstances be limited to the choice of only one specific means, if the effective protection of life cannot be achieved in any other way'.[100]

Up to this point, the structure of protective duties and thus also protective rights has been entirely straightforward and clear. The real problems start with further distinctions. The need to draw further distinctions arises for two reasons. The means of protection cannot simply be divided into two classes, effective and ineffective. There are more or less effective means of protection. On the other hand, protective duties have the character of principles, they require maximally extensive protection relative to what is factually and legally possible, which means that they can compete with other principles. Typical of the latter is the statement in the Schleyer Judgment that the Basic Law establishes 'a duty of protection not only as against the individual, but also against the entirety of all citizens'.[101]

The possibility of different degrees of effectiveness and of competing

---

[98] BVerfGE 39, 1 (42, 44); 46, 160 (164).
[99] BVerfGE 46, 160 (164) (emphasis added).
[100] BVerfGE 46, 160 (164 f.); similarly BVerfGE 39, 1 (46 f.).
[101] BVerfGE 46, 160 (165).

principles makes it necessary to refine the basic model considerably. A simple example will show how this is to be carried out. Assume that there are five means of satisfying protective duty P_1, namely M_1 to M_5, as well as a competing principle P_2. M_5 is totally ineffective. For that reason it is already excluded by the basic model. M_1 and M_2 are as effective as each other, as are M_3 and M_4. However, M_1 and M_2 are more effective than M_3 and M_4. On its own, P_1 requires M_1 or M_2. If one were proceeding on the basis of the basic model alone, the discretion of the basic model would apply in respect of M_1 and M_2. Suppose now that the competing principle P_2 is affected in its realization by the adoption of all four remaining means, but that it is more severely affected by M_1 and M_2 than by M_3 and M_4. In this case, the principles must be balanced to determine whether P_1 is so weighty as against P_2 that the use of M_1 or M_2 is still justified, and, should this not be the case, whether at least the use of M_3 or M_4 is justified. If neither is the case, the choice of all suitable means of satisfying the prima facie protective duty is definitively prohibited; if it is not true that neither is the case, because at least the adoption of M_3 or M_4 can be justified in the light of P_1 as against P_2, then the discretion of the basic model obtains with respect to M_3 and M_4. But this discretion can easily be limited, because while M_3 and M_4 may be equally effective with regard to P_1, M_4 may interfere with P_2 more intensively than M_3, so that the choice of M_4 would represent an unnecessary interference with P_2, which means that the use of M_3 can be justified as the least intrusive means with respect to P_2. There would then no longer be any discretion in respect of the realization of P_1, although there are several effective means, and indeed some of which are equally effective.

The discretion which has been referred to until now—it can be called '*structural discretion*'—gives rise in itself to no pressing problems as regards the issue of justiciability. However, the problems become pressing in connection with the closely implicated issues of balancing and effectivity. Structural discretion is related to two other quite different forms of discretion, namely with an *epistemic discretion* in respect of the normative problem of *balancing*, and an *epistemic discretion* in respect of the empirical problem of *effectivity*. The problem of effectivity is largely concerned with the effect of current measures in the future, that is, with problems of prognosis.[102] The assessment of the problem of justiciability is thus connected with the role that problems of balancing and prognosis play in the context of protective rights.

As has already often been pointed out, balancing principles is not odd in constitutional law. It is unavoidable in the context of defensive rights as well. If the problems of balancing in the context of protective rights are

---

[102] See K. J. Philippi, *Tatsachenfeststellungen des Bundesverfassungsgerichts* (Cologne, Berlin, Bonn, and Munich, 1971), 28 ff.

supposed to make them less justiciable than defensive rights, then they must have some special characteristics in that context. Schuppert's suggestion that one should distinguish between uni- and multidimensional liberty problems, relating this to different levels of reviewing competence by the Federal Constitutional Court and to different degrees of legislative discretion, points in this direction.[103] Unidimensional liberty problems arise when 'common interests and constitutionally protected individual interests' conflict. This is supposed to be the case with defensive rights. Schuppert takes the view that the required solution to such conflicts 'can be established with a high degree of plausibility through interpretation as already determined by the constitution'.[104] By contrast, multidimensional liberty problems are those in which 'common interests and constitutionally protected individual interests' do not conflict, but where 'the legal positions of individuals and groups, which can all equally appeal to a constitutional basis, or even constitutional rights' do. Unlike a unidimensional conflict, the solutions to these conflicts 'are not predetermined by the constitution'.[105] The consequences for the problem of justiciability are obvious.

Protective rights are largely concerned with delimiting the positions of different constitutional right-holders. If Schuppert's analysis works, this has far-reaching consequences for their justiciability. But Schuppert's analysis only works to a very minor degree. The first point is that the distinction between uni- and multidimensional liberty problems is only workable under certain conditions—Schuppert himself speaks in terms of a gradual shift.[106] Balancing in the context of defensive rights can take account not only of common interests but also the rights of others, and common interests can play a decisive role alongside the rights of others when balancing in the context of protective rights. This triadic structure (rights of x, common interests, rights of y_1, y_2 ...) lurks behind every constitutional rights problem. Thus an interference with legal liberty which is to be judged against defensive rights can be justified not only by reference to its necessity in protecting certain common interests, but also by reference to its necessity in protecting individual positions of others.[107] In reverse, the refusal to grant protection can be justified not only by the need to respect the individual positions of others, but also with reference to the need to protect common interests. One comment in the Müllheim–Kärlich Judgment is to be understood in this last sense. There, the Court speaks of the function of the state, 'having regard to *general needs*, to carry out an accommodation between the constitutional positions of endangered citizens on one hand and the industry on the other'.[108] Burdening endangered citizens with residual risk could

---

[103] Schuppert, *Funktionell-rechtliche Grenzen der Verfassungsinterpretation*, 38 ff.
[104] ibid. 41.   [105] ibid.   [106] ibid. 46.
[107] See BVerfGE 49, 24 (53 ff.).
[108] BVerfGE 53, 30 (57 f.) (emphasis added).

hardly be justified by the liberties of the industry *alone*. So it is no accident that the Court refers to the 'general interest in the provision of energy'.[109]

Thus the sharpness of the distinction between uni- and multidimensional problems is not that great. Nevertheless, one can say that the proportion of complex balancing exercises which the Federal Constitutional Court has to undertake is greater among those concerning protective rights than it is among those concerning defensive rights. But one cannot draw from this the conclusion—and this leads to the second weakness of Schuppert's argument—that defensive and protective problems are distinguished by the fact that the former are largely predetermined by the Constitution and the latter not. We will not consider the obscure concept of constitutional predetermination any further. We will simply assume that a constitutional question is predetermined by the Constitution if there is no reasonable doubt about the correctness of the answer for everyone who holds to the constitutional text and the rules of constitutional argumentation. Guided by this assumption, then even in the field of defensive rights there are innumerable questions which are not predetermined. A proponent of Schuppert's thesis could accept this, but deflect it with the observation that defensive rights are concerned with everyday legal controversy and uncertainty which remains within a certain zone of plausibility, whereas protective rights are concerned with doubts and disputes of a more fundamental nature. Even this distinction is dubious. There are problems in the area of defensive rights which extend far beyond the scope of jurisprudence to the most fundamental controversies—think, for example, of the right to demonstrate—and there are positions within the area of protective rights which no one ever seriously questions—think of the protection from bodily injury by the criminal law. This makes it clear that the boundaries of legislative discretion, and the competence of the constitutional court, cannot depend on structural distinctions such as that between defensive and protective rights, but solely on substantive issues. As can be stated on the basis of the general concept of a constitutional right formulated above, the substantive issue is whether a certain form of protection is so important from the perspective of constitutional law, that granting it or refusing to grant it cannot be left to simple parliamentary majorities.

This formula also contains the key to the solution of the prognosis problem. It is easy to see that each suggested solution to the prognosis problem implies a suggested division of competence between the constitutional court and the legislature.[110] The issue in each case is whether a means of protection M satisfies the protective duty D. According to prognosis Pg_1 it does;

---

[109] BVerfGE 53, 30 (58).

[110] See F. Ossenbühl, 'Die Kontrolle von Tatsachenfeststellungen und Prognoseentscheidungen durch das Bundesverfassungsgericht', in C. Starck (ed.), *Bundesverfassungsgericht und Grundgesetz*, i (Tübingen, 1976), 467 ff.; Schuppert, *Funktionell-rechtliche Grenzen der Verfassungsinterpretation*, 54.

according to prognosis Pg_2 it does not. The legislature adopts Pg_1. If the legislature has the competence to decide which prognosis to adopt, then the constitutional court cannot say that the protective duty has been breached. If the court has the competence to decide, then it could say that Pg_1 is false, Pg_2 correct, and that protective duty D is therefore not satisfied by M.

Discussion of prognosis competence reveals that all-or-nothing solutions are not appropriate. The legislature cannot proceed on the basis of any prognosis it pleases, but nor can the constitutional court replace the prognoses of the legislature with its own at will, and nor is there any simple rule which definitively delimits the competence of the legislature and the competence of the court in all cases.[111] Rather, as the Federal Constitutional Court rightly stated in the Co-determination Judgment, the solution lies in the outworking of 'differentiated standards . . . which extend from a review of evidence . . . through a review of plausibility, to an intensive substantive control'.[112] This is not the place to go into the structure and problems of such a gradated system of review. What is interesting is simply the justification for the requirement of gradation. Its starting-point is the recognition that the extent of constitutional rights protection by the Court, and thus the extent of the definitive constitutional rights positions existing in the legal system, depends to a significant extent on the extent of the prognostic discretion of the legislature. As regards the limiting of constitutional protection, prognostic discretion is *in outcome* no different from the competence to set limits. This reveals that its extent can only be determined by reference to the constitutional principle at issue in the case, the weight of which in the particular case is decisive.[113] It is in this sense that the Court stated in the Passengers Judgment, 'the more that statutory intervention affects elementary expressions of human freedom of action, the more carefully the reasons put forward for its justification have to be weighed against the basic claim of the citizen to liberty'.[114] Thus the prognosis problem becomes one of balancing relevant substantive constitutional principles with the formal principle of the democratically legitimated competence of the legislature to take decisions. The large number of other relevant aspects[115] are to be taken account of in the context of this balancing.

[111] See Ossenbühl, 'Die Kontrolle von Tatsachenfeststellungen und Prognoseentscheidungen', 503.
[112] BVerfGE 50, 290 (333). For a demand for a 'differentiated, substantive and thematically gradated control system', see also Ossenbühl, 'Die Kontrolle von Tatsachenfeststellungen und Prognoseentscheidungen', 501.
[113] For a reliance on the 'value' or 'strength' of the relevant constitutional right, see U. Seetzen, 'Der Prognosespielraum des Gesetzgebers', NJW 1975, 432 f.; Ossenbühl, 'Die Kontrolle von Tatsachenfeststellungen und Prognoseentscheidungen', 506 f.
[114] BVerfGE 17, 306 (314).
[115] These include, for example, 'the characteristics of the field in question' as well as the 'possibilities of forming a sufficiently certain judgment' (BVerfGE 50, 290 (333)).

The decisive point here is that the problem of balancing as it affects prognostic discretion appears equally in both defensive and protective rights. With protective rights it often has a greater weight on account of their special link to the future, but this only amounts to a difference of degree. We can therefore maintain the position that as regards justiciability, protective rights do not give rise to any problems which do not already arise with defensive rights.

III. RIGHTS TO ORGANIZATION AND PROCEDURE

1. ON THE CURRENT STATE OF DEBATE

No idea has attracted as much attention in recent discussion of constitutional rights as the thought that there is a connection between constitutional rights, organization and procedure. Key elements of the discussion are Häberle's suggestion of a *status activus processualis*, which is supposed to relate to the 'procedural side of constitutional liberty, "constitutional due process" '[116] and Hesse's thesis that 'organization and procedure often [turn out] to be the—sometimes only—means of bringing about an outcome compatible with the constitution, and thus realistically to secure constitutional rights in the light of modern problems'.[117] Goerlich has attempted to make the idea of procedure fruitful for an overarching concept of constitutional rights. It becomes clear just how far this goes when Goerlich speaks of 'material and formal constitutional rights as the procedural guarantee of the political, legal and even social processes of a society'.[118] The idea of procedure has not only attracted attention in German constitutional law. As far as the United States is concerned, the controversy between Ely[119] and Tribe[120] is a good example. In addition, the emergence of procedural ideas is not limited to jurisprudence, as the intensive discussion of procedural theories in modern ethics shows.[121] So constitutional rights doctrine seems here to have found a 'key word'[122] which first holds out the promise of a middle road between a comprehensive theory of values enforced by the constitutional court and allowing the legislature to do all

---

[116] P. Häberle, 'Grundrechte im Leistungsstaat', VVDStRL 30 (1972), 81.
[117] K. Hesse, 'Bestand und Bedeutung der Grundrechte in der Bundesrepublik Deutschland', EuGRZ 1978, 434 f.
[118] H. Goerlich, *Grundrechte als Verfahrensgarantien* (Baden-Baden, 1981), 203.
[119] Ely, *Democracy and Distrust*.
[120] L. H. Tribe, 'The Puzzling Persistence of Process-Based Constitutional Theories', Yale LJ 89 (1980), 1063 ff.
[121] See e.g. Rawls, *A Theory of Justice*; J. Habermas, 'Discourse Ethics: Notes on a Program of Philosophical Justification', in id., *Moral Consciousness and Communicative Action*, trans. C. Lenhardt and S. W. Nicholsen, (Cambridge, 1990), 43 ff.
[122] Häberle, 'Grundrechte im Leistungsstaat', 129.

the work on account of a subjectivistic value-scepticism, which secondly accords with the spirit of the age, and which thirdly leads to an area so familiar to lawyers.

In view of such far-reaching perspectives, it is hardly surprising that some have sounded a cautious note. Ossenbühl warns against a 'general constitutional rights-oriented procedural euphoria . . . which could have unforeseeable consequences and which will then lead in due course to unnecessary frustration, as so many other jurisprudential fashions have'.[123] Bethge speaks of a 'foreground plasticity' of the 'argumentation peg "realization and securing of constitutional rights through organization and procedure" ' and of a 'Passepartout-formula'.[124] In saying these things, neither writer rejects an (additional) interpretation of constitutional rights provisions in the light of the idea of procedure. What is being demanded is the drawing of distinctions, and this demand is justified. The idea of procedure so central to practical philosophy and jurisprudence[125] and the idea of constitutional rights concern such a variety of complex matters, that a simple transfer of *the* idea of procedure to *all* constitutional rights can at best lead only to trivial outcomes.

The case-law of the Federal Constitutional Court provides some examples of a differentiated application of the idea of procedure. It is interesting not least because the Court had worked through certain key weaknesses in procedural theory before it attracted so much attention. Large parts of the discussion about 'constitutional rights as procedural guarantees' are attempts to reproduce and conceptualize existing developments in judicial practice. The case-law of the Federal Constitutional Court will therefore stand right at the forefront of the discussion of the existence and structure of procedural rights.

2. THE CONCEPT OF A RIGHT TO ORGANIZATION AND PROCEDURE

The content of rights to organization and procedure is highly ambiguously described by that phrase. One has to ask whether the concept of rights to organization and procedure describes one connected complex of rights, or whether the term combines *two* separate complexes of rights to organization and rights to procedure, which could actually be treated separately.

It is noticeable that the phrase 'realization and securing of constitutional rights through organization and procedure',[126] which has in time come

---

[123] F. Ossenbühl, 'Kernenergie im Spiegel des Verfassungsrechts', DÖV 1981, 6.

[124] H. Bethge, 'Grundrechtsverwirklichung und Grundrechtssicherung durch Organisation und Verfahren', NJW 1982, 2.

[125] See R. Alexy, 'Juristische Argumentation und praktische Vernunft', in *Jahrbuch der Akademie der Wissenschaften in Göttingen*, 1982, 29 ff.

[126] Hesse, 'Bestand und Bedeutung der Grundrechte', 434; C. Starck, 'Die Grundrechte des Grundgesetzes', Jus 1981, 242; Bethge, 'Grundrechtsverwirklichung und Grundrechtssicherung', 1.

perpetually to be used, is regularly found as a heading for discussions which by no means distinguish strictly between rights to organization and rights to procedure. The distinctions which are drawn[127] do not follow a clear line between the concepts of procedure and organization, but quite different criteria. This makes it clear that the common usage of both expressions is relatively non-technical.

The reason for the relatively non-technical use of the term is easy to see. The range of its reference is very wide. It extends from rights to effective legal protection,[128] which no one would refuse to call 'procedural rights', to rights to 'organizational state measures'[129] such as those relevant to the creation of academic committees in universities. Putting such different things under one term, whether it carries a combined label or not, is only justified if they have commonalities which justify the combination. The justifying commonality of the combination is the idea of procedure. Procedures are systems of rules and/or principles for the production of outcomes. If the outcome is produced in observance of the rules or having regard to the principles, then it is from a procedural perspective to be treated positively. If it is not produced in this way, then it is from a procedural perspective faulty and to be treated negatively. This broad definition of procedure covers everything which falls under the phrase, 'realization and securing of constitutional rights through organization and procedure'. So in spite of obvious differences, under this definition both the norms of contract law and of legal procedure are procedural norms. The former set out how a contractual obligation can be produced, the latter, a judgment. At the same time, the wide concept of procedure shows what is relevant about the idea of procedure in the context of constitutional rights. Norms of procedure and organization should be formulated in such a way that the outcome is with adequate probability and to an adequate extent constitutional.[130] How far it is possible to establish such a connection between legal procedures and their outcomes can for the moment be ignored.

The idea of procedure justifies drawing the variety of phenomena found in the field of organization and procedure under one head. By contrast, the

---

[127] See e.g. Hesse, 'Bestand und Bedeutung der Grundrechte', 435 ff.; Ossenbühl, 'Kernenergie im Spiegel des Verfassungsrechts', 5 f.; Bethge, 'Grundrechtsverwirklichung und Grundrechtssicherung, 2 ff.

[128] See BVerfGE 34, 367 (401); 35, 348 (361); 37, 132 (148); 39, 276 (294); 44, 105 (120); 45, 297 (322); 45, 422 (431); 46, 325 (334); 48, 292 (297); 49, 220 (225); 49, 252 (256); 51, 150 (156); 52, 391 (408).

[129] BVerfGE 35, 79 (116).

[130] Procedural and organizational norms need not only have the character of means; they can be ends in themselves. A procedural norm N has the character of a constitutional rights end-in-itself, if N would still be constitutionally required, even if it could be established that were N to apply the outcome of the procedure would under no circumstances and in no respect be constitutionally more compatible than if N were not to apply. It is an open question whether there are any organizational and procedural norms which are constitutional rights ends-in-themselves.

terminological question is of secondary importance. Instead of rights to organization and procedure, one could simply talk about procedural rights on the basis of a wide concept of procedure which also embraces organizational norms. Use will regularly be made of this possibility purely for reasons of simplicity.

Even after all this there remains a fundamental ambiguity. Procedural rights could be both rights to the enactment of certain procedural norms, and also rights to a certain 'interpretation and concrete application' of procedural norms.[131] An example of the latter are the many decisions of the constitutional courts on the law of compulsory auctions, which are concerned with a constitutionally compatible interpretation of procedural norms.[132] The right to procedure in the form of a right to effective legal protection is in these cases addressed to the courts. Procedural rights, which have as their object the enactment of procedural norms, are by contrast addressed to the legislature as rights to law-making. Here we are principally concerned with these latter rights.

3. ON THE PROBLEM OF THEIR EXISTENCE

Answers to questions about the existence and structure of rights to organization and procedure all depend on what types of rights to organization and procedure we are concerned with. But in spite of the need to differentiate, it is a good idea to discuss the problem of their existence generally, before looking at the different types.

As regards the problem of their existence, the most important question is to what extent constitutionally based duties of the legislature to take responsibility for particular procedures and organization correspond to subjective rights of right-holders. While the literature deals with questions of organization and procedure for the most part without much thought as a problem of duties of the legislature,[133] and while an objectivist tendency is also argued for,[134] the case-law contains interesting references as regards the question of subjectification.

The common theme of the case-law is that regardless of the fact that the Basic Law contains direct procedurally related rights in the form of legal process rights (arts. 19(4), 101(1), 103(1), 104), and regardless of the fact that the Rule of Law can generally be used to ground requirements for the

---

[131] See BVerfGE 53, 30 (61).

[132] See e.g. BVerfGE 46, 325 (333 ff.); 49, 220 (225 ff.); 49, 252 (256 ff.); 51, 150 (156).

[133] See e.g. Bethge, 'Grundrechtsverwirklichung und Grundrechtssicherung', 2 ff.; W. Schmidt, 'Grundrechtstheorie im Wandel der Verfassungsgeschichte', 169 ff.

[134] See e.g. Rupp, 'Vom Wandel der Grundrechte', 176 ff.; 187 ff. as also, very decisively, U. K. Preuß, *Die Internalisierung des Subjekts* (Frankfurt a. M., 1979), 189 ff.; 194, for whom there is 'no legal claim against the legislature to the creation of liberal structures. The establishment of liberal structures is purely a function of the political process, and within that, a function of the legislature charged with enacting binding law.'

existence and formation of procedures, procedural rights are derived from substantive constitutional rights.[135] The start of the development is represented by the statement in the Lake-Regulations Judgment that 'according to the conception of the Basic Law, . . . effective legal protection securing property [is] an important element of the constitutional right itself'.[136] The right to legal protection, initially tied to the right to property, has been generalized in the further course of the case-law in two ways. First, it has been extended to ever more constitutional rights,[137] and secondly, the right to effective legal protection through the courts has been generalized to a right to constitutional protection by procedure *per se*.[138] Today, one can say that according to the case-law of the Federal Constitutional Court every substantive constitutional right contains a procedural right. But if substantive rights are subjective rights why not also the procedural rights? The anchoring of protection through procedure in the substantive right creates at any rate a prima facie argument for their subjectification.

Their subjective character gives rise to hardly any problems where we are concerned with rights addressed to the judiciary to a constitutionally compatible interpretation and application of broadly constitutional procedural norms, as in the Enforcement of Judgments Judgment.[139] Problems start arising by contrast when we come to rights that certain procedures should apply, that is, rights that norms be enacted in the field of organization and procedure. Reference will only be made here to the thoughts above concerning protective rights and to two interesting decisions in this connection. In the first one, the University Judgment, one can find a paradigm statement, which has already been often cited, of a subjective right to certain procedures addressed to the legislature. On the basis of the constitutional right in article 5(3) Basic Law, the constitutional right-holder has 'a right to such state measures, including organizational ones, which are indispensable in the protection of his constitutionally-secured sphere of freedom'.[140] It is easy to extrapolate a subjective right to procedural norms from the second decision, the judgment concerning the Hamburg Lake-Regulations. There the court for reasons of security of rights permitted a direct statutory expropriation only in exceptional cases.[141] This means that

[135] For some structural problems of this practice of derivation, see Bethge, 'Grundrechtsverwirklichung und Grundrechtssicherung', 6 f.; D. Lorenz, 'Der grundrechtliche Anspruch auf effektiven Rechtsschutz', AöR 105 (1980), 639 f.
[136] BVerfGE 24, 367 (401).
[137] On art. 14 Basic Law, see e.g. BVerfGE 35, 348 (361); 37, 132 (148); 45, 297 (322); 46, 325 (334); 49, 220 (225); 49, 252 (256); 51, 150 (156); on art. 12 Basic Law, see, e.g. BVerfGE 39, 276 (294); 41, 251 (265); 44, 105 (120); 45, 422 (431); 48, 292 (297); 52, 380 (388 ff.); on art. 2(1) Basic Law, see e.g. BVerfGE 52, 214 (219); 53, 30 (65); on art. 16(2)(2) Basic Law, see e.g. BVerfGE 52, 391 (407).
[138] BVerfGE 53, 30 (65).
[139] See e.g. BVerfGE 49, 220 (225 ff.); 49, 252 (256 ff.); 51, 150 (156 ff.).
[140] BVerfGE 35, 79 (116).   [141] BVerfGE 24, 367 (402 f.).

article 14 Basic Law contains a right that expropriation in non-exceptional cases only be carried out through the process of administrative expropriation. Both decisions make it clear that the constitutional court is not ruling out the existence of subjective rights addressed to the legislature to certain enactments in the field of organization and procedure. No more can be said at an abstract level. Everything else depends on the type of right at issue.

4. PROCEDURAL RIGHTS AND STATUS THEORY

One of the most interesting structural problems of procedural rights is whether they are really to be located in the positive status as rights to positive acts, or whether they do not rather belong to the negative or active status.

4.1 Procedural Rights and Negative Status

Earlier on, rights to the non-removal of legal positions were also described as rights to negative state action.[142] There are countless ordinary legal procedural positions on the basis of ordinary legal norms. To the extent that their existence is constitutionally required, and this is to a large degree the case, the procedural content of constitutional rights norms consists also in the prohibition of their removal, that is, they protect from acts of removal. Does this mean that it is false to deal with procedural rights, as here, in the context of the positive status?

The answer is no. It is indeed correct that the procedural content of constitutional rights norms consists to a large extent in the protection of existing procedural positions, either prohibiting their removal outright, or at least without substitute. It is also correct that the rights corresponding to these prohibitions are to be located in the negative status (in the wide sense),[143] which means that procedurally directed constitutional rights norms can to a large extent be discussed also in the context of negative status rights. But it does not follow from all this that it is inadequate, let alone false, to deal with procedural rights in the context of the positive status.

A first argument for this is that when state action is not a matter of securing the normative state of affairs, but of creating something new, the question is always whether the state has to *do* something (enact norms) or not. It is different in the case of rights of non-interference with actions and the non-affecting of (natural) states of affairs.[144] With them, the question is always whether the state has to *refrain* from doing something. The force of this argument is, however, limited. One could accept it and say that procedural rights concerned with new matters should be dealt with in the context of the positive status, but that the securing of already existing ordinary legal

---

[142] 125 ff.   [143] See above at 171.   [144] See above at 122 ff.

procedural positions is exclusively a question of the negative status, which would mean that the procedural aspect, to a large extent, would be dealt with under the negative status. To justify general treatment in the context of the positive status further argument is necessary.

That further argument is that rights to procedural positions are rights that certain things should exist which require positive acts to bring them into being. From this perspective, it is a matter of chance whether the acts leading to the existence of procedural positions in ordinary law have already been carried out or not. The fact that the legislative acts necessary to bring about these positions in ordinary law have already been carried out does not alter the truth that had they not been carried out, a right that they be carried out would still exist. This hypothetical right of enactment is more important than the right to non-removal. This can be seen among other things from the fact that an answer to the question of whether an ordinary legal procedural position is protected by a right to non-removal presupposes an answer to the question whether the occupant of the position has a right as against the legislature that it make the position available to him.

A third argument, which has already been referred to above, merely confirms this.[145] It is not impossible to see the maintenance of existing norms, as well as enactments and repeals, as acts of the legislature. If one adopts this way of looking at things, the problem of status has a simple solution. In respect of existing procedural positions under ordinary law, procedural rights are rights that the legislature carry out the positive act of maintaining them in force.

4.2 Procedural Rights and Active Status

Classing procedural rights with active status rights seems more plausible than classing them with negative status rights. In this sense, Häberle states, 'the *status activus processualis* is derived from the hitherto primarily substantive *status activus*'.[146]

At first sight, the fact that the field of procedure and organization consists primarily of *powers*,[147] and that the active status is made up of powers,[148] seems to count towards such a classification. But a second look shows that things are not quite so simple. Rights against the legislature to organization and procedure are not powers but rights to powers. As such there can be no doubt that they belong to the positive status.

Admittedly, this is not the last word on the connection between rights to organization and procedure, and the active status. As rights to organization

---

[145] 126.

[146] Häberle, 'Grundrechte im Leistungsstaat', 81.

[147] If it is a matter of powers, then it is also a matter of liabilities, as it also is of the opposites of powers and liabilities, namely disabilities and immunities; on these concepts see above at 155.

[148] See above at 172 f.

and procedure, the rights in question do not belong to the active status, but their objects, that is, organization and procedure, for the most part powers, can belong to the active status.

In some cases this is unproblematic, as an example will show. Article 38(1) Basic Law gives to the individual a subjective right to vote. Voting without some form of organization is impossible. So article 38(1) gives the individual a right against the state that it organize matters to make voting possible. Since the Basic Law does not prescribe any particular electoral system,[149] and since competing electoral principles have to be taken account of in structuring an electoral system, the legislature has a not inconsiderable discretion.[150] But not everything is at its disposal. The powers of the individual, which the state has to create under article 38(1) by ordinary legislation, and to the existence of which the individual has a subjective constitutional right, make up a significant part of his active status in Jellinek's classic sense.

The question is, how far this can be generalized. One example which makes the difficulties of generalization plain is the duty of the state under article 9(1) Basic Law to make available norms for the creation of incorporated associations, which is treated by everyone, and correctly, as an instance of 'the realization and securing of constitutional rights through organization and procedure'. The powers established by the law of incorporated associations do not belong to the classic active status, because they are not powers of 'participation in the state' in Jellinek's sense.[151] If one none the less wants to class them in the active status, one has to expand this concept. Such an expansion could occur in two ways, either in that one includes all legal powers of the individual, or that one extends it to all legal positions the realization of which in some way affects or could affect state decision-taking. But neither development is desirable. To put all the powers that an individual has within a legal system under one heading is doubtless interesting, but the concept of active status should not be used for it. The citizen–state relation to which Jellinek's system is directed would be destroyed. It also seems pointless to include all legal positions the realization of which could have some effect on state decision-taking, such as the legal liberty to express one's opinion, within the active status. The distinction which is so important for legal systems between legal powers which have as their object the process of state decision-taking, and legal liberty to have a factual influence on it, the maintenance of which is advisable even for those whose prime interest is in factual influence, would be blurred. This says nothing against the possibility of classing all rights which in the widest sense have (or are supposed to have) an influence on the process of forming public or state opinion under one heading. What is being argued

---

[149] BVerfGE 6, 104 (111). [150] BVerfGE 3, 19 (24 f.).
[151] Jellinek, *System der subjektiven öffentlichen Rechte*, 136 ff.

for is that in such a reclassification structural differences are not lost which are significant for the legal situation of the individual and on which his factual situation to a great extent depends. For these purposes a structurally oriented, and that means narrower, concept of active status is advisable. An appropriate term for the wider concept is that of 'political rights'.

And so some, but not not all, of the objects of rights to organization and procedure belong to the active status. This leads to the question of the existence of a borderline between the positions which belong to the active status and those which do not. The Müllheim–Kärlich Judgment[152] is a good one against which to clarify this problem, and above all on account of the different emphases which the procedure of approval under atomic energy law received from the majority of the Court and the dissenting opinion. The rules of procedure for atomic energy approval do not grant a power of co-determination. There would only be powers of co-determination, and thus participation in the state decision-taking process in Jellinek's sense, if endangered citizens or their representatives were members of a body voting on the granting of an atomic energy licence, or if endangered citizens, or groups of them, had a right of veto. But the procedural position of the citizen is limited to a bundle of rights to information and debate. The power of objection, the exercise of which gives rise to a duty on the part of the governmental licence administrator to engage in consultation (sects. 7(1), 8(1) Atomic Procedure Regulations), can be seen as a central part of this right. Whether and how the objections are taken account of is a matter for the government administration. So in broad outline the procedure follows the classic model of *audi alteram partem* and not a voting model. If one ties the structure of this procedure with the purpose to which it is directed, namely the protection of individual rights,[153] then one has an argument against classifying it under the active status in Jellinek's sense.

The dissenting opinion paints a somewhat different picture. Here too the purpose of protecting individual rights is emphasized, and it is also insisted that 'the decision-taking prerogative of the relevant official must be maintained'. But what is interesting is how the protective purpose is to be achieved while the decision-taking competence of the official remains, namely by a 'process of communication between the operators of power-stations, endangered citizens and officials responsible', which is supposed to secure 'a scientific regard for all relevant aspects'.[154] In this connection, the opinion speaks in terms of an influence of the participants on the decision.[155] These comments have been understood to have a tendency in the direction of a direct-democratic decision procedure, and have been criticized on the basis of an inconsistency between the idea of such process and

---

[152] BVerfGE 53, 30.　　　　[153] BVerfGE 53, 30 (64).
[154] BVerfGE 53, 30 (77).　　　[155] BVerfGE 53, 30 (76).

constitutional rights.[156] The general problem of the relationship between constitutional rights and procedure[157] which this raises will only be dealt with later on. Here we are simply interested in one point which the dissenting opinion correctly makes, as well as its consequences for the problem of the extent of the active status. The dissenting opinion correctly points out that the purpose of participation is to ensure influence on the decision through the process of communication. If there were no real possibility that alternative decisions might be made on the basis of participation, which would not have been made in its absence, then participation would be an unsuitable means relative to the purpose of protecting constitutional rights, and thus pointless. It could only be directed to purposes other than constitutional rights protection, or perhaps towards the dubious purpose of protecting constitutional rights by delaying the interference with rights, regardless of whether it is unlawful or not. Here, we shall proceed on the assumption that it is not pointless as regards the protection of constitutional rights. It can then be said that participation creates legally the factual possibility of having an influence on the state decision-taking process related to the protection of constitutional rights. This is less than a legal power of co-determination in the state decision-taking process, but it has more to do with state decision-taking than the private law power to make a contract. Thus this example makes it clear that while the concept of the active status in Jellinek's sense offers an indispensible starting-point for understanding procedural and organizational positions, distinctions drawn with the help of finer instruments are needed in areas not covered by it.

5. Types of Right to Organization and Procedure

The variety of forms and contents of organization and procedure in the field of constitutional rights corresponds to a variety of possibilities for their classification. A comprehensive classification, taking account of all types and aspects, would only be possible on the basis of a detailed doctinal analysis of rights to organization and procedure. This would be material enough for another book. Here, we only have space to emphasize those aspects useful and required in the context of a general theory of the structure of constitutional rights. From this perspective a division of the relevant rights into four groups seems appropriate: (1) private law powers, (2) court and administrative procedures (procedure in the narrow sense), (3) organization in the narrow sense, and (4) state decision-taking.

---

[156] See Ossenbühl, 'Kernenergie im Spiegel des Verfassungsrechts', 3, 6.
[157] See e.g. Rupp, 'Vom Wandel der Grundrechte', 183 ff.; C. Starck, 'Die Grundrechte des Grundgesetzes', 242 f.

5.1 Private Law Powers

Rights to private law powers are rights against the state that the state make available norms constitutive of private legal acts, and thus constitutive of the creation, alteration, and removal of private law positions. These rights can be related both to the requirement that such norms be valid at all, and to the requirement that they have a certain content. Examples of complexes of norms which belong to the field of such rights, and which are discussed in the context of the realization and securing of constitutional rights through organization and procedure,[158] are the norms of contract law, property law, marriage, inheritance, and the law of incorporated associations.

The complexes of norms mentioned are exactly those which traditionally and appropriately are called 'legal institutions'. This leads to two questions. (1) What have private law legal institutions to do with the idea of procedure? (2) Do constitutional rights to private legal institutions exist at all, or are private legal institutions merely protected by an objective institutional guarantee?

The connection between private legal institutions and the idea of procedure consists in the fact that private legal institutions are mainly composed of powers, which as such do not already substantively separate the legal spheres of private legal persons, but rather create the legal possibility of creating such a separation. But this means that they are procedures for the creation of law. As procedures for private and autonomous law-making they are variants of one of the basic procedural models, namely the model of contract.[159]

The question of whether there are subjective rights to the existence of private legal institutions, or whether these are only objectively protected as against the legislature is not so easy to answer.[160] Since the work of Martin Wolff[161] and Carl Schmitt,[162] the constitutional protection of private legal institutions has been discussed as a problem of objective institution-guarantees.[163] [164] Under the Weimar Constitution, in view of the dilemma of

[158] K. Hesse, 'Bestand und Bedeutung der Grundrechte' 434; C. Starck, 'Staatliche Organisation und staatliche Finanzierung', in id., *Bundesverfassungsgericht und Grundgesetz*, 485.

[159] See R. Dreier, 'Recht und Gerechtigkeit', in *Funkkolleg Recht, Studienbegleitbrief 2*, issued by the Deutsche Institut für Fernstudien an der Universität Tübingen (Weinheim and Basle, 1982), 28 ff.   [160] See on this already above at 157.

[161] M. Wolff, 'Reichsverfassung und Eigentum', in *Festgabe für W. Kahl* (Tübingen, 1923), 5 f.

[162] Schmitt, *Verfassungslehre*, 170 ff.; id., 'Freiheitsrechte und institutionelle Garantien der Reichsverfassung', in id., *Verfassungsrechtliche Aufsätze*, 2nd edn. (Berlin, 1973), 140 ff., 160 ff.; id., 'Grundrechte und Grundpflichten', in ibid. 215 ff.

[163] Following C. Schmitt, 'institution-guarantee' [*Institutsgarantie*] refers to the constitutional rights protection of private law institutions, which is to be distinguished from an 'institutional guarantee' [*institutionelle Garantie*], which refers to public law entities; see C. Schmitt, 'Freiheitsrechte und institutionelle Garantien', 143, 149, 160 ff.

[164] On the state of recent discussions, see E. Schmidt-Jortzig, *Die Einrichtungsgarantien der Verfassung* (Göttingen, 1979).

'meaninglessness on one hand, ineffectiveness on the other',[165] this theory carried the securing of the constitutional status of certain rights a stage further.[166] But with article 1(3) Basic Law, which also binds the legislature to constitutional rights as directly binding law, this reason for the adoption of merely objective institution-guarantees has fallen away. The route to a subjectification of constitutional protection for private law powers is thus opened, and it is required, as above all Kloepfer has demonstrated,[167] that we take it.[168]

The main argument for subjectification is that numerous constitutional rights conceptually presuppose the existence of private legal institutions. Without norms of property, there can be no property in the legal sense, without norms of marriage there can be no marriage in the legal sense, and so on. The Federal Constitutional Court correctly comments, 'the constitutional right of the individual presupposes the legal institution called "property" '.[169] A legislature which abolished legal institutions such as property and marriage would be taking from constitutional right-holders something which they have a constitutional right to.

The real question is, who has subjective rights to what on the basis of which norms? As a test case we can consider the norms enabling the creation of private legal positions, that is, those which give rise to powers such as the acquisition of property and the conclusion of marriage. To adopt Kloepfer's words, such norms do not protect states of affairs but secure their creation.[170] As far as marriage is concerned, the Federal Constitutional Court has given a clear answer. On the basis of article 6(1) Basic Law it has recognized a 'right of freedom to contract marriage'.[171] This is to be understood in the sense that article 6(1) Basic Law contains among other things a right to the power to contract marriage with a freely chosen partner. Things are not as simple with the power to acquire property.[172] Would a law making the acquisition of property unlawful also breach the article 14 constitutional rights of persons who have no real property? Kloepfer says

---

[165] Schmitt, 'Freiheitsrechte und institutionelle Garantien', 141.

[166] See W. Schmidt, 'Grundrechtstheorie im Wandel der Verfassungsgeschichte', *Jura*, 1983, 174 f.

[167] M. Kloepfer, *Grundrechte als Entstehenssicherung und Bestandsschutz* (Munich, 1970), 37 ff.

[168] That the idea of constitutional rights to private law powers is not so very unusual can be seen from some of the regional constitutions. So for example art. 45(1)(3) Constitution of Hesse states, 'each person is entitled to acquire and dispose of property according to law'. See also art. 60(1)(2) Constitution of Rhineland-Palatinate; art. 109(1)(2) Constitution of Bavaria as well as art. 111(2) Weimar Imperial Constitution.

[169] BVerfGE 24, 367 (389).

[170] Kloepfer, *Grundrechte als Entstehenssicherung und Bestandsschutz*, 24 ff.

[171] BVerfGE 36, 146 (161).

[172] For the state of the controversy, see Kloepfer, *Grundrechte als Entstehenssicherung und Bestandsschutz*, 37 ff.; P. Wittig, 'Der Erwerb von Eigentum und das Grundgesetz', NJW 1967, 2185 ff.

that it would on the grounds that 'the freedom to dispose of property would be inconceivable without the freedom to acquire it'.[173] But the argument from an indubitable subjective constitutional protection of the power to dispose of property[174] to a corresponding subjective protection of the power to acquire property is not strictly necessary. A subjective right to a power of disposal is consistent with a merely objective protection of the power of acquisition through an institution-guarantee. The decisive argument for subjectification arises rather from the idea of procedure. In that constitutional rights guarantee private legal institutions, they guarantee procedures for private autonomous formation of legal relations among equals. Both the thought of the fairness of procedure as well as individual liberty in the realm of property require that not only already existing private law positions, but also the legal possibility of attaining to such positions, should benefit from full constitutional protection. Article 14 Basic Law should therefore be interpreted so that it guarantees a subjective right to the power to acquire property.

That final remark should be generalized. It is not as if there are first of all objective institution-guarantees which serve the securing of constitutional rights via securing a basic set of norms, and then secondly constitutional rights as subjective rights which are secured in this way. Rather, there is a subjective right to the validity of those private law norms which are necessary to make possible what the constitutional right guarantees. The institution-guarantee as a doctrinal construction is unnecessary. This does not mean that there is no constitutional guarantee of private law institutions. The fact that x has a right against the state that norms $N_1, \ldots, N_n$ of legal institution I be valid, means that the state is obligated to x to ensure that $N_1, \ldots, N_n$ apply. But if the state is obligated to x to ensure that these norms apply, then it is simply obligated to ensure that the norms apply. So the view put forward here does not lead to any lesser protection for constitutional securing of private law institutions. It simply adds a subjective element to their objective securing. This addition is indispensable if constitutional rights are to be taken seriously as individual rights.

5.2 Court and Administrative Procedures (Procedure in the Narrow Sense)

Rights to court and admininstrative procedures are mostly rights to 'effective legal protection'.[175] The condition of effective legal protection is that the outcome of the procedure protects the substantive rights of the rightholder affected. The formula of the Federal Constitutional Court is to be

---

[173] Kloepfer, *Grundrechte als Entstehenssicherung und Bestandsschutz*, 47.
[174] BVerfGE 26, 215 (222).
[175] See BVerfGE 34, 367 (401); 35, 348 (361); 37, 132 (148); 39, 276 (294); 44, 105 (120); 45, 297 (322); 45, 422 (432); 46, 325 (334); 48, 292 (297); 49, 220 (225); 49, 252 (256); 51, 150 (156); 53, 30 (64 f.).

linked to the protecting of substantive rights, when it describes the function of procedural law as follows: 'procedural law serves the attainment of legal, and in this respect correct, but beyond that also within the scope of that correctness, just, decisions'.[176] All this points to the fact that in the field of procedure two aspects have to be put into relation with each other, a procedural and a substantive aspect.

There are two fundamentally different models of the relationship between procedural and substantive aspects. According to the first model, the correctness of the outcome depends solely on the procedure. If the procedure is correctly carried out, then the outcome is correct. There is no procedurally independent standard of correctness. On the second model, by contrast, there are procedurally independent standards of correctness. The procedure is a means of satisfying them to the greatest degree possible as well as a way of filling the discretion left by the standards.

A general procedural theory has to add further distinctions to this one, in particular those which relate to a hierarchy of procedures.[177] However, we are not concerned here with general procedural theory, but with assessing the relationship between legal procedure and constitutional rights. If we limit ourselves to this point, then we can say that the idea of constitutional rights is only satisfied by the second model. Constitutional rights are in some decisive respects non-procedural. This is sharply revealed by their relationship to the democratic legislative process. Not everything which is the outcome of discussion and voting in Parliament is constitutionally possible. It is true that constitutional rights directly and indirectly secure participation in the democratic process. To this extent they are procedural. But on the other hand they set substantive limits to this procedure, and in this sense they are non-procedural.

The thought that constitutional requirements for procedure cannot displace constitutional requirements for the outcome applies for all legal procedures. When the dissenting opinion in the Müllheim–Kärlich Judgment sees it as 'decisive' that 'official procedure on its own is suitable to lead to "correct" decisions from the point of view of safety',[178] then this cannot be taken to express the view that the atomic licensing procedure, even when its rules are interpreted as consistently as possible with the Constitution, guarantees *as a procedure* a constitutionally correct outcome. This can be seen among other things from the fact that the procedural rule in question first of all does not guarantee the formation of a consensus on the part of all participants, and secondly does not ensure that the approving official always reaches the constitutionally correct outcome after carrying out the procedure, that is, that citizens who at the end of the procedure

---

[176] BVerfGE 42, 64 (73); see also BVerfGE 46, 325 (333); 49, 220 (226); 52, 131 (153).
[177] See R. Alexy, 'Die Idee einer prozeduralen Theorie der juristischen Argumentation', *Rechtstheorie*, Beiheft 2 (1981), 178 ff.
[178] BVerfGE 53, 30 (76).

are still of a different opinion from the official have necessarily made a constitutional mistake. This does not mean that such procedures are unsuitable for the protection of constitutional interests. Even if the constitutionality of the procedure is not guaranteed by the outcome, at least the probability of a constitutionally consistent outcome is increased. For these reasons, procedures are constitutionally required as a means of constitutional rights protection. But it should be clear that merely increasing the probability of a constitutionally consistent outcome can never be a reason for abandoning judicial examination of the substantive consistency of the outcome with constitutional rights norms.

The fact that procedural norms cannot do everything in the field of constitutional rights does not mean that they are to be undervalued. Wherever procedural norms can raise the protection of constitutional rights they are prima facie required by constitutional principles. If no competing principles apply, then there is a definitive right to their application. So as far as the connection between constitutional rights and legal procedure is concerned, procedural and substantive aspects are to be combined into a dual model that guarantees the primacy of the substantive aspect.

A comparison of procedural rights in the narrow sense with rights to private law powers shows what different purposes are being pursued in the field of organization and procedure. While rights to private law powers secure above all the chance of carrying out certain constitutionally guaranteed acts at all, procedural rights in the proper sense serve primarily the protection of existing legal positions against the state and third parties. It is therefore also possible to consider the latter in the context of protective rights.[179] They are discussed here because their procedural aspect is more interesting from a theoretical perspective than their protective one.

5.3 Organization in the Narrow Sense

The third group of rights contains constitutional requirements for legal areas such as higher education law, broadcasting law, and co-determination law. The combination of such diverse things under the concept of organization in the narrow sense is justified by the fact that they have one thing in common. They regulate large numbers of people coordinated in pursuit of certain common aims.

One has to distinguish between organization as the result of legislative action, which is expressed in organizational norms, and organization in the sense of a legal entity. Here we are concerned with individual rights addressed to the legislature that certain organizational norms should apply. These rights should be distinguished both from rights of organizations against the legislature and also from rights of individuals against organizations. Individual organizational rights in the narrow sense addressed to the

---

[179] See above at 300 ff.

legislature are individual rights that the legislature pass certain organizational norms consistent with the constitution. Constitutionally consistent legislative organization can be secured not only by subjective rights but also by merely objective commands and prohibitions. Both can be found in the case-law of the Federal Constitutional Court. Once again, we are only interested here in the subjective/objective dichotomy within the wide field of problems concerning constitutionally required organization.

It is a view common within constitutional rights doctrine that constitutional rights have two sides, a subjective and an objective side. What exactly these two sides are is admittedly anything but clear.[180] The current context makes it necessary to keep two distinctions apart. The first is a distinction between *norms*, the second a distinction between *reasons* for norms.

Norms may grant subjective rights or they may not. As has been explained above,[181] subjective rights are legal relations between legal subjects. If x has a right against the state that it ensure the existence of a certain organization $(RxsG)$,[182] then the state has a duty to x to ensure that this organization exists $(OsxG)$. This relational duty[183] implies a non-relational duty. If the state has a duty to x to ensure that a certain organization exists $(OsxG)$, then it has the duty to ensure that the organization exists (OsG). Thus every subjective right implies the existence of a non-relational, and in this sense, objective, duty. By contrast, the reverse does not hold. It does not follow from the fact that the state has a duty (OsG) that there is a legal subject to whom this duty is owed. The principal question in the subjective/objective dichotomy can be formulated in the following way: to what extent is the constitutionally required organization required by norms which create subjective rights, and to what extent by norms which only give rise to objective duties?

The answer to this question depends on the possible reasons for organizationally related constitutional rights norms. The possible reasons can be divided into two groups. Reasons in the first group relate to the significance of the organization required by the constitutional rights norm for the *individual*, to his situation in life, his interests, his freedom. Reasons in the second group relate to the significance of the organization required by constitutional rights for the *collectivity*, that is, for common interests or collective goods. A justification of the first type can be called individualistic and in this sense '*subjective*', while a justification of the second type is non-individualistic and in this sense '*objective*'. If both groups are combined, the question is how the relationship between them is to be defined.

One could take the view that the relationship between both types of

180 See Schwabe, *Probleme der Grundrechtsdogmatik*, 286 ff.
181 120 f.
182 On this mode of representation, see above at 121.
183 See on this above at 131.

justification and both types of norm consists simply in the objective or subjective character of the justification bringing with it the objective or subjective character of the norm. However, the matter is not that simple. Those who base the duty of the legislature to ensure constitutionally consistent organization exclusively or principally by reference to common interests will conclude that they have a merely objective character. By contrast, those who justify it by reference to the freedom of the individual could conclude, as happened in the university organization judgment, that there is a subjective right of the right-holder 'to such state measures, including organizational ones, which are indispensible for the protection of their constitutionally secured sphere of freedom',[184] but one need not. One can try to base the acceptance of a merely objective constitutional rights norm in the face of a subjective justification in two ways. The first strategy adopts Häberle's distinction between constitutional rights interest and constitutional right.[185] What constitutionally required organizational norms are supposed to secure for the individual is in general only his constitutional rights *interest*. But to secure this, the granting of subjective rights to organization is as a rule not necessary. The second strategy also makes the point that while constitutionally required organization in the final analyis always serves the individual, it often does it for the individual *as a member of a collectivity* of individuals, and so in general it is not appropriate to talk in terms of individual subjective rights to organization.

To clarify the problems raised, it is worth considering the three Television Judgments of 1961, 1971, and 1981.[186] All three judgments accept the duty of the legislature to 'ensure broadcasting freedom by statutory intervention'.[187] By broadcasting freedom is therefore understood a *state of affairs* within the broadcasting system which consists in broadcasting being free from state control and pluralistic.[188] At the same time it is typical and appropriate when in the first Television Judgment legislative organization is described as a 'means' for reaching this 'end'.[189]

We cannot consider the many problems of broadcasting freedom associated with the three Television Judgments here. We shall only cast a glance at the different accenting of the objective and subjective side in the three judgments. In the first two judgments, the objective side is dominant. Broadcasting freedom is characterized as an 'institutional liberty'.[190] Talk is not only generally about its 'fundamental significance for the entire public, political and constitutional life of the Regions', but objective consequences are drawn from this argument, namely that the 'content of article 5 Basic Law' gives rise to a 'constitutional position of the member state within the

---

184 BVerfGE 35, 79 (116).   185 Häberle, 'Grundrechte im Leistungsstaat', 122.
186 BVerfGE 12, 205; 31, 314; 57, 295.   187 BVerfGE 57, 295 (322).
188 BVerfGE 12, 205 (265 f.); 57, 295 (323).   189 BVerfGE 12, 205 (261).
190 BVerfGE 12, 205 (261 f.); 31, 314 (326).

federal state' which consists of the Regions being able to demand the protection of broadcasting freedom by the Federation.[191] This has little to do with individual subjective rights. There is a further objective tendency with talk in the 1971 judgment of ' the special nature of broadcasting as an institution under obligations to the general public',[192] and when it is said that broadcasting bodies fulfil 'public functions'.[193]

By contrast, the 1981 judgment is characterized by a noticeable weakening of the objective side and a strengthening of the subjective side. In the field of broadcasting, the subjective side could have at least four roots: (1) individual rights to broadcast, (2) individual rights to acquire information and form opinions, (3) rights of those working in broadcasting, and (4) rights of social groups to express their views through broadcasting media. The variety of subjective components finds expression in the judgment when it is stated that the legislative structuring of broadcasting is concerned with reconciling conflicts of 'constitutional rights positions', and as an example of which is given 'the claim to comprehensive and truthful information arising out of freedom of information and on the other hand the freedom of expression of those who make the programmes, or whose views are broadcast.'[194] It is also noticeable that at a systematically central point, broadcasting freedom is no longer described as 'institutional' but as an '*instrumental* freedom'.[195] If one were to take this term out of context it could give rise to all sorts of confusion. Negative liberty, to do or not to do as one pleases within boundaries however narrowly drawn, is by definition not an instrumental liberty. Since constitutional liberty is for the most part negative liberty, the concept of instrumental liberty should not be abstracted from contexts in which it can be sensibly used. Such a context is given if one understands 'broadcasting freedom' as a state of existence free from state control and pluralistic, and sees this as a means serving the end of 'free formation of opinion'.[196] All this would have little to do with an emphasizing of the subjective, if all that was meant by 'free formation of opinion' were an objective process. But the Court makes it clear that this is not the case. It does not speak in terms of a 'free public' but a 'free individual and public formation of opinion'.[197] Furthermore it is instructive to compare the first television judgment with this one on the significance of broadcasting. Then, the Court spoke in terms of 'significance for the entire public, political and constitutional life'.[198] Now it talks in terms of 'significance for *individual* and public life'.[199] All this shows that the duty of the state to ensure freedom from state control and pluralism in the broadcast-

---

[191] BVerfGE 12, 205 (259).   [192] BVerfGE 31, 314 (328).
[193] BVerfGE 31, 314 (329); the dissenting judgment at BVerfGE 31, 314 (340 ff.) is critical at this point.
[194] BVerfGE 57, 295 (321).   [195] BVerfGE 57, 295 (320).
[196] ibid.   [97] ibid.   [198] BVerfGE 12, 205 (259).
[199] BVerfGE 57, 295 (emphasis added).

ing system is justified not only objectively, but also to an important extent
subjectively, whereby here, in order not to complicate matters further, only
the freedom to form opinions and freedom of information are to be considered as subjective reasons.

Does the justification of state duty, among other things with these arguments, imply a corresponding subjective right? Can one reason from the
'claim to comprehensive and truthful information arising from freedom of
information' which the Court speaks of,[200] to a right of the citizen against
the state that it so structure broadcasting that freedom from state control
and pluralism reign, a right that in its content need not be as extensive as
the duty, since this could be based on other (subjective and/or objective)
grounds, but which is enforceable through legal process? Opinions are split.
Bethge accuses the 'right of action in matters concerning the securing of
pluralism' of amounting to a public interest action. Such a right of action
would put the individual in the position of a 'functionary of the objective
legal order'.[201] By contrast, Rupp considers it at least possible that 'article
5(1)(2) Basic Law gives everyone a right to an organization of the public
informational monopoly which secures freedom' because 'a constitutionally
consistent organization of broadcasting does not simply serve the public
interest, but primarily the interest of each individual'.[202] Starck accepts a
judicially enforceable right of the citizen 'to an organization of broadcasting and a procedure for the composition of managing committees that
secures a balanced programme'.[203]

One can agree with the Federal Constitutional Court that constitutional
rights are 'in the first instance individual rights'. To use its own words, 'the
function of constitutional rights as objective principles consists in the principled strengthening of their application, but it has its roots in this primary
meaning. They cannot be detached from their real source to become an
independent system of objective norms, in which the original and permanent point of constitutional rights recedes.'[204] If one takes the thesis that
constitutional rights are in the first instance subjective rights seriously, then
a second thesis is unavoidable. Whenever individual freedom is constitutionally protected, then the protection must basically take the form of a
subjective right. But this means that the state's duty of organization must

[200] BVerfGE 57, 295.
[201] H. Bethge, 'Rechtsschutzprobleme eines rundfunkspezifischen Pluralismus', *Ufita*, 81
(1978), 92.
[202] H. H. Rupp, Comment on judgment, JZ 1979, 29.
[203] C. Starck, 'Teilhabeansprüche auf Rundfunkkontrolle und ihre gerichtliche
Durchsetzung', in *Presserecht und Pressefreiheit, Festschrift für M. Löffler*, (Munich, 1980),
388. Starck bases this right not merely on freedom of information, but also on the socializa-
tion of broadcasting freedom. In addition he argues for subjectification primarily in respect of
a right of socially relevant groups to representation on broadcasting councils (ibid. 384). Since
we are only concerned here with the general structure of subjectification, such further possibilities will not be followed up.
[204] BVerfGE 50, 291 (337).

correspond to individual rights to basically the same extent, because protecting the freedom of the relevant individual makes this necessary. So to the extent that an organization of broadcasting free from state control and pluralistic is constitutionally required by the freedom of the individual to form opinions and gain information, the state is not merely subject to an objective duty. Rather, this duty corresponds to a subjective right of the individual affected. But if there are subjective rights, the public interest action objection fails. The individual plaintiff is not acting as functionary of the objective legal order, but is enforcing his rights.

We are left with the two arguments mentioned above against moving from subjective justification (that is, reasoning from individual liberty) to a subjective norm (ie. a norm granting a subjective right). The first argument seeks to draw a line between constitutional rights interests and constitutional rights, and the second refers to non-individualizability.

The objection can be made to the first argument, that the importance of constitutional protection for the individual can be so minor and/or the effect on the individual by organization so indirect, that the recognition of a subjective right as the strongest form of protection is not required, but that protection by a merely objective norm is sufficient. At any rate, the acceptance of merely objective protection is in need of justification. In principle, a subjective right, at any rate in the form of a prima facie right, is to be recognized.

The second argument suggests that while constitutionally required organization always serves the individual in the final analysis, it often does this by serving the individual as a member of a collectivity of individuals, which excludes the recognition of an individual right. One aspect of this argument emerges in Ossenbühl's writings. He states, 'where *all* are equally affected, one can no longer speak in terms of *individual* effect'.[205] This sentence cannot mean that where all individuals in a given class are equally affected, then no single individual is affected, because the latter does not follow logically from the former. What could be meant is that the single individual is not affected alone, but along with other individuals. But this does not exclude the breach of individual subjective rights. By establishing a state television network in which only one social grouping could express its views, everyone would be affected. But it does not follow from this that there could be no breach of each individual's right to a pluralistic broadcasting system free from state control. Taking constitutional rights as individual rights seriously excludes all such arguing with collectivities. Thus the collectivity argument cannot undermine the thesis that if the individual is constitutionally protected, this is achieved in principle not merely through objective norms, but by subjective rights.

---

[205] Ossenbühl, 'Kernenergie im Spiegel des Verfassungsrechts', 7.

5.4 State Decision-Taking

The fourth group consists of rights against the state that it make participation in state decision-taking possible through procedures established by ordinary law. The main example is the right under article 38(1) Basic Law to a constitutionally compatible regulation in ordinary law of the power to vote. As has already been noted, the right to a power is a right within the positive, not the active, status. Its object is a normative act of the state. But this normative act consists in placing the individual legally in the situation in which he may exercise the power of voting, which belongs to the active status.

The difference between the right addressed to the legislature to regulate the power to vote by way of ordinary law and the power to vote itself makes the connection between constitutional rights and democratic procedure particularly clear.

On the basis of the power to vote, the possessor of this power is, albeit in an indirect way, a participant in legislation.[206] On the basis of a right to a constitutionally compatible regulation of the power under ordinary law, he could be the opponent of the legislature, because his constitutional right sets limits to its powers. This double aspect applies to all constitutional rights which are exercisable for the purpose of participation in the legislatively relevant process of forming state opinion, so it applies for example to the rights of freedom of expression, assembly, and association. On one hand they open up the possibility of constitutionally significant participation in the decision-taking process, and on the other hand as constitutional rights they set limits to the power of the legislature. To the extent that constitutional rights can be exercised for purposes other than participation in constitutionally relevant state decision-taking, they are only related to the latter function. This alone shows that constitutional rights which secure the democratic process express a trust in its rationality, but that this trust is not unlimited. There is thus both an internal connection as well as a tension between constitutional rights and the principle of democracy.

IV. ENTITLEMENTS IN THE NARROW SENSE (SOCIAL CONSTITUTIONAL RIGHTS)

1. CONCEPT AND STRUCTURE

Entitlements in the narrow sense are rights of the individual against the state to something which the individual could obtain from other private

---

[206] See in place of many F. Scharpf, *Demokratietheorie zwischen Utopie und Anpassung*, (Konstanz, 1970), 29 ff.

individuals, if only he had sufficient financial means, and if only there were sufficient offers on the market. When people talk about social constitutional rights, that is, rights such as rights to welfare, work, accommodation, and education, it is primarily entitlements in the narrow sense that they are referring to.

One must distinguish between expressly enacted entitlements, such as can be found in a series of regional constitutions, and interpretatively derived entitlements. Occasionally, the expression 'social constitutional rights' is reserved for the first category, while the latter are termed 'constitutional entitlements',[207] or 'social interpretations of rights to freedom and equality'.[208] The distinction between expressly enacted and interpretatively derived entitlements is doubtless an important one. On the other hand, there is extensive correspondence between the two categories as regards their content,[209] structure,[210] and the problems they give rise to.[211] This allows us to call all entitlements in the narrow sense 'social constitutional rights', and within the class of social constitutional rights to distinguish between expressly enacted ones and interpretatively derived ones.[212]

It has already been pointed out that the Basic Law, a few narrow exceptions apart, does not contain any expressly formulated social constitutional rights, but that nevertheless great energy has been expended[213] on whether and which social constitutional rights it guarantees.[214] This controversy, which has been well nourished by the case-law of the Federal Constitutional Court, is a controversy about whether it is required or prohibited to derive[215] norms granting social constitutional rights from constitutional rights provisions. Whether such derivations are required or impermissible from the perspective of constitutional law depends on whether the better constitutional reasons count for requiring or prohibiting this. One can only evaluate the quality of reasons if one knows what they are supposed to be reasons for, and so we shall consider first the candidates for derivation.

The norms which are derived from constitutional rights provisions under the title 'social constitutional rights' are very varied in nature. From a structural perspective they can be divided according to three criteria. First, they

[207] J. Lücke, 'Soziale Grundrechte als Staatszielbestimmungen und Gesetzgebungsaufträge', AöR 107 (1982), 31.
[208] W. Martens, 'Grundrechte im Leistungsstaat', VVDStRL 30 (1972), 12.
[209] ibid. 30.
[210] E.-W. Böckenförde, 'Die sozialen Grundrechte im Verfassungsgefüge', in E.-W. Böckenförde, J. Jekewitz, and T. Ramm (eds.), *Soziale Grundrechte* (Heidelberg and Karlsruhe, 1981), 12.
[211] J. P. Müller, *Soziale Grundrechte in der Verfassung?* 2nd edn. (Basle and Frankfurt, 1981), 166.
[212] See Isensee, 'Verfassung ohne soziale Grundrechte', 373.
[213] See the bibliography in K. Hernekamp (ed.), *Soziale Grundrechte* (Berlin and New York, 1979), 235 ff.
[214] See above at 293 ff.
[215] On the concept of derivation, see above at 33 ff.

could be norms granting *subjective* rights or they could be merely *objective* norms binding the state. Secondly, they could be *binding* or *non-binding* norms, and in this sense programmatic statements. A norm will be described as 'binding' when it is possible to establish that it has been breached before the Federal Constitutional Court. Thirdly, the norms could establish *definitive* or *prima facie* rights and duties, that is, they could be rules or principles. If one combines these criteria one ends up with eight norms of quite varied structure, which can be represented in the following table:

binding				non-binding			
subjective		objective		subjective		objective	
definitive	prim. fac.	definitive	prim. fac.	definitive	prim. fac.	definitive	prim. fac.
1	2	3	4	5	6	7	8

Binding norms granting definitive subjective entitlements (1) give the strongest protection, while non-binding norms imposing a merely objective prima facie duty of the state to provide goods (8) give the weakest. The many different theses proposed in the field of social constitutional rights can be clarified in the light of this table. Four examples: according to Hesse, an 'understanding of constitutional rights as the highest objective norms' gives rise, 'for the legislature' to 'a (positive) duty to do everything to realize constitutional rights, even where there is no subjective claim of the citizen to this'.[216] This must refer to binding objective prima facie duties (4). Von Mutius classifies the original 'participation rights' discussed in the first Numerus-Clausus Judgment as 'constitutional entitlements' which must be understood as 'leges imperfecta', as 'mere programmatic statements'.[217] This can be understood in the sense of a non-binding definitive subjective right (5).[218] The Federal Constitutional Court speaks of the 'right of entry to a degree programme of one's choice', which is held intrinsically by the qualified citizen, but which is subject to the 'bounds of possibility'.[219] This right is, as will be further explained below, a binding subjective prima facie right (2). Finally, the right to an existential minimum[220] is a binding subjective definitive right (1).

In addition to these structural differences, there are substantive ones. The difference between *minimal* and *maximal* content is particularly

---

[216] K. Hesse, 'Grundrechte: Bestand und Bedeutung', in E. Benda, W. Maihofer, and H.-J. Vogel (eds.), *Handbuch des Verfassungsrechts* (Berlin and New York, 1983), 95.

[217] A. v. Mutius, 'Grundrechte als "Teilhaberechte"—zu den verfassungsrechtlichen Aspekten des "numerus clausus" ', VerwArch 64 (1973), 193.

[218] Krebs's 'binding programmatic statements' should by contrast be seen as norms giving rise to binding objective prima facie obligations (see W. Krebs, *Vorbehalt des Gesetzes und Grundrechte* (Berlin, 1975), 92).

[219] BVerfGE 43, 291 (314 f.).   [220] See on this above at 290 f.

important.[221] A minimalist programme aims at securing 'for the individual mastery over a minimal scope for life and social status',[222] that is, it aims at what are called 'minimal rights' or "small" social rights'.[223] A maximalist content is being referred to when people speak of a 'full realization' of constitutional rights,[224] or the right to education as a 'claim to intellectual-cultural emancipation to individuality, autonomy, to socio-political coming of age'.[225]

The variety sketched in leads to the suspicion that problems of social constitutional rights cannot be a matter of all-or-nothing. A differentiated approach seems unavoidable.[226] Against this background, it is necessary to consider some of the arguments for and against 'social constitutional rights'. The term 'social constitutional rights' will be taken as an overarching concept for all norms of types 1 to 8. The aim is to work out a proposal for social constitutional rights which rests on the theory of principles,[227] is oriented towards the formal guiding idea set out above,[228] and which takes account of both sides of the argument.

2. ON THE ARGUMENTS FOR AND AGAINST SOCIAL CONSTITUTIONAL RIGHTS

The main argument for social constitutional rights is an argument from freedom. Its starting-point is composed of two theses.

The first thesis is that *legal* liberty, that is, the legal permission to do or not to do, is valueless without *factual* (real) liberty, that is, the factual possibility of choosing between permitted alternatives.[229] This thesis is formulated at a very general level. It is at any rate correct, if one interprets it to say that the legal liberty of x to perform act ϕ or not to perform it, is valueless for x in the sense of useless, if for factual reasons x does not have the possibility of choosing between the performance and non-performance of

---

[221] For this distinction, see Breuer, 'Grundrechte als Anspruchsnormen', 95, with further references.

[222] L. Wildhaber, 'Soziale Grundrechte', in Saladin and Wildhaber, *Der Staat als Aufgabe*, 385.

[223] Müller, *Soziale Grundrechte in der Verfassung?* 183. See also Lücke, 'Soziale Grundrechte als Staatszielbestimmungen und Gesetzgebungsaufträge', 18.

[224] K. H. Friauf, 'Zur Rolle der Grundrechte im Interventions und Leistungsstaat', DVBl 1971, 676; Krebs, *Vorbehalt des Gesetzes und Grundrechte*, 122.

[225] L.-R. Reuter, 'Soziales Grundrecht auf Bildung?' DVBl 1974, 12. See also K. Grimmer, *Demokratie und Grundrechte* (Berlin, 1980), 259; K.-D. Heymann and E. Stein, 'Das Recht auf Bildung', AöR 97 (1972), 189 ff.

[226] On the necessity of differentiating, see D. Lorenz, 'Bundesverfassungsgericht und soziale Grundrechte', JBl 103 (1981), 19 f.; W. Schmidt, 'Soziale Grundrechte im Verfassungsrecht der Bundesrepublik Deutschland', *Der Staat*, Beiheft 5 (1981), 22; Breuer, 'Grundrechte als Anspruchsnormen', 93.

[227] See on this above at 47 ff.

[228] 297 ff.

[229] On the concepts of legal and factual liberty, see above at 144.

ϕ.[230] This point is what is referred to by Lorenz von Stein when he writes, 'freedom is only real for him who possesses the conditions for it, the material and intellectual goods which are the prerequisite of self-determination',[231] or by the Federal Constitutional Court when it states, 'the right to freedom would be valueless without the factual prerequisites for being able to use it'.[232]

The second thesis argues that under the conditions of a modern industrialized society, the material foundation for the factual freedom of a large number of citizens is not to be found in a 'mastered sphere of life',[233] but depends essentially on state activities.[234] One can accept this thesis as well, a few qualifications aside.[235]

However, these theses represent little more than a starting-point for an argument for social constitutional rights. This can easily be seen from the fact that it is possible not only to accept the truth of both of them, but even to accept that the production of factual freedom is intended by the Constitution, without accepting the existence of social constitutional rights. One only needs to adopt a division of function between constitutional rights and the political process whereby the former is to ensure legal liberty

---

[230] The fact that the general thesis that legal liberty is valueless without factual liberty is in need of several qualifications can be shown, among other things, by the following observations: (1) The fact that everyone has the legal liberty to choose between ϕ and ~ϕ can be valuable for x, even if he himself does not have the factual ability to choose, because he profits from others having the choice. (2) A legal liberty of x's can be valuable for x, even if he does not have the factual ability at present to appropriate it, because he still has the chance of being able to appropriate it at some future date. (3) x can consider his legal liberty to choose between ϕ and ~ϕ to be valuable, even though it is useless on the grounds of his factual non-liberty. He considers legal liberty to be an end in itself. (4) The need for numerous further distinctions arises from the fact that factual liberty is often not a matter of all-or-nothing, but a matter of degree. It could well be that the choice between ϕ and ~ϕ is useless for x, who leads a normal life, but that if he were prepared to sacrifice much of what is normally considered part of normal life, he would have the factual ability to make this choice.

[231] L. v. Stein, *Geschichte der sozialen Bewegung in Frankreich von 1789 bis auf unsere Tage*, iii (ed. Salomon) (Munich, 1921, reprinted Darmstadt, 1959), 104.

[232] BVerfGE 33, 303 (331).

[233] E. Forsthoff, *Verfassungsprobleme des Sozialstaats* (Münster, 1954), 6.

[234] See in place of many E.-W. Böckenförde, *Staat, Gesellschaft, Freiheit* (Frankfurt a. M., 1976), 76 f.; id., 'Die sozialen Grundrechte im Verfassungsgefüge', 8 f.; U. Scheuner, 'Die Funktion der Grundrechte im Sozialstaat', DÖV 1971, 511.

[235] J. Schwabe's point (in *Probleme der Grundrechtsdogmatik*, 257 ff.) is important, that a loss of 'mastered sphere of life' can be established if one compares the ideal type of the nineteenth century bourgeois man with today's average citizen, but that there are difficulties if one compares the average citizen of the nineteenth century with that of today. While this gives rise to an objection to basing the necessity of social constitutional rights on the change in the situation of citizens from the nineteenth to the twenty-first centuries, it does not represent an objection to justifying them with reference to the situation of the individual in industrial society. One can go a step further. Even in non-industrialized societies, the 'mastered sphere of life' of many citizens can be so small, that there are grounds enough for seeking to secure their situation through social constitutional rights. However, this says nothing against the point that state activity is necessary in industrialized societies if the legal liberty which is secured there and factual liberty are not to diverge too widely from each other.

and the latter factual.[236] In order to complete the argument from freedom, one has to show why factual freedom has to be secured directly *as a matter of constitutional right*.

In order to do this it is not sufficient to say that constitutional rights are supposed to secure freedom, that factual freedom is also an element of freedom, and that constitutional rights are also therefore supposed to secure factual freedom. That is precisely the question, whether constitutional rights *are* supposed to secure factual freedom. In order to justify a derivation of social constitutional rights by way of an argument from freedom, one has to show that the freedom which constitutional rights are supposed to secure includes factual freedom.

There are, above all, two arguments which can be put forward for this. The first relies on the importance of factual freedom for the individual. To give but three examples, it is of existential significance for the individual that he is not obliged to live under the existential minimum, that he is not condemned to long-term unemployment, and that he does not find himself excluded from the cultural life of his times. For those who are in such a situation, constitutional rights are in no way totally useless.[237] It is precisely those without any means of support who often value constitutional rights such as those protecting them from forced labour and similar, and which give them the possibility of improving their situation through the political process. However, it cannot be denied that the removal of their situation of want is more important to them than legal liberties with which they can do nothing because of their lack of means, and which for them are thus an 'empty formula'.[238] If one adds to this the fact that it is precisely the point of constitutional rights to make things which are particularly important to the individual and capable of legal securing, to be legally secured, then the first argument for constitutional protection is in place.

The second argument links directly to the first. It suggests that factual freedom is not only important from the formal aspect of securing really important things, but that it is also constitutionally significant from a substantive perspective. The Federal Constitutional Court has seen the catalogue of constitutional rights as the expression of a system of values, 'that has its centrepoint in the freely developing human personality and its dignity in the social community'.[239] This is to be understood in the light of the theory of principles[240] to mean that constitutional rights, among other things, express principles which require that the individual be able freely to develop his dignity in social community, which presupposes a certain degree of factual freedom. The conclusion is irresistible that if the aim of constitutional rights

---

[236] See Klein, *Die Grundrechte im demokratischen Staat*, 48 ff.
[237] See Bleckmann, *Allgemeine Grundrechtslehren*, 162.
[238] Böckenförde, *Staat, Gesellschaft, Freiheit*, 77.
[239] BVerfGE 7, 198 (205).
[240] See above at 47 ff.

is the freely developing human personality, then they are also directed towards factual freedom, that is, they secure the prerequisites for the realization of legal liberties,[241] and thus are 'not only principles of legal permission, but also of factual *capacity to act*'.[242] The question is whether this assumption, which gains additional support from the social state principle[243] and the principle of factual equality,[244] can survive in the light of counter-arguments.

The most important of many objections to social constitutional rights can be combined into two complex arguments, a formal and a substantive one.

The *formal* argument points to a dilemma: if social constitutional rights are binding, then they transfer social politics from the competence of Parliament to the constitutional court; if they are not binding, this breaches the article 1(3) Basic Law which states that all constitutional rights are. The starting-point of this argument is the thesis that social constitutional rights are not justiciable, or only to a very small extent.[245] This thesis can rely on the point that the object of most social constitutional rights is highly unclear. What, for example, is the content of a constitutional right to work? The scale of conceivable interpretations extends from a utopian right of each person to any work he wishes, at any place and at any time, to a compensatory right to unemployment benefit (but how much?). The problems of other social constitutional rights are not much different. Even in the case of the simplest social constitutional right, the right to an existential minimum, establishing its precise content gives rise to some difficulties.[246] Now there is nothing unusual in case-law and jurisprudence about difficulties in determining the precise content of rights and clarifying unclear concepts. So the non-justiciability thesis has to maintain a second thesis alongside that of the semantic and structural vagueness of social constitutional rights, namely the impossibility of reaching an accurate determination of the content and structure of abstractly formulated social constitutional rights by way of specifically legal means. It must maintain

---

[241] See P. Saladin, 'Die Funktion der Grundrechte in einer revidierten Verfassung', ZSR NF 87 (1968), 553: 'The guarantee of liberty for individual autonomous action is only honourable and fruitful if at the same time the most important preconditions for the use of this liberty are secured, if the constitution makers ensure the protection not only of "liberté" but also of "capacité" '.

[242] P. Häberle, 'Das Bundesverfassungsgericht im Leistungsstaat: Die Numerus-clausus-Entscheidung vom 18.7.1972', DÖV 1972, 731.

[243] See K. H. Friauf, 'Zur Rolle der Grundrechte im Interventions und Leistingsstaat', 676; E. Grabitz, *Freiheit und Verfassungsrecht* (Tübingen, 1976), 41 ff.

[244] See above at 276 ff. as well as G. Leibholz, *Strukturprobleme der modernen Demokratie*, 3rd edn. (Karlsruhe, 1967, reprinted Frankfurt a. M., 1974), 131.

[245] See Müller, *Soziale Grundrechte in der Verfassung?* 5 f., 20 ff.; Starck, 'Die Grundrechte des Grundgesetzes', 241; T. Tomandl, *Der Einbau sozialer Grundrechte in das positive Recht* (Tübingen, 1967), 17 f.; Brunner, *Die Problematik der sozialen Grundrechte*, 17 f.; K. Korinek, 'Betrachtungen zur juristischen Problematik sozialer Grundrechte', in *Die sozialen Grundrechte* (Die katholische Sozialakademie Österreichs: Vienna, 1971), 12.

[246] See Bleckmann, *Allgemeine Grundrechtslehren*, 164.

that law contains no adequate standard for this. For if law does not contain an adequate standard, then deciding about the content of social constitutional rights is a matter of politics.[247] But this means that under the principles of the separation of powers and democracy, determining the content of social constitutional rights does not fall within the competence of courts, but of the 'legislature directly legitimated by the people'.[248] [249] Thereafter, in the field of social constitutional rights, the courts could only decide what had already been decided by the legislature.

The argument from competence gains particular weight on the grounds of the financial relevance of social constitutional rights. Because of the significant financial expenditure associated with satisfying social constitutional rights, the existence of judicially enforceable broad social constitutional rights would mean that budgetary politics would be to a large extent constitutionally determined.[250] Since the Federal Constitutional Court would have to control the observance of these requirements, budgetary politics would fall into the hands of the Court, which would breach the Constitution.

Anyone who wants to avoid this unsustainable outcome and still uphold social constitutional rights has—if one follows the formal argument—only one way out. Norms granting social constitutional rights have to be understood as non-binding norms, that is, as norms not subject to the control of the constitutional court, norms corresponding to positions 5 to 8 in the table above. But non-binding constitutional rights norms are incompatible with the article 1(3) Basic Law.[251] So if the formal argument works, the adoption of social constitutional rights runs up against the dilemma of unconstitutional shift of competence or breach of the binding-nature clause.

The *substantive* argument against social constitutional rights suggests that social constitutional rights are incompatible with substantive constitutional norms, or at least that they run up against them. To the extent that these substantive constitutional norms grant liberties, the substantive argument is an argument from freedom *against* social constitutional rights themselves supported by an argument from freedom.[252]

[247] D. Wiegand, 'Sozialstaatsklausel und soziale Teilhaberechte', DVBl 1974, 660.
[248] See the formula in the Aircraft Noise Judgment, BVerfGE 56, 54 (81).
[249] See e.g. W. Martens, 'Grundrechte im Leistungsstaat', 35 f.; E.-W. Böckenförde, 'Die sozialen Grundrechte im Verfassungsgefüge', 11 f.; Hesse, 'Bestand und Bedeutung der Grundrechte', 434; Grabitz, *Freiheit und Verfassungsrecht*, 46.
[250] See in place of many Starck, 'Staatliche Organisation und staaliche Finanzierung', 518.
[251] See Starck, 'Die Grundrechte des Grundgesetzes', 241; Klein, *Die Grundrechte im demokratischen Staat*, 58 f.; Mutius, 'Grundrechte als "Teilhaberechte" ', 193.
[252] For the thesis that social constitutional rights and classic liberty rights are incompatible, see H. Huber, 'Soziale Verfassungsrechte?' in E. Forsthoff (ed.), *Rechtsstaatlichkeit und Sozialstaatlichkeit* (Darmstadt, 1968), 9; Martens, 'Grundrechte im Leistungsstaat', 33; Klein, *Die Grundrechte im demokratischen Staat*, 64 f.; id., 'Ein Grundrecht auf saubere Umwelt?' 657 ff.; E. Forsthoff, *Der Staat der Industriegesellschaft*, 2nd edn. (Munich, 1971), 73, 78; H. Schambeck, *Grundrechte und Sozialordnung* (Berlin, 1969), 127 f.

The conflict between social constitutional rights and liberties is particularly obvious in the case of the right to work. In a free market economy, the state has only limited control over the object of this right.[253] If it wants to satisfy directly the right of each unemployed person to a job, then it must either employ all unemployed people in existing public services, or it must limit or remove the private economic power of disposal over places of work. The first possibility, at least as a general solution, is out of the question, since it would lead under the conditions presupposed to unemployment merely masked as public service. The second would lead either to a substantial limitation of private economic discretion, or to the removal of the private economy. But this would mean, among other things, interferences in the constitutional rights of those who control productive property.[254]

Conflicts between the social constitutional rights of one person and the liberties of another do not simply arise when the state only directly controls a limited amount of the object of the right in a market economy, such as the right to work. All social constitutional rights are extremely costly. In satisfying social constitutional rights, the state can only distribute what it has taken from others, perhaps in the form of income tax.[255] But this means that the much discussed limits of the ability of the state to deliver do not simply arise from what distributable goods are at hand, but to a large extent on what the state is allowed to take from the owners of these goods for the purposes of redistribution without breaching their constitutional rights.

It is often claimed not only that there is a conflict between social constitutional rights of one citizen and the liberties of another, but also that there is a conflict between social constitutional rights and liberties for the same person. It is claimed, for example, that a right to work carries with it a duty to work.[256] The combination of a right and a duty to work is admittedly common,[257] but it is none the less not necessary. The state which introduces

[253] See Brunner, *Die Problematik der sozialen Grundrechte*, 14 f.

[254] See T. Tomandl, *Der Einbau sozialer Grundrechte in des positive Recht* (Tübingen, 1967), 30 f.; Brunner, *Die Problematik der sozialen Grundrechte*, 14 ff.; Starck, 'Staatliche Organisation und staatliche Finanzierung', 519; id., 'Die Grundrechte des Grundgesetzes', 241; Isensee, 'Verfassung ohne soziale Grundrechte', 379 f.; R. Scholz, 'Das Recht auf Arbeit', in E.-W. Böckenförde, J. Jekewitz, and T. Ramm (eds.), *Soziale Grundrechte* (Heidelberg and Karlsruhe, 1981), 84 f.; Lücke, 'Soziale Grundrechte als Staatszielbestimmungen und Gesetzgebungsaufträge', 39. That the full realization of the right to work is not possible without interfering with the constitutional rights of the owners of productive property is also admitted by proponents of such a right, see for example W. Däubler, 'Recht auf Arbeit verfassungswidrig?' in U. Achten *et al.* (eds.), *Recht auf Arbeit—eine politische Herausforderung* (Neuweid and Darmstadt, 1978), 171, who proposes justifying the interference by way of art. 15 Basic Law. Generally on the right to work, see H. Ryffel and J. Schwartländer (eds.), *Das Recht des Menschen auf Arbeit* (Kehl, Strasbourg, and Arlington, 1983).

[255] See C. Schmitt, 'Nehmen/Teilen/Weiden', in id., *Verfassungsrechtliche Aufsätze*, 503; W. Leisner, 'Der Eigentümer als Organ der Wirtschaftsverfassung', DÖV 1975, 74.

[256] See Isensee, 'Verfassung ohne soziale Grundrechte', 380.

[257] See e.g. art. 24 of the 1968 GDR Constitution.

a right to work can dispense with a duty to work, even if it is interested in getting as many citizens to work as possible. The interest in working, above all in a wage, is an incentive for enough citizens to take up their right to work. It might be different, of course, if the right to an existential minimum were to put the individual in such a position that it is no longer attractive enough for him to work.

Finally, conflicts between social constitutional rights and other such rights, as well as conflicts between social constitutional rights and collective goods, should be mentioned. An example of the former is the conflict between a right to work and an individual environmental right. Conflicts between social constitutional rights and collective goods, such as defence, arise from the fact that the realization of both has significant budgetary consequences, that is, it arises from the financial effect of social constitutional rights already mentioned.

3. A Model of Social Constitutional Rights

When one considers the arguments for and against social constitutional rights, it becomes clear that both sides can put forward weighty reasons. The solution consists in a model which takes account of arguments both for and against. This model is an expression of the formal guiding idea stated above,[258] that the constitutional rights of the Basic Law are those positions which from the perspective of constitutional law are so important that their granting or non-granting cannot be left to simple parliamentary majorities. As applied to the current problem, this means that everyone has those entitlements as social constitutional rights which from the perspective of constitutional law are so important that their granting or non-granting cannot be left to simple parliamentary majorities.

According to this formula, the question of which social constitutional rights the individual definitively has, is a question of balancing between principles. On one side, there is above all the principle of factual freedom.[259] On the other side are the formal principles of the decision-taking competence of the democratically legitimated legislature and the separation of powers, as well as substantive principles relating above all to the legal liberty of others, but also to other social constitutional rights as well as collective goods.

The model does not determine which definitive social constitutional rights the individual has. But it says that he can have some, and tells us what is relevant to the question of their existence and content. The detailed answer to this question is the function of the doctrine of individual social

[258] 297 ff.
[259] If the principle of factual equality also requires an entitlement (see above at 278 ff.), then there is a double justification.

constitutional rights. Nevertheless, one can give a general answer here. One has to consider an entitling position guaranteed, if (1) the principle of factual freedom requires it very strongly, and (2) the principles of the separation of powers and democracy (including the budgetary competence of Parliament), as well as (3) competing substantive principles (in particular those relating to the legal liberty of others) are relatively slightly affected by the constitutional guarantee of the entitling position and the decisions of the constitutional court which take account of it. These conditions are satisfied, at any rate, by minimal social constitutional rights, such as the right to an existential minimum, to basic accommodation, to school education, to training for a job, and to a basic level of healthcare. In what follows, various objections to the model will be discussed.

Even minimal social constitutional rights, particularly when they are claimed by large numbers of people, are to a large extent financially significant. But this fact alone does not justify concluding that they do not exist. The power of the principle of budgetary competence on the part of the legislature is not unlimited. It is not an absolute principle.[260] Individual rights can outweigh reasons of the politics of finance. Thus in its decision concerning housing benefit for social welfare recipients, the Federal Constitutional Court expanded the scope of those entitled, with financial impact, for the purpose of removing an inequality,[261] and in its decision on the length of imprisonment for purposes of investigation, obliged the state to provide the means necessary for avoiding a disproportionately long imprisonment.[262] All constitutional rights of the Basic Law limit the competence of the legislature;[263] they often do this in an uncomfortable way; occasionally, as financially significant rights, they impact on its budgetary competence.

The extent of reliance on social constitutional rights rises during economic crises. But it is exactly then that it is important to redistribute. The objection that the existence of even minimal definitive social constitutional rights makes the flexibility necessary in times of crisis impossible and thus risks turning an economic crisis into a constitutional crisis is a real one.[264] But in reply it can be pointed out, first, that not everything currently existing as a social right is required as a matter of minimal social constitutional rights, secondly, that the balancing of principles necessary under the model proposed here can lead to different definitive rights under different circumstances, and, thirdly, that it is precisely in times of crisis that even a minimal constitutional protection of social positions seems indispensable.

---

[260] On this concept, see above at 62.   [261] BVerfGE 27, 220 (228 ff.).
[262] BVerfGE 36, 264 (275); see also Schwabe, *Probleme der Grundrechtsdogmatik*, 266. For an example of a clearly financially effective decision as regards the level of income in the field of classic defensive rights, see the judgment of the Federal Constitutional Court on compulsory loans, BVerfGE 67, 256 (274 ff.).
[263] See above at 158 f.
[264] Isensee, 'Verfassung ohne soziale Grundrechte', 381 f.

The objection of a lack of justiciability can be raised even against this model. However, the response is that the problems of justiciability which arise in the context of this model are essentially no different from those which arise in the case of traditional constitutional rights.[265] Liberties often give rise to very complex problems of balancing, the solutions to which have far-reaching consequences for the life of the community. Apart from that, it is the case that the existence of a right cannot depend exclusively on a conception of justiciability, however defined; rather, if a right exists then it is also justiciable. The fact that social constitutional rights need expressing through ordinary law is not a decisive objection; so also do competence and procedure. The same applies for other constitutional rights. Procedural grounds are also not capable of supporting the non-justiciability thesis. As the case-law of the Federal Constitutional Court has shown, a constitutional court is in no way helpless in the face of an inactive legislature.[266] The spectrum of its procedural possibilities stretches from a mere determination of a breach of the constitution,[267] through setting a deadline by which constitutionally consistent legislation must be passed,[268] to direct judicial expression of what is required by the constitution.[269] [270]

The model set out is a model of balancing. It is a hallmark of all balancing models that more is prima facie required than definitively. One could take the view that this construction is impermissible in the case of social constitutional rights. It would lead first to delusion and then to frustration.[271] As a general objection to the fact that constitutional rights might first protect something prima facie, but subsequently exclude it definitively from protection by way of limitations, this point has already been dealt with.[272] The case-law of the Federal Constitutional Court on the Numerus-Clausus issue is instructive in showing that the answer is also to be extended to social constitutional rights. The Court proceeds on the basis of a binding subjective prima facie right of admission of every qualified citizen to the degree programme of his choice. The prima facie character of the

---

[265] See F. Klein, in H. v. Mangoldt and F. Klein, *Das Bonner Grundgesetz*, i, *Vorbemerkung* A IV 3; Saladin, 'Die Funktion der Grundrechte in einer revidierten Verfassung', 553; Wildhaber, 'Soziale Grundrechte', 384; H. Steiger, *Mensch und Umwelt, Zur Frage eines Umweltgrundrechts* (Berlin, 1975), 40 ff.; D. Lorenz, 'Bundesverfassungsgericht und sozialer Grundrechte', JBl 103 (1981), 21.

[266] See W. Schmidt, 'Soziale Grundrechte im Verfassungsrecht der Bundesrepublik Deutschland', 19; Friesenhahn, 'Der Wandel des Grundrechtsverständnisses', G16.

[267] See e.g. BVerfGE 39, 316 (333). On the idea of the 'subjectification of determinations', see F. Müller, B. Pieroth and L. Fohmann, *Leistungsrechte im Normbereich einer Freiheitsgarantie* (Berlin, 1982), 165 ff.

[268] See e.g. BVerfGE 33, 1 (13).

[269] See e.g. BVerfGE 3, 225 (237 ff.); 43, 154 (169 f.).

[270] See on this in detail J. Ipsen, *Rechtsfolgen der Verfassungswidrigkeit von Norm und Einzelakt* (Baden-Baden, 1980), 132 ff.

[271] See Isensee, 'Verfassung ohne soziale Grundrechte', 382 f.; Rupp, 'Vom Wandel der Grundrechte', 177.

[272] 211 ff.

right is clearly expressed in that it states that the right belongs to the right-holder 'in principle'[273] and that it is limitable.[274] The fact that the right as a prima-facie right is binding and does not simply have programmatic character is clear when it states that the right 'does not depend in its normative applicability on the greater or lesser degree to which it can be realized'.[275] But the nature of the right as binding and prima facie means that the limiting clause of this right, the 'reservation of the realizable in the sense of what the individual can reasonably demand from society'[276] does not lead to its being meaningless. This clause simply expresses the need for the right to be balanced. As regards the similarity of all constitutional rights at this point, it is of the greatest systemic interest when the Federal Constitutional Court carries over the formula of the 'tension between individual and society' developed in the context of the general right to freedom of action to the entitlement discussed there.[277] Admittedly, the balancing undertaken in the Numerus-Clausus Judgment did not lead to a definitive right of each individual to be admitted to the degree programme of his choice, but it did none the less lead to a definitive right to a selection procedure giving him an adequate chance,[278] which points to a connection between social constitutional rights and the procedural rights discussed above. But in order to judge the procedural regulations by the constitutional right one cannot avoid proceeding on the basis of a binding prima facie right.

The structure of argumentation implied by prima facie rights is rational, because it is rational to carry out legal justification as an interplay of reason and counter-reason. But this means that the reasons on both sides are too extensive. The possibility can never be excluded that someone might only accept the validity of reasons on one side of the argument and thus arrive at over-extensive outcomes. But this is possible in the case of classic liberties as well as social rights. Someone who only accepts the validity of the principle of legal liberty reaches just as over-extensive outcomes as the person for whom there is only a principle of factual liberty. The fact that pieces can be abstracted from a rational structure of justification and used in an irrational way is not a reason for abandoning it in favour of a less rational structure of justification. Those who are not convinced by the model of necessary interplay between reason and counter-reason proposed here that there is no definitive constitutional rights protection are hardly likely to be convinced by assertions that what they want to see definitively protected is not protected 'to start with'. So abandoning the structure of justification required by the theory of principles cannot be supported on educative grounds either, and anyway it is highly questionable whether a scientific theory should be affected such arguments.

---

[273] BVerfGE 43, 291 (315).   [274] ibid.   [275] ibid.
[276] BVerfGE 43, 291 (314); 33, 303 (333).
[277] BVerfGE 33, 303 (334).   [278] See BVerfGE 43, 291 (316 ff.).

Finally, one could take the view that the model proposed here impermissibly suppresses the objective in favour of the subjective. This objection could be based on Häberle's thesis of the supervening character of constitutionally relevant objective norms. 'Thus constitutionally relevant objective law "overtakes" subjective rights in a state which is pro-active. There are constitutional "mandates" of "constitutional rights utility" that (still) do not correspond to any subjective public right.'[279] Thus Häberle pregnantly expresses what many say when they classify the problem of social constitutional rights primarily as a problem of purely objective state duties.[280] Here we will only refer to Hesse, who speaks of a positive state duty 'to do everything to realize constitutional rights, even when there is no subjective claim of the citizen to it'. In this way the legislature receives 'directives and impulses' from constitutional rights. However, 'a concrete duty of state organs to undertake particular measures' cannot generally be derived from this, and so control by the constitutional courts is limited.[281]

However, the objection of failing to take account of the significance of the objective does not apply to the model proposed here. On the contrary, it offers a basis for a more accurate evaluation of the relevant content of the thesis of objective supervenience. The key is the theory of principles.

According to the model, the individual has a definitive entitlement whenever the principle of factual freedom has greater weight than competing formal and substantive principles taken together. This is the case with minimal rights. Such definitive minimal rights could well be what are meant when enforceable subjective public entitlements are contrasted with a supervening objective content. By contrast with definitive rights, which are the result of balancing, prima facie rights which correspond to principles, of which the '*per se*' right of admission to a university degree programme is an example,[282] always have a supervening character. The concept of supervenience is not tied to the subjective/objective dichotomy.

The step from the model to an objective level is possible because prima facie rights correspond to prima facie duties. These duties are prima facie duties of the state to ensure that the legal liberties of subjects correspond to factual liberties. The objective level which arises in this way is admittedly no *merely* objective level, but it is an *additional* objective level.

By contrast to its definitive duties, the prima facie duties of the state have an obviously supervening character. That does not mean they are not

[279] Häberle, 'Grundrechte im Leistungsstaat', 108.
[280] See e.g. Rupp, 'Vom Wandel der Grundrechte', 177; Krebs, *Vorbehalt des Gesetzes und Grundrechte*, 122 ff.; Böckenförde, 'Die sozialen Grundrechte im Verfassungsgefüge', 12 ff.; Badura, 'Das Prinzip der sozialen Grundrechte', 27 f.; Scheuner, 'Die Funktion der Grundrechte im Sozialstaat', 513; Müller, *Soziale Grundrechte in der Verfassung?*, 192, 239 ff.
[281] Hesse, 'Bestand und Bedeutung', 95 f.
[282] BVerfGE 45, 291 (315).

binding. It would be a mistake to suppose that where prima facie duties do not also correspond to definitive duties, that is, in the area of supervenience, they are not legally binding or are merely programmatic statements. The fundamental distinction between prima facie duties and non-legally binding duties can be seen from the fact that prima facie duties have to be considered in the process of balancing, while legally non-binding duties do not. From a legal perspective there must be acceptable reasons for the non-satisfaction of a prima facie duty, but there need not be for the non-satisfaction of a non-legally binding duty. If there are no acceptable reasons for its non-satisfaction, a prima facie duty can give rise to a definitive duty, but a non-binding duty can never do this.

So although Häberle is right to reject the 'alternative of subjective right or programmatic statement'—the table shows that the alternative is incomplete[283]—it is misleading when he objects to the 'proposition: legally binding = judicial control'.[284] Under the Basic Law, legally binding does imply judicial control. If Häberle's observation is to work, then it must be understood as a reference to the peculiarities of the judicial control of objective prima facie state duties. There are two such peculiarities. First, the object of control cannot be whether everything required by the prima facie duty is satisfied, but only whether what remains as a definitive duty in the light of competing prima facie duties has been satisfied. Secondly, among the competing principles it is not only substantive but also formal principles which play a decisive role, above all the competence of the democratically legitimated legislature. Neither alters the fact that the object of control by the constitutional court is whether the prima facie duty has been sufficiently taken account of in the light of competing principles.

The competence of the court ends at the boundaries of what is definitively required. But principles contain normative requirements on the legislature even on the far side of that boundary. A legislature which satisfies constitutional principles beyond the bounds of what is definitively required, satisfies constitutional rights norms, even if it is not definitively obligated to do so, and thus cannot be forced to do so by a constitutional court.

---

[283] See above at 336.
[284] Häberle, 'Grundrechte im Leistungsstaat', 107 f.

10

Constitutional Rights and Constitutional Rights Norms in the Legal System

I. THE FUNDAMENTAL NATURE OF CONSTITUTIONAL RIGHTS NORMS

The significance of constitutional rights norms for the legal system is a result of two factors: their formally and their substantively fundamental nature.

Constitutional rights norms are *formally fundamental* as a result of their location at the top of the hierarchy of the legal system as law directly binding on the legislature, executive, and judiciary. What this means can be seen by contrasting two extreme models of the constitution, a purely procedural and a purely substantive model.

In the *purely procedural model*, the constitution consists entirely of organizational and procedural norms. As regards legislation, this means that nothing is directly excluded as the potential content of positive law. Everything that comes into being regularly and in accordance with established procedures and forms is positive law.[1] A purely procedural constitution can only have an indirect effect on the content of what becomes positive law. Indirect influence arises when different procedures, which in themselves do not require any particular outcome, lead to different outcomes on account of existing circumstances. Thus experience shows that a three-class electoral system leads to laws with a different content than an electoral system based on universal equality. However indirect influence is to be evaluated, under the purely procedural model the will of the legislature, its rationality or irrationality, and the limits of its freedom of action, is in the final instance decisive for the content of law. On the assumption that a legislature can have any characteristics, then positive law can have any content. This model corresponds to a theory of constitutional rights under which they have no binding force on the legislature, that is, under

---

[1] The purely procedural model corresponds to Kelsen's dynamic principle, see H. Kelsen, *Pure Theory of Law*, trans. M. Knight (Berkeley, 1976), 195 ff.

which the legislature has the competence to limit them at will, even if only in a certain form. Under such a theory, constitutional liberty becomes, as Georg Jellinek put it, 'freedom from unlawful force',[2] and the substantive significance of constitutional rights shrinks to nothing.

The counterpart to a purely procedural model is a *purely substantive model*. While a constitution conforming to the purely procedural model is entirely possible, the possibility of a purely substantive constitution ever existing must be doubted. Nevertheless, a glance at the purely substantive model is interesting for systemic reasons. Under the purely substantive model, the constitution consists entirely of substantive norms from which the content of every legal norm in the legal system can be derived by some sort of methodical operation.[3] Such a constitution would be what Forsthoff has called a 'juridical genome [*Weltenei*] . . . from which everything derives, from the Criminal Code to the law concerning the manufacture of medical thermometers'.[4] If there is a legislature at all, then its function is limited to declaring what is already determined by the constitution. What is resolved under the purely procedural model by *decision* within the terms of the constitution, is replaced in the purely substantive model by *recognition* of its content.

The constitution which is the Basic Law is neither purely substantive nor purely procedural, but has a *mixed substantive-procedural character*. Its substantive components include state purpose provisions as well as constitutional rights norms; the core of its procedural part is made up of the norms concerning legislative process.

The fact that a constitution combines procedural and substantive elements has far-reaching consequences for the entire legal system. It means that as well as legal content which is merely *possible* so far as the constitution is concerned, there is also *necessary* and *impossible* legal content relative to the constitution. The fact that constitutional rights norms establish necessary and impossible legal content relative to the constitution[5] constitutes the core of their formally fundamental character.

In addition to formally fundamental nature, there is *substantive fundamentality*. Constitutional rights and constitutional rights norms are substantively fundamental, because they incorporate decisions about the basic normative structure of state and society. This is quite independent of how much or how little content they are given. If they have less content, one

---

[2] G. Jellinek, *System der subjektiven öffentlichen Rechte*, 2nd edn. (Tübingen, 1905), 103.

[3] A purely substantive constitution corresponds to Kelsen's static principle, see Kelsen, *Pure Theory of Law*, 196 f.

[4] E. Forsthoff, *Der Staat der Industriegesellschaft*, 2nd edn. (Munich, 1971), 144.

[5] Further differentiation is necessary in the case of a constitution which protects certain norms from constitutional amendment, as the Basic Law does in art. 79(3). The legal system not only has a necessary and impossible content relative to the currently valid content of the constitution; it also has necessary and impossible content relative to the validity of the constitution *per se*.

delegates more to the legislature, which can be seen as the power indirectly to determine the basic normative structure of state and society. The fact that decisions about the content of constitutional rights norms include decisions about the basic normative structure of state and society results from what they regulate. Questions of freedom and equality are not questions about a special area of law. They appear in all areas. How they are resolved in particular areas of law is not a secondary matter concerning the area in question, but a basic issue. Even less abstract objects of constitutional regulation concern fundamental substantive issues. If we want to say what the constitutionally required protection of marriage and the family amounts to, or what the guarantee of property requires, we cannot avoid answering basic questions about the normative ordering of society.

The ideas of formal and substantive fundamentality assert that constitutional rights norms play a central part in the legal system. However, they do not say how they do this or what this means for the structure of the legal system. These questions must now be considered.

II. THIRD PARTY, OR HORIZONTAL, EFFECT

One can consider a legal system from many different perspectives. Different concepts of a legal system correspond to the different perspectives. Two are of significance here. One can conceive of a legal system as a system of *norms*,[6] one can also conceive of it as a system of legal *positions*[7] or *relations*.[8] The system of norms and the system of positions and relations are two sides of the same coin in that legal positions and relations always correspond to the norms which establish them. In spite of this correspondence, both perspectives have their own value. One of the advantages of the norm-oriented perspective is that it includes the possibility of abstracting out from positions and relations, which simplifies matters and can also be of systemic interest. The advantage of a perspective based on positions and relations lies in its power to draw distinctions. Since discussing the effect of constitutional rights and constitutional rights norms on the legal system is all about drawing distinctions, this viewpoint is in principle preferable here.

There would be a simple answer to the question of the effect of constitutional rights norms on the legal system if its influence were limited to the state–citizen relationship. The answer would be more or less complete if one said that constitutional rights norms influence the legal system in that they affect the legal relationship between state and citizen in the form of subjective rights against the legislature, executive, and judiciary. It is easy to

---

[6] On the concept of a norm, see above at 20 ff.
[7] On the concept of a position, see above at 114 ff.
[8] On the concept of a relation, see above at 131 ff.

see that this answer is incomplete. As has been shown above, the rights of the individual against the legislature include, among other things, rights to protection from fellow citizens and to a private legal order with a certain content.[9] This shows that constitutional rights norms have some influence on the relations between citizens. This influence is particularly obvious in the case of rights against the judiciary in private law matters. These rights include, among other things, rights that the content of their judgments should not infringe constitutional rights.[10] This implies some sort of effect of constitutional rights norms on the norms of private law, and thus on the relations between citizens.

The effect of constitutional rights norms on the state–citizen relationship has been repeatedly considered in the course of our investigation. Their effect on the relations between citizens, that is, their third party or horizontal effect, has by contrast never been examined. But it is precisely third party or horizontal effect which is particularly useful in clarifying the effect of constitutional rights and constitutional rights norms on the legal system. For that reason it will now be considered.

1. ON THE 'RADIATION' THESIS

The Federal Constitutional Court tries to encapsulate the 'radiating effect'[11] of constitutional rights norms on the entire legal system by appealing to the concept of an objective order of values. To cite the Court itself, 'according to the long-standing case-law of the Federal Constitutional Court, constitutional rights norms do not simply contain defensive rights of the individual against the state, but at the same time they embody an objective order of values, which applies to all areas of law as a basic constitutional decision, and which provides guidelines and impulses for the legislature, administration and judiciary'.[12] The central concepts of this formulation are those of value and objective. The question is how these are to be understood.

It was suggested above that the Federal Constitutional Court's value-theory could be reformulated as a theory of principles, which is either left unaffected by the large number of objections to the theory of values or which can be defended against them.[13] The concept of value in this quotation can therefore be replaced by that of principle.

The question of the sense in which principles are supposed to be objective is harder to answer. It is relatively easy to say what it cannot mean. It cannot mean that their objectivity consists in the fact that as the highest principles of the legal system constitutional rights principles have nothing

---

[9] See above at 301 ff., 324 ff.
[10] BVerfGE 7, 198 (203); see also BVerfGE 42, 143 (149), in which the judgment of a civil court was described as an 'interference' with the 'constitutional rights sphere of the subject'.
[11] BVerfGE 7, 198 (207); see also BVerfGE 34, 269 (280).
[12] BVerfGE 39, 1 (41).　　　　　　　　　　　　　　　　　　　[13] 89 ff., 93 ff.

to do with individual positions. This would contradict the basic orientation of constitutional rights towards the individual,[14] and it would also not be reconcilable with the Federal Constitutional Court's view that the objective order of values is an expression of a 'principled strengthening of the validity of constitutional rights',[15] then using it to justify individual rights.[16] Understanding objective character in the sense of 'merely objective' is out of the question.

Furthermore, objectivity cannot consist in the fact that constitutional rights principles, as the highest principles, influence the legal system. All constitutional rights norms do that in some way. What the Court says is that it is exactly *as* objective principles that constitutional rights principles influence the legal system.

Finally, an interpretation which sees something objective in the fact that constitutional rights norms not only affect the situation of the individual, but that of everybody, must also be excluded. This is true of all constitutional rights norms as well.

The only possible interpretation is one which says that the objective is what remains when the subjective side of constitutional rights principles is overlooked or abstracted. But even this is not satisfactory. Overlooking or abstracting from the subjective side undoubtedly means that we are left with something objective, which is different from the 'merely objective' in that at any time it can be expanded on its subjective side again, but this does not lead to highest objective principles formed in such a way that they are capable of generally influencing the entire legal system. This is shown by the following consideration: if x has a right to G against the state s $(RxsG)$, then s has a duty to x in respect of G $(OsxG)$.[17] Abstracting from the subjective side leads from a relational to a non-relational duty[18] of s in respect of G, that is, a pure duty of s in respect of G (OsG). The object of this duty, G, is exactly that of the right from which it is derived. Suppose it consists of refraining from interfering with freedom of expression. The objective principle which one ends up with when the subjective side has been abstracted has the content of a prima facie state duty to refrain from interfering with freedom of expression. This principle is too particular to have an effect on all areas of the legal system. It only covers the area of rights that the state refrain from interfering in freedom of expression.

But with this it should be clear how it is possible to give the principle general substantive effect on all positions in the legal system. Two further abstractions have to be carried out. In addition to abstracting from the right-holder (beneficiary), one has to abstract from the addressee (the subject) and from the specific characteristics of the object (here, refraining

---

[14] See above at 304, 325 f., 332 ff.

[15] BVerfGE 7, 198 (205); 50, 290 (337).

[16] See on this BVerfGE 35, 79 (116).

[17] See on this above at 131.

[18] On these concepts, see above at 132.

from state interference). This threefold abstraction turns the right of x against the state that it not hinder x's expression[19] into a pure good [*Gesolltsein*] of freedom of expression.[20] One suspects that such threefold abstracted principles are what is meant when the Court speaks of 'basic constitutional decisions',[21] 'evaluative guiding norms',[22] 'value-decisions'[23], and so on or simply of 'the ruling ideas of the Basic Law',[24] which are supposed to radiate to all areas of law. At any rate, such threefold abstracted principles are the most plausible reconstruction of this way of speaking. From now on they will be referred to as 'principles at the highest level of abstraction'.[25]

The adoption of principles at the highest level of abstraction has advantages and disadvantages. The advantages lie in their flexibility. They can be used as the starting-points of doctrinal justification for a great variety of structural and substantive constitutional requirements in all areas of law. The disadvantage lies in their vagueness. They invite one of the most obscure forms of legal justification, the 'deduction' or 'derivation' of concrete content from abstract principles.

Such a non-rational use is, of course, only a possibility associated with objective principles at the highest level of abstraction, not a necessity. It is equally possible to use abstract principles as a starting-point for rational justification in which more precise premises must be given and justified. Where this happens, their adoption promotes rationality and does not reduce it. The adoption of an objective order of values in the form of highest objective principles is thus not in itself non-rational, rather, it is something highly incomplete that can be used in both rational and non-rational ways. The thesis that highest principles which radiate into all areas of the legal system can be derived from the constitution is thus neither false nor inadequate. It just says very little. The question remains, in what form the influence takes place and what its content is. These questions must now be considered.

2. THE CONSTRUCTION OF HORIZONTAL EFFECT

The idea that constitutional rights norms affect the relations between citizens, and in this sense have a third party or horizontal effect, is accepted on

[19] Rxs (~hinder $s(\phi x)$); see on this above at 124, fn. 61.
[20] What gets lost structurally in the threefold abstraction becomes clear when one compares the structural form of the good of freedom of expression (E), namely OE, with the right from which it has been abstracted, namely Rxs (~hinder $s(\phi x)$).
[21] BVerfGE 7, 198 (205).   [22] BVerfGE 30, 173 (188).
[23] BVerfGE 42, 64 (73).   [24] BVerfGE 42, 64 (74).
[25] The concept of the *level* of abstraction thus relates to three aspects. As regards the object of a right, further *degrees* of abstraction can be distinguished. So the good of liberty has a higher degree of abstraction than the good of freedom of expression. But both are at the highest level of abstraction.

all sides today.[26] What is controversial is how and to what extent they do this. The question of *how* constitutional rights norms influence the relations between citizens is a problem of *construction*. The question of the *extent* to which they do this is a question of substance and indeed a problem of *conflict*.[27] Both the problem of construction and the problem of conflict are the result of a fundamental difference between state–citizen and citizen–citizen relations. The state–citizen relation is a relation between a constitutional right-holder and a non-right-holder.[28] By contrast, the relation between citizens is one between right-holders.[29]

2.1 Equivalence of Outcome in the Constructions

Three theories of the proper construction of horizontal effect can be distinguished: an indirect, a direct, and one mediated by rights against the state.

According to the theory of indirect horizontal effect, the main proponents of which are Dürig[30] and the Federal Constitutional Court,[31] constitutional rights influence the interpretation of private law as 'value-decisions', 'objective norms', 'constitutional rights values', in other words as *objective principles* in the sense just outlined. This influence is supposed to be realized above all in the concretization of private law general clauses,[32] but it can be applied beyond this in the interpretation of every private law norm, and in particular cases can extend to the justification of decisions against the literal meaning of the law.[33] In spite of this constitutional rights influence, the norms of private law remain private law norms and the rights and duties they establish remain private law rights and duties.[34] As far as the position of the judge is concerned, radiating effect

---

[26] See the account of the state of debate in F. Eckhold-Schmidt, *Legitimation durch Begründung: Eine erkenntniskritische Analyse der Drittwirkungs-Kontroverse*, (Berlin, 1974), 26 ff., 66 ff.

[27] See F. Gamillscheg, 'Die Grundrechte im Arbeitsrecht', AcP 164 (1964), 420; H. Bethge, *Zur Problematik von Grundrechtskollisionen* (Munich, 1977), 400.

[28] We are only interested here in this basic relation. Further differentiations are necessary in the case of problems such as whether public law legal persons have constitutional rights, and whether the state acting in its private capacity or churches are bound by constitutional rights; see on this A. Bleckmann, *Allgemeine Grundrechtslehren* (Cologne and Berlin, 1979), 77 ff.; 126 ff., 131 ff.

[29] See G. Dürig in T. Maunz and G. Dürig, *Grundgesetz Kommentar*, 5th edn. (Munich, 1983), art. 1 para. 130; also H. H. Rupp, 'Zum "Mephisto-Beschluß" des Bundesverfassungsgerichts', DVBl 1972, 67, who speaks of a 'structural distinction within constitutional rights between the relationship of personal liberty to personal liberty on one hand and personal liberty to state authority on the other'.

[30] G. Dürig, 'Das Eigentum als Menschenrecht', ZGesStW 109 (1953), 339 ff.; id., 'Grundrechte und Zivilrechtsprechung', in T. Maunz (ed.), *Festschrift für H. Nawiasky* (Munich, 1956), 157 ff.; id., in Maunz and Dürig, *Grundgesetz Kommentar*, art. 1 para. 127 ff., art. 2 para. 56 ff.; id., 'Zum "Lüth-Urteil" des Bundesverfassungsgerichts vom 15.1.1958', DÖV 1958, 194 ff.

[31] BVerfGE 7, 198 (203 ff.); 52, 131 (166); standing case-law.

[32] BVerfGE 7, 198 (206).   [33] See BVerfGE 34, 269 (279 ff.).

[34] BVerfGE 7, 198 (205).

establishes a duty to take account of the influence of constitutional rights on private law norms when interpreting them.

The theory of direct horizontal effect, maintained principally by Nipperdey[35] and the first senate of the Federal Labour Court[36] also accepts that 'constitutional rights in the classic narrow sense of subjective public rights are only directed against the state'.[37] As in the theory of indirect horizontal effect, the influence of constitutional rights norms on the private law is supposed to arise from 'their character as objective, binding, constitutional law'.[38] The difference is that the objective principles not only affect the relations between citizens by influencing the interpretation of private law norms, but in that 'subjective private rights of the individual flow directly [from them]'.[39] As Nipperdey says, 'the legal effect [of constitutional rights] is rather a directly normative one which modifies existing private law norms, or creates new ones, regardless of whether they concern obligatory or dispositive law, general clauses or specific norms, whether prohibitions, commands, subjective rights, protective laws or justifying reasons'.[40] In this sense, constitutional rights are supposed to have absolute effect.[41]

According to the third theory, the effect on relations between citizens is the consequence of the state being bound to constitutional rights as subjective public rights. Schwabe has put forward an extreme version of this theory. As has already been explained,[42] Schwabe takes the view that the state is a participant in potential infringements of constitutional rights interests by other citizens through private law because it has made the private law system available and enforces it. The state must accept that infringements are the responsibility of the state even though they are carried out by private actors.[43] The problem of horizontal effect can thus be resolved simply through conceiving of constitutional rights as state-oriented rights within the negative status.[44] It has already been pointed out[45] that the theory of state accountability for privately effected infringements underlying this construction is not sustainable. The only significant point in this context is that this weakness of Schwabe's version does not undermine the

---

[35] L. Enneccerus and H. C. Nipperdey, *Allgemeiner Teil des Bürgerlichen Rechts*, i, 15th edn. (Tübingen, 1959), 91 ff.; H. C. Nipperdey, 'Freie Entfaltung der Persönlichkeit', in K. A. Betterman and H. C. Nipperdey (eds.), *Die Grundrechte*, vol. 4.2 (Berlin, 1962), 747 ff.; id., 'Grundrechte und Privatrecht', in H. C. Nipperdey (ed.), *Festschrift für E. Molitor* (Munich and Berlin, 1962), 17 ff. See also W. Leisner, *Grundrechte und Privatrecht* (Munich, 1960), 356 ff.

[36] See e.g. BAGE 1, 185 (191 ff.); 4, 274 (276 ff.).

[37] Nipperdey, 'Grundrechte und Privatrecht', 24.   [38] ibid.

[39] ibid.   [40] ibid. 26.   [41] ibid. 24.

[42] Above at 305.

[43] J. Schwabe, *Die sogenannte Drittwirkung der Grundrechte* (Munich, 1971), 16 ff.; 149, 154 ff.; id., *Probleme der Grundrechtsdogmatik* (Darmstadt, 1977), 213 ff.

[44] id., *Die sogenannte Drittwirkung der Grundrechte*, 141 ff.

[45] Above at 305 ff.

general construction of horizontal effect achieved by way of rights against the state. This construction is not forced to work simply with negative status rights, but can also use positive status rights aiming at constitutionally required protection in the relationship between private individuals.

It can easily be seen that the extent of the three constructions is different. While indirect horizontal effect is aimed at the judges,[46] horizontal effect mediated by rights against the state is aimed at both the legislature[47] and the judiciary. Direct horizontal effect also applies primarily to the judiciary. In what follows, the judicial aspect will stand in the foreground.

The 'three constructions, in so far as they relate to adjudication, are outcome-neutral.[48] Two juridical constructions are outcome-neutral if every outcome which could be achieved in the context of one could also be achieved in the context of the other. That the creator of a new construction has developed it in order to achieve different outcomes from that achieved by existing constructions, that the proponents of one construction tend towards different outcomes from the proponents of different constructions, that one construction tends to favour some outcomes rather than others, all this does not affect outcome-neutrality. The only thing that matters is that in all cases the same outcome *can* be achieved.

None of the three theories transfers constitutional rights as state-directed rights by merely exchanging the addressee in the relations between citizens.[49] All three theories allow one to take account of the fact that both sides of the relation between citizens are beneficiaries of constitutional rights. Each one permits of degrees of influence. For all of them, the extent of the influence of constitutional rights on relations between citizens is in the final instance a matter of balancing interests.[50] According to the theory of indirect horizontal effect, the balancing of interests has to take place in the context of the application of currently valid private law, but it presupposes a concept of legal interpretation which in certain cases even permits decisions contrary to the literal meaning (e.g. teleological reduction),[51] [52]

---

[46] See on this H. H. Rupp, 'Vom Wandel der Grundrechte', AöR 101 (1976), 170.

[47] See on this BVerfGE 14, 263 (278); 38, 132 (140).

[48] The outcome-equivalence of different constructions of horizontal effect has often been remarked on; see e.g. Gamillscheg, 'Die Grundrechte im Arbeitsrecht', 404, 419; F. Bydlinski, 'Bemerkungen über Grundrechte und Privatrecht', ÖZöR 12 (1962/3), 441; Eckhold-Schmidt, *Legitimation durch Begründung*, 71 ff. According to C. Starck, 'Die Grundrechte des Grundgesetzes', JuS 1981, 243, it 'still has to be worked out in detail' if Dürig's construction leads to different outcomes from Nipperdey's.

[49] See Nipperdey, 'Grundrechte und Privatrecht', 23; Dürig, 'Grundrechte und Zivilrechtsprechung', 158 ff.; Schwabe, *Die sogenannte Drittwirkung der Grundrechte*, 75 ff.

[50] Nipperdey, 'Grundrechte und Privatrecht', 28, 32; Enneccerus and Nipperdey, *Allgemeiner Teil des Bürgerlichen Rechts*, 103; BVerfGE 7, 198 (210 ff.); Schwabe, *Die sogenannte Drittwirkung der Grundrechte*, 107 ff.

[51] See H. Brandenburg, *Die teleologische Reduktion* (Göttingen, 1983).

[52] See Dürig's 'closing the gaps in the protection of values', id., in Maunz and Dürig, *Grundgesetz Kommentar*, art. 1 para. 133.

and thus it does not definitively exclude outcomes possible under the other approaches. Even under the other approaches, a departure from literal meaning needs justification. The process of balancing under all three theories can lead to relatively general rules under which certain constitutional rights in certain areas of private law are entirely, or substantially, overridden. For example, none of the three constructions excludes the possibility that testamentary freedom is unaffected by the right to equal treatment. If one considers the matter in terms of the outcome, it is not the construction, but the evaluation with which it is combined which is the decisive issue. What follows will strengthen and extend this thesis.

2.2 A Three-Stage Model of Horizontal Effect

The fact that all three constructions are outcome-neutral does not make the question of which one is correct irrelevant. The question of how the effect of constitutional rights and constitutional rights norms on private law 'must be conceptualized in detail'[53] not only demands an answer because jurisprudence cannot be satisfied simply with getting the right or acceptable answers regardless of the way they are structured, but also because without the correct construction it is not possible to get an informative picture of the effect of constitutional rights and constitutional rights norms on the legal system.

The controversy about horizontal effect has up to the present been carried on as if one of the three constructions has to be right. This assumption is false. It is to be maintained that each of the three constructions correctly highlights some aspects of the complicated legal relations typical of horizontal effect cases, and only becomes inadequate when the aspects identified are taken to be a complete solution. A complete, and in this sense adequate, solution can only be provided by a model which embraces all aspects. The outline of such a model will now be sketched in.

The model divides into three levels: the level of state duties, the level of rights against the state, and the level of legal relations between private individuals. There is no relationship of degree between these levels, rather there is a relationship of mutual implication.

The theory of indirect horizontal effect is rooted in the level of state duties. The fact that constitutional rights norms are objective principles (an objective order of values) for all areas of law means that the state is obligated to have regard for them both in legislating in the private law field[54] and also in private law adjudication. As far as private law adjudication is concerned this is expressed in the Lüth Judgment in the following words, 'As a constitutional requirement, the judge must consider whether the

---

[53] Thus the appropriate formulation of the Federal Constitutional Court in BVerfGE 7, 198 (204).

[54] See BVerfGE 14, 263 (278); 37, 132 (140).

substantive private law provisions to be applied by him are influenced by constitutional rights in the way described; if they are, he must have regard for the modification of private law arising in this way when interpreting and applying these provisions'.[55]

The second level is that of horizontally relevant rights against the state. The fact that the judge has the duty to take account of the constitutional order of values when interpreting and applying private law norms does not mean that he necessarily breaches constitutional rights in the form of subjective rights when he breaches this duty. But there must be such a connection if the case-law of the Federal Constitutional Court on the influence of constitutional rights and constitutional rights norms on private law is to be consistent. If there were no such connection, the court could not have been permitted to establish in the course of the Lüth Judgment that the judgment of the private law court *infringed* the *constitutional right* of the plaintiff arising from article 5(1)(1) Basic Law.[56] It should have rejected the constitutional complaint, which presupposes a breach of constitutional rights in the form of subjective rights (article 93(1)(4a) Basic Law, § 90(1) Federal Constitutional Court Act) as impermissible.[57] As far as the Federal Constitutional Court is concerned, the connection seems to be unproblematic. As it states in the Lüth Judgment,

if he [that is, the private law judge, R.A.] disregards these standards and bases his judgment on ignoring this constitutional influence on private law norms, he is not simply breaching objective constitutional law, in that he fails to recognize the content of the constitutional rights norm (as an objective norm); rather, as a holder of public power, his judgment breaches the constitutional right, to the respecting of which even by the judiciary the citizen has a constitutional claim.[58]

The question is, in what does a constitutional right consist, which a civil court is capable of infringing by the content[59] of its judgment. This question is aimed at none other than the relationship between the first and second levels.

A right can only be infringed by those against whom it is held. If civil courts can infringe the constitutional rights of citizens by the content of their judgments, then the rights being breached must be rights of the citizen against the judiciary, that is, against the state. One could take the view that these rights are none other than defensive rights against the state, that is,

---

[55] BVerfGE 7, 198 (206).   [56] BVerfGE 7, 198 (199).

[57] This conclusion is drawn by H.-U. Erichsen, *Staatsrecht und Verfassungsgerichtsbarkeit I*, 2nd edn. (Munich, 1976), 65 ff. D. Merten, Comment on Judgment, NJW 1972, 1799 follows him. In the third edition (Munich, 1982) Erichsen has changed his mind on the grounds that the 'objective-legal content [serves] to secure and strengthen the subjective-legal content', which means that 'in breaching the objective-legal content of the constitutional rights norm, the subjective-legal regulating element [can] also be affected' (53). But the question must arise here as well for Erichsen how this connection is to be understood.

[58] BVerfGE 7, 198 (206 f.).   [59] See BVerfGE 7, 198 (203).

negative status rights. This is Schwabe's view, and it makes an important point, but it suffers from weaknesses which prevent it from applying as a general answer.

The Lüth Judgment[60] shows that the defensive right construction makes a valid point. The court in Hamburg had *forbidden* Lüth to make certain statements. This concrete legal prohibition removed a part of Lüth's legal liberty to express his opinion, which consists precisely in the fact that expressions of opinion are neither prohibited nor required. The fact that this prohibition concretizes an abstract-general norm (§ 826 Civil Code), and that this norm is a private law norm, does not alter the fact that the judicial prohibition, as such an act of public power, interferes with freedom of expression.[61] So the question is whether the interference is covered by the limitation clause of article 5(2) Basic Law, that is, by § 826 Civil Code as a general law in the sense of this provision.[62] This shows that cases like the Lüth case can be conceived by way of the defensive right construction. But this does not mean that the construction has no weaknesses.

A first weakness of this construction is that it is only applicable where we are dealing with commands and prohibitions, but not where a constitutional right-holder is objecting to express or implied *permissions* addressed to other beneficiaries. The *Blinkfüer* Judgment[63] makes this plain. The publishing house Springer had urged newspaper and magazine retailers to boycott the *Blinkfüer* magazine, and had combined their call with a threat of trade sanctions if it were not followed. The Federal Civil Court rejected the claim of *Blinkfüer*'s publisher to damages. In response to the constitutional complaint raised against this judgment, the Federal Constitutional Court quashed the judgment of the Federal Civil Court on the grounds that it breached the publisher's constitutional right under article 5(1) Basic Law. The rejection of the claim to damages by the Federal Civil Court implies that it considered the call for a boycott to be legally *permitted*. As was argued above,[64] this does not mean, as Schwabe contends, that the state is accountable for the call for a boycott as a state interference with press freedom because it permitted it and failed to impose any sanctions. By rejecting the action, the Federal Civil Court did not interfere with the constitutional right to press freedom. What it did was something quite different: it refused to grant the *Blinkfüer* publisher any *state protection* from the *private* actions of another. The breach of the constitutional right arising from article 5(1) Basic Law which the Federal Constitutional Court effectively establishes thus cannot be a breach of a negative status right. It is a breach of a positive status right against the state to be protected from interferences by

---

[60] See on this J. Schwabe, 'Bundesverfassungsgericht und "Drittwirkung" der Grundrechte', AöR 100 (1975), 443 ff.

[61] See BVerfGE 7, 198 (203).

[62] BVerfGE 7, 198 (211).

[63] BVerfGE 25, 256.

[64] 305 ff.

other private individuals.[65] This makes it clear that Schwabe's defensive right construction is not sufficient fully to grasp state-mediated constitutional influence on private law. The defensive construction has to be expanded with an entitlement-based[66] or protective right construction.

Even if one expands it in this way, the weakness remains that the mere combination of a defensive and protective construction does not result in a unified one. This weakness does not mean that the constructions stated are false or valueless. But it keeps the desire for a unified construction alive. We can create such a construction by adopting a right of the citizen against the civil courts that they take adequate account of the constitutional principles which support the position argued for by the citizen. If this right is breached, so also is the constitutional right to which the relevant constitutional principle belongs. This construction is explicitly related to *adjudication*.

Such a construction has two advantages. The first consists in the fact that the right adopted in it is more clearly related to problems relevant to horizontal effect cases. This is apparent in two respects. First, the civil court has to have regard for the constitutional principles which count in favour of the positions argued for by each party, but it also has to apply existing private law, to the extent that it is not inconsistent in every interpretation with constitutional principles. The fact that in horizontal effect cases not only constitutional principles but also private law rules have a role to play can be seen at once in the fact that in many cases constitutional principles permit a variety of possible solutions, and that the judge is not simply bound to substantive constitutional principles, but also to many other further obligations, such as those arising from the formal principles of respect for the decisions of the democratically legitimated legislature and regard for precedent. It is thus appropriate that the right against the civil courts proposed here requires account to be taken of constitutional principles 'to the appropriate extent'.

The second advantage is that the adjudication-related construction does not suppress the defensive and protective construction, but provides a foundation for it. Whenever a civil court breaches the adjudication-related right of the citizen, that is, whenever it fails to have due regard for a constitutional principle which counts in favour of the position he is arguing for, it also breaches a defensive or a protective right depending on the circumstances of the case.

The adjudication-related construction cannot be accused of an unjustifiable subjectification of adjudicative duties. It neither gives the individual a

---

[65] See on this point correctly E. Friesenhahn, 'Der Wandel des Grundrechtsverständnisses', in *Verhandlungen des fünfzigsten Deutschen Juristentages* (Hamburg, 1974; ii, Munich, 1974), G27: 'the breach lay in the fact that the Federal Supreme Court failed to grant this protection'.

[66] On the wide sense which this concept has in this context, see above at 294 f.

right that the outcome of adjudication be in all respects constitutionally compatible, nor does it give him a right that the outcome be intrinsically correct; it simply gives him a right that the constitutional principles counting for *his* position be taken adequate account of.

The third level is concerned with the constitutional influence on legal relations between private individuals. This raises the issue of direct horizontal effect. The first question is what is meant by direct horizontal effect. According to what has already been said, two possible meanings can be ruled out straight away. First, direct horizontal effect cannot mean that rights of the citizen against the state are also rights of the citizen against other citizens. This is excluded on conceptual grounds and is not maintained by any proponent of the theory of direct horizontal effect. As such, a right of the citizen against the state is, by definition, not a right of the citizen against another citizen. Secondly, direct horizontal effect cannot be achieved simply by exchanging the addressee of the right of the citizen against the state. This is partly impossible for conceptual reasons—a citizen cannot have a right against another citizen that he enact or not enact certain laws, for example—and it is partly excluded, as all proponents of the theory of direct horizontal effect point out, by the fact that constitutional rights norms in the relations between citizens have a different 'effective strength' from those in the citizen–state relation on account of the mutuality of the beneficiaries.[67]

A third possibility is meant by direct horizontal effect. It consists in the existence of certain rights and no-rights, liberties and no-liberties, powers and disabilities in the relations between citizens on the basis of constitutional reasons, which would not exist in the absence of these reasons. If we define the concept of direct horizontal effect in this way, then both the theory of indirect horizontal effect and that of state-mediated horizontal effect give rise to direct horizontal effect. This can be shown by using the *Blinkfüer* Judgment.

The Federal Constitutional Court starts by establishing that the objective order of values underlying the constitutional rights catalogue affects the question of what is unlawful for the purposes of § 823(1) Civil Code.[68] This corresponds to the theory of indirect horizontal effect. The Federal Civil Court came to the conclusion that the boycott called for by the Springer publishing house was not unlawful. This means that *Blinkfüer* has no right against Springer that it refrain from issuing the boycott call. This no-right of *Blinkfüer*'s is, as has been shown above, equivalent to a permission to Springer to carry out the boycott.[69] According to the Federal Constitutional Court, constitutional principles demand precisely the opposite outcome.

---

[67] See in place of many Nipperdey, 'Grundrechte und Privatrecht', 27.

[68] BVerfGE 25, 256 (263).

[69] See above at 136: $\sim Rxy \sim G \leftrightarrow PyxG$.

This means that *on the basis* of constitutional principles, *Blinkfüer* has a right against Springer that the latter refrain from calling for a boycott. This right is equivalent to an obligation on the publishing house owed to the other publisher to refrain from making the boycott call.[70] Thus constitutional principles lead to rights and duties between private individuals, which are necessary on account of these principles, but which would not be necessary in their absence. This is direct horizontal effect. The theory of indirect horizontal effect necessarily results in direct horizontal effect.[71]

The same is true of state-mediated horizontal effect. As has already been shown, the Federal Civil Court breached the right of the *Blinkfüer* publisher to protection in the relationship between private individuals. It breached this right because it failed to take adequate account of the constitutional principles counting for the position of the publisher. But this presupposes the existence of a definitive right of the publisher against the publishing house that it refrain from the boycott as required by constitutional principles.

So Leisner's maxim that 'horizontal effect will in the final analysis always be direct'[72] is correct. However, this maxim must not be taken to mean that there is only the level of direct horizontal effect in the sense outlined. There are all three levels. Each expresses an aspect of the same matter. Which is chosen in the process of legal justification is a question of utility. None of them can claim primacy over the others.

Against the form of direct horizontal effect set out here there is only one sustainable argument: the denial of any form of horizontal effect whatsoever. All other arguments against direct horizontal effect fail. It is easy to disarm the objection that each form of direct horizontal effect leads to an impermissible removal or limitation of private autonomy.[73] Private autonomy itself and not its limitation is the object of constitutional guarantee and thus of horizontal effect. It is a weakness of the discussion about horizontal effect that to a large extent the question of the limitation of private autonomy stood in the foreground, and that its protection was not dealt with as of equal significance. How the limits of private law powers are to be drawn is a question of substance and thus in the final analysis a problem of the balancing of interests. By establishing direct horizontal effect in the sense identified here, there is no prejudice in respect of this question of substance. It simply sharpens our perception of constitutional problems.

The objection that direct horizontal effect even in the sense defended here is incompatible with the role of the civil courts has to be taken more seriously. In its exaggerated form it claims that direct horizontal effect

---

[70] See above at 136: $Rxy{\sim}G \leftrightarrow Oyx{\sim}G$.
[71] See H. H. Klein, 'Öffentliche und private Freiheit', *Der Staat*, 10 (1971), 149.
[72] Leisner, *Grundrechte und Privatrecht*, 378.
[73] See Dürig, 'Grundrechte und Zivilrechtsprechung', 158 ff.

makes civil law redundant. If there is direct horizontal effect, the judges can resolve civil cases directly on the basis of constitutional rights norms. Why they should still have regard for private law is impossible to say.[74]

However, this objection overlooks the fact that constitutional principles in no way lay down precisely one solution in every case. There are innumerable private law cases in which more than one solution is constitutionally possible. In these cases private law norms have a constitutive significance. It also overlooks the fact that it is often unclear what constitutional principles require in a private law case. In this situation it is necessary that the civil courts are able to base themselves on authoritative sources, that is, on enacted norms, precedents, and commonly held doctrinal propositions in the interests of a consistent adjudicative practice which satisfies the requirements of legal certainty and equal treatment.[75] Private law adjudication which based each case solely on the text of the Basic Law, but apart from that decided on the basis of a normative *tabula rasa*, would never satisfy these requirements. The civil courts are thus prima facie bound to observe valid private law, whether in the form of statutes, precedents, or accepted doctrine. If they want to depart from this on the grounds of constitutional principle, then they bear the burden of argument.[76]

One could take the view that with the necessity of private law norms as an intermediate stage, the directness of horizontal effect collapses. This would be the case if directness of horizontality were taken to imply the redundancy of private law norms. Of course, one can define the concept of direct horizontal effect in this way, and thus reduce every instance of direct horizontal effect ad absurdum, or limit it to entirely new areas of private law, not even influenced by judicial law-making. But such a concept of direct horizontal effect would miss the decisive point. This consists in the fact that because constitutional principles influence the system of private law norms, they require or exclude the existence of certain rights and no-rights, liberties and no-liberties, powers and disibilities in the relations between citizens, which in the absence of constitutional principles, that is, on the basis of a private law system alone uninfluenced by constitutional principle, would not be characterized as constitutionally necessary or impossible. In this sense there is direct horizontal effect.

That last point leads to the question whether a private individual who breaches the right required for constitutional reasons which another private person holds against him breaches a constitutional right of the other. For example, did the Springer publishing house in the *Blinkfüer* case breach *Blinkfüer*'s constitutional right to press freedom? The answer turns on a

---

[74] See Schwabe, *Die sogenannte Drittwirkung der Grundrechte*, 140 ff.

[75] See on this R. Alexy, *A Theory of Legal Argumentation*, trans. R. Adler and N MacCormick (Oxford, 1989), 248, 250 ff., 274 ff.

[76] On the requirement for specal justification, see Starck, 'Die Grundrechte des Grundgesetzes', 245.

terminological distinction. One could say that a constitutionally necessary private right was breached, but one could also say that the right breached, because it is constitutionally required, belongs to the variegated bundle which makes up the complete constitutional right,[77] and that whenever one part of that bundle is breached, 'the constitutional right' is. The first way of putting it has the advantage that it prevents many misunderstandings and simplifications associated with the idea of a breach of constitutional rights by a private individual. The second has the advantage of doctrinal consistency. It seems advisable to keep both ways of putting it available, and where misunderstandings could arise to explain the second with the help of the first.

III. THE LEGAL SYSTEM AND CONSTITUTIONAL RIGHTS REASONING

1. CONSTITUTIONAL RIGHTS AND THE NATURE OF THE LEGAL SYSTEM

The influence of constitutional rights norms on all areas of the law, in which respect third party, or horizontal, effect covers one of the most problematic aspects, has far-reaching consequences on the character of the legal system. Three are of particular significance.

The first consists of the limitation of the possible content of ordinary law. Admittedly, as a mixed substantive-procedural constitution, in no way does it establish the entire content of ordinary law, but it does exclude certain content as constitutionally impossible and requires other content as constitutionally necessary. This applies for all law-making procedures within the system, that is, also for the constitutionally necessary power of private individuals to establish legal duties by way of contract. Thus on account of the validity of constitutional rights norms, the constitution gives the legal system a *substantively determined* character.

The second consequence arises from the type of substantive determination. Substantive determination would be entirely unproblematic if it were always clear what was required on the basis of constitutional rights norms. But this is not the case. The reason for this does not lie simply in the semantic and structural openness of constitutional rights provisions, but to a large extent also in the principled character of constitutional rights norms. Their principled character implies the necessity of balancing interests. The procedure of balancing is, of course, as has been shown,[78] a rational one, but it certainly does not lead to exactly one solution in every case. Which solution is regarded as correct after having balanced the interests depends upon

---

[77] See on this above at 159 ff.   [78] 100 ff.

value-judgments, which are themselves not controllable by the balancing procedure. In this sense, balancing is an open procedure. But the openness of balancing leads to an openness of the legal system, substantively determined by constitutional rights norms though it is. So on the basis of the validity of constitutional rights norms, the legal system gets—to some extent—the character of an *open* legal system.

The third consequence concerns the nature of this openness. The validity of constitutional rights norms means that the legal system is open *in respect of morality*. This is most obvious with the basic substantive concepts of constitutional rights, the concepts of dignity, freedom, and equality. These concepts are also basic to practical philosophy. In adopting them, the most important principles of modern natural law have been incorporated into the constitution and thus also into positive law.[79] The detailed application of these principles, and balancing them against each other, are problems of justice. Rawls's principles of justice,[80] which are none other than an attempt to relate freedom and equality, make this quite clear and in exemplary fashion. When the Federal Constitutional Court says that the constitution makers tried 'to realize the idea of justice in the Basic Law',[81] then this is related above all to principles of constitutional rights. Thus the influence of constitutional rights as positive law on all areas of the legal system implies an influence of the idea of justice on all areas of law, required by positive law.

2. On the Problem of the Controlling Competence of the Constitutional Court

Substantive determination through morally open standards leads to a whole series of questions. In a legal system such as the German one which has a constitutional court of comprehensive jurisdiction, problems for constitutional jurisdiction arising from substantive determination play a particular role. In the centre of the long-standing and time-consuming debate about the jurisdiction of the constitutional court[82] stands the balancing of the

---

[79] See R. Dreier, *Recht—Moral—Ideologie* (Frankfurt a. M., 1981), 124; M. Kriele, *Recht und praktische Vernunft* (Göttingen, 1979), 124.

[80] J. Rawls, *A Theory of Justice* (Cambridge, Mass., 1971), 302 f.

[81] BVerfGE 3, 225 (233). See also G. Robbers, *Gerechtigkeit als Rechtsprinzip: Über den Begriff der Gerechtigkeit in der Rechtsprechung des Bundesverfassungsgerichts* (Baden-Baden, 1980).

[82] On this, see on one hand the papers on the 'Nature and Development of State Adjudication' by H. Triepel and H. Kelsen at the 1928 conference of the Association of German Teachers of Public Law (VVDStRL 5 (1929), 2 ff., 30 ff.) and on the other hand the papers on 'Constitutional Adjudication in the System of State Functions' by K. Korinek, J. P. Müller, and K. Schlaich at the 1980 conference of the same association (VVDStRL 39 (1981), 7 ff., 53 ff., 99 ff.) as well as P. Häberle (ed.), *Verfassungsgerichtsbarkeit* (Darmstadt, 1976); K. Stern, *Das Staatsrecht der Bundesrepublik Deutschland*, ii (Munich, 1980), 933 ff.; J. Mackert and F. Schneider, *Bibliographie zur Verfassungsgerichtsbarkeit des Bundes und der Länder*, i, ii, iii (Tübingen, 1971, 1976, 1982).

competence of the court and the legislature. There would be a perfect solution in a rule-based system, which in every case would give precisely one answer to the question whether the court has exceeded its jurisdiction whenever it takes some form of action against the legislature. However, such a solution is not in sight, and one can ask whether in the light of the roots of the problem in fundamental questions there will ever be such a solution. However, for the present, one thing seems certain: general formulae such as 'judicial self-restraint' do not help us much. What is necessary is a differentiated solution.[83] The direction in which a solution is to be sought was well expressed by the Federal Constitutional Court in its Co-determination Judgment, when in the context of legislative prognoses it distinguished between 'evidential review', 'plausibility review', and 'intensive review of content'.[84]

It is not possible to discuss the problems of constitutional jurisdiction in more depth here. That would require opening up a new subject altogether. What is of interest is what can be learnt from a specifically constitutional rights-based perspective on these issues.

The starting-point is the fact that in so far as constitutional rights have the character of individual rights against the legislature, they are positions which by definition establish legislative duties and limit legislative powers. The mere existence of a constitutional court establishing legislative breaches of duty and abuse of powers for constitutional reasons is not sufficient to ground an objection of an unconstitutional transfer of competence from the legislature to the court. If the constitution grants to the individual rights against the legislature and intends there to be a constitutional court to uphold these rights (as well), then the activity of the constitutional court in the field of legislation to uphold these rights is not an unconstitutional assumption of legislative competence; it is not only constitutionally permitted, it is also required.

So the question of *whether* the constitutional court has controlling powers in the field of legislation is not open for dicussion; the only question is as to their *extent*. At this point it is absolutely necessary to distinguish three levels of argument: the substantive, the functional or competence-based, and the methodological and epistemological.

One is dealing with the *substantive* level, when, in the Co-determination Judgment mentioned, the Federal Constitutional Court makes the 'predictive prerogative' of the legislature, and thus the reviewing jurisdiction of the court, depend among other things on 'the significance of relevant legal

---

[83] For attempts in this direction, see J. Delbrück, 'Quo vadis Bundesverfassungsgericht?', in J. Delbrück, K. Ipsen, and D. Rauschning (eds.), *Recht im Dienst des Friedens, Festschrift für E. Menzel* (Berlin, 1975), 89 ff.; G. F. Schuppert, *Funktionell-rechtliche Grenzen der Verfassungsinterpretation* (Königstein, Ts., 1980), 1 ff.; H. P. Schneider, 'Verfassungsgerichtsbarkeit und Gewaltenteilung', NJW 1980, 2103 ff.

[84] BVerfGE 50, 290 (333).

interests'.[85] This means that one factor which plays a role in determing the extent of jurisdiction in concrete cases or in certain types of case is the weight of relevant substantive constitutional principles.

Arguments at the *functional* or *competence-based* level are being raised when reasons for allocating jurisdiction to decide constitutional rights issues are put forward resting on actual or supposed characteristics of the decision-takers, such as the stronger democratic legitimation of the parliamentary legislature, its greater capacity to evaluate complex factual situations adequately, the relative ease of correcting mistakes, and the greater degree of acceptance of its decisions, or the higher degree of impartiality of the constitutional court, its qualification to decide questions of rights, and its relative independence from the pressures of the moment.

Finally, arguments at the *methodological* or *epistemological* level are those put forward for or against the rational justifiability of constitutional rights decisions. The spread of these ranges from thorough-going methodological scepticism, according to which questions of doubt can only be resolved by a 'decision which authoritatively removes the doubt',[86] through to a thorough-going methodological rationalism, according to which there is one right answer in every question of rights.[87]

An adequate solution to the problem of the jurisdiction to review will only be possible if sufficient account is taken of arguments at all three levels. Recent attempts to arrive at a solution by way of a 'functional-theoretical method'[88] are blinkered. The fact that all three levels have a part to play and that there can therefore be no primacy for the functional level from a systemic perspective, but rather for the material and methodological levels, can be seen from the fact that whenever it can be established with sufficient certainty that a subjective right of the individual exists against the legislature, the reasons counting against the court's jurisdiction to review must be outweighed. Thus the reviewing jurisdiction of the court always depends substantially on the *certainty* with which the *existence* of a constitutional rights position can be justified. The problem of the certainty of constitutional rights justification will be considered in what follows. This problem leads to the relationship between argumentation and decision.

---

[85] BVerfGE 50, 290 (332 f.).

[86] C. Schmitt, 'Das Reichsgericht als Hüter der Verfassung', in id., *Verfassungsrechtliche Aufsätze*, 2nd edn. (Berlin, 1973), 81.

[87] R. Dworkin, 'Hard Cases' in id., *Taking Rights Seriously*, 2nd edn. (London, 1978), 81 ff.

[88] See Schneider, 'Verfassungsgerichtsbarkeit und Gewaltenteiling', 2104; see also Schuppert, *Funktionell-rechtliche Grenzen der Verfassungsinterpretation*, 38 ff.; G. Zimmer, *Funktion—Kompetenz—Legitimation* (Berlin, 1979), 68 ff.

3. ARGUMENTATION AND DECISION

The question of the certainty of constitutional rights justification expresses just one aspect of a more general problem, which is whether jurisprudence has access to criteria and rules which allow us to distinguish correct and false legal justification. It is the function of a theory of legal argumentation to give an answer to this question. A position has been taken in depth on the theory of legal argumentation in other work.[89] Here, we are only concerned with problems specific to *constitutional rights* argumentation. A few references to the general theory of legal argumentation will suffice for these purposes.

3.1 On the General Theory of Legal Argumentation

The starting-point of a general theory of legal argumentation is that legal justification is always ultimately concerned with practical questions, that is, with what is commanded, prohibited, or permitted. Legal discourse is thus a special instance of general practical discourse.[90] As a special instance of general practical discourse, it is characterized by the fact that legal argumentation takes place under a series of limiting conditions, which can be briefly denoted by the obligation to follow statute, precedent, and doctrine. However, these obligations, which can be expressed through a system of specific rules and forms of legal argumentation,[91] do not lead in every case to just one answer. In all moderately problematic cases, value-judgments are needed which do not emerge necessarily from authoritative pre-existing material. The rationality of legal discourse depends largely on whether and to what extent these additional value-judgments are capable of rational control.

Thus the question of the rationality of legal justification leads to the question of the rational justification of general practical or moral judgments. The discussion of this question has long been adversely affected by an unfruitful opposition of two basic positions, reappearing in ever new varieties, between subjectivist, relativist, decisionist, and/or irrationalist positions on one hand, and objectivist, absolutist, cognitivist, and/or rationalist positions on the other. But there is no need for such an all-or-nothing attitude. More recent ethical discussion, which has been significantly influenced methodologically by modern logic, linguistic philosophy, and theories

---

[89] Alexy, *A Theory of Legal Argumentation*; id., 'Die Idee einer prozeduralen Theorie der juristischen Argumentation', *Rechtstheorie*, Beiheft 2 (1981), 177 ff.; A. Aarnio, R. Alexy, and A. Peczenik, 'The Foundation of Legal Reasoning', in A. Aarnio and D. N. MacCormick (eds.), *Legal Reasoning*, i (Aldershot, 1992), 233 ff.

[90] Alexy, *A Theory of Legal Argumentation*, 15 ff., 212 ff., 287 ff.; see also M. Kriele, *Recht und praktische Vernunft* (Göttingen, 1979), 33 f.; N. MacCormick, *Legal Reasoning and Legal Theory* (Oxford, 1978), 272.

[91] Alexy, *A Theory of Legal Argumentation*, 221 ff., 300 ff.

of argumentation, decision, and knowledge, and which in terms of its content is strongly influenced by Kantian ideas,[92] has shown that while *substantive* theories of morality giving precisely one answer to every moral question with intersubjectively binding certainty are not possible, nevertheless, *procedural* moral theories are possible, which formulate rules or conditions for rational practical argument or decision.[93] One particularly fruitful version of a procedural theory of morality is that of rational practical discourse.[94]

The advantage of discourse theory lies in the fact that as rules of rational practical argument, its rules are much easier to justify than substantive moral rules. The price to pay for this is that the procedure of discourse as such is compatible with very different outcomes. Of course, there are discursively impossible and discursively necessary outcomes, but there is always a wide space for the discursively merely possible. At the level of moral theory, this fault cannot be removed. To remove it, moral theory has to be combined with a theory of law. Such a combination is possible by way of a four-stage procedural model.[95] The four stages of the model are: (1) general practical discourse, (2) legislative procedure, (3) legal discourse, (4) court procedure.

General practical discourse comprises the first stage. Its system of rules expresses something rather like a general code of practical reason,[96] but in no way leads in every case to exactly one answer. But the resolution of social conflict demands the establishment of just one answer. This makes an institutionalized procedure of law-making necessary at the second stage, in which not only are arguments made, but decisions taken.[97] A model example of such a procedure is the *legislative procedure* of a democratic state, defined by a system of rules which in relation to factually possible alternatives guarantees a significant level of practical rationality, and which to that extent is justifiable in terms of the first procedure.

But even a law-making procedure is not capable of establishing in

---

[92] See on this ibid. 33 ff.

[93] See id., 'Die Idee einer prozeduralen Theorie der juristischen Argumentation', 178 ff.; id., 'Juristische Argumentation und praktische Vernunft', *Jahrbuch der Akademie der Wissenschaften im Göttingen*, 1982, 29 f.

[94] id., *A Theory of Legal Argumentation*, 177 ff.; J. Habermas, 'Discourse Ethics: Notes on a Program of Philosophical Justification', in *Moral Consciousness and Communicative Action*, trans. C. Lenhardt and S. W. Nicolsen (Cambridge, 1989), 43 ff.

[95] Alexy, 'Die Idee einer prozeduralen Theorie der juristischen Argumentation', 185 ff.

[96] id., *A Theory of Legal Argumentation*, 188 ff; see on this M. Henket, 'Towards a Code of Practical Reason?' Lecture to the 11th World Congress of the International Association of Legal and Social Philosophy (Helsinki, 1983, recorded in the proceedings of the Congress).

[97] In addition to this argument for the institutionalization of a legal system, which is based on the limits of practical knowledge, there is an additional argument from force. This is based on the fact that even the assent of all within a discourse to a rule does not necessarily mean that they will all follow it. A combination of the arguments from knowledge and from force in the context of justifying the necessity of an institutionalized legal system can be found in I. Kant, *The Metaphysics of Morals*, trans. M. Gregor (Cambridge, 1991), 123 f.

advance just one solution to every case as both historical experience and conceptual considerations show. This gives rise to the necessity of a third procedure, that of *legal discourse*. Just like the first procedure, this one is not institutionalized in any strict sense, but unlike the first it has obligations to respect statute, precedent, and legal doctrine. This obligation has the consequence that the uncertainty of outcome of general practical discourse is to a significant extent reduced. But on account of the necessity of general practical argumentation in the context of legal argumentation, uncertainty of outcome is not totally eliminated. This leads to the necessity for a fourth, once again strictly institutionalized, procedure, namely that of *court process*, in which as in legislative procedure there is not just argument but also decision. The outcomes of these procedures are rational if their rules and enforcement satisfy the requirements of the first three procedures. The fact that questions of evaluation emerge during legal process, left open by pre-existing authoritative material, which are the subject-matter not only of argumentation but also of decision, does not mean that rationality has been abandoned. For one thing, these questions of evaluation are determined in the context of obligations, which as the model shows, are as such rational; for another thing, questions of evaluation can be determined on the basis of rational practical argumentation, which gives the decision a rational character, even if more than one decision is possible under the rules of rational practical argumentation.

3.2 The Basis of Constitutional Rights Argumentation

In order to cover constitutional rights argumentation, this model has to be extended. Constitutional rights discourse is not bound by decisions made during legislative procedure, but takes precedence over them. This means that the most important binding factor for legal argumentation, relatively concrete ordinary statute law, disappears. In its place are highly abstract, open, and ideologically loaded constitutional rights provisions. The question is what this means for the rational controllability of constitutional decision-taking. To answer this, it is a good idea to draw a distinction between the *basis* and the *process* of constitutional argumentation. The basis will be considered first.

The basis of constitutional rights argumentation can—a few significant distinctions aside—be identified in the same way as general legal argumentation under the headings, 'statute', 'precedent', and 'doctrine'. Here, only as much will be said under each heading as is necessary to show that constitutional rights argumentation is capable of being rational.

3.2.1 Text and Intention

By the obligation of constitutional rights argumentation to respect 'statute', is meant the obligation to the *text* of the constitutional rights provisions and the *will* of the constitution makers. The main expression of this obligation is

through the rules and forms of semantic and 'genetic' (origin-based) interpretation.[98] Subjective-teleological interpretation, which refers to the
purposes assigned to the constitutional rights provisions by the constitution
makers, is also to be included within genetic interpretation.[99] The rules and
forms of systematic, historical, and comparative interpretation can play an
additional role in establishing text and intention. What does not belong in
the context of the obligation to statute is objective-teleological interpretation, which is concerned with the purposes which the interpreter assigns to
the law.[100]

It has regularly and rightly been pointed out that the extent and power
of semantic and genetic arguments over constitutional rights argumentation
is limited.[101] The relatively small *extent* of control derives from the openness of constitutional rights provisions, as well as from the fact that the
record of their development in many cases reveals nothing or nothing
certain. The *force* of obligation is weakened by the fact that semantic and
genetic arguments, if they are relevant at all, do not always require the
outcome desired. They can be outweighed by other arguments. This makes
it clear that semantic and genetic arguments taken on their own are quite
inadequate to control constitutional rights argumentation. But it would be
a mistake to conclude from this that they have no contribution to make in
this respect at all.[102]

Much, but not everything, is compatible with the text[103] of constitutional rights provisions. The fact that the text requires or excludes a certain
interpretation is a very strong argument for or against it. An example of a
decision in which a semantic argument played a decisive role was the decision concerning bailiffs' powers of search, for which the constitutional
court required judicial approval, above all on account of the text of article
13(2) Basic Law ('Searches may only be authorized by a judge').[104] That the

---

[98] See R. Alexy, *A Theory of Legal Argumentation*, 235 ff.
[99] ibid., 203 f.
[100] See id., 'Teleologische Auslegung und Gesetzesbindung', in *Sprache und Recht, Loccumer Protokolle*, 31 (1980), 143 ff.
[101] See in place of many H. Huber, 'Über die Konkretisierung der Grundrechte', in P. Saladin and L. Wildhaber, *Der Staat als Aufgabe* (Basle and Stuttgart, 1972), 192 ff.; E.-W. Böckenförde, 'Die Methoden der Verfassungsinterpretation', NJW 1976, 2090 f.
[102] Huber, 'Über die Konkretisierung der Grundrechte', 195, thinks that 'traditional legal interpretation is out of place and no good'. If this means that the classical canons of semantic and genetic interpretation have no role to play in constitutional rights argumentation at all, then this is wrong. Admittedly, Huber limits the radical nature of his thesis: 'they are capable at most of preparing in a small way for the final understanding of constitutional rights'. But this permits at least a certain role for the classical canons. The same applies to Böckenförde, who emphasizes the 'inadequacy of classical rules of interpretation', but then lets them play their part in the constitutional theory which he considers decisive, which includes 'the application of the classic hermeneutical rules of interpretation' (id., 'Die Methoden der Verfassungs-
interpretation', 2091).
[103] On the possibilities and limits of semantic interpretation, see H.-J. Koch and H. Rüßmann, *Juristische Begründungslehre* (Munich, 1982), 126 ff.
[104] BVerfGE 51, 97 (106 f.).

semantic argument is a very strong one does not mean that it always wins. This is made clear by the Pharmacists Judgment, in which contrary to the text of article 12(1)(1) Basic Law, freedom of choice of profession was subjected to the regulatory power of article 12(1)(2).[105] None the less, this case still shows the force of the semantic argument. In order to overcome it, it is not sufficient to show that a solution contrary to the text is better than a consistent one; the reasons for a contrary solution must be so strong that from a constitutional perspective they justify a departure from the text.[106] In the Pharmacists Judgment, the Court was able to put forward such reasons. Thus the text of constitutional rights provisions binds constitutional rights argumentation in the sense that a burden of argumentation lies in its favour.

The same applies to the history of the Constitution's formulation. The Federal Constitutional Court has repeatedly maintained the thesis that 'the derivation of specific provisions of the Basic Law cannot be decisive in determining their interpretation'.[107] That genetic arguments have no decisive significance does not mean that they have no significance at all. The origins of provisions often do not give rise to a single interpretation. To base oneself on them means, in practice, to tread on uncertain ground.[108] But when something unambiguously for or against a proposed interpretation does emerge, then this is to be put forward as an argument, and if this argument is not to be followed, then reasons are necessary which justify this.

Thus the extent and force of the obligation of constitutional rights argumentation to respect 'statute' is limited, but it is there. This does not contradict the theory of principles. As has been shown above, constitutional rights norms have a double aspect as rules and principles.[109] To the extent that the constitution makers have taken decisions in the form of rules, then these are binding unless adequate constitutional reasons can be given for their not being binding.

3.2.2 Precedent

The second part of the foundation of constitutional rights argumentation is made up of precedent. Smend's words, 'the Basic Law applies for all practical purposes in the way the Federal Constitutional Court interprets it'[110] expresses its significance. This significance corresponds to the self-interpretation of the

---

[105] BVerfGE 7, 377 (400 ff.).
[106] See Alexy, *A Theory of Legal Argumentation*, 248; Kriele, *Recht und praktische Vernunft*, 79 ff.
[107] BVerfGE 51, 97 (110); 6, 389 (431); 41, 291 (309).
[108] See Dürig, 'Comment on Elfes Judgment', JZ 1957, 169.
[109] 84.
[110] R. Smend, 'Festvortrag zum Feier des zehnjährigen Bestehens des Bundesverfassungsgerichts am 26 Januar 1962', in *Das Bundesverfassungsgericht*, 2nd edn. (Karlsruhe, 1971), 16.

Court as the 'authoritative interpreter and guardian of the constitution'.[111]
As a matter of detail, a whole range of questions is admittedly still open, as
the discussion about the legal force of the Court's decisions, their binding
effect on state organs under § 31(1) Federal Constitutional Court Act, and
their having statutory effect as commanded in a series of cases under §
31(2) show.[112] Here, we are only concerned with the general precedential
force of decisions of the Federal Constitutional Court for constitutional
rights argumentation. The relationship between their general precedential
force, which they have in common with all judicial decisions, to their legal
force, their binding nature, and statutory effect under §§ 31(1) and (2)
Federal Constitutional Court Act need not be considered. Legal force arises
anyway only for identical cases,[113] the binding nature of judgments under
§ 31(1) does not, according to the case-law of the Court, extend to the
Court itself,[114] and therefore does not extend to the constitutional rights
argumentation which leads to Court decisions either, and statutory effect
under § 31(2), even if it is binding on the Federal Constitutional Court at
all,[115] does not establish any more extensive material obligation beyond
that of ordinary legal force.[116] If one follows the case-law of the Federal
Constitutional Court, general precedential force plays a considerable role
alongside the obligations established by the rules just cited; if one treats
general precedential force as included within these rules, above all in §
31(1) Federal Constitutional Court Act,[117] then although there is an additional positive-legal basis for it, there is in practice nothing new.

The two main rules for the use of precedent are:

(1)   If a precedent can be cited for or against a decision, then it is to be
      cited.

---

[111] BVerfGE 40, 88 (93).

[112] See in place of many M. Sachs, *Die Bindung des Bundesverfassungsgerichts an seine
Entscheidungen* (Munich, 1977); N. Wischermann, *Rechtskraft und Bindungswirkung verfas-
sungsgerichtlicher Entscheidungen* (Berlin, 1979); R. Zuck, 'Die Selbstbindung des
Bundesverfassungsgerichts', NJW 1975, 907 ff.; H. Maassen, 'Probleme der Selbstbindung des
Bundesverfassungsgerichts', NJW 1975, 1343 ff.; K. Vogel, 'Rechtskraft und Gesetzeskraft der
Entscheidungen des Bundesverfassungsgerichts', in C. Starck (ed.), *Bundesverfassungsgericht
und Grundgesetz*, i (Tübingen, 1976), 568 ff.; K. Lange, 'Rechtskraft, Bindungswirkung und
Gesetzeskraft der Entscheidungen des Bundesverfassungsgerichts', JuS 1978, 1 ff.

[113] BVerfGE 4, 31 (39); 20, 56 (86 f.). In addition, the Federal Constitutional Court also
considers the extent to which it is bound to be elastic when it has already ruled on a particular norm, as decisions on repeated references under art. 100(2)(1) Basic Law show; see
BVerfGE 33, 199 (203 f.); 39, 169 (181 f.).

[114] BVerfGE 4, 31 (38); 20, 56 (87).

[115] An idea rejected by H. J. Wolff and O. Bachof, *Verwaltungsrecht I*, 9th edn. (Munich,
1974), 127, and accepted with further references by Lange, 'Rechtskraft, Bindungswirkung
und Gesetzeskraft', 7.

[116] See BVerfGE 33, 199 (203 f.), as also Lange, 'Rechtskraft, Bindungswirkung und
Gesetzeskraft', 8.

[117] See e.g. M. Kriele, *Theorie der Rechtsgewinnung*, 2nd edn. (Berlin, 1976), 299 ff.; Sachs,
Die Bindung des Bundesverfassungsgerichts an seine Entscheidungen, 139.

(2) One who wants to depart from precedent bears the burden of argumentation.[118]

The justification for these rules, which has been set out elsewhere, will not be repeated here. The point will simply be made that the most important arguments relate to equality, legal certainty, the protection of reliance, reduction of workload, and stability as the basis of progress.[119] In the current context the only point of interest lies in the significance of these rules for the rational controllability of constitutional rights argumentation.

By using the principle of universalizability[120] it is possible to derive a more or less concrete rule from each decision of the Federal Constitutional Court which determines the case decided. A textbook example of such a decision-related rule is the rule in the Lebach Judgment referred to several times already: 'Thus to summarize, a repeated television report of a serious criminal act, no longer covered by the interest in up-to-date information, is at any rate impermissible if it endangers the resocialization of the criminal'.[121] Where cases are adequately similar, such decision-related rules are repeatedly applied. Thus in one of the many decisions on postal delays, it is stated, 'the Federal Constitutional Court has repeatedly decided in the context of procedural regulations concerning restitutionary damages that delays by the German Federal Post in transporting and delivering mail cannot be treated as the fault of the individual (BVerfGE 45, 360 (362); 46, 404 (406) with further references'.[122] The precedential force of the ratio is displayed not only in those cases in which the Court repeatedly applies a rule already established, but also precisely in those cases in which it extends it to cases with new characteristics, as well as in those cases in which it does not extend it on account of some new characteristic. An example of extension is provided by the decision concerning the continuation of investigative detention on account of the overburdening of a regional court. The Court refers first to a series of earlier decisions in which it decided that an extension of the time period in § 121(1) Law of Criminal Procedure was impermissible, if it was caused by the fact that 'the criminal investigative officials and the courts had not taken all reasonable measures to establish the facts as quickly as possible and to reach a judicial decision about the acts alleged to have been committed by the accused'. Then it goes on to say, 'the same must also apply where the reason for the time extension lies in the fact that after the main procedure has commenced, the start of the main hearing in a matter ripe for consideration is significantly delayed by avoidable faults or omissions in the organization of the court'.[123] An example of a refusal

---

[118] Alexy, *A Theory of Legal Argumentation*, 278.
[119] Kriele, *Theorie der Rechtsgewinnung*, 258 ff.; id., *Recht und praktische Vernunft*, 96 ff.; Alexy, *A Theory of Legal Argumentation*, 275 ff.
[120] See ibid. 222, 275 f.; MacCormick, *Legal Reasoning and Legal Theory*, 73 ff.
[121] BVerfGE 35, 202 (237).   [122] BVerfGE 53, 25 (28).
[123] BVerfGE 36, 264 (273).

to extend a ratio is the decision on the age limit for an orphan's benefit.[124] In an earlier decision, the Court had declared impermissible a limitation of the benefit to unmarried orphans;[125] now the question was whether an age limit of 25 was permissible. As far as precedential force is concerned, the point is that the Court referred to the earlier decision and gave a reason why the age limit was to be treated differently from the limitation to unmarried persons. This shows how the ongoing decision-taking practice of the Federal Constitutional Court leads to fixed points in constitutional rights argumentation.

If we bring together all the ratios of the Federal Constitutional Court, we end up with a relatively comprehensive and dense network of norms. Every new decision contributes to its density. One could therefore take the view that the precedential binding nature of this system of norms amounts to too much rather than too little. The objection that the law suffers from encrustation springs to mind. But this objection can be dealt with. First of all, reference can be made to the possibility of distinguishing and overruling.[126] However close the network of ratios is, new cases always display new characteristics which can be put forward as reasons for differentiation. In addition, the precedential force of ratios only gives rise to a prima facie obligation. A ratio can be abandoned if sufficient reasons can be put forward for this.[127] Secondly, one must also point out that behind the system of ratios, principles retain their validity. A dense and well-tried system of ratios makes a comprehensive balancing of principles unnecessary in easy cases, that is, in cases in which the principles suggest no other solution than the ratio. This explains the fact that as constitutional case-law gets older, so recourse to the underlying order of values gets less frequent.[128] But this does not mean that principles lose their validity. The moment doubts arise, they come into play again whereby they develop their ability to amend and overturn rules.

This alone makes clear that the rationally justifiable strengthening of constitutional rights argumentation through the precedential force of the decisions of the Federal Constitutional Court amounts to no encrustation. At the same time, this admittedly implies that the degree of certainty produced by precedent is limited. In addition, the degree of certainty is lessened by numerous standing formulae of the Federal Constitutional Court with a very open character. In the light of many of them, one could talk in

---

[124] BVerfGE 40, 121.   [125] BVerfGE 28, 324 (347).

[126] See Kriele, *Theorie der Rechtsgewinnung*, 275 ff.; MacCormick, *Legal Reasoning and Legal Theory*, 219 ff.

[127] The precedential force of decisions of the Federal Constitutional Court thus does not mean a 'canonisation of statements of the Federal Constitutional Court'; see on this K. Schlaich, 'Verfassungsgerichtsbarkeit im Gefüge der Staatsfunktionen', VVDStRL 39 (1981), 138.

[128] See K. Hesse, *Grundzüge des Verfassungsrechts der Bundesrepublik Deutschland*, 14th edn. (Heidelberg, 1984), para. 299.

terms of precedentially established uncertainty. Textbook examples are the principle of proportionality, the prohibition of arbitrariness, and the human nature formula. They mean that in respect of the precedentially bound nature of constitutional rights argumentation, it is not simply open in a negative sense on account of the inherent limits of precedent, but it is also positively held open.

The ongoing exclusion of possibilities which has been taking place since the first decisions of the constitutional court in 1951 thus has a double aspect. On one hand, much has been decided which could have been decided differently, but it has also been decided that the system of constitutional rights norms is a system open to the requirements of principle. Thus while precedent makes an indispensible contribution to the certainty of constitutional rights argumentation, it is not on its own sufficient to ensure the rational control of constitutional rights justification.

3.2.3 Substantive Constitutional Rights Theories

The third part of the foundation of constitutional rights argumentation was identified above under the term 'doctrine'. It was shown in Chapter 1 that three dimensions of legal doctrine can be identified: an analytical, an empirical, and a normative.[129] The question of the basis of constitutional rights argumentation refers to the normative dimension and to normative theories of constitutional rights doctrine.

Doctrinal theories can display a highly variable degree of abstraction.[130] Here, we are only interested in general normative theories of constitutional rights, that is, theories with a relatively high degree of abstraction. Such theories can be termed 'substantive constitutional rights theories'. Accordingly, purely analytical and purely empirical theories are not substantive constitutional rights theories, but nor are normative theories which only deal with individual constitutional rights provisions or certain issues of constitutional rights, and which are therefore not general.

One could ask whether it is right to count substantive constitutional rights theories as a foundation of constitutional rights argumentation. Substantive constitutional rights theories are of course to be justified by reference to the text of the Constitution, the will of the constitution makers, and the precedents of the Federal Constitutional Court, but since they are more than merely repetitions of text, empirically ascertainable intentions and precedents, they are supported neither directly by the authority of the Constitution nor directly by the precedents of the Court. If they are widely accepted, they gain the weight of dominant opinion,[131] but this can at any time be shattered in the course of argument. Statute, precedent, and

---

[129] See above at 6 ff.
[130] Dreier, 'Zur Theoriebildung in der Jurisprudenz', in id., *Recht—Moral—Ideologie*, 73.
[131] See H. Ehmke, 'Prinzipien der Verfassungsinterpretation', VVDStRL 20 (1963), 71 f.

doctrine represent a line of clearly diminishing authoritative force. Thus substantive constitutional rights theories have the character of basically non-authoritative, but argumentatively grounded foundations of constitutional rights argumentation. The concept of an argumentatively grounded foundation of argumentation is subject to the objection of circularity. But this objection can be met by reference to the distinction between basis and process. The idea that in the course of a process of argumentation a theory can be put forward, which is rejectable, but as long as it has not been rejected can itself form the basis for further argumentation has nothing circular about it. So the question is how such a substantive constitutional rights theory can be created and what it can contribute to the rational control of constitutional rights argumentation.

As a general normative theory of constitutional rights, a substantive constitutional rights theory is only possible as a theory of principles. It has been shown above that principles and values are the same thing, one in deontological, the other in axiological clothing.[132] If one works on the basis of a sufficiently broad concept of purpose, it is also possible to change this into the third category of practical concepts, namely the category of anthropological concepts,[133] and instead of, say, the principle of freedom, or the value of freedom, to talk of freedom as a purpose. Thus instead of theories of principles or theories of values, substantive constitutional rights theories can be expressed in terms of general theories of purposes.

According to Böckenförde, a constitutional rights theory is 'a systematically oriented view of the general character, the normative goals and the material extent of constitutional rights'.[134] As has already been said,[135] Böckenförde distinguishes five such theories, 'the liberal, or civic/Rule of Law theory of constitutional rights, the institutional theory, the value theory, the democratic-functional and the social state theory of constitutional rights'.[136] This division places categorically very different elements on one level. It thus has not so much a systematic character, but rather the

---

[132] 92 f.   [133] See above at 87 f.

[134] E.-W. Böckenförde, 'Grundrechtstheorie und Grundrechtsinterpretation', NJW 1974, 1529.

[135] 11.

[136] ibid. 1530. A similar division can be found in K. Kröger, *Grundrechtstheorie als Verfassungsproblem* (Baden-Baden, 1978), 15 ff. Other divisions are possible and maintained. Thus Scheuner distinguishes two 'basic approaches', one which follows the 'liberal tradition' and another which attempts to 'assert the validity of other, more strongly objectively formulated principles of constitutional rights protection, alongside the aspect of securing liberties' (U. Scheuner, 'Die Funktion der Grundrechte im Sozialstaat', DöV 1971, 507). Grabitz adopts a threefold division, according to which there are 'three principal patterns of interpretation' for constitutional rights, the theories of the liberal, substantive, and social states under the Rule of Law (E. Grabitz, 'Freiheit als Verfassungsprinzip', *Rechtstheorie*, 8 (1977), 4 ff.). Finally, a fourfold division can be based on Klein's 'four dimensions of the constitutional conception of liberty': 'freedom from the state', 'political self-determination', 'social participation', and a 'right to state protection from social power' (H. H. Klein, *Die Grundrechte im demokratischen Staat*, 48).

character of a presentation of general views represented in recent constitutional rights doctrine.

Three of the theories listed, the liberal, the democratic, and the social state theories, can easily be identified as general theories of the purpose or principles of constitutional rights. *Liberal* theories of the strongest form are propounded by those who see the sole purpose or 'sole protected interest'[137] of constitutional rights in individual freedom of action and decision in the sense of an absence of state interference, that is, by those for whom the principle of state oriented negative liberty is the only principle of constitutional rights.[138] Weaker versions of the liberal theory arise when this principle is not seen as the sole principle of constitutional rights, but only one, which prima facie takes precedence over other constitutional rights principles. One of the strongest variants of a *democratic* theory is maintained by Krüger, for whom constitutional rights, to the extent that they do not relate to the sphere of privacy and intimacy, 'represent above all positions of free participation in society'.[139] This means that democratic principles are included within constitutional rights principles and are at least given prima facie precedence.[140] The hallmark of a *social state* theory are theses such as the one that 'the freedom intended by constitutional rights . . . consists of real life chances and choices',[141] or that the function of constitutional rights is to be found in the 'maintenance or creation of social structures which guarantee the highest possible chance for personal development'.[142] This is asserting that the principle of factual liberty is a constitutional principle of at least equal status with the principle of legal liberty.

The two other theories listed by Böckenförde, the value theory and the institutional theory, differ fundamentally from these, which describe substantive purpose and weight. The fact that a theory is a theory of *values* says only that it is a theory about some sort of values, it does not say anything about which values it concerns. A theory of values pruned of its

---

[137] See H. H. Klein, *Die Grundrechte im demokratischen Staat*, 2nd edn. (Stuttgart, Berlin, Cologne, and Mainz, 1974), 64. See also E. Forsthoff, 'Zur heutigen Situation einer Verfassungslehre', in H. Barion, E.-W. Böckenförde, E. Forsthoff, and W. Weber (eds.), *Epirrhosis, Festgabe für Carl Schmitt* (Berlin, 1968), 195; C. Schmitt, *Verfassungslehre* (Munich and Leipzig, 1928) (5th edn. Berlin, 1970), 164.

[138] The principle of legal equality will not be considered in this context.

[139] H. Krüger, 'Der Wesensgehalt der Grundrechte', in J. Seifert and H. Krüger, *Die Einschränkung der Grundrechte*, xiii (Hanover, 1976), 45. See also W. Abendroth, *Das Grundgesetz*, 7th edn. (Pfullingen, 1978), 76; H. Ridder, 'Meinungsfreiheit', in F. L. Neumann, H. C. Nipperdey, and U. Scheuner (eds.), *Die Grundrechte*, ii (Berlin, 1954), 249 ff., 266.

[140] Smend can be considered the most important founding father of democratic theories, as indeed of other non-liberal, or not exclusively liberal, theories; see e.g. R. Smend, 'Bürger und Bourgeois im deutschen Staatsrecht', in id., *Staatsrechtliche Abhandlungen*, 2nd edn. (Berlin, 1968), 318 ff.

[141] W. Krebs, *Vorbehalt des Gesetzes und Grundrechte* (Berlin, 1975), 78.

[142] E. Grabitz, 'Freiheit als Verfassungsprinzip', *Rechtstheorie*, 8 (1977), 10. See also P. Häberle, 'Grundrechte im Leistungsstaat', VVDStRL 30 (1972), 99, 109.

unsustainable and superfluous assumptions can be formulated as a theory of principles.[143] It is also possible, even if this can easily lead to misunderstanding, to express it in terms of purpose if one uses a wide conception of purpose. The considerations put forward above have shown that a constitutional rights theory of principles and thus also a corresponding theory of values, is indispensable. This general structural thesis implies that regardless of what substantive theory of constitutional rights one supports, one has to presuppose a value theory. So for example the liberal theory of constitutional rights is not a competitor with *the* value theory, but is the expression of *one* value theory which has a certain content. Thus it cannot compete as such with value or principle or purpose theories, but only with such theories which have a different content. The same applies for the democratic or social state theory. Every normative theory of constitutional rights presupposes some sort of theory of values, principles, or purposes.

Things are not so simple in the case of *institutional constitutional rights theories*, which are the expression of a general institutional theory of law as it has been developed above all by Hauriou and Romano,[144] and which has been most comprehensively applied to constitutional rights by Häberle.[145] The institutional theory of constitutional rights consists of a bundle of theses, which are not easy to disentangle, concerning the purpose, the structure, and content of constitutional rights norms as well as theses which are supposed to support these arguments. Their *normative* basic thesis is that constitutional rights should be institutions.[146] What this means depends on the ambiguous concept of an institution.[147] From Häberle's extensive catalogue of conditions which have to be fulfilled if constitutional rights are to be what they ought to be (institutions), two can be isolated. To be institutions, constitutional rights must be (1) made use of in practice and continually by as many people as possible and (2) have as high a degree possible of stabilizing effect on 'the entirety of the constitution and the social order'.[148] Both can be seen as purposes the fulfilment of which is supposed

---

[143] See above at 86 ff.

[144] See on this the German editions with extensive bibliographies: M. Hauriou, *Die Theorie der Institution und zwei andere Aufsätze*, ed. R. Schnur (Berlin, 1965); S. Romano, *Die Rechtsordnung*, ed. R. Schnur (Berlin, 1975), as well as the compilation by R. Schnur (ed.), *Institution und Recht* (Darmstadt, 1968). Generally on institutional theory, see H. Schelsky (ed.), *Zur Theorie der Institution* (Düsseldorf, 1970).

[145] P. Häberle, *Die Wesensgehaltgarantie des Art. 19 Abs. 2 Grundgesetz* 3rd edn. (Heidelberg, 1983), 70 ff.

[146] ibid. 122.

[147] On the analysis of this, see e.g. B. Rüthers, *'Institutionelles Rechtsdenken' im Wandel der Verfassungsepochen* (Bad Homburg, Berlin, and Zurich, 1970), 34 ff., who distinguishes factual, metaphysical, and normative conceptions of institution.

[148] id., *Die Wesensgehaltgarantie*, 123. Both aspects clearly show the inheritance of Smend, according to whom constitutional rights 'follow the entire constituent purpose of constitutional law' which consists of the 'continual renewal and development of the common will of the state organization as a real living unity' (R. Smend, 'Das Recht der freien Meinungsäußerung', in id., *Staatsrechtliche Abhandlungen*, 90 f.).

to determine the interpretation of constitutional rights. Of course, these purposes are highly formal. The fact that a stable state of affairs should be produced and secured says nothing about the content of such a state nor how it is to be produced or secured. But it does say that supra-individual purposes, or as Häberle puts it, the 'supraindividual whole'[149] is to be given particular weight in interpreting constitutional rights provisions, which is the expression of a basic evaluative thesis about the relationship between individual and collective interests. The first condition can also be interpreted evaluatively without any difficulty. That as many as possible can in reality make use of constitutional rights refers to social state[150] and democratic[151] tendencies of the theory—a tendency which Häberle later pursued even further.[152] The idea that the normative content of the institutional theory of constitutional rights is to be interpreted as a theory of values has many further confirmations. Instead of 'constitutional rights ideas'[153] or 'guiding images',[154] which the legislature is supposed to realize, one can also talk in terms of values or principles. Häberle often speaks in terms of values and value-decisions in exactly this sense.[155] Finally, it has to be pointed out that the most telling identifying characteristic of both open and disguised theories of values or principles, the balancing of interests, plays a central role in Häberle's 'institutional theory'.[156]

It can therefore be said that the normative content of the institutional theory of constitutional rights consists of a theory of principles or values. The hallmark of the content of this theory of principles is that all relevant principles play a role in it, but that the liberal principle is relatively lightly valued and that principles relating to collective interests are relatively highly valued.

This quick glance at the five theories of constitutional rights confirms the correctness of the thesis that substantive constitutional rights theories are theories of principle. Thus the question is, which principled theory is the correct one. Three types of principled theory are possible, those which rest essentially on *one* principle of constitutional rights, those which proceed on the basis of a bundle of principles of equal status, and those which while they proceed on the basis of a bundle of constitutional rights principles nevertheless attempt to establish some degree of order between them.

Böckenförde's proposal of a liberal constitutional rights model modified by a social state purpose, that is, a non-constitutional rights principle, is an example of a theory resting on one principle of constitutional rights.[157] The

---

[149] *Die Wesensgehaltgarantie*, 164.   [150] ibid. 15 ff.   [151] ibid. 17 ff.
[152] id., 'Grundrechte im Leistungsstaat', 43 ff.
[153] id., *Die Wesensgehaltgarantie*, 105, 116.
[154] ibid. 182, 184.   [155] ibid. 7, 12 ff., 184, 221.
[156] ibid. 31 ff.
[157] See E.-W. Böckenförde, 'Grundrechtstheorie und Grundrechtsinterpretation', NJW 1974, 1538.

question is whether it can be shown to be the correct one.[158] According to Böckenförde, a constitutional theory, and thus a theory of constitutional rights, is 'only possible as a theory expressly or implicitly contained in the constitution, discoverable from the constitutional text and origins by rational means'.[159] Before it is asked whether a liberal theory is discoverable in the constitution by rational means on this basis, it must be made clear what this question is looking for. It is not concerned with whether the principle of legal liberty[160] and, as must be added, the principle of legal equality,[161] underlie the constitution as liberal constitutional principles or not. The question is rather whether these principles are the only constitutional rights principles to be expressed in the constitution.

There can be no doubt that principles of legal liberty and equality do underlie the constitution, but it can be doubted whether it is 'discoverable from the constitutional text and origins by rational means' that these are the only constitutional rights principles. It is precisely the openness of text and origins which make a substantive theory of constitutional rights seem necessary. But if this is so, then one cannot expect to derive a theory which removes the openness solely from text and origins. Rather, premises are necessary for its justification which are not necessarily derivable from text and origins. A hint of the character of these premises is given by Böckenförde's description of constitutional rights theories as 'the expression of certain views of the state and basic perspectives on the relationship of the individual to state community'.[162] This makes it plain that to the extent that each theory of constitutional rights is not necessarily grounded in pre-existing authoritative materials, it has to be based on a philosophy of state and society, which by contrast to attempts to ground them textually or immanently in the constitution gives rise to an objection of circularity:[163] The theoreticians derive their theory from the text, which is to be read according to their theory. Böckenförde meets this objection in that he characterizes his theory as an interpretative hypothesis, 'subject to a strong regard for the (normative) expressions, presuppositions and context of its derivation etc. of the concrete constitution' and about which an 'argumentative consensus'[164] is to be developed. As such, this response is acceptable, but after what has been said about the openness of text and origins it must be doubted whether the materials he suggests his theory is subject to, if one does not already interpret them in the light of that theory, which would

---

[158] On the critique of one-point theories generally, see above at 12.

[159] Böckenförde, 'Die Methoden der Verfassungsinterpretation', 2098.

[160] See on this above at 230 f.

[161] id., See on this above at 276 ff.

[162] id., 'Grundrechtstheorie und Grundrechtsinterpretation', 1537.

[163] See Dreier, 'Zur Problematik und Situation der Verfassungsinterpretation', in id., *Recht—Moral—Ideologie*, 126.

[164] Böckenförde, 'Die Methoden der Verfassungsinterpretation', 2098.

again be circular, only give rise to a purely liberal theory, that is, only fail to exclude this one.

If in this situation one does not want to move directly to the uncertain basis of political and social philosophy, the only alternative is to search for further authoritative material. Such can be found, in view of their precedential force, in the decisions of the Federal Constitutional Court. If one follows Böckenförde, the case-law of the Court is unproductive in the establishment of a substantive constitutional rights theory. Böckenförde justifies this by the fact that the Court bases itself 'changeably on different constitutional rights theories'.[165] If one uses Böckenförde's division, it is true that the Court prefers now one theory, now another. But one cannot draw from this the conclusion that the case-law of the Court has no underlying constitutional rights theory. The concept of a constitutional rights theory is not limited to theories which only express one principle, rather, as has already been stated, there is the possibility of a constitutional rights theory proceeding on the basis of a bundle of principles. If we orient ourselves by the case-law of the Federal Constitutional Court, we arrive at a combined theory which contains more constitutional rights principles than the liberal principle (legal liberty/legal equality).[166]

Against such combined theories the objection of uselessness is pressing. Thus Böckenförde thinks that they can be none other than catalogues of topoi which one can use at will.[167] In response, three considerations can be put forward: (1) On account of their logical structure, principles are more than topoi. (2) A certain ordering of principles through prima facie relations of precedence is possible; a combined theory can be a theory of principles of the third type identified above. (3) Not too much should be expected of a substantive constitutional rights theory.

(1) That principles are more than mere topoi is shown by the Law of Balancing.[168] Principles cannot be adopted or rejected at will. If they are relevant, then they must be taken account of. In a case of competing principles, balancing is necessary, in which the question is whether the importance of satisfying one principle justifies the necessary degree of non-satisfaction of the other. This does not establish the outcome, but the justification brings us a stage further in rational justification.

(2) It has been shown above that an ordering of principles or values leading in each case to exactly one outcome in an intersubjectively controllable way—such an ordering can be called a 'hard ordering'—is impossible.[169] However, what is possible is a soft ordering by way of prima facie precedence.

---

[165] ibid. 1536.
[166] See on this above at 290 ff. On the thesis that sets of purposes are to be derived from individual constitutional rights provisions, see M. Kriele, *Einführung in die Staatslehre* (Reinbek, 1975), 335 ff.
[167] Böckenförde, 'Die Methoden der Verfassungsinterpretation', 1537.
[168] 102.   [169] 96 ff.

The justifiable core of Böckenförde's proposed substantive constitutional rights theory is that, as has been shown above,[170] it is possible to demonstrate a prima facie precedence for the principles of legal liberty and legal equality, in other words a burden of argumentation in favour of these principles. The prima facie precedence of the principle of legal liberty corresponds largely to the 'basic presumption of liberty' of the Federal Constitutional Court[171] and the maxim 'in dubio pro libertate'.[172] Numerous objections have been raised against these principles, but they can be rejected. This can be seen by a quick glance at the six most important of them. The first objection states that the principles in question are impermissibly general,[173] excluding necessary differentiation.[174] This does not affect a prima facie precedence of the principle of legal liberty. It permits every possible differentiation, provided that the burden of argumentation is satisfied. A second objection states that the principles are too crude, because they relate to 'liberty' and thus fail to take account of the fact that the liberties of different constitutional right-holders can conflict, which could lead to the unjustified privileging of one person's liberty at the cost of another's.[175] In response, prima facie precedence exists only in relation to principles other than those of legal liberty and equality. If legal liberty opposes legal liberty or legal equality in different constitutional right-holders, then the prima facie relation does not apply. A third objection argues that in cases of doubt 'neither the more liberal nor the less liberal but only the correct answer' applies.[176] This objection fails to recognize that prima facie precedence is a means precisely of finding the correct solution according to the constitution. When in a case of conflict equally good reasons can be put forward for one solution or the other, then one cannot say which solution is correct without a rule of precedence. In *these* cases prima facie precedence tells us that the solution corresponding to the principle of legal liberty is the constitutionally correct one. A fourth objection states that prima facie precedence is incompatible with the optimizing function laid down by the idea of the unity of the constitution.[177] But prima facie prece-

---

[170] 283, 343 f.

[171] BVerfGE 6, 32 (42); 13, 97 (105); 17, 306 (313 f.); 32, 54 (72).

[172] See above all P. Schneider, 'In dubio pro libertate', in *Hundert Jahre deutsches Rechtsleben, Festschrift zum hundertjährigen Bestehen des Deutschen Juristentages 1860–1960*, ii (Karlsruhe, 1960), 279 ff.; id., 'Prinzipien der Verfassungsinterpretation', VVDStRL 20 (1963), 31 ff., as well as E. v. Hippel, *Grenzen und Wesensgehalt der Grundrechte* (Berlin, 1965), 18.

[173] P. Lerche, 'Stil, Methode, Ansicht', DVBl 1961, 698.

[174] R. Scholz, *Wirtschaftsaufsicht und subjektiver Konkurrentenschutz* (Berlin, 1971), 130.

[175] C. Graf v. Pestalozza, 'Kritische Bemerkungen zu Methoden und Prinzipien der Grundrechtsauslegung in der Bundesrepublik Deutschland', *Der Staat*, (1963), 446.

[176] A. Keller, *Die Kritik, Korrektur und Interpretation des Gesetzeswortlauts* (Winterthur, 1960), 279; Ehmke, 'Prinzipien der Verfassungsinterpretation', 87.

[177] Hesse, *Grundzüge des Verfassungsrechts*, para. 72; Krebs, *Vorbehalt des Gesetzes und Grundrechte*, 52.

dence in no way excludes optimization, which is necessary anyway on account of the structure of principles.[178] It only contains a rule for the solution of argumentative stalemates which can arise in attempting to optimize. A fifth objection states that prima facie precedence leads to an over-extensive interpretation of liberties (negative status rights)[179] and is the expression of an anarchistic individualism as well as an overblown economic liberalism.[180] This overrates the material significance of prima facie precedence. It does not exclude the subordination of the principle of legal liberty to competing principles. It simply requires that stronger reasons speak for the solution required by competing principles than for the principle of legal liberty. This leads to the one important objection, the sixth one. Prima facie precedence has a formal character. It brings to the theory of principles a tendency to legal liberty and equality, but it contains no standard[181] for determining the extent to which this tendency should be followed or not. This depends on the application of substantive criteria, which is structured, but not determined, by prima facie precedence. This limits the practical value of prima facie precedence, but it does not make it valueless. Not being able to have material determination is not a reason for abandoning structuring.

(3) What has just been said leads to the third point. Not too much should be expected from a substantive constitutional rights theory. The most developed form of a substantive constitutional rights theory would be one which provided one correct solution to each case. In recent times it is above all Dworkin who has tried to develop such a theory. He considers a 'soundest theory of law' to be possible, which contains those principles together with their relative weight,[182] which can best justify precedent and enacted norms,[183] and on which basis there is exactly one right answer in each case.[184] To see that such a programme for a substantive constitutional rights theory is destined for failure, one only has to ask what a theory of principles has to look like if it is to contain just one answer for each case. One first possibility, of cardinal or ordinal rankings of principles, has already been rejected above.[185] Prima facie precedence only leads to a structuring of argumentation which rests on principles, as has just been shown, and not to a hard ordering, which in each case leads necessarily to exactly

---

[178] See above at 47 ff.
[179] Ehmke, 'Prinzipien der Verfassungsinterpretation', 87.
[180] Keller, *Die Kritik, Korrektur und Interpretation des Gesetzeswortlants*, 279.
[181] Pestalozza, 'Kritische Bemerkungen zu Methoden und Prinzipien', 446.
[182] Dworkin, *Taking Rights Seriously*, 66.
[183] ibid., 116 f.
[184] ibid., 81; id., 'No Right Answer?', in M. S. Hacker and J. Raz (eds.), *Law, Morality and Society: Essays in Honour of H. L. A. Hart* (Oxford, 1977), 76 ff. See on this with further references R. Alexy, 'Zum Begriff des Rechtsprinzips', *Rechtstheorie*, Beiheft 1 (1979), 61 f., 82 ff.; A. Peczenik, 'Is There Always a Right Answer to a Legal Question?' in *Essays in Legal Theory in Honor of K. Makkonen, Oikeustiede Jurisprudentia*, 16 (1983), 241 ff.
[185] 96 ff.

one outcome. The only remaining possibility is that of an ordering by concrete relations of precedence, which express the relative weight of principles in specific cases or types of case. An example of a concrete relation of precedence is that of the Lebach Judgment according to which under the condition that one is dealing with a repeat television broadcast of a serious criminal act no longer covered by the interest in up-to-date information and which endangers the resocialization of the criminal, the principle of the protection of privacy takes precedence over broadcasting freedom.[186] As has been shown above, according to the Law of Competing Principles this relation of precedence implies a rule prohibiting the broadcasting of the programme if the conditions identified are met. But this shows the dilemma which every attempt to harden up a theory of principles by concrete relations of precedence faces. If maximum hardness, that is, the establishment of an answer for every conceivable case, is to be attained, the theory must contain a concrete relation of precedence for every conceivable constitutional rights case, and that means a ratio for every conceivable constitutional rights case. But this would mean the theory becoming a comprehensive list of ratios for every conceivable constitutional rights case. The limits of human imagination alone exclude the possibility of creating a list of this nature. In addition, the ratios contained in such a list could hardly meet with universal consent, for this would presuppose that for every constitutional rights case there is a solution which everyone agrees with. But the most important point is that the solutions contained in the list need justification. And the question of their justification leads back to the problem of a substantive constitutional rights theory, which the list is supposed to be a means of solving.

After all that, it can be said that a substantive constitutional rights theory which necessarily lays down the resolution of every constitutional rights case is not possible. But this gives us a reason for not expecting too much from a substantive constitutional rights theory from the very beginning. One can expect no more from it than that it rationally structure to the greatest extent possible constitutional rights argumentation in a substantively acceptable way. These requirements are satisfied by a principled theory which contains a bundle of constitutional rights principles, and which places these in a soft ordering by granting prima facie precedence to the principles of legal liberty and legal equality.

3.3 The Process of Constitutional Rights Argumentation

The discussion of the foundation of constitutional rights argumentation was designed to meet the question of the rational controllability of constitutional rights argumentation. The outcome is that constitutional rights argumentation is determined and structured to some extent in a rational

---

[186] BVerfGE 35, 202 (237).

way by its foundation, but that the degree and strength of control established by this is limited. A significant rationality gap remains. Into this rationality gap steps the process of constitutional rights argumentation: the discourse of constitutional rights.

The discourse of constitutional rights is an argumentative procedure which is concerned with arriving at correct constitutional rights outcomes on the basis set out.[187] Since constitutional rights argumentation is only incompletely determined by its foundation, general practical argumentation is a necessary component of constitutional rights discourse. This means that constitutional rights discourse, as indeed legal discourse generally, shares in the uncertainty of outcome of general practical discourse. The open-texture of the legal system caused by constitutional rights is thus inevitable. But it is an open-texture of a qualified sort. It is an open-texture not in the sense of the arbitrariness of mere decisionism. The foundation set out gives to constitutional rights argumentation a degree of stability, and the rules and forms of general practical and legal argumentation rationally structure the constitutional rights argumentation which takes place on its basis.[188]

The uncertain outcome of constitutional rights discourse leads to the necessity of authoritative constitutional rights decision-taking. If the parliamentary majority is not to regulate itself, which would mean its acting as judge in its own cause,[189] the only alternative is some sort of constitutional court. The fact that a constitutional court not only argues but also decides is not irrational. It is a general proposition that practical reason can only be realized in the context of a legal system which combines argumentation and decision in a rational way.[190] In the light of this insight, the institutionalization of constitutional adjudication, where decisions are capable and in need of justification and critique in the process of a rational constitutional rights discourse, is itself entirely rational.

---

[187] On the fact that constitutional rights discourse is not simply a matter for constitutional courts and constitutional lawyers, see P. Häberle, 'Die offene Gesellschaft der Verfassungsinterpreten', JZ 1975, 297 ff.

[188] See Alexy, *A Theory of Legal Argumentation*, 284 ff.

[189] See Dworkin, *Taking Rights Seriously*, 142 f.

[190] See Kriele, *Recht und praktische Vernunft*, 40 ff.

Postscript

The central thesis of this book is that regardless of their more or less precise formulation, constitutional rights are principles and that principles are optimization requirements. Since the *Theory of Constitutional Rights* first appeared in 1985, the optimization thesis has met with numerous objections. Some of these concern general problems in the theory of norms.[1] But most revolve around the question of whether the optimization thesis provides an appropriate model of constitutional rights. The critique moves between two poles or strands.

I.   TOO LITTLE AND TOO MUCH

The first strand of criticism argues that the model of principles based on the optimization thesis deprives constitutional rights of their force. This objection has been stated with most force by Habermas: 'If principles manifest a value that one should optimally realize, and if the norms themselves do not dictate the extent to which one must fulfill this optimizing prescription, then the application of such principles within the limits of what is factually possible makes a goal-oriented weighting necessary'.[2] This 'goal-oriented weighting' leads to the possibility that 'individual rights can be sacrificed at times to collective goals'.[3] But then constitutional rights would lose their firmness, which can only be guaranteed by way of a strict deontological structure, that is, by their having the character of rules. By contrast, giving them the character of principles destroys a 'fire wall'. 'For if in case of collision *all* reasons can assume the character of policy arguments, then the fire wall erected in legal discourse by a deontological understanding of legal norms and principles collapses.'[4] Balancing constitutional rights does not simply endanger their force in general. There is also the risk that they fall victim to 'irrational rulings',[5] for there are no rational standards for balancing. 'Because there are no rational standards for this, weighing takes place either arbitrarily or unreflectively, according to customary standards and hierarchies.'[6] In short: constitutional rights are first of all softened into opti-

---

[1] See on this R. Alexy, 'On the Structure of Legal Principles', *Ratio Juris*, 13 (2000), 294 ff.

[2] J. Habermas, *Between Facts and Norms*, trans. W. Rehg (Cambridge, Mass., 1996), 254.

[3] Id., 'Reply to Symposium Participants, Benjamin N. Cardozo School of Law', in M. Rosenfeld and A. Arato (eds.), *Habermas on Law and Democracy* (Berkeley, Los Angeles, and London, 1998), 429.

[4] id., *Between Facts and Norms*, 258.   [5] ibid. 259.

[6] ibid. 259.

mization requirements and then risk disappearing altogether in a maelstrom of irrational balancing.

One could call Habermas's critique an appeal to the danger of too little constitutional rights. The reverse, the danger of too much, stands in the centre of Böckenförde's critique. Böckenförde's starting-point is a distinction between constitutional rights as classic defensive rights of the citizen against the state and constitutional rights as basic provisions [*Grundsatznormen*]. Constitutional rights as basic provisions, or as Böckenförde calls them in reliance on the terminology of the Federal Constitutional Court, 'objective basic provisions', are supposed to correspond 'exactly' to what the theory of principles calls optimization requirements: 'Principle-norms are optimization requirements which can be satisfied to varying degrees and for which the required degree of satisfaction depends not only on factual but also on legal possibilities. They have a normative tendency to optimization, without however being fixed to any specific content; they are—necessarily—open to being balanced.'[7] Böckenförde concedes that this principled character 'is capable of serving as the basic doctrinal concept of constitutional rights, because it can embrace all the functions of constitutional rights and, in reverse, allow all such functions to be developed at random from it'.[8]

But this is supposed to have far-reaching and ultimately unacceptable consequences. The role of constitutional rights in the legal system changes fundamentally. While classic constitutional rights were limited to one part of the legal system, the relationship between state and citizen, constitutional rights as principles would have an effect throughout the entire system. There would be a radiating effect in all fields of law, which would necessarily lead to the third party, or horizontal, effect of constitutional rights, as well as to constitutional objects such as protection, social security, organization, and procedure, which require a positive act on the part of the state and are not limited to requiring state omissions, as are the classic liberties.[9] In this way, constitutional rights would become the 'highest principles of the entire legal system'.[10] As such, they would already contain everything in themselves; only concretization through balancing would be necessary: 'At the level of principles having an optimizing tendency, the legal system as a whole is already contained in the constitution. It simply needs concretising.'[11]

This corresponds precisely to what Forsthoff sarcastically called the 'constitution as juridical genome [*Weltenei*] . . . from which everything derives, from the Criminal Code to the law regulating the production of medical thermometers'.[12] Characterizing constitutional rights as optimization

---

[7] E.-W. Böckenförde, 'Grundrechte als Grundsatznormen. Zur gegenwärtigen Lage der Grundrechtsdogmatik', in id., *Staat, Verfassung, Demokratie* (Frankfurt a. M., 1991), 185.
[8] ibid.   [9] ibid. 168 ff.   [10] ibid. 188.   [11] ibid. 189.
[12] E. Forsthoff, *Der Staat der Industriegesellschaft*, 2nd edn. (Munich, 1971), 144.

requirements is supposed to lead to such a constitutional model, with fatal consequences. The parliamentary legislature loses all autonomy. Its function is exhausted in the mere establishing of what has already been decided by the constitution. The democratic political process would largely lose all significance,[13] and the 'shift from parliamentary legislative state to constitutional adjudicative state' would be irresistable:[14] 'For if constitutional rights are principles with an optimizing tendency, the constitutional court is required to ensure the enforcement of its normative content'.[15] There is thus for Böckenförde only one alternative: either one opts for constitutional rights as principles and thus for the adjudicative state, or for a reduction of constitutional rights to classic defensive rights and thus for the parliamentary legislative state.[16] The question is whether it is really true that only these possibilities exist.

II. FRAMEWORK AND FOUNDATION

The alternative between adjudicative state and legislative state is a contrast between two ways of dividing competences. Böckenförde combines this dichotomy at the level of competences with a choice concerned with the structure and content of constitutional norms and thus with the constitution as a normative object. This is the contrast between the constitution as a framework [*Rahmenordnung*] and the constitution as a foundation [*Grundordnung*]. The alternative of framework or foundation plays a central role in the controversy about the theory of principles. This can be seen already in the fact that the concept of a framework has become somewhat of a common rallying-cry for those who are, at the level of detail, highly diverse opponents of the idea of optimization. The theory of principles is thereby located under the opposing concept, that of a foundation. According to Böckenförde, a constitution is the 'legal foundation of society as a whole', if 'all legal principles and possibilities for compromise in developing the legal system are already contained in it *in nuce*'.[17] This corresponds to Forsthoff's genome, and it crudely, but effectively, expresses the target of all proponents of the framework conception.

On this basis, the theory of principles is an easy victim. If the theory of principles necessarily leads to a constitution which already contains the entire legal system, then the theory of principles condemns the legislature under the oversight of the judiciary simply to declaring what has already been decided by the constitution. The 'political creativity of the legislature' would be completely displaced by the 'pressure of constitutional optimiza-

---

[13] Böckenförde, 'Grundrechte als Grundsatznormen', 197.
[14] ibid. 190.   [15] ibid. 196.
[16] ibid. 198 f.   [17] ibid. 198.

tion'.[18] But that would be incompatible with the principles of democratic parliamentarianism and the separation of powers. These require that the democratically legitimated legislature have a quantitatively and qualitatively significant and autonomous part in structuring the legal system.

So everything boils down to the question of whether the theory of principles really does necessarily lead to a foundation in Böckenförde's sense, which excludes all legislative discretion. The answer to this question turns on the concepts of framework and foundation. The concept of a framework will be considered first.

1. THE CONCEPT OF A FRAMEWORK

The concept of a framework must be distinguished from the criteria by which its content is determined. A wide diversity of criteria have been suggested for determining its content. Three examples will suffice. The first is Böckenförde's framework. This is created by excising more recent dimensions of constitutional rights such as third party or horizontal effect and protective duties, and reducing constitutional rights to the classic defensive rights against public power.[19] One could call this a liberal constitutional reduction. Hain is among those who shy away from such a substantive proposal. He preserves all dimensions, but then reduces them all to a 'minimum standard'.[20] This could be described as a general material constitutional reduction. Particularly radical is the model of methodological constitutional reduction proposed by Jestaedt. According to this third way of determining the framework, the constitution only contains what can be established empirically as the historical intention of the constitution makers.[21]

The concept of a framework itself must be distinguished from such criteria for determining the content of a constitution as a framework. This concept is the same in the case of all conceptions of framework, and is to that extent formal. For reasons of simplicity, only the relationship between constitution and legislature will be considered here. Three basic scenarios can be distinguished.

In the first scenario, the constitution contains no substantive commands or prohibitions limiting the competence of the legislature. The latter is permitted and empowered to do anything, so long as it observes the constitutional provisions relating to its competence, procedures, and forms. This is the purely procedural model of a constitution.[22] In the purely procedural

---

[18] C. Starck, 'Review of Robert Alexy, Begriff und Geltung des Rechts', *Der Staat*, 32 (1993), 475 f.

[19] Böckenförde, 'Grundrechte als Grundsatznormen', 194 f.

[20] See K.-E. Hain, *Die Grundsätze des Grundgesetzes* (Baden-Baden, 1999), 32, 188 ff.

[21] M. Jestaedt, *Grundrechtsentfaltung im Gesetz* (Tübingen, 1999), 337, 361 f.

[22] See 349 above.

model there is by definition no substantive framework. The competence of the legislature is, as a matter of substance, unlimited. One can call the class of possible legislative decisions its 'discretion'. The statement that there is no substantive framework is thus equivalent to the statement that the discretion of the legislature is substantively unlimited.

The purely procedural model is incompatible with the legal obligation of the legislature to respect constitutional rights, since it is defined by the negation of every substantive legal obligation, including those imposed by constitutional rights. If one takes the perspective of a radical sceptic about balancing, then treating constitutional rights as principles results in such a negation of every substantive legal obligation. Radical scepticism about balancing is defined by the view that every outcome of a balancing process is considered possible. If, as the objects of balancing, constitutional rights exclude no possible outcome, then they cannot be binding. They are thus not capable of setting limits to the legislature, and cannot represent a framework. From the perspective of radical scepticism about balancing, the only thing they can do is to create the false impression of an existing framework. A constitutional court can use this to mask the arbitrary nature of its decisions, and on this view the legislature is not bound by the constitution, but sold out to the constitutional court. And there are no legitimate reasons for such a sale.

Radical scepticism about balancing is seldom maintained in its fullest expression, but it is often hinted at. This is the case, for example, with Habermas's thesis of the lack of rational standards for balancing and his picture of the collapse of a constitutional fire wall.[23] This establishes the first question in the context of the constitution as framework which must be put to the theory of constitutional rights as principles: is the theory of principles capable of creating a rational framework for the legislature?

The counterpart to a purely procedural model of the constitution is a purely substantive one. Here, the constitution contains a command or prohibition in respect of every conceivable legislative decision. This is the constitution of Forsthoff's genome. Under this model there is no statutory provision which the constitution permits the legislature to enact or not to enact as it chooses. Accordingly, all discretion is excluded. Now there can be no doubt that such a lack of discretion would contravene the principle of the decision-taking capacity of the democratically legitimated legislature. If Böckenförde's accusation that the theory of principles leads to the elimination of all independent legislative decision-taking capacity is correct, then the theory of principles would indeed have been shot through the heart.

In discussing the purely procedural model, the question was raised whether the theory of principles is capable of prohibiting something to the legislature, that is, whether it is capable of creating a framework in the

---

[23] Habermas, *Between Facts and Norms*, 258.

sense of a set of limits. A second question must now be added to this one: whether the theory can do this without removing all forms of discretion. This is the case if it is capable of commanding some things, prohibiting others, and neither commanding nor prohibiting still others. If something is neither commanded nor prohibited, then it is permitted to do or to refrain from doing it. If one is permitted to do or to refrain from doing something, then one has been left free.[24] Legislative discretion thus consists precisely of those alternatives in respect of which the legislature has been left at liberty. One could therefore also call this discretion the 'sphere of legislative freedom'.

Under the first scenario, the legislature is left at liberty in respect of everything, which corresponds to the purely procedural constitutional model. Under the second scenario, the legislature is not left at liberty in respect of anything, which expresses the purely substantive constitutional model. The third possibility consists in some things being left at liberty and others not, that is, others being commanded or prohibited. This corresponds to the substantive-procedural model.[25]

The metaphor of a framework can thus be rendered more precise as follows: what is commanded and prohibited constitutes the framework. What is left free, that is, neither commanded nor prohibited, is what can be found within the framework. In this way, what is left free defines the discretion of the legislature. This discretion is a structural one.[26] One could also talk in terms of a content-related discretion which arises from the structure of constitutional norms. What matters is that its extent is determined by what legally applies on the basis of constitutional norms. Structural discretion is constituted by the limits of what the constitution definitively commands and prohibits.

That last point distinguishes structural from epistemic or knowledge-related discretion. Epistemic discretion is not constituted by the limits of what the constitution commands and prohibits, but by the limits of our capacity to know on one hand what the constitution commands and prohibits and on the other what it neither commands nor prohibits, that is, what it leaves free. To exaggerate the point, one could say that epistemic discretion is constituted by the limits of our capacity to know what the limits of the constitution are. The limits of this capacity can be the limits of both empirical and normative knowledge. Whether the constitution allows for such epistemic discretion depends on the role of formal principles and will therefore only be discussed at that point. Here we are only interested in distinguishing structural and epistemic discretion.

Up to this point, the framework model has been described with the help of concepts of command, prohibition, and liberty. One could also do this using concepts of necessity, impossibility, and possibility. What is

[24] 131.   [25] 350.   [26] 310.

commanded by the constitution is constitutionally necessary, what is prohibited by the constitution is constitutionally impossible, and what has been left free by the constitution is on account of the constitution neither necessary nor impossible, that is, it is constitutionally merely possible. The problem of the constitution as a framework can thus also be formulated as a problem of the existence of a sphere of the constitutionally merely possible. The opponents of the optimization thesis assert that the existence of such a sphere is incompatible with the idea of optimization.

2. THE CONCEPT OF A FOUNDATION

Before the problem of the compatibility of framework and optimization is considered, the second concept in the arsenal of the opponents of the theory of principles needs clarification: the concept of a foundation. This concept can be understood quantitatively or qualitatively. A constitution is a foundation in a quantitative sense, if it leaves nothing free, that is, if it contains either a command or a prohibition in respect of everything. This is Forsthoff's genome, which leaves nothing undetermined, even in the case of medical thermometers. This quantitative concept of foundation is an exact counterpart to the concept of a framework.[27] It is not possible for a constitution to be simultaneously a foundation in the quantitative sense and a framework. The situation is quite different in the case of a qualitative concept of foundation. A constitution is a qualitative or substantive foundation when it decides issues which are foundational for society. This concept of foundation is compatible with a concept of framework. A constitution can decide basic questions, and in that sense be a foundational order, but leave a lot of matters open and in that sense be a framework. According to the theory of principles, a good constitution will do both. It must be both a foundation and a framework. This is possible, first, if it commands and prohibits some things, that is, if it creates a framework, secondly, if it leaves some matters free, that is, if it leaves some discretion, and thirdly, if its commands and prohibitions determine those basic questions within society which can and ought to be determined by a constitution. The question is whether these requirements can be satisfied if one assumes that constitutional rights have the structure of principles.

III. STRUCTURAL DISCRETION AND BALANCING

What constitutional norms neither command nor prohibit falls within the

---

[27] Apart from the one just discussed, there is a second exact counterpart to the concept of a framework. It is that of a constitution which determines nothing as a matter of substance, in other words, one corresponding to the purely procedural model.

structural discretion of the legislature. Structural discretion is considerably less problematic than epistemic discretion. That the legislature is free if the constitution contains no relevant obligations needs no justification. That it is free because there are problems knowing whether it is free or not, is by contrast not as obvious. This fact alone justifies us in considering structural discretion before epistemic discretion.

There are three types of structural discretion: end-setting discretion, means-selecting discretion, and discretion in balancing.

1. END-SETTING DISCRETION

In respect of any constitutional right, the legislature has an end-setting discretion whenever the constitutional right contains an authorization to limit its enjoyment which either leaves the reasons for the limitation open, or which while identifying the possible reasons for limiting the right, merely permits limitations for these reasons without requiring them. In the first case, the legislature can decide for itself whether and on the basis of which goals, ends, or principles it wishes to limit the enjoyment of the right.[28] In the second case, it is still left with the decision whether it wants to appropriate the goals, ends, or principles identified in the authorization and limit the right.

End-setting discretion is widest when the legislature can choose the ends justifying limitation itself. The case-law of the Federal Constitutional Court contains examples of ends such as the 'preservation and support of the manual crafts'[29] and the contribution of employers to the costs of unemployment benefit if former employees can find no new work on account of an agreement with their former employer not to engage in competitive practices.[30] A third example concerns the 'maintenance of a German merchant navy'. Article 27 Basic Law states that German trading vessels constitute a unified merchant navy. This could be understood to mean that the maintenance of a German merchant navy has 'the status of a constitutionally protected good'. Were this to be so, the legislature would be required to pursue that goal. There would then be no end-setting discretion. The Federal Constitutional Court has left the question of whether the collective interest in maintaining the German merchant navy is the subject of a constitutional principle open, and has limited itself to establishing that the legislature 'can' at any rate legitimately seek to pursue this goal.[31] Thus the maintenance of a German merchant navy is treated as a goal which the legislature may pursue, because it falls within its end-setting discretion.

Goals subject to end-setting discretion are usually collective goods. If an individual right can be put forward as a reason for limiting a constitutional

---

[28] 81 f. [29] BVerfGE 13, 97 (110).
[30] BVerfGE 99, 202 (212). [31] BVerfGE 92, 26 (43).

right, then constitutional principles are at play on both sides. There is then in that situation no end-setting discretion.

2. MEANS-SELECTING DISCRETION

The second type of discretion, means-selecting discretion, becomes relevant whenever constitutional rights norms not only prohibit interferences, but also require positive acts, such as granting protection.[32] This discretion arises from the structure of positive duties. If one is required to save a drowning person, and if this can be done by swimming out to them, by throwing them a life-ring or by sending out a boat, then the duty to save does not require the implementation of all three measures. The duty is fulfilled if the person is saved by one of them. It is different in the case of negative duties. The prohibition of homicide includes the prohibition of every form of killing.[33] If the various means are broadly equally suitable in reaching or supporting the goal, and if in respect of other goals or principles they have either no or negligible negative effects, means-selecting discretion is unproblematic. It is quite different if the various means promote the goal to varying extents, or if the extent to which they do this is unclear, or if the various means have varying negative effects on other goals or principles, or if the extent to which they do this is unclear.[34] A decision will then depend on balancing and the possibility of identifying the relevant actual degree of promotion and damage. This leads to new problems of discretion. The problem of structural discretion in balancing will be considered first.

3. DISCRETION IN BALANCING

One objection often made against the theory of principles begins with the thesis that the idea of optimization is connected with the idea of a highest point, and continues with the assertion that this excludes structural discretion. Thus Lerche writes that principles as optimization requirements are 'tied to the highest attainable state under the (legal, factual) circumstances' and 'thus, *in nuce, to an ideal point*'.[35] 'In the light of the wide-ranging, endlessly *competing* content' this implies an 'intensive and thorough binding of the legislature to the highest attainable point'. This is supposed to lack 'internal legitimation'.[36] Scherzberg makes a similar point. As optimization requirements, constitutional rights only permit 'those resolutions of conflict which represent the highest possible realization of all relevant

---

[32] See e.g. BVerfGE 46, 160 (164 f.).   [33] 308.

[34] See on this M. Borowski, *Grundrechte als Prinzipien* (Baden-Baden, 1998), 140.

[35] P. Lerche, 'Die Verfassung als Quelle von Optimierungsgeboten?' in J. Burmeister (ed.), *Verfassungsstaatlichkeit. Festschrift für Klaus Stern* (Munich, 1997), 205.

[36] ibid. 205 f.

constitutional rights interests'. This is taken—a few exceptions apart—
'structurally to exclude decision-taking discretion'.[37]

The highest point thesis amounts to the claim that in the field of principles there is always one right answer. If in addition one recognizes the fact
that the field of constitutional principles is practically unlimited on account
of general freedom of action and the general principle of equality as well as
the radiating effect on the entire legal system, it becomes clear that the highest point objection is none other than a special variant of the Forsthoff
genome critique applied to optimization.

Whether the highest point objection is valid depends on what is to be
understood by 'optimization' under the theory of principles. This turns on
the definition of principles. Principles are norms which require the greatest
possible realization of something relative to what is factually and legally
possible. It is one of the central theses of the *Theory of Constitutional
Rights* that this definition implies the principle of proportionality with its
three sub-principles of suitability, necessity, and proportionality in the
narrow sense, and that conversely the principled character of constitutional
rights follows logically from the principle of proportionality.[38] This equivalence means that the three sub-principles of the principle of proportionality define what the theory of principles understands by 'optimization'. The
question of whether optimization is incompatible with the framework
nature of the constitution is thus equivalent to the question whether the
principle of proportionality is similarly incompatible. To answer this question, the principles of suitability and necessity will be considered first.

3.1 Suitability and Necessity

The principles of suitability and necessity express the requirement
contained in the definition of principles for the greatest possible realization
relative to what is factually possible. This has little to do with 'highest
points'. This can be illustrated by way of two cases. The first case is
concerned with suitability. A hairdresser had installed a cigarette vending
machine on his property without permission. The administrative officials
threatened him with a fine on account of a breach of the law concerning
retail trade. This law required a permission which would only be granted if
the applicant could demonstrate, 'the necessary expertise'. The proof necessary could be supplied by an apprenticeship in commerce, a long period of
practice in a business, or through a special examination in which commercial knowledge was to be demonstrated.[39] The hairdresser sought legal
redress in the courts. The Upper Regional Court of Appeal in Saarbrücken,
which was the court of second instance, considered the requirement to

---

[37] A. Scherzberg, *Grundrechtsschutz und Eingriffsintensität* (Berlin, 1989), 174.
[38] 66 ff.
[39] BVerfGE 19, 330 (332 ff.).

prove commercial ability in the case of mere placing of vending machines unconstitutional and sought a ruling from the Federal Constitutional Court. The Federal Constitutional Court reached the conclusion that the requirement to prove competence for any trade in any goods, and thus also for the operation of cigarette vending machines, breached freedom of profession guaranteed in article 12(1) Basic Law. Its reasoning was based to a large extent on the fact that proving commercial competence in the case of operating a cigarette vending machine was not a suitable means of protecting the consumer from health or financial risks.[40] It was thus prohibited by the principle of suitability and in breach of the constitutional right of freedom of profession.

This argument is an expression of the idea of optimization. Two principles are in play, that of freedom of profession (P_1) and consumer protection (P_2). The means (M) adopted, proof of commercial competence, lack suitability and are thus not capable of promoting P_2, but they obstruct the realization of P_1. In this situation, there are no costs either to P_1 or P_2 if M is omitted, but there are costs to P_1 if M is adopted. Thus P_1 and P_2 taken together may be realized to a higher degree relative to what is factually possible if M is abandoned. So P_1 and P_2 *taken together* prohibit the use of M. This is none other than an expression of the idea of Pareto-optimality: one position can be improved without detriment to another.[41]

The simple example shows that one cannot avoid optimizing if one is not prepared to give up the principle of suitability. It also shows that the aspect of optimization located in the principle of suitability does not consist in attaining a highest point. Rather, the principle of suitability has the status of a negative criterion. It cuts out unsuitable means. Such a negative criterion does not settle everything, but it does exclude some things. It thus fits the idea of a framework very well. As an element of a framework it excludes some things, namely unsuitable things, without thereby settling everything.

A similar point can be made in respect of the principle of necessity. This requires that of two broadly equally suitable means, the one which interferes less intensively should be chosen. Once again, an example can be considered which concerns freedom of profession and consumer protection in competition with each other. A regulation issued by the Federal Minister for Youth, Family, and Health contained a prohibition on selling confectionery containing cocoa powder, but consisting substantially of puffed rice and thus not a genuine chocolate product. The purpose of this regulation was to protect consumers from mistaken purchases. The Federal Constitutional Court established that such a trade prohibition was entirely suitable to protect consumers. If a product may not be traded at all, the danger that it might be bought by mistake is slim. But the trade prohibition

---

[40] BVerfGE 19, 330 (338 f.).   [41] 105.

was not necessary. There was an equally suitable, less intensively interfering, means. A labelling requirement could meet the risk of confusion and deception 'in an equally effective, but less intrusive way'.[42]

The idea of optimization is clearly recognizable here as well. The principle of consumer protection (P_2) is broadly equally well satisfied by a duty to label (M_1) as by a trade prohibition (M_2). So for P_2 is it irrelevant whether M_1 or M_2 is adopted. This is not the case for freedom of profession (P_1). M_2 interferes much more intensively with P_1 than does M_1. In the light of what is factually possible $(M_1$ or $M_2)$, P_1 can be satisfied to a greater extent by choosing M_1 over M_2, without costing P_2 anything. So the optimization of P_1 *and* P_2 prohibits the adoption of M_2.

Thus the principle of necessity is an expression of the idea of Pareto-optimality as well. Because of the existence of a less intensively interfering and equally suitable means, one position can be improved at no cost to the other. Of course, at this point means are not simply being excluded as with suitability. However, the legislature is not categorically required to adopt the less intensively interfering means. The point is simply that if the legislature wishes to pursue its goal further, it may only use the less intensive of the means, or an equally mild means, or a still milder one. That is no optimization to the highest point, but simply a ban on unnecessary sacrifices of constitutional rights.

Of course, examining suitability and necessity is not always as simple as in the two cases just considered. There are many causes for this, of which two are particularly noteworthy. The first is that suitability and necessity are concerned with means–ends relations, which often throw up difficult problems of prognosis. In 1994 the Federal Constitutional Court had to decide whether criminalizing the production, trade, dissemination, and receipt of cannabis products was compatible with general freedom of action (art. 2(1) Basic Law) and freedom of the person (art. 2(2)(1) Basic Law). This gave rise to the question of whether the decriminalization of cannabis, as the less intrusive means as far as liberty is concerned, could not equally or even better meet the dangers arising from this drug and illegal trade in it as could a general criminal prohibition. The basis of the Court's answer can be found in the thesis that 'scientifically based knowledge, which necessarily points to the correctness of one or the other strategies' was not present.[43] In this situation, the decision of the legislature for criminalization had to be accepted, 'for in choosing between several potentially suitable routes to reaching a legal goal the legislature enjoys a prerogative of assessment and decision'.[44] This shows what a large role epistemic discretion can play in examining suitability and necessity. Granting the legislature the competence to assess empirical facts is in outcome equivalent to granting it the competence to

[42] BVerfGE 53, 135 (146). [43] BVerfGE 90, 145 (182 f.).
[44] BVerfGE 90, 145 (183).

limit constitutional rights.[45] The question of whether and to what extent such discretionary assessments can be justified does not belong in the context of structural discretion, but in the context of knowledge-related discretion. And this is for the most part a problem of formal principles.

The problem of epistemic discretion arises both in the case of suitability and in the case of necessity. The second cause for the complexity of what is intrinsically a simple structure only affects necessity. It lies in the possibility of cases arising in which not only two, but more than two, that is, at least three principles are relevant. It is often the case that the less intrusive means as regards the constitutional right it affects, which equally effectively promotes the goal pursued by the legislature, has the disadvantage that it affects some third principle or goal. An example is provided by a decision of the Federal Constitutional Court concerning a prohibition on the business of hiring out workers to building contractors for a fee. This practice led to numerous breaches of provisions of labour law, welfare law, commercial law, and tax law. But there were also companies who followed these provisions. These argued that totally banning their activity was not necessary, since the statutory goal, combating an illegal practice, could be attained by adopting a less intrusive means. All that was needed was more effective controls on building sites. In this way both their constitutional right to freedom of profession could be respected and the legislative goal reached. If it only depended on freedom of profession (P_1) and combating an illegal practice (P_2), assuming control (M_1) and prohibition (M_2) were equally effective, the argument would be compelling. The prohibition (M_2) would be prohibited. But now the Federal Constitutional Court brought a third principle into play, that of the sparing use of public resources (P_3). The individual was not permitted to expect that to avoid interferences with constitutional rights, 'public resources, whch are only limited, should be used beyond what can reasonably be expected of society to extend the official department responsible for combating these undesirable states of affairs'.[46] This fundamentally alters the situation. The question of whether M_1 should be adopted instead of M_2 is not to be decided merely on the basis of the relationship between P_1 and P_2. P_2 is neutral as regards the alternatives of M_1 or M_2, and thus irrelevant as regards the choice between these two means, since P_2 only requires that one or the other be adopted. The question of choice is decided solely between P_1 and P_3. Does the Constitution in the case at hand permit a relatively intensive interference with constitutional rights (M_2) in order to burden public resources less, or does it require a much greater burdening of public resources in order to realize the goal of combating an illegal practice (P_2) with a much less intensive interference with constitutional rights? This question takes us out of the field of optimization relative to what is factually possible, and into the

[45] 313.   [46] BVerfGE 77, 84 (110 f.).

greatest possible realization relative to what is legally possible. The question is whether P_2 and P_3 *taken together* justify the relatively intensive interference with P_1 contained in the prohibition (M_2). This is a problem of balancing and it takes us to the third stage of the principle of proportionality.

3.2 Proportionality in the Narrow Sense

As optimization requirements, principles demand not only the greatest possible realization relative to what is factually possible, they also demand the greatest possible realization relative to what is legally possible. This is determined mainly by competing principles. The principle of proportionality in the narrow sense as the third sub-principle of proportionality expresses the meaning of optimization relative to competing principles. It is identical with the Law of Balancing. This states: 'The greater the degree of non-satisfaction of, or detriment to, one principle, the greater must be the importance of satisfying the other'.[47] This expresses the point that optimization relative to competing principles consists of nothing other than balancing.

The Law of Balancing shows that balancing can be broken down into three stages. The first stage involves establishing the degree of non-satisfaction of, or detriment to, the first principle. This is followed by a second stage in which the importance of satisfying the competing principle is established. Finally, the third stage establishes whether the importance of satisfying the competing principle justifies the detriment to, or non-satisfaction of, the first.

Habermas's objection to the theory of principles would basically be justified if it were not possible to make rational judgments about, first, intensity of interference, secondly, degrees of importance, and thirdly, their relationship to each other. As principles, constitutional rights would then—the contribution of suitability and necessity to the exclusion of possibilities aside—permit any solution. There would be no framework, because there would be no limit. By contrast, Böckenförde's objection would basically be justified if balancing always required precisely one decision from the legislature, that is, if there were no structural discretion in balancing. Since talk of frameworks and discretion only makes sense if some sort of limits are possible, the problem which Habermas draws attention to will be considered first. If one takes literally his thesis that balancing lacks 'rational standards',[48] then it is saying that there is no case in which a result to a balancing exercise can be reached on a rational basis. To this thesis there are two antitheses, one radical and one moderate. The radical antithesis asserts that balancing leads in a rational way to one outcome in every case.

---

[47] 102.
[48] Habermas, *Between Facts and Norms*, 259.

The theory of principles has never maintained this thesis and has always emphasized that balancing is not a procedure which leads necessarily to precisely one outcome in every case.[49] Thus everything turns on the moderate antithesis. This maintains that one outcome can be rationally established through the use of balancing, not in every case, but in at least some cases, and that the class of these cases is interesting enough to justify balancing as a method.

It is easy to find examples in which rational judgments are possible about intensity of interference and degrees of importance, such that an outcome can be rationally established by way of balancing. The duty of tobacco producers to place health warnings about the dangers of smoking on their products is a relatively minor interference with freedom of profession. By contrast, a total ban on all tobacco products would be a serious interference. Between such minor and serious cases, others of moderate intensity of interference could be found. One example would be a ban on cigarette vending machines and restricting the sale of tobacco products to certain shops. In this way, a scale can be developed with the stages, 'minor', 'moderate', and 'serious'. Our example shows that valid assignations on this scale are possible. One only has to imagine somebody who treats a total ban on all tobacco products as a minor interference with the producer's freedom of profession, and the duty to put health warnings on the packaging as a serious interference. It would not be easy to take such judgments seriously.

A three-stage scale is also possible on the side of the competing reasons. The reason for the duty to put warnings on tobacco products is to protect people from health risks. The Federal Constitutional Court was not exaggerating when it stated in its decision on health warnings, that 'according to the current state of medical knowledge, it is certain' that smoking causes cancer and cardio-vascular disease.[50] The weight of the reasons justifying interference is therefore high. They weigh heavily. If in this way the intensity of interference is established as minor, and the degree of importance of the reason for the interference as high, the outcome is easy to see. The weighty reason for interference justifies the minor interference. The duty to place health warnings on tobacco products therefore does not breach the freedom of profession of tobacco producers guaranteed by article 12(1) Basic Law. This outcome of examining proportionality in the narrow sense is not merely plausible. In the light of the minor intensity of the interference and the great weight of the reason for interference, it can well be described, along with the Federal Constitutional Court, as 'obvious'.[51]

Now one could take the view that the example does not tell us very much. On one hand there is economic activity. Here, scales are entirely

[49] 100, 83, 105, 362. See also 364, 366, 383, 385, 386.
[50] BVerfGE95, 173 (184).
[51] BVerfGE 95, 173 (187).

possible, since at root they are based on considerations of cost. On the other hand there is life and death. If empirical investigation can show that the dangers here are reasonably great, locating the reason in the upper area of importance can be based on quantifiable facts. That might not be applicable to areas in which quantifiable factors such as costs and probabilities play no, or no significant, role.

To deal with this objection, a case will be considered which concerned a classic conflict between freedom of expression and personality rights. The widely published satirical magazine, Titanic, described a paraplegic reserve officer who had successfully carried out his call-up to a military exercise, first as 'né Murderer' and in a later edition as a 'cripple'. The Upper Regional Court in Düsseldorf ruled against Titanic in an action brought by the officer and ordered it to pay damages of DM 12,000. Titanic brought a constitutional complaint. The Federal Constitutional Court undertook 'case-specific balancing'[52] between the freedom of expression of those involved with the magazine (art. 5(1)(1) Basic Law) and the officer's general personality right (art. 2(1) in connection with art. 1(1) Basic Law). To this end the intensity of interference with these rights was determined and placed in relationship with each other. The judgment in damages was treated as 'lasting', or a *serious* interference with freedom of expression, even though it was the result of a civil and not a criminal judgment. This was justified above all by pointing out that damages could reduce the future willingness of those affected to produce their magazine as they had hitherto done.[53] The description, 'né Murderer', was then placed in the context of the satire published by the Titanic. In this, several persons had been described as having a surname at birth in a 'recognizably humorous' way, from 'puns to silliness'; for example, the then federal president, Richard von Weizsäcker, was described as 'né Citizen'.[54] This context made it impossble to see in the description an 'unlawful, serious, illegal breach of personality'.[55] The interference with the personality right was thus treated as having a moderate, perhaps even only a minor, intensity. Corresponding to this, the importance of protecting the officer's personality right through an award of damages was moderate, and perhaps only minor. These assessments complete the first part of the judgment. In order to justify an award of damages, which is a serious interference with the constitutional right of freedom of expression, the interference with the right of personality, which was supposed to be compensated for by the damages, would have to be at least as serious. But according to the assessment of the Federal Constitutional Court it was not. That meant that the interference with freedom of expression was disproportionate, which means that calling the officer 'né Murderer' was not a ground for awarding damages.

---

[52] BVerfGE 86, 1 (11).   [53] BVerfGE 86, 1 (10).
[54] BVerfGE 86, 1 (11).   [55] BVerfGE 86, 1 (12).

However, matters were different in the case of the description of the officer as a 'cripple'. This description was a '*serious* breach of the paraplegic's
personality right'.[56] The importance of protecting the officer by the imposition of damages was thus great. This was justified by the fact that describing a severely disabled person as a 'cripple' is generally taken these days to
be 'humiliating' and express a 'lack of respect'. So the serious interference
with freedom of expression was countered by great importance for the
protection of personality. In this situation the Federal Constitutional Court
came to the conclusion that it could 'see no flaw in the balancing to the
detriment of freedom of expression'.[57] Titanic's constitutional complaint
was thus only justified to the extent that it related to damages for the
description 'né Murderer'. As far as the description, 'cripple', was
concerned, it was unjustified.[58]

One can argue whether the description, 'né Murderer', really represents
only a moderate or a minor interference. Such doubts will be considered in
the context of formal principles. The significant point for present purposes
is that it can hardly be doubted that the award of damages and describing
someone as a 'cripple' are both very intensive interferences with the relevant
principles.

On the side of the severely disabled, one can characterize this even
further than the Court. The Federal Constitutional Court rightly held that
describing a paraplegic as a 'cripple' was humiliating and disrespectful.
Such public humiliation and lack of respect affects the dignity of the victim.
That is not merely serious, it is a very serious or an extraordinarily serious
violation. One has reached the area in which interferences can hardly ever
be justified by any strengthening of the reasons for the interference. This
corresponds to the law of diminishing marginal utility,[59] which is the fire
wall that Habermas misses in the theory of principles. The Titanic Case is
thus not only an example of the fact that scales which can intelligently be
put into relationship with each other are possible even in the case of imma-
terial goods such as personality and free speech, but it is also an example of
the power inherent in constitutional rights as principles to set limits by way
of the process of balancing, which while not rigid and ascertainable without balancing, are none the less firm and clear.

The Tobacco and Titanic Judgments show that rational judgments about
degrees of intensity and importance are possible and that such judgments
may be put into relationship with each other for the purposes of justifying
an outcome. Of course such judgments presuppose standards which are not
to be found in the Law of Balancing. Establishing that a judgment against
the Titanic to pay damages is a serious interference with freedom of expression makes assumptions about what threatens freedom of expression. On

---

[56] BVerfGE 86, 1 (13), emphasis added.   [57] ibid.
[58] BVerfGE 86, 1 (14).   [59] 103.

the other hand, the judgment that the description 'cripple' is a serious violation of personality makes assumptions about what it means to be a person and have dignity. But that does not mean, to use Habermas's words, that 'weighing takes place either arbitrarily or unreflectively, according to customary standards and hierarchies'.[60] The assumptions underlying judgments about intensity of interference and degree of importance are not arbitrary. Reasons are given for them which are understandable. It is also questionable whether these assumptions are made by the Federal Constitutional Court 'unreflectively, according to customary standards and hierarchies'. It is true that the standards follow a line of precedent. But talk of 'customary standards' would only be justified if the existence of precedent were the only relevant matter for the decision, and not their correctness. Furthermore, one could only talk of 'unreflective' application if this application did not take place in the course of argumentation. For arguments are the public expression of reflection. But there is no lack of argumentation. All this applies to the Tobacco Judgment as well.

Thus both decisions show that there are cases in which limits can be drawn to state activity in a rational way with the help of the Law of Balancing. This disproves the thesis that balancing in the final analysis permits anything because it lacks rational standards. To that extent the Law of Balancing survives Habermas's objections. Now we must pursue the question whether it can also do this against Böckenförde's objections. This presupposes that it is compatible with discretion to a sufficient extent. To answer the question of discretion in the field of application of the Law of Balancing, we have to take a closer look at the system underlying the classifications considered up to this point. All classifications follow a three-grade or triadic model. The three grades can be characterized by the terms 'light', 'moderate', and 'serious'. Representation is made easier if these stages are identified by the letters '*l*', '*m*' and '*s*' respectively. The letter '*l*' stands here not just for the common term 'light' but also for other expressions such as 'minor' or 'weak', and '*s*' includes 'high' and 'strong' as well as 'serious'.

Under the Law of Balancing, the objects of evaluation as l, m, or s are the degree of non-satisfaction of, or detriment to, one principle and the importance of satisfying another. Instead of 'degree of non-satisfaction or detriment' one could also talk in terms of the 'intensity of interference'. If one uses P_i as a variable for the principle the infringement of which is to be examined, one can represent the intensity of interference in P_i 'IP_i'. Interferences are always concrete interferences. Intensity of interference is thus always a concrete quantity. As such it is different from the abstract weight of P_i. For reasons of clarity it is important to make it plain whether

---

[60] Habermas, *Between Facts and Norms*, 259.

one is talking about an abstract or a concrete quantity. In the case of IP_i this is not intrinsically necessary, because intensity of interference is always necessarily concrete. But it is no loss to make the concreteness of IP_i explicit by adding 'C'. 'C' expresses the circumstances of the case which are relevant to the decision, and it plays a central role in the Law of Competing Principles.[61] To make this connection clear, 'IP_iC' stands for the intensity of interference (I) in P_i in the circumstances (C) of the case to be decided.

The second quantity in the Law of Balancing is the importance of satisfying the other principle. By contrast with intensity of interference, the degree of importance need not necessarily be exclusively considered a concrete quantity. One can create a concept of importance which combines concrete and abstract quantities. So, for example, human life has in the abstract a greater weight than the general liberty to do or not to do as one pleases. The importance of protecting life in a particular situation can thus be determined both by the abstract weight of life and the risks to life in the concrete situation. The possibility of such a combined concept of importance is, of course, no argument against distinguishing its components. That is true simply on analytical grounds. In addition, abstract weights only have an influence on the outcome of balancing if they are different. If they are equal, which in the case of competing constitutional rights is often the case, the only relevant factor is their concrete importance. Something like a concept of concrete importance is thus indispensable. This can be identified by taking 'S' for the importance of satisfying a principle, 'P_j' for the principle, and 'C' for the fact that what counts is importance on the facts of the case to be decided. The concrete importance of P_j can thus be represented by 'SP_jC'.

Of course, this does not answer the question of what the concrete importance of P_j actually is. It is only clear that this depends on the concrete circumstances of the case. The elements of the concrete case which are important for the decision are the measures to be evaluated and the effect which their implementation and non-implementation will have on the relevant principles. Non-implementation belongs here, because the question is whether the measure is constitutionally permitted or prohibited, and prohibition corresponds to omitting the measure. The meaning of this can be illustrated from the Titanic case. We are only concerned with the description of the paraplegic officer as a 'cripple'. In order to determine the intensity of interference with freedom of expression, one only has to ask how intensively the prohibition of this expression combined with an award of damages interferes with freedom of expression. That is what the constitution would require of this constitutional right if it were to permit the prohibition contained in the judgment of the Düsseldorf Upper Regional Court along with the award of damages. In order to establish the importance of

[61] 54.

satisfying the principle of protecting personality, one has to ask in reverse what omitting or not implementing the interference with freedom of expression, that is, treating the description, 'cripple', as permitted and not subject to damages, would mean for the protection of personality. But this is none other than the cost to the protection of personality if freedom of expression were to be preferred. The importance of the principle of protecting personality in the Titanic Case can thus be derived from the intensity with which non-interference in Titanic's freedom of expression would interfere with the officer's personality right. This can be generalized and stated as follows: the concrete importance of P_i is the same as the intensity with which the non-interference with P_i interferes with P_j.

In the light of this statement, one can now ask why one needs to speak in terms of the concrete 'importance' of P_i at all. This is a terminological problem. It would indeed be possible, even in the case of P_j, simply to speak in terms of the intensity of an interference, this time the intensity of the interference caused by not interfering with P_j. So the question is, which form is the more appropriate. Legal analysis should delve as deeply into its subject-matter as possible and not be put off even by the most complicated of structures. But when the analytical work is complete, the jurist must return to the surface and share his discoveries in the simplest and most familiar words possible. From this point of view, the concept of the concrete importance of the competing principle seems well suited to expressing the content of the concept of intensity of interference through non-interference, and it attaches to well-grounded and widespread intuitions. So in the context of the Law of Balancing we will continue to speak of the importance of satisfying the other principle. The counterpart to 'IP_iC' is thus 'SP_iC'.

The objects of evaluation as *l*, *m*, or *s* have now been established. In setting out the Law of Balancing, it was stated that it breaks the balancing process down into three steps. The first two in our triadic model can now be carried out: evaluating IP_iC as *l*, *m*, or *s* and evaluating SP_iC as *l*, *m*, or *s*. The question is now how the third step can be carried out, in which the evaluations are to be set in relationship with each other. If one considers the possible permutations in the triadic model, the answer is simple. There are three circumstances in which P_i takes precedence:

(1) $IP_iC : s / SP_iC : l$
(2) $IP_iC : s / SP_iC : m$
(3) $IP_iC : m / SP_iC : l$

In these cases the conditional relation of preference $(P_i \text{ P } P_j)C$[62] applies, just as in the Law of Competing Principles. These three cases of the precedence of P_i are matched by three cases of the precedence of P_j:

---

[62] 53.

(4) $IP_iC : l \,/\, SP_jC : s$
(5) $IP_iC : m \,/\, SP_jC : s$
(6) $IP_iC : l \,/\, SP_jC : m$

In these cases, $(P_j \mathbf{P} P_i)\, C$ applies. In addition to these six cases, which can be decided on the basis of the triadic scale, there are three stalemate situations:

(7) $IP_iC : l \,/\, SP_jC : l$
(8) $IP_iC : m \,/\, SP_jC : m$
(9) $IP_iC : s \,/\, SP_jC : s$

The three situations of balancing stalemate lead to structural discretion in balancing. To demonstrate this, the triadic model needs to be investigated in a little more depth.

The three classes of the triadic model represent a scale which attempts to systematize classifications which can be found both in everyday practice and legal argumentation. Such a three-class system is far removed from a metrication of intensities of interference and degrees of importance on a cardinal scale such as a scale from 0 to 1, and it has to be far removed, because intensities of interference and degrees of importance are not capable of metrication on such a scale.[63] The gradation in terms of light, moderate, or serious is often difficult enough as it is. In some cases one can still just about distinguish light and serious, and in some cases even that seems impossible. Legal scales can thus only work with relatively crude divisions, and not even that in all cases. Calculable measurements by way of a continuum of points between 0 and 1 cannot apply. Nevertheless, what is possible is an illustration of the structure underlying the triadic model with the help of numbers. Against this background, it is possible to create a formula which expresses the weight of a principle under the circumstances of the case to be decided, in short, its *concrete weight*. It goes:

$$WP_{i,\,j}C = \frac{IP_iC}{SP_jC}$$

This formula expands the Law of Competing Principles and the Law of Balancing. It can be called the 'Weight Formula'.[64] The one symbol it

---

[63] 99.

[64] The Weight Formula only includes concrete quantities. It therefore represents the situation in which only these are relevant. As has already been stated, that is the case when the abstract weights of the principles are the same. If they are different, then they must be included in the formula. To this end, WP_iA can stand for the abstract weight of P_i, and WP_jA for the abstract weight of P_j. The Weight Formula then has the following form:

$WP_{i,\,j}C = (IP_iC \,.\, WP_iA)/(SP_jC \,.\, WP_jA)$

This formula makes it clear why abstract weights are redundant when they are equal. They cancel each other out. The formula without abstract weights is thus no different from the formula with abstract weights, except with the cancelling out carried out.

contains which has not yet been introduced is 'W'. W stands for the concrete weight of P_i, that is, the weight of P_i under the circumstances of the case to be decided (C). The Weight Formula makes the point that the concrete weight of a principle is a relative weight. It does this by making the concrete weight the quotient of the intensity of interference with this principle and the importance of the competing principle. Relativity is expressed by using $P_{i,j}$. The concrete weight of P_i is the concrete weight of P_i relative to P_j. Now one can only talk about quotients in the presence of numbers, which is not the case in any direct sense with balancing. So concrete weight can only really be defined as a quotient in a numerical model which illustrates the structure of balancing. In legal argumentation it is only analogous to a quotient. But the analogy is an instructive one.

There are various possibilities for allocating numbers to the three values of the triadic model. One possibility which is relatively straightforward and at the same time highly instructive is to take the values 2^0, 2^1, and 2^2, that is, 1, 2, and 4.[65] On this basis, *l* has the value 1, *m* the value 2, and *s* the value 4. The concrete weight of P_i ($WP_{i,j}C$) is then established by inserting 1, 2, or 4 in the weight formula for IP_iC and SP_iC. The number to be

---

It is an interesting question whether cumulative effects can be built into the Weight Formula. This question arises, for example, if several principles can be appealed to in support of an interference with a constitutional right. One could extend the Weight Formula in the following way:

$$WP_i -_n C = (IP_iC \cdot WP_iA)/(SP_jC \cdot WP_jA + \ldots SP_nC \cdot WP_nA)$$

The adequacy of this expansion depends on whether the importance of reasons for limiting rights simply increases additively. This question will be left open at this point.

[65] One could also try to represent the three levels by three points on the scale of 0 to 1. One particularly obvious possibility is to divide this scale in three and to take the centre point of each part for *l*, *m*, and *s* respectively. The letter *l* would then be assigned the value $1/6$, *m* $1/2$, and *s* $5/6$. Since the difference between *l* and *m* on one hand and *m* and *s* on the other would be the same, this would create an arithmetical sequence. But this would lead to unacceptable distortions in creating *quotients*. In cases in which the interference in P_i is justified, these make a plausible enough impression. The sequence of values in this case is: $l/s = 1/5$, $l/m = 1/3$, $m/s = 3/5$. The fact that the value of l/m is smaller than than of m/s in spite of the identical difference between *l* and *m* and *m* and *s* could still be explained by the fact that principles are more resistant in cases of moderate interference than in cases of slight interference, that they gain in strength as the interference increases. But the same would have to be true on the other side as well, in the case of the values when P_i wins. But the sequence of values here is $s/m = 5/3$, $m/l = 3$, $s/l = 5$. According to this, P_i has less concrete weight (5/3) in a case of serious interference combined with a moderately important competing principle, than with a moderate interference justified only by a principle of minor importance (3). That contradicts the intuition that principles gain in strength as the intensity of interference increases. Such distortions can only be avoided in the case of arithmetical sequences if *differences* are calculated in place of quotients. If one adopts the sequence $1/6$, $1/2$, $5/6$, one ends up with the following values in cases in which P_i is outweighed: $l/m = -1/3$, $m/s = -1/3$, $l/s = -2/3$. In cases in which P_i wins, the following sequence arises: $s/m = 1/3$, $m/l = 1/3$, $s/l = 2/3$. In a case of stalemate (l/l, m/m, s/s) the value is always 0. This mode of representation has the virtue of simplicity. Its disadvantage is that unlike geometric sequences such as the one chosen in the text, it does not express the fact that principles gain in strength as interferences intensify. I am grateful to Luís Virgílio Alfonso da Silva for interesting comments on the problem of assigning numbers to *l*, *m*, and *s*.

inserted is determined by whether the intensity of interference or the degree of importance is judged to be light, moderate, or serious. In those cases in which P_i takes precedence, the concrete weight of P_i ($WP_{i,j}C$) is a result of inserting the relevant values: $s/l = 4$, $s/m = 2$, $m/l = 2$. This corresponds to the intuition that a principle is particularly weighty (4) when it is seriously interfered with (*s*) on relatively trivial grounds (*l*). The sense in which weight is relative is also clear. Relative weight sinks (2) if serious interference (*s*) takes place when it is moderately important (*m*) to satisfy a competing principle. The same outcome (2) applies whenever there is a moderate interference (*m*) for which only a minor reason can be given (*l*).

In all cases in which P_i takes precedence over P_j, the value of P_i is greater than 1. If it sinks below 1, this expresses the idea that P_j takes precedence. The three values for the outweighing of P_i are $l/s = \frac{1}{4}$, $m/s = \frac{1}{2}$, $l/m = \frac{1}{2}$. What has been said in respect of the values of the precedence of P_i applies here in reverse.

As regards the issue of structural discretion, the stalemate cases are of particular interest. In these, the concrete weight of P_i is always the same. This expresses the idea of the equal value of all stalemate situations. The equal value of stalemates in balancing is the basis for structural discretion in balancing. This can be demonstrated by way of a case.

The case was concerned with reports in the Hamburg magazine, *Stern*, in 1982 and 1983 about the investigations of the Bonn prosecutor's office in a case involving donations by businesses to a political party. The reports quoted from the transcripts of statements by witnesses and one accused person, as well as from defence submissions. These literal quotations took place before the files had been discussed in any public hearing. This is punishable by imprisonment for up to one year or a fine under § 353 *d* No. 3 Criminal Code. The court in Hamburg, before which the editors responsible were tried, considered this provision unconstitutional, because it was not sufficiently capable of achieving its purposes. The court referred the matter to the Federal Constitutional Court. The Federal Constitutional Court identified two purposes behind § 353 *d* No. 3 Criminal Code: first, the protection of those affected by the legal procedings, required by their right to personality under article 2(1) in connection with article 1(1) Basic Law along with the presumption of innocence contained in article 6(2) ECHR, and secondly, the protection of the impartiality of those taking part in the proceedings, required by the principle of impartial adjudication found expressed in articles 97 and 101 Basic Law.[66] The most significant difficulty for the decision was the fact that only literal quotation from the investigatory files is criminal, not more sensational non-literal reports. The Federal Constitutional Court came to the conclusion that because of the authenticity of literal repetition, such quotations could threaten the goals

[66] BVerfGE 71, 206 (216 f., 219).

just mentioned more seriously than non-literal reports.[67] While the protection achieved by the ban on literal quotations was 'incomplete' and thus 'marginal'[68] and 'minimally effective',[69] freedom of expression and of the press protected in article 5(1) Basic Law was also 'only limited to a small extent', because the press were still able to report without using literal quotations.[70] The Federal Constitutional Court summarized the outcome of its consideration of proportionality in the narrow sense in one sentence, which reads like an application of the Weight Formula applied to the values l/l: 'Accordingly [i.e. in the light of the minimal intensity of the interference, R.A.], the limitation of the liberties of article 5(1) Basic Law is not disproportionate to what it seeks to achieve: the—admittedly marginally effective—protection of the legal interests of § 353 d No. 3 Criminal Code'.[71]

In this sentence, the words 'not disproportionate' are of particular significance. The Court accepts the constitutionality of the interference with press freedom not just when the importance of the reasons for interfering exceeds the intensity of the interference, but already where there is a draw, in this case, the l/l-stalemate. Disproportionality in the narrow sense only arises if concrete importance sinks below the intensity of interference, that is, under the circumstances s/l, s/m and m/l. Now the legislature is permitted not to act in a situation of l/l stalemate. And in the light of the definition of discretion above as liberty either way, the fact that it is also permitted to act under these circumstances means that it has a discretion. Since this arises from what legally applies as a matter of constitutional rights, the discretion is a structural one.

The decision is significant for the theory of structural discretion in a second way which results from what is more or less a passing comment, in which the Court states that it is up to the legislature to decide whether it wishes to enact alternative regulations which might be better or more just.[72] A better solution as regards the protection of personality and adjudicative integrity could only be brought about by more intensive interferences with press freedom. If such interferences have a moderate intensity, the degree of importance of protection achieved must also reach a moderate level. Even a serious interference could be justified, if it is matched by a correspondingly high degree of importance for the protection achieved. This means that structural discretion runs along the line of stalemates.

The last point shows that a distinction must be drawn between two aspects of structural discretion in balancing. The first lies in the stalemate itself. If the reason for the interference is just as strong as the reason against it, the interference is not disproportionate. The decision in the *Stern* Case is an example of this. The same applies to the counterpart of interference, the

---

[67] BVerfGE 71, 206 (216). [68] BVerfGE 71, 206 (219).
[69] BVerfGE 71, 206 (221). [70] BVerfGE 71, 206 (220).
[71] BVerfGE 71, 206 (221). [72] BVerfGE 71, 206 (218).

failure to grant protection. If the reasons for failing to grant protection are as strong as the reasons for protection, non-protection is not disproportionate. This leads to a significant discretion in the area of third party, or horizontal, effect.[73] The second aspect of structural discretion in balancing is that stalemates at different levels are of equal value. The idea of a structural discretion in balancing therefore consists of a combination of two ideas: equality in a situation of stalemate, and equality between situations of stalemate. In no way does this answer every question, but it does make clear what is meant by the idea of a structural discretion in balancing.

Opponents of the theory of principles could argue that talk of a balancing stalemate is a trick, which is only plausible in the crude triadic model. This supposedly masks the fact that in reality there are no, or hardly any, stalemates. Some sort of small, or at least tiny, difference is always at hand. The only thing that should be conceded is that if there are stalemates they are extremely rare, or at least rare.[74] The basis of this objection is that finer gradations than those of the triadic model are possible. Such finer gradations can be created either by using a finer scale, or simply by asking directly in each case whether IP_iC or SP_jC is the greater, or whether they are both the same. The latter would be a weighting in the concrete case doing without scales altogether. First, we will consider the possibility of a finer scale.

It is very easy to create a plausible finer scale on the basis of the triadic model. One only has to apply the three classes to each in turn. In this way one can create a nine-stage double-triadic model, which can be represented as follows: (1) *ll*, (2) *lm*, (3) *ls*, (4) *ml*, (5) *mm*, (6) *ms*, (7) *sl*, (8) *sm*, (9) *ss*. This division expresses the idea that there are not only simply light, moderate, and serious interferences, but also very serious (*ss*), moderately serious (*sm*), and less serious (*sl*) interferences, moderate interferences at the top of the range (*ms*), in the middle of the range (*mm*), and at the bottom of the range (*ml*), and minor interferences in the upper (*ls*) and middle (*lm*) ranges, as well as very trivial interferences (*ll*).[75] There are many cases in which such divisions are plausible. Thus in the Titanic Case one could class the importance of protecting the officer from being called a cripple very highly (*ss*) and contrast this with a moderately serious interference (*sm*) with press freedom.

Such refinements of scale admittedly have limits. In principle, they can

[73] See on this BVerfGE 96, 56 (66), where the Federal Constitutional Court appropriately uses the term, 'discretion in balancing'.

[74] See Scherzberg, *Grundrechtsschutz und Eingriffsintensität*, 174.

[75] The nine classes of the double triadic model may be represented by the values 2^0 to 2^8. In this case, where there is a great divergence of value, the concrete weight of P_i ($WP_{i,j}C$) rises and falls dramatically. Where there is a very serious (*ss*) interference which can only be justified by a very minor (*ll*) reason, the concrete weight of P_i is 256. Conversely, a very minor (*ll*) interference justified by a very important (*ss*) reason reduces the value to 1/256. The number of stalemates triples to nine.

be carried ever further, but the system then quickly becomes incomprehensible. How is one supposed to understand 'seriously slightly moderate' for example? Apart from that, the nine grades can often only be applied to the subject-matter with difficulty. The question whether an interference in the context of the simple triadic model is slight or moderate, or moderate or serious, is already often not easy to answer. As the *Titanic* Case shows, refinements of the scale can resolve some stalemates. But in the light of the increasing problems in application accompanying each refinement, they cannot remove all stalemates.

The only question left is whether a radical removal of stalemate is possible by weighting in the context of each concrete case and doing without any scale at all. If in this process one is left with a relation of precedence, its converse, and a relation of equal rank, then one is left with a model which reduces the nine permutations of the simple triadic model to three: that in which IP_iC is greater than SP_jC, that in which SP_jC is greater than IP_iC, and that in which they are equal. But the last situation is identical with a stalemate. To prevent this, either the relation of equal weight must be excluded in advance as impossible, or it must be asserted that there is no case in which it arises. The former amounts to defining away what one does not want, which is hardly acceptable. The latter leads to the question whether constitutional rights principles and the constitutional argumentation relevant to their application have such a precise structure, that a difference of degree which excludes a stalemate is practically always at hand, making a stalemate so unlikely that it can be ignored for practical purposes. This would be the case if intensities of interference, degrees of importance, and abstract weights were really such that they could be represented on scales with an infinite number of classes. Such a representation would not simply be an idealized model,[76] but the reproduction of an actually existing structure. But there is little in favour of such a structure really existing. It is as true here as it is generally in practical matters that as Aristotle pointed out, 'we must . . . not look for precision in all things alike, but in each class of things such precision as accords with the subject-matter'.[77] Constitutional rights are not a subject-matter which is so finely distinguished that it excludes structural, that is, real balancing stalemates to such an extent as to make them practically insignificant. But that means that a discretion in balancing, as a structural discretion enjoyed by the legislature and the judiciary,[78] really does exist.

Behind this conclusion there lurks, admittedly, a problem. How can stalemates in balancing which are a result of what is, namely the normative structure of constitutional rights, be distinguished from stalemates in

---

[76] See on this N. Jansen, 'Die Abwägung von Grundrechten', *Der Staat*, 36 (1997), 29 ff.

[77] Aristotle, *Nichomachean Ethics*, trans. W. D. Ross, rev. J. O. Urmson, in J. Barnes (ed.), *The Complete Works*, 2 vols. (Princeton, 1984), 1098a.

[78] See on this BVerfGE 96, 56 (63 ff.).

balancing which are only a result of the limits to our possible knowledge? Only the former give rise to structural discretion. The latter can at most be the subject-matter of epistemic discretion. The fact that the question about the distinction between structural and epistemic stalemates in balancing can be asked without criteria for answering it lying readily to hand shows that the distinction between structural and epistemic discretion can be difficult. But the fact that it can be difficult does not mean that it does not exist. And if it does exist, then the admissibility of epistemic discretion is an issue. This is in the main a matter of formal principles.

IV. FORMAL PRINCIPLES

The relationship between substantive and formal principles is one of the most disputed aspects of the theory of principles. By way of preparing an answer to some of the objections of some critics, the position adopted by the theory of principles must first be clarified. This can be summarized in the thesis that the problem of epistemic or knowledge-related discretion can be resolved by balancing formal and substantive principles.[79]

1. Epistemic Discretion as the Outcome of Balancing

The question of the existence of epistemic discretion arises whenever knowledge of what is commanded, prohibited, or left free by constitutional rights is uncertain. Uncertainty can be caused by uncertainty about either empirical or normative premisses. Empirical uncertainty can be a problem in all constitutional justification. It plays a particular role when considering suitability and necessity. The Cannabis Judgment of the Federal Constitutional Court offers an example. Whether the legislature is allowed to prohibit cannabis products depends mainly on whether the interference with constitutionally protected liberty contained in the prohibition is suitable and necessary to combat dangers associated with the drug. If criminal prohibition were not suitable or not necessary it would be definitively prohibited on account of constitutional rights. One could take the view that the Federal Constitutional Court should only permit interference if the truth of those empirical assumptions on which suitability and necessity depend is established. But the court proceeds differently. It does not establish the truth of the legislature's empirical premisses, but their uncertainty: 'Scientifically based knowledge, which necessarily points to the correctness of one or the other strategies, is not available'.[80] None the less, it permits

---

[79] A thorough and instructive examination of this theme can be found in M. Raabe, *Grundrechte und Erkenntnis* (Baden-Baden, 1998).
[80] BVerfGE 90, 145 (182 f.).

the interference with the constitutional right. This is the result of giving the legislature a discretion as regards the knowledge of relevant facts, in other words an empirical epistemic discretion, and locating the legislature's empirical assumptions underlying the ban on cannabis within this discretion.

By contrast, normative epistemic discretion, or normative knowledge-related discretion, arises when it is not clear what the best weighting of the relevant constitutional rights is, and the legislature is given certain limits within which it can take decisions according to its own evaluation. One of the 1998 decisions of the Federal Constitutional Court on protection from redundancy is a good example. It concerned the question whether businesses with fewer than five employees could be exempted from the relatively strict redundancy provisions of employment law with the result that employees in such businesses being made redundant only enjoyed the relatively weak general protection of private law. Here, the employers' freedom of profession guaranteed by article 12(1) Basic Law as a defensive right competed with the state's protective duty, also arising from article 12(1), towards employees. The Federal Constitutional Court required these to be optimized: 'The competing constitutional rights positions are to be understood in the context of their effect on each other, and to be limited in such a way that they become as effective as possible for all concerned'.[81] At the same time, the Court granted the legislature a 'broad liberty of law-making', which embraced not only empirical assessments, but also 'the evaluation of the range of interests, in other words weighting opposing requirements and determining their need of protection'.[82] That means that a breach of the duty to protect employees could only be found if the limits of this discretion are exceeded. The Court denied that the limits had been exceeded by pointing out that employees could be granted the 'constitutionally required minimum protection'[83] through the general provisions of private law. In resolving competing constitutional rights, one can either grant what the constitution states must be granted at a minimum, or one can do more. If neither side is granted less than what must be granted at a minimum, the Constitution has by definition not been breached. That minimum protection was granted here was not only justified by the fact that 'weighty requirements' of the employee were countered by a right of the business 'worthy of protection to a high degree',[84] which points in the direction of a structural stalemate, but also by the fact that the interests of business were seen '*by the legislature* as particularly worthy of protection'.[85] This reference to the legislature's assessment points in the direction

---

[81] BVerfGE 97, 169 (176).   [82] ibid.
[83] BVerfGE 97, 169 (178).   [84] BVerfGE 97, 169 (177).
[85] BVerfGE 97, 169 (180), emphasis added.

of normative knowledge-related discretion.[86] This could be used in reverse. That would occur were the legislature to consider the interests of employees particularly worth protecting and to bring small businesses within the scope of the stronger redundancy provisions. If there is a discretion, that is not unconstitutional either, so long as the minimum position of businesses is not threatened. This marks out the other side of the discretion.

Epistemic discretion in balancing gives rise to particular problems on account of its proximity to structural discretion in balancing, which can also be found in the decision just discussed. Empirical epistemic discretion has in this respect a simpler structure, and will be considered first.

The Cannabis Judgment clearly exposes the main problem with all epistemic discretion. If the legislature is permitted to base its interferences with constitutional rights on uncertain premises, then it is possible that the protection afforded by constitutional rights will be refused on the basis of false assumptions, even though constitutional rights have in reality been breached. Constitutional rights would offer more protection if the legislature were to be refused an epistemic discretion.

The theory of principles can lock on to this general consideration of the structure of epistemic discretion almost automatically. Constitutional rights as principles require the greatest possible realization relative to what is factually and legally possible. Granting the legislature empirical epistemic discretion means allowing for the possibility that rights might not be realized to the greatest extent relative to what is factually possible. The adversely affected constitutional rights principle, as an optimization requirement, demands that no epistemic discretion be permitted. If this were the only relevant factor, a constitutional right could only be limited on the grounds of empirical premises the truth of which was assured. If truth is not ascertainable, one should only proceed on the basis of the empirical premises most favourable to the right in question, that is, those which cannot justify interference or the failure to grant protection.[87]

It is precisely at this point that the formal principle of the democratically legitimated decision-taking competence of the legislature comes into play.[88] This principle is a formal principle because it has no content, but rather states how content is to be established. Thus one could also call it a proce-

---

[86] One could also read this statement as referring to an end-setting discretion. The regulatory reservation of art. 12(1)(2) Basic Law does not identify any reasons for interference. As has been shown above, it therefore permits interferences on the basis of goals which are not prescribed by the Constitution. These include economic goals. End-setting discretion is admittedly not unlimited. In the final analysis its limits are set by balancing, and in doing this, problems of structural and epistemic discretion in balancing emerge. It is thus inevitable that end-setting discretion will merge into epistemic discretion in balancing. Setting the borderlines can be difficult. Nevertheless, as always, that is no reason for not distinguishing between them.

[87] Raabe, *Grundrechte und Erkenntnis*, 228, rightly speaks of a 'constitutional requirement at the epistemic level'. One could also use the concept of epistemic optimization.

[88] 313; see also 191 f.

dural principle. As a procedural principle it requires that the democratically legitimated legislature should take as many important decisions for society as possible.[89] Decisions such as the prohibition or permission of cannabis products are important for society. If the decision in this matter depends upon empirical assessments, then the decision-taking competence of the legislature demanded prima facie by the formal principle includes the competence to determine the issue even in a situation of uncertainty. And with this, the formal principle competes with the substantive constitutional rights principle. The latter prima facie excludes the competence of the legislature to base its decision on uncertain empirical premises unfavourable to the constitutional right; the former prima facie requires just this competence.

There are two extreme solutions to this competition, behind which ultimately the old tension between constitutional rights and democracy can be found.[90] The first consists of an absolute precedence for the substantive constitutional rights principle as against the formal principle in cases of epistemic uncertainty. This would have the consequence that the legislature could only interfere in any way with constitutional rights on the basis of empirical premisses the truth of which was assured. If there is a general right to freedom of action, practically all legislative decisions interfere with constitutional rights. But even apart from that right, most decisions must be evaluated in the light of constitutional rights. There is, for example, hardly a measure in commercial, employment, or environmental law which does not interfere with somebody's freedom of profession or property. Absolute precedence for the substantive constitutional rights principle would thus have the consequence that the legislature could only pursue its goals on the basis of empirical premisses which were reliably true. But the moment one is concerned with reasonably complex contexts, empirical knowledge of this quality is practically never available. Absolute precedence for the substantive constitutional rights principle would thus lead in wide areas to complete or nearly complete legislative paralysis. That cannot be the intention of a constitution which, first of all, has a legislature, and secondly, has a directly democratically legitimated one. The Federal Constitutional Court therefore made the point well: 'Uncertainty about the effects of a law in an uncertain future cannot exclude the power of the legislature to pass that law, even if it has a wide impact'.[91] Absolute precedence for the substantive constitutional rights principle before the principle of the decision-taking competence of the legislature is thus to be rejected. It would be compatible neither with the separation of powers nor with the principle of democracy.[92]

---

[89] 82.
[90] 297 f.; see also R. Alexy, 'Basic Rights and Democracy in Jürgen Habermas's Procedural Paradigm of the Law', *Ratio Juris*, 7 (1994), 227 ff.
[91] BVerfGE 50, 290 (332). [92] See BVerfGE 56, 54 (81).

The other extreme solution is not an option either. It would mean that the legislature could base even extremely intensive interferences in constitutional rights on highly dubious prognoses. Whereas with the absolute precedence of the constitutional rights principle the condition of certain truth would reduce the ability of the legislature to act to a minimum, with absolute precedence for the formal principle the limit of certain falsehood would increase it to a maximum. That cannot be the intention of a constitution which wants to protect constitutional rights. The Federal Constitutional Court is correct at this point as well: 'Conversely, uncertainty as such is not sufficient to give rise to a prognostic discretion on the part of the legislature immune from constitutional review'.[93]

If the extremes are to be rejected, the only potential solutions are moderating ones. These could either require the same degree of certainty in the case of all interferences with constitutional rights, or require different degrees of certainty in the case of different interferences. Only the second solution is compatible with constitutional rights as principles. As principles, constitutional rights require that the certainty of the empirical premises underlying the interference be greater, the more intensive the interference is. This leads to a second Law of Balancing. It goes,

> The more heavily an interference in a constitutional right weighs, the greater must be the certainty of its underlying premises.

Unlike the first Law of Balancing, this second law does not refer to the substantive importance of the reasons underlying the interference, but to their epistemic quality. The first Law of Balancing can therefore be called the 'substantive Law of Balancing', and the second the 'epistemic Law of Balancing'.

It is easy to see that the protases of the 'the-more-statements' of both Laws of Balancing are in substance identical. It is true that the substantive Law of Balancing in the form given above[94] only refers to the intensity of the interference (degree of non-satisfaction or detriment), while the epistemic Law of Balancing just given refers to the weight of the interference. But such variations can easily be clarified and comprehended with the help of the Weight Formula. The concept of the weight of an interference, which has up to now not been systematically introduced, is constructed from two variables in the Weight Formula: the intensity of interference (IP_iC) and the abstract weight of the relevant principle (WP_iA). One can define it as the product of these two values. In discussing the Weight Formula, it was shown that abstract weights can be cancelled out when they are equal.[95] When this applies, the aspect of abstract weight can be removed from the formulation of the epistemic Law of Balancing. The same applies if one is

[93] BVerfGE 50, 290 (332).
[94] 401.　　[95] 408.

only concerned with the relationship between intensity of interference and the certainty of the premisses underlying it. The epistemic Law of Balancing would then read,

> The more intensive an interference in a constitutional right is, the greater must be the certainty of its underlying premisses.

All this is only a matter of various different formulations, which are more or less useful in different circumstances, but which do not change the protases.

The identity of the protases is of great systematic significance. It shows that the substantive constitutional rights principle in issue represents an archimedean point. This common point of reference makes it possible to combine substantive and epistemic elements on the side of the reasons for interference. This combination follows the rule that the concrete importance of satisfying a competing principle (SP_jC) through a statutory measure M justifies the intensity of M's interference in P_i (IP_iC) the less, the more the certainty sinks that M really can achieve the sought-after satisfaction of P_j. Thus the concrete weight of a principle ($WP_{i, j}C$) rises with the degree of empirical uncertainty on the side of the realization of the competing principle.

All this presupposes that talk of degrees of certainty or uncertainty about the legislature's empirical premisses makes sense. This question raises the issue of scales on the epistemic side of the Law of Balancing as well.

In its Co-determination Judgment, the Federal Constitutional Court attempted to distinguish three different degrees of intensity of review: an 'intensive review of content', a 'plausibility review', and an 'evidential review'.[96] This brings a triadic epistemic model into play which has a high degree of formal similarity to the substantive triadic model set out above, and which can be built into the Weight Formula without any great difficulty.[97] It also shares a high degree of plausibility with the substantive three-class scale. It can hardly be doubted that a high intensity of interference demands a high degree of certainty about the underlying empirical premisses. This corresponds to the 'intensive review of content' which the Federal Constitutional Court carries out, for example, in the case of life imprisonment.[98] If both the intensity of interference and the degree of

---

[96] BVerfGE 50, 290 (333).

[97] To do this, 'R' is to be taken for the reliability of the empirical assumptions concerning what the measure in question means for the non-realization of P_i and the realization of P_j in the circumstances of the concrete case (C). This can then be denoted by 'RP_iC' and 'RP_jC'. In this way the Weight Formula can be expanded as follows:

$$WP_{i, j}C = (IP_iC . WP_iA . RP_iC)/(SP_jC . WP_jA . RP_jC)$$

The three epistemic classes of certain or reliable (r), maintainable or plausible (p), and not evidently false (e) can thus be assigned to RP_iC and RP_jC as the values 2^0, 2^{-1}, and 2^{-2}. Of course, a refinement of the triad is possible here as well.

[98] BVerfGE 45, 187 (238).

importance reach the highest degree, then merely moderate certainty on the side of the competing principle will not suffice to justify certain consequential loss on the side of the object interfered with. Moderate certainty arises when the premisses are plausible or maintainable. When in the Cannabis Judgment the Federal Constitutional Court considered it adequate that the empirical assumptions of the legislature were 'maintainable',[99] then it shows that in its view the interference was not at the highest level of intensity. The same applies when it is sufficient that the empirical premisses are not evidently false. In the simple triadic model, that is the lowest degree of certainty.

In this way, the relationship between formal and substantive principles can be relatively easily determined in the case of empirical epistemic discretion. Matters are not quite so easy in the case of normative epistemic discretion. On one hand this is to do with the concept of normative discretion and on the other hand with the difficulty of determining the relationship between structural and epistemic discretion in balancing. What is common to all discretion is that the legislature is free to decide within the scope of its discretion, and that the limits of discretion are set precisely by what the legislature is prohibited from doing and commanded to do. Now epistemic discretion is a discretion which arises from the fact that the knowledge of what is prohibited, commanded, and left free by constitutional rights is uncertain. Granting the legislature an epistemic discretion therefore means giving it the competence to a certain extent, namely the precise extent of knowledge-related discretion, to determine what constitutional rights command, prohibit, and leave free. In respect of empirical epistemic discretion there were plausible grounds for this. Is this also true in respect of normative epistemic discretion?

At first sight, normative epistemic discretion on the part of the legislature seems ruled out from the beginning because it dissolves the limits of structural discretion and thus the obligation of the legislature to respect constitutional rights. If the legislature were free in all cases to decide as judges in their own cause what they were commanded, prohibited, and permitted to do by constitutional rights, one could no longer talk in terms of a real, reviewable, obligation to respect constitutional rights. The legal normativity of constitutional rights could no longer be taken seriously. But such an all-embracing liberty, corresponding to an unlimited normative knowledge-related discretion, is not an option. Epistemic discretion is only an issue in cases of uncertainty. Since, as has been shown, there are numerous cases in which it is certain, or sufficiently certain, how balancing should be done, there are numerous cases in which epistemic discretion is excluded.

So normative epistemic discretion only arises, if at all, in cases of normative uncertainty. The most important case of normative uncertainty in the

---

[99] BVerfGE 90, 145 (182).

field of constitutional rights is uncertainty about balancing. The decisive question is how the relationship between structural and epistemic discretion in balancing is to be determined in cases of uncertainty about balancing.

As an example we can consider once again the decision of the Federal Constitutional Court on protection from redundancy. The fact that the Federal Constitutional Court speaks of a 'broad sphere of liberty in law-making' of the legislature in 'evaluating the interests at stake' does not necessarily mean that it is concerned with normative discretion in balancing. This also applies when it equates the evaluation of the interests at stake with the 'weighting of opposing requirements' and 'determining their need of protection'.[100] All that can easily be understood in terms of a structural balancing stalemate. One only has to class the interests of business and the interests of employees in the concrete situation as broadly equal to reach the conclusion that both excluding small businesses from strict protection against redundancy and including them lies within a structural discretion, and leaves the legislature free. This simply makes the assumption that in this case constitutional rights only admit of a crude classification, so that there is a broad balancing stalemate corresponding to a similarly wide structural discretion in which both the legislative measure and its omission falls. As evaluation and weighting within structural discretion, the 'evaluation of the interests at stake' by the legislature as well as the 'weighting' undertaken by it is then, by definition, not legal evaluation and weighting, but political. Its outcome is legally left free. Within structural discretion, constitutional rights principles can be the subject-matter of balancing, but they cannot determine the balancing on account of the structural stalemate. The reviewing competence of the constitutional court is then limited without the need for an epistemic discretion on the part of the legislature, since the competence of the court ends at the limits of the definitive Ought.[101]

It is of great significance that the same result can be reached by way of a normative epistemic discretion in balancing. The limits of structural discretion in balancing are in this respect identical with the limits of normative epistemic discretion in balancing. The distinction consists solely in the fact that legal considerations are not removed from the discretion. Rather, discretion is between various legal possibilities. On one hand it is considered as arguable, and in this sense possible, that constitutional rights permit, or even require, the extension of strict protection against redundancy to small businesses, as that they prohibit its extension, and on the other hand it is considered impossible to tell which of these two possibilities is the better justified. In this situation, since there are constitutional rights on both sides, there is an epistemic stalemate between them. Each of the two constitutional rights demands the solution more favourable to itself. But on account of the stalemate, neither has the power to determine

---

[100] BVerfGE 97, 169 (176).   [101] 348.

the dispute. The substantive constitutional rights situation is thus epistemically neutral. In this situation, substantive constitutional rights principles do not have the power to prevent the principle of the decision-taking competence of the democratically legitimated legislature from leading to an epistemic discretion in balancing. In the light of the fundamental tension between constitutional rights and democracy, any other solution would be unsustainable. To this extent one can say that there is normative knowledge-related discretion.

2. EPISTEMIC DISCRETION AND THE BINDING NATURE OF THE CONSTITUTION

If a decision may be taken because it falls within an epistemic discretion, then the possibility cannot be excluded that this decision may be false, even though it is permitted. Hitherto unperformed empirical investigations or hitherto unconsidered normative arguments may make the mistake apparent. Epistemic discretion is therefore necessarily bound up with the problem of the divergence between what is actually commanded, prohibited, and left free by constitutional rights, and what can be proved to be commanded, prohibited, and left free by them.[102] This divergence between what is, in other words the ontic, and what can be proved to be the case, in other words the epistemic, seems to lead from knowledge-related discretion to undemonstrable breaches of constitutional rights. The competence of the legislature on the basis of its epistemic discretion to prohibit something by statute, which on the basis of constitutional rights as they really are may not be prohibited, seems to correspond not only to a non-competence on the part of the constitutional court to invalidate the unconstitutional prohibition, but also to a constitutional prohibition on doing this. With this, the possibility of constitutional prohibitions which it is constitutionally prohibited to review seems to enter the scene. The justification of epistemic discretion on the basis of formal principles seems to lead inexorably to a distinction between action-norms [*Handlungsnormen*], that is, norms saying what the legislature is prohibited, commanded, and left free to do, and review-norms [*Kontrollnormen*], that is, norms which form the basis of the review of the legislature by the constitutional court.[103]

The most important critique of formal principles focuses on this divergence. It argues that the epistemic discretion created by formal principles is incompatible with the binding of the legislature to constitutional rights under article 1(3) Basic Law,[104] as it is generally with the binding of the

---

[102] See on this Raabe, *Grundrechte und Erkenntnis*, 147 ff.
[103] See Jestaedt, *Grundrechtsentfaltung im Gesetz*, 259.
[104] Scherzberg, *Grundrechtsschutz und Eingriffsintensität*, 175 f.; M. Gellermann, *Grundrechte in einfachgesetzlichem Gewande* (Tübingen, 2000), 71.

legislature to the constitution under article 20(3).[105] The legal hierarchy is thereby disrupted.[106] The 'backbone of the legal system' gets weakened into a 'process of normative osteomalacia';[107] in short, everything collapses into an uncontrollable mess.

In order to meet this objection, it is important to distinguish two questions. The first is, to what extent do formal principles lead to divergences at all? The second is, whether these divergences are really divergences. Let us start with the first question. Formal principles would have the greatest possible power to create divergences, first, if they were capable on their own of restricting constitutional rights, and secondly, if they were capable of doing this completely. Scherzberg gets close to this when he argues that the formal principle of the decision-taking competence of the legislature extends to making an exception for the legislature from the 'generally assumed normative structure'. The principled nature of constitutional rights, 'their character as optimization requirements' would 'thereby *itself* become a "*principle*" '.[108] Scherzberg seems to be saying with this that where principles compete, formal principles do not simply override substantive ones, they deprive them of their character as optimization requirements. There would then be practically nothing left on the substantive side.

Such a perspective fails to recognize that the formal principle of the decision-taking competence of the legislature on its own does not suffice to override a substantive constitutional rights principle. If this were not so, it would not be impossible to say, 'the interference with this constitutional right is very intensive, and there is not the slightest substantive reason justifying it, but it is none the less permissible because the democratically legitimated legislature can take more decisions when it is permitted to take this decision than when it is not'. If it is clear that a very intensive interference with constitutional rights is not justified by any substantive reason, then this interference unambiguously breaches the constitutional right on the basis of the Weight Formula. When the sentence just given is generalized, it leads to the following: 'breaches of constitutional rights are permissible, because if they are permissible, the legislature can decide more issues than if they are not permissible'. That has a hint of absurdity. It results from the fact that the formal principle of the decision-taking competence of the legislature on its own is being opposed to substantive constitutional rights principles. Procedural formal principles can override substantive constitutional rights principles only in connection with other substantive principles. One could call this the 'Law of Combination'. The Law of Combination makes it clear how easy it is to reduce formal principles ad absurdum when one opposes them to substantive principles in isolation.

[105] Jestaedt, *Grundrechtsentfaltung im Gesetz*, 223 f.
[106] Hain, *Die Grundsätze des Grundgesetzes*, 137.
[107] Jestaedt, *Grundrechtsentfaltung in Gesetz*, 246.
[108] Scherzberg, *Grundrechtsschutz und Eingriffsintensität*, 175.

Things look quite different where knowledge is uncertain. The issue of normative knowledge-related discretion only arises when the weight of competing principles is uncertain. Empirical knowledge-related discretion is only an issue when the empirical premises underlying an interference are unsure. In both cases, formal principles have the sole function of participating in the division of decision-taking competences in the case of uncertainties located in the relationship between substantive principles. The moment uncertainty disappears they go out of action again. This makes it impossible for a constitutional court to say that while the constitutional right has been breached, the competing legal interpretation of the legislature is to be respected on formal grounds.[109]

The admissibility of empirical knowledge-related discretion can hardly be disputed. Someone who demands its total removal is practically demanding the removal of the legislature's capacity to act. That is why this discretion is hardly discussed by the critics of formal principles. At the same time it represents an important example of their central role. Empirical knowledge-related discretion shows that formal principles threaten constitutional rights as little as competing substantive principles. Just as the latter are included within the substantive Law of Balancing, so the former are included in the epistemic Law of Balancing.

Things are similar in the case of normative knowledge-related discretion. Of course, a radical sceptic about balancing can assert at this point that the area of uncertainty about balancing is co-extensive with the area of balancing itself, so that if one grants the legislature a discretion in balancing whenever there is uncertainty, one can never set limits on the basis of balancing, which would severely reduce the binding force of constitutional rights. Against this view it has already been pointed out that rational determinations of intensities of interference and degrees of importance, and thus rational knowledge in the field of balancing, is possible.[110] We only need to add that as interference with a constitutional right increases, so also does not only its substantive resistance, but also the cognizability of gradual distinctions. There is something akin to an epistemic law of increasing marginal discriminability matching the substantive law of diminishing marginal utility. In everyday affairs one often cannot tell how intensive an interference is. As one strikes at the core of the matter, the ability to distinguish increases.

All in all, the degree of divergence involved in admitting the existence of knowledge-related discretion is limited and governable. There simply remains the question whether divergence is tolerable in itself. Should we not always demand the convergence of what applies as a matter of constitu-

---

[109] See on this J.-R. Sieckmann, *Regelmodelle und Prinzipienmodelle des Rechtssystems* (Baden-Baden, 1990), 163.
[110] 402 ff.

tional rights and what is to be taken as applying? This demand expresses none other than the postulate of acting only on the basis of ideal knowledge. Those who strive after this postulate in the field of action have to pay a high price. In constitutional law this price is the substantial incapacity of the legislature. Constitutions with constitutional rights are attempts simultaneously to organize collective action and secure individual rights. In the case of constitutional rights this double aspect is demonstrated by the possibility of legislative limitation of rights. The limitability of enacted constitutional rights is a part of what they are. Knowledge-related discretion adds an epistemic border to substantive limitation. This border is required by the constitution as a whole, in other words, on the grounds of a systematic constitutional argument. But from that perspective, the perspective of what the constitution as a whole requires, the divergence disappears. Knowledge-related discretion hides within constitutional rights. It becomes internalized. It is nevertheless true that the divergence remains as a thorn in the flesh of substantive constitutional rights principles.[111] But this thorn is the unavoidable tribute which the ideal of constitutional rights has to pay for the gain, which is hard to overestimate, of its institutionalization in the world as it is.

[111] See Raabe, *Grundrechte und Erkenntnis*, 171.

Appendix: The Constitutional Rights Provisions of the German Basic Law[1]

Article 1 [Protection of human dignity; human rights; binding nature of constitutional rights]

(1) Human dignity is inviolable. It is the duty of all public authorities to respect and protect it.

(2) For this reason, the German people are committed to inviolable and inalienable human rights as the basis of every human community, and of peace and justice in the world.

(3) The following constitutional rights bind the legislature, the executive, and the judiciary as directly applicable law.

Article 2 [Free development of the personality; right to life and bodily integrity; liberty of the person]

(1) Every person has the right to free development of their personality, to the extent that they do not infringe the rights of others or offend against the constitutional order or public morals.

(2) Every person has the right to life and bodily integrity. Liberty of the person is inviolable. These rights may only be interfered with on a statutory basis.

Article 3 [Equality before the law]

(1) All people are equal before the law.

(2) Men and women have equal rights. The state supports the factual realization of the equal rights of men and women and works towards the removal of existing discrimination.

(3) No person may be disadvantaged or advantaged on account of their sex, birth, race, language, national or social origins, faith, or religious or political opinions. No person may be disadvantaged on account of their disability.

Article 4 [Freedom of faith, conscience, and religion; conscientious objection]

(1) Liberty of faith and conscience and the freedom to confess a religion or worldview are inviolable.

(2) The undisturbed exercise of religion is guaranteed.

(3) No person may be forced into armed military service against their conscience. Details are subject to federal statute law.

---

[1] 23 May 1949, most recently amended by statute of 19 Dec. 2000.

Article 5 [Freedom of speech, press, and broadcasting; freedom of art and science]

(1) Every person has the right freely to express and disseminate their opinions in word, writing, or picture, and to acquire information from generally accessible sources without hindrance. The freedom of the press and the freedom of reporting through broadcasting and film are guaranteed. There is no prior censorship.

(2) These rights are limited by the requirements of the general law, by legal provisions for the protection of young persons, and by the right of personal dignity.

(3) Art and science, research, and teaching are free. Academic freedom does not absolve anyone from fidelity to the Constitution.

Article 6 [Marriage and family]

(1) Marriage and the family stand under the particular protection of the state.

(2) The care and upbringing of children are the natural right of parents and their primary duty. The state community oversees its fulfilment.

(3) Children may only be separated from their families against the will of their parents or guardians on the basis of statute law, where those charged with their upbringing neglect their duty or if the children are in danger of serious maltreatment for other reasons.

(4) Every mother is entitled to the protection and care of the community.

(5) Legislation shall ensure that illegitimate children are granted the same conditions of physical and mental development and social status as legitimate children.

Article 7 [School system]

(1) The entire school system is under the oversight of the state.

(2) Parents and guardians have the right to determine the participation of their children in religious education.

(3) With the exception of non-confessional schools, religious education is a regular subject in all state schools. Without prejudice to the state's right of oversight, religious education is delivered in conformity with the principles of religious communities. No teacher may be obliged to give classes in religious education against their will.

(4) The right to establish private schools is guaranteed. Private schools which are substitutes for state schools require state approval and are subject to the laws of the Regions. Approval is to be granted if the private schools are not inferior to state schools in their educational objectives, facilities, and the qualifications of their teaching staff, and if a segregation of pupils according to the financial means of their parents is not promoted. Approval is to be refused if the economic and legal status of teachers is not adequately secured.

(5) A private primary school is only to be permitted if the educational authority accepts that it meets a special educational need, or if, on application by the parents or guardians, it is to be established as a community school, a confessional school, or a world-view-specific school, and if a state primary school of this type does not exist in the neighbourhood.

(6) Preparatory schools remain abolished.

Article 8 [Freedom of assembly]

(1) All Germans have the right to assemble peaceably and without weapons without prior notification or permission.
(2) As regards assemblies in the open air, this right may be limited by statute or on a statutory basis.

Article 9 [Freedom of association]

(1) All Germans have the right to form corporations and associations.
(2) Associations whose purposes or activities contravene the criminal law, or which are directed against the constitutional order or good international relations, are prohibited.
(3) The right to form associations for the maintenance and enhancement of working and economic conditions is guaranteed to everybody and in respect of all occupations. Agreements which seek to limit or obstruct this right are void; measures directed to this end are illegal. Measures adopted under articles 12*a*, 35(2) and (3), 87*a*(4) and 91 may not be directed against employment disputes which are carried on for the maintenance and enhancement of the working and economic conditions of associations as understood in the first sentence of this paragraph.

Article 10 [Privacy of correspondence, post, and telecommunications]

(1) Privacy of correspondence, as well as privacy of post and telecommunications, are inviolable.
(2) Limitations may only be imposed on a statutory basis. If the limitation serves the protection of the free democratic basic order or the existence or security of the Federation or a Region, statute may provide that the affected party shall not be informed, and that in place of legal process there shall be a review by bodies and subsidiary bodies established by Parliament.

Article 11 [Freedom of movement]

(1) All Germans have the right to move freely within the entire federal territory.
(2) This right may only be limited by statute or on a statutory basis for cases in which persons do not have sufficient means of livelihood and their free movement would be particularly burdensome on the general public, or where necessary to avert an imminent danger to the existence of the free democratic basic order of the Federation or a Region, or in response to epidemics, natural disasters, or particularly serious accidents, to protect young people from serious maltreatment or to prevent the commission of criminal acts.

Article 12 [Freedom of profession]

(1) All Germans have the right to choose their profession, place of work, and training. The exercise of a profession can be regulated by statute or on a statutory basis.
(2) Nobody may be forced to do a particular job, except in the context of traditional general compulsory community service which applies equally to everyone.
(3) Forced labour is only permissible if a deprivation of liberty has been ordered by the courts.

Article 12*a* [Military and substitute service, other forms of obligatory service]

(1) From the age of 18, men may be obliged to perform service in the armed forces, in the Federal Border Guards, or in an organization for civil defence.

(2) Anyone who refuses to perform armed military service for reasons of conscience can be obliged to undertake substitute service. The duration of substitute service may not exceed that of military service. The details shall be regulated by statute law, which is not permitted to affect the freedom of conscientious decision, and which shall provide for the possibility of substitute service which is not connected with the armed forces or the Federal Border Guards in any way.

(3) Those who may be obliged to perform military service and who have not been called up for service under paragraphs 1 or 2, may be obliged by statute or on a statutory basis during a state of defence to perform civilian services or take on employment for the defence of the country, including the protection of the civilian population; obligations by way of public service are only permissible in respect of policing functions or such sovereign functions of public administration which could be undertaken in the context of public service employment. Contracts of employment under the first sentence can be justified in the case of the armed forces in the area of supplies and public administration; obligations undertaken in the context of contracts of employment to supply the civilian population are only permissible to cover essential needs or to secure their protection.

(4) If the need for civilian services in civilian and permanent military hospitals during a state of defence cannot be met on a voluntary basis, women from the age of 18 to 55 may be appointed to such services by statute or on a statutory basis. On no account may they perform armed service.

(5) For the period of time preceding a state of defence, obligations under paragraph 3 may only be imposed in accordance with article 80*a*(1). To prepare for services under paragraph 3 for which particular knowledge or abilities are necessary, participation at educational institutions can be made obligatory by statute or on a statutory basis. To this extent, the first sentence does not apply.

(6) If in a state of defence the need for manpower in the areas identified in the second sentence of paragraph 3 cannot be met on a voluntary basis, the liberty of Germans to exercise a profession or to give up a job may be limited by statute or on a statutory basis. Before the state of defence exists, paragraph (5)(1) applies correspondingly.

Article 13 [Inviolability of the home]

(1) The home is inviolable.

(2) Searches may only be authorized by a judge or, if delay is dangerous, by other bodies as provided for by statute law, and then only in the manner prescribed by the relevant law.

(3) If specific facts give rise to the suspicion that someone has committed a particularly serious criminal offence, specifically identified as such in a statute, technical means for the acoustic observation of accommodation in which the suspect is supposed to reside may be adopted on the basis of a judicial order if the discovery of the facts by other means is disproportionately difficult or with-

out hope of success. The duration of the measure is to be fixed. The order is made by a body constituted of three judges. If delay is dangerous, it can also be made by an individual judge.

(4) In order to combat serious dangers for public security, in particular a general danger or a threat to life, technical means for the observation of accommodation may only be adopted on the basis of a judicial order. If delay is dangerous, the measure can also by approved by another body determined by statute; a judicial decision is to be obtained afterwards without delay.

(5) If technical means are intended exclusively for the protection of persons involved in an operation on accommodation, the measure can be approved by a body determined by statute. Further use of the information acquired in this way is only permissible for the purposes of criminal investigation or the combating of dangers, and only if the legality of the measure has been judically established; if delay is dangerous, a judicial decision is to be obtained afterwards without delay.

(6) The Federal Government reports annually to the Federal Assembly on the use of technical means under paragraph 3, as well as under paragraph 4 to the extent that they are within the competence of the Federation, and under paragraph 5 to the extent that the measures require judicial oversight. A committee elected by the Federal Assembly exercises parliamentary control on the basis of this report. The Regions guarantee an equivalent parliamentary control.

(7) Apart from that, infringements and limitations may only be undertaken to prevent a general danger or a risk to the life of individuals on a statutory basis, also to guard against a pressing threat to public security and order, in particular for the removal of accommodation emergencies, to combat epidemics, or to protect young people in danger.

Article 14 [Property, inheritance law, and deprivation]

(1) Property and the law of inheritance are guaranteed. The content and limits of this right are determined by law.
(2) Property carries with it obligations. Its use must also serve the public interest.
(3) A deprivation of property is only permissible if it serves the public interest. It may only be carried out by statute or on the basis of a statute which regulates the type and amount of compensation. Compensation is to be determined by a fair balancing of the interests of the general public and the affected parties. In cases of dispute about the level of compensation, access to the ordinary courts remains open.

Article 15 [Nationalization, transfer into public ownership]

Land, natural resources, and the means of production may be transferred into public ownership or other forms of public management for the purposes of nationalization by a statute which regulates the type and amount of compensation. As regards compensation, articles 14(3)(3) and 14(3)(4) apply correspondingly.

Article 16 [Expatriation, extradition]

(1) German citizenship may not be withdrawn. Deprivation of citizenship may only take place on a statutory basis, and may only occur against the wishes of affected parties if it does not make them stateless.

(2) No German may be extradited to another country. An exception may be made by statute for extradition to a member state of the European Union or to an international court, so long as Rule of Law principles are respected.

Article 16*a* [Asylum]

(1) The politically persecuted enjoy a right of asylum.
(2) Any person arriving from a member state of the European Community, or from a third state in which the application of the Convention on the Legal Status of Refugees and the Convention for the Protection of Human Rights and Fundamental Freedoms is secured, may not appeal to paragraph 1. States outside of the European Community to which the preconditions contained in the first sentence of this paragraph apply will be identified by a statute which requires the consent of the Federal Council. In the situation envisaged in the first sentence, measures terminating residence can be enforced independently of any legal proceedings commenced in respect of them.
(3) States may be identified by a statute, which requires the consent of the Federal Council, in which on the basis of the legal situation, the application of law, and the general political circumstances, it appears to be guaranteed that neither political persecution nor inhuman or degrading punishment or treatment takes place. It will be presumed that immigrants from such a state are not persecuted, so long as they do not allege facts which give rise to the conclusion that contrary to the presumption they are politically persecuted.
(4) The enforcement of measures terminating residence in the situations envisaged in paragraph 3 and in other cases which are obviously unfounded or which must be treated as obviously unfounded, shall only be set aside by the court if there are serious doubts about the legality of the measure; the extent of review may be limited and late evidence disregarded. The detail shall be regulated by statute.
(5) Paragraphs 1 to 4 do not prevent the regulation of the competence to examine applications for asylum and mutual recognition of decisions in respect of asylum applications under international treaties between member states of the European Community and third party states, which have regard for obligations arising from the Treaty concerning the Legal Status of Refugees, and the Convention for the Protection of Human Rights and Fundamental Freedoms, implementation of which must be guaranteed in the third party states.

Article 17 [Right of petition]

Everyone has the right, individually or together with others, to address written requests or complaints to the appropriate authorities and to Parliament.

Article 17*a* [Limitations of constitutional rights during compulsory military and substitute service]

(1) Laws concerning compulsory military and substitute service may provide that during the period of military or substitute service, the constitutional rights of members of the armed forces or substitute services to express and disseminate their opinions by way of word, writing or picture (art. 5(1)(1) clause 1), freely to assemble (art. 8), and the right of petition (art. 17) in so far as it grants the right to address requests or complaints together with others, may be limited.

(2) Laws designed to defend and protect the civil population may provide that free-dom of movement (art. 11) and the inviolability of the home (art. 13) may be limited.

Article 18 [Forfeiture of constitutional rights]

Anyone who abuses their freedom of expression, in particular the freedom of the press (art. 5(1)), academic freedom (art. 5(3)), freedom of assembly (art. 8), free-dom of association (art. 9), the privacy of correspondence, post and telecommuni-cations (art. 10), property (art. 14) or the right of asylum (art. 16*a*) to fight against the free democratic basic order forfeits these constitutional rights. The fact of forfei-ture and its extent are to be determined by the Federal Constitutional Court.

Article 19 [Limitation and core content of constitutional rights, applica-tion to legal persons, guarantee of access to justice]

(1) To the extent that this Basic Law permits a constitutional right to be limited by statute or on a statutory basis, that law must apply generally and not for a specific case. Apart from that, the statute must identify the constitutional right by its article.
(2) In no case may the core content of a constitutional right be infringed.
(3) Constitutional rights are also valid for domestic legal persons, to the extent that their substance makes them so applicable.
(4) If any person's rights are violated by a public authority, they have access to the courts. If no other courts with jurisdiction are established, recourse may be had to the ordinary courts. Article 10(2)(2) remains unaffected.

Article 20 [Constitutional principles; right of resistance][2]

(1) The Federal Republic of Germany is a democratic and social federal state.
(2) All state authority proceeds from the people. It is exercised by the people in elec-tions and referendums and through specific legislative, exective, and judicial organs.
(3) Legislation is bound to the constitutional order; the Executive and Judiciary are subject to statute and law.
(4) All Germans have the right of resistance against any person who undertakes to set aside this order, if other remedies are unavailable.

Article 33 [Equality of all citizens, public service]

(1) Every German has the same civic rights and duties in every Region.
(2) Every German has the same right of access to every public office, according to their ability, skills, and expertise.
(3) The enjoyment of civil and civic rights, the admission to public office as well as the rights acquired in public service are independent of religious commitment. No one may be disadvantaged by their membership or non-membership of a religion or world-view.
(4) The exercise of sovereign authority as an ongoing function is generally to be delegated to members of the public service, who are employed in a public law relationship of service and loyalty.

[2] Note that the constitutional complaint procedure only permits reliance upon para. 4.

(5) Public service law is to be regulated with regard for the traditional principles of the professional civil service.

Article 38 [Federal Assembly, members, elections]

(1) Members of the German Federal Assembly are to be elected in general, direct, free, equal, and secret ballots. They are representatives of the entire people, not bound to mandates or instructions, subject only to their consciences.
(2) Those who have reached the age of 18 are entitled to vote. Those who have reached the age of majority are electable.
(3) Further details are regulated by federal statute.

Article 101 [Exceptional courts]

(1) Courts of exceptional jurisdiction are prohibited. Nobody may be deprived of access to their proper judge according to law.
(2) Courts for specific areas of jurisdiction may only be established by statute.

Article 103 [Right to a hearing; constitutional rights of accused persons]

(1) Everybody has a right to a hearing before the courts.
(2) An act may only be punished if its criminal nature is established by law in advance of its commission.
(3) Nobody may be punished under general criminal law more than once for the same act.

Article 104 [Legal guarantees in cases involving deprivation of liberty]

(1) The liberty of the person can only be limited on the basis of a formal statute and having regard to the requisite formalities therein. Detained persons may not be mistreated, either emotionally or physically.
(2) Only a judge may determine the admissibility and duration of a deprivation of liberty. In the case of every deprivation of liberty not based on a judicial order, a judicial decision must be reached without delay. The police are not permitted to hold anyone arrested on their own authority beyond the end of the day after the arrest. Details are to be regulated by statute.
(3) Any person provisionally detained on suspicion of having committed a criminal offence is to be brought before a judge at the latest on the day after the arrest, who will inform them of the reasons for their arrest, examine them, and provide them with an opportunity to make objections. The judge must without delay either issue a written detention order, giving reasons, or let the person free.
(4) A relative of the detainee or somebody he trusts is to be informed without delay of every judicial decision ordering or determining the duration of a deprivation of liberty.

The constitutional complaint: Article 93(1)(no. 4*a*) Basic Law

The Federal Constitutional Court shall rule . . . on constitutional complaints, which can be raised by anyone on the grounds that their constitutional rights, or their rights contained in articles 20(4), 33, 38, 101, 103, and 104, have been infringed by a public authority.

Bibiography

Aarnio, A., *Philosophical Perspectives in Jurisprudence* (Helsinki, 1983).
—— Alexy, R., and Peczenik, A., 'The Foundation of Legal Reasoning', in A. Aarnio and D. N. MacCormick (eds.), *Legal Reasoning*, i (Aldershot, 1992), 15–40, 233–81.
Abendroth, W., *Das Grundgesetz, Eine Einführung in seine politischen Probleme*, 7th edn. (Pfullingen, 1978).
Achterberg, N., 'Antinomien verfassungsgestaltender Grundentsscheidungen', *Der Staat*, 8 (1969), 159–80.
Adomeit, K., *Gestaltungsrechte, Rechtsgeschäfte, Ansprüche. Zur Stellung der Privatautonomie im Rechtssystem* (Berlin, 1969).
—— 'Zivilrechtstheorie und Zivilrechtsdogmatik—mit einem Beitrag zur Theorie der subjektiven Rechte', *Jahrbuch für Rechtssoziologie und Rechtstheorie*, 2 (1972), 503–22.
—— *Rechtstheorie für Studenten. Normlogik—Methodenlehre—Rechtspolitologie*, 2nd edn. (Heidelberg and Hamburg, 1981).
Aicher, J., *Das Eigentum als subjectives Recht: Zugleich ein Beitrag zur Theorie des subjektiven Rechts* (Berlin, 1975).
Albert, H., 'Erkenntnis und Recht. Die Jurisprudenz im Lichte des Kritizismus', *Jahrbuch für Rechtssoziologie und Rechtstheorie*, 2 (1972), 80–96.
Alchourrón, C. E., and Bulygin, E., *Normative Systems* (Vienna and New York, 1971).
Aldag, H., *Die Gleichheit vor dem Gesetz in der Reichsverfassung* (Berlin, 1925).
Alexy, R., 'Zum Begriff des Rechtsprinzips', *Rechtstheorie*, Beiheft 1 (1979), 59–87.
—— 'Die logische Analyse juristischer Entscheidungen', ARSP, Beiheft NF 14 (1980), 181–212.
—— 'Teleologische Auslegung und Gesetzbindung', in *Sprache und Recht, Loccumer Protokolle*, 31 (1980), 143–51.
—— 'Die Idee einer prozeduralen Theorie der juristischen Argumentation', *Rechtstheorie*, Beiheft 2 (1981), 177–88.
—— 'Juristische Argumentation und praktische Vernunft', *Jahrbuch der Akademie der Wissenschaften in Göttingen*, 1982, 29–32.
—— 'Rechtsregeln und Rechtsprinzipien', Lecture before the Eleventh World Congress of the International Association for Philosophy of Law and Social Philosophy (appears in the proceedings of the Congress) (Helsinki, 1983).
—— 'Das Gebot der Rücksichtnahme im baurechtlichen Nachbarschutz', DÖV 1984, 953–63.
—— *A Theory of Legal Argumentation*, trans. Ruth Adler and Neil MacCormick (Oxford, 1989).
—— 'Basic Rights and Democracy in Jürgen Habermas's Procedural Paradigm of the Law', *Ratio Juris*, 7 (1994), 227–38.
—— 'On the Structure of Legal Principles', *Ratio Juris*, 13 (2000), 294–304.
Amelung, K., *Rechtsgüterschutz und Schutz der Gesellschaft* (Frankfurt a. M., 1972).
Anderson, A. R., 'Logic, Norms and Roles', *Ratio*, 4 (1962), 36–49.

Anschütz, G., *Die Verfassung des Deutschen Reichs*, 14th edn. (Berlin, 1933) (reprint: Darmstadt, 1965).

Aristotle, *Nichomachean Ethics*, trans. W. D. Ross, rev. J. O. Urmson, in J. Barnes (ed.) *The Complete Works*, 2 vols. (Princeton, 1984), 1098a, 1729–1867.

—— *Politics*, trans. B. Jowett, in J. Barnes (ed.) *The Complete Works*, 2 vols. (Princeton, 1984), 1986–2129.

Arrow, K. J., *Social Choice and Individual Values*, 2nd edn. (New York, London, and Sydney, 1963).

Austin, J., *Lectures on Jurisprudence or The Philosophy of Positive Law*, i, 4th edn (London, 1873).

Austin, J. L., *How to do things with Words* (London, Oxford, and New York, 1962).

—— 'Performative Utterances', in id., *Philosophical Papers*, ed. J. O. Urmson and G. J. Warnock, 2nd edn. (London, Oxford, and New York, 1970), 233–52.

Bachof, O., 'Reflexwirkungen und subjektive Rechte im öffentlichen Recht', in O Bachof, M. Drath, O. Gönnenwein, and E. Walz (eds.), *Gedächtnisschrift für W. Jellinek* (Munich, 1955), 287–307.

—— 'Freiheit des Berufs', in K. A. Bettermann, H. C. Nipperdey and U. Scheuner (eds.), *Die Grundrechte*, vol. 3.1 (Berlin, 1958), 155–265.

—— 'Diskussionsbeitrag', VVDStRL 39 (1981), 175.

Badura, P., 'Das Prinzip der sozialen Grundrechte und seine Verwirklichung im Recht der Bundesrepublik Deutschland', *Der Staat*, 14 (1975), 17–48.

Baier, K., *The Moral Point of View* (Ithaca, NY and London, 1958).

Barry, B., *Political Argument* (London and New York, 1965).

Bayles, M. D., 'Courts vs Legislatures as Protectors of Human Rights', Lecture before the 11th World Congress of the International Association of Legal and Social Philosophy (appears in the proceedings of the Congress) (Helsinki, 1983).

Becker, E., 'Verwaltung und Verwaltungsrechtsprechung', VVDStRL 14 (1956), 96–131.

Becker, O., *Untersuchungen über den Modalkalkül* (Meisenheim and Glan, 1952).

Behrends, O., 'Institutionelles und prinzipielles Denken im römischen Privatrecht', *Zeitschrift der Savigny-Stiftung für Rechtsgeschichte, Romanistische Abteilung*, 95 (1978), 187–231.

Beinhardt, G., 'Das Recht der öffentlichen Sicherheit und Ordnung in seinem Verhältnis zur Eingriffs- und Leistungverwaltung', DVB1 1961, 608–13.

Benda, E., 'Die Menschenwürde', in E. Benda, W. Maihofer, and H.-J. Vogel (eds.), *Handbuch des Verfassungsrechts* (Berlin and New York, 1983), 107–28.

Bentham, J., *The Works of Jeremy Bentham*, ed. J. Bowring, facsimile of the 1835–43 edition, vol. iii (New York, 1962).

—— *An Introduction to the Principles of Morals and Legislation*, ed. J. H. Burns and H. L. A. Hart (London, 1970).

—— *Of Laws in General*, ed. H. L. A. Hart (London, 1970).

Berg, W., *Konkurrenzen schrankendivergenter Freiheitsrechte im Grundrechtsabschnitt des Grundgesetzes*, (Berlin and Frankfurt 1968).

Berlin, I., 'Two Concepts of Liberty' in id., *Four Essays on Liberty* (London, Oxford, and New York, 1969), 118–72.

Bethge, H., *Zur Problematik von Grundrechtskollisionen* (Munich, 1977).

—— 'Rechtsschutzprobleme eines rundfunkspezifischen Pluralismus', *Ufita*, 81 (1978), 75–96.

Bibliography

Bethge, H., 'Grundrechtsverwirklichung und Grundrechtssicherung durch Organisation und Verfahren', NJW 1982, 1–7.

Betterman, K. A., *Grenzen der Grundrechte* (Berlin, 1968).

Bierling, E. R., *Zur Kritik der juristischen Grundbegriffe* (Part 1, Gotha, 1877; Part 2, Gotha, 1883).

Blaesing, H., *Grundrechtskollisionen*, Diss. (Bochum, 1974).

Bleckmann, A., *Allgemeine Grundrechtslehren* (Cologne and Berlin, 1979).

Böckenförde, E.-W., 'Grundrechtstheorie und Grundrechtsinterpretation', NJW 1974, 1529–38.

—— 'Die Methoden der Verfassungsinterpretation—Bestandsaufnahme und Kritik', NJW 1976, 2089–99.

—— *Staat, Gesellschaft, Freiheit* (Frankfurt a. M., 1976).

—— 'Die Sozialen Grundrechte im Verfassungsgefüge', in E-W. Böckenförde, J. Jekewitz, and T. Ramm (eds.), *Soziale Grundrechte* (Heidelberg and Karlsruhe, 1981), 7–16.

—— 'Grundrechte als Grundsatznormen. Zur gegenwärtigen Lage der Grundrechtsdogmatik', in id., *Staat, Verfassung, Demokratie* (Frankfurt a. M., 1991).

Böckenförde, W., *Der allgemeine Gleichheitssatz und die Aufgabe des Richters. Ein Beitrag zur Frage der Justitiabilität von Art.3 Abs.1 des Bonner Grundgesetzes* (Berlin 1957).

Borowski, M., *Grundrechte als Prinzipien* (Baden-Baden, 1998).

Brandenburg, H., *Die teleologische Reduktion* (Göttingen, 1983).

Breuer, R., 'Grundrechte als Anspruchsnormen', in O. Bachof, L. Heigl, and K. Redeker (eds.), *Verwaltungsrecht zwischen Freiheit, Teilhabe und Bindung, Festgabe zum 25jährigen Bestehen des Bundesverwaltungsgerichts* (Munich, 1978), 89–119.

Brinkmann, K., *Grundrechts-Kommentar zum Grundgesetz für die Bundesrepublik Deutschland vom 23.5.1949* (Bonn, 1967).

Brinz, A., *Lehrbuch der Pandekten*, i, 2nd edn. (Erlangen, 1873).

Brunner, G., *Die Problematik der sozialen Grundrechte* (Tübingen, 1971).

Bucher, E., *Das subjektive Recht als Normsetzungsbefugnis* (Tübingen, 1965).

Bühler, O., *Die subjektiven öffentlichen Rechte und ihr Schutz in der deutschen Verwaltungsrechtsprechung*, (Berlin, Stuttgart and Leipzig, 1914).

Bydlinski, F., 'Bemerkungen über Grundrechte und Privatrecht', ÖzöR 12 (1962/3), 421–60.

Caemmerer, E. v., *Das Problem des Kausalzummenhangs im Privatrecht* (Freiburg, 1956).

Canaris, C.-W., *Systemdenken und Systembegriff in der Jurisprudenz*, 2nd edn. (Berlin, 1983).

Carnap, R., *Meaning and Necessity*, 2nd edn. (Chicago and London, 1956).

Chlosta, J., *Der Wesensgehalt der Eigentumsgewährleistung* (Berlin, 1975).

Christie, G. C., 'The Model of Principles', Duke LJ 1968, 649–69.

Coing, H., *Die juristischen Auslegungsmethoden und die Lehren der allgemeinen Hermeneutik* (Cologne and Opladen, 1959).

—— 'Zur Geschichte des Begriffs "subjektives Recht" ', in id., *Zur Geschichte des Privatrechtssystems* (Frankfurt a. M., 1962), 29–55.

Corbin, A. L., 'Legal Analysis and Terminology', Yale LJ 29 (1919), 163–73.

Däubler, W., 'Recht auf Arbeit verfassungswidrig?' in U. Achten *et al.* (eds.), *Recht auf Arbeit—eine politische Herausforderung* (Neuwied and Darmstadt, 1978), 159–80.

Davidson, D., 'The Logical Form of Action Sentences', in N. Rescher (ed.), *The Logic of Decision and Action*, (Pittsburgh, 1967), 81–95.

Degenhart, C., *Systemgerechtigkeit und Selbstbindung des Gesetzgebers als Verfassungspostulat* (Munich, 1976).

Degenkolbe, G., 'Über logische Struktur und gesellschaftliche Funktionen von Leerformeln', *Kölner Zeitschrift für Soziologie und Sozialpsychologie*, 17 (1965), 327–38.

Delbrück, J., 'Quo vadis Bundesverfassungsgericht?' in J. Delbrück, K. Ipsen, and D. Rauschning (eds.), *Recht im Dienst des Friedens, Festschrift für E. Menzel* (Berlin, 1975), 83–105.

Denninger, E., *Rechtsperson und Solidarität* (Frankfurt and Berlin, 1967).

—— *Polizei in der freitheitlichen Demokratie* (Frankfurt and Berlin, 1968).

—— *Staatsrecht*, i (Reinbek, 1973), ii (Reinbek, 1979).

Deutsch, E., *Haftungsrecht, Erster Band: Allgemeine Lehren* (Cologne, Berlin, Bonn, and Munich, 1976).

Dreier, R., *Zum Begriff der 'Natur der Sache'* (Berlin, 1965).

—— 'Bemerkungen zur Rechtserkenntnistheorie', in *Rechtstheorie*, Beiheft 1 (1979), 89–105.

—— *Recht—Moral—Ideologie* (Frankfurt a. M., 1981).

—— 'Das Menschenbild im Recht', in W. Böhme (ed.), *Was halten wir für Recht?*, *Herrenalber Texte*, 29 (1981), 87–94.

—— 'Recht und Gerechtigkeit' in German Institute for Distance Learning at Tübingen University (ed.), *Funkkolleg Recht, Studienbegleitbrief 2* (Weinheim and Basle, 1982), 11–37.

Dürig, G., 'Das Eigentum als Menschenrecht', ZGesStW 109 (1953), 326–50.

—— 'Der Grundrechtssatz von der Menschenwürde', AöR 81 (1956), 117–57.

—— 'Grundrechte und Zivilrechtsprechung', in T. Maunz (ed.), *Festschrift für Hans Nawiasky* (Munich, 1956), 157–90.

—— 'Ammerkung zum Elfes-Urteil', JZ 1957, 169–73.

—— 'Zum "Lüth-Urteil" des Bundesverfassungsgerichts vom 15.1.1958', DÖV 1958, 194–7.

Dworkin, R., 'No Right Answer?' in P. M. S. Hacker and J. Raz (eds.), *Law, Morality and Society: Essays in Honour of H. L. A. Hart* (Oxford, 1977), 58–84.

—— *Taking Rights Seriously*, 2nd edn. (London, 1978).

—— 'What is Equality? Part 1: Equality of Welfare', *Philosophy and Public Affairs*, 10 (1981), 185–246.

Eckhoff, T., 'Guiding Standards in Legal Reasoning', *Current Legal Problems*, 29 (1976), 205–19.

Eckhold-Schmidt, F., *Legitimation durch Begründung: Eine erkenntniskritische Analyse der Drittwirkungs-Kontroverse* (Berlin, 1974).

Edwards, P., *The Logic of Moral Discourse* (New York and London, 1955).

Ehmke, H., *Wirtschaft und Verfassung. Die Verfassungsrechtsprechung des Supreme Court zur Wirtschaftsregulierung* (Karlsruhe, 1961).

—— 'Prinzipien der Verfassungsinterpretation', VVDStRL 20 (1963), 53–102.

Ehrenfels, C. v., *System der Werttheorie*, i (Leipzig, 1897), ii (Leipzig, 1898).

Ehrlich, E., *Die juristische Logik* (Tübingen, 1918).

—— 'Freie Rechtsfindung und freie Rechtswissenschaft', in id., *Recht und Leben. Gesammelte Schriften zur Rechtstatsachenforschung und zur Freirechtslehre* (Berlin, 1967), 170–202.

Ely, J. H., *Democracy and Distrust* (Cambridge, Mass. and London, 1980).

Engisch, K., *Logische Studien zur Gesetzesanwendung*, 3rd edn. (Heidelberg, 1963).

Enneccerus, L., and Nipperdey, H. C., *Allgemeiner Teil des Bürgerlichen Rechts*, 2 vols., 15th edn. (Tübingen, 1959/60).

Erichsen, H.-U., *Staatsrecht und Verfassungsgerichtsbarkeit 1*, 2nd edn. (Munich, 1976), 3rd edn. (Munich, 1982).

Esser, J., 'Möglichkeiten und Grenzen des dogmatischen Denkens im modernen Zivilrecht', AcP 172 (1972), 97–130.

—— 'Dogmatik zwischen Theorie und Praxis', in F. Baur, J. Esser, F. Kübler, and E. Steinhoff (eds.), *Funktionswandel der Privatrechtsinstitutionen, Festschrift für L. Raiser* (Tübingen, 1974), 517–39.

—— *Grundsatz und Norm in der richterlichen Fortbildung des Privatrechts*, 3rd edn. (Tübingen, 1974).

—— and Schmidt, E., *Schuldrecht*, vol. 1.2, 5th edn. (Heidelberg and Karlsruhe, 1976).

Evers, H.-U., 'Zur Auslegung von Art. 2 Abs.1 des Grundgesetzes, insbesondere zur Persönlichkeitskerntheorie', AöR 90 (1965), 88–98.

Eyermann, E., 'Gleichheitssatz, Wurzel des Willkürverbots?' in *Verfassung und Verfassungsrechtsprechung, Festschrift zum 25-jährigen Bestehen des BayVGH* (Munich, 1972), 45–53.

Fechner, E., *Die soziologische Grenze der Grundrechte* (Tübingen, 1954).

Finnis, J., *Natural Law and Natural Rights* (Oxford, 1980).

Fitch, F. B., 'A Revision of Hohfield's Theory of Legal Concepts', *Logique et Analyse*, 10 (1967), 269–76.

Fohmann, L. H., *Konkurrenzen und Kollisionen im Verfassungsrecht* (Berlin, 1978).

Føllesdal, D., and Hilpinen, R., 'Deontic Logic: An Introduction', in R. Hilpinen (ed.), *Deontic Logic: Introductory and Systematic Readings* (Dordrecht, 1971), 1–35.

Forsthoff, E., *Verfassungsprobleme des Sozialstaats* (Münster, 1954).

—— 'Die Umbildung des Verfassungsgesetzes', in H. Barion, E. Forsthoff and W. Weber (eds.), *Festschrift für C. Schmitt* (Berlin, 1959), 35–62.

—— *Zur Problematik der Verfassungsauslegung* (Stuttgart, 1961).

—— 'Zur heutigen Situation einer Verfassungslehre', in H. Barion, E.-W. Böckenförde, E. Forsthoff and W. Weber (eds.), *Epirrhosis, Festgabe für Carl Schmitt* (Berlin, 1968), 185–211.

—— *Der Staat der Industriegesellschaft*, 2nd edn. (Munich, 1971).

Frankena, W. K., 'Value and Valuation', in P. Edwards (ed.), *The Encyclopaedia of Philosophy*, vii (New York and London, 1967), 229–32.

—— *Ethics* (Englewood Cliffs, NJ, 1963).

Frege, G., *Conceptual Notation*, trans. T. W. Bynum (Oxford, 1972).

—— 'Thoughts', in *Logical Investigations*, trans. P. T. Geach and R. H. Stoothoff (Oxford, 1977).

Freytag Löringhoff, B. v., 'Die logische Struktur des Begriffs Freiheit', in J. Simon (ed.), *Freiheit. Theoritsche und praktische Aspekte des Problems* (Freiburg and Munich, 1977), 37–53.

Friauf, K.-H., 'Zur Rolle der Grundrechte im Interventions und Leistungsstaat', DVBl 1971, 674–82.

Friedrich, M., 'Die Grundlagendiskussion in der Weimarer Staatsrechtslehre', *Politische Vierteljahresschrift*, 13 (1972), 582–98.

Friesenhahn, E., 'Der Wandel des Grundrechtsverständnisses', in *Verhandlungen des fünfzigsten Deutschen Juristentages* (Hamburg, 1974; ii, Munich, 1974), G1–37.

Gäfgen, G., *Theorie der wirtschaftlichen Entscheidung*, 3rd edn. (Tübingen, 1974).

Gallwas, H.-U., *Faktische Beeinträchtigungen im Bereich der Grundrechte* (Berlin, 1970).

Gamillscheg, F., 'Die Grundrechte im Arbeitsrecht', AcP 164 (1964), 385–445.

Geiger, T., *Vorstudien zu einer Soziologie des Rechts*, 2nd edn. (Neuwied and Berlin, 1964).

Geiger, W., 'Das Menschenbild des Grundgesetzes', in W. Böhme (ed.), *Was halten wir für Recht?*, Herrenalber Texte, 29 (1981), 9–23.

Gellermann, M., *Grundrechte in einfachgesetzlichem Gewande* (Tübingen, 2000).

Gentz, M., 'Zur Verhältnismäßigkeit von Grundrechtsteingriffen', NJW 1968, 1600–7.

Gerber, C. F. v., *System des Deutschen Privatrechts*, 2nd edn. (Jena, 1850).

Gerber, H., *Die weltanschaulichen Grundlagen des Staates* (Stuttgart, 1930).

Gewirth, A., 'Are there any Absolute Rights?' Phil Q 31 (1981), 1–16.

—— 'There are Absolute Rights', Phil Q 32 (1982), 348–53.

Gierke, O. v., *Die soziale Aufgabe des Privatrechts* (Berlin, 1889).

—— *Deutsches Privatrecht*, ii (Leipzig, 1905).

Giese, B., *Das Würde-Konzept. Eine norm-funktionale Explikation des Begriffes Würde in Art.1 Abs.1 GG* (Berlin, 1975).

Goble, G. W., 'Affirmative and Negative Legal Relations', Ill LQ 4 (1922), 94–106.

—— 'Negative Legal Relations Re-examined', Ill LQ 5 (1922), 36–49.

Goerlich, H., *Wertordnung und Grundgesetz* (Baden-Baden, 1973).

—— *Grundrechte als Verfahrensgarantien* (Baden-Baden, 1981).

Göldner, D. C., *Verfassungsprinzip und Privatrechtsnorm in der verfassungskonformen Auslegung und Rechtsfortbildung. Verfassungskonkretisierung als Methoden und Kompetenzproblem* (Berlin, 1969).

Götz, V., *Recht der Wirstchaftssubventionen* (Munich and Berlin, 1966).

Grabitz, E., 'Der Grundsatz der Verhältnismaßigkeit in der Rechtsprechung des Bundesverfassungsgerichts', AöR 98 (1973), 568–616.

—— *Freiheit und Verfassungsrecht. Kritische Untersuchungen zur Dogmatik und Theorie der Freiheitsrechte* (Tübingen, 1976).

—— 'Freiheit als Verfassungsprinzip', *Rechtstheorie*, 8 (1977), 1–18.

Grimmer, K., *Demokratie und Grundrechte* (Berlin, 1980).

Gross, H., 'Standards as Law', *Annual Survey of American Law 1968/69*, 575–80.

Haag, K., *Rationale Strafzumessung* (Cologne and Berlin, 1970).

Haas, D., 'Freie Entfaltung der Persönlichkeit', DÖV 1954, 70–2.

Häberle, P., 'Grundrechte im Leistungsstaat', VVDStRL 30 (1972), 43–141.

—— 'Das Bundesverfassungsgericht im Leistungsstaat. Die Numerus-clausus-Entscheidung vom. 18.7.1972', DÖV 1972, 729–40.

—— 'Die offene Gesellschaft der Verfassungsinterpreten', JZ 1975, 297–305.

Häberle, P., (ed.), *Verfassungsgerichtsbarkeit* (Darmstadt, 1976).
—— *Die Wesensgehaltgarantie des Artikel 19 Abs. 2 Grundgesetz*, 3rd edn. (Heidelberg, 1983).
Habermas, J., 'Discourse Ethics: Notes on a Program of Philosophical Justification', in *Moral Consciousness and Communicative Action*, trans. Christian Lenhardt and Shierry Weber Nicholsen (Cambridge, 1990).
—— *Between Facts and Norms*, trans. William Rehg (Cambridge, 1996).
—— 'Reply to Symposium Participants, Benjamin N. Cardozo School of Law', in M. Rosenfeld and A. Arato (eds.), *Habermas on Law and Democracy*, Berkeley, Los Angeles, and London, 1998).
Hain, K.-E., *Die Grundsätze des Grundgesetzes* (Baden-Baden, 1999).
Hamel, W., *Die Bedeutung der Grundrechte im sozialen Rechtsstaat. Eine Kritik an Gesetzgebung und Rechtsprechung* (Berlin, 1957).
Hare, R. M., *The Language of Morals* (London, Oxford, and New York, 1952).
—— 'Universalisability', *Proceedings of the Aristotelian Society*, 55 (1954/5), 295–312.
—— *Freedom and Reason* (Oxford, 1963).
—— 'Meaning and Speech Acts', in id., *Practical Inferences* (London and Basingstoke, 1971), 74–93.
—— 'Principles', *Proceedings of the Aristotelian Society*, 73 (1972/3), 1–18.
—— *Moral Thinking* (Oxford, 1981).
Harnischfeger, H., *Die Rechtsprechung des Bundesverfassungsgerichts zu den Grundrechten* (Hamburg, 1966).
Hart, H. L. A., *The Concept of Law* (Oxford, 1961).
—— 'Bentham's "Of Laws in General" ', *Rechtstheorie*, 2 (1971), 55–66.
—— 'Bentham on Legal Rights', in A. W. B. Simpson (ed.), *Oxford Essays in Jurisprudence*, second series (Oxford, 1973), 171–201.
Hartmann, N., *Ethics*, trans. S. Coit, 2 vols. (London, 1932).
Hatschek, J., *Deutsches und Preußisches Staatsrecht*, 2 vols., 2nd edn. (Berlin, 1930).
Hauriou, M., ed. R. Schnur, *Die Theorie der Institution und zwei andere Aufsätze* (Berlin, 1965).
Haverkate, G., *Rechtsfragen des Leistungsstaats* (Tübingen, 1983).
Heck, P., *Das Problem der Rechtsgewinnung*, 2nd edn. (Tübingen, 1932).
—— *Begriffsbildung und Interessennjurisprudenz* (Tübingen, 1932).
Hegel, G. W. F., *Lectures on the Philosophy of World History*, trans. H. B. Nisbet (Cambridge, 1975).
Heller, H., 'Die Krisis der Staatslehre' (1926), in id., *Gesammelte Schriften*, ii (Leiden, 1971), 3–30.
Henke, W., *Das subjektive öffentliche Recht* (Tübingen, 1968).
Henket, M., 'Towards a Code of Practical Reason?' Lecture before the 11th World Congress of Legal and Social Philosophy (appears in the proceedings of the Congress) (Helsinki, 1983).
Hensel, A., *Grundrechte und politische Weltanschauung* (Tübingen, 1931).
Herberger, M., and Simon, D., *Wissenschaftstheorie für Juristen* (Frankfurt a. M., 1980).
Hernekamp, K. (ed.), *Soziale Grundrechte* (Berlin and New York, 1979).
Hesse, E., *Die Bindung des Gesetzgebers an das Grundrecht des Art.2 Abs.1 GG bei der Verwirklichung einer 'verfassgsmäßigen Ordnung'* (Berlin, 1968).

Hesse, K., 'Der Gleichheitsgrundsatz in Staatsrecht', AöR 77 (1951/2), 167–224.

—— 'Bestand und Bedeutung der Grundrechte in der Bundesrepublik Deutschland', EuGRZ 1978, 427–38.

—— 'Grundrechte: Bestand und Bedeutung', in E. Benda, W. Maihofer and H.-J. Vogel (eds.), *Handbuch des Verfassungsrechts* (Berlin and New York, 1983), 79–106.

—— *Grundzüge des Verfassungsrechts der Bundesrepublik Deutschland*, 14th edn. (Heidelberg, 1984).

Heymann, K.-D., and Stein, E., 'Das Recht auf Bildung', AöR 97 (1972), 185–232.

Hilpinen, R., 'An Analysis of Relativised Modalities', in J. W. Davis, D. J. Hockney, and W. K. Wilson (eds.), *Philosophical Logic* (Dordrecht, 1969), 181–93.

—— (ed.), *Deontic Logic: Introductory and Systematic Readings*, (Dordrecht, 1971).

Hintikka, J., 'Some Main Problems of Deontic Logic', in R. Hilpinen (ed.), *Deontic Logic: Introductory and Systematic Readings* (Dordrecht, 1970), 59–104.

Hippel, E. v., *Grenzen und Wesengsgehalt der Grundrechte* (Berlin, 1965).

Hirschberg, L., *Der Grundstatz der Verhältnismäßigkeit* (Göttingen, 1981).

Hislop, D. J., 'The Hohfeldian System of Fundamental Legal Conceptions', ARSP 53 (1967), 53–89.

Hobbes, T. *Leviathan,* ed. M. Oakeshott (Oxford, 1960).

Hohfeld, W. N., 'Some Fundamental Legal Conceptions as Applied in Judicial Reasoning', in id., *Fundamental Legal Conceptions as Applied in Judicial Reasoning and Other Legal Essays* (New Haven, 1923), 23–64.

Holstein, G., 'Von Aufgaben und Zielen heutiger Staatsrechtswissenschaft', AöR 50 (1926), 1–40.

Honoré, A. M., 'Rights of Exclusion and Immunities against Divesting', Tul L Rev 34 (1960), 453–68.

Huber, E. R., 'Der Streit um das Wirtschaftsverfassungsrecht', DÖV 1956, 97–102, 135–43, 172–5, 200–7.

Huber, H., 'Soziale Verfassungsrechte?' in E. Forsthoff (ed.), *Rechtsstaatlichkeit und Sozialstaatlichkeit* (Darmstadt, 1968), 1–15.

—— 'Über die Konkretisierung der Grundrechte', in P. Saladin and L. Wildhaber (eds.), *Der Staat als Aufgabe: Gedenkschrift für Max Imboden* (Basle and Stuttgart, 1972), 191–209.

Hughes, G., 'Rules, Policy and Decision Making', Yale LJ 77 (1968), 411–39.

Husserl, E., *Logical Investigations*, trans. J. N. Findlay (London, 1970).

Huxley, A., *Eyeless in Gaza* (London, 1955).

Ihering, R. v., 'Unsere Aufgabe', *Jahrbücher für die Dogmatik*, 1 (1857), 1–52.

—— *Geist des römischen Rechts auf den verschiedenen Stufen seiner Entwicklung*, part 3, 5th edn. (Leipzig, 1906).

Ipsen, H. P., 'Gleichheit', in F. L. Neumann, H. C. Nipperdey, and U. Scheuner (eds.), *Die Grundrechte*, ii (Berlin, 1954), 111–98.

Ipsen, J., *Rechtsfolgen der Verfassungswidrigkeit von Norm und Einzelakt* (Baden-Baden, 1980).

Isensee, J., *Das legalisierte Widerstandsrecht* (Bad Homburg, Berlin, and Zurich, 1969).

—— *Wer definiert die Freiheitsrechte? Selbstverständnis der Grundrechtsträger und Grundrechtsauslegung des Staates* (Heidelberg and Karlsruhe, 1980).

Isensee, J., 'Verfassung ohne soziale Grundrechte', *Der Staat*, 19 (1980), 367–84.
—— *Das Grundrecht auf Sicherheit. Zu den Schutzpflichten des freiheitlichen Verfassungsstaates*, (Berlin and New York, 1983).
Jäckel, H., *Grundrechtsgeltung und Grundrechtssicherung* (Berlin, 1967).
Jestaedt, M., *Grundrechtsentfaltung im Gesetz* (Tübingen, 1999).
Jansen, N., 'Die Abwägung von Grundrechten', *Der Staat*, 36 (1997), 27–54.
Jellinek, G., *System der subjektiven öffentlichen Rechte*, 2nd edn. (Tübingen, 1905).
—— *Allgemeine Staatslehre*, 7th reissue of the 3rd edn. (1914) (Bad Homburg, 1960).
Jellinek, W., 'Grundrechte und Gesetzesvorbehalt', *Deutsche Rechts-Zeitschrift*, 1946, 4–6.
Kalinowski, G., 'Théorie des propositions normatives', *Studia Logica*, 1 (1953), 147–82.
—— *Einführung in die Normenlogik* (Frankfurt a. M, 1973).
Kanger, S., 'New Foundations for Ethical Theory', in R. Hilpinen (ed.,) *Deontic Logic: Introductory and Systematic Readings* (Dordrecht, 1970), 36–58.
—— and Kanger, H., 'Rights and Parliamentarism', *Theoria*, 32 (1966), 85–115.
Kant, I., *The Moral Law (Groundwork of the Metaphysics of Morals)*, trans. H. J. Paton (London, 1948).
—— *The Metaphysics of Morals*, trans. Mary Gregor (Cambridge, 1991).
Kasper, F., *Das subjektive Recht—Begriffsbildung und Bedeutungsmehrheit* (Karlsruhe, 1967).
Kaufmann, E., *Kritik der neukantischen Rechtsphilosophie* (Tübingen, 1921).
Kaufmann, E., 'Die Gleichheit vor dem Gesetz im Sinne des Art. 109 der Reichsverfassung', VVDStRL 3 (1927), 2–24.
Keller, A., *Die Kritik, Korrektur und Interpretation des Gesetzeswortlauts* (Winterthur, 1960).
Kelsen, H., *Hauptprobleme der Staatsrechtslehre entwickelt aus der Lehre vom Rechtssatze* (Tübingen, 1911).
—— 'Wesen und Entwicklung der Staatsgerichtsbarkeit', VVDStRL 5 (1929), 30–88.
—— 'Das Problem der Gerechtigkeit', in id., *Reine Rechtslehre*, 2nd edn. (Vienna, 1960).
—— *Pure Theory of Law*, trans. Max Knight (Berkeley, 1967).
—— *General Theory of Norms*, trans. Michael Hartney (Oxford, 1991).
Kirsch, W., *Einführung in die Theorie der Entscheidungsprozesse*, 3 vols., 2nd edn. (Wiesbaden, 1977).
Klami, H. T., *Legal Heuristics* (Vammala, 1982).
Klein, F., 'Zum Begriff und zur Grenze der Verfassungsgerichtsbarkeit', DÖV 1964, 471–6.
Klein, H. H., 'Öffentliche und private Freiheit', *Der Staat*, 10 (1971), 145–72.
—— *Die Grundrechte im demokratischen Staat*, 2nd edn. (Stuttgart, Berlin, Cologne, and Mainz, 1974).
—— 'Ein Grundrecht auf saubere Umwelt?' in H. Schneider and V. Götz (eds.), *Festschrift für W. Weber* (Berlin, 1974), 643–61.
Kloepfer, M., *Grundrechte als Entstehenssicherung und Bestandsschutz* (Munich, 1970).
—— 'Grundrechtstatbestand und Grundrechtsschranken in der Rechtsprechung

des Bundesverfassungsgerichts—dargestellt am Beispiel der Menschenwürde', in C. Starck (ed.), *Bundesverfassungsgericht und Grundgesetz: Festgabe aus Anlaß des 25jährigen Bestehens des Bundesverfassungsgerichts* (Tübingen, 1976), 405–20.

—— *Datenschutz als Grundrecht. Verfassungsprobleme der Einführung eines Grundrechts auf Datenschutz* (Königstein im Tannus, 1980).

—— *Gleichheit als Verfassungsfrage* (Berlin, 1980).

Knies, W., *Schranken der Kunstfreiheit als verfassungsrechtliches Problem* (Munich, 1967).

Koch, H.-J., *Über juristisch-dogmatisches Argumentieren im Staatsrecht*, in id. (ed.), *Die juristische Methode im Staatsrecht* (Frankfurt a. M., 1977), 13–157.

—— and Rüßmann, H., *Juristiche Begründungslehre* (Munich, 1982).

Kocourek, A., 'Non-legal-content Relations', Ill LQ 4 (1922), 233–9.

—— *Jural Relations*, 2nd edn. (Indianapolis, 1928).

Kommentar zum Bonner Grundgesetz (Bonner Kommentar), ed. H. J. Abraham *et al.*, 9 vols. (Hamburg, 1950)

Kommers, D. P., 'Der Gleichheitssatz: Neuere Entwicklungen und Probleme im Verfassunsgrecht der USA und der Bundersrepublik Deutschland', in C. Link (ed.), *Der Gleichheitssatz im modernen Verfassungsstaat* (Baden-Baden, 1982), 31–50.

Korinek, K., 'Betrachtungen zur juristischen Problematik sozialer Grundrechte', in *Die sozialen Grundrechte*, ed. The Catholic Social Academy of Austria (Vienna, 1971), 9–23.

—— 'Die Verfassungsgerichtsbarkeit im Gegüge der Staatsfunktionen', VVDStRL 39 (1981), 7–52.

Kraft, V., *Die Grundlagen einer wissenshcaftlichen Wertlehre*, 2nd edn. (Vienna, 1951).

Krauss, R. v., *Der Grundsatz der Verhältnismäßigkeit* (Hamburg, 1955).

Krawietz, W., 'Artikel: Begriffsjurisprudenz', in J. Ritter (ed.), *Historisches Wörterbuch der Philosophie*, i (Basle, 1971), cols. 809–13.

—— 'Was leistet Rechtsdogmatik in der richterlichen Entscheidungspraxis?' ÖzöR 23 (1972), 47–80.

—— (ed.,) *Theorie und Technik der Begriffsjurisprudenz* (Darmstadt, 1976).

Krebs, W., *Vorbehalt des Gesetzes und Grundrechte* (Berlin, 1975).

Kriele, M., *Einführung in die Staatslehre* (Reinbek, 1975).

—— *Theorie der Rechtsgewinnung*, 2nd edn. (Berlin, 1976).

—— 'Das Grundgesetz im Partienkampf', in id., *Legitimationsprobleme der Bundesrepublik* (Munich, 1977), 131–45.

—— *Recht und praktische Vernunft* (Göttingen, 1979).

—— *Befreiung und politische Aufklärung* (Freiburg, Basle, and Vienna, 1980).

Kröger, K., *Grundrechtstheorie als Verfassungsproblem* (Baden-Baden, 1978).

Krüger, H., 'Der Wesensgehalt der Grundrechte i.S.des Art.19 GG', DÖV 1955, 597–602.

—— 'Der Wesensgehalt der Grundrechte', in J. Seifert and H. Krüger, *Die Einschränkung der Grundrechte, Schriftenreihe der Niedersächsischen Landeszentrale für Politische Bildung, Verfassungsrecht und Verfassungswirklichkeit*, xiii (Hanover, 1976), 35–60.

Kutschera, F. v., *Einführung in die Logik der Normen, Werte und Entscheidungen* (Freiburg and Munich, 1973).

Laband, P., *Das Staatsrecht des Deutschen Reiches*, i, 2nd edn. (Freiburg, 1888).

Lange, K., 'Rechtskraft, Bindungswirkung und Gesetzeskraft der Entscheidungen des Bundesverfassungsgerichts', JuS 1978, 1–8.

Larenz, K., 'Rechtsperson und subjektives Recht', in G. Dahm *et al.*, *Grundfragen der neuen Rechtswissenschaft* (Berlin, 1935), 225–60.

—— *Allgemeiner Teil des deutschen bürgerlichen Rechts*, 1st edn. (Munich, 1967).

—— *Richtiges Recht* (Munich, 1979).

—— *Methodenlehre der Rechtswissenschaft*, 4th edn. (Berlin, Heidelberg, and New York, 1979), 5th edn. (Berlin, Heidelberg, New York, and Tokyo, 1983).

Laszlo, E., and Wilbur, J. B. (eds.), *Value Theory in Philosophy and Social Science* (New York, London, and Paris, 1973).

Lautmann, R., *Wert und Norm: Begriffsanalysen für die Soziologie*, 2nd edn. (Opladen, 1971).

Lazzer, D. de, 'Rechtsdogmatik als Kompromißformular', in R. Dubischar *et al.* (eds.), *Dogmatik und Methode, Festschrift für J. Esser*, (Kronberg and Taunus, 1975), 85–112.

Lehmann, H., *Allgemeiner-Teil des Bürgerlichen Gesetzbuches*, 13th edn. (Berlin, 1962).

Leibholz, G., *Die Gleichheit vor dem Gesetz* (1925), 2nd edn. (Munich and Berlin, 1959).

—— *Das Wesen der Repräsentation und der Gestaltwandel der Demokratie im 20. Jahrhundert*, 3rd edn. (Berlin, 1966).

—— *Strukturprobleme der modernen Demokratie*, 3rd edn. (Karlsruhe, 1967) (reissue, Frankfurt a. M., 1974).

Leibniz, G. W., 'Elementa Juris Naturalis' (1671), manuscript draft B (Hanover), manuscript final draft C (Hanover), reproduced in id., *Sämtliche Schriften und Briefe*, ed. Prussian Academy of Science, series 6, vol. 1 (Darmstadt, 1930), 465–80, 480–5.

Leisner, W., *Grundrechte und Privatrecht* (Munich, 1960).

—— *Von der Verfassungsmäßigkeit der Gesetze zur Gesetzmäßigkeit der Verfassung, Betrachtungen zur möglichen selbständigen Begrifflichkeit im Verfassungsrecht* (Tübingen, 1964).

—— 'Der Eigentümer als Organ der Wirstschaftsverfassung', DÖV 1975, 73–9.

Lenk, H. (ed.), *Normenlogik, Grundprobleme der deontischen Logik* (Pullach, 1974).

Lepa, M., 'Grundrechtskonflikte', DVBl 1972, 690–701.

Lerche, P., *Übermaß und Verfassungsrecht. Zur Bindung des Gesetzgebers an die Grundsätze der Verhältnismäßigkeit und der Erforderlichkeit* (Cologne, Berlin, Munich, and Bonn, 1961).

—— 'Stil, Methode, Ansicht', DVBl 1961, 690–701.

—— 'Review of Peter Häberle, Die Wesensgehaltgarantie des Art.19 Abs.2 Grundgesetz', DÖV 1965, 212–14.

—— 'Die Verfassung als Quelle von Optimierungsgeboten?' in J. Burmeister (ed.), *Verfassungsstaatlichkeit. Festschrift für Klaus Stern* (Munich, 1997).

Levinson, J., 'Gewirth on Absolute Rights', *The Philosophical Quarterly*, 32 (1982), 73–5.

Lindahl, L., *Position and Change: A Study in Law and Logic* (Dordrecht, 1977).

Link, C., *Herrschaftsordnung und bürgerliche Freiheit* (Vienna, Cologne, and Graz, 1979).

—— (ed.), *Der Gleichheitssatz im modernen Verfassungsstaat* (Baden-Baden, 1982).

Lorenz, D., 'Der grundrechtliche Anspruch auf effektiven Rechtsschutz', AöR 105 (1980), 623–49.

—— 'Bundesverfassungsgericht und soziale Grundrechte', JBl 103 (1981), 16–26.

Löw, K., 'Ist die Würde des Menschen im Grundgesetz eine Anspruchsgrundlage?' DÖV 1958, 516–20.

Luce, R. D., and Raiffa, H., *Games and Decisions. Introduction and Critical Survey* (New York, London, and Sydney, 1957) (reprint, 1967).

Lücke, J., 'Soziale Grundrechte als Staatszielbestimmungen und Gesetzgebungsaufträge', AöR 107 (1982), 15–60.

Luhmann, N., 'Zur Funktion der "subjektiven Rechte" ', *Die Funktion des Rechts in der modernen Gesellschaft, Jahrbuch für Rechtssoziologie und Rechtstheorie*, 1 (1970), 321–30.

—— *Rechtssoziologie*, 2 vols. (Reinbek, 1972).

—— *Grundrechte als Institution*, 2nd edn. (Berlin, 1974).

—— *A Sociological Theory of Law*, trans. E. King and M. Albrow (London, 1985).

Lyons, D., 'Rights, Claimants and Beneficiaries', Am Phil Q 6 (1969), 173–85.

Maassen, H., 'Probleme der Selbstbindung des Bundesverfassungsgerichts', NJW 1975, 1343–8.

MacCallum, G. C., 'Negative and Positive Freedom', *Philosophical Review*, 76 (1967), 312–34.

MacCormick, N., 'Law as Institutional Fact', LQR 90 (1974), 102–29.

—— ' "Principles" of Law', Jur Rev, 19 (1974), 217–26.

—— 'Rights in Legislation', in P. M. S. Hacker and J. Raz (eds.), *Law, Morality and Society, Essays in Honour of H. L. A. Hart*, (Oxford, 1977), 189–209.

—— *Legal Reasoning and Legal Theory* (Oxford, 1978).

—— 'Coherence in Legal Justification', in W. Krawietz, H. Schelsky, G. Winkler, and A. Schramm (eds.), *Theorie der Normen, Festgabe für O. Weinberger*, (Berlin, 1984), 37–53.

Mackert, J., and Schneider F., *Bibliographie zur Verfassungsgerichtsbarkeit des Bundes und der Länder*, 3 vols. (Tübingen, 1971, 1976, 1982).

Macpherson, C. B., 'Berlins Teilung der Freiheit', in id., *Demokratietheorie* (Munich, 1977), 159–94.

Mally, E., 'Grundgesetze des Sollens: Elemente der Logik des Willens' (Graz, 1926) reprinted in E. Mally, *Logische Schriften*, ed. K. Wolf and P. Weingartner (Dordrecht, 1971), 227–324.

Mangoldt, H. v., 'Grundrechte und Grundsatzfragen des Bonner Grundgesetzes', AöR 75 (1949), 273–90.

—— and Klein, F., *Das Bonner Grundgesetz*, i, 2nd edn. (Berlin and Frankfurt, 1957).

Martens, W., 'Grundrechte im Leistungsstaat', VVDStRL 30 (1972), 7–38.

Marx, K., 'The Constitution of the French Republic adopted on 4 November 1848', in K. Marx and F. Engels, *Works*, x (London, 1978).

Marx, M., *Zur Definition des Begriffs 'Rechtsgut'* (Cologne, Berlin, Bonn, and Munich, 1972).

Maunz, T., *Deutsches Staatsrecht*, 23rd edn. (Munich, 1980).

Maunz, T., and Dürig, G. *et al.*, *Grundgesetz Kommentar*, 5th edn. (Munich, 1983).

—— and Zippelius, R., *Deutsches Staatsrecht*, 24th edn. (Munich, 1982).

Merten, D., 'Urteilsanmerking', NJW 1972, 1799.

—— 'Das Recht auf freie Entfaltung der Persönlichkeit', JuS 1976, 345–51.

—— 'Handlungsgrundrechte als Verhaltensgarantien—zugleich ein Beitrag zur Funktion der Grundrechte', VerwArch 73 (1982), 103–21.

Meyer-Cording, U., *Kann der Jurist heute noch Dogmatiker sein? Zum Selbstverständnis der Rechtswissenschaft* (Tübingen, 1973).

Moritz, M., *Über Hohfelds System der juridischen Grundbegriffe* (Lund and Copenhagen, 1960).

Müller, F., *Normstruktur und Normativität* (Berlin, 1966).

—— *Normbereiche von Einzelgrundrechten in der Rechtsprechung des Bundesverfassungsgerichts* (Berlin, 1968).

—— *Die Positivität der Grundrechte. Fragen einer praktischen Grundrechtsdogmatik* (Berlin, 1969).

—— *Freiheit der Kunst als Problem der Grundrechtsdogmatik* (Berlin, 1969).

—— 'Thesen zur Struktur von Rechtsnormen', ARSP 61 (1970), 493–509.

—— *Juristische Methodik*, 2nd edn. (Berlin, 1976).

—— *Juristische Methodik und Politisches System. Elemente einer Verfassungstheorie II* (Berlin, 1976).

—— 'Rechtsstaatliche Methodik und politische Rechtstheorie', *Rechtstheorie*, 8 (1977), 73–92.

—— *Die Einheit der Verfassung. Elemente einer Verfassungstheorie III* (Berlin, 1979).

—— *Strukturierende Rechtslehre* (Berlin, 1984).

—— Pieroth, B., and Fohmann, L., *Leistungsrechte im Normbereich einer Freiheitsgarantie* (Berlin, 1982).

Müller, J., *Auswirkungen der unterschiedlichen Auffassungen zum Rechtscharakter des Art. 2 Abs. 1 GG und zu dessen Schranken* (Hamburg, 1972).

Müller, J. P., *Soziale Grundrechte in der Verfassung?* 2nd edn. (Basle and Frankfurt, 1981).

—— 'Die Verfassungsgerichtsbarkeit im Gefüge der Staatsfunktionen', VVDStRL 39 (1981), 53–98.

—— *Elemente einer schweizerischen Grundrechtstheorie* (Berne, 1982).

Münch, I. v., (ed.), *Grundgesetz-Kommentar*, i, 2nd edn. (Munich, 1981).

Mutius, A. v., 'Grundrechte als "Teilhaberechte"—zu den verfassungsrechtlichen Aspekten des "numerus clausus" ', VerwArch 64 (1973), 183–95.

Nagel, S. S., 'Issues regarding Tensions between Goals of Equality and Freedom', in G. Dorsey (ed.), *Equality and Freedom*, ii (New York and Leiden, 1977), 603–10.

Nawiasky, H., *Allegemeine Rechtslehre als System der rechtlichen Grundbegriffe*, 2nd edn. (Einsiedeln, Zürich, and Cologne, 1948).

Nieuwland, H. van, *Darstellung und Kritik der Theorien der immanenten Grundrechtsschranken*, diss.jur. (Göttingen, 1981).

Nipperdey, H. C., 'Grundrechte und Privatrecht', in H. C. Nipperdey (ed.), *Festschrift für E. Molitor* (Munich and Berlin, 1962), 17–33.

—— 'Freie Entfaltung der Persönlichkeit', in K. A. Betterman and H. C. Nipperdey (eds.), *Die Grundrechte*, vol. 4.2 (Berlin, 1962), 741–909.

Nozick, R., *Anarchy, State, and Utopia* (New York, 1974).

Opp, K.-D., *Soziologie im Recht* (Reinbek, 1973).

Ossenbühl, F., 'Die Interpretation der Grundrechte in der Rechtsprechung des Bundesverfassungsgerichts', NJW 1976, 2100–7.

—— 'Die Kontrolle von Tatsachenfeststellungen und Prognoseentscheidungen durch das Bundesverfassungsgericht', in C. Starck (ed.), *Bundesverfassungsgericht und Grundgesetz, Festgabe aus Anlaß des 27jährigen Bestehens des Bundesverfassungsgerichts*, i (Tübingen, 1976), 458–518.

—— 'Kernenergie im Spiegel des Verfassungsrechts', DÖV 1981, 1–11.

Otte, G., 'Komparative Sätze im Recht. Zur Lokik eines beweglichen Systems', *Jahrbuch für Rechtssoziologie und Rechtstheorie*, 2 (1972), 301–20.

Patzig, G., 'Artikel: Relation', in H. Krings, H. M. Baumgartner, and C. Wild (eds.), *Handbuch philosophischer Grundbegriffe*, iv (Munich, 1973), 1220–31.

Paulson, S., 'Zum Problem der Normenkonflikte', ARSP 66 (1980), 487–506.

Peczenik, A., 'Principles of Law: The Search for Legal Theory', *Rechtstheorie*, 2 (1971), 17–35.

—— 'On the Nature and Function of the Grundnorm', *Rechtstheorie*, Beiheft 2 (1981), 279–96.

—— *Grundlagen der juristischen Argumentation* (Vienna and New York, 1983).

—— 'Is There Always a Right Answer to a Legal Question?' in *Essays in Legal Theory in Honor of K. Makkonen, Oikeustiede Jurisprudentia*, 16 (1983), 241–58.

Perelman, C., *The Idea of Justice and the Problem of Argument*, trans. J. Petrie (London, 1963).

Perry, R. B., *General Theory of Value* (New York, 1926).

—— *Realms of Value* (Cambridge, Mass., 1954).

Pestalozza, C. Graf. v., 'Kritische Bemerkungen zu Methoden und Prinzipien der Grundrechtsauslegung in der Bundersrepublik Deutschland', *Der Staat*, 2 (1963), 425–49.

Peters, H., 'Die freie Entfaltung der Persönlichkeit als Verfassungsziel', in D. S. Constantopoulos and H. Wehberg (eds.), *Festschrift für R. Laun* (Hamburg, 1953), 669–78.

—— 'Elternrecht, Erziehung, Bildung und Schule', in K. A. Bettermann, H. C. Nipperday, and U. Scheuner (eds.), *Die Grundrechte*, vol. 4.1 (Berlin, 1960), 369–445.

—— *Das Recht auf freie Entfaltung der Persönlichkeit in der höchsrichterlichen Rechtsprechung* (Cologne and Opladen, 1963).

Philippi, K. J., *Tatsachenfeststellungen des Bundesverfassungsgerichts* (Cologne, Berlin, Bonn, and Munich, 1971).

Plato, *The Laws*, trans. Trevor J. Saunders (London, 1970).

Podlech, A., 'Wertungen und Werte im Recht', AöR 95 (1970), 185–223.

—— *Gehalt und Funktionen des allgemeinen verfassungsrechtlichen Gleichheitssatzes* (Berlin, 1971).

—— 'Recht und Moral', *Rechtstheorie*, 3 (1972), 129–48.

Popper, K. R., *The Open Society and its Enemies*, i, 5th edn. (London, 1966).

Preuß, U. K., *Die Internalisierung des Subjekts. Zur Kritik der Funktionsweise des subjektiven Rechts*, (Frankfurt a. M., 1979).

Quine, W. V. O., *Methods of Logic*, 2nd edn. (London, 1962).

Raabe, M., *Grundrechte und Erkenntnis* (Baden-Baden, 1998).

Radbruch, G., *Legal Philosophy*, 3rd edn., trans. Kurt Wilk (Cambridge, Mass., 1950).

Radbruch, G., *Rechtsphilosophie*, 8th edn. (Stuttgart, 1973).

Raiser, L., 'Der Stand der Lehre vom subjektiven Recht im Deutschen Zivilrecht', JZ 1961, 465–73.

—— 'Wozu Rechtsdogmatik?' DRiZ 1968, 98.

Ramsauer, U., *Die faktischen Beeinträchtigungen des Eigentums* (Berlin, 1980).

—— 'Die Bestimmung des Schutzbereichs von Grundrechten nach dem Normzweck', VerwArch 72 (1981), 89–106.

Raphael, D. D., 'Tensions between the Goals of Equality and Freedom', in G. Dorsey (ed.), *Equality and Freedom*, ii (New York and Leiden, 1977), 543–58.

Rauschning, D., 'Staatsaufgabe Umweltschutz', VVDStRL 38 (1980), 167–210.

Rawls, J., 'Justice as Fairness', *Philosophical Review*, 64 (1958), 164–94.

—— *A Theory of Justice* (Cambridge, Mass., 1971).

Raz, J., *The Concept of a Legal System* (Oxford, 1970).

—— 'Legal Principles and the Limits of Law', Yale LJ 81 (1972), 823–54.

—— *Practical Reason and Norms* (London, 1975).

Rehbinder, M., *Rechtssoziologie* (Berlin and New York, 1977).

Rescher, N., *The Coherence Theory of Truth* (Oxford, 1973).

—— *Cognitive Systematization* (Oxford, 1979).

Reuter, L.-R., 'Soziales Grundrecht auf Bildung? Ansätze eines Verfassungswandels im Leistungsstaat', DVBl 1974, 7–19.

Ridder, H., 'Meinungsfreiheit', in F. L. Neumann, H. C. Nipperdey, and U. Scheuner (eds.), *Die Grundrechte*, ii (Berlin, 1954), 243–90.

—— *Die soziale Ordnung des Grundgesetzes. Leitfaden zu den Grundrechten einer demokratischen Verfassung* (Opladen, 1975).

Robbers, G., *Gerechtigkeit als Rechtsprinzip. Über den Begriff der Gerechtigkeit in der Rechtsprechung des Beundesverfassungsgerichts* (Baden-Baden, 1980).

Rohlf, D., *Der grundrechtliche Schutz der Privatsphäre* (Berlin, 1980).

Rokeach, M., *The Nature of Human Values* (New York, 1973).

Romano, S., *Die Rechtsordnung*, ed. R. Schnur (Berlin, 1975).

Römer, P. (ed.) *Der Kampf um das Grundgesetz* (Frankfurt a. M., 1977).

Ross, A., *On Law and Justice* (London, 1958).

—— *Directives and Norms* (London, 1968).

Ross, W. D., *The Right and the Good* (Oxford, 1930).

Rottleuthner, H., *Rechtswissenschaft als Sozialwissenschaft* (Frankfurt a. M., 1973).

—— *Rechtstheorie und Rechtssoziologie* (Freiburg and Munich, 1981).

Rubel, R., *Planungsermessen* (Frankfurt a. M., 1982).

Rüfner, W., 'Überschneidungen und gegenseitige Ergänzungen der Grundrechte', *Der Staat*, 7 (1968), 41–64.

—— 'Grundrechtskonflikte', in C. Starck (ed.), *Bundesverfassungsgericht und Grundgesetz, Festgabe aus Anlaß des 25jährigen Bestehens des Bundesverfassungsgerichts*, ii (Tübingen, 1976), 453–79.

Rupp, H. H., *Grundfragen der heutigen Verwaltungsrechtslehre. Verwaltungsnorm und Verwaltungsverhältnis* (Tübingen, 1965).

—— 'Das Urteil des Bundesverfassungsgerichts zum Sammlungsgesetz—eine Wende in der Grundrechtsinterpretation des Art. 2 Abs.1 GG?' NJW 1966, 2037–40.

—— 'Zum "Mephisto-Beschluß" des Bundesverfassungsgerichts', DVBl 1972, 66–7.

—— 'Grundrechtlicher Freiheitsstatus und ungesetzlicher Zwang', DÖV 1974, 193–5.

—— 'Vom Wandel der Grundrechte', AöR 101 (1976), 161–201.

—— 'Urteilsanmerkung', JZ 1979, 28–9.

Rüthers, B., *'Institutionelles Rechtsdenken' im Wandel der Verfassungsepochen* (Bad Homburg, Berlin, and Zurich, 1970).

Ryffel, H., 'Review of M. Kriele, "Theorie der Rechtsgewinnung" (Berlin, 1967) and F. Müller, "Normstruktur und Normativität" (Berlin, 1966)', DVBl 1971, 83–5.

—— and Schwartländer, J. (eds.), *Das Recht des Menschen auf Arbeit* (Kehl, Strasbourg, and Arlington, 1983).

Sachs, M., *Die Bindung des Bundesverfassungsgerichts an seine Entscheidungen* (Munich, 1977).

—— 'Zur dogmatischen Struktur der Gleichheitsrechte als Abwehrrechte', DÖV 1984, 411–19.

Saladin, P., 'Die Funktion der Grundrechte in einer revidierten Verfassung', ZSR (NF) 87 (1968), 531–60.

—— *Grundrechte im Wandel*, 2nd edn. (Berne, 1975).

Sattler, A., 'Die Pflicht des Gesetzgebers zum Erlaß von Vorschriften über die Organisation der Hochschulen', in H. Schneider and V. Götz (eds.), *Festschrift für W. Weber* (Berlin, 1974), 325–44.

Savigny, E. v., Neumann, U., and Rahlf, J., *Juristiche Dogmatik und Wissenschaftstheorie* (Munich, 1976).

Schätzel, W., 'Der internationale Schutz der Menschenrechte' in *Festschrift für F. Giese* (Frankfurt a. M., 1953), 215–30.

Schambeck, H., *Grundrechte und Sozialordnung* (Berlin, 1969).

Schapp, J., *Das subjektive Recht im Prozeß der Rechtsgewinnung* (Berlin, 1977).

Scharpf, F., *Demokratietheorie zwischen Utopie und Anpassung* (Konstanz, 1970).

Scheler, M., *Formalism in Ethics and Non-formal Ethics of Values*, trans. Manfred S. Frings and Roger L. Funk, 5th edn. (Evanston, Ill., 1973).

Schelsky, H. (ed.), *Zur Theorie der Institution* (Düsseldorf, 1970).

Scherzberg, A., *Grundrechtsschutz und Eingriffsintensität* (Berlin, 1989).

Scheuner, U., 'Pressefreiheit', VVDStRL 22 (1965), 1–100.

—— 'Die Funktion der Grundrechte im Sozialstaat. Die Grundrechte als Richtlinie und Rahmen der Staatstätigkeit', DÖV 1971, 505–13.

Schlaich, K., 'Die Verfassungsgerichtsbarkeit im Gefüge der Staatsfunktionen', VVDStRL 39 (1981), 99–146.

Schlink, B., *Abwägung in Verfassungsrecht* (Berlin, 1976).

Schmidt, J., *Aktionsberechtigung und Vermögensberechtigung. Ein Beitrag zur Theorie des subjektiven Rechtes*, (Cologne, Berlin, Bonn, and Munich, 1969).

Schmidt, W., 'Die Freiheit vor dem Gesetz zur Auslegung des Art.2 Abs.1 des Grundgesetzes', AöR 91 (1966), 42–85.

—— 'Soziale Grundrechte im Verfassungsrecht der Bundesrepublik Deutschland', *Der Staat*, Beiheft 5 (1981), 9–28.

—— 'Grundrechtstheorie im Wandel der Verfassungsgeschichte', *Jura*, 1983, 169–80.

Schmidt-Assmann, E., 'Anwendungsprobleme des Art. 2 Abs. 2 GG im Immissionsschutzrecht', AöR 106 (1981), 205–17.

Schmidt-Jortzig, E., *Die Einrichtungsgarantien der Verfassung. Dogmatischer Gehalt und Sicherungskraft einer umstrittenen Figur* (Göttingen, 1979).

Schmidt-Rimpler, W., Gieseke, P., Friesenhahn, E., and Knur, A., 'Die Lohngleichheit von Männern und Frauen. Zur Frage der unmittelbaren Einwirkungdes Art.3 Abs.2 und 3 des Grundgesetzes auf Arbeits und Tarifverträge', AöR 76 (1950/1), 165–86.

Schmitt, C., *Unabhängigkeit der Richter, Gleichheit vor dem Gesetz und Gewährleistung des Privateigentums nach der Weimarer Verfassung* (Berlin and Leipzig, 1926).

—— *Verfassungslehre* (Munich and Leipzig, 1928) (5th edn. Berlin, 1970).

—— *Über die drei Arten des rechtswissenschaftlichen Denkens* (Hamburg, 1934).

—— 'Die Tyrannei der Werte', in *Säkularisation und Utopie, Festschrift für E. Forsthoff* (Stuttgart, Berlin, Cologne, and Mainz, 1967), 37–62.

—— *Verfassungsrechtliche Aufsätze aus den Jahren 1924–1954. Materialien zu einer Verfassungslehre*, 2nd edn. (Berlin, 1973).

Schmitt Glaeser, W., *Mißbrauch und Verwirkung von Grundrechten im politischen Meinungskampf* (Bad Homburg, Berlin, and Zurich, 1968).

—— 'Die Freiheit der Forschung', *Wissenschaftsrecht, Wissenschaftsverwaltung, Wissenshaftsförderung*, 7 (1974), 107–34, 177–92.

Schnapp, F. E., 'Grenzen der Grundrechte', JuS 1978, 729–35.

—— 'Die Verhältnismäßigkeit des Grundrechtseingriffs', JuS 1983, 850–5.

Schneider, Hans, 'Zur Verhältnismäßigkeits-Kontrolle insbesondere bei Gesetzen', in C. Starck (ed.), *Bundesverfassungsgericht und Grundgesetz, Festgabe aus Anlaß des 25jährigen Bestehens des Bundesverfassungsgerichts*, ii (Tübingen, 1976), 390–404.

Schneider, H.-P., 'Verfassungsgerichtsbarkeit und Gewaltenteilung', NJW 1980, 2103–11.

Schneider, Harald, *Die Güterabwägung des Bundesverfassungsgerichts bei Grundrechtskonflikten* (Baden-Baden, 1979).

Schneider, L., *Der Schutz des Wesensgehalts von Grundrechten nach Art.19 Abs.2 GG* (Berlin, 1983).

Schneider, P., 'In dubio pro libertate': in *Hundert Jahre deutsches Rechtsleben, Festschrift zum hundertjährigen Bestehen des Deutschen Jusristentages 1860–1960*, ii (Karlsruhe, 1960), 263–90.

—— 'Prinzipien der Verfassungsinterpretation', VVDStRL 20 (1963), 1–52.

Schnur, R. (ed.), *Zur Geschichte der Erklärung der Menschenrechte* (Darmstadt, 1964).

—— (ed.), *Institution und Recht* (Darmstadt, 1968).

Scholler, H., *Die Interpretation des Gleichheitssatzes als Willkürverbot oder also Gebot der Chancengleichheit* (Berlin, 1969).

Scholz, R., *Die Koalitionsfreiheit als Verfassungsproblem* (Munich, 1971).

—— *Wirtschaftsaufsicht und subjektiver Konkurrentenschutz* (Berlin, 1971).

—— 'Das Grundrecht der freien Entfaltung der Persönlichkeit in der Rechtsprechung des Bundesverfassungsgerichts', AöR 100 (1975), 80–130, 264–90.

—— 'Nichtraucher contra Raucher—OVG Berlin, NJW 1975, 2261 und VG Schleswig, JR 1975, 130', JuS 1976, 232–7.

—— 'Das Recht auf Arbeit. Verfassungsrechtliche Grundlagen, Möglichkeiten und Grenzen der Kodifikation', in E.-W. Böckenförde, J. Jekewitz, and T. Ramm (eds.), *Soziale Grundrechte* (Heidelberg and Karlsruhe, 1981), 75–89.

Schreckenberger, W., *Rhetorische Semiotik. Analyse von Texten des Grundgesetzes und von rhetorischen Grundstrukturen der Argumentation des Bundesverfassungsgerichts* (Freiburg and Munich, 1978).

Schulz-Schaeffer, H., *Der Freiheitssatz des Art. 2 Abs. 1 Grundgesetz* (Berlin, 1971).

Schuppert, G. F., *Funktionell-rechtliche Grenzen der Verfassungsinterpretation* (Königstein im Taunus, 1980).

Schwabe, J., *Die sogenannte Drittwirkung der Grundrechte* (Munich, 1971).

—— 'Mißdeutungen um das "Elfes-Urteil" des BVerfG und ihre Folgen', DÖV 1973, 623–30.

—— 'Bundesverfassungsgericht und "Drittwirkung" der Grundrechte', AöR 100 (1975), 442–70.

—— *Probleme der Grundrechtsdogmatik* (Darmstadt, 1977).

—— 'Grundrechtlich begründete Pflichten des Staates zum Schutz gegen staatliche Bau- und Anlagegenehmigungen?' NVwZ 1983, 523–7.

Schwäble, U., *Das Grundrecht der Versammlungsfreiheit* (Berlin, 1975).

Schwacke, P., *Grundrechtliche Spannungslagen* (Stuttgart, Berlin, Cologne, and Mainz, 1975).

Schwan, E., 'Datenschutz, Vorbehalt des Gesetzes und Freiheitsgrundrechte', VerwArch 66 (1975), 120–50.

Schwark, E., *Der Begriff der 'Allgemeinen Gesetze' in Artikel 5 Absatz 2 des Grundgesetzes* (Berlin, 1970).

Schweiger, K., 'Zur Geschichte und Bewertung des Willkürverbots', in *Verfassung und Verfassungsrechtsprechung, Festschrift zum 25-jährigen Bestehen des BayVGH* (Munich, 1972), 55–71.

Scitovsky, T., *Welfare and Competition: The Economics of a Fully Employed Economy* (London, 1952) (reissue, 1964).

Searle, J. R., *Speech Acts* (Cambridge, 1969).

—— 'Prima Facie Obligations', in J. Raz (ed.), *Practical Reasoning* (Oxford, 1978), 80–90.

Seetzen, U., 'Der Prognosespielraum des Gesetzgebers', NJW 1975, 429–34.

Selmer, P., 'Generelle Norm und individueller Grundrechtsschutz. Gedanken zum Thema Recht und Individualität', DÖV 1972, 551–60.

Shuman, S. I., 'Justification of Judicial Decisions', in *Essays in Honour of Hans Kelsen*, Cal L Rev 59 (1971), 715–32.

Siebert, W., *Verwirkung und Unzulässigkeit der Rechtsausübung* (Marburg, 1934).

—— 'Vom Wesen des Rechtsmißbrauchs. Über die konkrete Gestaltung der Rechte', in G. Dahm *et al.*, *Grundfragen der neuen Rechtswissenschaft* (Berlin, 1935), 189–226.

Sieckmann, J.-R., *Regelmodelle und Prinzipienmodelle des Rechtssystems* (Baden-Baden, 1990).

Simitis, S., 'Die Bedeutung von System und Dogmatik—dargestellt an rechtsgeschäftlichen Problemen des Massenverkehrs', AcP 172 (1972), 131–54.

Simonius, A., 'Über Bedeutung, Herkunft und Wandlung der Grundsätze des Privatrechts', ZSR, NF 71 (1952), 237–73.

Singer, M. G., *Generalization in Ethics* (New York, 1961).

Smend, R., *Staatsrechtliche Abhandlungen und andere Aufsätze*, 2nd edn. (Berlin, 1968).

—— 'Festvortrag zur Feier des zehnjährigen Bestehens des Bundesverfassungsgerichts am 26 Januar 1962', in *Das Bundesverfassungsgericht*, 2nd edn. (Karlsruhe, 1971), 15–29.

Sontheimer, K., 'Zur Grundlagenproblematik der deutschen Staatsrechtslehre in der Weimarer Republik', ARSP 46 (1960), 39–71.

Spinoza, B. de, 'Ethics', *Collected Works*, trans. and ed. E. Curley (Princeton, 1985).

Starck, C., *Der Gesetzesbegriff des Grundgesetzes. Ein Beitrag zum juristischen Gesetzesbegriff* (Baden-Baden, 1970).

—— 'Empirie in der Rechtsdogmatik', JZ 1972, 609–14.

—— 'Das "Sittengesetz" als Schranke der freien Entfaltung der Persönlichkeit', in G. Leibholz *et al.*, *Menschenwürde und freiheitliche Rechtsordnung, Festschrift für W. Geiger*, (Tübingen, 1974), 259–76.

—— 'Staatliche Organisation und staatliche Finanzierung als Hilfen zu Grundrechtsverwirklichungen?' in C. Starck (ed.), *Bundesverfassungsgericht und Grundgesetz, Festgabe aus Anlaß des 25jährigen Bestehens des Bundesverfassungsgerichts*, ii (Tübingen, 1976), 480–526.

—— 'Teilhabeansprüche auf Rundfunkkontrolle und ihre gerichtliche Durchsetzung', in *Presserecht und Pressefreiheit, Festschrift für M. Löffler* (Munich, 1980), 375–89.

—— 'Die Grundrechte des Grundgesetzes', JuS 1981, 237–46.

—— 'Noch einmal: Die Grundrechte des Grundgesetzes', JuS 1981, 644.

—— 'Die Anwendung des Gleichheitssatzes', in C. Link (ed.), *Der Gleichheitssatz im modernen Verfassungsstaat* (Baden-Baden, 1982), 51–73.

—— 'Menschenwürde als Verfassungsgarantie im modernen Staat', in L. Lombardi Vallauri and G. Dilcher (eds.), *Christentum, Säkularisation und modernes Recht* (Baden-Baden and Milan, 1982), 805–29.

—— Review: 'Robert Alexy, Begriff und Geltung des Rechts', *Der Staat*, 32 (1993), 475–76.

Steiger, H., 'Institutionalisierung der Freiheit? Zur Rechtsprechung des Bundesverfassungsgerichts in Bereich der Grundrechte', in H. Schelsky (ed.), *Zur Theorie der Institution* (Düsseldorf, 1970), 91–118.

—— *Mensch und Umwelt Zur Frage eines Umweltgrundrechts* (Berlin, 1975).

Stein, Ekkehart, *Staatsrecht*, 8th edn. (Tübingen, 1982).

Stein, Erwin, 'Werte und Wertewandel in der Gesetzesanwendung des öffentlichen Rechts', in J. Esser and E. Stein, *Werte und Wertewandel in der Gesetzesanwendung* (Frankfurt a. M., 1966), 40–74.

Stein, L. v., *Geschichte der sozialen Bewegung in Frankreich von 1789 bis auf unsere Tage*, 3 vols., Salomon edn. (Munich, 1921) (reprinted Darmstadt, 1959).

Steinberger, H., *Konzeption und Grenzen freiheitlicher Demokratie* (Berlin, Heidelberg, and New York, 1974).

Steiner, J. M., 'Judicial Discretion and the Concept of Law', CLJ 35 (1976), 135–57.

Stenius, E., *Wittgensteins Trakat. Eine kritische Darlegung seiner Hauptgedanken* (Frankfurt a. M., 1969).

Stern, K., *Das Staatsrecht der Bundesrepublik Deutschland*, i (Munich, 1977), ii, (Munich, 1980).

—— 'Menschenswürde als Wurzel der Menschen und Grundrechte', in N. Achterberg, W. Krawietz, and D. Wyduckel (eds.), *Recht und Staat im sozialen Wandel, Festschrift für H. U. Scupin* (Berlin, 1983), 627–42.

Stevenson, C. L., 'Persuasive Definitions', *Mind*, 47 (1938), 331–50.

—— *Ethics and Language* (New Haven and London, 1944).

Stoll, H., *Kausalzusammenhang und Normzweck im Deliktsrecht* (Tübingen, 1968).

Stone, J., *Legal System and Lawyers' Reasonings* (London, 1964).

Strawson, P. F., 'Ethical Institutionism', *Philosophy*, 24 (1949), 23–33.

Struck, G., 'Dogmatische Diskussionen über Dogmatik', JZ 1975, 84–8.

Stuhlmann-Laeisz, R., *Das Sein-Sollen-Problem. Eine modallogische Studie* (Stuttgart and Bad Cannstatt, 1983).

Suhr, D., *Entfaltung der Menschen durch die Menschen* (Berlin, 1976).

Tarski, A., *Einführung in die mathematische Logik*, 2nd edn. (Göttingen, 1966).

Taylor, C., 'What's Wrong with Negative Liberty?' in A. Ryan (ed.), *The Idea of Freedom, Essays in Honour of Isaiah Berlin* (Oxford, New York, Toronto, and Melbourne, 1979), 175–93.

Thoma, R., 'Grundrechte und Polizeigewalt', in H. Triepel (ed.), *Festgabe zur Feier des fünfzigjährigen Bestehens des Preußichen OVG* (Berlin, 1925), 183–223.

—— 'Die juristische Bedeutung der grundrechtlichen Sätze der deutschen Reichsverfassung im allgemeinen', in H. C. Nipperdey (ed.), *Die Grundrechte und Grundpflichten der Reichsverfassung*, i (Berlin, 1929), 1–53.

—— 'Ungleichheit und Gleichheit im Bonner Grundgesetz', DVBl 1951, 457–9.

Thon, A., *Rechtsnorm und subjektives Rechte* (Weimar, 1878).

Thul, E. J., 'Die Denkform der Rechtsdogmatik', ARSP 46 (1960), 241–60.

Tomandl, T., *Der Einbau sozialer Grundrechte in das positive Recht* (Tübingen, 1967).

Topitsch, E., 'Die Menschenrechte. Ein Beitrag zur Ideologiekritik', JZ 1963, 1–7.

Tribe, L. H., 'The Puzzling Persistence of Process-Based Constitutional Theories', Yale LJ 89 (1980), 1063–80.

Triepel, H., *Goldbilanzenverordung und Vorzugsaktien* (Berlin and Leipzig, 1924).

—— 'Wesen und Entwicklung der Staatsgerichtsbarkeit', VVDStRL 5 (1929), 2–29.

Urmson, J. O., 'Einstufen', in G. Grewendorf and G. Meggle (eds.), *Seminar: Sprache und Ethik* (Frankfurt a. M., 1974), 140–74.

Viehweg, T., 'Zwei Rechtsdogmatiken', in U. Klug (ed.), *Philosophie und Recht, Festschrift für C. A. Emge* (Wiesbaden, 1960), 106–15.

Vogel, K., 'Rechtskraft und Gesetzeskraft der Entscheidungen des Bundesverfassungsgerichts', in C. Starck (ed.), *Bundesverfassungsgericht und Grundgesetz, Festgabe aus Anlaß des 25jährigen Bestehens des Bundesverfassungsgerichts*, i (Tübingen, 1976), 568–627.

Volkmar, D., *Allgemeiner Rechtssatz und Einzelakt* (Berlin, 1962).

Wälde, T. W., *Juristische Folgenorientierung* (Kronstein, 1979).

Walter, R., 'Das Spannungsverhältnis der sozialen Ziele Freiheit und Gleichheit', in G. Dorsey (ed.), *Equality and Freedom*, ii (New York and Leiden, 1977), 583–602.

Wasserstrom, R. A., *The Judicial Decision* (Stanford, Calif. and London, 1961).

Weber, M., *Economy and Society*, ed. G. Roth and C. Wittich, 5th edn. (Berkeley, 1968).

Weber, W., 'Die verfassungsrechtlichen Grenzen sozialstaatlicher Forderungen', *Der Staat*, 4 (1965), 409–39.

Wehrhahn, H., 'Systematische Vorfragen einer Auslegung des Art. 2 Abs.1 des Grundgesetzes', AöR 82 (1957), 250–74.

Weinberger, C., and Weinberger, O., *Logik, Semantik, Hermeneutik* (Munich, 1979).

Weinberger, O., 'Úrahy o logice normativnich vĕt', *Filosofický časopis*, ČSAV 4 (1956), 918–26.

—— 'Gleichheit und Freiheit: Komplementäre oder widerstreitende Ideale', in G. Dorsey (ed.), *Equality and Freedom*, ii (New York and Leiden, 1977), 641–52.

—— *Logische Analyse in der Jurisprudenz* (Berlin, 1979).

—— 'Das Recht als institutionelle Tatsache', *Rechtstheorie*, II (1980), 427–42.

Wendt, R., 'Der Garantiegehalt der Grundrechte und das Übermaßverbot', AöR 104 (1979), 414–74.

Wertenbruch, W., 'Der Grundrechtsbegriff und Art. 2 Abs.1 GG', DVBl 1958, 481–86.

Wieacker, F., *Zur rechtstheoretischen Präzisierung des § 242 BGB* (Tübingen, 1956).

—— *Privatrechtsgeschichte der Neuzeit*, 2nd edn. (Göttingen, 1967).

—— 'Zur praktischen Leitung der Rechtsdogmatik', in R. Bubner, K. Cramer, and R. Wiehl (eds.), *Hermeneutik und Dialektik, Festschrift für H.-G. Gadamer*, ii (Tübingen, 1970), 311–36.

Wiegand, D., 'Sozialstaatsklausel und soziale Teilhaberechte', DVBl 1974, 657–63.

Wildhaber, L., 'Soziale Grundrechte', in P. Saladin and L. Wildhaber (eds.), *Der Staat als Aufgabe, Gedenkschrift für M. Imboden* (Basle and Stuttgart, 1972), 371–91.

Wilhelm, W., *Zur juristischen Methodenlehre im 19. Jahrhundert* (Frankfurt a. M., 1958).

Williams, G., 'The Concept of Legal Liberty', in R. S. Summers (ed.), *Essays in Legal Philosophy* (Oxford, 1968), 121–45.

Willke, H., *Stand und Kritik der neueren Grundrechtstheorie. Schritte zu einer normativen Systemtheorie* (Berlin, 1975).

Windscheid, B., *Lehrbuch des Pandektenrechts*, 9th edn., ed. T. Kipp, i (Frankfurt a. M., 1906).

Winters, G., 'Tatasachenurteile im Prozeß richterlicher Rechtssetzung', *Rechtstheorie*, 2 (1971), 171–92.

Wintrich, J. M., *Zur Problematik der Grundrechte* (Cologne and Opladen, 1957).

Wischermann, N., *Rechtskraft und Bindungswirkung verfassungsgerichtlicher Entscheidungen* (Berlin, 1979).

Wittgenstein, L., *Philosophical Investigations*, trans. G. E. M. Anscombe, 2nd edn. (Oxford, 1958).

Wittig, P., 'Der Erwerb von Eigentum und das Grundgesetz', NJW 1967, 2185–8.

—— 'Zum Standort des Verhältnismäßigkeitsgrundsatzes in System des Grundgesetzes', DÖV 1968, 817–25.

Wolf, J. G., *Der Normzweck im Deliktsrecht* (Göttingen, 1962).

Wolff, H. J., 'Rechtsgrundsätze und verfassungsgestaltende Grundentschiedungen als Rechtsquellen', in O. Bachof, M. Drath, O. Gönnenwein, and E. Walz (eds.), *Festschrift für W. Jellinek* (Munich, 1955), 33–52.

—— and Bachof, O., *Verwaltungsrecht I*, 9th edn. (Munich, 1974);

Verwaltungsrecht II, 4th edn. (Munich, 1976); *Verwaltungsrecht III*, 4th edn. (Munich, 1978).

Wolff, M., 'Reichsverfassung und Eigentum', in *Festgabe für W. Kahl* (Tübingen, 1923), section IV, 1–30.

Wright, G. H. v., 'Deontic Logic', *Mind*, 60 (1951), 1–15.

—— *Logical Studies* (London, 1957).

—— *Norm and Action* (London, 1963).

—— *The Logic of Preference* (Edinburgh, 1963).

—— *The Varieties of Goodness* (London and New York, 1963).

—— *An Essay in Deontic Logic and the General Theory of Action* (Amsterdam, 1968).

Wróblewski, J., 'The Problem of the Meaning of the Legal Norm', in id., *Meaning and Truth in Judicial Decision* (Helsinki, 1979), 1–26.

—— 'Three Concepts of Validity of Law', *Tidskrift, utgiven av Juridiska Föreningen i Finland* (1982), 406–19.

Wronkowska, S., Zieliński, M., and Ziembiński, Z., 'Rechtsprinzipien: Grundlegende Probleme', in id., *Zasady prawa* (Warsaw, 1974), 225–9.

Wülfing, T., *Grundrechtliche Gesetzesvorbehalte und Grundrechtsschranken* (Berlin, 1981).

Yoshino, H., 'Zur Anwendbarkeit der Regeln der Logik auf Rechtsnormen', in *Die Reine Rechtslehre in wissenschaftlicher Diskussion*, Schriftenreihe des Hans Kelsen-Instituts, vii (Vienna, 1982), 142–64.

Zacher, H. F., 'Soziale Gleichheit', AöR 93 (1968), 341–83.

—— *Sozialpolitik und Menschenrechte in der Bundesrepublik Deutschland* (Munich and Vienna, 1968).

Zeidler, W., 'Die Aktualität des Gleichheitssatzes nach dem BGG', DÖV 1952, 4–7.

Zimmer, G., *Funktion—Kompetenz—Legitimation. Gewaltenteilung in der Ordnung des Grundgesetzes* (Berlin, 1979).

Zippelius, R., *Wertungsprobleme im System der Grundrechte* (Munich, 1962).

Zuck, R., 'Die Selbstbindung des Bundesverfassungsgerichts', NJW 1975, 907–11.

Zuleeg, M., 'Hat das subjektive öffentliche Recht noch eine Daseinsberechtigung?' DVBl 1976, 509–21.

Index